W9-BGT-098

KONG
歸英
SH

We are Hong
We have a choice to
just like Gibraltar & th
我地係香港
我地同直布羅陀同祖
有選

Colonialism

Praise for
Colonialism: A Moral Reckoning

'This scrupulous, fair-minded and scholarly analysis of the morality of colonialism offers welcome relief from the polemicists. It is vital reading both for historians and political theorists'

VERNON BOGDANOR, Professor of Government, King's College London and author of *The Strange Survival of Liberal Britain: Politics and Power before the First World War* (2022)

'In these days of academic group think, a vindictive cancel culture and a largely morally supine intelligentsia, few have the courage to wade in without fear or equivocation to tell uncomfortable truths that hysterical mobs scream down. With an open mind and indefatigable curiosity, in this brilliant and immensely readable book, Nigel Biggar looks with a clear eye at the good as well as the bad in unfairly traduced British Empire'

RUTH DUDLEY EDWARDS, historian and author of *The Seven: The Lives and Legacies of the Founding Fathers of the Irish Republic* (2016)

'Nigel Biggar fearlessly goes where few other scholars now venture to tread: to defend the British Empire against its increasingly vitriolic detractors. He does not ignore the many blemishes on the face of British rule, but he demonstrates that there were profound differences between Britain's empire and the totalitarian empires of Stalin and Hitler, against whom Britain fought all but alone in 1940 and 1941. Those who wish to accuse the Victorians of genocide – who seek gulags in Kenya or Holocausts in the Raj – will probably not risk being "triggered" by reading this book. But they really should. Not so much a history as a moral inquest into the colonial past, Biggar's book simply cannot be ignored by anyone who wishes to hold a view on the subject'

NIALL FERGUSON, Milbank Family Senior Fellow at the Hoover Institution, Stanford University, and author of *Empire: How Britain Made the Modern World* (2003)

'A hugely impressive ethical map of empire, based on an encyclopaedic reading of events and the literature around them. A very timely riposte to the ethically flawed and unhistorical campaign by Black Lives Matter and its apologists to conflate benevolent empire with slavery and, worse still, with Nazism'

ZAREER MASANI, former BBC producer, historian,
author of *Macaulay: Liberal Imperialist* (2013)
and son of an Indian nationalist father

'A view of history that one set of modern voices will find outrageous, another considers obvious and reasonable. Nigel Biggar offers here a persuasive assessment of the British empire as exhibiting good and bad, light and shade, selfish and unselfish motives. His moral analysis has enraged many academics and frightened some publishers. As a not-uncritical child of empire, I think his assessment is fair and accurate. Judge for yourself, but accept that it is important that this case should be put'

MATTHEW PARRIS, columnist for
The Times newspaper, born in Swaziland

'It is a damning indictment of the state of freedom of speech in this country that a work of true scholarship as well-researched, rigorously argued and well written as Nigel Biggar's *Colonialism: A Moral Reckoning* should have been nearly cancelled by a publisher. Any objective reader not blinded by woke prejudice will recognize that this important book is a serious and substantial contribution to one of the great debates of our times: whether we should be ashamed of our forefathers'

ANDREW ROBERTS, the Roger and Martha Mertz Visiting Fellow
at the Hoover Institution at Stanford University, Visiting Professor
at the War Studies Department at King's College London,
and author of *George III* (2021)

'A scrupulously honest reassessment of a controversial episode in world history, *Colonialism* is a refreshing addition to a historiography that has recently degenerated into a series of unexamined judgments and partisan narratives. With careful research, compelling arguments, and a text free from rhetoric, this impressive and very well-written book should further the debate on colonialism in a sensible way'

TIRTHANKAR ROY, Professor of Economic History at the London School of Economics and author of *The Economic History of India 1857–1947* (2020) and *The Economic History of Colonialism* (2020)

'The British Empire has recently become the focus of a divisive campaign to rewrite British and Western history as a story of slavery, racism and shame. This is too important an issue to be ignored. In this uncompromising and compelling book, Nigel Biggar contests damaging falsehoods and provides a searching discussion of the core ethical questions that arose from the complex experience of empire, and which still trouble us today'

ROBERT TOMBS, Professor Emeritus of History, University of Cambridge, and author of *The English and Their History* (2014)

Colonialism

A Moral Reckoning

Nigel Biggar

WILLIAM
COLLINS

William Collins
An imprint of HarperCollins*Publishers*
1 London Bridge Street
London SE1 9GF

WilliamCollinsBooks.com

HarperCollins*Publishers*
Macken House
39/40 Mayor Street Upper
Dublin 1
DO1 C9W8
Ireland

First published in Great Britain in 2023 by William Collins

23 24 25 26 27 LBC 8 7 6 5 4

HB ISBN 978-0-00-851163-0
TPB ISBN 978-0-00-851164-7

Typeset in Bulmer MT Std by Palimpsest Book Production Ltd, Falkirk, Stirlingshire

Printed and Bound in the US by Lakeside Book Company

This book is produced from independently certified FSC™ paper
to ensure responsible forest management.

For more information visit: www.harpercollins.co.uk/green

Contents

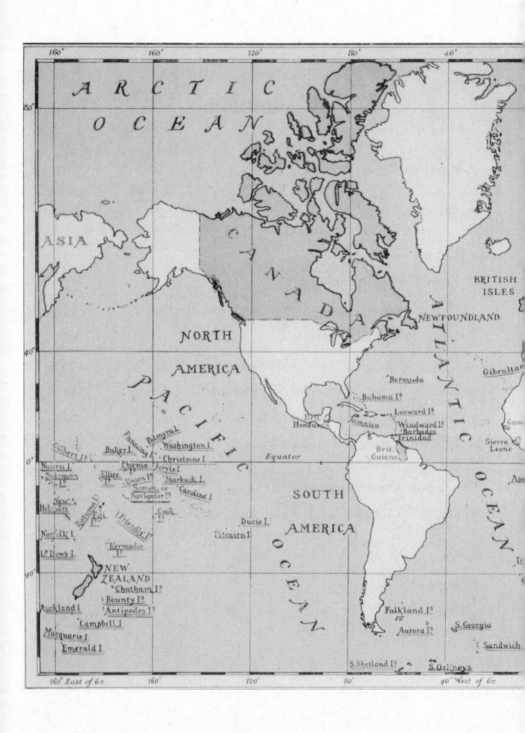

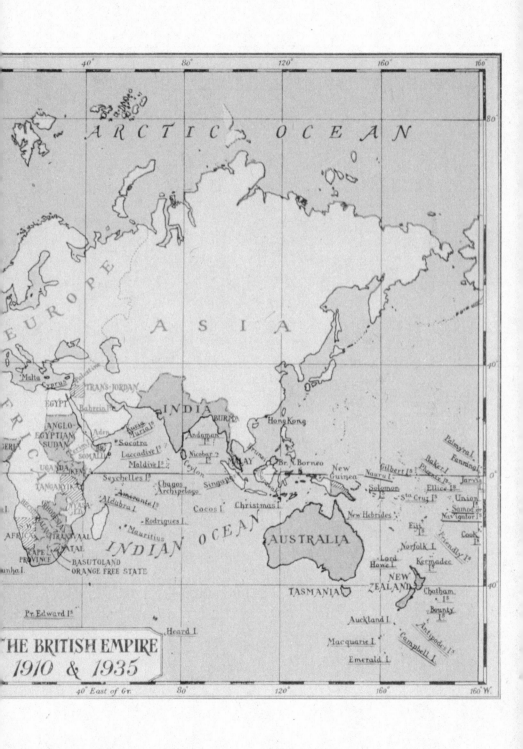

THE BRITISH EMPIRE
1910 & 1935

Acknowledgements

I n September 2017, playing truant from a conference in Rome, I sat down at a sunny table outside a café on the edge of Trastevere. After ordering an Americano, I pulled out of my briefcase a copy of Bruce Gilley's article 'The Case for Colonialism' and started to read it. I read it once and then I read it again. I found my heart lifting because Gilley had dared to give bold voice to unfashionable things that I had long thought but (largely) suppressed. 'This may be dynamite,' I said to myself, 'but it's not at all stupid.' A month later, inspired, I published an article in *The Times* newspaper that commended Gilley. The following week all hell broke loose, as I found myself plunged into the 'culture war' over colonialism. Since that hell inadvertently gave birth to this book, my first set of thanks must go to Bruce for setting such an example of intellectual integrity and moral courage. Only because he first stood out – at no small cost – was I moved to follow.[1]

Next, I must thank Robin Baird-Smith of Bloomsbury Publishing, for it was he who suggested in February 2018, in the wake of my baptism of fire, that I write a book on the subject of colonialism. Initially, I doubted that I was ready for the task. But as time passed, I warmed to the idea and decided to take the risk. I am now glad that I did.

After reading the manuscript in January 2021, Robin commented, 'I consider this to be a book of major importance.' It then entered the copy-editing process and a cover was designed. In March, however, I received an email from the very top of Bloomsbury announcing that they had decided to delay publication indefinitely, because 'public feeling' was 'not currently favourable'. I asked them to specify which 'public feeling' they were referring to, and what would have to change to make conditions favourable to publication, but they declined to give answers. Instead, they informed me that they were cancelling our contract. Happily, William Collins has rescued what Bloomsbury chose to jettison, and for that I warmly thank the following: William Shawcross, constant friend; Matthew Hamilton, assiduous literary agent; David Roth-Ey, executive publisher, Arabella Pike, publishing director, and Iain Hunt, painstaking senior editor at William Collins.

In the course of writing this book, I have accumulated debts of gratitude to many other people, whose help deserves acknowledgement here. The following read and commented either on the whole manuscript or on parts of it: Ali Ansari, Mehmet Çiftçi, Brad Faught, Niall Ferguson, Bruce Gilley, Tim Hare, Donald Hay, Stewart Herman, Robert Jackson, Simon Kingston, Victoria Kingston, John Lloyd, Richard Luce, Zareer Masani, Kenneth Morgan, Charlie Newington-Bridges, Gwyn Prins, Tripurdaman Singh, Doug Stokes, David Stroud and Simon Walters. The following gave advice on particular matters: John Anderson, Paul Bew, Vernon Bogdanor, Sarah Carter, Ping-cheung Chan, Ann Curthoys, James Daschuk, Patrice Dutil, John Gascoigne, David Gilmour, Therese Feiler, Graham Gudgin, Christopher Hallpike, Ashley Jackson, Lawrence James, Rob Johnson, Andrew Lambert, Robin Law, Donal Lowry, Richard Luce, Robert Lyman, Allan Mallinson, Stephen Prince, Craig Robinson, Tim Rowse, Tirthankar Roy, William ('Barry') Sheehan, Donald Smith, John Stenhouse, Robert Tombs, Charles Townshend, W. E. ('Bill') Vaughan and Nicholas Wood. Some advice I took, some I did not; the responsibility for the result is entirely mine.

For the first time in my life, I wrote a book to meet a deadline. I began writing on 6 July 2020 and finished the original manuscript with under twelve hours to spare, on 31 December 2020. One of the historians whom readers will meet in the pages that follow is G. H. L. Le May, who tutored me in modern history when I was an undergraduate at Oxford in the early 1970s. Of all the end-of-term reports I received, he wrote the only one I remember, since he urged 'Mr

Biggar to cease arriving at tutorials with ink dripping from his fingers'. On this occasion, almost fifty years later, I fear that the ink was barely dry. Still, I arrived on time. I could not possibly have done so, however, without the grant of a period of research leave comprising Michaelmas Term 2020. For this, I am very grateful to the Faculty of Theology at the University of Oxford, as well as to my colleague Professor Joshua Hordern, who readily assumed some of my academic responsibilities during my absence. Equally, I am grateful to fellow members of Christ Church Cathedral Chapter, who covered my cathedral duties while I was away.

I must also thank the McDonald Agape Foundation for enabling me to spend more time on research and writing in recent years, by providing me with two excellent colleagues to help take the strain of teaching and administration: Dr Ashley Moyse, the McDonald Post-Doctoral Fellow in Christian Ethics and Public Life, and Dr Dafydd Daniel, the McDonald Departmental Lecturer in Christian Ethics.

A little of what follows has already appeared in print elsewhere. A considerably abbreviated version of a penultimate draft of Chapter 2 was published online by Briefings for Britain on 26 November 2020. Several paragraphs in Chapter 3, section VII, bear a close resemblance to Chapter 8, section VI, of *What's Wrong with Rights?* (OUP, 2020). Chapter 3, section XI, is a fuller version of an article that was published online by *UnHerd* under the title 'How Racist Was the British Empire?', on 20 May 2021. The paragraphs on the Treaty of Vereeniging in Chapter 4, section VII, draw heavily from 'Compromise: What Makes It Bad?', *Studies in Christian Ethics*, 31.1 (February 2018), pp. 41–3. And a shortened version of the second half of Chapter 8, section VI, which examines the British military expedition to Benin in 1897, was published online by *The Critic* magazine under the title 'Whites and Wrongs: Dan Hicks, *The Brutish Museums: The Benin Bronzes, Cultural Violence and Cultural Restitution*', on 18 March 2021. Accordingly, I thank Briefings for Britain, Oxford University Press, Sage Publications, *The Critic* and *UnHerd* for their kind permission to use these materials in the present work.

Finally, I thank my wife, Ginny, for cheerfully keeping the world running and enduring long periods of my distracted presence and silent absence, while I did little but ruminate and write. Truly, without her, nothing much at all.

Nigel Biggar
Christ Church, Oxford
31 July 2022

Introduction

I

It was early December 2017 and my wife and I were at Heathrow airport, waiting to board a flight to Germany. Just before setting off for the departure gate, I could not resist checking my email just one last time. My attention sharpened when I saw a message in my inbox from the University of Oxford's Public Affairs Directorate. I clicked on it. What I found was notification that my 'Ethics and Empire' project had become the target of an online denunciation by a group of students, followed by reassurance from the university that it had risen to defend my right to run such a thing. So began a public row that raged for the best part of a month. Four days after I flew, the eminent imperial historian who had conceived the project with me abruptly resigned. Within a week of the first online denunciation, two further ones appeared, this time manned by professional academics, the first comprising fifty-eight colleagues at Oxford, the second, about two hundred academics from around the world. For over a fortnight, my name was in the press every day.

What had I done to deserve all this unexpected attention? Three things. In late 2015 and early 2016 I had offered a qualified defence of the late-nineteenth-century imperialist Cecil Rhodes during the first Rhodes Must Fall campaign in Oxford.[1] Then, second, in late November 2017, I published a column in *The Times* newspaper, in which I referred approvingly to Bruce Gilley's controversial article 'The Case for Colonialism', and argued that we British have reason to feel pride as well as shame about our imperial past.[2] Note: pride, *as well as shame.* And a few days later, third, I finally got around to publishing an online account of the 'Ethics and Empire' project, whose first conference had in fact been held the previous July.[3] Contrary to what the critics seemed to think, this project is not designed to defend the British Empire, or even empire in general. Rather, it aims to select and analyse evaluations of empire from ancient China to the modern period, in order to understand and reflect on the ethical terms in which empires have been viewed historically. A classic instance of such an evaluation is St Augustine's *The City of God*, the early-fifth-century AD defence of Christianity, which involves a generally critical reading of the Roman Empire. Nonetheless, 'Ethics and Empire', aware that the imperial form of political organisation was common across the world and throughout history until 1945, does not assume that empire is always and everywhere wicked, and does assume that the history of empires should inform – positively, as well as negatively – the foreign policy of Western states today.[4]

II

Thus did I stumble, blindly, into the Imperial History Wars.[5] Had I been a professional historian, I would have known what to expect, but being a mere ethicist, I did not. Still, naivety has its advantages, bringing fresh eyes to see sharply what weary ones have learned to live with. One surprising thing I have seen is that many of my critics are really not interested in the complicated, morally ambiguous truth about the past. For example, in the autumn of 2015 some students began to agitate to have an obscure statue of Cecil Rhodes removed from its plinth overlooking Oxford's High Street. The case against Rhodes was that he was South Africa's equivalent of Hitler, and the supporting evidence was encapsulated in this damning quotation: 'I prefer land to n---ers . . . the natives are like children. They are just emerging from barbarism . . . one should kill as many n---ers as possible.'[6] However, initial research discovered that the Rhodes Must Fall campaigners had lifted this quotation verbatim from a book review by Adekeye Adebajo, a former Rhodes Scholar who is now director of the Institute for Pan-African Thought and Conversation at the University of

Johannesburg. Further digging revealed that the 'quotation' was, in fact, made up from three different elements drawn from three different sources. The first had been lifted from a novel. The other two had been misleadingly torn out of their proper contexts. And part of the third appears to have been made up.[7]

There is no doubt that the real Rhodes was a moral mixture, but he was no Hitler. Far from being racist, he showed consistent sympathy for individual black Africans throughout his life. And in an 1894 speech he made plain his view: 'I do not believe that they are different from ourselves.'[8] Nor did he attempt genocide against the southern African Ndebele people in 1896 – as might be suggested by the fact that the Ndebele tended his grave from 1902 for decades. And he had nothing at all to do with General Kitchener's 'concentration camps' during the Second Anglo-Boer War of 1899–1902, which themselves had nothing morally in common with Auschwitz. Moreover, Rhodes did support a franchise in Cape Colony that gave black Africans the vote on the same terms as whites; he helped to finance a black African newspaper; and he established his famous scholarship scheme, which was explicitly colour-blind and whose first black (American) beneficiary was selected within five years of his death.[9]

However, none of these historical details seemed to matter to the student activists baying for Rhodes' downfall, or to the professional academics who supported them. Since I published my view of Rhodes – complete with evidence and argument – in March 2016, no one has offered any critical response at all. Notwithstanding that, when the Rhodes Must Fall campaign revived four years later in the wake of the Black Lives Matter movement, the same old false allegations revived with it, utterly unchastened. Thus, in the *Guardian* newspaper, an Oxford doctoral student (and former editor of the *Oxford University Commonwealth Law Journal*) was still slandering Rhodes as a 'génocidaire' in June 2020.[10]

This unscrupulous indifference to historical truth indicates that the controversy over empire is not really a controversy about history at all. It is about the present, not the past.[11] An empire is a single state that contains a variety of peoples, one of which is dominant. As a form of political organisation, it has been around for millennia and has appeared on every continent. The Assyrians were doing empire in the Middle East over four thousand years ago. They were followed by the Egyptians, the Babylonians and the Persians. In the sixth century BC the Carthaginians established a series of colonies around the Mediterranean. Then came the Athenians, followed by the Romans and after them the Byzantine rump. Empire first appeared in China in the third century BC and, despite periodic collapses, still survives today. From the seventh century AD Muslim Arabs invaded east as far as Afghanistan and west as far as central France. In the fifteenth century empire proved very popular: the Ottomans were doing it in Asia Minor, the Mughals in the Indian subcontinent, the Incas in South America and the Aztecs in Mesoamerica. Further north, a couple of centuries later, the Comanche extended their imperial sway over much of what is now Texas, while the Asante were expanding their control in West Africa. And in the 1820s King Shaka led the highly militarised Zulus in scattering other South African peoples to several of the four winds, conducting at least one exterminationist war.

Set in this global historical context, the emergence of European empires from the fifteenth century onwards is hardly remarkable. The Portuguese were first off the mark, followed by the Spanish, and then, in the sixteenth century, by the Dutch, the French and the English. The Scots attempted (in vain) to join their ranks in the 1690s and the Russians did so in the 1700s. What is remarkable, however, is that the contemporary controversy about empire shows no interest at all in any of the non-European empires, past or present. European empires are its sole concern, and of these, above all others, the English – or, as it became after the Anglo-Scottish Union of 1707, the British – one.[12] The reason for this focus is that the real target of today's anti-imperialists or anti-colonialists is the West or, more precisely, the Anglo-American liberal world order that has prevailed since 1945. This order is supposed to be responsible for the economic and political woes of what used to be called the 'Developing World' and now answers to the name 'Global South'. Allegedly, it continues to express the characteristic 'white supremacy' and 'racism' of the old European empires, displaying arrogant, ignorant disdain for non-Western cultures, thereby humiliating non-white peoples. And it presumes to impose alien values and to justify military interference. So, since British colonialism is the main target of contemporary critics, that will be the focus of this book – though much that obtained in the British case also obtained in the other European ones, too.

The anti-colonialists are a disparate bunch. They include academic 'post-colonialists', whose bible is Edward Said's *Orientalism* (1978) and who tend to inhabit university departments of literature rather than those of history.[13] For one expression of their view, take Elleke Boehmer, professor of world literature in English at the University of Oxford, whose departmental web-page presents her as 'a founding figure in the field of colonial and postcolonial studies':

> Is killing other people bad? Yes. Is rapacious invasion bad? Absolutely. And so it must follow that empires are bad, as they typically operate through killing and invasion. Across history, empires have involved the imposition of force by one power or people upon others. That imposition generally involves violence, including cultural and linguistic violence, such as the suppression and subsequent loss of native languages . . . [E]mpire requires exclusion to operate . . . spawning wars and genocides . . . [N]o empire sets out to bring law and order to other peoples in the first instance. That is not empire's primary aim. The first motivating forces are profit and more profit.[14]

How historically accurate, politically realistic and morally sophisticated such a view is, readers may judge for themselves in the light of what follows in this book. But whatever its intellectual merits, academic 'post-colonialism' is not just of academic importance. It is politically important, too, insofar as its world-view is absorbed by student citizens and moves them to repudiate the dominance of the West.

Thus, academic post-colonialism is an ally – no doubt, inadvertent – of Vladimir Putin's regime in Russia and the Chinese Communist Party, which are determined to expand their own (respectively) authoritarian and totalitarian power at the expense of the West. In effect, if not by intent, they are supported by the West's own hard left, whose British branch would have the United Kingdom withdraw from NATO, surrender its nuclear weapons, renounce global policing and retire to free-ride on the moral high ground alongside neutral Switzerland. Thinking along the same utopian lines, some Scottish nationalists equate Britain with empire, and empire with evil, and see the secession of Scotland from the Anglo-Scottish Union and the consequent break-up of the United Kingdom as an act of national repentance and redemption. Meanwhile, with their eyes glued to more domestic concerns, self-appointed spokespeople for non-white minorities claim that systemic racism continues to be nourished by a persistent colonial mentality, and so clamour for the 'decolonisation' of public statuary and university reading lists.

In order to undermine these oppressive international and national orders, the anti-colonialists have to undermine faith in them. In his novel *The Man Without Qualities,* which lay unfinished at his death in 1942, Robert Musil mused on the decline of the Austro-Hungarian Empire before the First World War: 'However well founded an order may be, it always rests in part on a voluntary faith in it . . . once this unaccountable and uninsurable faith is used up, the collapse soon follows; epochs and empires crumble no differently from business concerns when they lose their credit'.[15] One important way of corroding faith in the West is to denigrate its record, a major part of which is the history of European empires. And of all those empires, the primary target is the British one, which was by far the largest and gave birth to the United States, Canada, Australia and New Zealand. This is why the anti-colonialists have focused on slavery, presenting it as the West's dirty secret, which epitomises its essential, oppressive, racist white supremacism. This, they claim, is who we really are. This is what we must repent of.

Politically, this makes good sense. If you want to make others obey your will, it is surely useful to subvert their self-confidence and exploit their guilt. If Henry Kissinger is to be believed, ever since Sun Tzu's *Art of War* in the fifth century BC, China's *Realpolitik* has placed a premium on gaining psychological advantage.[16] Certainly, its agents are looking to gain that now. In 2011 a British diplomat in China was told, 'What you have to remember is that you come from a weak and declining nation.'[17] And when, in July 2020, Britain criticised the Chinese regime for running roughshod over the Sino-British Joint

Declaration of 1984, in which China had agreed to respect Hong Kong's relative autonomy and liberal rights, Beijing's ambassador was quick to dismiss the criticism as colonial interference.[18] Similarly, when the hard left wants to undercut Britain's role as a major supporter of the post-1945 liberal international order, or when Scottish separatists want to deepen alienation from the United Kingdom, it is politically useful to recount the history of the British Empire as a litany of ugly racial prejudice, rapacious economic exploitation and violent atrocity.[19]

This all makes good sense politically – provided that the end justifies any means and you have no scruples about telling the truth. Historically, however, it does not make good sense at all. As with Cecil Rhodes, so with the British Empire in general, the whole truth is morally complicated and ambiguous. Even the history of British involvement in slavery had a virtuous ending, albeit one that the anti-colonialists are determined we should overlook. After a century and a half of transporting slaves to the West Indies and the American colonies, the British abolished both the trade and the institution within the empire in the early 1800s. They then spent the subsequent century and a half exercising their imperial power in deploying the Royal Navy to stop slave ships crossing the Atlantic and Indian oceans, and in suppressing the Arab slave trade across Africa.[20]

There is, therefore, a more historically accurate, fairer, more positive story to be told about the British Empire than the anti-colonialists want us to hear. And the importance of that story is not just past but present, not just historical but political. What is at stake is not merely the pedantic truth about yesterday, but the self-perception and self-confidence of the British today, and the way they conduct themselves in the world tomorrow. What is also at stake, therefore, is the very integrity of the United Kingdom and the security of the West. That is why I have written this book.[21]

III

What I have written is not a history of the British Empire but a moral assessment of it. Whenever historians write about empire what they say is coloured by their moral values and principles. I do not criticise them for that, since it is inevitable. Even if we are absolutely scrupulous in finding out and acknowledging all of the relevant facts, when those facts involve human actions or their institutional results, our interpretation of them – our very choice of words in which to make sense of them, the manner in which we build a coherent story out of them – is bound to reflect our moral judgements. So historians cannot reasonably be criticised for expressing a moral point of view in their thinking and writing.

However, what sometimes deserves criticism is their lack of awareness of it. For example, in their letter of protest against my 'Ethics and Empire' project in December 2017, the fifty-eight Oxford academics (some of whom were historians) declared that 'Good and evil may be meaningful terms of analysis for theologians. They are useless to historians.'[22] If they meant that historians are not primarily in the business of making moral assessments, then they were quite correct: historians are not trained to do that. However, their dismissive tone suggests that they were saying something more: that the making of moral judgements was professionally beneath them, something that lesser, unscientific mortals indulge in. In that, they were both wrong and blind. Their own letter was rife with moral assumptions and judgements, but, not knowing much about ethics, they were unaware of it. Consequently, their judgements were merely asserted, not argued.

IV

In contrast, let me put my ethical cards on the table, face up, so that readers do not have to waste time puzzling over what they might be, and so that they know where to deploy pinches of sceptical salt, if they so wish, in the pages that follow.

First of all, it is often said about colonialism that we ought not to judge the past by the present. That is, I think, both true and untrue. It is untrue, if it means that we should not judge at all. We are moral beings; we cannot help but make moral judgements and react negatively, say, to historic instances of excessive violence. If we pretend not to judge, we will judge anyway, but obliquely.

On the other hand, it is true that we should not judge the past by the present, if it means one of two things. One is that human beings are always in the process of learning morally, and that some moral truths that are obvious to us were just not obvious to our ancestors. To us, for example, it is obvious that slavery is wrong, because it makes one person the absolutely disposable property of another. However, to most of our ancestors up until the second half of the eighteenth century, slavery was a fact of life – an institution that had existed all over the world since time immemorial. There could be good or bad forms of it – some granting slaves certain rights, others not; some being merciful, others being cruel – but the institution itself was taken for granted.[23] We should forgive our ancestors for not perceiving some moral truths quite as clearly as we do, just as we shall surely need forgiveness from our grandchildren for our own moral dullness.

The second sense in which it is true that we should not judge the past by the present is that the circumstances of the past were often very different from our own, and that good moral judgements will take that into account. The peace and security that most people in the early twenty-first century West take for granted as normal are, historically, quite extraordinary. We may hold, for example, to the moral principle that violence should only be used when necessary and kept to a minimum. Yet violence that would be excessive in the peaceful circum-stances of contemporary Britain, and in a world governed by the post-1945 international legal order, might not have been excessive in the unstable circumstances of weak nineteenth- or early-twentieth-century states or in conflicts between peoples representing vastly different cultures and restrained by no commonly recognised conven-tions. We cannot help but judge the past by our present ethics. We can make sure, however, that our present ethics are informed by a sensitivity to human limits and frailty and by a historical imagination that enables us to enter sympathetically into the moral constraints and demands of circumstances very different from our own. That is, we can ensure that our morality is not self-righteously, rigidly moralistic.

The next thing to say is that I am a Christian by conviction and a theologian by profession, so my ethics are shaped, first and foremost, by Christian principles and tradition. That does not mean that readers who are not Christian need find my moral views entirely alien. I am also a human being and I share a more or less common world with other humans. What is more, as a Christian I am inclined to believe that that common world is structured by universal moral principles, and my study of ethics, both in the West and outside it, has confirmed that that is indeed so. For example, when, in 2013, I attended a conference on the ethics of war in Hong Kong, I discovered that ancient and medieval Confucian tradition had developed a concept of 'just war' that was very similar to the one developed in the Christian West – in spite of the fact that Chinese civilisation and Christendom had developed almost entirely independently of each other until the early modern period. What they had in common, they had not borrowed from each other.

My Christian ethical viewpoint can be characterised in two general senses as 'realistic'. First, it involves the belief that there is an objective moral reality that precedes, frames and dignifies with significance all human choices: there are universal moral principles.

Second, in my ethical thinking I aspire to be honest about human limitations, about the enveloping fog that not infrequently blurs the sharpest eyes, about the inevitability of risk and about the relative intractability of historic legacy. When Joseph Chamberlain, British colonial secretary, commented on imperial policy in South Africa in 1900, 'We have to lie on the bed which our predecessors made for us', he spoke with an admirable practical wisdom that academics – including ethicists – and student activists typically lack.[24] Not having such wisdom, they lack a compassionate appreciation of the constraints under which human beings so often have to act. Consequently, they also lack forgiveness for honest error and tragic failure.

More specifically, my ethics include the belief that all human beings are basically equal. This bears thinking about, because in so many respects human beings are unequal – in beauty, intelligence, moral virtue, physical strength, material resources, political power, opportunity and, yes, potential. Social engineering can reduce some of those inequalities, but not all of them. I could say that humans are nevertheless equal in 'dignity', but that really would not get us very far, so long as the meaning of 'dignity' remains obscure. The best I can do to clarify it is to say that I believe all humans share the dignity of being accountable for the spending of their lives to a God who looks with compassion upon their limitations and burdens.

Belief in the basic equality of human beings does not imply that all cultures are equal. A culture that can write is superior *in that technical respect* to one that cannot. A culture that knows that the earth is round is superior *in that intellectual respect* to one that does not. A culture that abhors human sacrifice to the gods and female infanticide is superior *in that moral respect* to one that practises them.

Nor does belief in basic equality mean that I consider social hierarchy to be immoral. Any large-scale human society will need to work out a division of labour, whereby some sit in a planning office while others dig ditches. The moral challenge is to prevent a functional hierarchy, where relations of authority and subordination are justified by organisational efficiency, from ossifying into an essential one, where those relations are thought to be natural.

Even if human beings were all saints, government would still be needed to organise them. But since human beings are not all saints, since all of us are sometimes inclined to break common rules and abuse our neighbours, government is needed to maintain law and order. This remains its basic moral responsibility, even when it acquires other responsibilities for promoting the welfare of its citizens, since without law and order nothing human can flourish – unless you think that the unconstrained power of the warlord is a form of flourishing.

I am not a pacifist. I do think that the maintenance of just law and order sometimes requires physical coercion. The fact that the need for such coercion is regrettable, even lamentable, does not lessen its necessity.

As I see it, whether or not a policy that involves killing – or any other policy, for that matter – is morally right or wrong is not determined simply by its effects or consequences. What decides its moral quality are the motive and intention of the agent, and the proportionality of its means to its ends. Let me explain. In order to be morally right, a policy must primarily want or intend something good or valuable. Not infrequently, however, circumstances confront us with a dilemma: we cannot achieve one thing that is valuable without (at least the risk of) causing damage to another thing that is also valuable. In such a situation, it might be morally right for us to proceed, knowing that we will probably or even certainly damage the latter. Whether such a choice is morally justifiable depends on the valuable quality of our ultimate goal, but not on that alone. It also requires that the means that might or will cause damage are 'proportionate' – that is, best fitted to achieve the valuable goal, while calibrated to risk minimal damage *en route*.

The pursuit of what is valuable or good is basic to the moral rightness of anything we do, even if it is not sufficient for it. What is good for us is in our genuine interest. Therefore, there is nothing at all wrong with pursuing our own *genuine* interests – indeed, we have a duty to do so. As with individuals, so with governments. Governments have a responsibility to look after the interests of their people. As the French political philosopher Yves Simon wrote during the Abyssinia crisis of 1935, 'What should we think, truly, about a government that would leave out of its preoccupations the interests of the nation that it governs?'[25] This duty is not unlimited, of course. There cannot be a moral obligation to pursue the interests of one's own people by doing an injustice to others. Still, not every pursuit of national interest does involve injustice; so the fact that national interests are among the motives for a government's policy need not make it immoral.

Sometimes individuals and governments can be well motivated to achieve an important good, and they can choose their means of getting there conscientiously, and yet, through the bad fortune of relentlessly adverse circumstances, *they can still fail*. Not all failure to do good or avoid evil is immoral and culpable. Some of it is honest and tragic. Where that is so, the fitting response is not blame, but compassion.

History contains an ocean of injustice, most of it unremedied and now lying beyond correction in this world. Even with respect to recent crimes, the attempt at human justice is haphazard and its achievement fragmentary. Those sober facts oblige realism. Yet human beings seem to have a deep instinct for justice that will not let us settle for less, obliges us to hope against hope and drives us to our knees. The resultant posture, situated between cynicism and utopianism, is well captured by Reinhold Niebuhr's famous prayer: 'God give us grace to accept with serenity the things that cannot be changed, courage to

change the things that should be changed, and the wisdom to distinguish the one from the other.'[26]

V

Before I release the reader into the main body of this book, four things
remain to be done. First, let me make a couple of terminological points.
'Imperialism' and 'colonialism' are often used as synonyms to refer
loosely to the phenomenon of empire. Strictly speaking, however, a
distinction should be made between them, since sometimes empire
did not involve colonisation. Much of British India, for example,
comprised the 'princely states' that were largely autonomous, but
subject to British imperial 'advice' or supervision. They were never
colonised in the sense of having Britons permanently take over their
direct administration or settle in dominating numbers on their territory.
As it happens, I am inclined to avoid using either word, since the
suffix 'ism' connotes an ideological system or practical unity and
essence that does not do justice to the changing variety that was actually the British Empire.

I should also explain my choice of words to denote the peoples that
met the British when they first arrived in North America, the Caribbean,
Africa and Asia. As a rule, I refer to them, in the first instance, as
'native peoples'. However, where overuse would sound clumsy I deploy
'natives' instead. As I use it here, the word 'native' does not connote
cultural primitiveness any more than it does when I describe myself
as 'a native of Scotland' or when, later in this book, I refer to the
'natives' of Britain in the 1940s. I could have used the word 'indigenes'
instead, but I decided not to simply because it is less familiar. When
it comes to the native peoples of Australia and Tasmania, however, I
use the word 'aboriginals', partly because it is customary and partly
because, unlike most of the native peoples elsewhere, they really were
the original inhabitants of the territory on which the British found
them.

VI

Next, I have consigned most of my skirmishes with historians to the endnotes. However, at several points in the main text readers will find themselves presented with what is, in effect, a critical review of a particular book or report. The purpose in each case is the same: to lay bare the gap between the data and the reasons given on the one hand, and the anti-colonialist assertions and judgements made on the other. The exposure of this gap naturally raises the question, Why? – or more precisely, What? That is to say, what is it that has propelled assertion and judgement to run out ahead of their supporting data and reasons? The obvious answer is moral and political conviction. There is nothing wrong, of course, with moral and political conviction animating historical interpretation. Indeed, as I have already said, I think it inevitable, and it certainly obtains in my own case. What is wrong, however, is when moral and political motives refuse to allow themselves to be tempered or corrected by data and reason. For then, the motives distort and mislead; and when they distort and mislead repeatedly and wilfully, they lie. I consider this issue further in the Epilogue.

VII

Third, for those readers whose knowledge of the history of the British Empire is sketchy, let me offer the framework of a bare chronology. The English Empire began with the expansion of the Kingdom of Wessex during the ninth and tenth centuries to create a unitary state encompassing roughly the territory now called 'England'. States do not exist naturally; they have to be founded. And after being founded, they usually grow in territorial extent and wider influence. That growth can reasonably be called 'imperial'. Empire, then, is a phase in the history of many a nation-state.

In 1066 the Anglo-Saxon Kingdom of England was incorporated by conquest into the Norman Empire, which at its height included Sicily and enclaves on the shores of North Africa. Just over a hundred years later, the Normans established a foothold in Ireland around

Dublin. In the late 1200s, their Plantagenet successors conquered Wales.

In the 1580s English Protestants were encouraged to establish 'plantations' or settlements in Munster, the south-western part of the island of Ireland, and in the early 1600s Scottish Protestants were encouraged to settle in Ulster, the northern part.[27] The same period saw the beginning of English colonisation of the eastern seaboard of North America and the West Indies.

In 1707 the Kingdoms of England and Scotland were united by treaty, and the 'English' Empire became the 'British' Empire. In 1713 at the end of the War of the Spanish Succession, Britain acquired Newfoundland and what became known as Nova Scotia (as well as Gibraltar). Fifty years later in 1763, at the conclusion of the worldwide Seven Years' War with France (whose North American component is known as the 'French and Indian Wars'), Quebec was added to Britain's possessions in North America. Two decades later in 1783, following the American War of Independence, the British Empire lost all of its North American colonies south of the Great Lakes, retaining only what became known as 'Canada'.

The growth of Britain's commercial involvement with India (and points further east, such as Malaya, Singapore and China) was marked by the founding of the East India Company (EIC) in 1600. From 1757 for a hundred years the EIC not only traded with Indian merchants but came to rule vast swathes of Indian territory. After the Indian Mutiny of 1857, the company's 'Raj' (or rule) passed to the British Crown.

The British first established a colony in Australia in 1788. They purchased the leasehold right to establish a trading post in Singapore in 1819. They formally incorporated New Zealand into the empire at Māori request in 1840. And they acquired Hong Kong by treaty with imperial China in 1842.

The first imperial perch in Africa was established at its southernmost tip, the Cape of Good Hope, in 1814, when the Dutch surrendered it. (In the same year, Malta also joined the empire.) In West Africa British influence grew along the coast, and then into the interior, from the 1870s, eventually founding colonies in the Gold Coast (Ghana) and

Nigeria. Twenty years later the same happened in East Africa (Uganda and Kenya), during which period Cecil Rhodes' British South Africa Company pushed north from the Cape into what became Rhodesia. After the Second Anglo-Boer War, the Union of South Africa was created in 1910, bringing the two formerly Dutch Afrikaner republics of the Orange Free State and the Transvaal under British imperial sovereignty. In 1922 Tanganyika came under British rule according to a League of Nations' mandate.

In the later 1870s a financial crisis brought British administration to Egypt. The aftermath of the Russo-Turkish War brought it to Cyprus in 1878, and the First World War brought it to Palestine and Iraq.

Meanwhile the so-called 'white settler colonies' were acquiring greater autonomy within the empire. In 1867 Canada was the first to be granted the status of a 'dominion', followed by Australia, New Zealand and South Africa in the opening decade of the 1900s. Despite attempts to woo them into a federal system, the dominions were granted almost complete legislative independence in 1931. The community comprising Britain and the dominions, in which members enjoyed formal independence but shared cultural ties and political interests, was described as the 'British Commonwealth of Nations'.[28]

After two and a half years of violence between militant nationalists on the one hand, and the British state and its supporters on the other, southern Ireland accepted the status of a dominion within the empire in 1922, only to exchange it for that of a republic in 1949. Egypt also gained independence in 1922, Iraq in 1932, India and Pakistan in 1947, and Palestine (as the State of Israel) in 1948. All of Britain's remaining African colonies became independent states between 1956 and 1965. Hong Kong was handed back to China in 1997.

Today, two direct vestiges of the British Empire remain. First, there are the fourteen 'Overseas Territories' that retain a constitutional link with Britain, which continues to bear responsibility for defence and foreign relations. Most of these are islands in the Caribbean Sea, the Mid- and South Atlantic, and the Indian and Pacific oceans. Others are Gibraltar, the two Sovereign Base Areas on Cyprus, and the British Antarctic Territory. The other imperial vestige is the Commonwealth of Nations, which comprises fifty-four independent countries in Europe, the Americas, Africa, Asia and the Pacific. The vast majority of these used to be parts of the British Empire, but the two most recent members were not: Mozambique (1995) and Rwanda (2009).

VIII

Finally, as I have said, what now follows is not a history of the British Empire, but a moral evaluation of it. Accordingly, the book is not ordered chronologically. Rather, each chapter addresses a set of moral questions that the history of the empire raises: Was imperial endeavour driven primarily by greed and the lust to dominate? (Chapter 1); Should we speak of 'colonialism and slavery' in the same breath, as if they were the same thing? (Chapter 2); Was the British Empire essentially racist? (Chapter 3); How far was it based on the conquest of land? (Chapter 4) Did it involve genocide? (Chapter 5); Was it driven fundamentally by the motive of economic exploitation? (Chapter 6); Since colonial government was not democratic, did that make it illegitimate? (Chapter 7); and, Was the empire essentially violent, and was its violence pervasively racist and terroristic? (Chapter 8). In the Conclusion, I summarise my moral evaluation of the British colonial past. And in an Epilogue, I consider the nature and motives of anti-colonialism and its bearing upon the British future.

1

Motives, Good and Bad

I

Anti-colonialists often talk about 'the colonial project', as if an empire such as the British one was a single, unitary enterprise with a coherent essence. Then they characterise that supposed essence in terms of domination, despotism, oppression, racism, white supremacism, exploitation, theft or unconstrained violence. In this way they imply that its driving motives were lust for power, delight in domination, racial contempt and greed.[1]

Such a description does not fare well in the light of history. No one woke up one sunny morning in London and said, 'Let's go and conquer the world.' In that sense, the British Empire was not from its inception a coherent project, methodically developed out of some original plan. It was not started by a single agent or like-minded group of agents. Therefore, it was not the fruit of a single motive or cluster of motives, such as the desire to dominate and exploit, or even to improve and civilise. There was no essential motivation behind the British Empire.[2]

While that has been true of most empires, it has not been true of all of them. Most notoriously, the brief but extensive European empire of the Nazi regime in Germany, which lasted a mere seven years from the Anschluss with Austria in March 1938 to Germany's surrender to the Allies in May 1945, was the fruit of a single mind, supported and qualified by a group of political allies. More than any other, Adolf

Hitler and his spellbinding vision of things generated a coherent Nazi project, driven by a set of powerful motives: revenge upon France for the military defeat of 1918 and the humiliating peace terms of 1919; the yearning to see Germany recover its rightful, dominant position in European and world affairs; the hatred of Bolshevism, cosmopolitan capitalism, America and, above all, Jewry; and the concomitant desire to purge the world of these evils. Therefore, of the Nazi empire, which at its height in 1942 ran from the Atlantic coast of France to the River Volga in Russia, and from Finland to Libya, one can say that it had an essence of leading motives: resentment, vengeance, hatred and racist loathing. Most empires, however, were not so unitary, deliberate and coherent.

The British Empire was certainly neither a single project nor animated by a single aim. The main motive that propelled the imperial expansion of the Kingdom of Wessex over England and then of Norman England over Wales was, as is often the case, the desire of a state for security against, respectively, Danish enemies who threatened its autonomy and Welsh raiders who disturbed the peace of its borders. But sometimes it was a case of royal authority sanctioning the gains of private knightly enterprise after the fact, in order to maintain a measure of control over potential rivals – as when the rule of Henry II of England followed Norman knights in the hire of Irish chiefs to Ireland. The Tudor foundation of colonies in North America was also driven by the desire to secure England against the dominant power of imperial Spain. (Not for the first or last time would the beginnings of an empire be 'anti-imperialist'. So was the Revolutionary origin of the later, nineteenth-century western empire of the United States.) Resistance to dominant power is not its own justification, however. Some dominant powers deserve to be accepted. So England's resistance to Spanish imperialism in the sixteenth century needs to give an account of itself.

That justifying account comes in terms, first of all, of religion, but then also of liberty. England was Protestant and Spain was Catholic, and under Philip II Spain was committed to eliminating Protestantism and recovering Protestant Europe for the Roman Church – if need be, by force of arms. Accordingly, Spanish armies waged war against the

Dutch, off and on, for eighty years. But the 'religious' war between Catholics and Protestants was not simply an arcane, if bloody squabble over different views of the Eucharist; it was bound up with opposing views of authority and autonomy, both in the church and in wider society. Protestantism typically elevated the conscience of the individual, promoted the notion of the priesthood of all believers and accordingly downgraded the authority of the ecclesiastical hierarchy. Insofar as the Christian Church was held to be a model for a Christian society as a whole, this Protestant anti-authoritarianism had political implications. The 'Reformation Wall', which was opened in the grounds of the University of Geneva in 1909, inscribes in statuary and stone what those implications amounted to: 'liberty', whether in Switzerland, Scotland, England or New England. Tudor England under its Protestant queen, Elizabeth I, was no democracy, of course. However, intent on sparing her kingdom the bloodshed being spilled over religion on the other side of the English Channel, Elizabeth set about creating a comparatively broad Church of England that was a somewhat Catholic version of Protestantism. It is true that non-conformists, whether Protestant or Catholic, were subject to penalties, which, when enforced in times of foreign threat or political crisis, could be very severe indeed. Nevertheless, from the beginning, the Anglican Church was marked by a certain liberal strain, as expressed by its great sixteenth-century apologist, the Christian humanist Richard Hooker, when he wrote, 'We must acknowledge even heretics themselves to be, though a maimed part, yet a part of the visible Church.'[3] England's resistance to imperial Spain's domination, therefore, was a defence not only of Protestantism, with its seeds of anti-authoritarian politics, but also of a relatively liberal ecclesiastical arrangement, which was designed to prevent civil war.

So among the reasons for the earliest English colonisation of North America were the desires to defend national autonomy, the freedom to be Protestant and a broad Church designed to prevent bloodshed on the streets. Subordinate to these were other motives, too. 'Privateers' such as Sir Francis Drake and Sir Walter Raleigh were licensed by the Crown to raid Spanish shipping and ports for silver and gold, and to establish colonies in order to mine for them. For the privateers, this held the prospect of amassing fabulous private wealth; and for the Crown, the prospect of augmenting revenue by taking a 20 per cent cut of the proceeds.

The extension of English – and after 1707, British – control over territories in distant parts of the globe was often a consequence of international rivalry and war, and the associated need to gain a competitive advantage. In the late sixteenth and early seventeenth centuries, the main rival was Spain. From the late seventeenth to the early nineteenth centuries it was France. Initially, France represented the authoritarian Catholicism and monarchical absolutism that England had repudiated. After 1793, it represented terroristic revolution imposed by military force, and then, under Napoleon, the scarcely less frightening prospect of invasion and foreign domination. In the second half of the nineteenth century, Russia became a strategic threat to British interests in the Near East and in India; and in 1914–18 Germany's illegal invasion and ruthless occupation of Belgium and France posed a direct threat to the security of Britain itself. In the course of each of these international struggles, Britain acquired more territory in the Americas, Africa, the Middle East and the Indian subcontinent.

II

The desire of self-defence and therefore advantage in international competition or war was often the leading imperial motive of those who ruled Britain, whether from the throne or from Parliament. More widespread, popular motives were the need to make one's way in the world, the intention to trade and the excitement of foreign adventure. Take, for example, John Malcolm. Born to a tenant farmer in rural south-west Scotland in 1769, Malcolm left home at the age of twelve with a parochial school education and travelled south. He did this because his father had gone bankrupt and could no longer afford to feed his seventeen children. Once in London, Malcolm obtained a place in the Madras Army of the East India Company (EIC), and just over a year later sailed east. In the course of the remaining fifty years of his life, Malcolm fought battles against the Marathas, learned Persian, led three diplomatic missions to the Shah of Persia, wrote a *History of Persia* that Goethe is known to have borrowed three times from Weimar's State Library and ended up as governor of Bombay. Malcolm's case fits perfectly into the category of 'hard-luck stories of men travelling to the Subcontinent for perfectly decent motives and without any desire to fleece its inhabitants'.[4] Thus, the necessity of making his own way in the world and earning a living, the lure of adventure, the need to exhibit martial prowess, earnest fascination with foreign culture and eventually the ambition to exercise his talents in ruling: all of these propelled Malcolm, first of all, into the British Empire, and then into confirming and expanding it.[5]

The variety of Malcolm's own personal motives, however, were channelled through those of the institution that he spent his adult life in serving. As its name suggests, the East India Company was a commercial corporation, which had received a royal charter from Queen Elizabeth I in 1600. This charter granted the company a monopoly on English trade with all countries east of the Cape of Good Hope and west of the Straits of Magellan – the monopoly being designed to offset the very high risks attending seaborne trade in an era of small, wooden ships and pirates roaming unpoliced oceans. Twelve years later, the EIC won permission from the Mughal emperor to establish its first trading post at Surat on the west coast of the Indian subcontinent. Making profit out of trade and giving the shareholders a decent return on their investment, therefore, was the company's primary motive.

Then as now, however, prosperous trade depended upon political peace, and from the middle of the seventeenth century central and northern India became increasingly disturbed. The Muslim Mughals had come to rule in northern India after invading from Afghanistan in the 1520s, and especially from the 1550s onward their empire expanded until it covered almost all of India. From the early 1680s, however, this empire was weakened internally by a series of insurrections against oppressive taxation. Then in 1739–40 a Persian invasion defeated the emperor and occupied his capital, Delhi. Thereafter, the Mughal Empire disintegrated into a plurality of states that were virtually independent, while paying lip service to imperial authority, and whose rivalry often escalated into armed conflict. Some territories became virtually stateless.[6] Imperial weakness allowed northern India to be invaded four times by the Afghans between 1748 and 1761. One consequence of these foreign raids was to enlarge the market for professional, mercenary cavalrymen, who sold their 'protection' to the highest bidder and lived off the peasantry between contracts. In this situation, '[l]ocalised anarchy hindered the exchange of goods. Throughout this period the British, French, and Dutch trading companies grumbled about the losses they suffered from an upsurge in brigandage and coastal piracy.'[7] The EIC's commercial interests naturally entailed an interest in security, and since the Mughal imperial authorities were not providing that security, the company – along with its European counterparts – set about securing itself by developing a private armed force, mostly by hiring and training Indians. In 1755, to bolster this commercial protection on the eve of what would turn out to be seven years of worldwide war with France, the British government in London decided to send a Royal Navy squadron and regular British troops to supplement the EIC's forces. This pattern of initial endeavour in private trade eventually involving public naval and military support is a common refrain in the history of the British Empire: it appeared again, for example, in the case of Hong Kong.[8]

So the logic of trade led, through the need for security, to the acquisition of military power. It also led to control over territory, but not – as is commonly assumed – through conquest. As Tirthankar Roy has written:

> Turning the emergence of the empire . . . into a battle between good and evil creates melodrama; it invites the reader to take sides in a fake holy war. But if good soap opera, it is bad history. The empire was not an invasion. Many Indians, because they did not trust other Indians, wanted the British to secure power. They preferred British rule over indigenous alternatives and helped the Company form a state . . . The empire emerged mainly from alliances. It emerged from lands 'ceded' to the Company by Indian friends, rather than lands it 'conquered' . . . The Company came to rule India because many Indians wanted it to rule India.[9]

Rival Indian rulers were keen to enlist British military expertise and British-trained and -led troops, with a view to prevailing in local wars. In return, they often paid the company in land and the right to tax, sometimes even handing over a port and its revenue.[10] Since the primary interest of the company was to make money for its shareholders, and since a further interest of its usually underpaid agents was to make their private fortunes on the side, the combined effect was sometimes ruinous during the first decade of its rule in Bengal. (While it does not exonerate their early excesses, it does put them in perspective to note that the company's men were not alone in their rapacity, since they were almost invariably aided by local collaborators, especially the predominantly Hindu banking and business elites.) In this fashion from the 1740s, and especially the famous victory of Robert Clive at the Battle of Plassey in 1757, to the resignation of Warren Hastings as de facto governor-general in 1785, the EIC's Indian empire grew without any sense of imperial mission and without any grand plan, and simply in ad hoc response to commercial and money-making opportunities and the consequent requirements of security.

In an anarchical situation where there is no law that overarches states, or no authority capable of enforcing it, anxiety and fear predominate, allied to the urgent need to preserve one's life, liberty and property. In extreme situations, of course, such preservation depends on having the military wherewithal to vanquish enemies on the field of battle, but in the intervening periods of peace it depends on deterrence, convincing enemies that open conflict is really not worth contemplating. Effective deterrence depends on maintaining military prestige, that is, a discouraging reputation for overwhelming enemies and punishing them. Thus, the logic of defence entails, if not random aggressiveness, then active pugnaciousness. In order to stay still, one has to move forward; in order to keep what you have got, you must expand. As John Malcolm put it in 1805:

It was a true saying which the great Lord Clive applied to the progress of the British Empire in India – 'To stop is dangerous; to recede ruin'. And if we do recede . . . – nay, if we look as if we thought of receding – we shall have a host of enemies, and thousands who dare not even harbour a thought of opposing the irresistible tide of our success, will hasten to attack a nation which shows by its diffidence in its own power that it anticipates its downfall.[11]

Four decades later, James Abbott, army officer and administrator in the Punjab, echoed Malcolm exactly when he wrote:

Delay, when a fearful and instant retribution is everywhere expected, will be attributed to timidity. We hold our position in the Punjab wholly by force of opinion, by the general belief in our superior courage and resources. Our Empire in India has the same foundation, and one or both may pass away if we evince any symptoms of hesitancy.[12]

On this Lawrence James has commented astutely: 'In India, as on the Anglo-Scottish marches, war had a momentum of its own.'[13]

It would be quite misleading, however, to suppose that the agents of the EIC were all about making a profit for shareholders, amassing fortunes for themselves and intimidating Indian opponents. John Malcolm was not the only company man to take a serious interest in learning about his cultural environment. Warren Hastings, for example, achieved fluency in Bengali and had a decent working knowledge of Urdu and Persian. Fascinated by India's Hindu and Buddhist past, which had faded from sight during seven centuries of Muslim rule, he pioneered the revival of Sanskrit and sponsored the first ever English translation of the Bhagavad Gita. In 1784 he supported the prodigiously polyglot Sir William Jones in founding the Calcutta Asiatic Society, which became the centre of a cultural revival that would blossom into the Bengal Renaissance, especially in the late nineteenth and early twentieth centuries.[14] So great was Hastings' cultural enthusiasm that he once declared, 'In truth, I love India a little more than my own country.'[15]

Post-colonialist disciples of Edward Said brush this aside as so much 'Orientalist' cultural 'appropriation', which is designed to confirm Westerners' sense of their own superiority and to impress on those they rule a corresponding sense of inferiority.[16] But this fails to do justice to the phenomenon. In general, when people encounter a foreign culture, they are bound to try and understand it in their own, familiar terms. In so doing, they become aware of elements that do not fit and at that point they recognise cultural difference, which might alarm and repel them, but equally might fascinate and attract them. In this particular case, Hastings clearly admired what he encountered. Besides, it is quite hard to see how his translation of the Bhagavad Gita served to entrench British domination.[17] On the contrary, the comparative philology developed by William Jones undermined the Eurocentric assumption of the primacy of Graeco-Roman language and civilisation.[18] According to Nirad Chaudhuri, in rescuing classical Sanskritic civilisation from oblivion, Hastings, Jones and other European Orientalists 'rendered a service to Indian and Asiatic nationalism which no native could ever have given. At one stroke it put the Indian nationalist on a par with his English ruler.'[19] It gave him the material out of which to build 'the historical myth' of a Hindu civilisation that was superior to Europe's.[20]

III

One thing that never happened in British India was the mass immigration of Britons. This was largely because India was already a long-settled country, but also because the EIC discouraged European immigration, lest it cause social friction and create political trouble. The number of Britons in India was always tiny. In 1830 there were no more than 36,400 white soldiers in the whole of the vast country.[21] That had risen to only 65,000 by 1900, when the British portion of the population amounted to a mere 154,691 individuals out of a total of nearly 300 million.[22]

The situation in Africa was similar. In spite of attempts in the late nineteenth and early twentieth centuries to encourage whites to settle there – especially in South Africa and Kenya – the numbers always remained relatively small. One reason was the inhospitable climate and the threat of disease, but another was the prospect of making a better life by settling elsewhere in the world.

Nevertheless, in the eighteenth century about 500,000 people emigrated from the British Isles. And from 1815 to 1924 the number rocketed to 25 million during a period when mass migration became a global phenomenon, involving about 35 million continental Europeans, 7 million Russians, and (from 1846 to 1940) 50 million Chinese and 30 million Indians.[23] The preferred destination for British and Irish emigrants was North America, followed by Australia. From 1810 to 1860 the number of settlers in Australasia shot up from 12,000 to 1.25 million, expanding a hundredfold in fifty years. From 1790 to 1860 the population of British North America grew from about 250,000 (mostly French) to 3.25 million (mostly Anglophone), and from 1891 to 1911 the four provinces of western Canada grew sevenfold from 250,000 to 1.75 million.

The motives of migrants, then as now, were various. Some had no choice in the matter. Until the American colonists won their independence in 1783, Britons convicted of crimes judged not deserving of hanging were transported across the Atlantic to serve out their sentences on the far side. From 1788 their destination changed to Australia, where an estimated 168,000 convicts were shipped until penal transportation ceased in 1868. Of those who chose to migrate, some went in search of religious freedom – most famously, the 'Pilgrim Fathers', who sought to escape the Church of England and landed on the coast of what would become Massachusetts in 1620. Others fled a victorious enemy: in 1783 about 50,000 loyalists left the emergent United States for what remained of British North America – mostly to Nova Scotia, where they inadvertently and suddenly tripled the settler population, upsetting its *modus vivendi* with the native peoples.[24] Emigrants from Ireland and Highland Scotland were typically driven to escape dire poverty – most notably during the Great Famine in 1840s Ireland – but their counterparts from Lowland Scotland and England were probably less pushed by misery than pulled by the prospect of betterment – freehold farms, a life with leisure as well as work, an egalitarian social environment and (for men) the right to vote.[25] As James Belich has put it, 'Settlers wanted a life as well as a living.' What is more, they 'were not ogres. They were whining bundles of hopes and fears just like us.'[26]

IV

For most Britons who emigrated, 'empire' meant primarily the opportunity of a better life for themselves and their families. However, for many, from the early decades of the nineteenth century onward, 'empire' also meant the opportunity to make a better life for other people. As we shall see in more detail in the next chapter, inspired by a Christian ideal of basic human equality, a popular, national movement arose in late-eighteenth-century Britain to bring about the abolition, first, of the trade in slaves from Africa across the Atlantic to the Caribbean and the American colonies, and subsequently of the institution of slavery itself throughout the empire. Thereafter, Christians and other humanitarians called for the British government to intervene in faraway parts of the world – especially West, South and East Africa – to suppress slavery. For example, in the early 1860s the famous Christian missionary, physician and explorer David Livingstone lobbied for the establishment of British imperial administration in the Shire Highlands of what is now Malawi, in order to provide a stable political environment for the development of cash crops and commerce as a necessary alternative to the trade in slaves.[27]

After the abolition of slavery in the British Empire in 1834, humanitarians turned their attention to the plight of native peoples as they suffered the large-scale influx of European migrants in British North America, Australia and New Zealand. So, in 1837, led by Quakers such as Thomas Hodgkin, they founded the Aborigines Protection Society, which flourished for the next seventy years. Merged with the Anti-Slavery Society in 1909, it lives on today as Anti-Slavery International.[28]

Meanwhile the same Christian, humanitarian, 'improving' spirit had taken hold of British government in India. Disquiet over the unscrupulous means by which agents of the EIC were making their fabulous fortunes, over their parliamentary influence and over the company's lack of public accountability led to the passing in 1784 of the India Act, which placed the EIC's territories under the dual government of the old court of directors and a new Board of Control, whose president was a member of the Cabinet and answerable to the British Parliament.[29] Two years after the Act was passed, a new ruler of British India was appointed: Charles, the Marquess Cornwallis, not long returned from the far side of the Atlantic, where he had been forced to surrender his troops to the American rebels at Yorktown. Determined to end the corruption of public government by private interests, Cornwallis stopped the EIC's agents trading on their own accounts and using the company's ships to dispatch their own goods back to Britain, and he raised their salaries generously in compensation. He also introduced measures to protect native weavers against commercial exploitation, and set about building a coherent system of law out of the confused legal and judicial mêlée he had inherited. To that end, he oversaw the translation into English of classic texts of Muslim and Hindu law, and in 1791 he supported the founding of a Sanskrit College in Benares, which survives to this day as Sampurnanand Sanskrit University. According to Lawrence James, Cornwallis 'was in every way a model Governor-General', being 'an upright, well-intentioned soldier whose interior life had been touched by the ideals of contemporary Evangelical Christianity'. Moreover, '[h]is successors, Minto, Hastings, Lord William Bentinck, Auckland, Hardinge, and the Earl of Dalhousie were all, in different ways, inspired by the same creed . . . They saw themselves not as India's conquerors but as its emancipators.'[30] Francis, 1st Marquess of Hastings, for example, who was governor-general from 1813 to 1823, expressly dedicated himself to promoting the 'happiness of the vast population of this country'.[31]

V

Up until the 1870s British interests in Africa were largely limited to the coast, which provided a base for action against the slave trade, a staging post for India and the East, and entrepôts for primary resources. The expensive control of more extensive territory, often disease-ridden, held little appeal. Thereafter, however, the attraction grew for several overlapping reasons.[32] There was the need to disrupt the inland trade in slaves, partly by developing alternative forms of commerce. Allied to this was the desire to curb the southern expansion of militant Islam, lest it revive the trade. Hence the need to protect Uganda and Nyasaland from Arab incursions.[33]

Also allied was the concern to put a stop to constant internecine warfare, partly to cut off the source of the supply of slaves, partly to relieve the human misery caused by chronic conflict and partly to foster trade. Conflict was being seriously exacerbated by the uncontrolled arms trade. It is estimated that the Zulu probably had 8,000 guns by 1879 (the year they massacred the British at Isandlwana) and that the Shona and Ndebele probably had 10,000 guns by 1896 (the year they rose up in revolt against the British South Africa Company). In the seven years from 1895 to 1902 an estimated 1 million firearms entered German and British East Africa alone. An additional exacerbation was concession-hunting by private European adventurers. King Mbandzeni of Swaziland, for example, had conceded more land than the total area of his kingdom, and the incendiary tangle of overlapping concessions was such that the British government felt bound to intervene in 1884 and 1894, appropriate the land and supervise its re-apportionment. And when the high commissioner for Southern Africa, Hercules Robinson, supported Rhodes' establishment of a British presence in what became Rhodesia, he argued that it would 'check the inroad of adventurers', since the rush of concessionaires to Matabeleland had 'produced a condition of affairs dangerous to the peace of that country'.[34]

Of all the various interests that Britain had acquired in pacifying large swathes of Africa, however, the one most urgently felt in London was probably the need to avoid the embroilment of European nations in local conflicts escalating into direct war between them.[35] As the prime minister, Lord Salisbury, declared in 1890, during a debate on the Anglo-German Agreement Bill:

> The Governments of Germany and England have been on the most friendly terms, and I think have been able to impart at least a considerable portion of their own friendliness and moderation to those who served under them, but it is impossible to impart it to those not under their control, though they share our nationality . . . It is impossible to restrain them. It is impossible to prevent the danger of collisions, which might be murderous and bloody; and then when those collisions took place, the echo of them would be heard here, they would be recounted

and magnified in newspapers in both countries, they would be pressed
upon popular passion until even the Governments themselves might
not be able to resist the contagion of the feeling evoked.[36]

VI

In addition to suppressing the inland slave trade, curbing the influence
of militant Islam and imposing *Pax Britannica*, from the late 1880s
Britain also acquired a strategic interest in the 'inter-lacustrine' region
between Lakes Victoria, Kyoga, Albert, Edward and Tanganyika in
East Africa. This was because whoever controlled the sources of the
Nile could threaten Egypt's agricultural surplus, finances and ability
to service its debt.[37] And why did the British care about that? Because
in the late 1870s they had arrived in Cairo to save European investments
by sorting out the finances of the state, which was tottering on the
verge of bankruptcy. They ended up staying for decades to establish
a wider set of administrative and economic reforms and to attempt
cosmopolitan nation-building.

Isma'il Pasha, khedive (or Ottoman viceroy) of Egypt from 1863 to
1879, had borrowed large sums to enable his ambitious programme of
modernisation, the most expensive item of which was the construction
of the Suez Canal, but which also included the building of railways,
irrigation canals, schools and a Royal Opera House.[38] In addition, the
khedive needed money to fund an expansionist war with Ethiopia.
With the end of the American Civil War in 1865, American cotton
re-entered the European market, causing a sudden fall in the price of
Egyptian cotton and a concomitant drop in government revenue.
Desperate to finance his loans, the khedive resorted to short-term
measures such as the *muqabala* ('exchange'), which allowed those
liable to land tax to make a one-off payment amounting to six times
their annual rate in return for perpetual relief from half their tax burden.
Notwithstanding this, by 1876 Egypt's international debt amounted to
more than £68 million, consuming 60 per cent of the state's revenue
in interest payments. Blocked from raising more tax by a consultative
assembly dominated by landowners, the khedive turned to European
powers for help. The result was the institution of European control

of Egypt's public finances, which began as a joint Anglo-French responsibility, but subsequently became solely British.

The British comptroller-general in Egypt, Evelyn Baring – known later as Lord Cromer – put it on record to Lord Salisbury, then the foreign secretary, that even though he had been appointed by the British government, he saw himself as having responsibilities to the Egyptian government that might conflict with those of Britain. In such a case, he said, he considered his Egyptian responsibilities as paramount. Salisbury agreed: 'You have duties to the Egyptian sovereign and people which we have not,' he wrote, 'and you cannot be guided entirely by the political interests of England as we shall be.'[39] Above all, Cromer considered himself duty-bound to aid the Egyptian peasant, and he believed that bondholders should have the 'permanent interests' of Egypt at heart and should not press the peasantry too hard.[40] Accordingly, he reduced the tax burden on them, and compensated for the loss of public revenue by restricting the khedive's personal expenditure, virtually abolishing the *muqabala*, and increasing the burden on lightly taxed large landowners.

Among the groups threatened by these reforms were native Egyptian Army officers, who, with the halving of the military budget, were faced with compulsory early retirement. Partly because of this, but also to impose constitutional constraints on the khedive, to end the domination of government by Turco-Circassians and reform it on Islamic principles, Colonel Ahmed 'Urabi led an attempted coup in 1882. Alarmed that this might lead to a default on Egypt's debts and Egyptian seizure of the Suez Canal, and with the encouragement of the khedive, the generally intervention-shy British government of William Gladstone authorised a military response, leading to the Royal Navy's bombardment of Alexandria and the British Army's defeat of 'Urabi's forces at the Battle of Tel El Kebir.

Initially, Cromer argued strongly that the subsequent British occupation of Egypt should not be prolonged, and he opposed the imposition of a protectorate. 'I do not see what the Egyptians, considered as a nation, have done to forfeit their right to self-government,' he said. 'There remains nothing in the area of fiscal reform that can't be done by the Egyptians themselves.'[41] His views were music to the ears of the government in London, which had no desire to take on the burden and risks of administering yet another territory. When the Ottoman sultan offered Gladstone the exclusive control and administration of Egypt, he refused it.[42]

As time went on, however, Cromer became increasingly concerned about the durability of his reforms, worrying that if the British were to evacuate too soon, the country would quickly relapse into the chaos that had required foreign intervention in the first place. By 1887 he had come to the firm view that it would take at least a decade to secure what had been achieved. The previous year he had written to the Earl of Iddesleigh, foreign secretary: 'The idea that we can put matters right, and then leave our work to be continued by native agents, is, in my opinion, erroneous.'[43] In the meantime, mindful of the need to make foreign occupation less irksome, Cromer supported the repair of the Delta Barrage and the canals flowing off it, which greatly augmented the availability of irrigation water for the peasantry, and doubled the cotton crop. He also rescinded the call-out of the deeply resented *corvée* – that is, forced labour for public works – and moved towards substituting the use of paid labour for canal cleaning.

By the time the predicted decade was complete, however, Cromer was less optimistic about the necessary timetable, because he had become more ambitious about what needed to be done. In response to the nationalist mantra 'Egypt for the Egyptians!' he answered, 'Who is the true Egyptian?'[44] Cromer observed that the actual people of Egypt were not just the Muslim peasants, landowners and clerics, but also the Armenian, Syrian and Coptic Christians, and the Turks. Accordingly, he wrote, 'The only real Egyptian autonomy . . . which I am able to conceive as either practicable or capable of realisation without serious injury to the various interests involved, is one which will enable all the dwellers in cosmopolitan Egypt, be they Moslem or Christian, European, Asiatic, or African, to be fused into one self-governing body.'[45] However, if that was ever to happen, government would have to transcend ethnic biases and serve 'the true interests of the dwellers in Egypt, of whatsoever nationality or creed they may be'.[46] Cromer was not persuaded that Egyptians by themselves were yet capable of doing this, and not without good reason. After all, on one occasion he had had to intervene and override the preference of the Armenian prime minister, Nubar Pasha, for appointing his Christian confrères, by insisting upon the dismissal of two incompetent Coptic judges.

Cromer's biographer, Roger Owen, has observed that 'many of [his] Egyptian contemporaries . . . were much more ready to acknowledge some of the positive effects of his rule than most of those who followed', and that he had acted 'with great personal integrity and with a practical concern for the economic well-being of the poorer Egyptians was freely acknowledged in Cairo as well as London'.[47] One of those contemporaries was an exuberant Muslim who wrote to Cromer in 1906, exclaiming, 'He must be blind who see not what the English have wrought in Egypt: the gates of justice stand open to the poor; the streams flowing through the land are not stopped at the order of the strong; the poor man is lifted up and the rich man pulled down; the hand of the oppressor and the briber is struck when outstretched.'[48] Another contemporary was the moderate nationalist Ahmad Lutfi al-Sayyid, who wrote in 1907 of the 'magnificent results' of Cromer's financial reforms, while criticising him for failing to establish the foundations of a 'productive and serviceable' system of public education, using Britons rather than Egyptians to effect his reforms and preferring to create an 'internationalist' nationality in Egypt instead of attending to the true, native one.[49] And one exception to the rule of diminished subsequent appreciation is al-Sayyid's own niece, the historian Afaf Lutfi al-Sayyid-Marsot. In 1968 Professor al-Sayyid-Marsot dismissed nationalist exaggeration of Cromer's errors, noted his 'affection for Egypt' and commented that his

financial policy . . . – low taxation, efficient fiscal administration, careful expenditure on remunerative public works, and minimum interference in the internal and external traffic of goods – plus Egypt's powers of recuperation, due to her fertile soil, had by 1890 brought prosperity to the country. The real *per capita* income during the first decade of [the twentieth] century was higher than at any time in modern Egyptian history, with the possible exception of the early 1920s.[50]

She continued: 'Although Cromer had turned Egypt into a British
dependency in all but name, yet materially and in the best colonial
tradition, he had given the Egyptians much . . . [I]n spite of all its
shortcomings, British rule in Egypt was benevolent . . . British justice
in Egypt was at least better than the justice meted out by the Khedive.'[51]

Cromer left Egypt in 1907, but it took another half-century before
the last British troops followed him. The reasons for such a prolon-
gation of the British occupation were various, but the leading ones
were the persistence of the perceived need to continue supervising
the embedding of good government, stiffened by the enlarged importance for British imperial strategy of Egypt as a Mediterranean military
base and as guardian of the route to India and the east. Thus, a British
presence that had been welcomed by many Egyptians in the 1880s
and 1890s as a temporary expedient became increasingly irksome to
the swelling ranks of nationalists as time moved on but the British did
not. In 1914, when the Ottoman Empire allied itself to Germany, the
British formally declared Egypt a 'protectorate'. However, rising
nationalist pressure persuaded them to restore Egypt to its status as
an independent kingdom in 1922. Nonetheless, British influence on
Egypt's domestic government, and control over its defence and the
Canal Zone, continued for a further three decades. The last British
troops left Egypt in June 1956, returning only briefly later that year
during the ill-fated Suez Crisis.

VII

Whereas state insolvency brought the British to Egypt, it was the
vicissitudes of war that brought them more deeply into other parts of
the Middle East. Had the Ottoman Empire not decided to throw in
its lot with Germany in 1914, and had British imperial troops not
(eventually) defeated it in 1918, Britain would never have come to rule
Palestine and Iraq. But as we have seen in the case of Egypt, to arrive
is one thing, to stay, another.

Senior military figures lobbied strongly in favour of evacuating
Palestine after the end of the war, doubting the benefits and foreseeing
the military liabilities of staying. General Sir Henry Wilson, chief of

the imperial general staff, wrote in May 1919, 'The problem of Palestine is exactly the same . . . as the problem of Ireland, namely, two peoples living in a small country hating each other like hell', and whereas what was needed was 'an overriding authority so strong that it can enforce its will on both opposing parties', he doubted that Britain was in a position to provide it in Palestine 'for the simple reason that we have not got the troops'.[52]

Wilson's voice and others like it were overridden for a cluster of reasons. Not least among them was the so-called Balfour Declaration of November 1917, addressed on behalf of the British government by Arthur Balfour, foreign secretary, immediately to Lord Rothschild and ultimately to the Zionist movement. The statement was as brief as it was to prove fateful:

> His Majesty's Government view with favour the establishment in Palestine of a national home for the Jewish people, and will use their best endeavours to facilitate the achievement of this object, it being clearly understood that nothing shall be done which may prejudice the civil and religious rights of existing non-Jewish communities in Palestine, or the rights and political status enjoyed by Jews in any other country.

The declaration was made partly because Balfour, reportedly moved to tears by Chaim Weizmann's stories of Jewish suffering from antisemitism, had been won over to the Zionist vision of the undoing of an ancient wrong by restoring a people, long exiled and yearning to return home, to their native land.[53] The British Cabinet as a whole, however, was more moved by the urgent need to win the First World War, a conflict of unprecedented cost in blood and treasure, whose victorious conclusion was still not in sight after three gruelling years of fighting. Cabinet members had been persuaded that the international community of Jews was a powerful force in world affairs, wielding considerable political influence both in Washington, DC, and in Moscow after the February Revolution, and that therefore the British government's support for Zionist ambitions would win it American favour and help keep Russia in the war. Reinforcing this ad hoc, wartime concern for political advantage was a set of strategic factors, in which the protection of the Suez

Canal featured, but not decisively.[54] Also operative were vaguer considerations such as the common view that Ottoman rule had been corrupt
and oppressive and deserved to be supplanted; the obligation to provide
Arab allies, who had revolted against that rule, with an alternative; the
need to prevent another rival power from filling the vacuum left by the
departed Ottomans and becoming predominant in the region; and confidence in the civilising virtues of British government. As Lord Robert
Cecil, assistant secretary of state for foreign affairs, said in 1918: 'From
the point of view of the inhabitants we should almost certainly [govern
the region] better than anybody else and therefore it would be better
for us to do it.'[55] Others were much more doubtful. General Sir Walter
Congreve, who commanded the Egyptian Expeditionary Force from
1919 to 1923, remarked of British support for the Zionist project that
'we might as well declare that England belongs to Italy because it was
once occupied by the Romans'.[56]

The wording of the Balfour Declaration left open the question of
what *kind* of 'national home' for the Jewish people the British would
facilitate in Palestine, and how this would be made compatible with
the political aspirations of the Arabs already resident there. During the
quarter of a century from 1923 to 1948 when they were bound by
the League of Nations' mandate to administer Palestine with a view
to establishing a Jewish homeland and an independent state, the British
considered a variety of permutations to satisfy the conflicting political
interests of Jew and Arab – including a semi-autonomous Jewish
province within a larger Arab state (under British suzerainty), a Jewish
state within an Arab federation and a bi-national state. Had the rate
of Jewish immigration been moderated earlier, had Jewish immigrants
been more open to retaining Arab labour on the land they purchased
and less inclined to segregation, had Zionists been more willing to
settle for something short of a fully Jewish state, and had consequent
Arab resentment at their displacement not exploded into violence,
then a peaceful political compromise might have been possible.[57]

However, the policy of the British government had radically underestimated the incendiary cultural friction that was likely to result when
town-dwelling Jews from Eastern Europe suddenly found themselves
rubbing shoulders with Arab peasants. As one immigrant from Poland

put it in 1928: 'Here and there you run into Arab villages – they live like real pigs . . . If you saw how and what they eat and where they sleep, you'd feel real revulsion at touching them.'[58] Moreover, British policy had also underestimated the political challenge of reconciling the conflicting political interests. Some members of the government did have their eyes wide open. Cabinet member and former viceroy of India, Lord Curzon, for example, asked in 1918, '[W]hat would happen to the present Muslim population? . . . They will not be content either to be expropriated for Jewish immigrants or to act merely as hewers of wood and drawers of water to the latter.'[59] But Balfour's astonishing insouciance prevailed. As he wrote in August 1919, 'in Palestine we do not propose even to go through the form of consulting the wishes of the present inhabitants of the country . . . Zionism, be it right or wrong, good or bad, is rooted in age-long traditions, in present needs, in future hopes, of far profounder import than the desires and prejudices of the 700,000 Arabs who now inhabit that ancient land.'[60] At the time of his declaration in 1917, those Arabs had amounted to 93 per cent of the population.[61]

The consequence of this 'colossal blunder', as High Commissioner Sir John Chancellor later called it,[62] was that the British found themselves locked into an impossible situation. Ronald Storrs, who was governor of Jerusalem from 1917 to 1926, expressed their frustration with characteristic wryness: 'Two hours of Arab grievances drive me into the Synagogue, while after an intensive course of Zionist propaganda I am prepared to embrace Islam.'[63] Eventually, after twenty-five years of failing to buy Arab political consent with improved infrastructure and reduced judicial corruption,[64] after searching in vain for a compromise to which both Jews and Arabs would agree, after attracting violence from both sides, after fighting an exhausting Second World War, in the wake of the dislocation of European Jewry by the Holocaust, and in the face of pressure from the United States not to delay in establishing a Jewish state, the British Empire unilaterally surrendered its mandate to the United Nations in February 1947 and evacuated Palestine. In the following November, the UN voted in favour of two states with Jerusalem under international control. The United Kingdom abstained.[65]

VIII

On the eve of the First World War, the Ottoman Empire stretched from the Bulgarian border down to the foot of the Red Sea and then over to the Persian Gulf. When the Ottomans entered the war as an ally of Germany in the autumn of 1914, Anglo-Indian troops quickly seized control of Basra in Lower Mesopotamia, to protect the oil fields and control the Gulf. The following year the British moved north to capture Baghdad, for the sake of what Field Marshal Lord Kitchener, secretary of state for war, called 'prestige'[66] – that is, demonstrating military ascendancy, demoralising and distracting the Turks, and encouraging the Arabs to rise up against them. The campaign was a disaster, ending in the British being besieged in Kut and surrendering in April 1916. Within twelve months the humiliating defeat was avenged, however, when General Maude marched into Baghdad in March 1917.

Thus, the British arrived in the capital city of the Ottoman *vilayet* (or province) of Baghdad. And there they stayed for the next sixteen years. Why? *Pace* Marxist historians, the main reason was not oil.[67] Certainly, there were strategic reasons. In the Sykes-Picot Agreement of 1916 Britain and France had defined their respective spheres of influence in a post-Ottoman future, partly to prevent friction between them and partly to stem the spread of Russian influence.[68] Accordingly, when the war's end raised the need for some 'civilised power', as Lord Curzon put it, to oversee the post-Ottoman construction of self-standing states, Britain stood ready to assume responsibility for the whole of Mesopotamia.[69] Part of that responsibility, which was of major concern to the League of Nations, was the protection of minorities, not least Christians and Jews.[70] This sense of moral responsibility was reinforced by the conviction of Arabists such as the famously intrepid Gertrude Bell – whose death in 1926 even the Iraqi nationalist press would mourn[71] – that putting an end to capricious and incompetent Turkish rule would be a humanitarian blessing.[72] More specifically, there was the motive of keeping the British promise to Hussein bin Ali al-Hashimi, the sharif of Mecca, that, in return for his revolt against the Turks, they would support his leadership in building an Arab state out of the ruins of the Ottoman Empire.[73] In fulfilment of this promise, they facilitated the installation of his third son, Faisal, as the first king of Iraq – and of Abdullah, Hussein's second son, as the first emir of Transjordan (and, from 1946, the king of Jordan).

Early on, there was also the ambition of the government of India, which had supplied most of the troops for the campaign, to seize first Basra and then Baghdad, to make Mesopotamia an Indian colony, developing irrigation canals, increasing the productivity of food and supporting some of India's surplus population from the Punjab. That plan, however, was short-lived. Despite notable improvements in agricultural development, public health, law and finance,[74] widespread rebellion broke out in July 1920, provoked, ironically, by the sudden efficiency of British administration, whose 'thoroughness [especially in raising taxes] and even . . . probity were unfamiliar, irksome, and unnecessary'.[75] In the aftermath of the rebellion, a strategy of more modest, light-touch and cheaper indirect rule was pursued under the shrewd and not unpopular direction of Sir Percy Cox. According to Ali Allawi, Cox, who was high commissioner and then ambassador to Iraq from 1920 to 1923,

> was a patient, determined and insightful man, and his knowledge of Arab affairs was probably greater than that of any other person . . . He also had the rare ability to see into the motives of people from a radically different culture . . . He was quite liked by ordinary Iraqis, who saw him as kindly, wise and tolerant, and many parents named their children 'Kawkuss' . . .[76]

A fundamental problem with imperial policy was that the British could not identify their own interests with much clarity or conviction. The costs of intervention in money and blood were a constant concern and limitation. In the run-up to the signing of the Anglo-Iraqi Treaty of October 1922, Winston Churchill, then secretary of state for the colonies, threatened immediate evacuation, much to King Faisal's alarm, who wrote to him, 'I can tell you with certainty . . . the dangers and injuries to myself and my country which would result from sudden and unnatural abandonment.'[77] But that did not stop the former prime minister, Herbert Asquith, from arguing in Parliament the following

February that Britain had no vital interests in Iraq and should withdraw forthwith.

Nevertheless, the British stayed for a further decade, fending off external aggressors, securing internal peace, protecting the rights of minorities, and giving Faisal time to pick his way between Shi'a clerics, radical nationalists and Kurdish separatists while trying to build up the institutions of a new, viable, effective and non-sectarian state. In June 1930 a second Anglo-Iraqi Treaty was signed, in which Britain recognised Iraq's independent responsibility for internal order and external defence, promised to withdraw all its forces, and undertook to train and supply the Iraqi Army. In return, the British were granted the right to be consulted about foreign policy and the use of two air bases for twenty-five years. This treaty came into force when the British Mandate came to an end upon Iraq's admission into the League of Nations as an independent state in October 1932. According to Ali Allawi, '[t]he overwhelming tenor of opinion in other Arab countries, especially in the Levant, was to contrast Iraq's political progress favourably with the travails of those countries still under French rule'.[78] Twelve months later, however, King Faisal died and was succeeded by his only son, Ghazi. In 1936 General Bakr Sidqi led the first of a succession of military coups, and in 1958 Faisal's twenty-three-year-old, Harrow-educated grandson, Faisal II, was murdered and the Hashemite monarchy overthrown in favour of a republic. While Britain had succeeded in establishing the new Iraqi state, its increasing independence necessarily reduced British control over its destiny.

IX

Thanks to Woodrow Wilson, president of the United States as it was emerging onto the international scene as a major power, the principle of national self-determination had come to direct the decision-making of the Paris Peace Conference in 1919. Consequently, that principle became integral to the mandate system of the League of Nations that the Treaty of Versailles established. According to Article 22 of the League's charter, 'the well-being and development' of those colonies and territories which, because of the recent Great War, had ceased to be under the sovereignty of the states formerly governing them, and 'which are inhabited by peoples not yet able to stand by themselves under the strenuous conditions of the modern world', was assigned as 'a sacred trust of civilisation' to 'advanced nations who by reason of their resources, their experience or their geographical position can best undertake this responsibility'.[79]

The post-war idea that 'advanced nations' were provisional trustees, charged with the responsibility of promoting the development of certain peoples to the point where they could stand on their own feet in the modern world, impressed itself upon the British Empire. But the idea was no novelty. The American War of Independence at the end of the eighteenth century had taught the British that their Empire should cede an increasing degree of autonomy to its constituent parts. Accordingly, colonies such as Canada, Australia, New Zealand and South Africa, where white settlers had come to dominate, were granted the status of dominions between 1867 and 1910 and became fully autonomous between the two world wars. However, the idea that autonomy was the destiny of colonies was not confined to the 'white dominions'. As far back as the 1820s Sir Thomas Munro, governor of Madras from 1819 to 1827, had written of the British presence in India to the EIC's Court of Directors:

Your rule is alien and it can never be popular. You have much to bring to your subjects, but you cannot look for more than passive gratitude. You are not here to turn India into England or Scotland. Work through, not in spite of, native systems and native ways, with a prejudice in their favour rather than against them; and when in the fullness of time your subjects can frame and maintain a worthy government for themselves, get out and take the glory of the achievement and the sense of having done your duty as the chief reward for your exertions.[80]

Munro's wise opinion was common among his peers. Exactly the same view was voiced by his fellow Scots, Mountstuart Elphinstone, governor of Bombay from 1819 to 1827, and Sir John Malcolm, his successor as governor from 1827 to 1830.[81]

So the effect of Woodrow Wilson's successful promotion of the principle of national self-determination at Versailles was not to impress upon the British Empire something novel and alien. Rather, it was to strengthen and push to the front a liberal rationale for empire that had long been present. After the First World War, therefore, and especially after the Second World War, when the view of the state as an agent of welfare was ascendant in Britain, colonial governments, supported by London, became increasingly intent upon economic, educational and political development.

X

There was no essential motive or set of motives that drove the British Empire. The reasons why the British built an empire were many and various. They differed between trader, migrant, soldier, missionary, entrepreneur, financier, government official and statesman. They sometimes differed between London, Cairo, Cape Town and Calcutta. And the reasons that dominated differed from one time to another. Almost all of the motives I have unearthed in this chapter were, in themselves, innocent: the aversion to poverty and persecution, the yearning for a better life, the desire to make one's way in the world, the duty to satisfy shareholders, the lure of adventure, cultural curiosity, the need to make peace and keep it, the concomitant need to maintain martial prestige, the imperative of gaining military or political advantage over enemies and rivals, and the vocation to lift oppression and establish stable self-government. There is nothing morally wrong with any of these. Indeed, the last one is morally admirable.

Good motives can be corrupted by vices, of course, and we have already seen evidence of greed and imprudence. Yet some degree of moral corruption is an invariable feature of human affairs, infecting even the noblest of endeavours. Moral malice or weakness is universal, but it need not be central or systemic. The charge of the anti-colonialists, however, is that the British colonial 'project' was systemically vitiated. Different systemic vices are proposed by different advocates for the prosecution, but the most common is the sheer love of lording it over inferior races. That is the overarching topic of the next two chapters, the first on slavery and the second on racism.

2

From Slavery to Anti-slavery

I

Colonialism and slavery – there is a connection between them, of course. Yet the reason for current interest in the topic assumes something much stronger – not merely a connection, but an equation. Contemporary agitators in the cause of 'decolonisation', whether campaigning for Rhodes Must Fall or Black Lives Matter, clamour that white Britons need to learn more about their ancestors' involvement in the slave trade and slavery, because the anti-black racism allegedly endemic in contemporary British society derives from the 'white supremacism' used to justify the enslavement of blacks in the seventeenth and eighteenth centuries. White Britons in the third decade of the twenty-first century, so it is claimed, view blacks now essentially as white slavers and planters did in the early eighteenth century. Racist colonialism is what connects them, and it needs to be exposed, confessed and repudiated through cultural decolonisation. This is the thesis that this chapter will test, as we explore the actual nature of the connection between the British Empire and slavery.

II

First, however, we should pause to think about what we mean by 'slavery'. Historically, there have been a variety of slaveries, various not only in their legal status and actual form, but also in their moral quality. For us, however, 'slavery', like 'torture' and 'genocide', refers to something simply, irredeemably and intolerably evil. What is it that we have in mind? What are the features of slavery that are simply evil?

One feature is hard labour. Yet many kinds of work are laborious, even soul-destroyingly tedious, without amounting to enslavement. Sometimes laborious work is performed under the terms of an unfair indenture or contract, to which the employee has consented only under duress – and yet an exploited employee does not quite make a slave.[1] Even 'forced labour' can fall well short of slavery. There is nothing necessarily wrong with requiring members of a community, by law or custom, to spend some of their time and energy on public works or in public service.

What distinguishes and specifies slavery as the simple evil that we now understand it to be is not hard labour, or an unfair contract, or legal compulsion. What specifies it is that the slave's time and employment are owned, not voluntarily under certain conditions for certain purposes and for a certain length of time, but absolutely. The slave is the slave-owner's disposable property, to be put to whatever use the owner decides, and to be bought and sold – and perhaps even killed – at will. That is the pure form or 'paradigm' of slavery, and it is the treatment of another human being as absolutely disposable property that makes it categorically worse than other forms of unjust employment.[2]

Nevertheless, it is important to remember that, historically, not everything that went by the name of 'slavery' lived down to this simply evil form. In different times and places the condition of the slave differed.[3] Sometimes there were legal or customary constraints on what owners were permitted to do with their human property: the right to ownership was not always absolute. For example, an owner was sometimes forbidden to strike or kill his slave, or obliged to grant him his freedom, under certain conditions. And where a failure of proprietorial duty was liable to incur legal penalties, and where those penalties were applied, there the slave had an enforceable right. Yet even where there were no legal constraints and no corresponding rights, slave-owners whose consciences retained a measure of sensitivity may have felt morally obliged to use their legal freedom humanely – say, by not selling a slave apart from his wife and children, if they could possibly avoid it.

However, when all the qualifications have been duly made, it remains the case that where a slave was radically dependent upon the will of his master for his livelihood, his family and even his life, and where that will was subject to little or no effective legal constraint, the institution of slavery was highly objectionable. For even if it did happen to occasion decent treatment, it did not secure it, and it also permitted the most dreadful abuse.

III

Slavery was not only various, but ancient. From the earliest times, victors in battle chose to enslave the vanquished rather than slaughter them. Counter-intuitive though it may be, therefore, slavery represented a moral advance. As the late-nineteenth-century moral philosopher David Ritchie put it, slavery was

> a necessary step in the progress of humanity . . . [since] [i]t mitigated the horrors of primitive warfare, and thus gave some scope for the growth, however feeble, of kindlier sentiments towards the alien and the weak . . . Thus slavery made possible the growth of the very ideas which in course of time came to make slavery appear wrong. Slavery seems to us horrible . . . It used not to seem horrible.[4]

Not only was it ancient; it was universal. Across the globe societies have employed forced labour in agriculture, mining, public works and even as troops. All the ancient Mesopotamian civilisations practised slavery in one form or another, starting with Egypt in the third millennium BC. To the west, around the shores of the Mediterranean Sea, the ancient Greeks, Carthaginians and Romans followed. To the east, slavery could be found among the Chinese from at least the seventh century AD, and subsequently among the Japanese and Koreans. In the Americas, the peoples on the northern Pacific coast practised it from before the sixth century AD,[5] the Incas and the Aztecs extracted forced labour from subject peoples from the fifteenth century, and the Comanches ran a slave economy from the eighteenth century.

From the time of Muhammad in the 600s onward, slavery was practised throughout the Islamic world. In the eighth and ninth centuries the Vikings supplied slave markets in Arab Spain and Egypt with slaves – *white* slaves – from eastern Europe and the British Isles. In the 1600s corsairs or pirates from the Barbary Coast of North Africa raided English merchant ships, and even villages in Cornwall and west Cork, for slaves. One estimate has it that raiders from Tunis, Algiers and Tripoli alone enslaved between 1 million and 1.25 million Europeans from the beginning of the sixteenth century to the middle of the eighteenth century.[6] Another estimate reckons that the Muslim slave trade as a whole, which lasted until 1920, transported about 17 million slaves, mostly African, exceeding by a considerable margin the approximately 11 million shipped by Europeans across the Atlantic.[7]

Meanwhile Africans had been enslaving other Africans for centuries, mostly by capturing them in war or raids, sometimes taking them in lieu of debt. Often slaves were destined for profitable export, first to Roman markets and then to Arab ones. But they also had their local uses, which included supplying victims for human sacrifices. The practice of human sacrifice in West Africa was attested as early as the tenth century by Ibn Hawqal,[8] and by Europeans four hundred years later. Human sacrifices – as distinct from the judicial execution of criminals – served a variety of purposes: sometimes to appease the gods, but more often to supply a deceased master with servants in the afterlife, to make a conspicuous display of extravagant wealth and to intimidate onlookers. Although wives, favourites, women and foreigners were also liable to serve as victims, slaves – usually war captives – were the main source. Commonly, their fate, especially at funerals, was to be buried alive. One report in 1797 has it that between 1,400 and 1,500 people were sacrificed at royal funerals in Asante.[9]

IV

Slavery and the slave trade, then, were alive and well in Africa long before Europeans arrived to develop the export market. The Portuguese

were the first to seek slaves from West Africa in the 1440s, to make up
for a labour shortage in Portugal and to man sugar plantations on their
Atlantic island possessions, not least Madeira. Between 1525 and 1866
the Portuguese Empire is reckoned to have shipped 5,841,468 slaves
out of Africa, amounting to 46.7 per cent of the total of African slave
exports of 12,508,381. After the Portuguese came the English – or, from
1707, the British – with 3,259,443 slaves exported, or 26.1 per cent of
the total, mostly between 1660 and 1807.[10] The exporting was primarily
done by merchants operating under the charter of the Royal African
Company, which had been granted not only a monopoly, but the right
(and obligation) to establish forts and 'factories' (trading posts), maintain troops and exercise martial law on the West African coast.[11] In fact,
the company was never able to secure its monopoly against interlopers,
and in 1698 that monopoly was formally withdrawn.[12]

The conditions under which slaves were transported across the
Atlantic were infamously dreadful, with the human cargo tightly packed
below decks, initially shackled, starved of daily fresh air and sunlight
for all but an hour or two, malnourished, dehydrated and prey to
disease for a voyage lasting up to six weeks. One African witness, who
survived the ordeal in the mid-1750s, described it thus:

> The stench of the hold . . . now that the whole ship's cargo were
> confined together . . . became absolutely pestilential. The closeness of
> the place, and the heat of the climate, added to the number in the ship,
> which was so crowded that each of us had scarcely room to turn himself,
> almost suffocated us. This produced copious perspirations, so that the
> air soon became unfit for respiration, from a variety of loathsome smells,
> and brought on a sickness among the slaves, of which many died . . .
> This wretched situation was again aggravated by the galling of the
> chains, now become insupportable; and the filth of the necessary tubs
> [latrine buckets], into which the children often fell, and were almost
> suffocated. The shrieks of the women, and the groans of the dying,
> rendered the whole a scene of horror almost inconceivable.[13]

General mortality statistics lay bare the scale of the suffering. According
to one estimate, of the African slaves shipped by British traders in

1672–87 a full 23 per cent were 'lost in transit'.[14] It seems that conditions became less dreadful later, since, according to another estimate, over the much longer period 1662–1807 13.2 per cent died before they reached the shores of the Americas.[15] However, even if this does represent a comparative improvement, it still amounts to the terrible loss of about 450,000 souls.

Most of those who survived the sea journey were deposited in the Caribbean, especially Barbados and Jamaica. Some were taken beyond to the coast of the American colonies, mostly south of New Jersey. There they were sold at auction as pieces of property or 'chattels', often separated from their families.[16] In the West Indies and southern American colonies they were put to work on plantations, probably producing sugar, though perhaps tobacco or rice. Organised into regimented gangs, they were subject to severe discipline, which was too often cruel. In 1654 a French priest, Antoine Biet, reported how one master in Barbados whipped a slave 'until he was all covered in blood', and then 'cut off one of his ears, had it roasted, and forced him to eat it'.[17] In 1680 an English clergyman berated Barbadian planters for inflicting on their slaves punishments such as castration, amputation and 'even Dissecting them alive'.[18] Punishment for rebellion could be even more sadistic. In 1675 after a failed slave revolt, several of the ringleaders were executed by being burned alive.[19] In 1741 the leader of the 'Great Negro Plot' in New York City suffered the same dreadful fate.[20] And in 1763 runaway slaves who were supposed to have confessed to the murder of two whites were burned alive 'by a slow fire behind the Court House' at Savanna-la-Mar in Jamaica.[21]

The treatment of slaves was not always so horrific. Sometimes masters regarded them with a certain benevolence as members of their extended household, taking a kindly interest in their lives. Sometimes slaves were manumitted, usually by paying an agreed price, less often by getting baptised or being granted their freedom in their master's last will and testament.

Notwithstanding that, the slave remained radically dependent on his master's will and accordingly vulnerable. Because slavery had not existed in England for centuries, the common law was completely silent on the status and treatment of slaves. Thus, the colonies were left free to formulate their own codes, which typically gave owners almost complete control over the movements of their slaves, whose company they kept and how they behaved. Unlike indentured servants, they 'effectively had no legal redress against maltreatment'.[22]

Further, the conditions of work were very harsh, especially on the sugar plantations. Slaves commonly toiled for their owners for up to twelve hours a day, six days a week, without pay. They were malnourished, labouring in a very debilitating climate and prey to a wide array of diseases. Not unsurprisingly, they suffered a high rate of mortality. As a result, before the ending of the slave trade, none of the sugar colonies in the West Indies managed to achieve a natural increase in the slave population. That is why they had to keep on bringing in fresh supplies of slaves. Even so, Jamaica, which had imported 575,000 Africans in the course of the eighteenth century, still only had 348,825 in 1807.[23]

V

Not every investor made money out of the slave trade. The Royal African Company, for example, struggled to make a profit partly because of its obligation to maintain forts on the coast of West Africa. Still, between 1770 and 1792 average profits per venture in the Bristol trade amounted to 7.6 per cent, and in the second half of the eighteenth century Liverpool shareholders could expect, in a normal year, a return of 8–10 per cent.[24]

Famously, in his seminal *Capitalism and Slavery* (1944), the Trinidadian historian Eric Williams argued that profits from the slave trade provided a major source of capital for financing Britain's world-leading industrial revolution and made 'an enormous contribution to Britain's industrial development'.[25] This thesis has been controversial. Williams himself was quite clear in not claiming that the slave trade was 'solely and entirely responsible for industrial development'.[26] So the controversy has concerned its effect relative to other factors. In the late 1960s Roger Anstey minimised its effect by calculating that the profits from the slave trade fell far below Williams' estimate and could not have financed the industrial revolution to a significant extent.[27] Anstey's general view has been confirmed more recently by David Richardson, who estimated that profits from the slave trade probably contributed under 1 per cent of total domestic investment around 1790.[28] In 2010, David Brion Davis, the distinguished historian of slavery and its abolition in the Western world, confidently pronounced the last rites on Williams' thesis, declaring that it 'has now been wholly discredited by other scholars'.[29]

The slave trade is one thing; slavery itself is another. Some argue that, of all economic sectors, the Atlantic slave-based economy – especially sugar production – made the most significant contribution to Britain's industrial development.[30] Yet David Eltis and Stanley L. Engerman are highly sceptical: 'Sugar was just one of hundreds of industries in a complex economy; and while sugar was one of the larger industries, its linkages with the rest of the economy and its role as an "engine" of economic growth compare poorly with textiles, coal, iron ore, and those British agricultural activities which provided significant inputs to industry.'[31] Another economic historian, Joel Mokyr, agrees: 'In the absence of West Indian slavery, Britain would have had to drink bitter tea, but it still would have had an Industrial Revolution, if perhaps at a marginally slower pace.'[32]

Nevertheless, the slave economies of British colonies did serve to fuel the growth of external trade and thereby generate the accumulation of further capital. The growing demand for sugar on the part of British consumers stimulated increased production in the West Indies, which in turn stimulated the importation of clothing and equipment from Britain and slaves from Africa. The economic historian Kenneth Morgan reports an argument that Caribbean-based demand might have been responsible for about 35 per cent of the growth of total British exports between 1748 and 1776, and for about 12 per cent of the growth in British industrial output in the third quarter of the 1700s. He then comments judiciously:

> The growth in English exports supplied to the Americas in the mid-eighteenth century helped to expand production in the textile, metal, and hardware industries in Britain. The need to provide such export goods at an accelerating rate may well have aided the diffusion

of technical innovation, notably in cotton spinning, to the British textile industry. And so it is likely that the main stimulus of the slave trade to the British economy lay in the channels of increasing demand. It would be incorrect to claim that the wealth flowing home from the slave trade was a major stimulus for industrialization in Britain, but it would not be unfair to claim that the slave-sugar complex strengthened the British economy and played a significant, though not decisive part, in its evolution.[33]

VI

As the effects of colonial slavery upon Britain are controversial, so are its effects on Africa. And they are likely to remain so, since data on trends in output and population in pre-colonial Africa are scarce. Some argue that the Atlantic slave trade made little difference to most of Africa, though it might have had a greater impact on the population and wealth of societies along its Atlantic coast.[34] Others hold that it had devastating consequences, causing widespread depopulation and economic dislocation, undermining the socio-political fabric of African societies, and propagating forms of slavery and servitude hitherto unknown.[35]

Although it is impossible to calculate the costs to Africa of the slave trade with any precision, it makes sense to suppose that British (and European) demand for slaves stimulated African endeavour to supply – and thereby an increase in war and slave-raiding in West and Central Africa. While the British investors and merchants bear responsibility for that, so do their African suppliers. Commercial and political elites in West and Central Africa 'appear to have made large profits from helping to meet the American demand for slave labour'.[36]

VII

The British were actively involved in the slave trade for about one hundred and fifty years until 1807, and in employing slave labour for almost three decades beyond that, until 1834. Before about 1770, few condemned the institution of slavery as such. Even the maroons – runaway slaves who hid out in the forested interiors of Jamaica and elsewhere – were prepared to secure their own autonomy in 1739 by agreeing to stop freeing slaves and to assist white settlers in suppressing slave revolts.[37] They also kept slaves of their own.[38] Nevertheless, in the second half of the eighteenth century both the trade and the institution came under mounting public criticism in Britain. Two main intellectual streams fuelled the opposition. One was a body of Enlightenment philosophers, which included the Baron de Montesquieu and Adam Smith. In his highly influential *De l'esprit des lois* (1748, translated into English two years later), the former objected to slavery because of its demoralising effects on both parties: by robbing the slave of his freedom, it makes it impossible for him to act 'through a motive of virtue', and because, 'by having an unlimited authority over his slaves [the master] insensibly accustoms himself to the want of all moral virtues, and from thence becomes fierce, hasty, severe, choleric, voluptuous, and cruel'.[39] Smith went further, romanticising Africans in his *Theory of Moral Sentiments* (1759) and attributing to the slave a superior moral dignity:

There is not a Negro from the coast of Africa who does not . . . possess a degree of magnanimity which the soul of his sordid master is too often scarce capable of receiving. Fortune never exerted more cruelly her empire over mankind than when she subjected those [African] nations of heroes to the refuse of the gaols of Europe, to wretches who possess the virtues neither of the countries which they come from, nor of those which they go to, and whose levity, brutality, and baseness, so justly expose them to the contempt of the vanquished.[40]

The second, more popular, intellectual catalyst for the emergence of the movement to abolish the slave trade and slavery in the late eighteenth century was Christian. Anti-slavery sentiment flourished widely among English Dissenters or Nonconformists – especially the Quakers – and the Methodist or evangelical wing of the Church of England. John Wesley, Anglican priest and founder of Methodism, prefaced his *Thoughts upon Slavery* (1774) with a quotation of the tenth verse of the fourth chapter of the Book of Genesis: 'And the Lord said

– What hast thou done? The voice of thy brother's blood crieth unto me from the ground' (Genesis 4:10). The context is Cain's murder of his brother Abel and the implication is clear: African and Englishman, slave and master, are brothers, common children of the same God. In what follows Wesley counters the argument that slavery rescues Africans from an even worse plight, by presenting evidence, first, of the prosperity, culture and high social organisation of West African peoples, and then of the barbaric treatment meted out to them as slaves by their English masters. As he draws to a close, Wesley addresses readers who have inherited slaves:

> Perhaps you will say, 'I do not *buy* any negroes: I only *use* those left me by my father.' – So far is well; but is it enough to satisfy your own conscience? Had your father, have *you*, has any man living, a right to use another as a slave? . . . It cannot be, that either war, or contract, can give any man such a property in another as he has in sheep and oxen. Much less is it possible, that any child of man, should ever be *born a slave*. Liberty is the right of every human creature, as soon as he breathes the vital air. And no human law can deprive him of that right, which he derives from the law of nature.
>
> If therefore you have any regard to justice, (to say nothing of mercy, nor of the revealed law of GOD) render unto all their due. Give liberty to whom liberty is due, that is to every child of man, to every partaker of human nature. Let none serve you but by his own act and deed, by his own voluntary choice. – Away with all whips, all chains, all compulsion! Be gentle towards men. And see that you invariably do unto every one, as you would he should do unto *you*.[41]

Anti-slavery sentiment acquired practical, political focus in 1787 with the founding of the Society for the Abolition of the Slave Trade in London. Among its founding members was Thomas Clarkson, who promoted the sale of the autobiography of Olaudah Equiano, a former slave from West Africa,[42] and who collaborated with William Wilberforce and other members of the Clapham Sect in mounting and sustaining a campaign both inside and outside Parliament.[43] Extra-parliamentary agitation was considerable: in 1791 about 30 per cent of the adult male population of Britain signed anti-slavery petitions.[44] Events overseas also played an important part in shaping public opinion at home. The 1791 rebellion of slaves in Saint-Domingue, which neither the French nor the British could suppress and which culminated in the foundation of the independent, black-led Republic of Haiti in 1804, helped to give abolition the appearance of historical inevitability.

The efforts of the campaigners finally bore fruit in 1807, when Parliament legislated to abolish the slave trade. It took a further twenty-six years to achieve the empire-wide abolition of the institution of slavery itself, initially because the leading abolitionists were politically conservative and assumed that cutting off fresh supplies of slaves would doom the slave-based economies to wither naturally, gradually, and with minimal disruption. Even most black abolitionists were gradualists until the 1820s.[45]

However, when the plantations proved more resilient than had been expected, agitation to hasten abolition picked up steam. In an attempt to slow things down, the government presented the colonial legislatures with proposals to ameliorate the condition of the slaves in 1823. These included granting the right to present evidence in court, removing hindrances to manumission, establishing savings banks for slaves and imposing legal restrictions on punishments. Yet whereas the government's proposals could bind the Crown colonies, they could not oblige the older ones such as Barbados and Jamaica, which enjoyed the right to self-government and had their own legislative assemblies. There London's efforts at amelioration ran into fierce resistance.[46] This was one factor in converting cautious, conservative minds to the cause of immediate abolition. Another was the savage retribution meted out to black rebels (and their white missionary supporters) in the slave revolts in Demerara in 1823 and Jamaica in 1831–2. In July 1832, Lord Howick, under-secretary of state for the colonies, wrote to the new governor of Jamaica: 'The present state of things cannot go on much longer . . . Emancipation alone will effectually avert the danger.'[47] The following year Parliament passed the Slavery Abolition Act, which came into effect twelve months later. Thus, on 1 August 1834 slaves throughout the British Empire were formally emancipated.

VIII

One controversial feature of the process of abolition was the agreement to compensate slave-owners for their loss of property to the tune of £20 million, which was paid by the government and funded by metropolitan taxpayers. That concession is controversial today and it was controversial then. The government was already committed to abolition, but it preferred to win the consent of the West Indian planters rather than have to coerce them. The shadow of the French Revolution and its Terror was long and made unthinkable the idea of the state riding roughshod over the right to property. The payment of compensation to the slave-owners was considered a distasteful but necessary political compromise.[48] The Anti-Slavery Society, which had been founded by Wilberforce and Clarkson in 1823, was not happy with many aspects of the Slavery Abolition bill, but supported it rather than jeopardise the momentum towards emancipation. Clarkson was quite unapologetic about the compensation, viewing it 'not as an indemnification but as money well paid for procuring the cooperation of the West India Planters and Legislators, without which the abolition of slavery might have been materially obstructed and retarded, if not prevented'.[49]

Also controversial at the time was the requirement that, as a transitional arrangement, all slaves over the age of six should first become apprenticed labourers bound to perform unpaid work for their former masters for between forty and forty-five hours a week, for up to six years. Only work undertaken over and above that would be paid. Upon completion of this period of apprenticeship, the slaves would be fully emancipated. Although special imperial magistrates were appointed to supervise the system and ensure fair play, they were too few, too underpaid and too weak vis-à-vis the colonial assemblies to be effective. The result was that planters were able to hinder black apprentices from developing economic independence, and to continue exploiting their labour. However, revived abolitionist agitation in Britain, combined with signs of unrest among apprentices in the British Caribbean, persuaded the government to end the transitional system two years early on 31 July 1838. In Jamaica, Trinidad and British

Guiana, many emancipated slaves found unsettled land on which to subsist, but in smaller colonies such as Antigua and Barbados, where free land was not readily available, employment on the plantations remained the only option.

In recent times the greatest controversy attending the abolition of the slave trade and of slavery itself has stemmed from another thesis proposed by Eric Williams, whom we met earlier. In *Capitalism and Slavery* (1944) not only did Williams hold that profits from the trade had financed Britain's industrial revolution, he also argued that the trade and the institution had been abolished because they were no longer profitable. This second thesis has been quite as contentious as the first. Against Williams, Roger Anstey demonstrated in 1975 that, in terms of economic interest, 1806–7 was the worst possible time for Britain to abolish its slave trade, embroiled as it was in a long war with Napoleon.[50] Two years later Seymour Drescher published *Econocide: British Slavery in the Era of Abolition* (1977), which presented a mass of empirical evidence that abolition amounted to an act of suicide for a major part of Britain's economy.[51] Drescher showed that the value of trade between the West Indies and Britain had increased sharply from the early 1780s to the end of the eighteenth century, and that the West Indies' share of total British overseas trade did not enter long-term decline until well after the flow of fresh supplies of slave labour had been cut off by Parliament. Although Williams continues to have his supporters, it is fair to say that the weight of judgement among contemporary historians falls heavily against him.[52]

IX

The strength of abolitionist feeling in Britain was so great that it did not relax after Parliament had been persuaded to abolish the slave trade and slavery within the British Empire; it went on to persuade the imperial government to adopt a permanent policy of trying to suppress both the trade and the institution worldwide. One sign of this enduring commitment was the emergence in the Foreign Office of a separate Slave Trade Department from 1819, which was in fact the Office's largest department in the 1820s and 1830s and maintained its independence until 1883, when it was incorporated into the Consular and African Department.[53] During the Congress of Vienna in 1814–15 Britain used its diplomatic clout to try to secure support for a general abolition treaty between all the major European powers, but in vain. Before and after the congress, however, it did succeed in getting nearly all the states still involved in the Atlantic slave trade to agree in principle to end it – including Portugal, Spain, France, Brazil and the United States. However, none would consent to a reciprocal right to search suspect shipping, which was required to give practical bite to the principle. Nevertheless, the British government persisted to such an extent that in 1842 the foreign secretary, Lord Aberdeen, saw fit to describe anti-slavery diplomacy as a 'new and vast branch of international relations'.[54]

In addition to the diplomatic velvet glove, the British also deployed the naval hard fist. Up to ten ships of the Royal Navy were stationed off the coast of West Africa to disrupt the export of slaves until 1833. Over the next ten years their number rose as high as nineteen, and from 1844 to 1865 it seldom fell below twenty, for several consecutive years stayed at over thirty, and twice reached a peak of thirty-six. At its height, the West African station employed 13.1 per cent of the Royal Navy's total manpower.[55] From 1839 naval patrols extended south of the Equator, and in 1845 the Slave Trade Act authorised the Navy to treat as pirates Brazilian ships suspected of carrying slaves, to arrest those responsible and to have them tried in British Admiralty courts. In 1850 Navy ships began trespassing into Brazilian territorial waters to accost slave ships, sometimes even entering its harbours and on one occasion exchanging fire with a fort. In September of that year Brazil yielded to the pressure, enacted legislation comprehensively outlawing the slave trade and began to enforce it rigorously. Shortly before his death in 1865 Lord Palmerston, twice prime minister, wrote that 'the achievement which I look back on with the greatest and purest pleasure was forcing the Brazilians to give up their slave trade'.[56]

Meanwhile, back in West Africa, the British employed a variety of means to achieve the same end. The thesis of Sir Thomas Fowell Buxton – proposed in his 1839 book *The African Slave Trade and Its Remedy*[57] – that the key to ending the slave trade and slavery in Africa was to promote alternative, 'legitimate' commerce had found wide acceptance. This led to the setting up of trading posts, and then, when the merchants complained of the lack of security, a more assertive colonial presence on land.[58] The year after strong-arming Brazil, the British attacked Lagos and destroyed its slaving facilities, having tried in vain to persuade its ruler to terminate the commerce in slaves. In 1861, when an attempt was made to revive the trade, they annexed Lagos as a colony.

On the other side of the continent the British brought persistent diplomatic pressure to bear upon the Sultanate of Zanzibar, which was the main port for the Great Lakes slave trade, but which also depended on the Royal Navy to protect its shipping from pirates in the Indian Ocean. Treaties were signed banning trade in slaves to the Americas in 1822 and to the more important Persian Gulf in 1845. In 1873 the sultan gave way when Sir Bartle Frere, governor of Bombay and a resolute opponent of the East African slave trade, threatened a naval blockade unless the export of slaves from the African mainland ceased altogether and the slave market was shut down once and for all. Bit by bit the trade in slaves was throttled. The institution of domestic slavery, however, was tolerated until Zanzibar became a British protectorate in 1890. Between then and 1909 a series of measures gradually emancipated slaves, first of all granting them rights against maltreatment and of self-redemption, then adding a right to obtain freedom on application to the courts. Here, too, slave-owners were compensated for their loss, partly in recognition that domestic slavery was sanctioned by Islamic law, but also to minimise the economic disturbance and political opposition.[59]

The humanitarian motive to suppress the slave trade and slavery remained a common reason for imperial endeavour in Africa from the late nineteenth century into the twentieth. It caused the British government to lean upon the khedive of Egypt to sign the Anglo-Egyptian Slave Trade Convention in 1877. It propelled General Charles Gordon into the Sudan in the same year. It found expression in the principles of the Imperial British East Africa Company, when it was founded in 1888. It featured among the reasons for establishing a British protectorate in Nyasaland in 1891. And it was one reason for the invasion of the Sokoto Caliphate (now northern Nigeria) by Frederick Lugard in 1903.

Imperial intentions to stop the slave trade in the Atlantic and Indian oceans were comparatively easy to realise through the Royal Navy's command of the seas. Success in suppressing the trade across the African mainland was more difficult to achieve, because it required the control of large swathes of territory. The elimination of the practice of slavery was also difficult, because it often involved interfering with a long-established and deeply embedded social institution, hallowed by custom, and legitimated by law and religion. Therefore, it risked causing major economic disruption, provoking fierce political opposition and having to compel compliance with resources that were usually very limited. For those reasons, some officials in the East India Company opposed action against slavery in India.[60] Notwithstanding this, the company eventually passed the Indian Slavery Act in 1843, which forbad officers in the discharge of their public duties from being involved in the trading of slaves or from enforcing rights of property in slaves, and which granted slaves the right to own property and equality under the penal law. Eighteen years later, the Indian Penal Code of 1860 proceeded to make the enslavement and trading of persons criminal offences.[61]

Further east in what is now Malaysia and Indonesia, however, the company was much bolder. Shortly after the Slave Trade Act was passed in 1807, in the person of Sir Stamford Raffles it summarily abolished the importation of slaves and slavery itself on the island of Penang. Subsequently, Raffles banned slave importation in Java, and in 1818–19 he emancipated the slaves in Bencoolen and established a school for their children.[62]

X

The task of estimating the cost of all the empire's various efforts to abolish the slave trade and slavery at sea and on land, worldwide, over the course of a century and a half, would present – at the very least – a major challenge both in scale and in complexity. No one, to my knowledge, has tried it. Some, however, have developed an estimate of the expense of transatlantic suppression alone. David Eltis reckoned that this cost British taxpayers a *minimum* of £250,000 per annum – which equates to £1.367–1.74 billion, or 9.1–11.5 per cent of the UK's expenditure on development aid, in 2019 – for half a century.[63] Moreover 'in absolute terms the British spent almost as much attempting to suppress the trade in the forty-seven years, 1816–62, as they received in profits over the same length of time leading up to 1807. And by any more reasonable assessment of profits and direct costs, the nineteenth-century costs of suppression were certainly bigger than the eighteenth-century benefits.'[64]

Chaim Kaufmann and Robert Pape took a broader view. In addition to the costs of naval suppression, they considered the loss of business caused by abolition to British manufacturers, shippers, merchants and bankers who dealt with the West Indies. They also factored in the higher prices paid by British consumers for sugar, since duties were imposed to protect free-grown British sugar from competition by foreign producers who continued to benefit from unpaid slave labour. Overall, they 'estimate the economic cost to British metropolitan society of the anti-slave trade effort at roughly 1.8 per cent of national income over sixty years from 1808 to 1867'.[65] Although the comparisons are not exact, they do illuminate: in 2021 the UK spent 0.5 per cent of GDP on international aid and just over 2 per cent on national defence. Kaufmann and Pape conclude that Britain's effort to suppress the Atlantic slave trade (alone) in 1807–67 was 'the most expensive example [of costly international moral action] recorded in modern history'.[66]

XI

Set in the context of the history of the world, or even just of Europe, Britain's involvement in slavery was nothing out of the ordinary. Everyone was involved, including, as we have seen in the case of the maroons, self-emancipated slaves. Moreover, British slave-owners were not universally sadistic and inhumane. Nevertheless, it remains true that the transatlantic transportation of slaves, and the treatment of them in the sugar fields, was usually brutal, often cruel and invariably life-shortening. In general, the injustice was grave, systemic and massive.

In this case, as in so many others, by 1807 and 1834 most of those who had suffered the injustice were dead and their grievance lay far beyond remedy, short of some God-given Final Judgement. The British could not undo the past, but they did do the next best thing: they repented of it and liberated the still living. And with due respect to Eric Williams, they did not just repent when it was economically convenient to do so. They did so because many of them had come to believe that making another human being one's disposable property both corrupted the owner and violated the dignity of the owned – because they had come to view slavery as morally repugnant. They abolished the slave trade within the empire, in spite of the advantage they were thereby handing commercial rivals, who would continue to benefit from employing cheap, wage-free labour in sugar production, and in spite of the loss of business to English exporters to the West Indies. And they abolished slavery itself, in spite of the higher price that British consumers would have to pay for freely produced sugar, and in spite of the cost to the taxpayer of compensating the slave-owners for the loss of their property in the sum of £20 million, which was about 40 per cent of the government's budget at the time. For sure, enslaved and freed Africans played important parts, too – through the example of the creation of the black Republic of Haiti, through the eloquent witness of Equiano and others, and through the slave rebellions that exposed the savagery of their masters. But the fact of black agency does not displace the fact of white agency. Both were in play.

The decision to compensate the slave-owners in 1833 is often used by anti-colonialists to discredit the abolition movement today, as Eric Williams' thesis sought to discredit it in 1944. There is no denying that it was a political compromise, but peaceful politics usually requires compromise, and some compromises are morally justified, even obligatory. Besides, the planters claimed that they faced ruin without compensation and, given the (to them) novel, additional cost of paying wages to previously slave labour, that claim is plausible. Even with compensation, many planters sold up within twenty years of emancipation, which suggests that their business model was indeed precarious. In 1834, for example, there were 670 sugar plantations in Jamaica; by 1854 that number had dropped by over half to 330.[67] From this it is reasonable to infer that, without compensation in 1833, at least some plantations would have gone bankrupt, with the consequent loss of employment opportunities for those free slaves, who, for one reason or another, could not find land of their own on which to subsist – especially on Antigua and Barbados. Many ex-slaves chose to stay working on plantations after the end of apprenticeship, because of the housing, medical care and food provided.

Subsequent attempts by the British Empire to suppress slavery were often attended by political compromise, because however powerful the empire was, its power was not infinite. It did not have the resources to send ships or troops to every part of the globe, in order to impose its will. And even when it did send troops, it sometimes came off worst. Notoriously, in 1842 a British army of 4,500 (plus 12,000 camp followers) was annihilated in its retreat from Afghanistan. In 1879 1,300 British and colonial troops were overwhelmed by Zulu warriors at Isandlwana in South Africa. And in 1883 an 8,000-strong Anglo-Egyptian army was massacred at El Obeid in the Sudan by the forces of the Mahdi, the purported redeemer of Islam. In this last case, the suppression of the slave trade was among the grievances of the Mahdists.[68] Lacking the power always to impose, the empire often had to act against slavery by increments, being careful not to excite too much opposition. Basil Cave, who was consul-general in Zanzibar when domestic slavery was finally abolished in 1909, bore witness to this when he reflected with satisfaction on the local history of British efforts at abolition:

> . . . all the time British influence was being steadily brought to bear upon the Sultan . . . Whenever an opportunity presented itself, when the Sultan appealed for political, financial, or personal assistance, when some benefit was offered or conferred . . . occasion was always taken to introduce some fresh anti-slavery measure and to move one more step forward towards final abolition.[69]

As a result, 'the whole of the servile population of East Africa has been freed from bondage without a hand, and almost without a voice, being raised in protest'.[70]

The desire to avoid provoking political opposition was not the only reason for moving gradually: there was also the recognition that the practice of domestic slavery in the Islamic world was generally not as inhumane as the plantation slavery of the West Indies. As Lord Cromer, the British reformer of Egyptian government from 1877 to 1907, put it, domestic slavery could command 'mitigating pleas', which, while not justifying its existence, should 'temper the zeal of the reformer who aspires towards its immediate abolition'. He believed that as a general rule, slaves in Egypt were well treated, and 'it may be doubted whether in the majority of cases the lot of slaves in Egypt is, in its material aspects, harder than, or even as hard as that of many domestic servants in Europe'. Indeed, whereas the latter could be thrown out of employment at any moment, '[c]ustom, based on religious law, obliges [an Egyptian master] to support his slave', if the latter chose not to emancipate himself. Besides, almost all the slaves in Egypt were women, and when they left the harems, they had no means of supporting themselves. Therefore, to have summarily abolished the legal status of slavery would have been 'in the highest degree imprudent'.[71] And imprudence is a moral vice.

XII

The basic problem with the anti-colonialists' equation of British colonialism with slavery, and their consequent demand for cultural 'decolonisation', is that it requires amnesia about everything that has happened since 1787. It requires us to overlook how widely popular in Britain was the cause of abolition from the closing decades of the eighteenth century onward. For example, referring specifically to the project to settle freed loyalist slaves from the American colonies in Sierra Leone in 1787, Stephen Braidwood concludes: 'the great majority of newspaper items [covering the expedition] . . . were sympathetic in tone. The fact of intermarriage and the good public response to the Committee's appeal for money to help poor blacks also indicate that racial hostility may have been less common than has often been assumed.'[72] Commenting on the following century, John Stauffer confirms this conclusion. 'Almost every United States black who travelled in the British Isles,' he writes, 'acknowledged the comparative dearth of racism there. Frederick Douglass noted after arriving in England in 1845: "I saw in every man a recognition of my manhood, and an absence, a perfect absence, of everything like that disgusting hate with which we are pursued in [the United States]."'[73]

Between the slave trade and slavery of the eighteenth century and the present lie a hundred and fifty years of imperial penance in the form of costly abolitionist endeavour to liberate slaves around the globe. For the second half of its life, *anti-slavery*, not slavery, was at the heart of imperial policy. The vicious racism of slavers and planters was not essential to the British Empire, and whatever racism exists in Britain today is not its fruit.[74]

3

Human Equality, Cultural
Superiority and 'Racism'

I

The British Empire cannot be equated with slavery, since, during the second half of the empire's life, imperial policy was consistently committed to abolishing it. It follows that whatever racism persists in Britain today cannot claim direct descent from the inhumane mentality of slave-owners and -masters in the eighteenth and early nineteenth centuries. However, that alone does not acquit the empire of the charge of predominant racism, since other causes might have generated it. So, notwithstanding its anti-slavery efforts, was the British Empire centrally, essentially racist?

II

As with slavery, so with racism, before considering its bearing on the empire, we first need to reflect on what we mean by it. All the more so, because the meaning of 'racism' has so expanded in recent times that it obscures several morally significant distinctions and is made to apply to some phenomena that do not deserve it. An uncontroversial, formal definition of 'racism' would be 'a pejorative attitude of a member of one race for all members of another race'. So understood, what is objectionable about 'racism' is what is objectionable about any prejudice directed at other people – whether they are members of a race, a nation, a social class or a religion – namely, that it *pre-judges* the individual by regarding him or her simply as a member of a group, automatically attributing to the individual that group's supposed characteristics, which are stereotyped in unflattering terms. So the sins of racism are two: first, the racial group is viewed in relentlessly negative terms; and second, the individual is not permitted to appear as anything other than a member of such a group. The group is simplified negatively, and the dignity of individuality is brushed aside.

What distinguishes racism from other kinds of prejudice such as social snobbery, or national chauvinism, or religious bigotry, is that its object is not simply a class of people within a society, or a body of citizens of a state, or a religious community. Its object is 'a race'. In this context, what is meant by 'a race' is not susceptible of precise definition. In the late nineteenth and early twentieth centuries, for example, there was a lot of talk of 'the Anglo-Saxon race', that is, people who share an English cultural and political heritage, sometimes even including Americans. More commonly nowadays 'race' is used, even more imprecisely, to lump together all people who have white or non-white skins, obliterating all manner of finer distinction between different kinds of white or black. The safest definition of a 'race' is still a vague one: it refers to an ethnic group marked by distinctive physical and cultural features.

Nowadays the sin of 'racism' has been loosened and broadened to mean any negative judgement made by a member of one race upon the culture of another, but especially by a 'white' person upon a 'black' culture. This assumes a basic cultural equality and a radical moral relativism and is designed to contradict Western assumptions of superiority. Insofar as all cultures are supposed to be equal in their different kinds of sophistication and their moral systems, no member of one culture can stand in moral judgement upon any other. Yet when I as a twenty-first-century Briton look back at my medieval forbears, it seems obvious that my culture is superior to theirs in a wide array of respects – scientific knowledge, medical practice, economic productivity, social equality, political freedom and public safety. And the common colloquial tendency to use the word 'medieval' as a synonym for 'barbaric' suggests that I am not alone in that perception. But if it is permissible to stand in judgement on a previous phase of one's own culture and reckon it inferior in certain respects, why would it suddenly become impermissible to stand in judgement on an analogous phase in a foreign culture? Thus, when Cecil Rhodes landed in South Africa in 1870 and encountered Bantu Africans, it was manifestly obvious to him that British civilisation at the time was superior – in natural science, technology, finance, communications, commerce, naval power and liberal political institutions – and common sense surely tells us that he was not wrong. Cultures have always judged one another in this fashion. In the medieval period Muslim Arab geographers and philosophers compared their own cultural sophistication favourably to what seemed to them the more primitive cultures of white northern Europeans and black Africans, attributing the natural inferiority in both cases to an intemperate climate, respectively too cold and too hot.[1] In the late eighteenth and early nineteenth centuries the imperial Qing dynasty in China regarded the British – and other Westerners – as barbarians, without any embarrassment at all. And in the 1940s, Gerald Hanley, then an officer in the British Army, found Somalis unshakeable in their prejudice against other black peoples:

> I had once tried hard to get the Somalis to give up their contempt for Bantu people . . . 'We cannot obey slaves', Somalis told me. 'It is impossible for us to live under slave people even when they are in [British] uniform and have arms' . . . I . . . could not change . . . the memory they [the Somalis] had of a time when these Bantu people were slave material for the Muslim world to the north. That was the trouble, the curse of race, looks, noses, lips, eyes, legends. Colour has little to do with it.[2]

There may be solid grounds for reckoning one's own culture superior to another in certain respects. As a rule, however, it is unwise to suppose that superiority to be absolute. No culture is perfect: and no culture is entirely lacking in merit. There were plenty of Britons whose imperial self-confidence did not prevent them making discriminate judgements and recognising virtue and value when they came across

them in America, Africa and Asia. For one famous example, take David
Livingstone's assessment of Africans in 1857: 'I have found it difficult
to come to a conclusion on their [Africans'] character. They sometimes
perform actions remarkably good, and sometimes as strangely the
opposite . . . After long observation, I came to the conclusion that they
are just a strange mixture of good and evil as men are everywhere
else.'[3] Similar sentiments were expressed a century later by David
Lovatt Smith, who served as a field intelligence officer during the Mau
Mau uprising in colonial Kenya in the 1950s. In his novel, *My Enemy:
My Friend*, he writes of his fictional counterpart, George Harris, that
he

> believed passionately that it was erroneous, patronising and downright
> dangerous to make comparisons between Africans living in Africa and
> Western man, because they had advanced on parallel but completely
> different planes; one neither higher nor lower than the other and one
> neither superior nor inferior to the other. Because their environment
> differed so greatly, they were aiming at entirely different goals . . . where
> would he [an African] be if, throughout history and up to colonial
> times, in the harsh environment of Africa, he had shown compassion
> towards neighbouring tribes and all those that were a threat to him
> and to his family? If he had borne the same compassion as Westerners,
> he could never have endured the environment where only the strong
> and the fittest survived.[4]

Moreover, even imperfect, relative superiority is never forever: whatever
advantage was won yesterday can be lost tomorrow.

III

The making of adverse judgements about another people's culture
need not be racist, if it is discriminate. Nor need it be racist, if it
attributes cultural inferiority to a lack of development, rather than
biological nature. To attribute it to biology is to regard a people as
incapable of development, as naturally inferior, and as fit always to be
ruled by others and never to participate in self-government. As

observed in previous chapters, the Christian view of all humans, white and black, as fellow children of God, fuelled criticism of the inhumane treatment of African slaves and propelled efforts to Christianise, civilise and modernise indigenous peoples in the first half of the nineteenth century. In the second half, however, the disappointment of early hopes of rapid improvement under colonial tutelage helped to put wind in the sails of the pessimistic, natural, biological explanation for the underdeveloped state of indigenous peoples.[5] Nonetheless, even in the final years of the century those were still not the terms in which the likes of Rhodes saw Africans. As we saw in the Introduction, he made this clear in a parliamentary speech given in 1894, when he declared: 'Now, I say the natives are children. They are just emerging from barbarism. They have human minds . . . we ought to do something for the minds and the brains that the Almighty has given them. *I do not believe that they are different from ourselves.*'[6] Because he believed in the possibility of African cultural development, Rhodes never sought to overturn the liberal, colour-blind franchise that had existed in Cape Colony since 1853, and which had given rise to a small black electorate.[7] And when in 1899 the Cape government proposed legislation that would have disenfranchised most native people, Rhodes protested, arguing that he had 'always differentiated between the raw barbarians and the civilised natives' and that the vote should be extended to Africans under the principle of 'equal rights to every civilised man south of the Zambesi'. The previous year, when asked to clarify what he meant by 'civilised man', he had added 'a man, white or black . . . who has sufficient education to write his name, has some property, or works. In fact, is not a loafer.'[8]

Rhodes' view echoed that of J. S. Mill, the great patriarch of Victorian liberalism, who, during the American Civil War, proved himself one of the most uncompromising and outspoken critics of slavery in the American south. Nevertheless, in the opening chapter of his classic 1859 treatise *On Liberty*, Mill wrote: 'Those who are still in a state to require being taken care of by others, must be protected against their own actions as well as against external injury . . . Despotism is a legitimate mode of government in dealing with barbarians, provided the end be their improvement, and the means justified by actually effecting that end.'[9] However patronising and uncompromising that sounds, it did not condemn barbarians as naturally barbaric; it affirmed the possibility of their change, improvement, civilisation. The barbarian's human *potential* was no less than anyone else's. In that basic respect, the barbarian and the civilised person were equally human. The difference was cultural, not natural. As Henry Melvill, principal of the East India Company College, wrote in 1846: 'Am I the keeper of the Hindu, the Indian, the Hottentot? . . . Is the savage my brother? If all have sprung from the same parents then the wild wanderer, the painted barbarian, is thy brother, though civilisation may have separated you by so wide an interval that you can scarcely seem to belong to the same race.'[10]

IV

Still, even if Mill's and Rhodes' views were not biologically racist, they will probably strike the contemporary reader as insufferably patronising. Yet even if that is a problem, it cannot be considered a racist problem in Rhodes' case at least, since he was indiscriminate in regarding other people as like children in needing guidance. In 1899, for example, he referred to the Fellows of Oriel College as 'children' (in financial management), when he stipulated that they should consult trustees about managing his benefaction.[11]

What is more, it surely cannot always be patronising to believe that foreign people need help, guidance or protection. Sometimes they do in fact need help, and sometimes they themselves know it. In 1919 the League of Nations believed that certain peoples formerly governed by the ousted Turks needed the support of an 'advanced nation' to 'stand by themselves under the strenuous conditions of the modern world'.[12] And King Faisal of Iraq – a man quite secure in his own self-respect – agreed, which is why he rebuked Winston Churchill when he threatened British withdrawal in 1922. What, then, makes a belief that others need one's help 'patronising'? The *Oxford English Dictionary* tells us that to patronise is to 'treat with an apparent kindness which betrays a feeling of superiority'. In an obvious sense, however, anyone in a position to help *is* in fact superior, whether in knowing more or having more resources, and a precondition of offering help is that they are first aware of their own superiority. So it cannot be the awareness or feeling of one's own superiority as such that makes the offer of help patronising. What does make it so is the abuse of the factual relation of superior to inferior, so as to make the beneficiary feel generally incapable and worthless. The difference is captured in the English language by the distinction between 'dominating' and 'domineering', and between 'being a lord' and 'lording it over someone'. A patronising benefactor is one who talks a lot and listens little, who thinks he has things to teach but not to learn, who always gives but never receives.

Did the imperial British patronise native people? Yes, they often did. Faisal and others were not infrequently irritated by the high-handed manner of British officials. But the British did not always patronise those they were trying to help. Sometimes they paid them the respect of making a serious investment in getting to know them well, learning their languages and customs, spending time among them and learning from them. For that reason, even if they did not always agree with them, Arabs in nascent Iraq of the 1920s respected, admired and trusted the likes of Gertrude Bell and Percy Cox.

As for Rhodes twenty-five years earlier, however one judges his choice of metaphor in referring to uncivilised black Africans and Oriel's dons as children, he was generally not the kind of man to stand on his own status and lord it over others.[13] Famously, in 1896 towards the end of the uprising of Ndebele and Shona against the oppressive rule of the British South Africa Company (BSAC), Rhodes and five companions ventured unarmed into hostile territory and parlayed with the rebels face to face for several days.[14] Robert Rotberg, who regards this as his subject's finest hour, describes the scene: 'Although the Africans were armed, and most of the whites exceedingly nervous, Rhodes appeared casual, even crossing from the white side of the gathering to the African side, and sitting with them and taking their part.' In the course of the negotiations, he learned about the natives' humiliations and realised that the white settlers had brought down retribution upon their own heads. The settlers and the imperial author-ities wanted the rebels' unconditional surrender, but Rhodes, knowing this would provoke them to take up arms again, resisted, responding,

'If necessary, tell the Secretary of State that I am prepared to go and live in the Matopos [hills] with the rebels.' Instead, he promised to reform the BSAC's administration, which moved the leading Ndebele chief to call him 'Umlamulanmkunzi' ('The bull who separates the two fighting bulls'), that is, 'Peacemaker'. Rhodes also realised that he had made a serious mistake in leaving his subordinates at liberty to misgovern Matabeleland and Mashonaland after the war of 1893, when the BSAC had defeated and overthrown the Ndebele kingdom. As a token of his intention to put things right, he bought back a hundred thousand acres of prime farming land and invited the Ndebele rebels to occupy large parts of it in perpetuity, on condition that residents work on his farms for three months of each year. Thousands of rebels took up his offer.[15] Later that year he resolved to make the building of trust between white and black part of his work.[16] Tragically, he did not have much time to come through on his promise, since he died six years later. But he did have time enough to stipulate in his final will of July 1899 that the scholarships that would famously bear his name should be awarded without regard for 'race'.[17]

V

In India, relations between imperial Britons and native populations changed over time and became more aloof. During the eighteenth century and well into the following one, it was not uncommon for the British to mix with native people socially, even to the point of taking Indian women as mistresses or wives, having children with them and sometimes bringing their Indian families back to live in Britain. The list of founder-members of the quintessentially 'establishment' Bengal Club, set up in Calcutta in 1827, shows no signs of racial exclusivity.[18] However, with the rising influence of evangelical Christianity and modernising utilitarianism in the early nineteenth century, and their lack of sympathy, respectively, for pagan culture and traditional ways, social mixing declined and the two peoples became generally more estranged. Up until 1833 Hindu and Muslim holy men had blessed the colours of sepoy regiments,[19] and the British took part in Hindu ceremonies and festivals. Thereafter, such practices were discouraged.[20]

The bloody Indian Mutiny of 1857 had contradictory effects on racial relations. On the one hand, it made Queen Victoria, 'Empress of India' from 1877, highly sensitive to the feelings of her Indian subjects. In 1888 she rebuked her prime minister, Lord Salisbury, when he referred to Dadabhai Naoroji, who would become Britain's first Indian MP, as 'a black man', and ten years later she urged her viceroy, Lord Curzon, to '*hear for himself* what the *feelings* of the Natives really are', and to be careful not 'to trample on' them or 'make them *feel* that they are a conquered people'.[21] On the other hand, it made the tiny minority of Britons in India acutely aware of their vulnerability, as the wife of an expatriate civil servant vividly testified in 1884, when she wrote that she always felt as if she were living on a volcano, 'with the elements of an eruption . . . seething below the surface'.[22] After 1857, British troops in India carried weapons into church services.[23] A minority that feels itself beleaguered naturally becomes defensive, and if it is a ruling minority, one way of defending itself is to impress its own natural superiority upon the ruled majority. Part of making that impression involves keeping one's distance, avoiding the equality of intimacy.

Nonetheless, aloofness need not be entirely a means of generating power. It can also be the innocent result of a natural preference for mingling with one's own kind, where a body of shared assumptions and social codes oils the wheels of social intercourse. Racial distance increases, therefore, when the number of expatriates enables them to form a socially self-sufficient society, since immigrants arriving en masse naturally form ghettos.[24] Ronald Storrs observed that racial relations in Egypt during the British occupation were better when the number of Britons was lower: 'Those of the 'eighties and 'nineties had left a fine tradition . . . of tactful dealing and happy relationships.' By 1910, however, the number had risen to the point where the British were mixing increasingly less with Egyptians and more with each other.[25] Yet, wrote Storrs, '[i]t would be unfair to ascribe these neglects and abstentions entirely to condescension or indifference. Between persons of different race, climate, language and religion the conversational going is not always easy, largely because of a lack of common ground.'[26] Writing of British members of the Indian Civil Service (known as 'Civilians') around the same time, David Gilmour makes a similarly benign judgement: 'Civilians may have been racially aloof and even dismissive, but they were not racist in the sense that they considered racial differences to be permanent and innate. They believed that they belonged not to a superior race but to a more advanced civilisation . . . Anglo-Indians may have stuck together in civil lines and had holidays together in the hill stations, but most of them were fond of the people they ruled.'[27]

Besides, not all Civilians were aloof and dismissive; some were fascinated. Jibbing against Edward Said's post-colonial caricature of Western attempts to understand eastern cultures as exercises in imperial control that violate their subject, Gilmour writes:

> No serious survey of the scholars of the ICS could conclude that they were a body of men who employed their skills to define an Indian 'Other' and create a body of knowledge for the purpose of furthering colonial rule . . . most were like the German orientalists, who had no colonialist agenda of their own, men motivated by pure curiosity and a desire to learn. Such people investigated in a mood of inquiry, not in the spirit of James Mill trying to find faults that demanded correction. Some might even admire what they studied, the character of the Buddha, the vernacular literatures, the empires of Asoka and Akbar, the architecture of Agra and Fatehpur Sikri. What imperialist use could be made of [John Faithfull] Fleet's work on the inscriptions of the Gupta kings or [Evelyn Berkeley] Howell's translation of the Mahsud ballads or [Arthur Coke] Burnell's catalogues of the Sanskrit manuscripts in the Palace of Tanjore? How, one wonders, are such works 'imbricated with political power'? How do they fit in with Edward Said's theory that 'all academic knowledge about India . . . is somehow tinged and impressed with, violated by, the gross political fact' of British domination?[28]

Moreover, insofar as aloofness was a trait of the British, they did not possess a monopoly of it. Conservative Hindus, in reaction against British attempts to abolish customs such as those of child marriage and female infanticide, became more emphatic in their Brahminical insistence on purification, especially in the preparation and consump-

tion of food. This made it difficult for the British to interact socially
with them: 'The British memsahibs wondered how they were expected
to form friendships when Indians would not eat with them, invite them
to their houses or allow them to meet – or even discuss – their wives
and daughters.' And understandably, 'lesser officials did not find it
easy to be friendly with a man who would wash his hands and change
his clothes after their greeting and then refuse to eat his food if he
thought their shadows had fallen across it'. If Indians resented British
high-handedness, the British found it difficult to warm to Indians who
treated them like Untouchables.[29]

While some forms of racial estrangement were understandable and
innocent, even if tragically unfortunate, others had no redeeming or
mitigating qualities. Edward Thompson, who worked as a teacher and
translator in India from 1910 to 1923, reported that in the 1860s the
commercial development of tea and coffee cultivation, the cotton and
jute industries, and foreign trade brought to India a 'flood' of English
planters and businessmen, who had been influenced by the wave of
anti-Indian feeling after 1857. These people were indiscriminately
'contemptuous of all things Indian' and had 'a far stronger sense of
racial superiority than their predecessors'. They were also sufficient
in number to develop a communal sense and bring corporate pressure
to bear upon the Indian government, most infamously emasculating
the Ilbert Bill's proposal in 1883 to extend the presidency of Indian
magistrates over the trials of Europeans, by allowing the accused to
opt for trial by a jury composed of half or a majority of Britons.[30] Even
during the Second World War casual racist contempt was alive and
well. Looking back on his experience as a young officer in the Royal
Indian Navy, B. C. Dutt recalled the attitude he and his Indian
comrades met in their British counterparts:

> . . . if we came into contact, their attitude, their talk, their language,
> there was no question of hiding it. The greeting was: 'Hi, black bastard!'
> It was so made that in my regiment or group, which consisted of
> practically all the communities of India, including 'Anglo-Indians' who
> had been very pro-British, every single one of us by the time we came
> back from the battlefront were all anti-British.[31]

There was a significant difference in racial attitudes between Britain itself and its colonies. Indians were often struck by the contrast between the friendliness of the British at home and their aloofness in India.[32] Renuka Ray, who was educated in England before proceeding to convent school in Calcutta in 1912, claimed that she 'never knew that there was such a thing as colour prejudice' until she returned to India.[33] Two decades earlier, Mohandas Gandhi had had the same experience. During the two and a half years he spent in London, studying to qualify as a barrister, he had experienced nothing but kindness from the English.[34] However, after a brief sojourn back in India, he travelled to South Africa to take up a position there in 1893. A few days after landing in Durban, sitting in a first-class train compartment for which he had bought a ticket, a white passenger objected to his presence as a 'coloured' person. When he refused to change compartments, a policeman was called, who pushed him out onto the platform, followed by his luggage. The train went on its way without him.[35]

The contrast in attitudes between the empire's mostly liberal metropolis and its colonial periphery often manifested itself in how those sent out to govern India reacted to what they found there. Lord Curzon, who arrived in India as viceroy in 1899, was appalled at the maltreatment of native Indians by soldiers and planters. 'The racial pride and the undisciplined passions of the inferior class of Englishman,' he wrote, threatened the very survival of British rule.[36] If the abuse appalled him, the indulgence with which magistrates and military authorities looked upon it moved him to outrage. Shortly after taking office, he discovered that at least twenty men from the Royal West Kent Regiment in Rangoon had raped an elderly Burmese woman, who subsequently lost her mind and died. Since their officers had sought to protect the culprits, he insisted that the entire regiment be punished. The West Kents were duly expelled to Aden, where they languished for two years without leave.[37] Similarly, after becoming the governor of Bombay in 1913, Lord Willingdon arrived at the Royal Bombay Yacht Club, of which he was patron, with the Maharaja of Patiala. To his dismay, his guest was refused entry because he was Indian. Five years later the Willingdon Club first opened its deliberately colour-blind doors.

VI

Not all racial exclusion was clearly racist in motivation, however. When he first arrived in Egypt in 1877, Lord Cromer's task was simply to put the country's finances on a sound footing. The further he progressed in this task, the greater his conviction became that the longevity of his financial reforms required a wider transformation of government. Alfred (later Lord) Milner, who served as Cromer's under-secretary of finance for three years, put it thus in his 1894 apologia, *England in Egypt*:

> . . . if we determined to base order, not upon mere external force, but upon internal stability, then there was nothing for it but to reconstruct radically the whole administrative machine, to overhaul the government in all its branches, to stamp out the corruption which lay at the root of Egypt's misfortunes and to secure to all its citizens at least some elementary form of justice . . . [T]he better way of restoring order . . . implied long years of toilsome effort . . .[38]

But such a radical overhaul could not just be organisational or technical; it also had to be cultural, even moral:

> For what was the good of recasting the system, if it were left to be worked by officials of the old type, animated by the old spirit? . . . Our task, therefore, included something more than new principles and new methods. It ultimately involved *new men*. It involved 'the education of the people to know, and therefore to expect, orderly and honest government – the education of a body of rulers capable of supplying it' . . . the wit of man has not yet discovered the means to accelerate a moral revolution. And it is the *moral revolution* which is the essence of the business.[39]

The problem, at root, was not bureaucratic organisation, but the moral quality of the culture of the ruling classes. As Cromer wrote to the foreign secretary, Lord Rosebery, in 1886: 'I have never yet come across an Egyptian who was not inordinately afraid of taking responsibility and who, particularly if some slight unpopularity is to be incurred, was not only too anxious to shift the responsibility of coming to a decision on to the shoulders of someone else.'[40] Milner shared his master's judgement. 'Where are the Egyptians who can govern Egypt?' he asked.

> What the upper-class Turk generally possesses is courage, dignity, good manners, the habit and air of command. What he generally lacks is energy, industry, public spirit, a sense of duty ... For centuries the idea of power has been dissociated from that of the performance of duty. Power was a thing to be aimed at for the benefit of yourself and your friends, not a trust to be discharged for the benefit of those below you ... Governing capacity, readiness to assume command and to take responsibility, are qualities scarce among Egyptians ... That the majority of Egyptian officials enormously prefer civilized methods of government, that they would rather live under a reign of legality, principle, and probity, than serve as agents of the old system of tyranny, muddle, and corruption, there can be no doubt whatever. But left to themselves, they do not possess the strength of character, the independence, or the *esprit de corps*, to resist the gradual return of the former evils ... It is easier for the younger men, who have never been trained in habits of suppleness and servility, to develop the virtues of firmness and self-reliance. But it will take a long time before these qualities permeate the whole body ... But all this requires time – time – time.[41]

Consequently, the government of Egypt could not be entrusted entirely to Egyptians for the time being. As Cromer wrote in his annual report for 1906: 'To suppose that, whilst the occupation lasts, we can leave these extremely incompetent Egyptians to do what they liked about local affairs is little short of madness'; 'it will not take years, but probably generations, to change the moral character of the Egyptian people'.[42]

Making a pejorative generalisation about another people is a dangerous business, because it can be racist, either because it is an unfair description of the group or because it blinds one to individual exceptions to the general rule. Whether or not Milner's and Cromer's characterisation of Egypt's ruling class at the turn of the twentieth century was in fact unfair and racist is an empirical question. It is possible that it was generally accurate, since human groups do develop cultures with characteristic strengths and weaknesses. Certainly, Faisal thought so, when he was struck by a public spiritedness in the English aristocracy that he found wanting in its Arab equivalent. In February 1921, he spent a weekend at Chatsworth, the seat of the Duke of Devonshire, where he met a young aristocrat (probably the duke's son). He was amazed to learn that this young man, the only son of the governor-general of Canada, had fought at Gallipoli and in Palestine, and that 'a huge number' of his relatives had been lost in the recent Great War. Faisal commented: 'Would any of our rich people do something like that? We deserve the [League of Nations] mandate. When one sees such things, one feels small indeed. That is how real nations live and are governed. If such a fortune was held by any one of our wealthy people he would move heaven and earth to make sure that none of his family was conscripted.'[43]

Faisal's Arabs, of course, were not the same as Cromer's or Milner's Egyptians. But there is Egyptian testimony that goes some way to confirming the judgement of the two Englishmen. The historian Afaf Lutfi al-Sayyid-Marsot, niece of Ahmad Lutfi al-Sayyid, the moderate nationalist founder of Egypt's first political party, agreed that '[l]ong years of Turkish misrule had not encouraged a spirit of initiative'.[44] She also thought that Cromer was entirely correct in his view of the khedive and his clique, who '*were* indeed thoroughly incompetent'.[45] Reporting that Cromer considered the emergent political leaders of native peasant origin 'for the most part exceedingly ignorant and . . . devoted exclusively to the furtherance of their own personal interest', she agreed that 'some . . . were undoubtedly as he described them' – although there were two notable exceptions: Saad Zaghlul, who later became prime minister, and Shaykh Muhammad Abduh, Egypt's 'greatest religious reformer'. Yet this qualification is one that Cromer himself would readily have accepted. He admired Zaghlul and had him appointed minister of education. He also had a very high regard for 'my friend Abdu', describing him as 'a man of broad and enlightened views': 'He admitted the abuses which have sprung up under Oriental Governments. He recognised the necessity of European assistance in the work of reform . . . [He] was a somewhat dreamy and unpractical, but nevertheless, genuine Egyptian patriot . . . In my Annual Reports I frequently spoke of him in high terms, and no one regretted his premature death more sincerely than myself.'[46]

Cromer's pejorative characterisation of the Egyptian capacity for good government and political leadership was not indiscriminate, and it did not prevent him from recognising exceptions to the rule. The same is even truer of Milner, who wrote:

> For my own part, I have found – and I believe it is the experience of most of my countrymen who have had many of these men [Egyptian civil servants] under them – that, if treated properly, they are far more capable and trustworthy than anybody would think possible at first sight . . . At bottom the Egyptian is intelligent and adaptable. He is by nature no more inclined to be dishonest than other people . . . Among those who have taken a foremost part in the regeneration of Egypt . . . have also been many natives. This is the most hopeful element of the situation. It is not only, or principally, upon what Englishmen do for Egypt that the case for England rests. It is upon what England is helping the Egyptians to do for themselves. And the great body of native reformers are perfectly aware of this. They are conscious of their own weakness. They want to do right. They thoroughly understand the essential principles of good government, and desire to see them applied to their own country . . . the true nature of British influence . . . is not exercised to impose an uncongenial foreign system upon a reluctant people. It is a force making for the triumph of the simplest ideas of honesty, humanity, and justice, to the value of which Egyptians are just as much alive as anybody else.[47]

If Cromer and Milner thought it wise to exclude native people from the highest, controlling echelons of government, it was only provisionally until such time as they had become trained in the necessary habits and virtues. 'As native governing capacity develops, as natives come forward who are fit for responsible posts now held by Englishmen,' averred Milner, 'these posts should be resigned to them.'[48]

VII

One of the many evils supposed to issue from the imperial presumption of one's own superiority is the licence to interfere in the affairs of inferior others, for the sake of what you – but not they – consider 'improvement'. Today's anti-colonialist critics portray this as essentially arrogant, disruptive and destructive – thereby aligning themselves, ironically, with yesterday's conservatives. Before he famously turned his eloquent ire onto the French Revolution, Edmund Burke inveighed against what, according to reports given him, he supposed to be the unaccountable, rapacious, interfering rule of the East India Company. India, Burke argued in the 1780s, 'does not consist of an abject and barbarous populace; much less gangs of savages . . . but a people for ages civilized and cultivated; cultivated by all the arts of polished life, whilst we were yet in the woods'.[49] Further, 'their morality is equal to ours, in whatever regards the duties of governors, fathers, and superiors; and I challenge the world to show in any modern European book more true morality and wisdom than is to be found in the writings of Asiatic men in high trust, and who have been counsellors to princes'.[50]

Nevertheless, anti-colonialists cannot argue that we do not have moral duties to foreign peoples, since they clearly (and rightly) think that we have a duty to stop oppressing the colonised. But if we have a duty to stop oppressing them ourselves, might we not also have a duty – sometimes – to try to stop them oppressing each other? Human rights activists (who are typically also anti-colonialist) must think so, since they protest vigorously both against foreign states when they violate the right of their own citizens to be free from arbitrary violence and against foreign societies when they tolerate the abuse of women and domestic slavery. And such activists commonly call upon their own governments to intervene in some fashion. Yet in doing this they inadvertently mirror the Christian missionaries and humanitarians of the nineteenth century, when they protested against such things as slavery, female infanticide and child marriage, and appealed to the British government to use its imperial power to suppress them.

In fact, the imperial government was often reluctant to interfere, because of the financial cost and the risk of provoking a violent reaction – which should attract the approval of contemporary anti-colonialists, but does not. In its early days, the EIC barred the entry of Christian missionaries, because it saw them as cultural irritants and so threats to the peace. EIC officers were indeed horrified by native practices they sometimes encountered, but they often preferred to tackle them patiently and gradually. Thus Captain John Campbell, posted to the remote uplands of southern Orissa in the late 1830s, found that female infanticide and child sacrifice (*meriah*) were practised among the semi-nomadic Konds. He reasoned, however, that '[t]he superstition of ages cannot be eradicated in a day ... Any increase of coercion would arouse the jealousy of the whole race.' Consequently, he proceeded with great forbearance and persistent persuasion and by the late 1840s his patient methods had borne fruit: female infanticide had vanished and incidents of *meriah* were declining rapidly. A man of 'outstanding perseverance and humanity', Campbell entered into Kond folk memory as a saviour.[51] Sir John Malcolm's approach was similarly cautious and in 1822 he instructed his staff thus:

> You are called upon to perform no easy task; to possess power, but seldom to exercise it; to witness abuses which you think you could correct; to see the errors if not crimes, of superstitious bigotry, and the miseries of misrule, and yet forbear, lest you injure interests far greater than any within the sphere of your limited duties, and impede or embarrass, by a rash change and innovation that may bring local benefit, the slow but certain march of general improvement.[52]

When it came to the practice of *sati*, whereby widows immolated themselves on the funeral pyres of their deceased husbands (thus saving relatives from having to bear the expense of taking them in), Malcolm opposed the proposal that the Calcutta government should abolish it summarily.[53] Instead, allying himself with a Hindu holy man,

Sahajanand Swami, he resolved upon a campaign to abolish *sati* by moral persuasion. Meanwhile, however, the governor-general, Lord William Bentinck, supported by Hindu reformers such as Dwarkanath Tagore and Raja Ram Mohan Roy, who assured him that the practice had no basis in the Hindu sacred scriptures, had decided to abolish it.[54] This he did in Bengal in 1829, extending the law to Madras and Bombay in 1830.[55] As it happened, the social and political disturbances that Malcolm and others had feared were minimal.

Elsewhere, colonial challenges to native practices did kindle a fierce reaction. In the 1920s Christian missionaries in central Kenya launched a concerted campaign against the custom of female circumcision – known by its opponents as female genital mutilation (FGM) – that caused serious upset among Kikuyu Christians. One consequence of this may have been that, in January 1930, a sixty-three-year-old female missionary was attacked in her bed at Kijabe and forcibly circumcised before she was murdered.[56] Not violently, but still bitterly, the contemporary Kenya-born, now US-based professor of law, Makau wa Mutua, has railed against European missionary colonialism, whose ignorant racist prejudice, he believes, has done arrogant violence to traditional African cultures. Female circumcision, he argues, plays an important social function, which needs to be taken into account before it is modified or discarded.[57] However, while we might regret the disruption that inevitably accompanies social change, there are two reasons that should make us hesitate before accepting Mutua's view. First of all, his defence of a traditional practice on the ground of its important social function was one that Ottoman authorities used to deflect British pressure to abolish slavery. In 1840 Lord Ponsonby, British ambassador to Istanbul, wrote to Lord Palmerston, then British foreign secretary, that his urging the Ottomans to act against slavery and the slave trade had been greeted 'with *extreme astonishment and a smile* at the proposition of destroying an institution closely interwoven with the frame of society'.[58] Second, while Mutua might retain a fondness for female circumcision, because of its function in promoting social solidarity, other Africans strongly disagree. For example, the Sudanese El-Obaid Ahmed El-Obaid and the Ghanaian Kwadwo Appiagyei-Atua, also academic lawyers, regard it as 'unacceptable, even repulsive'.[59]

Mutua goes on to mount a more general argument in favour of a culture's 'right to be left alone'. As he sees it, the 'messianic faiths' or 'imperial religions' that are Christianity and Islam are guilty of something approaching 'cultural genocide' through their destruction of traditional African religion. Because that religion is closely bound up with social norms and cultural identities, its destruction has 'robbed Africans of essential elements of their humanity'. [60] To illustrate his point, Mutua invokes *Things Fall Apart*, the famous 1958 novel by Chinua Achebe, which tells a story about the encounter between, on the one hand, Okonkwo, guardian of Igbo culture and religion, and on the other, colonial administrators and missionaries. The story is propelled to its tragic climax when Okonkwo's son is converted to Christianity by an Igbo Christian, who congratulates him with the words, 'Blessed is he who forsakes his mother and father for my sake.' Beholding the train of events, a tribal elder laments that the white man 'has put a knife on the things that held us together and we have fallen apart'. Mutua comments that the encounter between Christianity and the Igbo religion involved 'the recruitment of converts, usually from among the social "rejects"', and that missionary schools 'usually preyed on the youth, capturing them and tearing them from their cultural moorings'. [61] Against this Western assault on traditional African culture, Mutua argues for a 'right against cultural invasion . . . the right [of indigenous beliefs] to be respected and left alone by more dominant external traditions'. [62]

Mutua's fierce critique of 'Western human rights' is motivated by a deeply felt sense of dismay and anger at the destruction of traditional African values and customs: 'It is this loss that I mourn,' he confesses, 'and for which I blame Christianity and Islam.'[63] While his grief deserves some sympathy, his reasoning merits critical scrutiny. First of all, notice how he operates with a very loose concept of coercion and violence, which, however common it may now be among anti-colonialists, is dubious. He tells us that Christianity's entry into Africa was just as 'violent' as Islam's, 'coming as it did in partnership with the colonial imperial powers'. [64] This is historically simplistic, however. As we have seen, British colonial administrators often actively discouraged Christian missionary activity, precisely because they wanted to avoid the political unrest that cultural interference tended to cause.[65] Nonetheless, as we have also seen, British colonial involvement in West and East Africa in the closing decades of the nineteenth century was considerably motivated by the missionary-inspired aim of suppressing the slave trade. This was no doubt regarded as unwarranted interference by the African sellers and the Arab buyers, but presumably not by the slaves – or by those treated like them. Looking back on the period 1890–1904, Baba of Karo, a Muslim African woman in what is now Nigeria, had this to say:

> We Habe wanted them [the Europeans] to come, it was the Fulani who did not like it. When the Europeans came the Habe saw that if you worked for them they paid you for it, they didn't say, like the Fulani, 'Commoner, give me this! Commoner, bring me that!' . . . the Europeans said that there were to be no more slaves; if someone said 'Slave!' you could complain to the *alkali* who would punish the master who said it . . . The first order said that any slave, if he was younger than you, was your younger brother, if he was older than you he was your elder brother – they were all brothers of their master's family. No one used the word 'slave' any more . . . In the old days if the chief liked the look of your daughter he would take her and put her in his house; you could do nothing about it. Now they don't do that.[66]

What is more, Africans were not, in fact, forced to convert to Christianity at the point of a British colonial gun. Indeed, Mutua himself admits as much, when he contends that there should be a right against 'coerced conversion', even when that occurs indirectly 'through the manipulation and destruction of other cultures', and that the most fundamental right of self-determination should disallow 'imposition by external agencies through acculturation'.[67] The 'coercion' he is talking about is not, in fact, physical violence at all, but the power of cultural attraction. In Chinua Achebe's story no one compels Okonkwo's son to convert; and Mutua does not claim that missionary schools literally took African youths captive. And while Mutua appears to disdain the missionaries' recruitment of 'social rejects' – rather as Indian Brahmins disdained the Christian recruitment of Untouchables, or Jewish pharisees Jesus' recruitment of sinners – presumably the rejects themselves would have a different story to tell. To talk, as Mutua does, of the conversion of Africans to Christianity as a form of 'violence', 'coercion' or even 'imposition' is exaggerated and misleading. It also betrays a rather low view of the agency of (non-conformist) Africans. Mutua reports Elizabeth Isichei's observation that '[t]oday most Igbo have been baptized, and traditional religion is the preserve of a small aging minority'.[68] To suppose that 'most Igbo' are merely gullible sheep would not only show a lack of curiosity, it would also patronise.[69] Far from being reluctant converts, many Africans were attracted to Christianity as a source of liberation. Writing in 1959, Ndabaningi Sithole asserted that

> one of the unique teachings of the Bible, especially the New Testament, is the worth and dignity of the individual in the sight of God . . . the Bible is redeeming the African individual from the power of supersti-tion, individuality-crushing tradition, witchcraft, and other forces that do not make for progress . . . The Bible-liberated African is now re-asserting himself not only over tribal but also over colonial authority, since these two are fundamentally the same.[70]

Deep down, Makau Mutua's complaint against the destruction of traditional African religion is part of a larger complaint against 'modernisation' – against the 'process of de-Africanization . . . and the wholesale subversion of traditional values and structures', which has been fuelled by industrialisation and urbanisation.[71] This may be a process that Western colonialism started, but, as Mutua himself laments, it is also one that post-colonial African rulers have often been very happy to adopt.[72] Indeed, in the 1950s and 1960s nationalist movements were frequently hostile to the 'feudal' customs and tradi-tions of their own peoples, and post-colonial states were at the forefront of UN activity to eradicate cultural practices considered harmful to women.[73] Again, while it is possible that African elites were slavishly going with the flow of what appeared to be 'progress', it is also possible that they had perceived in modern, Western ideas such as human rights, values that seemed to them good and worthy of embrace. Maybe, on first encounter, those ideas seemed absolutely novel and alien; more likely, they resonated with elements already present in traditional culture, while giving them a novel articulation, emphasis and force. More likely, they were at once somewhat familiar and somewhat novel: familiar enough to grasp, novel enough to propel fresh, critical lines of thought. Cultures are seldom entirely separate and are normally in the process of negotiating with each other. Even if it were right to preserve them in a state of quarantine, it is usually not possible. But while we might agree that there should be a right of individuals not to be forced against their will to adopt foreign beliefs and practices, we might doubt that there should be a right of communities to prevent members from choosing to adopt such ideas. If so, we would share that doubt with plenty of Africans.[74]

One such African was Ndabaningi Sithole; another was Chinua Achebe. Despite his reputation as a leading African nationalist, Achebe's assessment of British colonial rule in his native Nigeria was nuanced, even equivocal. On the one hand, he wrote that '[i]n my view, it is a gross crime for anyone to impose himself on another, to seize his land and his history, and then to compound this by making out that the victim is some kind of ward or minor requiring protection'.[75] On the other hand, he wrote very appreciatively of Christian missionaries, some of whom had converted his father: 'I also salute my father, Isaiah Achebe, for the thirty-five years he served as a Christian evangelist and for all the benefits his work and the work of others like him brought to our people. I am a prime beneficiary of the education which the missionaries had made a major component of their enterprise. My father had a lot of praise for the missionaries and their message, and so have I.'[76] And of the cultural disruption caused by the irruption of colonialism, his nonchalance could not have been further removed from Mutua's outrage:

The Igbo culture was not destroyed by Europe. It was disturbed. It was disturbed very seriously, but this is nothing new in the world. Cultures are constantly influenced, challenged, pushed about by other cultures that may have some kind of advantage at a particular time . . . a culture that is healthy will often survive. It will not survive exactly in the form in which it was met by the invading culture, but it will modify itself and move on.[77]

Six months before his death in 2013, when asked by an Iranian journalist whether his views of colonialism had changed since he wrote *Things Fall Apart*, Achebe said: 'The legacy of colonialism is not a simple one but one of great complexity, with contradictions – good things as well as bad.'[78]

VIII

Sometimes the sense that imperial Britons had of their own superiority was justified. Sometimes it consisted of the conviction that native people needed help that they could give, and sometimes that conviction was correct, the natives agreed with it and it did not patronise. Sometimes the sense of imperial superiority was confident enough not to vie with giving credit where credit was due, and with recognising native wisdom, beauty and virtue when it presented itself.

At other times, however, imperial superiority did take the racist form of unfair, disparaging prejudice against native peoples, which too often manifested itself in humiliating contempt, physical brutality, gratuitous social exclusion and racial segregation. This occurred much less at the imperial centre in London than at the colonial periphery, and less among governors, civil servants and missionaries than among soldiers, merchants, settlers and planters. Besides, unjust prejudice against members of social groups was hardly peculiar to the British. Indians were perfectly familiar with caste and religious prejudice, and were wont to take a disparaging view of Africans; Africans were quite capable of racist contempt among themselves; and the imperial Chinese regarded all Westerners as 'barbarians'. Moreover, racial segregation in the British Empire was sometimes as much the tragic result of native attitudes as of British ones, and even when Britons were its main cause, it was motivated more by the natural desire to move easily among one's own people than by a positive disdain for aliens. Once segregation had set in, however, racial alienation and disdain could easily follow, and it did.

Yet, as we saw in the case of Egypt under Lord Cromer, professional exclusion from the higher ranks of administration was not always motivated by racism, but by the need to wait for cultural change to embed itself in the character and habits of native civil servants – a need that native people themselves sometimes acknowledged. Of course, the longer the provisional exclusion was stretched out, the more frustration and resentment built up. But if some natives resented the cultural changes thrust upon them by colonial power as disruption, others welcomed them as liberation. On the eve of decolonisation, the British often found themselves criticised on both sides – by conservative natives for violating tradition and by progressive natives for not changing it enough.

In sum, the British Empire did contain some appalling racial prejudice, but not only that. It also contained respect, admiration and genuine, well-informed, costly benevolence. Indeed, from the opening of the 1800s until its end, the empire's policies towards slaves and native peoples were driven by the conviction of the basic human equality of the members of all races. It cannot fairly be said, therefore, that the empire was centrally, essentially racist.

IX

Yet however well historically grounded, that is not a conclusion that anti-colonialist axioms allow.

On 21 April 2021, the Commonwealth War Graves Commission published the report of its Special Committee to Review Historical Inequalities in Commemoration. This revealed that up to 54,000 Indians and Africans who had died in the service of the British Empire during the First World War had been commemorated 'unequally', and at least a further 116,000 had not been commemorated either by name or at all.[79] The report attributed the inequality of treatment ultimately to 'imperial ideology', that is, 'the entrenched prejudices, preconceptions and pervasive racism of contemporary imperial attitudes'.[80] The fateful phrase 'pervasive racism' was then picked up and broadcast by the press from the *Guardian* to *The Times*, and by television stations from the BBC to Al Jazeera.[81] Commenting on the report, David

Olusoga, professor of public history at the University of Manchester, said: 'It's *apartheid* in death. It is an absolute scandal. It is one of the biggest scandals I've ever come across as an historian.'[82] Casual onlookers worldwide could readily be forgiven for walking away convinced that British colonialism was racist at heart, and that the sooner the British 'decolonise' themselves, the better.

Yet closer inspection reveals a very different story. The report makes it clear that the Imperial War Graves Commission (as it was known then) was committed to the principle of the equal treatment of all the empire's fallen troops in the commemoration of their sacrifice, whatever the colour of their skin. As Sir Frederick Kenyon wrote in his seminal 1918 publication *War Graves – How the Cemeteries Abroad Will Be Designed*, 'no less honour should be paid to the last resting places of Indian and other non-Christian members of the empire than to those of our British soldiers'. Eight years later, the IWGC's founder, Sir Fabian Ware, reaffirmed this view, writing that 'all the soldiers of the empire should be treated alike'.[83] The report also makes clear that this principle was consistently realised in Europe – as can easily be confirmed by a visit to the Menin Gate in Ypres, where the names of Indians with no known grave join British ones in cascading down the walls, or to the cemetery at Noyelles-sur-Mer, where the burials of members of the Chinese Labour Corps are marked by individual headstones, just like those of British soldiers elsewhere.

Outside Europe, however, this egalitarian policy was sometimes compromised. Many Indian and African casualties were commemorated not with individually marked graves, but collectively with their names inscribed on memorials or in memorial registers. Other, mainly East African and Egyptian personnel received no commemoration by name and perhaps none at all. This deviation from the norm in Europe, the commission's report tells us, was due to 'problems largely born out of distance, communication, local conditions, and on-going instability'.[84] In East Africa many graves had not been marked during the fighting, and both there and in Mesopotamia,

climate and inhospitable terrain made some burials impossible to reach, while the destruction of wooden markers by termites or the theft of metal plaques could rob the dead of their identity. The sun could also bleach lettering from name boards, and wild animals and the weather could destroy the evidence of someone's final resting place.[85]

Practical obstacles, however, were not always the reason for unequal treatment. There was also the view that, since most of the African dead came from peoples that were not accustomed to burying the deceased and so would not appreciate marked graves, they should be commemorated on collective memorials. Thus, Major George Evans, the officer commanding the Graves Registration Unit in East Africa, wrote in January 1920 that most Africans 'do not attach any sentiment to marking the graves of their dead'. So, too, in May 1923, F. G. Guggisberg, governor of the Gold Coast, is reported to have said that 'the average native of the Gold Coast would not understand or appreciate a headstone'. And in May 1927 Lieutenant-Colonel A. E. Norton, commanding officer of the West African Regiment, wrote that 'the marking of . . . graves with headstones does not appeal to the West African soldier'.[86]

The report's comment on this and similar perceptions is stern: 'Sweeping judgements such as these, which chose to ignore the intricacies of faith, culture, and customs in Africa outside Christian and Islamic traditions, played a significant role in shaping the IWGC policies that led to unequal treatment.' Worse, they were not just innocently sweeping, for their failure to do justice to cultural particularities was rooted in an 'overarching imperial ideology' that was based on ideals of progress and civilisation that generated hierarchies of race and religion. Here, then, is where 'pervasive racism' is supposed to appear.[87]

Yet it is notable that the report does not actually say that the views of the officials were empirically mistaken. That was only wise, since it seems that the authors had not read any authority on the funerary customs of Africans. No such work appears in the report's select bibliography. Moreover, had they confirmed their hunch, they would not have written, weakly, that 'the advice sought from British colonial administrators and military officials took little or no heed of what *must have been* extremely broad ethnic customs'.[88] 'Must have been' suggests tentative speculation, not firm knowledge.

In fact, the ethnography of the period indicated that African peoples did often eschew burying their dead in marked graves. As reported in Volume IV of the 1911 edition of James Hastings' classic *Encyclopedia of Religion and Ethics*, 'the Masai, whose reason for not burying ordinary persons is said to be that the bodies would poison the soil, bury [only] their medicine-men and rich men'; 'Some African tribes, as the Latuka and the Wadjagga, leave the slain warrior unburied'; 'In many places . . . the dead cannot be buried until his debts are paid; and among the Fantis . . . he who has the temerity to bury a man becomes liable for his debts'; and 'the Barotse . . . bury in secret, from which we may probably infer that the object is to leave no clue as to the burial place lest it be violated by wizards'.[89] The Masai and the Wadjagga belonged to East Africa, the Latuka to the Sudan, the Fanti to West Africa and the Barotse to South Africa.

Whereas the commission's report is quick to attribute the colonial officials' view of African burial customs to imperial disdain for 'primitive' peoples, in fact it might well have been born of close attention to them in the form of ethnographic research and direct experience. In their African colonies the British were so thin on the ground that their rule was only sustainable by persuading native peoples to cooperate or at least acquiesce. Indeed, the policy of 'indirect rule' had become something of a model by the 1920s. But in order to be persuasive, the British had to make themselves well-informed. For sure, African custom varied a lot over a vast continent, but if the quoted colonial officials were in fact mistaken about the burial customs of their war dead, the report's authors have not shown it. Moreover, in their suggestion that any deviation from the European norm was unjust, they seem to set themselves against concessions to local African custom. They might even betray an assumption that all cultures must surely value the individual as highly as Christian cultures do. But that would be 'Eurocentric' – and 'Eurocentricity', we are told, is a sin.

However, allegedly ignorant, even dismissive, claims by colonial officials about African burial customs are not the only evidence of the 'pervasive racism' that the report claims to have exposed. Lying beneath them are the theoretical 'hierarchies of race and religion that underpinned empire'.[90] There is no doubt that the officials did regard the cultures of many African peoples as 'primitive', and the report quotes some of them as saying so. But I doubt they deserve blame for that, since – whether in terms of science, technology or medicine – African cultures were, compared to European ones, obviously less developed in the 1920s. Moreover, when it came to deciding to commemorate the wartime sacrifice of native Africans collectively rather than with individual headstones, the reason was often respect for native custom, rather than disdain for it.

Further still, it is most remarkable that discrimination was usually religious *rather than racial*. Thus, the IWGC treated non-white members of the West India Regiment, the British West Indies Regiment and South African units as Europeans, because they were presumed to be Christian (or Muslim) monotheists, and it accorded them individually named commemoration wherever possible.[91] For example, Lord Arthur Browne, the IWGC's principal assistant secretary, thought that the South African 'Cape Boys' should be treated as British soldiers and receive headstones, whereas native African soldiers should be commemorated only on collective memorials.[92]

Divergence from the norm in Europe because of serious practical difficulties or out of deference to native religious custom was not racist. What would have been racist is the differential commemoration of African or Indian dead because they were regarded as less worthy than their British or European counterparts simply on account of their ethnicity or race. Did that occur? The report does not present much unequivocal evidence of this, but it may present some. So, for example, at the Beira Christian cemetery in Portuguese East Africa, the graves of eighteen named native African soldiers were intentionally left unmarked – since the deceased were to be commemorated on the nameless Dar es Salaam African Memorial – while the marked graves of white South Africans and Europeans now remain.[93] Another possible example also occurred in Portuguese East Africa. When outlying cemeteries there were abandoned because of their remoteness, the British burials were concentrated in permanent cemeteries and given individual headstones, whereas non-European casualties in adjoining cemeteries were commemorated on a variety of memorials. If any of these non-European dead were Christian or Muslim and had a marked grave in the outlying cemeteries, but were then denied a grave with a headstone when concentrated, then their unequal treatment would have been racist. But the report does not clearly say that this is what happened.[94]

In sum, then, what the commission's report actually shows is this. Operating out of the metropolitan heart of the British Empire, the IWGC was committed to the racially egalitarian policy of commemorating all the fallen soldiers of the empire alike. This it did consistently in Europe, marking the known graves of individuals while naming those with no known grave on collective memorials, regardless of their race. Outside of Europe this policy was sometimes adjusted out of practical necessity or respect for native religious custom, with good moral justification. In certain cases, it may have been unjustifiably compromised by racist preference for Europeans. If that did happen, it was lamentable. But it still does not add up to evidence of 'pervasive' – far less, systematic – '*apartheid* in death'.

Parts of the report actually tend towards the same conclusion. To assert the success of the policy of equal commemoration in Europe, it tells us, 'is not to say that it was only there that the IWGC realised this goal or where it worked to make it a reality'.[95] That is to say, the egalitarian policy did sometimes prevail in Africa and the Middle East, too. As for those occasions when it was set aside, the report comments that '[i]n many ways it is understandable that IWGC operations during and following the First World War were not perfect'.[96] Deviation from the European norm was due – as we have already seen – to 'problems *largely* born out of distance, communication, local conditions, and on-going instability'.[97] Nonetheless, '*in a small number of cases* where Commission officials had greater say in the recovery and marking of graves, overarching imperial ideology connected to racial and religious differences were used to divide the dead and treat them unequally in ways that were impossible in Europe'.[98]

However, the report never quite manages to bring into clear focus the truth that not all inequalities are unjust – and that it pays no less respect to African or Indian fallen who would have received a headstone in northern France, to deny it to them in Africa or the Middle East, not because of their skin colour, but because of the dangerous remoteness of where they fell and were originally buried or out of deference to what was believed to be native custom. Because of its unresolved confusion on this ethical point, the report insinuates guilt where it should not, as when it writes that the IWGC was 'complicit' in decisions that compromised its principles and treated the dead unequally.[99]

When, to this ethical confusion is added the axiom of post-colonialist theory that the British Empire was informed by a single 'imperial ideology', which involved thinking of race and religion in terms of a fixed hierarchy of (white) superiority and (non-white) inferiority, the judgement is reached that the IWGC's inequalities of commemoration were ultimately attributable to 'pervasive racism'.

Except that, as we have seen, that is not what the data actually say. So this judgement does not follow from the evidence; it precedes it. It is, precisely, an anti-colonialist pre-judgement – a prejudice.

4

Land, Settlers and 'Conquest'

I

Innocent motives and good intentions can still be vitiated by acts of injustice. While there is nothing wrong per se with emigrating in pursuit of a better life, were that pursuit to involve trampling over the rights of others, then it would become wrong. One important right that the British Empire is often accused of violating is that of native peoples to land, for it is commonly assumed that the empire expanded simply by seizing territory through superior force of arms – that is, by naked conquest.

As 'slavery' and 'racism' have deserved some critical reflection, so does what we mean by 'a right'. A right is an institution that provides social backing for the protection of some important element of human flourishing – some human good. One such element is the freedom to use, develop and build a life out of a set of material things. Where we live in proximity to other people, and where material things are not abundant, those people pose a threat to our freedom, since what we currently have in our hands they might well like to take into theirs. Such a situation is vulnerable to constant conflict, and since constant conflict does not allow for much flourishing at all – except in the case of thugs and warlords – human societies have learned the wisdom of creating rules about who should have the freedom to use particular things, and to back those rules up by threatening to punish anyone who violates that freedom. These social rules or laws, supported by social authority and the threat of punishment, create rights to own things – rights to property. To have a right to property, therefore, means that one's freedom of use is relatively secure, thanks to the support of social institutions.

Suppose, then, a situation where members of two different societies encounter one another for the first time. Since these societies have made no treaties with each other, there is no international law to govern their interaction and no international authority to enforce the law. With respect to each other, therefore, the freedom to use things such as land is highly insecure, neither party having a legal right to property. So, were members of one society to trespass on the territory of the other, taking it and settling on it for their own purposes, no right would have been violated.

Nevertheless, an injustice may have been done. If that is so, it is only because, beyond the rules or laws that societies invent for them-selves and between themselves – beyond legal rights – there is also natural morality. That is to say, there are moral principles built into the rational nature or minds of all human beings, wherever they are located, which carry moral authority even where there is no law. One such principle is that one usually ought not to take from other people things in which they have invested their time and energy, or on which their social life has come to depend, or which they need to survive. 'Usually', of course, implies that there are exceptions. According to a major tradition of Western thought, which I generally endorse, one exception is when other people have more than they need to survive, and you are destitute. In such a situation it may be morally permissible for you to take what you need from their surplus without their permis-sion. The reason for this is that those who have more than they need are morally obliged to supply those who have less than they need; and if they fail to do their moral duty, those in need may do it for them.[1]

While natural moral principles such as these do provide some framework for ordering interactions apart from commonly recognised law, they are much more contingent, much less stable than legal rights. Whether or not I think that I should respect your freedom or invade it, depends on whether I estimate that you have more than you need and I have less. Even if I make my estimate conscientiously, your estimate might well differ from mine, and there is no overarching authority to arbitrate between us. The conscientious appreciation of the principles of natural morality will often restrain us in our treatment of foreign people and what they have, but that restraint will not be nearly as strong as a social system of law and rights. What is more, not everyone is conscientious and some will be propelled by greed or by the unfair, egoistic assumption that the life of someone else is worth less than their own. To this already unstable mix must be added the incomprehension, the lack of certainty, the dearth of trust and the fear that naturally arise when two alien peoples, speaking entirely different languages, stumble across one another. Under such volatile conditions – and in the absence of any commonly restraining law – friction, conflict, attack, invasion and conquest are, tragically, all too likely.

II

When British migrants first entered America, Africa and Australia, it was uncertain whose freedom to use land obliged respect. Adding to this uncertainty was often the migration of native peoples themselves. Some contemporary representatives of indigenous peoples hold that the land that they occupied when European migrants first appeared had been in their possession since time immemorial. Thus Tracey Lindberg, a member of the Cree 'First Nation' in Canada and professor of law at the University of Ottawa, has written: '"The earth is our mother". No one can own your mother . . . [T]here is no possibility that someone whose bones, histories, and laws were not birthed or placed in that land over thousands of years could come and "take it".' The native peoples, therefore, had – and still have – 'an inherent right' to the land, which is 'inviolable'.[2] This, however, is fanciful. According to Tom Flanagan, there was no human habitation of Canada before 12,000 BP ('Before Present', the present being 1950), since it was almost totally covered in glacial ice.[3] '[T]he direct ancestors of the Indians living in Canada (other than coastal British Columbia) at the time of contact with European explorers,' he writes, 'could not have arrived at those locations earlier than a few thousand years before; otherwise their languages would have become more divergent.'⁴ 'European settlers are, in effect, a new immigrant wave, taking control of land just as earlier aboriginal settlers did.'⁵

Further, some aboriginal spokespeople downplay the extent of conflict between native peoples. Thus, Georges Erasmus, a member of the Dene Nation and former national chief of the Assembly of First Nations, has claimed that 'our people were not a war-like people, but they did defend their interests. Our territorial boundaries were clearly defined. Although First Nations had many disputes with neighbours, they eventually arrived at peaceful arrangements with one another.'⁶ This, too, is fanciful and altogether softens the historical record. From the sixteenth century onward, there is strong evidence that aboriginal peoples 'contested with each other for control of territory and that conquest, absorption, displacement, and even extermination were routine phenomena'.⁷ In the south-west of North America, the Comanches launched 'an explosive expansion', which in three generations obliterated Apache civilisation from the Great Plains and carved out 'a vast territory that was larger than the entire European-controlled area north of the Río Grande at the time'.⁸ From 1750 to 1850 their empire dominated the region, building 'the largest slave economy in the colonial Southwest'.⁹ Meanwhile to the north, in the second half of the sixteenth century the Iroquois were displaced from the St Lawrence valley by the Algonquian-speaking Montagnais, but then returned in the seventeenth century, reconquered it and expanded west as far as present-day Illinois; in the eighteenth century the Ojibwa also pushed west into what are now Minnesota and Dakota; and in the seventeenth and early eighteenth centuries the Cree moved onto the prairies and encountered the Blackfoot, who were being pushed north and east by other tribes.¹⁰ 'These population movements were not caused by aboriginal people losing their own lands to white settlers, but by taking advantage of new technology [European guns] secured through trade.'¹¹ Therefore, judges Flanagan, Erasmus' account

hardly does justice to the war of extermination waged by the Iroquois against the Huron, or to the ferocious struggles between the Cree and the Blackfoot over access to the buffalo herds. The historical record

clearly shows that, while aboriginal peoples exercised a kind of collective control over territories, the boundaries were neither long-lasting
nor well defined and communities must have been repeatedly formed,
dissolved, and reconstituted with different identities.[12]

It follows that whatever property rights aboriginal peoples might have
had, they could not justifiably claim them by virtue of their occupation
of certain lands from time immemorial, for '[i]n many cases, the
patterns of habitation upon which the land-surrender agreements of
the nineteenth century were based were only a few decades old'.[13]

As in Canada, so in South Africa, where Adekeye Adebajo has
claimed that Rhodes 'dispossessed black people of their ancestral lands
. . . through armed conquest'.[14] The truth is altogether muddier. In
1888 Charles Rudd, acting on behalf of Rhodes' British South Africa
Company (BSAC), secured from the Ndebele king, Lobengula, a signed
concession granting the exclusive right to mine for minerals in
Mashonaland, which lay on the periphery of his realm. Ndebele rule
over Mashonaland involved little or no provision of any public goods,
but instead the constant, destabilising threat of raiding parties aimed
at abducting Shona men into military service, together with the extraction of tribute on pain of summary retribution.[15] If ever there was a
pure example of predatory colonial economics, this was it. In return
for his concession, Lobengula would receive a monthly payment of
£100 in perpetuity, 1,000 Martini–Henry breech-loading rifles and
100,000 rounds of ammunition, which would help him resist Boer
incursions from the Transvaal Republic. (This commitment to arm
the Ndebele surely suggests that Rhodes was not intending to wage
war on them himself.) There is some evidence that Rudd may have
been less than scrupulous in explaining all that was intended by the
agreement, and that when Lobengula subsequently claimed to have
been deceived by it, his claim had some ground.[16]

Nevertheless, in June 1890 Rhodes' men – numbering 186 whites,
supported by more 350 African labourers – cautiously skirting around
the edges of the Ndebele heartland, began to exploit the concession
anyway and Lobengula tolerated their intrusion, because he did not
want war.[17] Nor did Rhodes. However, three years later, in July 1893,

violence broke out after the white settlers of Salisbury woke up one morning to find their Shona servants being slaughtered on their door-steps by a punitive Ndebele raiding party (who were disobeying their chief's orders to keep clear of the whites).[18] In the ensuing conflict, the settlers prevailed, aided by their liberal use of Maxim guns.[19] In this way, the BSAC came to rule the territory of what would become Rhodesia (now Zimbabwe) by means of conquest. But the conquest was provoked by a violent Ndebele raiding expedition *three years after* the BSAC's ambiguous ingress, which Lobengula had tolerated.

Moreover, *pace* Adebajo, the conquered territory was hardly 'ances-tral'. The lands occupied by the Ndebele in the 1890s they themselves had seized by conquest about fifty years before, having broken off from the militaristic Zulu empire and migrated westward to found their own 'militarised state', scattering other African peoples before them.[20] The Shona, whose lands they occupied, were reduced to the status of vassals, subject to indiscriminate torture, slaughter and laying waste upon failure to pay tribute. On entering a Shona village shortly after its punishment by the Ndebele, one missionary reported: 'Fastened to the ground was a row of bodies, men and women, who had been pegged down and left to the sun's scorching by day and cold dews by night, left to the tender mercies of the pestering flies and ravenous beasts.'[21] If the Ndebele had some moral claim to the territory they ruled, it was based neither on their possession since time immemorial nor on the beneficence of their rule.

III

It is true that settlers, eager to better their lives and knowing what could be achieved with land associated with native peoples, were often frustrated by the latter's failure to make it more productive and by the apparent squandering of resources. Thus, an editorial in the *Sarnia Observer* addressed the natives of Canada in 1868, saying, 'You must either fall into the ranks of progress, or sell your lands at the high value which our labour and enterprise has given them; and stand aside so that others can perform the work for the public good.'[22] Frustration tends to be the mother of impatience, impatience that of greed and

greed that of injustice – and too often they were, notwithstanding
colonial governments' attempts at regulating the transfer of land.

Whether a people are morally justified in refusing to develop land,
both to their own benefit and to the benefit of the other people it can
be made to sustain, is an ethical question that does not command a
simple answer. The political philosophers John Locke (in the seventeenth century), Emer de Vattel (in the eighteenth century) and David
Gauthier (in the twentieth century) have all argued that they are not
justified.[23] And at his treason trial in Regina in 1885, Louis Riel, 'the
great Canadian symbol of aboriginal resistance', recognised the
cogency of their argument, saying:

> . . . civilization has the means of improving life that Indians or half-breeds
> have not. So when they come in our savage country, in our uncultivated
> land, they come and help us with their civilization, but we helped them
> with our lands, so the question comes: Your land, you Cree or you half-
> breed, your land is worth today one-seventh of what it will be when the
> civilization will have opened it? Your country unopened is worth to you
> only one-seventh of what it will be when opened. I think it is a fair share
> to acknowledge the genius of civilization to such an extent as to give,
> when I have seven pairs of socks, six, to keep one.[24]

However, whatever the force or otherwise of such arguments, British
colonial policy did not generally sanction the seizure of native lands
just because settlers thought they could make better use of them.

IV

When British colonists first landed on the shores of America, South
Africa, Australia or New Zealand, they carried with them the authority
of the government in London. With that authority came instructions
on how to treat whatever native people they met. One of those instructions was to declare sovereignty over the territory on which they had
set foot, according to the so-called 'doctrine of discovery'. This asserted
the right of the first European country to discover a territory to exclude
all other rival European powers from it, and especially from buying

land in it. On the one hand, this did presume that Christian nations were justified in limiting the right of native people to make whatever alliances, and sell whatever territory, they pleased – on the grounds of a qualitatively superior civilisation and quantitatively superior coercive power. We may assume that the natives recognised at least the latter, otherwise they would not have accepted the colonisers' declaration of sovereignty at all – as they often did. On the other hand, the doctrine of discovery defined distinct spheres of influence, in order to prevent friction and war between European nations – which sometimes served native interests, too.[25] It was also designed to assert an overarching authority to govern relations between Europeans and natives. As Tom Flanagan writes,

> Consider . . . what would have happened if the European states had initially refrained from asserting their sovereignty but their subjects had privately pursued the alluring opportunities for exploration, trade, mining, forestry, and agriculture in the New World. Private parties and companies would quickly have taken up arms to defend themselves against depredations both by other colonists and the aboriginal inhabitants. The ensuing violence would have drawn in the European sovereigns whether they had originally wanted to be involved or not.[26]

What is more, the doctrine did actually recognise that native peoples should have a legal right, based on the international consensus of European nations, to possess, occupy and use their lands, and that therefore Europeans could only come to possess them by consent.[27] Remarkably, the European colonisers *unilaterally* decided to bind themselves in their treatment of native land *by their own law* – out of recognition of universal natural justice.

In North America, the legislative assemblies of all thirteen American colonies enacted laws affirming their right of pre-emption, requiring individual colonists to obtain licences to buy, lease or occupy Indian lands, in order to prevent an anarchic and incendiary free-for-all and to make expansion orderly and peaceful. For the same reason, they asserted sovereignty over commercial relationships between colonists and native peoples, hoping 'to control the trade of weapons and alcohol to Indians and to prevent fraudulent trade practices because these activities often caused friction and conflicts'.[28] In 1763, responding to the Indian uprising against territorial encroachment known as Pontiac's War, King George III issued a Royal Proclamation, which declared that the native tribes in the territory west of the Appalachian and Allegheny Mountains as far as the Mississippi river 'live under our protection', and that it was essential to the security of the colonies that the Indian nations not be 'disturbed in the possession of such part of our dominions and territories as, not having been ceded to or purchased by us, are reserved to them'. Even though the Royal Proclamation – because of its constraint upon westward colonial expansion – was one of the irritants that incited the American colonists to revolt against the British Empire twelve years later, the new-born United States adopted the doctrine of discovery that it expressed. So in 1787 the Confederation Congress' Northwest Ordinance, which sought to govern the opening up of the western lands for European settlement, declared: 'The utmost good faith shall always be observed towards the Indians, their lands and property shall never be taken from them without their consent; and in their property, rights, and liberty, they shall never be invaded or disturbed, unless in just and lawful wars.'[29] Two years later, Henry Knox, President George Washington's secretary of war, wrote along similar lines that '[t]he Indians being the prior occupants, possess the right to the soil. It cannot be taken from them unless by their free consent, or by right of conquest in case of a just war. To dispossess them on any other principle, would be a gross violation of the fundamental laws of nature.'[30]

Authoritative public statements of principle are important, since they both express what a government intends and provide a standard by which it can be held to account. At an assembly at Niagara in 1764 the Royal Proclamation was formally accepted by a number of native peoples, who expected its terms to be kept and enforced. Of course, principle is one thing and implementation another, and in human affairs the former seldom finds complete realisation in the latter. In the colonies on the north-eastern seaboard, on the one hand, governments took the view that all the land rights of the Mi'kmaq and Maliseet had been extinguished by the French, who had ceded Acadia to the

British in 1713, while, on the other hand, the natives maintained that they had granted the French only the right to use the land.[31] Moreover, when fifty thousand loyalist refugees – including native, Mohawk allies – arrived in Nova Scotia at the end of the American War of Independence, they did not consider themselves bound by the provisions of the proclamation at all.[32] In at least one case, a native people did not survive: by 1829 the Beothuk people of Newfoundland had become extinct. Yet settlers' encroachments on their territory is only one of several mooted causes of their demise, which include European diseases, the Beothuk withdrawal into the interior and conflicts with other native peoples. The fate of the Beothuk was a matter of earnest concern to British governors, naval officers, settlers and merchants, who feared that 'the English nation, like the Spanish, may have affixed to its Character the indelible reproach of having extirpated a whole race of People'.[33] Meanwhile in Upper Canada the principles of the Royal Proclamation were adhered to and between 1781 and 1812 land was obtained to accommodate loyalists and, later, settlers by treaties with the native peoples.[34] Nonetheless, by the mid-1780s the Mississauga had been reduced by infectious diseases and weakened by widespread alcohol abuse, and by 1820 settlers outnumbered them by eighty to one.[35]

In the 1870s, when European settlement in western Canada was heralded by the construction of a railway heading towards the Pacific coast, seven 'Numbered Treaties' were made with native peoples (followed by a further four from 1899 to 1921 covering the northern territories). In these treaties both parties claimed common, equal kinship under the Crown, with Alexander Morris, lieutenant-governor of Manitoba, addressing the assembled native chiefs during the making of Treaty 6 in 1876, saying, 'You are, like me and my friends who are with me, children of the Queen. We are of the same blood, the same God made us and the same Queen rules over us.'[36] Facing the end of their traditional way of life with the imminent extinction of the bison, the native peoples of the west formally ceded vast tracts of land in return for retaining the right to hunt and fish outside of settlements, the assignment of land reserves held by the Crown for their use and benefit, the granting of annual payments, a cash bonus per capita, the supply of implements and cattle for farming and ranching, the provision of schools and government aid in time of famine.[37] Unfortunately, the collapse of the bison herds two years later and the ensuing famine happened so suddenly that the government was caught off guard and its provision of aid proved less than sufficient.[38]

Both in the case of the Beothuk and Mississauga in the east and of the tribes of the plains in the west, the vulnerability of native peoples to the diseases inadvertently imported by immune Europeans goes a long way towards explaining the speed with which they were displaced by settlers.[39] As James Daschuk writes:

> The importance of introduced infectious disease cannot be overstated in the history of indigenous America. In the Canadian northwest, epidemics of introduced contagious diseases swept through the region with regularity from the 1730s to the 1870s . . . [T]he spread of foreign diseases among highly susceptible populations comprised a tragic, unforeseen, but largely organic change. Those who place human agency and greed and the expansionism of colonial powers at the centre of decline of indigenous nations in the western hemisphere are missing half the story; the role played by biology cannot be ignored. It was a fundamental principle in the history of indigenous America.[40]

V

As in Canada, so in New Zealand British sovereignty and settlement expanded by way of treaty-making. The background was this. The islands that became known as New Zealand were first populated by Polynesian explorers who arrived in the thirteenth century.[41] So began what has been called 'the Māori colonial era', which, by introducing rats and dogs, led to the extinction of several species of native wildlife.[42] In the fifteenth and sixteenth centuries increased competition for resources gave rise to intertribal warfare, which was often indiscriminate (killing the elderly, women and children), involved the enslavement of the vanquished and sometimes cannibalism, and resulted in vendettas lasting generations.[43] After Captain James Cook re-discovered New Zealand in 1769, European trade with the Māori developed, initially via sealskins for the Chinese market, but by the 1830s through timber and flax for the Royal Navy.[44] On the Māori side, the trade was for muskets. These then fuelled three decades of intertribal 'Musket Wars' from 1807, which reached their peak in 1822–36 and caused the virtual extermination of some small tribes. By the early 1830s the Māori were trading 'the smoked heads of slain enemies' for muskets, with some slaves being killed specifically to supply the heads for this grisly market.[45] At least 20,000 Māori perished in these wars, which, together with disease, caused the native population to drop from about 110,000 in 1769 to 70,000 in 1837.[46] '[I]f any chapter in New Zealand history has earned the label "holocaust",' wrote Michael King, 'it is this one.'[47] The bloodshed ended thanks in part to the influence of Christianity, which forbad cannibalism and slavery, and whose influence was spread by Māori evangelists, many of them former slaves.[48]

By the 1830s, therefore, the Māori had been decimated by war and disease. In addition, they were being increasingly disturbed by the lawless attempts of growing numbers of settlers to acquire their lands. So in 1831 thirteen northern Māori chiefs twice sent letters to King William IV, asking the British Crown to protect them from interference by settlers and French seamen.[49] Although initially reluctant to get involved – as it often was – the British government eventually accepted that rapid and extensive settlement by British migrants was inevitable, and that annexing the territory would secure commercial interests and fend off the French while at the same time serving the humanitarian purpose of protecting the native peoples.[50] According to Michael King, successive governors of New South Wales and Colonial Office officials – their evangelical humanitarian convictions stiffened through lobbying by the Anglican and Wesleyan missionary societies and the Aborigines Protection Society – were 'the only authorities outside New Zealand who revealed themselves to be genuinely interested in the welfare of Māori, and in particular how well Māori were faring in their interaction with Europeans'. This concern was 'genuine and profound'.[51]

In 1832, therefore, a British resident was appointed to help introduce a settled form of government among the Māori, involving collective native sovereignty, in order to end intertribal warfare. After he had arrived, he found himself in receipt of native appeals to adjudicate

land disputes.[52] Subsequently, in 1835 thirty-four Māori chiefs signed
the Declaration of the Independence of New Zealand, in which the
British Crown was invited to protect a notional Māori nation. The
British, in turn, recognised the declaration. Initially, the evangelical
secretary of state for war and the colonies, Lord Glenelg, was minded
to protect the Māori by resisting pressure from private enterprise in
the form of the New Zealand Association (later, the New Zealand
Company) to permit organised colonisation, but by 1838 colonisation
had come to be regarded as inevitable.[53] The protective task then
became to manage it humanely.

In 1839 the first lieutenant-governor was instructed to gain 'the free
and intelligent consent of the Natives according to their customary
usages' for 'the recognition of Her Majesty's sovereign authority over
the whole or any part of those islands which they may be willing to
place under Her Majesty's dominion',[54] and in 1840 the Treaty of
Waitangi was signed by 540 Māori chiefs from both North and South
Islands. In the English-language version of the treaty the Māori ceded
to the British Crown both 'sovereignty' and the right of pre-emption
to buy whatever land the Māori might wish to sell, in return for full
property rights over their lands, forests and fisheries, as well as the
rights and privileges of British subjects. Quite what British 'sovereignty'
would amount to and what kind of Māori autonomy it would allow,
however, was left unclear and became a hostage to later interpretative
fortune.

According to Claudia Orange, author of the standard account of
the Treaty of Waitangi and its ramifications:

> By 1850 the balance sheet of benefits and disadvantages of British
> administration might well have appeared favourable to many Maori.
> There appeared to be a place for Maori people in a variety of colonial
> activities. They profited from the increased pace of development as
> settlement expanded . . . Through government employment on road
> and other public works, as well as through private contracts, Maori
> earned considerable amounts in cash . . . In some instances, Maori
> took the initiative – a hotel . . . townships . . . flour mills . . . Money
> earned by Maori contributed in no small measure to the welfare of

both Maori and settler . . . Many Maori also participated in the social life of the colony. In the capital, they took part in regattas, attended levees and socials at Government House, celebrated the Queen's birthday and the colony's anniversary day with feasts provided at government expense . . . The new authority in the land also gradually overcame some of the old tribal antagonisms and made it possible for tribes to mix and communicate more freely . . . Under [Governor George] Grey's administration, some of the long-promised welfare benefits were provided: hospitals were opened . . . and the Education Ordinance provided for Maori education.[55]

Nevertheless, disquiet over the implications of British 'sovereignty' continued to disturb. On the one hand, the British needed sovereignty in the form of supreme authority to impose law and order on both Māori and non-Māori, not least by controlling the sale of land. On the other hand, as recognised by James Stephen, permanent under-secretary in the Colonial Office, subjection to British sovereignty and to English law were not 'convertible terms', and the difference allowed space for Māori legal autonomy – short of customs such as cannibal-ism.[56] But the uncertain difference also allowed for friction. So when, in 1841, Governor William Hobson forbad the felling of kauri trees, to stop the wanton destruction of forests, and when the first Māori accused of multiple murders was apprehended, native resentment at perceived British overreach stirred.[57]

Some Māori interpreted the indeterminate meaning of British 'sover-eignty' so as to permit autonomous political institutions that would strengthen the protection of native custom and the representation of native interests to the government. So, in 1853, began a movement to set up a Māori 'king' at the apex of a loose federation, and in 1860 a conference at Kohimarama affirmed the co-existence of the traditional jurisdictions of native chiefs under a 'sovereign', protective British one.[58] In 1892 this pursuit of native autonomy blossomed into a Māori parliament, albeit one intended to supplement, rather than supplant, its New Zealand counterpart.

Not all Māori supported this political direction, however. The 1852 constitution had granted the franchise to any male aged twenty-one or over who could meet the property qualification, regardless of race, and from 1867 the property restriction was lifted and special Māori constituencies returned four members to the New Zealand legislature in Wellington. Just as the experiment in a native parliament petered out in the opening years of the twentieth century, the Young Māori Party emerged in Wellington, comprising Māori MPs who regarded separatist demands for 'Absolute Maori Authorities' as 'wishful thinking', and who were 'convinced that survival for the Maori race lay in shedding those aspects of the traditional way of life that retarded Maori acceptance of the modern world'.[59]

Native autonomy was not the only issue; native land was another. By the late 1850s the Māori were beginning to feel overwhelmed. In 1858 the settler population had burgeoned to 59,000 (from 2,000 in 1840), outnumbering the native people.[60] The gold rushes of the 1860s sucked in more immigrants, not only from Europe but also from China.[61] The newcomers' hunger for land intensified disputes. Frustrated by the constraints of the Treaty of Waitangi upon land sales and purchase, settlers preferred a narrow reading of the treaty's guarantee of Māori land, restricting it to what was occupied and cultivated. London, however, refused this.[62] Māori, on the other hand, were irritated at the government's use of the right of pre-emption to buy cheaply from the natives, sell dearly to the settlers and then use the profits to finance administration and development.[63] Sometimes settlers and natives claimed to differ in their understanding of what had been purchased. So when in 1844 a settler attempted to remove manganese from land he had bought, the local chief objected that he had sold the land but not the stones. Claudia Orange comments that 'it is difficult to know whether he [the chief] was simply "giving it a try"'.[64] In 1860 war broke out over a land sale by one Māori chief, to which a superior chief (within his customary rights) objected, but which the governor insisted should proceed.[65] Thus began a series of 'New Zealand Wars' that lasted until 1872, in which the Māori tribes involved sometimes met with considerable success, and which left large areas of the inland North Island under their effective control.[66]

The government's policy of punitive confiscation often took away the most desirable land and failed to discriminate between tribes that had fought against the Crown and those that had not, thus generating long-standing grievances.[67] Church of England missionaries led a campaign to uphold Māori rights under the Treaty of Waitangi, both in New Zealand and in Britain.[68] However, New Zealand had been made a self-governing colony in 1852, partly because of the difficulty of trying to rule effectively from London at a distance of 11,000 miles (as the crow flies), partly to save the British Treasury the costs of direct rule and partly – no doubt – tutored by the experience of the American Revolution.[69] While it is true that the constitution reserved any legislative enactment of the colonial parliament on specifically Māori affairs for the Crown's assent, on the principle that it was the Crown's duty to stand between settler and Māori, native affairs were difficult to isolate in practice.[70] As a consequence, the London government tended to consider that it had no right to interfere in the self-governing colony's affairs.[71] The battle for Māori rights had to be fought in New Zealand. There, in the last quarter of the twentieth century, it won some strategic victories. Māori appeals to the Treaty of Waitangi for redress led to the establishment in 1975 of the Waitangi Tribunal, with the power to rule on alleged breaches. Ten years later, the tribunal was empowered to consider cases reaching back to 1840. By the end of the twentieth century, almost a thousand claims had been registered, some attracting settlements involving compensation of NZ$170 million.[72]

VI

The humanitarian concern that moved the British government to assert its sovereignty over New Zealand was fuelled in no small part by what had happened to the aboriginal peoples of Australia. Before Captain Cook set sail for the Antipodes in 1768 he was instructed that, should he find the land inhabited, he was to 'endeavour by all proper means to cultivate a friendship and alliance with [the native peoples]' and 'with [their] consent . . . to take possession of convenient situations in the country in the name of the King of Great Britain'.[73] However, when the British reached Australia in 1770, they discovered a territory that seemed to them very sparsely populated and then only with foragers, not farmers settled on bounded land.[74] It also seemed that there were no established political authorities among the natives with whom treaties could be made. So, in 1788, when the first fleet of convict ships arrived on the coast of what would become New South Wales, British settlement proceeded on the assumption that the land was *terra nullius* – belonging to no one.[75]

It soon became clear that that was not the view of the aboriginals, who, when they saw that the foreigners intended to stay, began to attack them.[76] The frontier violence that flared up over subsequent decades, being subject to no common rules of war, was accordingly unrestrained and embittering. Colonial governors nevertheless strove to impose order by asserting the Crown's right of pre-emption in the matter of land purchase, and by asserting the rule of law equally over both settlers and aboriginals, treating violence between them as a matter for the courts. On occasions when they felt themselves compelled to manage indigenous violence by dispatching punitive expeditions composed of settlers, they found themselves reprimanded by London. In 1835, for example, the secretary of state for war and the colonies, Lord Glenelg, rebuked Governor Stirling of Western Australia for authorising such an expedition, and reminded him that aboriginal law-breakers should be arrested and punished according to the law. And two years later Glenelg reminded Governor Bourke of New South Wales that it was wrong to regard the aboriginal people 'as Aliens with whom a War can exist, and against who H.M.'s troops may exercise belligerent right', rather than as fellow subjects of the Crown. The Colonial Office's view was well expressed by Governor Gipps soon after his arrival in New South Wales in 1838:

> As human beings partaking of our common nature – as the aboriginal possessors of the soil from which the wealth of the country has been principally derived – and as subjects of the Queen, whose authority extends over every part of New Holland – the natives of the colony have an equal right with the people of European origin to the protection and assistance of the law of England.[77]

Unfortunately, Gipps, like so many colonial governors in the nineteenth century, found that his power to convert British policy into colonial practice was limited.[78] By the 1830s the devastating impact of British settlement upon native peoples had impressed itself upon the imperial centre and inspired Parliament to set up a Select Committee on Aboriginal Tribes. In its 1837 report, the committee concluded that '[w]hatever may have been the injustice of this encroachment [in New Holland, that is, mainland Australia], there is no reason to suppose that either justice or humanity would now be consulted by receding from it'.[79] Since it appeared to them that there was no going back, the only way was forward: to protect and educate native peoples. In fact, colonial government had anticipated that more than twenty years earlier, when Gipps' predecessor as governor, Lachlan Macquarie, had established a school for aboriginal children and set aside land for adult settlement and cultivation.

VII

Expanding empire without making treaties was a recipe for bitter conflict. At its best, treaty-making allowed empire to grow peacefully with the consent of many native peoples, which was given in the expectation of certain benefits. Sometimes, however, the British were less than scrupulous in explaining the terms to which agreement was sought. As we saw in section II earlier, it is possible that, in 1888, Charles Rudd was economical with the truth about what Lobengula's concession would entail. While the written text had been translated and explained to the king several times, there is testimony from a missionary-interpreter that Rudd, desperate to secure an agreement, added a set of verbal assurances 'that they would not bring more than 10 white men to work in his country, that they would not dig anywhere near towns, etc., and that they and their people would abide by the laws of his country and in fact be his people'.[80] If that is so, Rudd's promise – at least about the number of white immigrants – was not kept. It is, therefore, possible that the king was deceived on this point, as he later claimed to have been. However, quite how decisive were Rudd's alleged verbal qualifications in gaining his consent, we do not know. What we do know is that Lobengula was no fool and had had long experience of signing concessions to white men. Moreover, he was under siege by competing pressures – from the Boers, the Portuguese, the British and some of his own people who were urging him to authorise the annihilation of the whites. So it might be that he *did* know what he was doing when he signed the 'Rudd Concession', but, under pressure from one quarter or another, subsequently got cold feet and reneged on it. Whatever the cause, Lobengula later repudiated what he had put his hand to.

Sometimes treaties were made in less than good faith. At other times, while acting in good faith, the parties differed in their understanding of the terms. Thus, as we have also seen, the British and the Māori understood different things by 'sovereignty' in the Treaty of Waitangi. In the case of Canada, a common claim now made is that the natives could not conceive of the permanent alienation of land, and that when they made agreements with the British, they understood themselves to be 'sharing' land, not simply giving it away. Sarah Carter, for example, writes of the nearly seven million acres of land ceded by treaties between 1815 to 1825 that, while the British understood them to confer complete title, aboriginal tribes '*most likely* had a different conception of these agreements, not believing that the land was sold once and for all, but rather agreeing to share their land'.[81] She bases this tentative claim on 'the oral history of Aboriginal people'.[82] Similarly, Tracey Lindberg writes of 'the impossibility of cession of land by Indigenous peoples'.[83] In support, she invokes the present-day testimony of Leroy Little Bear, a member of the Blackfoot people, who has claimed that 'the standard or norm of the aboriginal peoples' law is that land is not transferable and therefore is inalienable. Land and benefits may be shared with others, and when Indian nations entered into treaties with European nations, the subject of the treaty, from the Indians' viewpoint, was not the alienation of the land but the sharing of the land.'[84]

There are, however, a number of problems with this account. First of all, the claim being made about how native people – *all* of them, *every*where, *throughout* history? – understood ownership is not merely historical, but political: it is being made in order to support contemporary legal cases asserting rights and demanding restitution or compensation. Of itself, that does not make the claim false, but it does signal that it is not disinterested.

Second, the native peoples of North America had been in contact with Europeans since the 1600s, some of them even visiting Europe. It seems implausible, therefore, to suppose that they had no idea at all of how Europeans understood property and its transfer – and therefore no idea of what the British understood by a treaty to cede land.

Third, the natives had had plenty of experience of the alienability of land, since they were intermittently pushing each other off it.

Fourth, if Flanagan is correct, the natives themselves were not lacking a concept of exclusive ownership. Plains Indians such as the Comanche, notwithstanding the fluidity of their situation, had institutions of private ownership. Forest hunters such as the Ojibwa recognised an exclusive right to harvest certain species in defined territories. And fishing peoples along the Pacific coast conferred a right to the private landownership of salmon runs at particular sites.[85]

Fifth and finally, oral testimony is not always reliable. As the Byzantine historian Mark Whittow has written:

> [S]ince at least the 1950s anthropologists have demonstrated how fluid and adaptable oral history can be . . . [T]he oral history of a tribe was primarily concerned to explain the present, and to this end would adapt and shape its view of the past . . . creating stories with supporting details to explain and justify present circumstances. Even under settled conditions an accurate memory of the past effectively lasted no more than two generations; in times of migration and other social upheaval change is quicker and more profound.[86]

What Whittow wrote with early medieval Arabic sources mainly in mind finds corroboration from anthropological experts on the native peoples of North America. Bruce Trigger, a Canadian anthropologist, has written of the 'tendency for lore to be refashioned as circumstances change'.[87] And another Canadian, Alexander von Gernet, who has made a special study of the use of oral traditions in litigation, has written: 'When independent evidence is available to permit validation, some oral traditions about events centuries old turn out to be surprisingly accurate . . . [However,] there is . . . overwhelming evidence that many oral traditions do not remain consistent over time and are either inadvertently or deliberately changed to meet new needs.'[88] Some of those 'new needs' are political.

VIII

A crucial factor in determining the nature of the encounter between British migrants and native peoples in Canada, South Africa, Australia and New Zealand was the power of the imperial and colonial governments – or, to be exact, the *limits* of that power. While both imperial and colonial governments encouraged emigration to Canada, Australia and South Africa at various times in the nineteenth and early twentieth centuries, most of it 'happened outside of government control'.[89] On an early occasion when the imperial government sought to stop the migration of European settlers, it famously failed. After the end of Pontiac's War, and in enforcement of the Royal Proclamation of 1763, the British stationed ten thousand troops along the Appalachian and Allegheny Mountains to stop settlers moving west into native territory, leaving the interests of the western tribes in the care of two super-intendents – Colonel John Stuart who was married to a Cherokee, and Sir William Johnson who was married to a Mohawk.[90] The British were perfectly sincere in their attempts to preserve the peace and rights of the native population. As the commander-in-chief of British forces in North America, Thomas Gage, commented in 1767, 'I find everywhere that the Soldiers agree perfectly well with the Indians, and they seem to look upon them at present, as People who are to protect them from Injurys.'[91] However, the best intentions of the redcoat cordon did not suffice. The following year, Gage wrote that '[a]t present there is a total Dissolution of Law and Justice on this head, amongst People of the Western Frontier; and the Indians can get no Satisfaction but in their own way, by retaliating on those who unhappily fall into their hands'.[92] Not only did the imperial government's attempt at restricting migration fail, it also so irritated both settlers and land speculators (among them, George Washington) that it became a major cause of American colonists' wholesale rejection of imperial authority in 1775.[93] That is why so many native people fought alongside the imperial

British during the American War of Independence: to resist the westward expansion of an alternative, American colonial empire. As the Mohawk chief Joseph Brant (Thayendanegea) put it: 'the Rebels . . . in a great measure begin this Rebellion to be sole Masters of this Continent'.[94]

After the colonists had won the war, the new US government did not even try to stop the migration, seeking only to manage it. As Thomas Jefferson remarked, frontier folk 'will settle the lands in spite of everybody'.[95] He understood what had eluded the British: that 'American leaders needed to ride, rather than resist, the settler wave heading west'.[96] But even riding proved difficult. When, in 1790, the first federal Congress enacted the Indian Trade and Intercourse Act, prohibiting the sale of tribal lands without the consent of the federal government, the original thirteen states proceeded to violate the law with impunity.[97]

As the US federal government struggled to control the federated states, so the British imperial government struggled to control its colonies. We have already noted in Chapter 2 how London, its fingers burned by the American War of Independence, was loath to override the autonomy of legislative assemblies in the West Indies on matters to do with slavery in the opening decades of the 1800s. A similar case arose at the dawn of the following century in South Africa. The year 1902 saw the signing of the Treaty of Vereeniging, which brought to an end the Second Anglo-Boer War between the British and the two Afrikaner (or Boer) republics of the Transvaal and the Orange Free State. The war had been launched in 1899 by the Boers with an invasion of Natal and Cape Colony. Yet their invasion was pre-emptive, because they perceived, with some good reason, that the British were angling for a showdown.

Much historical controversy has attended the issue of the primary motives and intentions of the British. These varied among the leading agents, but, with due respect to Marxist historians, seizure of the diamond and gold mines in Witwatersrand was not foremost among them. British policy was driven by Sir Alfred Milner – whom we last met in Egypt – who was an ardent Apostle of the superior virtues of fair, efficient and modernising British administration. Milner wanted to give South Africa the benefit of such virtuous government, and to secure regional peace, first between Afrikaner and British, and then between white and black, by creating an imperial confederation of states, as had recently been achieved in Canada. Initially, Milner had hoped to woo the Boers to his scheme, but eventually he came to the conclusion that it would either have to be forced upon them or abandoned altogether. One of the reasons that the Boer republics resisted absorption into the British Empire, even with confederal autonomy, was that they deeply resented British criticism of their mistreatment of black Africans and correlative interference by the imperial authorities to secure African rights. Cape Colony had granted black Africans the vote, under the same conditions as whites, as early as 1853. And in the 1881 Convention of Pretoria, which ended the First Anglo-Boer War, the British had insisted on the sovereignty of the empire, partly to secure the right of imperial authorities to intervene in defence of black Africans.[98]

However, in Article 8 of the Treaty of Vereeniging the British agreed to let the issue of the granting of the franchise to black Africans in the Boer republics be decided 'after' the republics had been removed from post-war imperial supervision and granted confederal autonomy. That is, it was agreed that the Boers should decide the matter for themselves. Some have seen this as demonstrating that the British had never really cared about African rights in the first place, exposing their humanitarian claims as mere rhetoric. One such was Thomas Pakenham, who, commenting on Milner's proposal to defer the granting of the native franchise, wrote: 'This . . . meant, in effect, that [he] . . . was proposing that they should make the exclusion permanent. Once self-governing, no Boer state would give the vote to Africans.' Colonial Office officials at the time agreed. One argued that '[t]he native franchise . . . is the only point worth hesitating about. As clause 9 [which became Article 8 in the final version] stands the native will never have the franchise. No responsible Govt. [that is, no self-governing colony] will give it to him'; while another wrote that 'it would not be in accordance with the traditions of British policy in South Africa to use words implying a doubt whether any civilized native would ever receive the franchise'. Eventually, however, the Cabinet yielded to Milner, leading Pakenham to make the damning judgement that the retention of '[t]he crucial word "after"... in Clause 9... made mockery of Chamberlain's claim that one of Britain's war aims was to improve the status of Africans'.[99]

Pakenham, however, is unfair.[100] He would have been correct, if Clause 9 (or Article 8) had expressed a simple or casual abandonment of African rights. However, there is a very plausible, alternative interpretation, which rests on a realistic appraisal of the limits of imperial power. The Second Anglo-Boer War had taken the British far longer, and cost them far more, to win than they had expected. In its latter stages it had moved into a guerrilla phase, involved ruthless counter-insurgency methods, and was accordingly very bitter indeed. The Boer republics had attracted a lot of international sympathy, and the British a correlative amount of opprobrium. At its end, both Milner and Herbert Kitchener, the senior British military commander, were extremely keen to make a sustainable peace and to bind up the deep wounds inflicted upon the relationship between Afrikaner and Briton. They perceived that to insist on African rights would be to pour salt in those wounds, and could result in the resumption of war. They also perceived that for the imperial authorities to try and enforce such rights in the republics would require a level of military and financial commitment that could not command domestic political support. So they compromised. But they did not compromise for trivial reasons: they wanted to avoid the resumption of bitter war and the futile imposition of military occupation. Nor did Milner simply surrender the cause of African rights. Rather, he compromised in the hope that, long-term, once the Boer republics had settled down in the British Empire and discovered the benefits of its administration, and once immigration had increased the British proportion of their populations, the issue of the rights of black Africans could be successfully addressed by political means.[101] His compromise was an instance of *Realpolitik* or 'realistic policy', but it did not simply jettison principle.[102]

As it turned out, Milner's assiduous attempts to increase British immigration were largely unsuccessful and the Afrikaner element therefore came to predominate in the new Union of South Africa, which was launched in 1910. The ultimate consequence was the abolition of the native franchise in 1934 and the loss of what Pakenham calls 'that priceless Liberal legacy: the no colour-bar tradition of the Cape'.[103]

But Milner and the British can only be blamed for that consequence, if, all things prudently considered, they could have stopped it. The limits of Britain's power – even at the very apogee of the British Empire – were such that they could not. Sometimes bad things happened to native peoples, not because the empire was too strong, but because it was too weak.

IX

There is no doubt that the native peoples with whom British colonists came into contact were invariably disturbed by the encounter, and sometimes they suffered grievously from it. In North America, Australia and to a lesser extent New Zealand this was because the number of immigrating settlers was overwhelming. There and in Africa, it was also because the disparity in cultural – and especially technological – development was great, much greater than that between Europeans and Indians. And while imperial pacification was beneficial in ending constant intertribal warfare, it also had the demoralising and socially destabilising effect of making native warrior classes redundant.[104] But, above all, the colonial encounter was destructive because of the susceptibility of the natives to imported diseases, which ravaged them.[105] Yet while the British and other Europeans were often the carriers, they were not the only ones. The deadliest killer of Australian aboriginals is reckoned to have been smallpox, some of which was probably transmitted by fishermen from what is now Indonesia.[106]

Sometimes native peoples lost territory to colonists because the latter mistook land that was unoccupied or uncultivated for land that was unowned. Sometimes the natives lost it because they were conquered by ungoverned settlers in war that easily flared up on lawless frontiers, where fear was abundant and trust rare. However, where British imperial authorities succeeded in asserting their 'sovereignty' over territory in North America, Australasia or Africa, native title to land was recognised and its transfer to settlers regulated – in principle and sometimes in practice – for the sake of justice and of peace. As Ronald Hyam has written, 'It is easy to condemn the extension of Western rule as sheer acquisitiveness. But the brutal alternative would have been rule by irresponsible European adventurers, armed with all the resources of their civilisation to work their selfish will as they wished, without any superior control at all.'[107] The normal imperial means of land transfer, therefore, was not by conquest but by treaty. Sometimes both parties shared the same understanding of what was agreed; sometimes they did not. Sometimes treaties were kept; sometimes they were broken. But even a broken treaty can provide the ground for legal remedy – as the Treaty of Waitangi has been doing in New Zealand since 1975.

5

Cultural Assimilation
and 'Genocide'

I

When the people of one culture meets another and dominates it in number and power, only three outcomes are possible: either the dominant people annihilates the dominated one, or the latter adapts and assimilates, or the two peoples separate. As we have seen with the Beothuk of Newfoundland, British colonial settlement did sometimes cause the annihilation of a native people. Whether such a phenomenon really was the result of human choice and ought to be called 'genocide' – as many are now wont to do – is a question we shall consider later in this chapter. The third option, separation – of which Afrikaner *apartheid* or 'separateness' was a version – was not British imperial policy.[1] Whether in Canada, Australia, New Zealand or South Africa, imperial policy was assimilation, even when provisional separation or segregation was countenanced.[2] The view that native peoples were essentially equal to Britons, possessed of the potential to become equally civilised, predominated in the imperial metropolis, even when some settlers on the colonial periphery doubted it.

Policies of assimilation usually started with such things as the creation of land reserves, the provision of native schools, the conversion of collective ownership into private property, the introduction of wage-labour and the promotion of agriculture. The consignment of indigenous people to reserves did involve segregation, of course, but it was viewed only as an interim measure. 'We must remember that they are the original owners of the soil, of which they have been dispossessed by the covetousness or ambition of our ancestors,' said John A. Macdonald, prime minister of Canada, to the House of Commons in May 1880. 'All we can hope for is to wean them [the natives], by slow degrees, from their nomadic habits, which have almost become an instinct, and by slow degrees absorb them or settle them on the land. Meantime they must be fairly protected.'[3] Segregation therefore was seen as a necessary step towards gradual assimilation: 'The reserve system was thought of as a protected training school in which Indians, sheltered from harsh contact, could be readied for membership in the larger society.'[4]

As a result, many native people did adapt. Supported by Upper Canada's policy of providing reserve-natives with land, seed, agricultural implements and 'religious improvement, education and instruction in husbandry',[5] the Algonquians rapidly adopted farming, while seeking to maintain their cultures and societies.[6] By the 1890s, agriculture on the reserves in the southern part of eastern Canada involved the systematic use of animals and farm machinery and production on a commercial scale. Some native people became fully integrated into the modern wage-earning economy and 'a small but important' number acquired a formal education and entered professional careers.[7] Adaptation on the prairies was more difficult, because of the sudden collapse of the bison and the lack of an agricultural tradition. Nonetheless, the chiefs of the native peoples of the western plains understood the necessity of change and so viewed the Numbered Treaties of the 1870s 'first and foremost as a bridge to a future without bison', deliberately extracting from the confederal government pledges of assistance in converting to agriculture.[8] As a consequence, by the 1920s, agriculture was quite well established on many prairie reserves: when the Hobbema Cree settled on their reserves around 1880 'they had virtually nothing', but by the late 1920s they had 'come close to self-sufficiency'.[9]

Nonetheless, there had been moves to deviate from this general pattern in the direction of permanent segregation. For example, Sir

Francis Bond Head, lieutenant-governor of Upper Canada from 1836 to 1838, regarded attempts to convert native people to farming as so much wasted effort, and proposed the removal of the Anishinabeg to Manitoulin Island, where they could continue their traditional way of life: 'The greatest Kindness we can perform toward these intelligent, simple-minded People, is to remove and fortify them as much as possible from all Communication with Whites.'[10] However, Head's proposal was abandoned in the face of a storm of protest from native leaders, missionaries and the Aborigines Protection Society in London, bolstered by native support for the Crown during the rebellions of 1837–8.[11]

The ascendancy of the policy of assimilation was signalled by the title of a piece of legislation passed by the Assembly of the Canadas in 1857: the 'Gradual Civilization Act'. This was explicitly designed to bring about the ultimate integration of native people and to remove all legal distinctions between them and other Canadians. To begin with, however, natives would have a distinct legal status as wards of the government, who were denied the franchise. However, any native adult male judged by a special board of examiners to be educated, free from debt and of good moral character would be free to apply for full legal rights and so become enfranchised. After a successful three-year trial period, he could acquire ownership of fifty acres of land, which would be removed from the reserve. At that point, the applicant would cease to be a member of a native people (in the eyes of the law).[12] Just under three decades later, the 1885 Electoral Franchise Act gave the vote to all adult male Indians in Eastern Canada who met the necessary property requirements, and allowed some male 'status Indians' in Eastern and Central Canada to vote without giving up their own laws, language and system of government.[13] This was welcomed by natives such as Chief Charles Big Canoe and band councillor James Ashquabe, who wrote to Prime Minister Macdonald to thank him for his 'earnest efforts to promote the welfare of the Indian people throughout the whole Dominion . . . We appreciate your difficulties in dealing with our less civilized brother in the Northwest who had not had the advantages we in Ontario have had . . . we thank you most cordially for the gift of franchise'.[14] In 1886 Macdonald wrote to Peter Jones

(Kahkewaquonaby), a Mississauga chief and Methodist minister, 'I hope to see some day the Indian race represented by one of themselves on the floor of the House of Commons.'[15]

This political assimilation was not unique in the British Empire and Canada was not the first part to enfranchise native people. As we have noted, in South Africa's Cape Colony black Africans were given the parliamentary vote on the same terms as whites in 1853, that is, on condition of ownership of property worth at least £25 or an annual income of £50 or more.[16] Before the creation of the Union of South Africa, this produced only a small black electorate of eight thousand, but that is reckoned sufficient to have had a decisive influence in seven of the thirty-seven constituencies in the general election of 1890.[17] Meanwhile in New Zealand the vote was extended to all Māori adult males in 1867, twelve years ahead of being given to their European counterparts, when the property qualification was abolished.[18] Indeed, from 1887 to 1894 an Irish-Māori MP, James Carroll (known to Māori as 'Timi Kara'), twice served as acting prime minister.[19]

Mistakes were made, of course, and there were failings. In Canada the Indian Act of 1876, for example, sought to preserve the territorial integrity of the native reserves by making real and private property immune from seizure by off-reserve creditors. By the same token, however, it made it impossible for natives to raise capital for investment, since they could not offer their property as security against loans.[20] In the west the home farm policy for developing agriculture on the reserves was ill-conceived and, launched in 1879, was abandoned only a few years later.[21] The administration of native affairs during the famine of the late 1870s and early 1880s was rife with corruption, and the company contracted to deliver rations to starving natives abused its privileged position to deliver substandard food.[22]

II

However, the instrument of assimilation that now attracts the fiercest opprobrium was Canada's system of residential schools. The motivation for establishing these schools was basically humanitarian, namely, to enable pupils to adapt and survive in a world that was changing radically.[23] This was a general need that many native people themselves acknowledged, as they found themselves unable to sustain their traditional hunting-and-gathering economy. As Chief Paulus Claus of the Bay of Quinte Mohawk said at the July 1846 conference at Orillia (in what is now southern Ontario), 'we cannot be a people unless we conform ourselves to the ways of the white man'.[24] Consequently, native leaders actively lobbied missionaries to set up schools that would teach their children agricultural skills, English language and Christian religion.

By the 1840s the Anglican and Methodist churches, having experimented with different kinds of schools, both independently reached the conclusion that boarding schools were likely to be most efficacious.[25] The rationale for this was that the induction of young native people into English- or French-speaking farming culture would be advanced by entirely abstracting them from their inherited environment. Thus, in 1835, the Methodist missionary Peter Jones, himself a mixed-blood Mississauga who 'believed fervently that European ways and Christianity were . . . for the benefit of the Ojibwa', advocated the removal of Indian children from their homes to boarding schools.[26] Nine years later the report of the governor-general's ('Bagot') Commission on the Affairs of Indians in Canada recommended a policy of promoting residential schools. Participation was entirely voluntary until 1894 and voluntary as a rule until 1920, when the government acquired the authority to compel the attendance of any child.[27] Between 1883 and 1996, when the last of the schools closed, about 150,000 children attended them. This amounted to only a third of native school-age children.[28]

Unfortunately, the reality of the schools not infrequently fell short of their humanitarian ideal. Too often, the discouragement of speaking native languages was unnecessarily strict, native culture was generally denigrated and indiscriminately suppressed, the promotion of Christianity was aggressive, the time devoted to manual labour was excessive and the time reserved for classroom education was inadequate. The diet, clothing and provision of medical services were generally poor – although 'students . . . were conscious that the conditions from which they had come to the school were often no better, or even worse'.[29] There was also corporal punishment, bullying and sexual abuse – this last perpetrated sometimes by members of staff, but more often by other pupils.[30]

Quite how extensive these failings were is difficult to determine. Certainly, they were not universal. In 1886, for example, Red Crow, a powerful chief in the Blood nation of the Blackfoot Confederacy, together with several of his fellow chiefs, 'had been greatly impressed by the attainment of Indian youths at the Anglican Mohawk Institute'.[31] Moreover, had there not been a significant record of success, 'numerous Indian groups' would not have lobbied, as they did, for the establishment of residential schools well into the twentieth century – for example, among the Methodist missions of central Alberta and the Anglican Diocese of Keewatin.[32] As for first-hand testimony, it is equivocal. As J. R. Miller, author of the standard history of the residential schools, has commented:

> While there are many former students who testify to the damage that
> the suppression of their language and other things did to them and to
> people they knew, there are also former students who firmly deny that
> their school experience scarred them or their fellow students . . . Too
> many ex-pupils have spoken positively of the experience as a whole,
> or of particular school workers who befriended them, or even of the
> balance of positive consequences that they struck after weighing both
> sides to justify ignoring or downplaying such memories . . . Too many
> . . . argue that the schools were important sources of knowledge and
> preparation for them to trivialize all positive recollections as the prod-
> ucts of individual peculiarities.[33]

Consequently, Miller concludes, '[t]he verdict on the full effect of residential schools on Native identity must . . . be given in muted and equivocal tones'.[34]

Those, however, are not at all the tones in which the verdict is now almost universally given. Nowadays the residential school system in Canada is commonly represented as the expression of 'a conscious racist strategy to exterminate aboriginal peoples'[35] and as a form of 'cultural genocide'.[36] To take one eminent example, the Truth and Reconciliation Commission of Canada opened the 'summary' volume of its final report in 2015 thus:

> For over a century, the central goals of Canada's Aboriginal policy were to eliminate Aboriginal governments; ignore Aboriginal rights; terminate the Treaties; and, through a process of assimilation, cause Aboriginal peoples to cease to exist as distinct legal, social, cultural, religious, and racial entities in Canada. The establishment and operation of residential schools were a central element of this policy, which can best be described as 'cultural genocide'.[37]

The historical connotations of 'genocide' encourage identification with the Nazi paradigm, and some have exploited this. So, in their 1997 book *The Circle Game*, Roland Chrisjohn and Sherri Young compared the residential school experience to the Holocaust, equating it with Hitler's attempts to create an Aryan master race.[38] More recently, the attention drawn to unmarked graves in cemeteries associated with the residential schools has been broadcast by native representatives, the Canadian press, the *New York Times* and Al Jazeera as the 'discovery' of 'mass graves', with all the connotations of mass murder such as the Nazis perpetrated.[39]

The assertion of judgements as extreme and misleading as this has been aided by the deliberate suppression of evidence to the contrary. Writing of the early 1990s, Miller observed that '[w]hat is sometimes disturbing is that at least some former pupils with positive memories tried unsuccessfully to place their positive recollections before the public via the press and electronic media, only to be rebuffed or ignored. For the most part, former students and former staff members who wish to provide a positive recollection or introduce some balance into the media depictions of residential school life have been relegated to the pages of denominational publications.'[40]

Yet even Miller, who is scrupulous enough to introduce a measure of balance into his account and who rejects the description of 'genocide', tends to exaggerate the sins of the residential schools.[41] This is mainly because of his undifferentiated understanding of 'racism', which he asserts was 'pervasive' in Euro-Canadian society.[42] A large part of what he means here is that European Canadians judged native ways by their own standards and, finding them wanting, were confirmed in their own 'racial superiority'.[43] Yet surely every people judges a foreign people by its own standards, and surely sometimes a people recognises foreigners as superior *in certain respects* – and is quite correct to do so. Many native people, observing European culture, recognised its superiority in terms of writing, technology, agriculture and medicine. That is why they wanted schools where their children could learn from it, so that future generations might share in its benefits. And those natives who chose to convert to Christianity presumably found something attractive in its world-view that was lacking in their inherited religion. Since it really is possible for one culture to be superior to another in certain respects, it cannot be racist to recognise it. And since native people sometimes agreed with Europeans that the latter's culture was superior in certain respects, it can hardly have been racist for Europeans to suppose it.[44]

What would have been racist is the European view that there was nothing at all redeeming in native culture and a consequently dismissive regard for it. It seems that this was in fact the view of some missionaries, who showed a patronising lack of sympathy for the inherited culture of their native pupils and sometimes presented a stark Manichaean dichotomy between European Christian virtue and native pagan vice.[45] It was this attempt at total cultural 'assimilation', as distinct from partial 'adjustment' or 'adaptation', that Miller rightly objects to.[46] Yet such an indiscriminate attitude was not universal, as he himself observes:

Clerics and bureaucrats frequently commented on the 'mental quickness' or the natural intelligence of the Indian, and they often noted as well the admirable ethical qualities of Aboriginal society in its undisturbed state . . . The deputy minister responsible for Indian policy at the time the industrial schools were developed thought that 'Indians as a rule are as intelligent and amenable to reason as White men' [Edgar Dewdney, 1884].[47]

What would have been even more deeply racist is the view that native peoples were biologically inferior, forever destined by nature to occupy a lower level of existence. Miller occasionally suggests that this was the prevalent view, as when he tells us that Christian thinking in Canada, the US and Britain 'had become suffused with racist preconceptions, partially as a result of "scientific racism"', which he associates with social Darwinism.[48] But this is quite wrong, for the Christian humanitarianism that dominated so much colonial thinking in the wake of the abolition of slavery was based on the premise of the fundamental equality of all races under God, which implies that such racial inequality as exists is merely developmental, not essential. And this Christian view was not generally eclipsed by its social Darwinist rival in the English-speaking world. As Colin Kidd writes:

> ... even at the high noon of nineteenth century racialism, theological imperatives drove the conventional mainstream of science and scholarship to search for mankind's underlying unities. The emphasis of racial investigation was not upon divisions between races but on race as an accidental, epiphenomenal mask concealing the unitary Adamic origins of a single extended human family ... quietly, subtly and indirectly, theological needs drew white Europeans into a benign state of denial, a refusal to accept that human racial differences were anything other than skin deep ... Theological factors, more than any others, dictated that the proof of sameness would be the dominant feature of western racial science.[49]

Nor was the Christian view displaced in Canada. From his analysis of debates in the Canadian House of Commons from 1880 to 1925, Glen Williams concludes that '[a]lthough it was growing in influence in the [sic] late nineteenth century Canadian political life, biological determinism never had the field entirely to itself... it was scarcely possible to stand in the House to make a speech denigrating a "race", without someone rising in principled objection to remarks that they considered unBritish, unchristian, illiberal, or just plain prejudiced'.[50] Miller himself obliquely admits this, when he writes that, had 'scientific racism' dominated Christian Canada, there would have been no experiment in Indian schooling at all, let alone the ambitious industrial schools after 1883. 'What,' he asks, 'would have been the point?'[51] Whereas missionaries took for granted native infanthood, they also took for granted native 'potential for an admirable adulthood'.[52]

Notwithstanding this, Miller is inclined to see racist oppression where he need not. So attempts by the schools to discourage pupils from speaking their native tongues he describes as 'linguistic repression' and as an 'attack on Native languages'.[53] Yet anyone who has tried to learn a foreign language knows that by far the most efficient means is learning by immersion – by being entirely extracted from one's familiar linguistic environment and plunged into the foreign one. No doubt, by our early twenty-first-century standards, the methods of language teaching employed in Canada's residential schools in the 1800s and early 1900s were crude and unimaginative, and no doubt punishment for transgression was severe.[54] However, Miller tells us that 'the missionaries themselves opposed a total ban on the use of Inuktitut or Indian languages', that many schools permitted the use of native languages in specified situations and that '[p]erhaps the only safe generalization' about the decree of the Department of Indian Affairs that native languages not be used was summed up in rule of conduct no. 12, which was laid down by the inspector of Indian schools of British Columbia in 1905: 'We must not talk Indian except when allowed'.[55]

It may be, as Miller holds, that the common practice of the 'half-day system', whereby pupils spent half their time in manual labour, either for the school itself or for some local farmer, became exploitative, 'extracting free labour' and amounting to 'involuntary servitude'.[56] The fact that the Ojibwa of Shoal Lake took care to negotiate a contract with the Presbyterians in 1902, which stipulated that schoolchildren under the age of eight not be given heavy work and that older children engage in classroom work at least half of each school day, does imply that the proportions of academic education and practical work did sometimes get out of balance.[57] Yet, as Miller himself admits, part of the cultural re-education of the children of hunter-gatherer parents involved making them accustomed to the world of farming, which has always involved a lot of hard manual labour.[58]

The root of many of the failings of the residential schools lay in the inadequacy of their funding, which was exacerbated by a change of confederal policy in 1892. Resolved to reduce the rising demand upon the public purse, which was fuelled by the expansion of the number of schools in 1883, the government terminated the policy of full funding and introduced a new system of per capita grants, which remained in place until the 1950s.[59]

This tighter financial regimen had the unhappy effect of making school administrators desperate to recruit and retain pupils, even sick and contagious ones, and of worsening their diet and increasing their manual labour.[60] It also inclined schools to employ under-trained teachers.[61] In 1907 a report by the chief medical officer of the Department of Indian Affairs, Dr P. H. Bryce, revealed appalling health and mortality statistics. As a consequence, three years later an agreement was reached between the government and the missionary societies, which increased public funding, improved living conditions, enhanced medical facilities, and tightened government inspection and enforcement.[62] Nonetheless, the death rates in the schools between 1921 and 1950 remained far higher than in the general Canadian population of school-aged children.[63]

Miller is generally scathing about the 'parsimonious bureaucrats in Ottawa', whose agenda was set by 'the bottom line',[64] and he hints that racist bias lay at the bottom of their parsimony: 'The importance of educating and training Indians as a means of "civilizing" them was always lower in government priorities than other proposed expenditures . . . the malignant neglect of a federal government that did not care enough about the welfare of children who were its legal wards'.[65] No doubt Ottawa could have cared more and spent more, and no doubt the welfare of native children was not at the top of its agenda. But governments then, as now, were subject to a multiplicity of claims upon public funding, whose total demand always outstripped supply. They had to prioritise, both according to their consciences and according to political constraints. It is probably true that the confederal government *could* have spent more on residential schools, but the question of whether it *should* have done – given all its other responsibilities – is a moot point. And an answer to that question would require a careful argument, which Miller does not provide. Moreover, one obstacle in the way of his hypothesis about racist parsimony is that, at least according to some experts, Ottawa's funding of relief for western natives during the famine of 1882 was in fact a 'substantial segment of overall government expenditure'.[66]

The wholesale damnation of the residential school system in Canada is overwrought and unfair.[67] Notwithstanding their failings, and the suffering caused by them, the schools were founded on a belief in essential racial equality and consequent faith in the capacity of native people to learn, adapt and develop. Moreover, as the Canadian political scientist Frances Widdowson and her partner Albert Howard have written:

> [W]hat would have been the result if aboriginal people had not been taught to read and write, to adopt a wider human consciousness, or to develop some degree of contemporary knowledge and disciplines? Hunting and gathering economies are unviable in an era of industrialization, and were it not for the educational and socialization efforts provided by the residential schools, aboriginal people would be even more marginalized and dysfunctional than they are today.[68]

No culture has a moral right to be immune to change or even to survive.[69] Feudal culture in Europe had no just claim to be preserved against agricultural improvement, industrialisation and urbanisation in themselves – as distinct from the sometimes brutal manner of their development. Not much more now remains of the culture of eighteenth- or nineteenth-century rural England than the walls of cottages, Morris dancing, and the folk songs that Percy Grainger and others assiduously recorded just before the singers died out in the early 1900s. And as for the Palaeolithic and Neolithic peoples of the British Isles, who were the cultural equivalents of some of the native peoples that Britons first encountered in North America, Africa and Australia, not much more remains of them than stone arrow-heads and burial mounds.[70] That may be sad, but it was not unjust.

III

At best, 'cultural genocide' is a metaphor: whatever its harm, it does not kill.[71] There are claims, however, that the British Empire did preside over real, lethal genocide, most infamously in Tasmania (or Van Diemen's Land) in the early 1800s. As Robert Hughes put it, the eradication of the first Tasmanians was the 'only true genocide in English colonial history'.[72] This is highly contested territory, containing controversies over the number of aborigines who died, the reasons for their dying and whether or not their near extinction amounted to 'genocide'.[73]

Estimates of the size of the aboriginal population in Tasmania, when the British first arrived in 1803, vary from just under two thousand to six thousand.[74] Estimates of the number of aboriginals killed in the so-called 'Black War' of 1825–32 vary from four hundred to one thousand. In his provocatively titled book *The Fabrication of Aboriginal History* (2002), Keith Windschuttle has argued with considerable cogency that the scale of aboriginal deaths has been exaggerated by recent historians.[75] Like Tom Flanagan in Canada, he contends that aboriginal oral history, uncorroborated by original documents, is 'completely unreliable, just like the oral history of white people'.[76] That does not mean, of course, that oral testimony of the killing of aboriginals by settlers is necessarily untrue, but it does mean both that we cannot be sure that it is true and that it is likely that some of it is not. And most of the allegations of the killings of aboriginals are based on testimony, not documentation.[77] On the other hand, given that the settlers had an interest in under-reporting how many aboriginals they had killed, it is also very likely that the number of documented deaths is too low.

Windschuttle's accusations of exaggeration have been met with indignant rebuttals from the accused, but the authoritative witness of Geoffrey Blainey suggests that they have largely found their target. In a review of *The Fabrication of Aboriginal History*, Blainey writes of the author that he operates 'with impressive thoroughness', and of those he criticises that 'many of their errors, made on crucial matters, beggared belief. Moreover, their exaggeration, gullibility, and what his book calls "fabrication" went on and on.' Had the errors been politically equitable, one might infer 'an infectious dose of inaccuracy', rather than bias; but '[m]ost of the inaccuracies . . . are used to bolster the case for the deliberate destruction of the Aborigines'.[78] While Blainey rejects the description of the aboriginal Tasmanians as backward, mentally and morally, as Windschuttle sometimes depicts them, he endorses 'the dominating theme of the book – that the evidence for "genocide" or deliberate "extirpation" appears frail or false'.[79]

While the violence of white settlers was indubitably responsible for some aboriginal deaths, probably in the mid-to-low hundreds, disease and intertribal war were to blame for many others. Even before the arrival of the British, according to 'strong oral tradition', the aboriginal population of Tasmania had been struck by a 'catastrophic epidemic', possibly caused by contacts with passing ships, which annihilated entire tribes.[80] Further, as Blainey writes,

[W]hile epidemics came irregularly, armed fights were more an annual event in many parts of the continent and Tasmania. Violent death . . . was a restraint on the growth of the population . . . The casualties might not, at first sight, seem large . . . [But an] aboriginal fight could . . . involve a far higher proportion of able-bodied males than any war of the twentieth century could possibly involve.[81]

Even on a 'very cautious' reading of the evidence, he deduces that 'the annual death rate in warfare equalled 1 for every 270 in the population. That death rate was probably not exceeded in any nation of Europe during any of the last three centuries.'[82]

At one point, however, Windschuttle's own argument surely surpasses credibility. He claims that when aboriginals in Van Diemen's Land responded violently to settlers, it was not because the latter were invading their territory, since they had no concept of land as fixed, exclusive property.[83] Accordingly – as '[a]ll the orthodox historians except [Lyndall] Ryan agree' – for the first twenty years of European settlement, relations between the aboriginals and the settlers were peaceful.[84] Nor, when the aboriginals fought, were they engaged in guerrilla war, since that would require a political objective and a form of political organisation to achieve their end. Yet '[t]he fact that they

never in twenty-five years made any political approaches to the British
... and never attempted any kind of meeting, bargaining, or negotia-
tion with them, speaks of a people who not only had no political
objectives but no sense of a collective interest of any kind'.[85] So, he
concludes, aboriginal violence was simply in aid of the criminal theft
of goods.[86]

Since native societies contain moral vice just like any other, this was
no doubt true in some cases. Thus, while the Port Davey aboriginals
were one of the most active bands in murdering and robbing white
settlers in 1829, no one had taken their land or disturbed their hunting
grounds.[87] Nevertheless, Windschuttle himself admits the aboriginals
did have 'very fluid versions of their territory', which changed with the
seasons', 'an emotional affinity' to certain territories, and a notion that
game and other fruits of the land belonged to them.[88] Understandably,
when settlers began to occupy lands in such a way as to deprive them
of their food supply, violence erupted.[89] It is surely not a coincidence
that the violent period of 1825–32 was also one that saw a boom in white
immigration. In 1827 Governor William Sorrell introduced free land
grants and assigned convict labour, in order to attract moneyed settlers.
His 'intention seems to have been to lower the cost of the convict system
rather than to transform Tasmania into a booming colony of free settlement'.[90] As a consequence, between 1828 and 1840 about 15,000 free
settlers and 25,000 fresh convicts entered the colony – four times the
number during the previous twenty-five years – tripling the population.[91]

So while it may be true that the Tasmanian aboriginals lacked
political organisation with fixed territorial boundaries, and that they
did not particularly object to immigrants settling on land where they
had sometimes gathered or hunted food, so long as they could gather
and hunt elsewhere nearby, when expanding settlement obstructed
their gathering and hunting, they did object, violently. Therefore, while
Windschuttle is right that the settlement did not amount to an invasion
of land as such, he is wrong to overlook the fact that when settlement
posed a threat to food sources, it did amount to an invasion of a tribe's
ability to subsist.

The most notorious incident during the 'Black War' was Lieutenant-
Governor George Arthur's prosecution of the policy of the 'Black

Line' in October and November 1830. This involved a cordon of up to 2,200 settlers attempting to corral aboriginals onto the Tasman Peninsula, as a precursor to relocating them to reserves on offshore islands. The policy failed, with only two natives being caught in the net.[92] Nevertheless, Henry Reynolds, a specialist in the history of frontier conflict between settlers and aboriginals, holds that the 'Black Line' had 'similarities with the modern practice of forced removal of peoples and "ethnic cleansing", recently defined as the "planned and deliberate removal from a certain territory of an undesirable population distinguished by one or more characteristics such as ethnicity, religion, race, class or sexual preferences"'.[93] The policy was adopted, he tells us, because Arthur feared the 'eventual extirpation of the Colony'.[94]

But this is not true, for Reynolds misquoted. As Windschuttle has pointed out, what Arthur really wrote was that he feared 'the extirpation of the aboriginal race itself'.[95] The line was not intended to exterminate aboriginals, but to end the cycle of frontier violence by driving the two 'most sanguinary' tribes from the settled areas of the midlands and the south-east into uninhabited country, deliberately leaving five of the other seven tribes out of its ambit.[96] The ultimate goal was to put the two tribes targeted onto a closed reserve – 'containing many thousands of acres of most unprofitable soil for Europeans, [but] well suited for the purpose of savage life' – where they could practise their traditional way of life, but pose no threat to settlers.[97] Whatever the rights and wrongs of the policy, it was not 'ethnic cleansing', because those corralled were selected not because of their ethnicity, but because of their violent resistance. Other aboriginals were left alone – indeed, some mission aboriginals assisted the British.[98]

Nor did the policy intend extermination. Arthur was a convinced evangelical humanitarian, who had declared himself 'a perfect Wilberforce as to slavery' when serving as acting paymaster-general in Jamaica.[99] And while in Tasmania he was assiduous in trying to curb the abuse of native people by whites, issuing a government notice in August 1830 urging settlers to restrain their convict servants from 'acts of aggression against these benighted beings' and 'whenever the

Aborigines appear without evincing a hostile feeling, that no attempt shall be made either to capture or restrain them, but, on the contrary, after being fed and kindly treated, that they shall be suffered to depart whenever they desire it'.[100] The following day he issued another notice, warning settlers and convicts that 'any wanton attack or aggression against the Natives' that came to the attention of the government would be punished.[101]

To be fair to Reynolds, he did not claim that the colonial government intended extermination. Indeed, he has admitted that 'there is no available evidence at all to suggest that it was the intention of the colonial government to effect the extinction of the Tasmanians'.[102] Nevertheless, he is among those historians who reckon that exterminationist views became ascendant among settlers, as distinct from government officials: '[s]harpened conflict called forth increased demands for extermination. They became common, for perhaps the first time, in Tasmania between 1828 and 1830.'[103] Commenting on twelve statements from prominent settlers and newspapers of the colony, he observes, 'What is certainly true is that prominent settlers felt no compunction about publicly expressing their genocidal desires and intentions and apparently had no concern about courting public disapproval or social ostracism by advocating extermination.'[104] For example, Edward Curr, the manager of the Van Diemen's Land Company, 'argued that Aboriginal hostility was so serious that the colonists would either have to abandon the island "or they must undertake a war of extermination"'.[105]

But Reynolds misleads again. As Windschuttle points out, the full statement that Curr made to Governor Arthur's Aborigines Committee in his letter of April 1830, from which Reynolds quotes an excerpt, is in fact a pessimistic prediction of what *might* happen *if* aboriginal violence continued, not advocacy in favour of exterminating the natives.[106] Curr went on to say:

These opinions I am sure will shock the feelings of the committee: it is a dreadful thing to contemplate the necessity of exterminating the aboriginal tribes. But I am far from *advising* such a proceeding. All that I say is that I think it will come to that. My own hands however shall be guiltless of blood, and I shall discountenance it as far as my authority extends, except under circumstances of aggression or in self-defence.[107]

Of the eight settler opinions that Reynolds offers in support of his extirpation thesis, Windschuttle convincingly shows that 'only two of them . . . unambiguously count in his favour'.[108]

In March 1830 the Aborigines Committee circulated a list of questions to 'Gentlemen of experience and long residence in the Colony', and elicited fourteen responses. Based on these, Brian Plomley, the ethnological historian of the Tasmanian aborigines, asserts that the settlers who gave evidence were 'extirpationists almost to a man'.[109] But Windschuttle's methodical examination of all the data shows that this is not so.[110] It is true that Edward Curr was the only one who tried to see the situation through aboriginal eyes:

> . . . it is probable they see no difference between our taking their Kangaroos and their taking our flour and sugar. What ideas can such men have of property? And how are they to understand the distinction between an imperfect property as their Kangaroos, and a proper one as our flour etc? . . . To steal what is of use to them may be consistent with their notions of amity . . .[111]

Still, 'a clear majority' of respondents thought that the whites – especially remote stock-keepers and bushrangers – were to blame for causing aboriginal hostility. Seven of the fourteen settlers thought that conciliation was still worth trying; the other seven thought that the time for conciliation had passed. Of these latter, three suggested removing the aboriginals to a location where they could no longer harass the settlers, while the other four recommended a resort to arms, one as a means of forcing the aboriginals to conciliate, only two with the intention to annihilate, all else having failed.[112] Windschuttle does not claim that exterminationist sentiment was entirely absent from the settlers, but rather that it was kept in check by the evangelical humanitarianism that was unusually influential among the founders of the colonies of New South Wales and Van Diemen's Land.[113] For this view he finds support from John Gascoigne and Patricia Curthoys, who observe that, in the first half of the nineteenth century, the 'visceral unscientific racism [of the lower orders] was, to some degree, kept in check by elite opinion, whether a Christian or an Enlightenment-based anthropology which generally emphasised the unity of humankind'.[114]

However, Gascoigne and Curthoys do point out the gap that often opened up between intention and implementation: 'the vastness of Australia and the parsimony of the Colonial Office' meant that the governors often lacked any practicable way of enforcing their writ.[115] James Boyce makes the same point, when he criticises Windschuttle for assuming 'a level of official control outside the major centres that simply did not exist' and asserts that '[t]he gap between the law and its implementation was everywhere apparent' (although he does imply that the governor had adequate military forces from the mid-1820s).[116] This seems a reasonable point, from which we may infer that, notwithstanding the humanitarian endeavours of the colonial government and the tender consciences of many settlers, the indiscriminate killing of aboriginals by some settlers and convicts with exterminationist intent probably did occur. With that qualification, however, Windschuttle's overall conclusion about the extermination of the Tasmanian aboriginals seems fair: 'The historic record shows that this prospect divided the settlers deeply, was always rejected by government and was never acted upon.'[117]

Whatever the motives and intentions of colonial officials, settlers and convicts vis-à-vis the aboriginal peoples of Tasmania, by the early 1830s only three or four hundred remained out of a population of at least two – and maybe six – thousand in 1803.[118] In a further attempt to protect them from the violence of whites, Governor Arthur endorsed the majority recommendation of his Aborigines Committee that the remaining aboriginals be removed to an offshore sanctuary, especially Flinders Island. From 1831 to 1836 between two and three hundred aboriginals were assembled on the mainland and taken across the sea.[119]

While some have chosen to describe the reserve on Flinders Island as a 'concentration camp',[120] it is significant that Henry Reynolds, who is seldom to be found on the same side as Windschuttle, strongly disagrees. He shows that Governor Arthur had no wish 'more sincerely at heart than that every care should be afforded these unfortunate people' and that he 'begged and entreated' George Augustus Robinson, the commandant of the aboriginal settlement on Flinders Island, to 'use every endeavour to prevent the race from becoming extinct'. Reynolds also argues that Arthur matched his words with deeds, ensuring that the aboriginals were better provided for – not least in medical care – than other welfare recipients in Tasmania such as orphans, paupers and convicts.[121] Indeed, the 'protectorate' on Flinders Island – intent upon shielding aboriginals from violence by separating them from whites, inducting them into agriculture and gradually educating them into civilisation – became something of a model for later aboriginal policy in Australia and even impressed imperial policy-makers in London.[122] This well-intentioned endeavour was not sufficient, however, to prevent most of the aboriginal people on Flinders Island from dying, mainly from respiratory diseases imported from Europe.[123] The experiment ended in 1847 with the relocation of forty-seven survivors.[124]

IV

It has become common, in some circles, to claim that the Nazi extermination of the Jews was merely a late expression of the genocidal intent that had always characterised European colonialism. Thus, Russell Thornton writes that '[i]n fact, the holocaust of North American tribes was, in a way, even more destructive than that of the Jews, since many American Indian peoples became extinct'.[125] And a collective of Canadian authors has claimed, 'Queen Elizabeth, King Ferdinand, Queen Victoria, King Louis and so on were the "Adolf Hitler's" [sic] of their day. "Auschwitz" was an everyday reality for many people across the world during the years of colonialism and the years that followed.'[126] A prime exhibit in the case for the prosecution of British colonialism is the extinction of the Tasmanian aboriginals.

So how well does the label 'genocide' fit what happened in Tasmania in the first half of the nineteenth century? If 'genocide' is to a whole people what 'homicide' is to an individual, then it must be deliberate and intentional. Indeed, that is how the 1948 UN Convention on the

Prevention and Punishment of the Crime of Genocide understands it – as comprising a set of 'acts committed *with intent* to destroy, in whole or in part, a national, ethnical, racial or religious group, as such' (Article II).[127] In that case, we can say – not only with Keith Windschuttle, but also with Henry Reynolds[128] – that what happened in Tasmania in general was clearly not a case of genocide, even if individual settlers and convicts did sometimes kill with racist motive and genocidal intent. During the first three decades of settlement, the aboriginal population of Tasmania – like the Beothuk of Newfoundland – declined for a variety of reasons, including intertribal warfare and, above all, disease. Even if the British immigrants brought the disease, and so indirectly caused aboriginal deaths through it, they did so inadvertently and cannot be blamed for it. The virtual, if not quite actual, annihilation of the Tasmanian aboriginals was far more tragedy than atrocity.[129]

Nevertheless, the absence of genocidal intention alone does not get the British entirely off the moral hook, for an action can also be made morally wrong through the negligent or complacent acceptance of evils that could have been feasibly avoided, even when they were not intended. In the case of Tasmania, colonial governors were certainly not negligent or complacent in that they strove consistently to save aboriginal people from the evil effects of white colonisation. However, what neither they nor their masters back in London tried to do was to stop the colonisation altogether, as some now suggest they should have done.[130] Tom Lawson, for example, writes that, while British officials 'disavowed, and indeed even regretted, the exterminatory impacts of their presence, yet they never faltered, never sought to roll back colonial development'.[131] The most obvious reason why they did not do so was their confident belief in the possibility of human progress. The 1830s and 1840s lay in the middle of what has been called the 'Age of Improvement'.[132] Medical science had invented the first vaccine against smallpox, engineering had produced ocean-going steamships and a boom in the building of railways, and Christian humanitarianism had not only abolished slavery within the British Empire but was engaged in securing legislation to protect the welfare of industrial workers at home. Colonial Office officials in London and colonial governors in Australia genuinely believed that inducting native peoples into progressive British civilisation would improve their lives.[133] That was one reason why they did not pause the process of colonisation. Another reason was that, since there had been little or no violence between settlers and aborigines for the first two decades of the colony's life, by the time it became clear that the presence of the British posed a mortal threat to the natives, colonial settlement had already taken root. What is more, the lethal diseases, once transmitted, could not be recalled. Further still, there seemed to be reason to hope that the dilemma could be resolved by creating protective reserves for the natives, where, in a secure environment, they could gradually adapt to the modern world growing up around them.

Still, could the British simply have stopped colonisation in Tasmania altogether, if they had wanted to? Certainly, the example of North America was not encouraging: the imperial government's attempt to stop settlers from intruding on native lands out west after 1763 had provoked a revolt that led to its complete loss of control over the American colonies twenty years later. To stop and reverse colonisation in Tasmania might well have required an early nineteenth-century government to fight a second (smaller) war against colonists, but this time not just on the other side of the Atlantic, rather on the far side of the globe. It would have been a highly hazardous undertaking and British officials can be forgiven, I think, for not contemplating it. And if the British had succeeded in vacating Tasmania, the vacuum would likely have been filled, sooner or later, by the French or even the Americans.

I do not think, therefore, that the British as a whole can be fairly blamed for what befell the Tasmanian aboriginals, although no doubt individual Britons committed grave crimes against them. However, even if the British were not culpable, they were responsible, in that their presence (largely) inadvertently caused the aboriginals' demise. They recognised and lamented that, and they did more than just wring their hands; they developed ameliorative policies and sought to implement them. The fact that their efforts were to little avail was tragic.[134]

V

In North America, Australasia and Africa the policies of the imperial government in London, and consequently those of the colonial governments beneath it, were based on the Christian and Enlightenment conviction of the basic human equality of members of all races, and driven by the humanitarian desire to enable less advantaged – less privileged – peoples to survive, develop and flourish. In 1837, the Select Committee on Aboriginal Tribes declared in its report:

> The British Empire has been signally blessed by Providence, and her eminence, her strength, her wealth, her prosperity, her intellectual, her moral and her religious advantages, are so many reasons for peculiar obedience to the laws of Him who guides the destinies of nations. These were given for some higher purpose than commercial prosperity and military renown . . . He who has made Great Britain what she is, will inquire at our hands how we have employed the influence He has lent to us in our dealings with the untutored and defenceless savage; whether it has been engaged in seizing their lands, warring upon their people, and transplanting unknown disease, and deeper degradation, through the remote regions of the earth; or whether we have, as far as we have been able, informed their ignorance, and invited and afforded them the opportunity of becoming partakers of that civilization, that innocent commerce, that knowledge and that faith with which it has pleased a gracious Providence to bless our own country.[135]

In addition to metropolitan humanitarians, colonial officials – as well as missionaries and many soldiers, traders and settlers – were also distressed at the evidently destructive impact of their presence on native peoples and they sought to ameliorate the effects. Having decided that they could not stop the mass migration of European settlers or reverse the process of colonisation, they sought to manage it humanely.[136] If they adopted policies of racial segregation, it was almost invariably as a temporary measure to protect native people from harmful encounters with settlers and to enable them to begin to adapt to a new, modern way of life. They were separated in order to be assimilated, and they were assimilated in order to be saved.

Not infrequently native people themselves recognised the need to adapt and they sought help in doing so. Regrettably, the education offered them was sometimes racist, denigrating native culture indiscriminately. Nevertheless, many natives did learn to survive and flourish in the new, modern, colonial world. Others perished, however, even as whole peoples. Certain historians have chosen to exaggerate the role of settler violence in causing such extinction, and some have gone so far as to equate the actions of colonial authorities with those of the Nazis, casually deploying such emotive and provocative words as 'concentration camp', 'holocaust' and 'genocide' in describing British policies. Such language is misleading to the point of slander. In fact, the colonial authorities strove to avoid the extinction of native peoples. That they too often failed was not a sign of their covertly genocidal intention, but rather a manifestation of human tragedy.

6

Free Trade, Investment and 'Exploitation'

I

The 'theft' of ancestral land from native peoples is only one of several economic crimes that anti-colonialists commonly lay at the feet of the British Empire. Others are the exploitation of natural and human resources, the use of slave labour, the destruction of native industry, the draining of profits from the colonial periphery to the imperial centre and the retardation of native economic development. All of these claims are highly controversial, partly because of competing economic theories, partly because there is very little reliable statistical information before 1950, and partly because the counterfactual question – whether there was a plausible alternative to the encounter with the West, which would have been better or worse – can only be given a highly speculative answer.[1]

II

Without doubt there were moments of economic oppression in the British Empire. In eighteenth-century India, for example, the East India Company (EIC) cooperated with leading Bengali financiers in deposing the Nawab – the viceroy or deputy ruler – of Bengal by way of the Battle of Plassey in 1757. As a consequence, the company came to dominate Bengal, profiting from land taxes imposed on the Bengali 'ryots' (tenant farmers) and, with the collaboration of the Armenian and Hindu merchants who were their factotums, using coercive methods to dominate markets and create monopolies. After the three years of 'unbridled and systematic economic exploitation' following Plassey, the Bengal state lay in financial ruins.[2] To be properly understood, however, the exploitation of the early years of the EIC's rule needs to be put in context. The contemporary Bengali poetic narrative, Gangaram's *Maharashtrapuran* (1751), recounts in detail how Maratha mercenaries – described by the eminent historian of the Mughal dynasty Sir Jadunath Sarkar (1870–1958) as 'human locusts' – raided western Bengal in the 1740s, tortured merchants, raped women and perpetrated a genocide. 'The truth is,' writes Tirthankar Roy, 'most Indian powers in this time lived on predation as freely as the East India Company officers did. The difference was the Company consisted of merchants and Indian merchants trusted them, flocking to Calcutta to seek their protection.'[3]

On other occasions, the economic hardship caused by the EIC's rule was a side-effect of good intentions. In 1786 Lord Cornwallis arrived in India, charged with completing the work of rooting out corruption that had begun during Robert Clive's second term as governor-general in 1765–6 and had continued under Warren Hastings, and also with overhauling the EIC's administration.[4] The need for such an overhaul lay in the decay of the Mughal systems and customs under Maratha rule, which the company had inherited.

After circumspect consideration, Cornwallis proceeded with a major reform of land taxation, known as the Permanent Settlement. This was intended to relieve the prevailing agrarian crisis and distress by doing two related things: on the one hand, benefiting the 'zamindars' (landholders and tax collectors) by giving them property rights in the land, fixing the amount of annual tax payable and allowing them to keep surplus revenue; and on the other hand, benefiting the ryots by giving the zamindars an interest in developing their lands as well as secure surpluses to invest in them, thereby improving the condition of their tenants. As Cornwallis wrote, 'It is immaterial to government what individual possessed the land, provided he cultivates it, protects the ryots, and pays the public revenue.'⁵ Unfortunately, that is not how it worked out. By creating an open market for land, the settlement resulted in large estates being sold at auction to distant urban buyers, who were more interested in milking their tenants for tax revenue than investing in agricultural improvements. As a consequence, ryots were often driven into debt, brigandage or revolt. As Lawrence James has written, 'Agricultural stagnation, investment paralysis and social tension were the direct results of the Company's land taxation.'⁶

Against this, however, need to be set the general economic benefits of the peace that the EIC brought to communities that had languished under Maratha instability. In September 1818 John Malcolm wrote to his wife of 'the blessings I obtain from the poor inhabitants . . . it joys my heart to find myself the instrument of punishing freebooters, and restoring great provinces to a prosperity they haven't known for years'. And the following month, he wrote to Mountstuart Elphinstone that '[t]he countries of the young prince Holkar are advancing to prosperity with a rapidity that looks almost miraculous to those unacquainted with the industry of the Ryots of India. They actually have reappeared in thousands, like people out of the earth, to claim and recultivate lands that have been fallow for twenty years.'⁷

III

Economic rapacity on the part of those responsible for governing did occur in the early decades of the EIC's rule in India, although Cornwallis put a stop to it. Policies such as the Permanent Settlement in Bengal sometimes did cause hardship for the poor, albeit not intentionally. In addition, imperial policy damaged some native industries, while opening up opportunities for others.

From 1846 the British Empire was committed to free trade, although it became increasingly protectionist from the First World War onwards.⁸ During the liberal period, traditional industries such as the Indian spinning and weaving of muslins were rendered uncompetitive by the untaxed import of cheap, machine-made cottons from Britain. However, even Karl Marx viewed this economic disruption and destruction as the inevitable side-effect of technological development and economic progress.[9] And according to the Marxist economist Bill Warren, imported cottons only caused a relative decline in local handicrafts, since there was in fact 'an *absolute* rise in the volume and number of items of traditional production, because the market underwent a massive expansion during this period'.[10]

What is more, free trade did enable native business to develop along novel lines, allowing Indian entrepreneurs to visit England in the later 1800s, observe the workings of manufacturing industry, import machinery and expertise to India, build factories employing Indians and then outcompete Manchester.[11] Since 1944 international institutions such as the World Bank and the International Monetary Fund have promoted free trade, just as the British Empire did, as the best strategy for economic growth and development. The extraordinary early economic success of settler countries such as Canada, Australia and New Zealand suggests that, at least under certain conditions, that is so.

A combination of the effects of the First World War, demands from the settler dominions for a system of imperial preference and the Great Depression moved the British Empire to adopt a policy of imperial protectionism from 1932 to the early 1950s. The results were mixed. Colonial consumers, of course, sometimes lost out. But the dominions benefited, as did colonies producing luxury goods such as sugar. Indeed, according to David Fieldhouse, imperial preference 'saved the West Indies, Fiji, and Mauritius from disaster'.[12]

During the Second World War, Britain bought commodities from its colonies at a fixed price, initially to ensure markets during the wartime disruption of international trade, but eventually to secure the supply of vital raw materials and to enable the earning of foreign exchange by resale. This led to the setting up of state marketing boards, to purchase commodities in West and East Africa and then use the profit from the margin between the price paid to the producer and that paid by British ministries to build up reserves. Out of these reserves, producers could be compensated after the war for the predicted large fluctuations in commodity prices. 'While the original intentions were certainly honourable, if possibly misguided, once these boards came under the control of local politicians they were used to extract surplus from the rural producer, notionally for development purposes, in practice largely for party and personal advantage. Probably nothing that the British did concerning agriculture in West Africa had more serious effects in the longer term than this system.'[13] Note, however, that the problem lay not in the colonial system itself, but in the post-colonial abuse of it.

IV

On the whole, colonial governments did not act in the interests of British business. 'By and large,' Fieldhouse writes, 'those who were responsible for controlling the colonies . . . tended to act as defenders of colonial interests as they saw them, if necessary against those of greedy compatriots . . . This was true throughout most of the modern period.'[14] For example, when, in the mid-1870s, the viceroy of India, Lord Northbrook, found himself pressed by Lord Salisbury, the secretary of state for India, to concur with the imperial policy of free trade and remove Indian duties on British textiles, he commissioned an inquiry. This reported that the existing 5 per cent tariff was 'not absolutely prohibitive' of the purchase of imported coarse cloth. In response, and without first consulting London as expected, Northbrook proposed what would become the Indian Tariff Act 1875, which reduced duties on most imported items but still left those on cotton yarn and cotton cloth at 3.5 per cent and 5 per cent, respectively. Thus, the British viceroy refused 'to amend a tariff policy which, as he was righty convinced, was seen in India itself as a defence of Indian industry against a powerful British interest'.[15] It is true that the imperial policy of free trade came to prevail from the 1880s to the 1920s, when India was persuaded not to protect its own cotton industry against the cotton manufacturers and exporters of Lancashire. Even so, British cloth imports accounted for only a sixteenth of India's needs and did not deter Indian entrepreneurs from opening textile factories in Bombay and Ahmedabad, or prevent British India from becoming the world's fourth greatest cotton manufacturing nation by 1914.[16]

It is also true that, in Egypt, Lord Cromer did disadvantage the development of a native cotton factory industry by imposing an 8 per cent excise duty on home-made textile products. However, his motive in doing so was not to boost the profits of British business, but rather to rescue the Egyptian government from insolvency. This the development of a native industry would have hindered, by reducing government revenue from the matching 8 per cent duty on imported cotton goods. In addition, 'like all free traders, he did not believe that this [the development of local industry] should be at the expense of the cheap imports which helped to clothe the large numbers of very poor people living in ... predominantly peasant societies'.[17] Yet Cromer's policies did not stop the founding of the Egyptian Cotton Mills Company in 1901, with managers and technical staff imported from Lancashire and Egyptian workers trained to operate the machinery.[18]

V

If growing markets abroad for the export of British manufactures was one motive of British imperial endeavour, so was growing the production abroad of commodities for export to British markets. Overseas production required an overseas labour force. Sometimes this was provided by white migrants, but even when this was the case, local workers were usually needed to make up most of the required number – as in the gold mines of the Witwatersrand in South Africa from the 1880s. In Africa, many native peoples were generally pastoralists, hunters or warriors and unaccustomed to industrial forms and habits of work – toiling for long, fixed hours, in return for earning wages. Moreover, the prospect of labouring in mines or on plantations often far away from home was not immediately attractive.

This presented would-be employers with a problem of incentivisation. In nineteenth-century Europe the incentive to enter the industrial labour force was usually natural necessity: population growth, combined with an increasingly mechanised agriculture, forced the rural unemployed to seek industrial work in the towns – not least down the coal mines – in order to survive. In late nineteenth- and early twentieth-century Africa, however, the population did not outgrow the limits of potential agricultural land. In the absence of natural incentives, therefore, the colonial state, needing capitalist business to generate public revenue, intervened to create artificial ones. These commonly took the form of head- or hut-taxes payable only in cash. This was certainly a form of pressure, but it was not forced labour in the strict sense of labour that was legally obliged and unpaid – as in Portuguese Mozambique.[19] Moreover, it did sometimes command a benevolent motive. In 1894 Cecil Rhodes spoke in support of the Glen Grey Bill in the parliament of Cape Colony, which proposed a tax of ten shillings on any African who had not worked outside of his district during the previous twelve months. The rationale he gave was this. Before the imposition of white rule over native peoples, young African men had been employed mainly as warriors. By suppressing intertribal war, white government had robbed them of their traditional employment and rendered them redundant. As a consequence, many had turned to alcohol. Therefore, Rhodes asserted, 'it is our duty as a Government to remove these poor children from this life of sloth and laziness and to give them some gentle stimulus to come forth and find out the dignity of labour'.[20] The patronising tone he used may grate and, no doubt, the stimulus was less gentle in fact than Rhodes let on. What is more, economic interest almost certainly featured among his unspoken motives, given the persistent problem of the undersupply of labour in the gold mines. Nevertheless, the problem of the enforced and debilitating unemployment of large numbers of young black African men was a real one, to which Rhodes was offering a practical solution. It is also noteworthy that Rhodes proposed to spend the proceeds of the tax on 'industrial schools' for training Africans.[21]

Besides, in addition to the artificially imposed need to pay colonial tax in cash, Africans had motives of their own for engaging in wage labour, which included earning money to buy cattle to use as a bride price, or ploughs to improve their commercial farming, or guns to protect their people against settlers. In the mines of South Africa, for example, they would opt in and out of work, staying for three- or six-month periods, making their purchases and then returning home. Some made this an annual custom; others never came back. For the young men who most frequently undertook it, wage labour offered access to an attractive new source of resources and the prospect of higher social status.[22]

Such irregularity and unpredictability, of course, did not suit those trying to run the mines, who sought ways of increasing their control over the African labourers and retaining their acquired skills for longer.[23] One main way was the introduction of closed compounds. Starting at the mines at Kimberley in 1885, unskilled Africans on short, three-month contracts were required to be confined in compounds, to stop them leaving in breach of contract, smuggling diamonds out and gaining access to enervating alcohol. Other, more skilled, less transitory African workers were housed in accommodation of their own construction, with more or less help from the mining companies.[24] The discriminating criterion, therefore, was not primarily race, but skill, length of contract and reliability.[25] Conditions varied from mine to mine. In 1902 Gardner Williams, the general manager of De Beers, offered this description of the largest compound:

Fully four acres are enclosed by the walls of De Beers' Compound, giving ample space for the housing of its three thousand inmates, with an open central ground for exercise and sports. The fences are of corrugated iron, rising ten feet above the ground, and there is an open space of ten feet between the fence and the buildings . . . Iron cabins fringe the inner sides of the enclosure, divided into rooms 25 feet by 30 feet, which are lighted by electricity. In each room twenty to twenty-five natives are lodged. The beds supplied are ordinary wooden bunks, and the bed clothing is usually composed of blankets which the natives bring with them, or buy at the stores in the compound, where there is a supply of articles to meet the simple needs of the natives. Besides these stores there is a hospital and dispensary . . . In the centre of the enclosure there is a large concrete swimming bath.[26]

Certainly, Williams had an interest in painting as agreeable a picture as possible, but his testimony is corroborated by that of other witnesses – one a physician – who visited the compounds in 1885 and 1895 and found them remarkably decent.[27] Indeed, in 1906 John Tengu Jabavu, the founder-editor of South Africa's first African-language newspaper, *Imvo Zabantsundu* ('Black Opinion'), declared the compound system 'as near perfection as it was possible to make it'.[28] Against those historians who have likened the system to a prison, Patrick Harries argues that

> the function of the compound, unlike the prison, was not to punish men convicted of misdemeanours by separating them from society; its function was rather to discipline a voluntary force of migrant labourers . . . The compounds had to attract men from competing areas of employment such as the gold mines, and, to do this, management and labour had to negotiate working conditions that were acceptable to both parties. Shangaans, Chopis, and Inhambane Tongas who, by the end of the 1880s, again made up the major part of the work force, came from an area almost entirely free of European control. As they were not yet compelled to sell their labour by a colonial government, they had to be attracted to the diamond fields by competitive working conditions. The mine owners were dealing with volunteers, not prisoners . . . migrant workers chose to subject themselves to a voluntary and often lengthy incarceration in these confined spaces . . . It was . . . with some justification that the manager of De Beers claimed in 1888 that 'our natives are better paid than the miners in any of the European countries' . . . It is clear that the mine owners . . . raised wages in an attempt to coax workers to give up their freedom of movement, accept the increased discipline and danger of underground labour, the new restrictions on the theft of diamonds . . .[29]

Moreover, according to the medical officer of health in 1895, 'the death rate of persons employed in the mines is . . . about . . . 30 per cent lower than that of the coloured population of the town', because 'in the compounds every care is taken to keep the men in good health, they have good food, good quarters, plenty of opportunities for personal cleanliness. Then there is the absence of liquor, and they enjoy proper care and attention during illness.'[30] What obtained at Kimberley, however, did not always obtain elsewhere. It seems that the compounds subsequently constructed in the mines of southern Rhodesia were worse – uncomfortable, overcrowded, with little or nothing by way of medical facilities, and often brutally policed.[31] Yet, thanks mainly to state regulation, ultimately driven by the Colonial Office, conditions did gradually improve, so that the annual death rate – mainly from disease rather than accidents – declined by 80 per cent from a dreadful 75.94 per thousand in 1906 to 11.50 in 1933.[32]

Despite assiduous attempts to attract and retain native labour, local supply often still fell short of demand. Recourse was had, therefore, to the importation of indentured labour from abroad. The terms and conditions of indentures (contracts) varied, but they would commonly involve an agreement to work for a specified number of years without pay (to discharge a debt) or for a fixed wage, in return for free transport to a colony, board and lodging, and perhaps the opportunity to settle. Young, able-bodied men signed indentures in order to escape poverty at home and in hope of better prospects abroad. This form of labour was not confined to those with non-white skins. Between 1650 and 1780, 50–66 per cent of Europeans migrating to North America did so under contracts of indentured servitude.[33] And the practice continued long after the War of Independence: for example, the Delaware and Raritan Canal in New Jersey was built by indentured labourers from Ireland between 1830 and 1834.[34] In the nineteenth and early twentieth centuries, however, the British Empire sought to make up for local shortages of labour by authorising the recruitment of indentured labourers from Asia, mainly India. In 1834 more than 41,000 Bengalis were conveyed as indentured labourers to Mauritius, but reports of abuse moved the Indian government to stop such shipments in 1838. Four years later they were resumed after a Protector of Emigrants had been appointed to make sure that the labourers had sufficient space, food, water and ventilation on the journey. From then until 1916 indentured labourers were transported from India to the West Indies, South Africa and East Africa.

The use of indentured labour was strongly opposed by British liberals such as the political philosophers L. T. Hobhouse and Gilbert Murray, who considered it to be de facto slavery.[35] So when, in the aftermath of the Second Anglo-Boer War, the imperial government decided to authorise the recruitment in China of labourers for work in the gold mines of South Africa's Witwatersrand, controversy erupted. The immediate reason for the decision was to save the mining industry, which faced a 66 per cent shortfall in labour.[36] But upon that industry depended the post-war recovery of the economy, and upon that recovery depended the post-war peace in South Africa. In addition, Lord Milner, then governor of the Transvaal and the Orange River Colony, was concerned to pre-empt an alliance of Boers and British mine-owners demanding that Africans be subjected to *truly* forced labour. As he wrote to Colonial Secretary Joseph Chamberlain in July 1903, 'I am quite certain, if the labour strain continues very much longer, we shall have, *among the meaner sort of British*, a clamour, not in so many words for slavery but "for some means or other of making the n---er work", and for self-government to accomplish this.'[37]

Between 1904 and 1906 over 63,000 Chinese were recruited in China for work in South Africa.[38] Their indentures were of three years' duration, renewable for a further period, and they required the labourer to return home at the end of his period of service. They stated the working hours, the nature of the work, the rate of wages, the rations and the right to free medical attendance. Recruiting agents were duty-bound to make sure that recruits fully understood the terms to which they were subscribing and a superintendent was appointed to run an administration to look after the interests of the labourers in South Africa.[39] It is true that the Chinese labourers were also confined to compounds, but this was largely in the interest of avoiding racial strife with both Europeans and Africans, not least the kind that had erupted earlier in California, when white workers discovered that Chinese workers were outcompeting them.[40] Liberal metropolitan indignation was overwrought, for this was no 'Chinese slavery'.

Nonetheless, the British general election of December 1905 ensured the end of the scheme, when it returned the Liberals to power. The new government's first step to end the use of indentured labour from China was to offer to fund the early repatriation of those labourers who wanted it. Tellingly, 'few opted to return voluntarily'.[41]

VI

The introduction of new technologies and techniques and their impact on the nature of work and society is usually disruptive, destroying the old ways in order to make way for the new. Invariably, the power of government to control the process and mitigate the evils is limited. That is true even of today's strong Western states; it was true in spades of their nineteenth- and early-twentieth-century predecessors. For example, in late eighteenth- and nineteenth-century Scotland one of the effects of agrarian reform was to increase rural unemployment, and sometimes the best thing that landlords and government could think to do was to facilitate the emigration of hundreds of thousands of Scots, mostly to North America: 'emigration across the Atlantic, where land was cheap and abundant, offered an alternative to those who feared rack renting, dispossession, and the loss of social status'.[42] This was highly distressing for those affected, but agrarian improvement was a social necessity, not an individual luxury. As the population of Scotland had risen, more people had come to earn a living in industry, mining and urban employment. Without a massive increase in food productivity, the cost of sustenance would have driven many people to starvation: 'It was the reformed agricultural system which delivered the enhanced supply of food and, together with some foreign imports, helped to avoid such a disaster. Thus the agrarian transformation was of vital human benefit, but it also came with some social costs and one of them was the dispossession of numerous families whose ancestors had lived and worked on the land since time immemorial.'[43]

Given the vast disparity in cultural development between late-nineteenth-century Europeans and most of their African contemporaries, the disruption to traditional ways caused by the colonial opening up of Africa to worldwide trade, and the development of a capitalist economy to produce exports to feed it, was bound to be tremendous. Nevertheless, if there were costs, there were also gains. Many Africans benefited from the change. Among them were those who would have been traded as slaves, had alternative goods for trade not been developed, together with new routes for export – as Sir Thomas Fowell Buxton had advocated from 1839, followed by Livingstone.[44]

Further, while the economic changes did impoverish some native people, the more enterprising learned to exploit the new markets and made themselves wealthy capitalists in the process:[45] 'At every stage from the first European occupation Africans attempted to protect their interests and to benefit from opportunities. It proved very difficult to move them from their own land or to modify their social and economic processes. Conversely, they were usually quick to spot and exploit new economic opportunities, provided these offered a satisfactory return.'[46] For example, even before formal colonisation in West Africa, native people were taking advantage of access to the expanding overseas markets opened up by colonial powers, producing an industry of thousands of tonnes of groundnuts and palm oil – and from the 1880s, rubber – for sale to European merchants.[47] And from the 1870s Africans in Nigeria and the Gold Coast pioneered the adoption of cocoa beans from South America, outcompeted European producers and rapidly made the Gold Coast the world's largest cocoa producer.[48] Meanwhile in South Africa from the 1860s to the 1880s some Africans 'adapted *more* effectively to economic change than white landowners', farming for the market, hiring themselves out as labourers and getting into the wagon-transport business that dominated the movement of freight until the mass advent of rail in the 1880s.[49] Prominent among these native entrepreneurs were the Mfengu (or Fingo) and the blacks of Natal, sometimes educated by missionaries, who entered with gusto into the new capitalist economy, supplying the Cape and Kimberley with transport, workers and goods: 'Like Kansas farmers – or, for that matter, like the White settlers of Natal – African Christians acquired a boom mentality.'[50]

Whether through African or British endeavour, native prosperity and health improved during the colonial period, although in some cases only towards the end. For example, in Nairobi real wages are estimated to have risen from a value of 1.3 'family subsistence baskets' in the 1900s to 1.8 in the 1950s; in Kampala, from 1.2 to 1.7; and in Accra, from 2.4 to 4.1. In Kenya annual infant mortality among Africans declined from 300–500 deaths per thousand live births in the 1920s to 145 in the 1950s; in Uganda from 245 to 126; and in the Gold Coast from 206 to 115. It is true that consistent improvement in infant mortality was not to be found everywhere on the continent. In Southern Rhodesia, for example, infant mortality rose from 202 to 267 between 1910 and 1940. Still, by 1960, it had fallen to 178.[51]

VII

While traditionalist critics damn the British colonial presence for disrupting pre-modern economies and societies in North America, Australasia and Africa, modernist critics damn it for arresting native capitalist development. The British, so they claim, were interested only in expanding the land available for the production of cash crops and extracting minerals for export, neglected prudent economic diversification, and discouraged technological improvement and the development of manufacturing:

> ... at least since the later nineteenth century critics of imperialism have blamed lack of industrialization for the limited economic development of colonial and other Third World countries, seeing this as the deliberate policy of the already industrialized West which wanted to preserve Third World markets for its own products ... Thus colonialism was mainly exploitative, extracting value from Africa and making no significant contribution to economic development.[52]

The question of when economic activity becomes 'exploitative' does not command a straightforward answer. It seems right that foreign investors, who have ventured their capital and, if successful, made economic growth possible in a colony, should receive an appropriate return on their investment. Indeed, it is not only just but prudent, since investors who do not receive what they consider to be appropriate returns will cease to invest. It is also prudent that some of the profits should be invested back into the business, to enable it to survive and grow. Then, of course, employees should be fairly remunerated. However, exactly what is 'appropriate', 'prudent' and 'fair' will vary from case to case, and opinions will differ. In West Africa, for example, it is true that much of the profit from exports accrued to European and American firms that bought, exported and speculated in tropical commodities. But without the capacity to invest large sums of capital and to suffer a delay in returns, and without expert knowledge of highly speculative international markets, long-distance commodity trading would not have been possible, nor the native employment it created.[53]

Did the overseas firms take home too much profit and pay their African employees too little? In 1904 the average cost of European labour in the Witwatersrand mines was £295 per head, while the equivalent for African labour was £46. On the assumption that the main factor in these costs was remuneration, we can infer that Europeans were paid six times more than Africans.[54] Sometimes the differential was ten times.[55] Initially, it might have been that the greater experience and skill of imported European miners merited higher remuneration than that offered to inexperienced Africans, but as time went on, the difference in experience – at least between Europeans and *some* Africans – would have disappeared. Beyond that point, how could the persistence of a pay differential between European and African be justified? What could explain it other than racism?

While it is possible that dogged racial prejudice trumped economic interest in the minds of the mine-owners, it is not likely. After the end of the Second Anglo-Boer War, the mines were desperate for labour: in early 1904 the number of miners needed was estimated at 197,000, while the number actually available was only 68,280.[56] One alternative, non-racist explanation for the wage differential lies in a distinction between labour markets. Unless one thinks that a given quantity of work has an absolute value in itself, which is impervious to market conditions – and I do not – then it might not be unfair to remunerate different people differently for the same work. In the case of late nineteenth- and early twentieth-century South Africa, Europeans and Africans, coming from dramatically different cultures, would have entertained very different expectations and required different market incentives, giving the same quantity of cash a different value in their respective eyes. In that case, different remuneration might have been culturally fitting and morally just. Britons who were minded to emigrate far preferred to go to the United States than to the imperial frontier: between 1881 and 1910, 49.3 per cent of migrants from England and Wales preferred the US, 20.7 per cent British North America, 12.3 per cent Australasia and only 17.5 per cent all other non-European destinations – including South Africa.[57] Therefore, in order to attract Britons to work in African mines, the rewards would have to have been attractively high. At the same time, there was also a need to offer Africans sufficiently attractive remuneration too, since artificial, coercive incentives such as the need to pay hut tax had failed to produce an adequate supply of labour – and mining companies did raise wages and improve conditions accordingly.[58]

VIII

The exploitative extraction of value is one of the main sins of which colonialism is accused; the failure to invest is another. The failure was certainly not absolute, since Britain invested far more capital overseas than any other nation. The leading exporter of capital from the mid-nineteenth century to at least 1929, Britain invested over a third of its overseas capital in the empire between 1865 and 1914.[59] While 70 per cent of that went to the white-settled colonies or dominions, a not-insubstantial 19.29 per cent was directed to India and a further 10.48 per cent to 'dependent colonies'.[60] Between 1919 and 1938 the proportion of capital invested in the empire rose to over two-thirds.[61]

Where there was limited investment before 1939, it was not because of a deliberate policy of keeping the native populations down. Rather, it was partly because investing in tropical agriculture was generally unattractive, whether due to environmental obstacles such as the precariousness of soil fertility in a context where supplies of water and fertiliser were unreliable and costly, or (as in West Africa) due to social and political factors that made plantations impracticable. It was also because investing in industrial production outside the mining industries of Southern and Central Africa was often unprofitable, since limited colonial markets favoured importation rather than local manufacture, especially during the long period when faith in the free market militated against protection.[62] It was even sometimes because colonial officials actively barred foreign investment: thus, in 1910–11 Lever Brothers was prevented from acquiring concessions in Nigeria on which to establish palm-oil processing mills with widespread hinterlands, since Africans were already producing for the world markets and generating tax revenue and because the alienation of large areas of land risked provoking native opposition.[63]

Besides, the fact that there was any overseas investment at all was because colonial states provided sufficient political stability and legal certainty to make the risks of financial ventures worth taking.[64]

However, even where there was investment, it is claimed, the economic benefit of the colonial presence was limited, because there was little transfer of skills from Europeans to natives. In some cases, this might be attributable to doubts – whether realistic or racist – about competence. But it was also partly because trading firms were largely controlled by expatriates and so offered little opportunity for native employment at the higher levels, and partly because the export production sector – such as mining – was so highly specialised that its skills had little broader relevance to native society.[65] On the other hand, as we have already noted, Indian entrepreneurs were able to import technology and know-how from Britain at the end of the nineteenth century and to establish native textile and steel industries that succeeded in outcompeting the imperial centre. In 1874 the Elphinstone College-educated Jamsetji Tata opened the first steam-powered cotton mills in Nagpur; and in 1907 his son, the Cambridge-educated Dorabji Tata, officially incorporated the Tata Iron and Steel Company in Bombay.

It is true that neither the imperial government in London nor its colonial counterparts engaged directly in economic planning and development before 1945, and those who think that the state should have a leading or important role in such development have been accordingly critical. However, until the turn of the twentieth century that was not widely thought – in Britain or elsewhere – to be government's business, which was instead supposed to be the maintenance of external defence, the keeping of internal peace and the administration of justice.[66] The doctrine of free trade reigned – then, as it generally does now, notwithstanding rising criticism of economic globalisation.

Nevertheless, as early as 1895 the colonial secretary, Joseph Chamberlain, had proposed the idea that Britain had a public duty to promote colonial development: '[it is] not enough to occupy certain great spaces of the world's surface unless you can make the best of them – unless you are willing to develop them. We are landlords of a great estate; it is the duty of a landlord to develop his estate.'[67] While

Chamberlain's vision did not gain much traction at the time, he did succeed in having legislation passed that made it cheaper and easier for colonies to raise capital on the London money market.[68]

It was the experience of an existentially threatening war in 1939-45, combined with socialist - or at least Keynesian - doctrine, that began the era of central government planning of the economy. What applied to the imperial centre applied to the colonial periphery, too, with London supplying the colonies with huge loans and grants for economic development. This led to 'the greatest boom period in African and Caribbean economic history during the 1950s and 1960s'.[69] Unfortunately, economic intervention by colonial governments also had a downside: policies designed to promote agricultural improvement in Kenya provoked resentment among those attached to their traditional practices, which was one of the causes of the bloody Mau Mau rebellion in 1952-60. Colonial officials who cautioned against too much change, too fast, were not always being thoughtlessly conservative.[70]

In his book *Economic Growth in the Third World: 1850-1980*, the American economist Lloyd Reynolds offered an overall assessment of European colonialism's economic record, whose conclusions, David Fieldhouse reports, 'are replicated by many other non-dogmatic commentators'.[71] His overall judgement (as Fieldhouse summarises it) is this: '[c]olonies could probably have grown faster had development been the primary imperial objective, which it very seldom was before the later 1940s . . . Conversely there is no certainty that any of these colonial economies would have done much better had they remained independent: the record of the few non-colonial Third World countries outside Latin America during the modern period was unimpressive.'[72] Reynolds' general point is given sharp focus by a comparison of Ethiopia and Southern Rhodesia in 1960. Whereas the latter had been subject to European rule for seventy years, the former had retained its independence except for a brief period of Italian occupation in 1935-41. Yet, with only one sixth the size of the other's population, Rhodesia outperformed Ethiopia dramatically in terms of modern development:

	Ethiopia	Southern Rhodesia
African schoolchildren	224,934 (1959–60)	552,000 (Africans only)
Hospital beds for Africans	5,823 (1959)	8,759 (1959)
Railways	683 miles (1963)	1,345 miles
Manufacturing plants	200 (1959)	1,059 (1961)[73]

IX

India was a case apart. Unlike most of Africa, the subcontinent had been host to a succession of highly civilised societies, and unlike North America and Australasia very few Britons emigrated there and fewer stayed. Moreover, the first considered native critique of colonial economics was developed by Indians. The claim that India had been a prosperous society, which British exploitation impoverished, circulated through academic and political circles from 1900 onward, especially in the Indian National Congress, and has found recent expression in Shashi Tharoor's 2016 *Inglorious Empire: What the British Did to India.*[74] The British, so the argument goes, destroyed much of the native peasant textile industry and prevented the development of manufacturing industry, in order to benefit British traders and manufacturers. In addition, they drained India's resources by making it pay for British military expenses, the salaries of British officials, and the interest due on British loans and investments. In sum, the charge against the Raj is that its 'combined effect was to condemn India to perpetual poverty as a nation forced to remain a primary producing country that was bled of the surplus which might have provided investment for modernization'.[75]

The truth about the Indian economy during the colonial period is not easy to determine, since, as David Washbrook wryly puts it, 'the most basic issues of empirical fact – population levels, GDP growth, per capita incomes – remain subject to frenzied dispute, especially for the first century of British rule when, it might be thought, the available data are too fragile to withstand the grandiose theoretical constructions often put upon them'. Even though the sources of evidence become firmer from the second half of the nineteenth century, they remain 'very inadequate by modern standards'.[76] Nevertheless, Washbrook offers some support to the nationalist narrative of the predatory draining of resources in his account of the East India Company's policies from the 1810s until 1858, when the government of India was taken out of its hands by the Crown after the Indian Mutiny: namely, the relentless pursuit of revenue maximisation through taxation in most of its territories outside of Greater Bengal and the ruthless asser-tion of monopolies in many of the most valuable commercial trades (opium, salt, betel and alcohol).[77]

On the other hand, the Bengali-born, liberal economic historian Tirthankar Roy is sufficiently confident to declare that, overall, the nationalist critique of the kind expressed by Tharoor does not stand up: 'generations of historians . . . have shown that it is not [true]'.[78] *Pace* Tharoor and others, the statistic that India produced 25 per cent of world output in 1800 and 2–4 per cent in 1900 does not prove that India was once rich and became poor; '[i]t only tells that industrial productivity in the West increased four to six times during this peri-od'.[79] Roy's argument is supported by the fact that uncolonised China suffered exactly the same fate as colonised India during this period.[80] The view of 'pessimistic' neo-Marxism that colonialism was essentially about the predatory extraction of colonial surplus owes more to economic dogma than historical or empirical data: 'The proposition that the Empire was at bottom a mechanism of surplus appropriation and transfer has not fared well in global history.'[81] In India, the insti-tutionalisation of extractive power by means of the seizure of land and the imposition of labour servitude was 'largely absent'. In its property law, the Raj 'consistently maintained an attitude of regard towards the peasant', and on land rights it did not discriminate between people by the ethnicity of the right holder:

> If anything, expatriate land-holding rights were weak compared with indigenous rights until well into the nineteenth century. Europeans could not own or purchase farm lands, for example, until the late

1830s, 80 years after colonisation had begun . . . In the case of labour servitude, the British imperial rule consistently legislated in favour of contractual rather than servile labour, though in practice the distinction could be hard to maintain . . . Indigenous labour practices in India had institutionalised servitude by means of the caste system. The slow but steady rise of contractual labour weakened traditional servitude . . .[82]

In their overriding aim to maintain free markets in commodities and factors of production the British found common cause with many Indian capitalists, at least up until the global economic crisis between the two world wars. Among these was the Tata family, whose business grew into India's largest conglomerate today by exploiting the opportunities created by the global economy sponsored by the British Empire.[83]

Moreover, in Roy's view, critics such as Tharoor are 'ill informed' on the record of Indian economic growth during the colonial period:

National income statistics do not show that during British rule the Indian economy became steadily poorer. They show that Indian agriculture stagnated, while manufacturing and trade prospered. Tropical heat and water shortages were to blame for the stagnation of agriculture, while the failure of monsoon rains was the main cause of repeated famines.[84] Similarly, free trade, and the customs union the empire created, in fact helped trade and industry. The volume of long-distance trade in India grew from roughly one million tons in 1840 to 160 million in 1940 . . .[85] As profits in trade were reinvested, India led the developing world in two leading industries of the industrial revolution, cotton textiles and iron and steel.[86] For example, in 1928, 48 per cent of the cotton spindles installed outside Europe, North America and Japan were in India . . . In 1935 50 per cent of the steel produced outside Europe, North America and Japan was produced in India . . . Not only factory industries like steel and cotton, but even the handicraft industries did well in the early twentieth century . . . [I]f free trade had been so damaging for Indian handicrafts, how was it that ten million artisans survived in 1950?[87]

Indeed, Indian nationalists such as B. R. Ambedkar, Rabindranath Tagore and Mahatma Gandhi all held that Indian society, not the British Empire, was mainly responsible for India's poverty: 'As a society that had invented the idea that the touch of another person could cause pollution, India did not need the British to know how to oppress and degrade other people. British rule, being an imposition from the outside, unleashed forces of change that weakened this home-grown cruelty. "The Depressed Classes welcome the British", Ambedkar said, "as their deliverers from age long tyranny and oppression by the orthodox Hindus".'[88]

Further, while it is true that the Raj spent much of its resources on sustaining a large standing army – in 1852-3 somewhere between one third and half of the annual budget[89] – this served to keep the peace within British India, secure its external borders and control its seaboard, all of which fostered domestic and overseas trade. Consequently, many Indian merchants in the nineteenth century, 'whose businesses spanned from Aden to Bombay to Hong Kong, would not agree' that the expense of an imperial army was a drain on India. Besides, the British taxpayer subsidised imperial defence, and through it secure overseas communications, to a considerable extent.[90]

Further still, the 'huge literature' investigating the origins of modern economic growth 'quickly dismisses ... [the idea] that the British enriched themselves at the expense of their colonies'.[91] If the main purpose of the colonial state had been to enrich Britain at the expense of India, major sectors of British business would not have complained of their frustration at government-imposed constraints on trade, investment and settlement in India, which were sometimes designed to stop free-market economics from threatening traditional rural society.[92] Nor would the colonial rulers have permitted the world's fourth largest cotton textile mill industry to emerge in Bombay and Ahmedabad in direct competition with Manchester. British arguments in favour of the empire rested far more on strategic needs than material gains.[93]

Roy's main criticism of British rule in India is not that it drained away surplus value or that it suppressed the development of native manufacturing industry. That 'nationalist narrative,' he writes, 'has not stood up to test all that well'.[94] Instead, he argues, British investment in development and welfare was too low. Commenting on the EIC's record up until 1857, he writes:[95]

> Its effect upon strengthening markets . . . was far greater than its impact on public welfare . . . Merchants . . . gained; the . . . Indian farm servant did not gain much. More than any pre-British state in India, this state aided market integration. Its capacity to change India more or less exhausted there . . . its greatest failing [was] an inability to transform rural livelihoods . . . agriculture remained poor, trapped in low yield, and mainly rainfed. A change came only in a few areas where the government invested money in canal irrigation, and the geography permitted such constructions. The best defence of that dismal record is that the Mughals or the Marathas were no better at meeting that challenge.[96]

The record did not change much after 1857 under the Raj.[97] The reason was that its government was small, certainly compared to Britain's, but also compared to those of other emerging economies at the time, such as Imperial Russia and Meiji Japan. As a consequence, after defence spending was seen to, not much public money remained to invest. Between 1920 and 1930 the government of the Federated Malay States spent on average more than ten times the money spent in British India per head, and that of Ceylon more than three times.[98]

While that may be so, it would be wrong to conclude that the British colonial state in India was entirely negligent of the need to invest in public infrastructure – even during the reign of the EIC. In 1851, partly to feed the ever-thirsty cotton-spinning and textile industry, the company began the creation of an artificial lake near Bombay, whose area 'was four times greater than any reservoir constructed in Europe or North America'.[99] Canals and dams were important, however, not only for industrial purposes, or for irrigation and therefore agricultural productivity, but also for the relief of unemployment and famine. The large projects were financed directly by public funds, the smaller ones with private money, both British and Indian.[100] The first section of what would become the 495-mile-long Cochrane (later, Buckingham) Canal was completed in 1806. The Western and Eastern Jumna Canals were restored in 1817–30. Restoration of the Grand Anicut (dam) began in 1834. Construction of the Ganges Canal began in 1842. The Godavari Anicut was completed in 1852.[101] And the East Coast Canal was extended for famine relief after the 1876–8 famine.[102] Reflecting on the achievement of completing the Ganges Canal, the *Calcutta Engineer's Journal* opined in 1864, 'One of the greatest difficulties in administrating the speedy relief to the famishing population of the regions, and the tardiness and cost of conveyance, has been eliminated.'[103] By the turn of the century British India had the largest irrigation system in the world.[104] Between 1885 and 1939 the acreage under irrigation more than doubled.[105] By 1942 the area of irrigated land in India stood at 57 million acres, of which 32 million were irrigated from public works. Under the British 25 per cent of all land became irrigated, compared to only 5 per cent under the Mughals.[106] 'Today,' writes Kartar Lalvani, 'water management remains one of the great testaments to British rule in India.'[107]

And then, more famously, there were the railways. While the sources of the necessary investment for building them were private, the government encouraged these to invest by generous subsidies that guaranteed profit. The British built more railways in India alone than the US, France, Germany and other European colonialists built in all their colonies – for commercial, military and famine-relief purposes. One estimate has it that when the railway network was extended to the average district, real agricultural income rose by about 16 per cent.[108] The first train ran along Indian tracks in 1853. Thirty years later India had 10,822 miles of railway; by 1922, 37,266 miles; and by 1947, 45,000 miles.[109] In comparison, China and Japan had only 292 and 3,855 miles of railway track, respectively, in 1900.[110] In 1952 China still had only 17,570 miles.[111]

What is more, there is at least one case where the Raj promoted railway-building deliberately in aid of the development of Indian-owned industry: Lord Curzon, viceroy from 1899 to 1905, arranged for vital railway track to be laid to the site of the Tatas' new steel plant in Bombay.[112]

X

Whether or not the long reign of the doctrine of free trade within the British Empire, the consequent refusal of some colonial governments to protect nascent native manufacturing industries, and their late conversion to the state's planning and direction of the economy positively arrested the economic development of colonies in Africa and India, or merely caused them to develop more slowly than they might have done, they certainly did not hinder the economic development of the settler colonies of Canada, Australia and New Zealand. These all developed their economies on the basis of the specialised production of commodities for export to the European or American markets within an initially free trade world economy. They also developed internationally competitive industries and became highly affluent.

Take Australia, for example. It was 'dependent' in the sense that its economic specialisation was determined by the international economy. Nevertheless, according to Fieldhouse, Australia's settlers 'brought with them a basket of attitudes, experiences and expectations that reflected those of contemporary Europe', including an 'instinctively capitalist' mode of production, which disposed them (and their native-born successors) to take hold of the opportunities for developing the wool industry with 'great energy and inventiveness'. And, unlike their counterparts in Africa, they were not hampered by the need to modernise a preponderant pre-capitalist native population.[113]

In addition to this and their 'capitalist' mentality, Australians also enjoyed the signal advantage of prudent government. In contrast to many Latin American countries before 1914, foreign investment – initially, mainly British – was 'wisely used in durable and economically rewarding facilities such as railways, ports, improvements to pastoral holdings, and urban housing. It was almost never used to make good budgetary deficiencies.' Accordingly, Australia's creditworthiness was high among British investors: 'Australian public credit was impeccable. By marked contrast with some Latin American countries, no Australian colony reneged on its public debt . . . Australia was thus able to retain its excellent record of financial probity and to finance its development by tapping into the best and cheapest money market in the world.'[114] As a result, Australia was 'the richest society in the world between the 1860s and the 1890s', and by the 1990s it had developed import-substituting industries that were internationally competitive, while remaining one of the world's most efficient agricultural producers.[115]

XI

The issue of the economic effects of colonialism is, and probably always will be, controversial. What is beyond reasonable controversy, however, is that the suppression of the trade in slaves, the exposure of markets to cheap manufactured imports, the spread of the practice of wage-earning work, and the introduction of modern technologies and agricultural practices were economically disruptive and socially disturbing. Nor can it be denied that British settlers or businessmen were sometimes moved by racial prejudice or greed to remunerate native workers unfairly, to abuse them verbally and physically, and to neglect their welfare. And it is arguable that the imperial government and its colonial counterparts' direct investment in education and economic development was more limited than it should have been.

In mitigation, we should observe that economic change, however improving, is often socially disturbing, sometimes terribly so. And, as we have seen, it disturbed eighteenth-century rural Scots as much as it disturbed later nineteenth- and early twentieth-century Africans. Observing the ill effects of modernisation, colonial officials sometimes sought to moderate change or shield native peoples from it altogether. While that won them the approval of traditionalists, it attracted the opprobrium of modernisers, both white and black.[116]

Besides, we should not forget that change, while disturbing, can bring welcome improvements. In 1959 the African nationalist Ndabaningi Sithole wrote, 'Millions no longer have to own livestock for their subsistence. They can sell their labour . . . As one African Nyasalander once put it: "Today all people do not need to have goats, cattle and sheep in order to live. They only need money . . . Money

... is a very good cow. You can milk it any time. You can eat and drink it any time. It is a cow that does many things for us.'"[117]

We should also observe that the view that the state has a major direct role in providing public goods beyond national security and the administration of justice began to gain momentum in Britain only in the late nineteenth century and achieved lift-off only after 1945. Further, given that the demand for the provision of welfare is virtually limitless, while the state's resources are invariably limited, there will always be a shortfall. In theory, more *could* always be done. Whether, in practice, it *should* be done depends on what is possible, given a state's multiple responsibilities. For revenue-rich states more is possible, for poorer ones, less. Colonial states were usually revenue-poor.

As for greed, racial contempt, the abuse of superior power and consequent injustice, these deserve our indignation and moral condemnation. But they are not peculiar to colonial states or societies.

Moreover, it should now be clear that there are many good reasons to think that the typical accusations commonly levelled against the economics of British colonialism owe more to political dogma than historical or empirical reality. To summarise the economic effects of the British Empire in terms of the exploitation of natural and human resources, the use of slave labour, the destruction of native industry, the draining of profits from the colonial periphery to the imperial centre and the retardation of native economic development is at best historically simplistic, at worst a slander upon the past. The Swiss historian Rudolf von Albertini, whose work was based 'on exhaustive examination of the literature on most parts of the colonial world to 1940',[118] reached a cautious but definite conclusion: 'one can state that colonial economics cannot be understood through concepts such as plunder economics and exploitation'.[119]

On the contrary, by promoting free trade around the world, the imperial government in London sometimes gave native producers opportunities – and native consumers, advantages – that they would not otherwise have had. And while the maritime routes of international trade were being policed by the *Pax Britannica* in the form of the Royal Navy, colonial governments fostered material prosperity and domestic trade by pacifying the territories under their control. Further, by subjecting the encounter of European adventurers, merchants and settlers with native peoples to supervision and regulation, they helped to moderate the disturbing impact of economic modernity. And by providing stable government and the rule of law – especially the English common law[120] – they encouraged foreign investment that, being risk averse, would otherwise have gone elsewhere. Between 1870 and 1935 over three-quarters of all foreign capital invested in sub-Saharan Africa went to British colonies.[121]

Writing of the economic effects upon India of incorporation into the British Empire, Tirthankar Roy reaches a positive conclusion overall:

> Without the eighteenth-century transformation of Bombay, Calcutta, and Madras, without the emerging trades in cotton and grain, without the extension of [East India] Company power inland, without Indian businesses migrating to the port cities, without the enterprise of the private traders in indigo or opium, and without the institutional conse-quences of Indo-European trade, it would be hard to explain the emergence of a nineteenth-century economic system in India that was modern in two senses, in enabling the prospect of one of the most impressive episodes of industrialization outside Europe, and in estab-lishing India as a trading power in a globalizing world.[122]

Looking beyond India in particular to the 'Third World' (or 'Global South') in general, David Fieldhouse arrives at a similar judgement. In his view, the modern experience of several former colonies in South-West and East Asia suggests that colonial rule and foreign trade 'almost invariably' laid the foundations for much more dramatic economic development as part of the international division of labour.[123] 'There seems no doubt,' he writes,

> that virtually every Third World country that has not been devastated by war, civil war or crass governmental incompetence is now richer in real terms than it was before its integration [into the international economy]. By other standards also there has been very considerable

improvement, notably in life expectancy, health, and literacy . . . there is little evidence to support belief in the general or inevitable immiseration of the Third World as a result of its incorporation into the international division of labour.[124]

In the nineteenth and early twentieth centuries, the leading vehicle for such incorporation was the British Empire.

7

Government, Legitimacy and Nationalism

I

As we observed in Chapter 1, anti-colonialist references to 'the colonial project' connote a unitary endeavour that was concerted. They thereby further imply a central agent that did the concerting, presumably the imperial government in London. Since it is assumed that 'the colonial project' was oppressive and exploitative, it is also assumed that the London government – together with allied capitalists – concerted the empire in the selfish interests of the British against the interests of the native peoples they ruled. Imperial rule, therefore, was bad rule. How does this account fare when it meets the historical data?

II

The government of the British Empire was not highly centralised, in part because, for much of its history, it could not be. Until the third decade of the nineteenth century, communication between the centre and the periphery was by sailing ship. During that period, it took four to six weeks to carry a message across the Atlantic, up to six weeks down to Cape Town and three to six months over to Bombay. With the application of steam power to maritime transport from the 1820s, however, communication became more rapid: ten days across the Atlantic by the 1880s, nineteen days down to South Africa by the 1890s and a month over to India by the 1870s. The invention of the telegraph transformed overland communications, and its development was sufficiently far advanced in India by 1857 to play a decisive part in suppressing the Indian Mutiny. Then the construction of durable undersea cables enabled communication to be telegraphed across the Atlantic in 1866 and to India in 1870, making it possible for London to speak to Calcutta and get a response within twenty-four hours rather than weeks.[1]

Slow communication with London was certainly one factor making for relatively autonomous government in distant colonies. In the seventeenth century, the governors of Bermuda were appointed by the Somers Isles Company until the Crown revoked its royal charter and took over the administration in 1684. However, the shock of losing the American War of Independence in 1783 impressed upon London the need to grant colonial governments, with their superior knowledge of local conditions, considerable freedom of manoeuvre. As a consequence, the white settler colonies became increasingly independent from the second half of the nineteenth century, with Canada acquiring 'dominion' status in 1867, followed by Australia, New Zealand and South Africa in the opening decade of the 1900s. The dominions obtained almost complete legislative independence in 1931. Given the major differences in geographical, demographic and economic context between Britain and its far-flung possessions, and given the limited amount of attention that ministers and legislators in Westminster could pay to the needs of each colony, it was not only wise but necessary for London to devolve power. While colonial authorities were bound by imperial policy and their legislation was subject to imperial approval, 'for the rest – and that meant on most matters of purely domestic concern – colonies did their own thing'.[2] However, as we have seen, devolution did have a downside: the more independence colonial governments acquired, the less power London retained to supervise their treatment of native peoples and protect native interests.

III

Government in the colonies was not 'democratic'. There was no universal adult suffrage anywhere in the British Empire, but then there was no universal adult suffrage in Britain itself until 1928 – less than twenty years before India gained its independence and less than forty before the main period of decolonisation.[3] It might be that electoral democracy is the best way of creating a government. It makes every citizen feel that they have an opportunity to help shape the choice of those who will rule them, so that even those whose party fails at the polls can at least be reassured by the knowledge that their voice was expressed and that the prospect remains of working politically to reverse the result at the next election. This makes political defeat more palatable and so helps to civilise political resentment, reducing the risk of it exploding into physical violence. The creation of a government by popular election also makes that government sensitive to the felt needs of electors, since it knows that if it wishes to survive at the next election, it cannot afford to lose the support of too many voters. Electoral democracy is, therefore, perhaps the ideal way to ensure that rulers do not become too distant from the ruled, and to tame political frustration. Nonetheless, it is no guarantee of political well-being.[4] Healthy democracy depends on well-informed and virtuous citizens. In fact, however, voters are usually less than fully informed rational actors, and sometimes they are susceptible to the charms of dangerous charlatans – as when they elected the Nazi Party into a leading position in the German Reichstag in July 1932 with 37 per cent of the vote. And while democratic accountability keeps governments on their toes, it can also cause them to avoid telling unpopular home truths and making difficult decisions. It tends to make them prefer the short-term over the long-term, too. As Winston Churchill famously – and realistically – said, 'Many forms of Government have been tried, and will be tried in this world of sin and woe. No one pretends that democracy is perfect or all-wise. Indeed, it has been said that democracy is the worst form of Government except for all those other forms that have been tried from time to time.'[5]

Still, whatever the virtues of democratically accountable government, it is simply not plausible to suppose that sufficiently good or just government first graced the earth with the granting of universal suffrage. All rulers suffer constraints. All are constrained by the need not to provoke such opposition as will remove them from power: only a reckless – and short-lived – ruler will simply ignore what others think and feel. And some are also constrained by their consciences to prefer the public to the private good and to serve the genuine interests of their people. Consequently, most rulers recognise the need to listen, whether just because they want to survive or because they want to discern what the public good might be.

If this is true of most rulers, it was especially true of colonial ones in places like India and Africa. That is because the number of British rulers was swamped by the number of native peoples ruled: the former could not have governed at all without the widespread consent and cooperation of the latter. As Lord Hardinge, viceroy and governor-general of India from 1910 to 1916, once candidly remarked: 'If each black man took up a handful of sand and by united effort cast it upon the white-faced intruders, we should be buried alive.'[6] The total population of the Indian subcontinent has been estimated at 139–214 million in 1800 rising to 183–247 million in 1850.[7] In 1830 India was garrisoned by 36,400 white soldiers (both British and East India Company) and 187,000 EIC sepoys and cavalry; in 1844 there were 50,000 white and 201,300 Indian troops.[8] In 1901 the native population numbered nearly 300 million while the number of British in India was 154,691.[9] The British members of the Indian Civil Service, who ran the higher echelons of the administration, were never more than twelve hundred.[10] Similarly, in Africa the ratio of white administrative officials to native people in the 1930s was 1:19,000 in Kenya and 1:54,000 in Nigeria. In circa 1939 the 43,114,000 inhabitants of the whole of British tropical Africa were presided over by a total of 938 white police and army personnel, 1,223 administrators and 178 judges, making an overall ratio of 1:18,432.[11]

Colonial rule was often indirect, mainly because the empire in Africa and India lacked the manpower, but also because it was cheaper and because it disturbed customary political institutions less, and so reduced the likelihood of violent unrest. Championed by Frederick

Lugard as the model for British colonial rule on the basis of his experience in northern Nigeria in the first two decades of the twentieth century, indirect rule left traditional native rulers in place, while bringing them under an overarching colonial system. Within certain broad constraints, native rule retained a high degree of autonomy.[12] According to Margery Perham, who made herself intimately acquainted with British colonial Africa between the two world wars and became the foremost expert on it, this system of government, which was careful to adjust itself to different social structures, absorbed the shock of Western annexation, kept the peace and 'induced a sympathetic, inquiring attitude in colonial officials towards African society'.[13] No doubt this was one reason why, in her experience, in the opening decades of colonial rule in early twentieth-century Nigeria, the Gold Coast, Uganda, Kenya, Nyasaland, Northern Rhodesia, Tanganyika and the Sudan, African peoples were 'almost, or even entirely passive in the hands of their new rulers . . . I travelled much in Africa between the wars . . . And yet I never saw any overt signs of discontent or antagonism; everywhere I met friendliness and eager curiosity. Colonial officials often accompanied me, but they never hesitated for a moment to let me trek and camp alone.'[14]

Before this, a form of indirect rule had long been operative in the subcontinent, where British India co-existed with hundreds of states ruled by native princes, who, subject to the advice of their British resident, were autonomous in internal, domestic policy so long as they did not so misrule as to destabilise their own state and thereby disturb their neighbours. Since imposing regime-change and annexing states had been one of the irritants that sparked the Indian Mutiny, the British were generally reluctant to intervene after 1857. As Mortimer Durand said in 1887: 'We must of course put down gross and systematic oppression, because we do not allow rebellion, which is the natural check upon repression, but I do not think it is our business to look too closely into administrative details, so long as the people are reasonably satisfied with their chief and he behaves well to us.'[15] Notwithstanding this, the British did depose the Nawab of Tonk in 1867 and the Khan of Kalat in 1893 for murder.[16]

In British India itself the views and interests of the native subjects of British rule were represented to their colonial rulers mainly through the thousands of Indians who, from the 1830s, dominated the middle and lower ranks of the government's administration as deputy collectors, assistant magistrates and subordinate judges.[17] In the courts the great majority of cases were tried by Indian judges. As viceroy, George Canning appointed an Indian judge to the Calcutta high court as soon as it was constituted in 1862; Alfred Lyall did the same in Allahabad on becoming lieutenant-governor of the North-West Provinces in 1882.[18] In 1874, the viceroy, Lord Northbrook, believing that 'native opinion has been too much ignored in recent legislation', took to inviting Indians to small dinner parties and visiting them in their homes, and appointed a non-aristocrat, Ramanath Tagore, to the Imperial Legislative Council, which had been enlarged in 1861 to include unofficial members of both races.[19] Lord Ripon, who was viceroy from 1880 to 1884, had been a Christian Socialist as a young man and had worked assiduously for the nascent cooperative movement and to promote working-class education in Britain. In India he became intent on promoting liberal reforms, including the development of local self-government through decentralisation.[20] Accordingly, 1892 saw the creation of municipal authorities, which were elected by rate-payers, opened up political responsibility to the still small but growing class of educated Indians and were balanced so as to ensure the representation of non-Hindu minorities. By 1911 there were 715 of these, commanding a combined budget of £2.5 million for spending on public works.

In 1908 the incorporation of Indians into government was taken a stage further with the Morley-Minto reforms. These involved the election of sixty Indian representatives to the viceroy's executive council, and between thirty and forty to the provincial legislative councils: 'Indian admission to these enclaves marked an end to their domination by senior [British] members of the ICS [Indian Civil Service], who had always claimed that they spoke for the silent masses of India.' The Indian National Congress welcomed the reforms – except for their accommodation of minority interests.[21] In August 1917 secretary of state for India Edwin Montagu announced to the House of Commons that government policy was that of 'the increasing association of Indians in every branch of the administration and the gradual development of self-governing institutions, with a view to the progressive realisation of responsible government in India as an integral part of the British Empire'.[22]

In India, Africa and the Middle East, British administrators' acute sense of public duty, especially to the impoverished and illiterate masses, was often allied to a deep scepticism about parliamentary politics. In this Lord Cromer was typical. Having acquired a low opinion of the quality of representatives in the colonial assemblies he had witnessed in Corfu, Valletta (Malta) and Spanish Town (Jamaica), he expected elected elites in India and Egypt to busy themselves with serving the interests of their own class, rather than the interests of the vulnerable and oppressed.[23] Instead, his ideal was of government run by a small cadre of expert and selfless administrators who, inspired by the 'granite rock of the Christian moral code', would pursue such policies as the suppression of slavery and *sati*, rather than introduce an electoral system that would enable a 'small minority of natives to misgovern their countrymen'.[24] As he put it, '[N]o assurance can be felt that the electors of Rajputana, if they had their own way, would not re-establish suttee [*sati*] . . . Christianity is our most powerful ally. We are the sworn enemies of the slave-dealer and the slave-owner.'[25] Cromer's ideal was undoubtedly autocratic, but it was also earnestly humanitarian. And in practice, the autocrat's natural temptation to ignorant arrogance was curbed by the necessity of native collaboration.

Meanwhile in the settler colonies legislative assemblies were set up, in which whites were represented, but usually not native peoples. Cape Colony in South Africa was the earliest exception with its colour-blind franchise from 1853 – sixteen years before the Fifteenth Amendment to the US Constitution – which had given rise to a small but influential black electorate of eight thousand voters by the end of the century.[26] Still, the view there, as elsewhere, was that the right and responsibility of voting should only be given to those who were fitted for it, for example, by possessing a certain amount of property and a certain level of education. If that seems patronising, it was not racist, since the same principle was applied to the franchise in Britain. The 1867 Reform Act granted the vote to all male householders in the boroughs, as well as lodgers who paid rent of £10 a year or more, and to agricultural landowners and tenants with very small amounts of land. Throughout the 1890s only 28 per cent of the adult (aged twenty-one and above) population of Britain were regarded by the law as fit to vote. Even now, the franchise is not unconditional: one only acquires the right to vote upon reaching a certain level of maturity, for which age is a crude proxy.

Notwithstanding the fact that blacks, like whites, in Cape Colony had to meet certain conditions before they could acquire the right to vote, the assumption prevailed that native people could become fit to vote, given time to develop.[27] Thus, when the Cape government proposed a bill in 1899 that would have disenfranchised most Africans, Cecil Rhodes protested, arguing that he had 'always differentiated between the raw barbarians and the civilised natives' and that the vote should be extended to Africans under the principle of 'equal rights to every civilised man south of the Zambesi'.[28] As we saw in Chapter 3, when asked to clarify what he meant by 'civilised man' in the previous year, he had replied, 'a man, white or black . . . who has sufficient education to write his name, has some property, or works. In fact, is not a loafer.'[29] Similarly, as we saw in Chapter 4, in New Zealand the Māori Representation Act of 1867 gave the vote to all native men over the age of twenty-one, while in Canada the Electoral Franchise Act of 1885 gave the federal vote to all adult male Indians in Eastern Canada who met the necessary property requirements, and allowed some male 'status Indians' in Eastern and Central Canada to vote without giving up their own laws, language and system of government.[30] The following year, as we saw in Chapter 5, Prime Minister John Macdonald wrote to a Mississauga chief, saying, 'I hope to see some day the Indian race represented by one of themselves on the floor of the House of Commons.'[31]

One common reason that colonial governments dragged their heels on introducing electoral democracy was concern about putting racial minorities at the mercy of majority tyranny. In Egypt the minorities were not at all the British, but the Mediterranean Christians – Copt, Syrian, Armenian and Greek – as well as the Turks. In India, the main minority comprised Muslims. And in Kenya, it was made up not just of British settlers, but of a larger number of Arabs and Indians. In 1922 the Colonial Office in London had declared that '[p]rimarily Kenya is an African territory' in which 'the interests of the African natives must be paramount'.[32] Especially after 1945 the colonial government pursued the goal of a multiracial polity where the different peoples would share power, after developing a sense of common citizenship by working together and learning to compromise rather than resort to violence. Accordingly, it sought gradually to reduce the predominant political power of the white settlers, upon whose taxes depended the funding for social welfare and economic development policies.[33] Up until 1948 the settlers held a majority of the elected seats on the Legislative Council, but then only half of them, and from 1958 a dwindling minority, a year after Africans were first elected on a restricted franchise. The Mau Mau uprising of 1952–60 derailed this gradualist policy, however, and thereafter the government sought instead to educate African leaders in the wisdom of political compromise before holding the first elections under universal suffrage in February 1961.[34]

IV

One of the gravest criticisms levelled against the undemocratic form of colonial government targets its relative imperviousness to the needs of those threatened by famine. The original critic, Amartya Sen, put it thus: 'One of the major influences on the actual prevention of famine is the speed and force with which early hunger is reported and taken up in political debates. The nature and freedom of the news media, and the power and standing of opposition parties, are of considerable importance in effective prevention of famines.'[35] It does make sense to suppose that electoral democracy, with its free press, is likely to communicate popular distress from the ruled to the rulers more efficiently than other political systems. However, we should note that British colonies, not least India, while lacking much in the way of wide suffrage and popular elections, often did have a press free enough to be ferociously critical of the government.

Moreover, communication of the problem is one thing; consensus over the solution, quite another. A major cause of the nature – and, some would say, inadequacy – of colonial governments' responses to the threat of famine was the persistent reign of the doctrine of free trade. This was not merely economic; it was also moral, attracting wide support from religious groups, trade unions and peace campaigners. As Richard Cobden wrote in 1842, free trade was 'the only human means of effecting universal and permanent peace'; it was 'the grand panacea', which would generate an international division of labour to everyone's benefit, foster economic interdependence and make war redundant.[36] But it was economic, too, and the ruling class – not only in Britain, but also in France – was persuaded by the theory of political economists that free trade in grain would naturally result in a national balancing of supply and demand, even in years of dearth.[37] They continued to be persuaded of this even in the face of harrowing reports of human suffering.

The best known – in some eyes, most infamous – case of famine that afflicted the British Empire was the Great Famine that befell Ireland in 1846–9. In this, about one million people – 12.5 per cent of the population – are estimated to have died of starvation and epidemic disease, and as a result of it about one and a quarter million are estimated to have emigrated between 1845 and 1851.[38] Together this amounts to a loss of more than a quarter of the total population. Some Irish nationalists, following John Mitchel (1815–75), blame the catastrophe on a distant (imperial) British government, in thrall to the dogma of free trade, motivated by racist contempt and intent on genocide.[39] As prime evidence they point to the fact that Charles Trevelyan, secretary of the Treasury and 'the most important force in British famine policy',[40] believed that that famine was God's judgement upon the feckless Irish, and that, during the famine, grain continued to be exported from Ireland.

The truth is more complicated and somewhat more forgiving. From 1815 the Corn Laws had imposed tariffs on grain imported into Britain, in order to keep prices high and support domestic landowners and farmers. Since this also kept the price of bread artificially high for consumers, it was naturally unpopular among the rapidly growing urban working class and led to agitation for the abolition of the tariffs. When the potato crop in Ireland failed disastrously in 1845, the

Conservative prime minister, Robert Peel, resolved to repeal the Corn Laws and lower the price of grain. This he achieved in June 1846 – but only with help from his Whig opponents and at the bitter cost of splitting his own party and forcing his eventual resignation. His Whig successor, Lord John Russell, was a leading advocate of repeal. Given these circumstances, it is not difficult to appreciate how politically unthinkable it was for the Russell government to contemplate interfering in the Irish market for grain to stop exports. Besides, the deficiency in food caused by the loss of the potato crop in 1846–8 was so great that, had all the exported Irish grain been retained, it would only have made up one-seventh of the lack.[41] Roy Foster comments: 'The idea that food produced in the country should not be exported was not adopted anywhere, and would have been considered an economic irrelevance at the time. It would also have required the assumption of powers that no contemporary government possessed, and inevitably caused violent resistance among the farmer classes; in any case, from 1847 Ireland was importing five times as much grain as she was exporting.'[42]

The British response to Irish distress did include elements of racist contempt, but, according to Paul Bew, those did not represent mainstream opinion: 'mainstream writers insisted on Irish qualities of hard work and intelligence, proved, above all, by Irish success outside the island, especially in the United States; an assumption of ethnic Irish laziness is not the decisive clue to English attitudes during the famine.'[43] Nor is it true, as Jennifer Hart's seminal claim runs, that Charles Trevelyan thought that the famine was 'the punishment of God on an indolent and unselfreliant [sic] people, and as God had sent the calamity to teach the Irish a lesson, that calamity must not be too much mitigated: the selfish and indolent must learn their lesson so that a new and improved state of affairs would arise'.[44] On the contrary, Trevelyan repeatedly urged his officials 'that People cannot under any circumstances be allowed to starve'.[45] It is true that in his 1848 book *The Irish Crisis*, he described the famine as 'a direct stroke of an all-wise and all-merciful Providence', which exposed 'the deep and inveterate root of social evil'. But the evil he was referring to was Ireland's agrarian economy with its – as he saw it – irresponsible landlords presiding over smallholders as they eked out subsistence in precarious dependence on the potato. It was this 'evil' economic system that he believed the famine had shown to be unsustainable and ripe for reform for the sake of a better future. As he wrote at the bottom of the same page and in the very last sentence of his book: 'God grant that the generation to which this opportunity has been offered, may rightly perform its part, and that we may not relax our efforts until Ireland fully participates in the social health and physical prosperity of Great Britain, which will be the true consummation of their union.'[46]

Ironically, if anything discouraged the delivery of aid to the starving Irish, it was as much Irish nationalist indignation as British racism.[47] As John Mitchel put it in the October 1847 issue of *The Nation*: 'We scorn, we repulse, we curse all English alms. Give us our rights and keep your charity.'[48] The implicit argument was this: that the root of Irish ills was 'a foreign parliament – ignorant, vain, headlong, insolent and selfish, who will take no heed of anything that is Irish – who will treat landlord and peasant, merchant and artisan, with indiscriminate insolence';[49] that to accept British aid would confirm Ireland's dependence and undermine the case for self-government (not least by acknowledging that the Westminster parliament was in fact less selfish, less insensitive and therefore less 'foreign' than asserted); and that, therefore, for the sake of the nationalist cause – and the long-term future of Irish freedom – the present Irish people should be let starve.

Undeterred by nationalist protests, Trevelyan and the British government were initially assiduous in providing aid in the form of paid employment through an extensive programme of public works. However, while this had proved effective in dealing with local famines before, it proved inadequate in 1846–7, partly because the price of food outstripped the wages paid. So February 1847 saw the introduction of soup kitchens, which offered direct aid in the form of the distribution of food, mostly free, to millions. Nevertheless, not even this was enough, since no amount of food could cure the disease that was then ravaging.[50] However, wary of the demoralising, 'pauperizing' effects of welfare dependence and expecting a better potato harvest, the government fatefully – some say, heartlessly – shut down the soup kitchens in August 1847, and expected most of the aid in future to be provided by the normal 'poor law' means of workhouses funded by local landowners and other rate-payers. With some good reason, the British tended to think that these had not borne as much of the burden as their civic duty obliged.[51] The great flaw in this policy was to assume that, however well such a system of poor relief worked in England, it could be expected to work adequately in Ireland, which had half England's population but only a fifth of its rateable property value and proportionally five times as many paupers.[52]

The overall judgement of A. M. Sullivan, a Young Ireland activist with direct experience of relief efforts, seems fair: 'It would be utter injustice to deny that the government made exertions which, judged by ordinary circumstances, would be prompt and considerable. But judged by the awful magnitude of the evil then at hand or actually befallen, they were fatally tardy and inadequate.' Ironically, Sullivan then went on to suggest that the Irish Famine was one of those 'calamities which the rules and formulæ of ordinary constitutional administration were unable to cope with, and which could be efficiently encountered only by the concentration of plenary powers and resources in some competent "despotism" located in the scene of disaster'.[53] The irony here lies in an Irish nationalist recommending as an emergency measure the kind of benevolent despotism that British colonial administrators such as Cromer championed as a rule in parts of the world afflicted by endemic and widespread agrarian poverty.

V

What Charles Trevelyan has long been to Irish nationalists, John A. Macdonald has become to contemporary Canadian anti-colonialists. When James Daschuk's *Clearing the Plains: Disease, Politics of Starvation, and the Loss of Aboriginal Life* was first published in 2013, it 'had all the effect of a well-placed bomb'.[54] That was because Daschuk argues that Macdonald, Canada's first prime minister, was culpable for the 'sinister' mismanagement of relief during the western famine of the 1880s and accuses him of 'outright malevolence'.[55] Elsewhere, Daschuk has implied that Macdonald's policies amounted to 'genocide'.[56] Daschuk does acknowledge that the primary causes of human distress and death were natural: the collapse of the bison population, the climatic effects of the volcanic explosion of Krakatoa in August 1883 and the spread of tuberculosis.[57] Nevertheless,

> [t]he most significant factor under human control was the failure of the Canadian government to meet its treaty obligations and its decision to use food as a means to control the Indian population to meet its development agenda rather than as a response to a humanitarian crisis . . . officials quickly turned the food crisis into a means to control [the hungry indigenous population] to facilitate construction of the railway and opening of the country to agrarian settlement.[58]

In particular, the provision of rations to distressed native peoples was made conditional upon their removal to reserves, so as to make way for the Canadian Pacific Railway and European settlement. This 'ethnic cleansing'[59] was necessary to enable the transition of the prairies 'to a new economic paradigm from which the overwhelming majority of treaty people were excluded'.[60] In addition, the provision of food was also made conditional upon the recipients working 'for the sake of the moral effect' and to prevent them thereafter 'expecting gratuitous assistance from the Government', as the deputy superintendent of Indian affairs, Lawrence Vankoughnet, put it.[61] Worse, the main company contracted to deliver rations abused its privileged position to deliver substandard food to reserves, 'probably with the collusion of government officials'.[62] Accordingly, Daschuk concludes that his 'study has shown that the decline of First Nations' health was the direct result of economic and cultural suppression. The effects of the state-sponsored attack on indigenous communities that began in the 1880s haunt us as a nation still.'[63]

Such a conclusion, however, is not supported by the evidence, much of it provided by Daschuk himself. First of all, strictly speaking, the Canadian government did not renege on its treaty obligations. Treaty No. 6. (1876), for example, reads thus:

> That in the event hereafter of the Indians comprised within this treaty being overtaken by any pestilence, or by a general famine, the Queen,

on being satisfied and certified thereof by Her Indian Agent or Agents, *will grant to the Indians assistance of such character and to such extent as Her Chief Superintendent of Indian Affairs shall deem necessary and sufficient* to relieve the Indians from the calamity that shall have befallen them.[64]

The government did exactly as it had promised to do. Tragically, it underestimated what was 'necessary and sufficient'.

Second, the government did not use the need of native people for food as an opportunity to advance its development agenda *rather than* as a reason for a humanitarian response; it did both – just as Trevelyan had done in Ireland. As Daschuk himself writes, 'Within months [of the outbreak of famine in the spring of 1878] large quantities of goods were being shipped north from Fort Benton, Montana'[65] and '[r]ations kept many from starving'.[66] He even quotes Macdonald as saying in 1882, 'We cannot allow them [the natives] to die for want of food'.[67] Appropriations for food relief alone to treaty populations 'shot' up from $157,572 in 1880 to $607,235 in 1882, and from 1882 to 1884 expenditures by the Department of Indian Affairs in Manitoba and the North-Western Territories exceeded $1 million per annum.[68] In the view of another historian who has analysed Ottawa's accounts for 1882, 'looking at the scope and range of government activity in that era, it is . . . important to acknowledge that Ottawa's 1882 half-million dollar response in emergency famine aid was – in its own way – impressive and humane'.[69]

Third, the Conservative government's 'development agenda' encompassed future native well-being. Given the sudden disappearance of the bison, which had been the main source of food for the peoples of the western plains, their survival necessitated a radical change in their way of life. Their leaders recognised this, seeing the Numbered Treaties 'first and foremost as a bridge to a future without bison', and they deliberately sought assistance in converting to agriculture.[70] That this was the route to salvation had been confirmed by the experience of the Canadian Dakota who, having taken up farming in the early nineteenth century, no longer depended on bison as their primary food source and so did not suffer the terrible decline of their western brethren.[71] One sign that the government intended to include native peoples in its 'new economic paradigm' was the introduction of the home farm programme to develop reserve agriculture. In implementation, however, it was 'hastily contrived' and an 'abysmal failure'.[72] Whether this failure was the consequence of culpable negligence, which casts doubt upon the sincerity of intention, rather than of ignorance or impotence, Daschuk does not show. He does admit, however, the general weakness of the confederal government: 'Other than the North-West Mounted Police [NWMP], the Canadian presence in the west at the time was minuscule. When the hunger began, Canada simply did not have the people or infrastructure to meet the demand for food.'[73] In the mid-1880s the NWMP numbered only about a thousand, while carrying the responsibility for enforcing Canadian law everywhere outside of Ontario and Quebec.[74]

Finally, whatever the failures in relief, whether culpable or not, we need to put them in perspective. If Patrice Dutil's reading of Daschuk's data is correct, the number of native deaths attributable to starvation on the Canadian plains from 1879 to 1883 was somewhere in the region of forty-five.[75]

No, that is not a typographical error.

VI

It seems unlikely to be a coincidence that one of the members of the Indian Civil Service who made himself an outstanding expert on Indian famines was Antony MacDonnell, a Catholic native of County Mayo, who had been born in 1844, the year before disaster struck his native land. In 1876 MacDonnell wrote a meticulous *Report on the Food-grain Supply and Statistical Review of the Relief Operations in the Distressed Districts of Behar and Bengal during the Famine of 1873-74*.[76] And when he was lieutenant-governor of the North-Western Provinces in the 1890s he gave district officers the discretion to spend money in emergencies without waiting for permission, telling their supervising commissioner to impress on them 'their personal responsibility in regard to starvation deaths. The system is ready and they have the funds. They cannot be held free from blame if starvation deaths occur.'[77]

However, notwithstanding the intense professional attention that MacDonnell and his like paid to analysing the problem and working out solutions, the Indian government's record on famine relief as a whole was 'a mixed one, ranging from the very successful to the wholly disastrous'. In 1865, adherence to the doctrine of the free market obstructed the importation of rice into Orissa, where almost one million people died of starvation and resultant disease. Overreacting (understandably) nine years later when famine threatened parts of Bihar and Bengal in 1874, the government imported vast – and, as it happened, excessive – quantities of rice from Burma. It succeeded in staving off starvation not only by distributing food to the sick and the elderly, but also by providing work for the able-bodied, mainly in the form of road and railway construction. Success, however, then bred complacency when, in 1876–8, the viceroy, Lord Lytton, responded to famine in the south of India parsimoniously, trying to avoid a repeated wastage of rice but consequently allowing millions to die. This disaster led to the drawing up of a Famine Code in 1880, whose recommendations included further irrigation- and railway-building in areas prone to drought. The government also set aside a substantial annual sum as famine insurance. That was still not sufficient to prevent further disastrous famines in 1896–7 and 1899–1900, but by the spring of 1900 the government had loosened its purse strings and was providing relief to five million people at a cost of £8.5 million, 'a gigantic effort reflected in a decline in the mortality rate to only just above the average'.[78] Tirthankar Roy writes of 'the disappearance of famines after 1900' because of 'better distribution of foodgrains, improvements in knowledge and information about agricultural conditions, and famine relief'.[79]

Next to the calamity suffered by Ireland in the late 1840s, the famine within the British Empire that attracts the greatest infamy is the one that killed between 1.5 and 3 million people in Bengal in 1942–4. In this case, the cause of famine, it is widely thought, was not a shortage of food but a failure to distribute it.[80] It is true that a series of tidal waves and rice-crop disease had damaged the late autumn harvest in 1942, that grain supplies from Burma had been cut off by Japanese occupation and that the government's evacuation of coastal areas in case of invasion had reduced the availability of fish.[81] Yet the late autumn harvest in 1942 still amounted to 83 per cent of the 1941 yield, the Burmese supply of grain would only have amounted to 1–200,000 tons and food stocks in 1943 were in fact 13 per cent higher than in 1941 while the population had only increased by 9 per cent.[82] The basic problem was the price of grain, which rose six-fold in eighteen months from January 1942 to August 1943 and so made food unaffordable for the rural poor.[83] The reasons for this price inflation were several. One was the extraordinary demand for resources generated by the war effort, intensified by the sudden influx of at least half a million Indian refugees from Japanese-invaded Burma. Another was the hoarding of stocks by those with the capital to speculate, when the authorities intervened in the market to fix the price of rice in the summer of 1942. And a third was corruption in the provincial and largely Indian-run government.[84]

Things began to improve when, thanks to Churchill, the former field marshal Lord Wavell took over as viceroy in October 1943. What he found was a demoralised administration. As he wrote in November, 'In the old days the senior members of the ICS were to some extent public figures ... regarded as ministerial. They held themselves morally and personally responsible for the welfare of the people in their charge, and would no more have tolerated in Calcutta, than you would tolerate in London, the disgraceful episode of the destitutes ... The officials do not seem to me to be conscious of the disgrace brought upon the administration.'[85] Immediately, he set out to tour Bengal and within a week he had deployed the army, despite its military priority of clearing the Japanese from Burma. By January 1944 he had established 347 civil emergency hospitals and 18 large military hospitals and deployed 1,700 extra public health staff. By then the worst of the crisis appeared to be passing, although many people would continue to die over the next year from disease facilitated by persistent malnutrition.

In the next month, Wavell pressed Churchill to release scarce Allied shipping from vital wartime duties in order to transport grain to Bengal, but the prime minister refused – and is now widely and fiercely condemned for it. Some have attributed his refusal to racist antipathy towards Indians, but the dilemma of whether or not to compromise the war effort against Nazi Germany and Imperial Japan at a time when victory was by no means secure, when Allied shipping was already being stretched to breaking point in supplying the invasion of Sicily and then of the Italian mainland, and when preparations were being made for the hazardous seaborne invasion of Normandy, was surely the prevailing reason.[86] Others accept this, but still blame Churchill for his 'lack of political will' in preferring the war effort to famine relief.[87] However, that overlooks the fact that the moral dilemma was a genuine one, in which it was not clear that famine relief *should have* been preferred to defeating the Nazi Germans and the imperial Japanese. In any case, Churchill's refusal was beside the point, insofar as there were in fact adequate stocks of food and that the real problem was one of distribution and price – as Churchill himself thought.[88] Moreover, by the end of 1944 Wavell had got the one million tons of grain he had demanded at the beginning.[89]

All things considered, whether in India or Canada, the record of the British imperial and colonial governments in relieving famine is not unfairly represented by Hugh Kearney in his judgement upon the British government's performance in 1840s Ireland: it 'may have lacked foresight and generosity, and have been guilty of grossly underestimating the human problems involved, but it was not guilty of either criminal negligence or of deliberate heartlessness . . . For all this catalogue of errors and rigidity, the tale is not one of deliberate extermination.'[90]

Moreover, the historical record does not bear out the claim that inadequacies in colonial governments' efforts at famine relief were ultimately attributable to the lack of democratic representation. In none of the cases we have reviewed were the imperial and colonial governments insensitive to the extent and depth of human distress caused by famine. On the contrary, they were committed to relieving it. Insofar as their commitment failed to meet the challenge, the causes were various: the unprecedented scale of natural disaster, limited public infrastructure and manpower, failure to appreciate the limits of local resources, parsimony in overreaction to previous wastage, wartime exigencies and dilemmas, competing claims on public funding, the unintended effects of intervention in the market (that is, hoarding) and local corruption. Indeed, since 1935 the Indian provinces had been ruled by elected governments and in 1943 the Bengal administration was a democratic one. And it was the *elected* minister of civil supplies in the Bengal government, Huseyn Shaheed Suhrawardy, whom Wavell suspected of corruption.[91] Moreover, famine did not suddenly cease to afflict the Indian subcontinent with the arrival of political independence and electoral democracy in 1947: the Bangladesh famine of 1974 is estimated to have caused the deaths of up to 1.5 million people.

VII

A second point on which the policy of British colonial governments has frequently attracted criticism was its failure to promote education sufficiently. To take one example, the moderate Egyptian nationalist Ahmad Lutfi al-Sayyid, while praising the 'magnificent results' of Lord Cromer's financial reforms, complained in 1907 that he had failed to establish the foundations of a 'productive and serviceable' system of public education.[92] Six decades later, the historian Afaf Lutfi al-Sayyid-Marsot echoed her uncle when she wrote that '[t]o the Egyptians, education and self-rule were Cromer's greatest failures in Egypt, just as his restoration of Egyptian finances was his greatest success'.[93] In his defence, however, we should note that the state's direct involvement in the provision of education was almost unknown in Britain itself until the Elementary Education Act of 1870, only seven years before Cromer arrived in Egypt.[94] Even then, within the national system created by the Act, many of the schools actually providing education were private, church foundations. (Indeed, that remains so to this day.) It should also be remembered that conservative Egyptians, not least Muslims, were hostile to Western education, especially that of women.[95] It is true that Cromer, following accepted wisdom in India, resisted educating more people than there were openings in government service, fearing that the combination of over-education and under-employment would serve to produce political agitators.[96] Yet given the combustible political record in Egypt and elsewhere of combining large numbers of students with unemployment – both during the colonial period and long after it – Cromer's anxiety was not ground-less.[97]

However, even if colonial governments did not promote education as much as they could and should have done, they nevertheless did promote it, first indirectly and then directly. For example, the East India Company – especially under Lord Elphinstone – supported the private foundation by alliances of Indians and Britons of modern, English-language institutions such as the Hindu College in Calcutta in 1817, a reconstituted Delhi College in 1828, the Elphinstone Institution in Bombay in 1835 and Madras University High School in 1841. Under EIC rule engineering colleges sprang up in Madras in 1803, Poona in 1834 and Roorkee in 1854, and by 1947 'well over 250,000 students were placed into engineering courses'.[98] The Madras Medical School was founded in 1835, followed by equivalents in Calcutta (1835) and Bombay (1845).[99] In 1911 British India had 186 colleges of higher education, and by 1939 that number had doubled.[100]

Meanwhile in Africa, colonial governments first of all permitted the setting up of schools and colleges by Christian missionaries and then, after the First World War, became directly engaged in promoting education. Chinua Achebe reports that in the decade after the war the colonial government in Nigeria established two 'first class' boarding schools for boys, one of which 'played a conspicuous role in the development of modern African literature'.[101] From the mid-1930s the imperial government in London became increasingly persuaded of the need to educate Africans for self-rule – as well as to provide an alternative to politically subversive higher education in the anti-colonialist US.[102] In the wake of the ('Asquith') *Report of the Commission on Higher Education in the Colonies*, which was published in June 1945, universities were established in Ibadan, Nigeria (1948); Accra, Ghana (1948); Khartoum, Sudan (1951); and Harare, Rhodesia and Nyasaland (1955). And in June 1963, just after Tanzania and Uganda had gained independence, and months before Kenya acquired it, the Federal University of East Africa was created out of Makerere College, Kampala (1922), the Royal College of Nairobi (1960) and the University College of Dar es Salaam (1961).

VIII

It is vital to the well-being of a political community that rulers govern in the interests of the public good. This does not mean, of course, that they should always govern in the perceived interests of all those they rule. That is impossible, since among the ruled are different, sometimes conflicting, felt interests, which cannot all be promoted at the same time, however individually worthy they might be. Rulers have to judge what is the overall public good and, in the light of that, select which felt interests of the ruled to promote. Nonetheless, in order to make wise judgements, rulers must first know what the felt interests of the ruled are, and that means that the latter must be represented to them, *somehow*. It may be that electoral democracy is generally the best way to make that happen. But even if it is the best way, it is not the only way.

Besides, the representation of the ruled to the ruler is not the only necessary ingredient of good government. There is also the effective rule of law and consequent security, without which human flourishing is barely possible, as well as the probity of officials. In 1883 the seventeen-year-old Sun Yat-sen ran away from home in China and arrived in the British colony of Hong Kong, where he proceeded to complete his secondary school education and then train at the Hong Kong College of Medicine for Chinese. During his sojourn there, protected by the colonial authorities from (Chinese) imperial demands for extradition and stimulated by a free press, he became involved in revolutionary plotting aimed at regime change in China.[103] His efforts eventually came to fruition in 1911, when the Qing dynasty was overthrown in favour of a republic. Twelve years later, Sun returned to the colony and gave an address at his old college (which had become Hong Kong University), in which he explained what had inspired his turn to republican revolution:

> I got those ideas in Hong Kong. I spent a great deal of my spare time walking the streets of the colony. Hong Kong impressed me a great deal, because there was orderly calm, and because there was artistic work being done without interruption. I went to my home in Xiangshan

twice a year and could immediately notice the great difference. There was disorder instead of order, insecurity instead of security . . . I began to wonder why it was that foreigners have done such marvellous things with this barren rock of Hong Kong in only seventy or eighty years, whilst China with several thousand years of civilization has not even one place like Hong Kong . . . I found that among the government officials [in the colony] corruption was the exception and purity the rule. It was the contrary in China, where corruption among officials was the rule . . . I was told by elders that the good governments in England and in Europe were not at first natural to those places, but that men had brought about a change in themselves. In England years ago there was just the same corruption, just the same forgeries in the courts, and the same cruelty, but that Englishmen loved liberty and that Englishmen had said, 'We shall no longer stand these things, we shall change them.' Then I got the idea in my head. 'Why can we not change it in China?' . . . My fellow students, you and I have studied in this English colony and in an English university and we must learn by English examples. We must carry this English example of good government to every part of China.[104]

After 1945 several million fellow Chinese endorsed Sun's view, when they chose to flee mainland anarchy for a better life under colonial government. But it was the rule of law and social order that drew them, not the right to vote. The colony still did not grant universal adult suffrage.[105]

Halfway around the globe and ninety years later, a famous Nigerian nationalist bore witness strikingly similar to Sun Yat-sen's. A year before his death in 2013, Chinua Achebe published *There Was a Country: A Personal History of Biafra*,[106] in which he reflected on the colonial rule under which he had been brought up: 'Here is a piece of heresy,' he wrote. 'The British governed their colony of Nigeria with considerable care. There was a very highly competent cadre of government officials imbued with a high level of knowledge of how to run a country . . . British colonies were, more or less, expertly run . . . One was not consumed by fear of abduction or armed robbery.'[107] As a result,

One had a great deal of confidence and faith in the British system that
we had grown up in, a confidence and faith in British institutions. One
trusted that things would get where they were sent; postal theft,
tampering, or loss of documents were unheard of. Today [in Nigeria],
one would not even contemplate sending off materials of importance
so readily, either abroad or even locally, by mail.[108]

Along the same lines, Achebe had earlier opined in 1962, only two
years after Nigeria's independence, 'Before [under colonial rule],
justice may have been fierce but it could not be bought or sold . . .
Now all that is changed.'[109] This remark touches on a further truth
about a vital condition of political health: that the sense of order
that elicits a people's trust in their political environment, and so
liberates them to invest in building lives, families and businesses,
depends crucially on the personal probity of public officials. Margery
Perham bore witness to the typical public-spiritedness of colonial
officers on the ground in early twentieth-century Africa, when she
wrote that

> the office of District Commissioner should stand out in history as one
> of the supreme types developed by Britain to meet a special demand
> . . . The D.C. . . . could be relied upon to be humane, uncorrupt,
> diligent . . . They generally loved their district and were nearly always
> eager to point out the virtues rather than the faults of the people under
> their charge . . . I have not forgotten the letter I had from one of the
> first Africans to become an Assistant District Commissioner and who
> was posted to some remote sub-station. 'I marvel', he wrote, 'that an
> English graduate can endure to live alone in such a place for £400.'[110]

More recently in 2010, the head of the Disasters Emergency Committee,
Brendan Gormley, who had extensive experience working for Oxfam
in Africa, has commented that administrators in the colonial period
showed more dedication to their task and had a greater understanding
of local peoples than their successors in today's 'aid period'.[111] Native
testimony can be found to corroborate both his view and Perham's.
Da'ud 'Abd al-Latif, who served as a senior member of the Sudan

Civil Service under the British in the 1950s, said of his colleagues: 'The British had a tremendous sense of mission, most of them, a real sense of mission, and were really idealistic . . . [They] lived amongst a people who respected them and, many times, loved them and whom they loved . . . The British Administrator['s] . . . allegiance was not to the British Government. His allegiance was to the Sudan Government.'[112]

However, by far the most famous examples of official probity in the British Empire were the 'covenanted' members of the Indian Civil Service, otherwise known as 'Civilians'.[113] Back in the closing decade of the eighteenth century, Lord Cornwallis' insistence that officials in the East India Company should live on their salaries, give up private trading and resist bribes 'helped to create a civil service that became widely regarded as incorruptible and just, one that even Indian nationalist newspapers would later regard as "absolutely above suspicion" and "the high water mark of morality in the public service of the country", and as beyond being "bribed to do anything"'.[114] One retired Civilian observed of his fellow recruits in the 1920s that 'most of us believed that we were following a vocation not just a career'. As a district officer in Ceylon in the opening decade of the 1900s, Leonard Woolf found himself rarely able to think 'of anything else except the District and the people, to increase their prosperity, diminish the poverty and disease, start irrigation works, open schools. I did not idealise or romanticise the people or the country; I just liked them aesthetically and humanly and socially.'[115] And a serving officer wrote this in 1938: 'To lead life-giving streams to thirsty fields, to foster mighty forests, to build roads and bridges, to minister to the sick, to spread the light of learning, to dispense justice, to maintain peace and order, to strive for the welfare of hundreds of thousands, perhaps millions of people – these are tasks which by their mere fulfilment provide ample recompense for any hardships that may be involved in their performance.'[116] If we are tempted to think, uncharitably, that all this is just so much self-idealisation by patronising colonial do-gooders, we should heed not only the witness of the nationalist press, but also of the Irish-American Charles Westwater:

In 1956 I was in the ranks of many who left the United States to rebuild a war-torn world. Assigned as spiritual and temporal leader of some impoverished village settlements in the newly created Thal Development Authority of the Punjab province in Pakistan, I found my Boston Irish ancestry unprepared for what I would encounter of British colonialism. It quickly became evident that the people tolerated me as a direct consequence of their prior experience with the British.

In 14 years I heard nothing but praise for the English colonial rulers, even from those who had served time in prison for one reason or another. When the suggestion was made that, given the choice, the people might have voted for the British to leave, an office *peon* corrected me with: 'You're wrong, sahib. Ninety-five per cent of the people would have voted for the British to stay.' . . .

In small hamlets with but traces of civilisation, I was approached by people to adjudicate a particular grievance. Whatever judgement was rendered would invariably be accepted by both parties, such was the aura accorded to a white man coming in the wake of British colonialism. An offhand remark by a Punjabi farmer who knew me as an American is an encomium I treasure: 'He's like an *angrezi sahib* – an Englishman.'[117]

And if Kartar Lalvani is to be believed, there are many older Indians who share Chinua Achebe's mature view of British colonial rule: 'It is a common refrain among the older generations that governance was then [during the British days] not so decrepit, bribery not so rampant, favouritism not so common, corruption and plunder of public funds not so pervasive, injustice not so blatant, and bureaucracy not so partisan as today.'[118]

The witness of subjects of colonial rule such as Sun Yat-sen, Chinua Achebe, Da'ud 'Abd al-Latif and Charles Westwater's Punjabi villagers testifies to the truth, as the American political scientist Michael Hechter has put it, that 'good alien governance may be better than bad native governance'. All rulers, whether native or foreign, legitimate their rule in the same basic ways: by enabling, defending and promoting public goods, and by distributing them fairly to the ruled.[119] Hechter offers three examples of foreign rule that clearly achieved such legitimation, two of them British. First, there was the (Chinese) Imperial Maritime Customs, which, with a predominantly British-staffed bureaucracy under the control of successive Chinese central governments, supplied public goods such as domestic customs administration, postal administration, harbour and waterway management, weather reporting and anti-smuggling operations from 1854 to 1950. Then there was the Sino-Foreign Salt Inspectorate, the British-dominated agency which collected an average of 25 per cent of Chinese central government receipts from 1928 to 1937 and whose 'rigorously fair and effective policies . . . generated legitimacy in an extremely nationalist environment'. The same was true, third, of the Ottoman Public Debt Administration, which, run by Europeans from 1881 to 1918, produced greater tax revenue for the imperial government by reducing bureaucratic corruption and, by raising the confidence of Western investors in the regime's fiscal responsibility, contributed to the development of infrastructure, especially railways.[120] It is because foreign rulers can achieve such legitimation, that '[r]esistance to alien rule is hardly universal'.[121]

IX

Nevertheless, whatever the good intentions of British colonial rulers, and however efficient and incorruptible they were, the fact is that their rule provoked – at different times and places – a 'nationalist' reaction that brought it to an end after the Second World War. When set against 'imperialism' or 'colonialism', 'nationalism' immediately acquires a positive connotation among us, signifying native liberation from foreign oppression. But the truth about 'nationalism' is much more complicated. Nationalist self-consciousness is usually formed in reaction: I become conscious of belonging to 'us', because I have become aware of my difference from 'them' – or, more exactly, because 'they' have made me aware of the difference. Often that difference is resented, and the reaction defensive. Sometimes what is defended is cultural – say, the survival of a language, religion or social system – and what is sought is a measure of autonomy against a dominant culture that threatens to overwhelm and extinguish. Sometimes, of course, more is sought – some lesser or greater degree of political autonomy. 'Lesser or greater', because there is no such thing as absolute autonomy; every human individual suffers constraints and exists in various kinds of dependent relationships. The same is true of polities.

Maybe there have been times when historical reality has brought the stereotype to life and a native people has been united in nationalist opposition to a colonial oppressor. Usually, however, nationalism has been divisive. Those who have sided with the colonial rulers have commonly been dismissed as dupes, collaborators, or at least as standing on the losing side of History. However, not only does that imply an inevitability about the direction of events that does not actually obtain, it also patronises many native people. No doubt 'loyalists' can be ignorant and self-interested, but so can 'nationalists', and sometimes the former have good reasons not to align themselves with the latter.

When a revolutionary elite among Irish nationalists decided to launch their famous Easter Rising in central Dublin in April 1916, they did so not as an expression of widespread popular opposition to Ireland's connection with Britain and its Empire, but in a violent attempt to disrupt growing contentment with it. This contentment was not stupid; it recognised that most of Ireland's historic grievances had been addressed.[122] In 1829 the Catholic Emancipation Act had ended the legal exclusion of Catholics from public office. By the close of the century Protestant control of government in Ireland was loosening its grip.[123] In 1901, when Catholics comprised 74 per cent of the population as a whole, at least three of the leading judges were Catholic, as were 43 per cent of barristers, 27 per cent of resident magistrates, 31 per cent of district inspectors and 74 per cent of police.[124] In 1903 the Wyndham Act had addressed the chronic vulnerability of tenant farmers by providing them with government funds to purchase land from their landlords, allowing a majority of them to become landowners. Further, Ireland was enjoying a cultural renaissance; and while its per capita national product was less than two-thirds that of the rest of the United Kingdom, it was higher than that of Norway, Sweden, Italy and Finland, and only 7.6 per cent behind that of France.[125] Notwithstanding this, judging by the memoirs of one of the rebels of

1916, Desmond FitzGerald, the revolutionaries were disturbed that '[t]he Irish people recognised themselves as part of England' and, according to the revolutionaries' own '"mystical" doctrine . . . that an elect few would ultimately leaven the whole country', they decided that 'extreme action must be taken'.[126]

The rising resulted in 450 lethal and 2,614 wounded casualties – the majority of whom were civilians – together with the destruction of much of Dublin's city centre.[127] Understandably, citizens who had found them-selves embroiled in the heart of the fighting around the General Post Office tended to be hostile to the rebels, and in the judgement of a leading constitutional nationalist, John Dillon, the Easter Rising was 'the first rebellion that ever took place in Ireland where you [the British government] had the majority on your side'.[128] Had it not been for General Sir John Maxwell's draconian decisions, after the fighting was over, to have armed troops conduct mass arrests, to hold courts-martial of the suspected ringleaders without access to defence counsel and then to execute the convicts,[129] Ireland might have continued on its peaceful, constitutional way to a form of home rule within the British Empire, rather than lurch into more widespread revolutionary violence in 1919 and thence to a more radical form of independence.

Nationalists seldom represent all of the actual people, usually acting instead in the name of an ideal people; and sometimes in the name of the latter, they terrorise and kill the former. Peter Godwin was brought up in colonial Rhodesia from the late 1950s and briefly taught African children in a Catholic school in the early 1970s. On one occasion he wrote on the blackboard of his class of black boys a question for discussion, 'Do you think that Rhodesia should have majority rule?', and then waited for a response:

> Eventually one boy raised his hand. 'No! I! Do! Not!' he sang out and then sat down.
> 'Why not?'
> He . . . replied, 'Because the tribes will keell each udder' . . .
> 'Do you really think that? Or are you just saying that because you think that's what I want to hear, because I'm a *mukiwa* [a European]?'
> They all laughed, and another boy said, 'We always used to keel

each udder before the white man came. The Matabele would come up and steal our cows and keel us, and we had to hide in caves.'[130]

Unfortunately, this African boy was not suffering from colonialist false consciousness. Shortly after this classroom exchange, Godwin, aged seventeen, was conscripted into the security forces during what is now known as the Zimbabwean War of Liberation, but was in fact a vicious civil war. In 1973 he found himself in Matabeleland, walking about a village that had been visited by Zimbabwe African National Liberation Army guerrillas:

> I walked around a hut and saw an old woman in a red dress, sitting against the wall, her knees drawn up against her chest, her head resting on her knees. When I called to her she didn't reply. I touched her gently on the shoulder, to wake her. Still no reply. Then I realized her dress had not originally been red, it was soaked in blood. I lifted her head. Her throat had been cut. Two others had been similarly dispatched . . . From them on, there were lots of incidents like that. And worse. Incidents that I try not to remember. Women impaled on stakes. Whole families burned to death inside their own huts, their hands tied behind their backs with wire. People accused them of being 'sell-outs', killed 'to make an example'.[131]

Later Godwin asked his black comrade, Sergeant-Major Gondo, "'But don't you sympathise a little bit with the aim of the terrs [terrorists], to get black rule?" . . . "These people are just communists", he spat, "they are being used by the Russians. They are just greedy for power . . . they are not fit to rule this country. They kill old men. Women even. You see what they do. They are cowards. I don't want to be ruled by them." '[132] Was the black sergeant-major merely a dupe? Was he a blind, unprincipled lackey of the ruling power? I doubt it.

X

Nationalism, even when it opposes colonial rule, is not its own justification. It is morally accountable and sometimes its account does not add up. On other occasions, the genesis of nationalist resentment against foreign, colonial rulers is quite understandable – and it often involved soldiers. In Ireland mass arrests and military executions in the wake of the Easter Rising might have seemed to General Maxwell an appropriately decisive response to an armed rising at Britain's back door, while the country – aided by more than two hundred thousand Irishmen in British uniform – was in the midst of fighting a horren-dously bloody world war with Germany, but it was a political disaster. The brutal military overreaction did indeed disturb growing Irish contentment with British government – just as the revolutionaries had intended. In 1919, as we shall see in the next chapter, General Dyer's murderous overreaction in Amritsar had the same alienating effect on Indian opinion.

Egypt's equivalent to Amritsar involved less the disproportionate violence of soldiers than a clumsy attempt at self-entertainment, combined maybe with the arrogance of foreigners, and capped with a miscarriage of justice. It was more tragedy than atrocity. In June 1906 five British officers and their battalion's doctor decided to amuse themselves by shooting pigeons at Dinshawai, as they had done the previous two years. On this occasion, however, they neglected to obtain official permission from the village headman. Their shooting caused a pile of grain to catch fire, which led, first, to an altercation, then to the accidental wounding of five villagers and finally to the accidental death of one of the officers. A special tribunal was set up to try the case, comprising two British and two Egyptian judges under the pres-idency of Butros Ghali, the acting minister of justice. After examining fifty-two accused people in thirty minutes,[133] the court reached its judgment and sentenced four of the convicted to hang for the 'inten-tional' murder of the officer, with a further eight to be flogged and twelve to suffer various lengths of penal servitude. Lord Cromer, who had left Cairo for London before the trial began, was appalled at the outcome, not least because public hangings had been officially abolished and he had been vaunting the British role in ending the use of the heavy whip to flog taxes out of the rural population. The Dinshawai judgment attracted fierce criticism in Britain, being described by one MP in the House of Commons as an act 'of mere revenge ... unworthy of the traditions of the British Empire'.[134] According to Afaf Lutfi al-Sayyid-Marsot, whose uncle had served as defence counsel for the accused peasants, the 'Dinshawai incident' 'became a turning-point in Anglo-Egyptian relations'.[135] It became the prism through which many Egyptians came to view British rule, breaking their faith in it, just as the massacre at Amritsar would do in India thirteen years later.

XI

Nationalist resentment against colonial rule was often crystallised and exacerbated by particular events, which excited outrage and, whether rightly or wrongly, were perceived as symptoms of a deeper constitutional malaise. But the crystallised and heightened resentment drew its material from deeper intellectual and emotional streams. One of these was sometimes Western political philosophy. So, for example, the views of turn-of-the-twentieth-century, non-Islamic Egyptian nationalists owed a lot to Ernest Renan, Jean-Jacques Rousseau and Herbert Spencer.[136] And the Indian nationalist Jawaharlal Nehru was steeped, first in the British liberalism of J. S. Mill and William Gladstone, and then in the European socialism of Karl Marx, Bertrand Russell and V. I. Lenin.[137]

Another deeper current of nationalist sentiment was the idealism of the young and their impatience with the old. As the Baghdad-born historian Elie Kedourie once put it, 'These [national] movements are ostensibly directed against the foreigner, the outsider, but they are also the manifestation of a species of civil strife between the generations; nationalist movements are children's crusades; their very names are manifestoes against old age.'[138] For example, al-Sayyid-Marsot writes of the emergence in Egypt at the end of the nineteenth century of an educated younger generation, some of whom had imbibed Western principles of liberty while studying at university abroad, others of whom had learned them in secondary schools and from newspapers. The result was a 'group of disoriented youngsters [who] needed a *raison d'être*, and they found it in the nationalist movement'.[139] In particular, they found it in Mustafa Kamil's mystical patriotism, which 'stimulated nationalist feelings in the young. These were the Egyptians who were most influenced by Kamil, for his message was based on an emotional appeal that could not fail to strike the imagination of the young, whereas at times it roused the cynicism of the old.'[140]

The same youthful features characterised the revolutionary nationalists in Ireland before and after the First World War. 'Like revolutionary leaderships elsewhere,' observes Tom Garvin, 'the Sinn Féin elite . . . was young.'[141] In the Introduction to his book-length study of the 'revolutionary generation', Roy Foster writes that '[t]he Irish radicals . . . saw themselves, like their Russian contemporaries, as building and inhabiting a different world from that of their parents. The previous generation was often the perceived enemy every bit as much as the British government.'[142] Then follows the opening chapter, which bears the title 'Fathers and Children'. Peter Hart, in his study of the Irish Republican Army (I.R.A.) in County Cork, also devotes a chapter to the role of generational conflict ('Youth and Rebellion'), in which he wrote:

> I.R.A. members were highly conscious of their youth. Being part of 'the younger generation as they called themselves' was central to their sense of identity and with their youth came nobility and purity: 'all that was brave and virile, all that was chivalrous, unselfish and high-spirited in the best of the young manhood of the nation' . . . Nearly all [the ex-I.R.A. men Hart talked to] took pleasure in remembering the defiance of their fathers (and clerical and political father figures).[143]

The purist idealism of youth was one of the deeper propellants of nationalist opposition to colonial rule; so was the frustration of the ambitions of the educated: 'In Ireland, as elsewhere, discontented and energetic young men and women, whose education often left them facing limited opportunities with a sense of frustration, turned their attention to critically assessing the status quo.'[144] Elsewhere, frustration became mixed with racial indignation. By the second half of the nineteenth century Indians were playing a more considerable role in the judiciary than in the executive branch, and in 1877 restrictions on Indian judges and magistrates trying British subjects in the three presidency cities of Calcutta, Bombay and Madras were removed. Three years later, after the arrival of the liberal viceroy Lord Ripon, two educated Indians, Behari Lal Gupta and Romesh Chandra Dutt, lobbied for an end to the lingering discrimination that prevented Indians from trying Britons outside the three cities. The idea was taken up in 1883 by the legal adviser to the Viceroy's Council, Sir Courtenay Ilbert, who proposed it in his Criminal Procedures Amendment Bill. However, the reaction from the European community – especially the non-official professionals, entrepreneurs, railway employees and the notoriously racist tea and indigo planters – was so furious that the viceroy caved in. The watered-down version of the Ilbert Bill that was finally enacted in 1884, while maintaining the principle of Indian judges trying British subjects, largely negated it in practice by conceding to the accused the option of insisting on trial by jury, at least half of whose members would be British. The shocking sight of the government being forced to compromise its vaunted commitment to racial equality under the law was a major stimulant of Indian nationalist consciousness. In May 1883, the Lahore *Tribune* had declared that '[t]he Ilbert bill . . . has brought together the people of India of different races and creeds into one common bond of union . . . the growing feeling of national unity which otherwise would have taken us years to form, suddenly developed into strong sentiments'.[145] When the bill failed to achieve its original, egalitarian aim, those nationalist sentiments organised themselves into what became the Indian National Congress in 1885.[146]

The failure to integrate educated native elites into government – up until the very eve of independence – was perhaps the greatest cause of nationalist resentment against British rule.[147] In Egypt, '[t]he canker of dissatisfaction lay in the civil service', which was the only area of advancement open to the average educated Egyptian. However, as the number of Egyptians with university degrees increased, so did the number of imported British graduates. In 1905 only 28 per cent of higher government posts were occupied by Egyptians, 42 per cent being taken by the British, and 30 per cent by Armenians and Syrians.[148] Three decades later educated natives in West and East Africa experienced the same thing:

From the 1930s some ... Africans [who had been educated in US universities] returned home from the United States to seek entry into the colonial structure (their only employment option) only to discover that the British had no role for them under the indirect rule system which the African 'traditional' chiefs served well. Consequently they became antagonized by the racism that rejected them hence began to oppose British rule strongly [*sic*]. To some extent, it could be safely argued that it was mainly British rejection of the educated Africans which drove them into 'radical' nationalist camp [*sic*].[149]

By refusing American-educated graduates jobs in the civil service, the colonial governments created 'an aggrieved elite [which] turned to create a new journalism "which was racy, irreverent, often ungrammatical, but which would be read by the mass products of the mission schools who had no higher education"'.[150] Had the British been more accommodating, in the judgement of the Nigerian-born historian Apollos Okwuchi Nwauwa, 'it would have been difficult to say whether mass nationalisms of the late 1930s and 1940s would have erupted when they did'.[151]

XII

The presumptuousness of a revolutionary elite, rebel terrorism, brutal military overreaction, wartime pressures, the arrogance of foreigners, the miscarriage of injustice, Western political principles, youthful idealism, the contempt of the young for the old, frustrated ambition, racial inequality and the exclusion of Western-educated natives from careers in government: these were the various sparks that kindled the flames of nationalist opposition to colonial rule. And there were others, which we met earlier in this book, such as the disruption of traditional ways and challenges to established religion. But perhaps the most incendiary was the sense of humiliation. Augustine Birrell, who as chief secretary for Ireland from 1907 to 1916 prepared the ground for self-government with a series of vital reforms, perceived at the heart of England's troubled relationship with Ireland wounded Irish self-respect. In 1890 he wrote:

Let an Englishman . . . sincerely ask himself what it is that makes him take pride in his nationality . . . He will find that it is the sense of self-esteem generated by knowing the figure which his nation makes in history; by considering the achievements of his nation in war, government, arts, literature, or industry . . . This is admirable, but not . . . exhaustive. The love of country is something a little more than mere *amour propre*. You may love your mother, and wish to make a home for her, even though she never dwelt in king's palaces, and is clad in rags. The children of misery and misfortune are not all illegitimate. Sometimes you may discern amongst them high hope and pious endeavour . . . 'The luxury of self-respect'. It is a wise phrase. To make Ireland and Irishmen self-respectful is the task of statesmen.[152]

As with Irishmen, so with Indians. Writing in 1926, Nirad Chaudhuri commented, 'There is one source from which bitterness against Europe is being replenished constantly. It is wounded national and personal self-respect.'[153] So, too, with Egyptians. It is not difficult to appreciate how it must have felt for the sixty-year-old prime minister, Nubar Pasha, who prided himself on his financial acumen, to suffer fiscal mentorship from a twenty-eight-year-old British financial adviser in the mid-1880s. Nor is it difficult to understand why '[t]he [Egyptian] Governor of a province, the *mudir*, who was often twice the [British] Inspector's age, resented any suggestions coming from a foreigner who barely spoke his language, and who could scarcely have mastered fallah folkways and mores (even had he been so inclined) during his brief period of training'.[154] As with Egyptians in particular, so with Africans in general. Margery Perham wrote with deep sympathy about the 'shattering experience' of shame and wounded pride often suffered by Africans who came to study in Britain and then returned home:

The student would return to Africa. What might he meet there? The fact of the subjection of his people to a few white officials, which he would now see with quite new eyes. He would also have the shock of seeing, again, with new eyes, the poverty and, by Western standards, the ignorance, of his own people. Yet, had he not proved by his own academic achievement the intellectual equality of his race? A further blow might befall him, either the refusal of the good official post he felt he had so strenuously earned, or appointment to a white man's post with inferior pay and conditions. The discrimination, especially in the early days, might have had some reasons behind it. But perhaps no single grievance has been so effective in deepening the already deep enough bitterness of the new intelligentsia. They might find escape from their almost intolerable anger or sorrow by projecting not a part, but perhaps the whole, blame for their problems upon the white man, and especially, of course, upon the ruling power.[155]

Equal in insight, though surpassing in eloquence, was the remark made by Faisal (before he became king of Iraq) to T. E. Lawrence ('of Arabia') sometime during the Arab Revolt in 1916–17: 'And though I know the British do not want it [the Hijaz], yet what can I say, when they took the Sudan, also not wanting it. They hunger for desolate lands, to build them up . . . [F]orced good . . . will make a people cry with pain. Does the ore admire the flame which transformsit? . . . Our race will have a cripple's temper till it has found its feet.'[156] Yet Faisal was an unusually wise man. Not only did he have the courageous honesty to confess the sense of shame that dependence can provoke, he also had the courageous humility to recognise the fact of being a temporary cripple in real need of support. So when in 1922 Churchill threatened to remove the British crutches that upheld his rule in Iraq, Faisal was mature enough to plead with him not to.[157] His was a patient nationalism.

XIII

To describe British colonial government as simply or generally oppressive and exploitative, as is commonly done, may satisfy certain ideological prejudices but it obscures the complicated historical truth. Colonial rule would not have been possible at all without the widespread acquiescence, participation and cooperation of native peoples. The motives for native cooperation were various, and while the temper of it ranged from reluctant to eager according to circumstances, it was not always or usually rendered under duress or illusion.

Indeed, it was often elicited by the liberating attractions of security, the rule of law and the honesty of officials.

The radical dependence of the colonial government on native support was bound to make it sensitive to popular views and needs, notwithstanding the absence or paucity of democratic elections. Besides, both in India and in Africa, colonial officials typically understood that their duty involved defending and promoting the interests of the rural poor. Notwithstanding this, government policy and its execution were sometimes inadequate to the task of relieving severe and widespread distress. The reasons for this were several, but racist malevolence or negligence were not generally among them, and so the failures, however disastrous, did not amount to anything approaching the Nazi Holocaust.

Within the limits of their resources, colonial governments provided something of a controlled environment for modernising economic, social and political change, which was bound to come anyway and would otherwise have been anarchical and even more disruptive and violent. Acutely aware both of their limited power to control and of the threat to public order posed by popular outrage or distress, the governments often sought to work with the grain of traditional native societies, moderating the pace of change. On the one hand, this pleased cultural conservatives, who were hostile to Western interference. On the other hand, it frustrated cultural modernisers, usually natives who had received a Western education.

It was because of their sympathy for conservative, rural people that British colonial officials tended to be suspicious of their educated, urban cousins. Insofar as that suspicion fed their refusal to admit educated native people into the higher echelons of government, it was fateful. Colonial rejection inspired nationalist consciousness, which, set ablaze by the happenstance of the deployment of disproportionate military force or an act of egregious injustice or a disastrous failure of famine relief, hardened into implacable anti-colonialist resentment. Then, as Margery Perham observed of post-1945 Africans, once they 'had been fully stirred in racial self-consciousness and political awareness, prematurely though this may be in their own interests, there was little more that foreign rulers could do for them . . . With her standards of efficiency and her sense of obligation to minority groups British governments wanted to see the transfer of power carried out by gradual and orderly stages . . . It was the African leaders who . . . forced the pace.'[158] Perham makes it clear that she considered that pace, however irresistible, to be tragically excessive and thought that Africans needed more time to prepare for self-government.[159]

Was she being patronising? The year before Perham published her view in *The Colonial Reckoning* (1961), the Montenegro-born political philosopher John Plamenatz had observed that the claim that colonised Asians and Africans 'are not yet fit for democracy and freedom because they have not learnt to work the institutions which make them possible . . . is often bitterly resented. Yet it may be well founded.'[160] It is clear, implicitly, that the widespread education he thought necessary to make democratic institutions work was not merely procedural but moral, concerning habits of behaviour: 'Freedom is difficult to establish, and is not to be had for the asking. It depends on institutions and habits that do not emerge of themselves as soon as a colony gets independence . . . a subject people . . . may fail to get freedom for getting independence too soon.'[161] Such habits include 'standards of decent behaviour in the making, resisting, and compromising of claims', which are enabled by the virtue of 'moderation'.[162] 'The essence of democracy,' he wrote, 'is competition for power and influence by persons and groups who respect each other's equal right to compete. This respect is not easily learnt.'[163]

If it was true in 1960 that Asian and African peoples had yet to acquire the virtues that make democratic politics work, it is equally true in 2022 that, thanks to illiberal 'cancel culture', British and other Western peoples stand in danger of losing them. Cultural advantage, however hard won, can always be lost again, since what has been learned can always be forgotten. Progress can roll backwards.

8

Justified Force and 'Pervasive Violence'

I

So far, we have assessed the following accusations levelled against 'the colonial project' in terms of the history of the British Empire: that it was motivated predominantly by greed and the sheer lust to dominate; that it was equivalent to slavery; that it was essentially racist; that it was based on the theft of land; that it was guilty of genocide; that it was fundamentally about economic exploitation; and that colonial government served British rather than native interests and, being undemocratic, was illegitimate. Now in this final chapter, we consider the charge that the empire was pervasively violent, and that its violence was essentially racist and terroristic.[1]

II

All states use physical force, sometimes to lethal effect. The reasons for this are basic and threefold: the primary duty of a state is to suppress disorder within society and to fend off threats from without; a secondary duty may be to defend foreign innocents from unjust aggression; and sometimes neither of these duties can be discharged without forcing those causing internal disorder, posing external threats or perpetrating injustice upon foreigners to desist, perhaps by killing them. Strong states operating in an international order governed by international law, which is backed by more or less effective international institutions, have less need to use force than weak states operating in an unpredictable, anarchical international environment. Compared to their twenty-first-century counterparts, Western states in the eighteenth, nineteenth and early twentieth centuries were weak, able to call upon fewer resources of intelligence, money and manpower, and, therefore, commanding less control. Force that would be unnecessary for a strong state to deploy, since it has a firmer grasp of the scale of the threat and is more confident of being able to meet it, could be necessary for a weak state, which, unable to see the threat clearly and less confident of its ability to fend it off, cannot afford to be conservative in its initial reaction. As we have seen, British colonial states were often weak.

The use of lethal force by a state is a costly and hazardous thing. It is financially expensive, consumes lives and causes grief, and can therefore provoke political unrest among the state's own people. It also breeds bitter resentment among the enemy's people that endures for generations, and, once begun, is often difficult to stop, with consequences unforeseeable. Famously, wars do *not* end by Christmas. Further, in societies that have learned to value the lives of human individuals highly, killing is a morally dangerous thing to do and should not be done unless really necessary. For those reasons, societies develop ethics of lethal force to restrain and govern its use.

In the West the dominant ethic has been the tradition of 'just war' reasoning, which developed in Christian Europe up until the early seventeenth century and has enjoyed a revival since the Vietnam War in the 1960s and especially since the wars of humanitarian intervention in the 1990s. This ethic has developed criteria for determining the justice of going to war and the justice of waging it. In order to justify a decision to go to war, there should be 'just cause', that is, an injustice to rectify. Next, war must be a 'proportionate' response, that is, the injustice needs to be sufficiently grave to warrant war's costs and risks and to make war a fitting means to stop it. Further, the state must have a 'right intention' in going to war, that is, it must genuinely aim to rectify the injustice rather than use it as a pretext for doing something quite different, such as plundering resources; and it must be ready to replace the status quo with something better. Finally, going to war must be a 'last resort', all other peaceful options having been exhausted.

As for the morally justified waging of war, there are two conditions: the lethal means must be 'discriminate', distinguishing between combatants and innocents (literally, the 'non-harming'), and not intentionally targeting the latter; and they must be 'proportionate', fit to achieve the military objective and no more than necessary to do so.[2] These last two criteria rule out terroristic violence, which deliberately attacks those known to be innocent with unrestrained violence, in order to terrify a population into submission.

This 'just war' ethic is the one to which I subscribe, and I shall use its criteria in assessing Britain's colonial wars and counter-insurgency operations. While the ethic's classical sources were not widely known in Britain during the colonial period, British statesmen and military officers often showed themselves aware of the principles of just cause, last resort, discrimination and proportionality.

The British Empire was frequently violent, but, as John Darwin has observed, that is hardly remarkable: 'Plainly, [the empire's] authority depended ultimately (and sometimes immediately) upon the use of violence. But then so has that of almost every state in history, precolonial, colonial and postcolonial (and things are not getting any better). To say that violence played a central part in Britain's imperial history is not to add much to the sum of knowledge.'[3] Still, there are a number of occasions when British imperial violence is widely believed to have been grossly immoral, and there are some who argue that *immoral* violence – racist and terroristic – lay at the empire's heart. In this chapter I have chosen to focus on six instances of imperial belligerency that have become infamous: the First Opium War of 1839–42, which Chinese nationalists accuse of inaugurating China's 'century of humiliation'; the vindictive repression of the Indian Mutiny of 1857; the disproportionate massacre in Amritsar in the Punjab of 1919, which some consider to be symptomatic of the 'racialised violence' essential to the Raj; the military takeover of Benin City in West Africa in 1897 and its appropriation of the famous 'Benin Bronzes', which is commonly held up as an icon of imperial rapacity; the Second Anglo-Boer War in South Africa of 1899–1902, allegedly fought for gold and sheer imperial supremacy by means that included the 'holocaust' of 'concentration camps'; and the counter-insurgency against the Mau Mau rebellion in Kenya in East Africa in the 1950s, damned by some as Britain's 'dirty war', involving an equivalent of the Soviet Union's 'gulag'.[4]

III

Among the most infamous chapters in the Chinese Communist Party's nationalist narrative of 'the century of humiliation' is the so-called First Opium War of 1839–42. Britain's interest in China lay primarily in trade and only in such territory as facilitated it. In the late eighteenth century, the East India Company had discovered that one of the few commodities for which it could find a Chinese market was opium. Long established in the culture of the Chinese elite, the social diffusion of the recreational use of opium had created strong demand.[5] At the same time, however, fearing the growth of drug addiction and its deleterious social effects, the authorities of the Qing Empire had outlawed its sale. The discovery in 1832 that Chinese imperial troops engaged in suppressing the revolt of the Yao had been incapacitated by opium can only have stiffened their resolve.[6]

Nevertheless, the official ban created commercial opportunity, and a lucrative black market was created when the EIC imported opium to its warehouses ('factories') in Canton and sold it to Chinese smugglers, who then bribed corrupt officials. In 1839 the Chinese authorities blockaded the British in Canton, forcing the chief superintendent to surrender the stocks of warehoused opium, which were then destroyed. Later that year the government in London decided to respond by deploying military force primarily 'to secure redress for insult'[7] – which, given what we learned in the previous chapter about the political potency of national self-esteem, should not surprise us.[8] From June 1840 the Royal Navy proceeded to inflict a series of defeats on Chinese forces, which led to the signing of the Treaty of Nanking in 1842. This extracted reparations for the merchants' loss of property, ceded the island of Hong Kong to Britain in perpetuity and opened five ports along the Chinese coast – including Shanghai and Canton – to British trade and residence.

It is true that the conflict was inflamed by what the British perceived as the humiliating, racist contempt of Chinese officials, who regarded them as 'barbarians' and refused direct contact with them.[9] It may be true that addiction to opium was not nearly the epidemical threat to physical and social health that the imperial authorities took it for, and that '[s]moking was a complex social ritual with inbuilt restraints on the amount of opium which could be consumed: it had no serious consequences for the health or life expectancy of the vast majority of consumers'.[10] And it may also be true that the Qing imperial policy of outlawing drug use was counterproductive, merely diverting demand and supply into a black market – then, as now.

Notwithstanding all these qualifications, however, it remains true that the Chinese imperial authorities had the right to ban the sale of opium within their borders and to demand that foreign merchants on its own soil stop supplying smugglers. However much they felt that their dignity had been insulted by the Chinese blockade of their merchants and detention of their officials, the British should not have dispatched the gunboats in 1840. *The Times* and a young William Gladstone were both thinking along the right lines when the former opposed the naval expedition as an 'engine of evil'[11] and the latter declared in the House of Commons that '[a] war more unjust in its origins, a war more calculated in its progress to cover this country with permanent disgrace, I do not know and have not read of'.[12] The mere slighting of honour is no just cause for war.

That said, when compared to the evils culpably inflicted on China within living memory by Chairman Mao in his Great Leap Forward of 1958–62 with its consequent deaths of more than 45 million, according to one authoritative estimate, and the Cultural Revolution of 1966–76 with its consequent deaths of at least 400,000 and perhaps 3 million, those inflicted by the British one hundred and eighty years ago fade into insignificance.[13]

IV

On 10 May 1857 the East India Company's sepoys in Meerut mutinied, killing British officers who resisted them, together with some women and children and Indians who came to their aid. What began as a mutiny then expanded into a rebellion that took hold of large areas of the North-West Provinces and Oudh. Thus, erupted the Indian Mutiny.[14]

The original cause lay in a set of professional grievances on the part of mercenary soldiers. These included a general deterioration in the terms and conditions of service; the threat posed to the social and religious status of Rajputs, Brahmins and well-born Muslims by the admission of Gurkhas and Sikhs into the army; religious objections from high-caste Hindus to the modernising withdrawal of their privileged exemption from overseas service; racial irritation at the indignity of the most senior Indian officers being subordinate to a junior – and sometimes arrogant – British officer; and professional frustration at the consequent ceiling over promotion.[15] In addition, the relationship between British officers and Indian troops had become more distant. This was partly because of the influence of evangelical morality, which frowned upon the taking of Indian mistresses, but also because of the alienating effect of an increase in British numbers – an unhappy consequence we have encountered before.[16] According to Sir Charles Napier, the root of the problem was that officers were 'now more numerous than formerly, and associate apart. All old officers of name in the Company's service . . . have complained that the younger race of Europeans keep aloof from Native officers.'[17]

Once the mutiny spread, it grew into a more general rebellion by becoming a focus for wider grievances. Among these were the insecurity of dynastic princes in general created by the 'doctrine of lapse' since the late 1840s, whereby the company would annex the territory of any Hindu ruler who died without a natural heir; the particular annexation of Oudh in 1856, which by severely reducing the royal household and army caused sudden and massive unemployment; and fears of the imposition of Christianity.[18] Then there was the 'racial arrogance [that] had been on the increase in India for at least a decade before the Mutiny, its spread being reflected in the everyday use of the word "n---er" for Indian, a term which, during the Mutiny, regularly appeared in print'.[19]

Although the Indian Mutiny did spread and expand, it never became universal. As colonial rebellions often did, it divided the natives and was as much a civil war as a war against the British. The rebels drew their support more from rural peasants, landowners and warlords than from urban clerks, teachers, traders, bankers and intellectuals, many of whom 'had embraced English education and the cosmopolitanism of the Company town and rejected the tropes of the old regime that found a brief revival during the rebellion'.[20] Supporters of the rebellion were mainly Hindus, sometimes Muslims; Sikhs and Pathans generally remained loyal to the company. Indeed, during the campaign to relieve Lucknow, Sikh troops enjoyed 'a warm and intimate camaraderie with Scottish Highland troops . . . whose echoes may be heard today as Indian and Pakistani regiments parade with bagpipes playing'.[21]

While the rebellion was ascendant, the British suffered two notorious, indiscriminate massacres. The first took place on 27 June, when approximately 450 British men, women and children, who had been promised safe passage out of besieged Cawnpore, were attacked as they tried to board boats. To what extent the attack was planned remains unclear, but more than half of the refugees were killed – shot, hacked or drowned. Nevertheless, about two hundred women and children survived and were imprisoned in a building called the Bibighar. On 15 July, when news reached the rebels that a British relief column was about to arrive, those prisoners who had not already died were cut to pieces and, whether dead or dying, thrown into a well.[22]

The British recovered from the initial shock, regained their footing and went on the offensive, capturing Delhi at the end of September 1857, followed by Lucknow and Jhansi in March, and Gwalior in June 1858. Their mood was often ferocious. Nothing loosens moral constraints on soldiers' violence than the enemy's atrocities, and the dreadful sight of the results of the massacres at Cawnpore – especially the murder of women and children – incited instincts of revenge.[23] When the relief column first arrived, its commander, Sir Henry Havelock, restrained his troops from wanton retaliation with a 'firm hand',[24] issuing an order to them that read, 'A Provost-Marshal has been appointed, with special instructions to hang up, *in their uniform*, all British soldiers that plunder. This shall not be an idle threat. Commanding officers have received the most distinct warnings on the subject.'[25] However, after Havelock had departed for Lucknow, Brigadier-General James Neill let loose the dogs of vengeance. Some captured rebels were forced to lick the blood from the stained floors of the Bibighar, and Muslims were sewn into pig-skins, before being hanged. Sepoys convicted by drumhead courts-martial were tied to the mouths of cannon and blown to pieces. Whole communities suffered merciless, indiscriminate reprisals, with villages being burned to the ground.[26] Much of the British and Anglo-Indian press clamoured for revenge.

Indian nationalist critics, and anti-colonialists following them, often claim that this unrestrained, vindictive violence opened a window onto the heart of the Raj. Rudrangshu Mukherjee, for example, has written that '[v]iolence . . . was an *essential* component of the British presence in India', that 'Imperial rule in India could *only* perpetuate itself by a deployment of terror' and that excessive violence was 'a product of . . . the *nature* of British rule'. As supporting evidence, he cites 'brutal floggings' and 'recalcitrant elements being blown from cannons'.[27] However, against this view stand, first, two general points: that the threat of violence and its use are essential components of any state, and that the deterrence of others through fear is a standard rationale for punishment. Then, more particularly, whatever one thinks of 'blowing from a gun' as a method of execution, it was not indiscriminate, insofar as the victim had been judged guilty of some crime. Further still, Barbara English has observed that 'flogging of Indian soldiers in the Bengal army had ceased by the 1850s, while it was retained for British soldiers until 1881' and that 'being blown apart by cannon was not a method of execution invented by the British, but was used by Indian powers such as the Marathas, and possibly the Moghuls; it was practiced by the rebel forces on fellow Indians within Cawnpore'.[28]

Moreover, the full story of the British response to the vindictive violence meted out in the course of the mutiny's suppression makes it clear that the heart of the Raj actually repudiated it. In his three-volume *History of the Sepoy War in India*, Sir John William Kaye wrote:

> An Englishman is almost suffocated by indignation when he reads that Mrs Chambers or Miss Jennings was hacked to death by a dusky ruffian. But in Native histories or, history being wanting, in Native legends or traditions, it may be recorded against our people, that mothers and wives and children ... fell miserable victims to the first swoop of English vengeance; and these stories may have as deep a pathos as any that rends our own hearts.[29]

Kaye dedicated his work to Lord Canning, who was governor-general of India during the mutiny. This was fitting, since Canning would certainly have endorsed Kaye's judgement. Just as the British were beginning to regain control, he issued what became known as the 'Clemency Resolution' of 31 July 1857. In this he urged the discrimination of sepoys belonging to regiments that had mutinied and committed bloodshed from those apprehended unarmed and whose regiments were innocent of atrocities; that deserters or mutineers in these last categories be tried by formal military tribunals; and that provision be made for those who could prove they were not present when a particular murder or outrage took place.[30] In December he told Lord Granville, 'As long as I have breath in my body, I will pursue no other policy than that which I have been following – not only for the reason of expediency ... but because it is just. I will not govern in anger.' In this, Canning had the full support of his monarch, Queen Victoria, who had written to him the previous month:

> Lord Canning will easily believe how entirely the Queen shared *his* feelings of sorrow and indignation at the unchristian spirit shown ... by the public towards Indians and towards Sepoys *without discrimination*. It is however not likely to last and comes from the *horror produced* by the *unspeakable* atrocities perpetrated against the innocent women and children which really makes one's blood run cold. For the perpetrators of these awful horrors *no* punishment can be severe enough, and, sad as it is, stern justice must be dealt out to all the guilty

men. But to the native at large, to the peaceable inhabitants, to the many kind and friendly ones who have assisted us, sheltered the fugitives and been faithful and true – these should be shown the greatest kindness. They should know there is no hatred of brown skin.[31]

Notwithstanding the vindictive clamour of the press, the gross violence meted out by some Britons in India in 1857–8 provoked a lot of self-criticism at home: 'the Mutiny called forth from writers of the day a voluminous discourse of dissent that often evoked . . . what can only be called a profound anguish of conscience and a profound disaffection from the war and from its sustaining ideology'.[32] This soul-searching led to major changes in government policy. On 1 November 1858 in Allahabad, Canning published Queen Victoria's Proclamation to the Princes, Chiefs and People of India. Following the India Act (1858), this announced that henceforth India would be governed not by the East India Company, but by the Crown through a secretary of state. In addition, it directly addressed some of the main grievances that had enabled the mutiny to spread:

> We desire no extension of Our present territorial Possessions; and . . . We shall sanction no encroachment on those of others . . .
>
> Firmly relying Ourselves on the truth of Christianity . . . We disclaim alike the Right and the Desire to impose Our Convictions on any of Our subjects. We declare it to be our Royal Will and Pleasure that none be in any wise favored, none molested or disquieted by reason of their Religious Faith or Observances; but that all shall alike enjoy the equal and impartial protection of the Law: . . .
>
> And it is Our further Will that, so far as may be, Our subjects, of whatever Race or Creed, may be freely and impartially admitted to Offices in Our Service, the Duties of which they may be qualified, by their education, ability, and integrity, duly to discharge.[33]

The very heart of the Raj had disowned the unrestrained violence of the counter-insurgency and sought to address what had caused the insurgency in the first place. Terrorism was not integral to the nature of British rule.

V

At about 5 p.m. on the afternoon of Sunday, 13 April 1919, General Reginald Dyer marched fifty Gurkha and Indian (Baluch and Pathan) soldiers armed with rifles, and forty Gurkhas armed only with their trademark *khukuris* or knives, into a walled park called the Jallianwala Bagh in the city of Amritsar in the Punjab. There he found a large crowd of civilians – in fact, although he could not have known it, they were mostly unarmed and numbered about 25,000 – and, without warning, ordered his troops to open fire on them. The shooting continued for between six and fifteen minutes, after which, without tending to the wounded, Dyer withdrew his men. They had used about a third of their ammunition and left behind them at least 379 dead and approximately 1,200 wounded.[34]

The political context of the 'Amritsar Massacre' was this. The British government was publicly committed to preparing India for self-government along the same lines as Canada, South Africa, Australia and New Zealand. As noted in the previous chapter, in August 1917 the secretary of state for India, Edwin Montagu, had announced to the House of Commons that government policy would be that of 'the increasing association of Indians in every branch of the administration and the gradual development of self-governing institutions, with a view to the progressive realisation of responsible government in India as an integral part of the British Empire'.[35] This general intention found specific expression in the reforms proposed in the Montagu-Chelmsford Report in 1918, which would inform the Government of India Act in December 1919.

However, Lord Curzon's decision to partition Bengal in 1904 had been deeply resented by Bengali Hindus and had spawned terrorist activity during the First World War, which continued after its end.[36] In response to this, the government of India passed the Anarchical and Revolutionary Crimes (or 'Rowlatt') Act on 18 March 1919. This prolonged for three years the powers that had been granted under the 1915 Defence of India Act: to detain political suspects without charge or trial for up to a year, renewable; and to try charges of sedition in private with three judges rather than a jury.[37] Indian opinion was outraged (if not always well informed) and Gandhi was stirred into launching his campaign of mass *satyagraha* ('soul force'), despite warnings by leaders of the Indian National Congress that his incitement of the masses would issue in violence.[38]

Congress was right. Whether incited by the Rowlatt Act, wartime price rises or the influenza epidemic of 1918–19 that overwhelmed the medical system and killed 12–17 million people, violence erupted in Delhi on 30 March 1919.[39] The police, subjected to a barrage of stones and brickbats by a large mob, fired a warning volley over their heads. When this had no effect, they proceeded to shoot eight rioters dead and wound two.[40] The arrest of Gandhi on 9 April was followed by further violence in Ahmedabad in Gujarat on 10 and 12 April. Confronted by rioters armed with *lathis* (sticks bound by iron rings), sticks, bill-hooks, swords and kerosene oil, the police gave notice twice to disperse, but in vain. They then fired one volley of buckshot, again in vain, followed by a further volley of ball ammunition, which finally made the crowd fall back. The claustrophobic, narrow streets meant that the police were too close to rioters to use less violent means of dispersal.[41]

In Amritsar itself, on 10 April, a huge crowd of fifty thousand people streamed out of the city towards the military district where the British lived. The troops panicked and opened fire, killing several rioters. The mob then beat a British railwayman and the garrison electrician to death, doused three British bank managers with kerosene and set them alight, and beat and left for dead Miss Marcella Sherwood, superintendent of the Mission Day School for Girls.[42] On 11 April the district magistrate issued a proclamation banning all public gatherings and warning that troops had orders 'to use all force necessary' and that 'All gatherings will be fired upon.' Nonetheless, Hans Raj, the twenty-three-year-old joint-secretary of the Satyagraha Sabha ('Non-violent Resistance Association'), who had been present when the mob attacked the National Bank, planned a public assembly for 13 April, to debate resolutions including: 'This grand meeting of the inhabitants of Amritsar looks with extreme indignation and disapproval on all those revolutionary actions which are the inevitable result of the inappropriate and inequitable attitude on the part of the

Government, and entertains apprehension that this despotic conduct of the Government might prove deleterious to the British Government.'[43]

On the morning of 13 April General Dyer paraded around Amritsar to issue a proclamation at nineteen key locations. Part of it read: 'No procession of any kind is permitted to parade in the streets in the city or any part of the city or outside it at any time. Any such processions or any gathering of four men will be looked upon and treated as an unlawful assembly and dispersed by force of arms, if necessary.' The proclamation itself was in English and Urdu, but was explained in Punjabi and Hindustani. Printed copies of the Urdu text were distributed. Nigel Collett comments that 'there is no doubt that the news spread by word of mouth throughout city'.[44] When Obadullah, the sub-inspector of police, overheard talk of holding a meeting in the Jallianwala Bagh anyway, he warned that 'they would be fired on'. But the response was defiant: 'let us be fired on'.[45] Shortly after these public proclamations, young boys were observed beating tin cans and advertising the unauthorised assembly in the Jallianwala Bagh at 4 p.m.[46]

So when Dyer brought his troops into the walled park that afternoon, he knew that he faced direct defiance of martial law and he feared that he faced full-scale insurrection. He saw his task, therefore, not merely as that of dispersing an unlawful assembly, but of meting out exemplary punishment in order to nip in the bud a reprise of 1857. Operating in aid of the police to suppress sectarian violence in Belfast in 1886, Dyer had seen the chaos that threatened when the authority of civil government dissipated; and, two years later, he had served in Burma with General Sir Frederick Roberts, whose instructions to commanding officers read: 'Resistance overcome without inflicting punishment on the enemy only emboldens him to repeat the game, and thus, by protracting operations, costs more lives than a severe lesson promptly administered.'[47] When later accused of trying to 'strike terror' in Amritsar, Dyer responded, 'Call it what you like. I was going to punish them . . . I wanted to reduce their *moral*, the *moral* [sic] of the rebels', thereby preventing 'more bloodshed, more looting, more lives lost'.[48] That is one reason why he kept on firing after his initial fear of being overwhelmed had subsided. Another reason was that the crowd was not clearly dispersing, because the exits from the park were so few and constricted – something that Dyer also did not know.[49] Six days after the shooting in the Jallianwala Bagh, on 19 April, Dyer issued his 'crawling order', which required that anyone wishing to proceed along the street in which Ms Sherwood had been assaulted, between the hours of 6 a.m. and 8 p.m., should crawl its 150-yard length.

When news of what had happened in Amritsar spread, the British reaction was mixed. On the one hand, the British press in India and Britain tended to support Dyer as having averted a second Indian Mutiny.[50] In September the Imperial Legislative Council passed an Indemnity Bill, preventing any future court case, civil or criminal, against anyone who had acted to restore order.[51] And on 19 July 1920 the House of Lords passed a motion backing Dyer by 129 votes to 86.

On the other hand, as soon as the viceroy, Lord Chelmsford, heard of Dyer's 'crawling order', he ordered it to be cancelled. On the back of the report of the Disorders Inquiry ('Hunter') Committee in March 1920, the government of India rejected Dyer's claim that he had been faced with an insurrection and severely censured him for not promulgating the prohibition of assemblies more widely, not issuing a warning before opening fire and not ceasing fire when the crowd had begun to disperse. It rejected Dyer's justification of prolonged firing as intending to intimidate law-breakers, because it 'greatly exceeded the necessity of the occasion', and concluded: 'We can arrive at no conclusion other than at Jallianwala Bagh General Dyer acted beyond the necessity of the case, beyond what any reasonable man could have thought to be necessary, and that he did not act with as much humanity as the case permitted.'[52] Addressing the House of Commons on 8 July 1920, the secretary of state for India lamented Dyer's conduct in the Jallianwala Bagh as 'indulging in frightfulness' and his 'crawling order' as 'enforcing racial humiliation'.[53] In the same debate, Winston Churchill, then secretary of state for war, said that a commander had to 'confine himself to a limited and definite objective, that is to say to preventing a crowd doing something they ought not to do', whereas Dyer had laid himself open to the charge of 'frightfulness', by which he meant 'the inflicting of great slaughter or massacre upon a particular crowd of people, with the intention of terrorizing not merely the rest of the crowd, but the whole district or country . . . We have to make it absolutely clear, some way or other, that this is not the British way of doing business.'[54] The commander-in-chief then summarily deprived Dyer of his command and informed him that he would be offered no further employment. In response, Dyer formally resigned. Compensation payments were made to the families of those killed. In April 1921, when the Duke of Connaught opened the new legislative assembly that the Montagu-Chelmsford reforms had instituted, he expressed 'deep regret' at 'these improper actions' at Amritsar and promised India that 'any repetition would be forever impossible'. And in the same month, the new viceroy, Lord Reading, made Amritsar and the Jallianwala Bagh his first visit after arriving in post, and ordered an increase in compensation to its victims.[55]

With the exception of Muslim landlords, the Hindu business elite and the Sikhs, who made Dyer an honorary member in Amritsar's Golden Temple, the Indian reaction was overwhelmingly condemnatory.[56] Moreover, it marked a radicalisation of nationalist temper and aspiration. The Indian press saw Amritsar – not least the 'crawling order' – as a manifestation of the true, racist nature of British rule.[57] By January 1920 Gandhi had abandoned his belief in dominion-style self-government for India within the empire: 'I can no longer retain affection,' he declared, 'for a Government so evilly manned as it is now-a-days.'[58] In March 1920 the three Indian lawyers on the Hunter Committee issued a minority report that compared Dyer's action to the 'Prussianism' that the British had just finished fighting in Belgium and Flanders.[59] And after observing the parliamentary debates in London in July 1920, Rabindranath Tagore concluded:

> The result of the debates in both Houses of Parliament makes painfully evident the attitude of mind of the ruling classes of this country towards India . . . The unashamed condonation of brutality expressed in their speeches and echoed in their newspapers is ugly in its frightfulness. The feeling of humiliation about our position under Anglo-Indian domination had been growing stronger every day for the last fifty years or more; but the one consolation we had was our faith in the love and justice of the English people, whose soul had not been poisoned by

that fatal dose of power which could only be available in a Dependency where the manhood of the entire population had been crushed down into helplessness. Yet the poison has gone further than we expected, and it has attacked the vital organs of the British nation.

However, were Indian nationalists then – and anti-colonialist historians now – really correct to read General Dyer's excessive violence as a revelation of the toxic essence of the British Empire in India?[60] In particular, was it a symptom of 'pervasive' and 'racialised' colonial violence?[61] After all, the British government, the government of India and the commander-in-chief in India were all unanimous in repudiating Dyer's actions. What is more, the principle of using the minimal necessary force had long been impressed on British army officers. One of Dyer's peers at Staff College in Camberley in 1896–7 recalled that the students had all received instruction in military law, which required that 'no more force must be used than is absolutely necessary: thus in the case of a riot, if called on to fire by a magistrate, first only a single round should be fired; if this has no effect, five rounds might be fired; and so on'.[62] On this point, the law did not distinguish between unlawful assembly, riot and insurrection.[63] As we have seen, troops faced with large, violent mobs in Delhi and Ahmedabad earlier in April 1919 had responded in a carefully calibrated, proportionate fashion. And after April 1919 they would adopt even greater caution, thereby perhaps contributing, tragically, to the failure to stop the murderous sectarian slaughter that occurred during Partition in 1947.[64]

Further, whatever Dyer's motives, racial contempt or hatred does not seem to have been among them. His biographer, Nigel Collett, has observed that his 'tendency to co-opt young men ran across racial boundaries. Idu, the aristocratic Reki . . . stayed with Dyer till the end'; that he resigned from the Jullundur Club in 1919 in support of the admission of Indian officer members; that when making his final departure from the garrison at Jullundur for the railway station, the Dyers 'found their path lit up by flares under which stood sepoys of all the Indian regiments in the station standing at the salute. In the station forecourt was a large guard of honour of all the garrison's NCOs who had gathered without order. The station was thronged.

"Large numbers of officers, British and Indian . . . were at the station to see them off."' In sum, Dyer

> related to his Indian soldiers in a way that few of his contemporaries could emulate. That, as well as the undeniable fact that he was a brave man, was why they liked and even venerated him . . . He felt truly Indian, and loved both the country and its natives, though the latter only so far as they were loyal subordinates . . . He had no racial prejudice, rather the reverse, and does genuinely seem to have preferred the company of inferiors in rank of any race.[65]

Finally, General Dyer's excessive use of force was not something peculiarly colonial. In June 1984, when the post-colonial government of India launched Operation Blue Star to suppress Sikh nationalist unrest in the Punjab, culminating in the storming of the Golden Temple in Amritsar, it deployed more than just a few dozen riflemen; it wheeled artillery and tanks into a congested urban area. The consequence was an official tally of 83 military, and 493 Sikh militant and civilian, fatalities, but at least one witness, a serving soldier, claimed 1,500 deaths and other reports raise the number even higher to 3,000 and beyond.[66] After Amritsar was taken, the Punjab was subjected to the 'President's Rule', which permitted police to detain suspects without trial for up to two years. It was also alleged that students and staff at Punjabi University, Patiala, were ordered to get on their knees and crawl before Indian soldiers.[67]

VI

Twenty-two years before the massacre at Amritsar, in February 1897, a British naval expedition had launched an attack on Benin City, the capital of the Edo (or Beni) people in West Africa. Commanded by Rear Admiral Harry Rawson, the British forces amounted to 1,200 marines, sailors and Niger Coast Protectorate (NCP) troops, most of the latter being Africans of the Hausa people. These were supported by about 2,000 Itsekiri carriers. In the course of the operation eight troops were killed and fifty wounded in action, with a further five dying of disease. Perhaps up to two hundred carriers became casualties, whether from the fighting or from smallpox. On the other side, the Edo probably suffered several hundred killed, with many more wounded.[68] The result was that the British prevailed, most of the city was burned to the ground and at least two thousand major *objets d'art* were taken away as spoils of war, among them the famous 'Benin Bronzes', plaques depicting the history of the Royal Court of Benin and cast from brass 'manillas' acquired through trade with Europeans that included the sale of slaves.[69] In the aftermath, those Edo chiefs accused of provoking war were put on trial – according to Edo, not British, law – and three were executed by firing squad.[70] Overami, the Oba (king) of Benin, was himself acquitted and offered a leading role in a form of indirect colonial rule. After he attempted to escape, however, he was exiled for life. In this way the kingdom of Benin was incorporated into the British Niger Coast Protectorate. Initially, the change of regime created a power vacuum outside of the immediate vicinity of Benin City, which led to a breakdown in law and order. By 1914, however, Benin had begun to prosper from the commercial growing of timber and rubber trees. In that year, when Overami died, his eldest son succeeded him as Oba of Benin, which was then part of the new colony of Nigeria.[71]

What motives lay behind this extension of colonial control? At the time, the kingdom of Benin was widely regarded by the British as an epitome of cruel tyranny. Correlatively, military intervention aimed at ending it was widely thought to be justified on humanitarian grounds. What eyewitnesses reported after entering Benin City in February 1897 confirmed this view. For example, before the end of that year, Commander R. H. Bacon, the expedition's intelligence officer, published an account of his experience in a book tellingly entitled *Benin: The City of Blood.* 'Truly has Benin been called The City of Blood', he began. 'Its history is one long record of savagery of the most debased kind.' On the immediate approach to the city, he reported that the expedition had come across two human sacrifices, presumably designed to ward off their attack. One of them comprised 'a young woman horribly mutilated, a rough wooden gag tied in her mouth was clenched tightly by her teeth'. 'Truly, as I heard a sailor remark, "It is

just about time someone did visit this place." These were our first
signs of Benin, and they did not improve our temper towards the
natives.' Once inside the city, Bacon and his comrades discovered
several compounds with long altars for human sacrifice. In one case,
'[t]he altar was deluged in blood, the smell of which was too over-
powering for many of us'. Indeed, '[t]he one lasting remembrance of
Benin in my mind is its smells. Crucifixions, human sacrifices, and
every horror the eye could get accustomed to, to a large extent, but
the smells no white man's internal economy could stand. Four times
in one day I was practically sick from them.' Then there were the
burial pits: 'And these pits! . . . out of one a Jakri [Itsekiri] boy was
pulled with drag-ropes from under several corpses; he said he had
been in five days'. 'Blood was everywhere; smeared over bronzes, ivory,
and even the walls'. And there was also the 'crucifixion tree with a
double crucifixion on it, the two poor wretches stretched out facing
the west, with their arms bound together in the middle . . . At the base
were skulls and bones, literally strewn about . . . Down the avenue to
the right was a tree with nineteen skulls . . . and down every main
road were two or more human sacrifices.'[72]

Bacon's account commands confidence partly by its own nature: it
is not unmeasured and displays a capacity for discriminating judgement. He recognised that Benin was no longer the centre of the slave
trade it had once been. He also made moral distinctions: 'Human
sacrifice undoubtedly differs in criminal degree.' For example, it is not
uncommon in some parts for a chief to kill a slave to take a message
to his father 'in the realm of shades'. 'Again, the killing of wives and
slaves to accompany the dead man to the next world is not without
its redeeming side.' But 'the atrocities of Benin' were of a different
quality altogether. And yet, notwithstanding all this horror, he was
able to write, 'the town was not without beauty of a sort'.[73] Confidence
in Bacon's veracity gathers further strength from corroborating testimony. The expedition's surgeon, F. N. Roth, for example, wrote in his
diary:

It is a misnomer to call [Benin] a city. It is a charnel house. All about
the houses and streets are dead natives, some crucified and sacrificed

on trees, others on stage erections, some on the ground, some in pits, and amongst the latter we found several half-dead ones ... As we neared Benin city we passed several human sacrifices, live women-slaves gagged and pegged on their backs to the ground, the abdominal wall being cut in the form of a cross, and the uninjured gut hanging out. These poor women were allowed to die like this in the sun ... As our white troops passed these horrors ... many were roused to fury.[74]

Most confidence-inspiring of all is the fact that while subsequent critics have challenged the significance of what Bacon and Roth described, none has undermined the general accuracy of their description. While Philip Igbafe insinuates fiction and lurid embellishment when he writes of 'stories of human sacrifice going on in Benin' and 'the gruesome pictures painted' of the city after its capture, he provides no substantiation.[75] Robert Home, in his own authoritative, book-length account of the expedition, judges Bacon's book 'a sober account' and repeats without demur much of the testimony of the eyewitnesses.[76]

Nevertheless, Home does go on to comment that 'the extent [of human sacrifice in Benin] has been exaggerated and the purpose of the practice little understood by Europeans ... It now seems that human sacrifice took place at only very few religious occasions at Benin, and that it was partly in the nature of public execution of criminals.' The sacrifice of a hundred or so victims was 'wrongly interpreted [by Bacon and his comrades] as proof that such wholesale killing was an everyday occurrence, while in fact it was a last desperate attempt to ward off the invasion'. Moreover, the crucifixion trees were places of public execution, 'where criminals were not left to die lingering deaths from crucifixion, but were garrotted and their bodies left as a sign to the gods. It was not so many years since criminals in Britain were executed and their corpses left to public view on the gibbet, and before that they were publicly drawn and quartered as well.'[77]

That said, Home does concede that '[t]here is no doubt that human sacrifice did take place at Benin'. Indeed, '[t]here is some evidence that the practice became more common in the nineteenth century'.[78] (In fact, according to Robin Law, 'the evidence is convincing for a substantial increase in the scale of human sacrifice in Benin from around the 1830s to the 1880s', and while Overami's accession to the throne in 1888 was followed by a decline, it was only 'temporary'.[79]) Home also affirms that the victims were not always justly convicted criminals. Some were supposed to be witches and wizards. Others were enemies of the Oba, hostages seized from dissident areas, unauthorised traders and unwanted slaves.[80] As we shall see, on at least one occasion they were also uninvited diplomats. Late Victorian Christians and humanitarians can surely be forgiven for finding such a practice as horrendous as their early twenty-first-century 'progressive' counterparts. And the fact is that colonial intervention, sometimes military, was necessary to stop it. As the Nigerian-born historian Olatunji Ojo has written: 'Most writers agree that protests from the potential victims, Christian missionaries and interventionist colonial regimes were crucial to the end of human sacrifice.'[81]

All this, however, is beside the point of the immediate motivation for the military intervention in 1897, for it was not the inhumanity of the Benin regime that decided it. Some argue that the basic motive was economic ambition. Thomas Uwadiale Obinyan, for example, attributes the expedition to 'the cruel itch for the selfish devastation and callous exploitation of the resources of other peoples . . . British avarice'.[82] More soberly, Igbafe argues in his influential article that it 'was prompted by economic rather than humanitarian considerations', being designed primarily to remove the Oba's obstruction of free trade, especially the commercial development of timber.[83]

Yet commerce was still not the decisive factor. Significantly, the expedition is usually described as 'punitive', for it was an act of retaliation for the massacre of an unarmed mission. The sequence of events was as follows. In the autumn of 1896, having arrived to take up the post of acting consul-general in the Niger Coast Protectorate, James Robert Phillips had consulted with both European and African (Itsekiri) traders. They told him of their long-standing frustrations with the Oba of Benin's power to stop trade from the interior at will, whenever he considered the terms to be unfavourable – and with his continuing to do so despite the treaty he had signed with Captain Henry Gallwey, vice-consul of the Benin River Station, in 1892, which committed him to permit free trade.[84] On 16 November 1896 Phillips wrote to the Foreign Office in London, arguing that, since all peaceful means of securing freedom of trade with the interior had been exhausted, he should be allowed to lead an armed expedition into Benin to depose the Oba and 'open up' the country.[85] Almost two months later, on 8 January 1897, the Foreign Office telegrammed its response to Phillips, instructing him to postpone any expedition 'to another year'.[86] By then, however, it was too late: Phillips was dead. While waiting to hear back from London, he had organised an unarmed mission to Benin, with the aim either of persuading the Oba to sign a new and stricter treaty or, should he refuse, of increasing pressure on the Foreign Office to authorise a military solution.[87] He informed the Oba of his intentions and set off, persisting in spite of a warning by the Itsekiri chief, Dogho, that it 'will be death to go on'. The Oba, who was involved in the ritual seclusion required by the Ague-Osa ceremony, declined to see the British party straightaway. Yet Phillips forged ahead, perhaps because he was anxious to prevent human sacrifices associated with the ceremony.[88] Left to himself, Overami would have received the mission: 'Perhaps they are coming to play [that is, trade],' he told his chiefs. 'You do not know. You must allow them to come and if it is war we will find out.' But the Oba was over-ruled by an impatient faction, who, having decided that war was inevitable, proceeded to lay an ambush. Their own messengers confirmed that the eight white men were unarmed, their revolvers locked up in boxes. Nevertheless, the Edo belligerents did not limit themselves to blocking the mission's progress or arresting its members. They attacked it, killing at least two of the Britons immediately and capturing up to four, whom they later sacrificed. (Two escaped.) In addition, they corralled about a hundred Itsekiri carriers for enslavement.[89]

It was only in response to this massacre of the acting consul-general's unarmed embassy that the British government was compelled – resentfully, according to Home – to authorise military intervention in Benin, in order to maintain its 'prestige' and thereby deter any repetition of the offence.[90] That was the proximate and decisive cause. Certainly, there were commercial interests that had been pressing for intervention – including the African ones of Chief Dogho – and for many traders those interests were, no doubt, predominant. However, for Christian or humanitarian traders, naval personnel, civil servants and government ministers, commercial interests were not simply commercial. 'Legitimate' trade was designed, in part, to replace the trade in slaves. Moreover, with free trade what Commander Bacon called 'the . . . seeds of civilisation' were supposed to circulate freely.[91] Reinforcing this point is the content of the 1892 treaty between the British and Overami. This bound the Oba to permit not only free trade between Benin and the outside world (Article VI), but also the freedom of Christian missionaries to reside and 'exercise their calling' (Article VII). It is also remarkable that the commitment to free trade comes sixth in a list of seven stipulations. Article I bound the Oba to refrain from entering into relations with any foreign power without British consent, and Article IV bound him to refer to British arbitration and decision any disputes between Benin and other parties – be they native chiefs or European individuals – that could not be settled amicably.[92] In other words, peace – international and internal – was the primary concern.

Some argue that, while the Edo 'hawks' handed the British a convenient pretext for invasion in January 1897, the British had already decided to invade anyway.[93] That is not so. It is true that the consul-general of the NCP, Ralph D. R. Moor, was convinced that only force would be effective – and he probably encouraged his deputy Phillips to take assertive measures in relation to Benin, while he himself was absent in London.[94] And it does seem that, by the end of December 1896, he had managed to persuade the Foreign Office of the need for a military expedition in principle. In written communication from the War Office to the Colonial Office on 24 December 1896, according to C. W. Newbury, 'the Foreign Office agreed and arranged the expedition with the War Office'.[95] Nonetheless, the Foreign Office advised Moor against the immediate undertaking of a military expedition against Benin, on the practical ground that the NCP force could not be reinforced with troops from Lagos and the Gold Coast.[96] Moreover, the telegram sent to Phillips on 8 January 1897 instructed him to postpone the expedition to 'another year' – the vaguest of terms.[97] This suggests a degree of equivocation, even prevarication. It seems that London had not quite made up its mind. Certainly, there were influential people within the Foreign Office who were sceptical of Moor's pleas to be allowed to use armed force in order 'to open up the country to civilisation and trade and to prevent the horrible human sacrifices and cruelties which were continually taking place therein'.[98] In particular, the head of the African Section in the Foreign Office, Sir Clement Hill, was 'unconvinced by Moor's professions of sympathy for the sufferings of the Benin people or his propaganda about the tyrannical Oba, fanatical juju priests, and human sacrifices of the city of blood', and repeatedly urged upon him 'a peaceful policy'.[99] Indeed, there is reason to suppose that Moor's reputation for advocating aggressive policies cost him his career.[100] So while recent events such as Moor's coercive deposition of the Itsekiri chief Nana of Brohimi in 1894 did give the Oba of Benin reason to fear that he would be the next target of British force, London had not in fact decided to shoot. Therefore, had it not been for the tragic collision of James Phillips' impetuosity with the impatience of some Edo chiefs, the British invasion of Benin may never have happened.

Apart from the moral justification of the punitive expedition against Benin in 1897, its other controversial feature was the looting of works of art from the Oba's compound. This is the issue on which Robert Home loses his characteristic dispassion. He laments that the British made no catalogue of the items they took and no record of where they were found, and that they broke the artistic tradition of the Edo by destroying the workshops of the guild craftsmen and their main client, the Oba's palace. And in a unique rhetorical flourish, he writes: 'For all their assumptions of racial superiority, the British at Benin did their best to destroy a remarkable artistic achievement, like the Mongols when they pillaged medieval Baghdad.'[101] But Home's description is too impassioned, for the evidence indicates that most of the city was destroyed by an accidental fire, not an intentional one. It is true that in the two days after the British had taken control on 18 February, they destroyed two compounds and the Queen Mother's House by fire, and demolished part of the King's House. Bacon tells us that this last demolition was for the purpose of military defence. He also tells us that the two compounds stood where roads entered the city, and that one of them belonged to 'the general who guarded the Ologbo and Sapobar Road'.[102] This implies that the compounds were located at strategic points and suggests that they, too, were destroyed for defensive purposes.[103] Whether or not that was also the case with the Queen Mother's House is not clear. Bacon comments that through its destruction was burned 'one more of the head-centres of vice in the city', but it may be that that was a morally satisfying side-effect of what was centrally a military intention.[104] It is significant that Bacon also reports that the demolition of part of the King's House was difficult, because 'the danger of firing the thatch from large charges [of gunpowder] was a risk not to be run'.[105] Evidently, the British sought to avoid a general conflagration.

Nevertheless, that is what happened the following day on 21 February. Home reports the British claim that it was inadvertent: two African carriers, drunk on cheap brandy in one of the huts, accidentally fired off some gunpowder, which set light to the palm-thatch roof. A strong breeze then caused the fire to spread rapidly and raze most of the town and the rest of the King's House in about an hour. Home also reports that the Edo did not believe this account.[106] Since his choice of words – 'did their best to destroy' – implies a deliberate, intentional action, he appears to align himself with Edo scepticism, although he does not tell us why. The evidence, however, is against him. Commander Bacon's account, which Home himself describes as 'sober', tells us that during preparations for a parade on 21 February, three days after the city had been taken, 'an alarm of fire was raised'. It started in the compound right next to the expedition's field hospital and spread so rapidly that the sick were evacuated and ammunition removed from buildings just in time. Bacon himself records that he 'lost everything except what I stood in and my blanket'.[107] Other eyewitness accounts corroborate his account.[108] The evidence that the British themselves were surprised by the fire, to the point where many of them lost all their belongings to it, strongly suggests that they did not deliberately start it. Home's suggestion of intentional destruction is unfounded, therefore, and Igbafe's statement that 'the troops burnt most of Benin City' is misleading.[109]

However, Home's accusation of deliberate destruction refers not just to the damage done to works of art and their means of production by the blaze, but also to their uprooting from their original cultural context. Yet this did not destroy the works themselves – at least no more than the extraction of religious paintings and sculptures from their original liturgical context in medieval churches for display in museums 'destroys' them. On the contrary, their removal had the fortunate effect of saving them from the fire, once it got going.[110] Still, it did involve the destruction of the artworks as parts of an ensemble in the context of particular buildings used for particular cultural purposes. But given the phenomena of human sacrifice – and, in many cases, the reality of it – that they had met upon entering Benin City, given the sense of outrage that this had provoked among them and given that many of the buildings containing the works of art were associated with such sacrifice, the British may well have felt that those artistic ensembles did not deserve to remain intact, sanctifying the horror with their beauty. Certainly, this was how Commander Bacon felt when the accidental fire began to consume the city: 'this head-centre of iniquity, spared by us from its suitable end of burning for the sake of holding the new seat of justice where barbarism had held sway . . . fire only could purge it, and here on our last day we were to see its legitimate fate overtake it'.[111] I, for one, find it hard to blame him.

It is true that the British unilaterally removed several thousand objects from Benin as 'spoils of war'. This was not 'looting', understood as the unauthorised seizure of items for private purposes by troops running amok, which was outlawed in the British Army and Royal Navy. At Benin Admiral Rawson took care to reserve all the major items as government property. As Captain Herbert Walker recorded in his diary on 20 February 1897, 'All the stuff of any value found in the King's palace and surrounding houses has been collected in the *Palave* house . . . Two tusks and two ivory leopards have been reserved for the Queen. The Admiral and his staff have been very busy "safeguarding" the remainder, so I doubt if there will be much left for smaller fry.'[112] One critic thinks that such removal, which he consistently misnames 'looting', could only have one, immoral purpose, namely, 'to denigrate and to shame the enemy beyond the present moment', to generate 'alterity'.[113] But that was not the admiral's driving aim. After he had taken the spoils back to London, some items were distributed as 'prizes' among the naval officers in proportion to rank, but most were auctioned by the Admiralty and bought up by the British Museum, General Pitt-Rivers and especially German museums.[114] William Fagg, 'a dominant figure in the twentieth-century history of the Benin Bronzes', claimed in 1981 that the proceeds of this sale were then used 'to defray the cost of pensions for the [expedition's] killed and the wounded'.[115] Although some think that Fagg's claim was 'pure fabrication', the devotion of the spoils of war to a relief fund was customary.[116] However the Admiralty deployed the money it raised in this case, it is reasonable to assume that it was for public, not private purposes. There are two contemporary clues as to what these might have been. In November 1896 James Phillips had suggested to the Foreign Office that were it to authorise a military expedition against Benin, 'sufficient ivory may be found in the King's house to pay the expenses incurred in removing the King from his Stool'. And in February 1897 Charles Hercules Read, keeper of British and medieval antiquities and ethnography at the British Museum, wrote that the Benin booty would be 'sold for the benefit of the Protectorate'.[117] While it is true that from July 1899, when Britain signed the Hague Convention (II), '[a]ll seizure or destruction of . . . works of art' became illegal, regardless of motive, it was not illegal in February 1897.[118]

Before I leave the topic of the punitive expedition against Benin in 1897, I am going to examine a book-length contradiction of the interpretation I have just given. I have already skirmished with it a little, but I want to confront it directly here, partly to show how my interpretation withstands the contradiction and partly to display more completely another example of how the moral-political axioms of some anti-colonialist academics distort their reading of the evidence. The book concerned is *The Brutish Museums: The Benin Bronzes, Cultural Violence and Cultural Restitution*, and its author, Dan Hicks, is professor of contemporary archaeology at the University of Oxford, where he is also curator at the Pitt Rivers Museum.[119]

Hicks' thinking is structured by a number of abstractions: 'corporate extractive capitalism', 'militarism', 'racism' and 'proto-fascism'.[120] All of these are used to characterise 'colonialism' and are morally laden in a pejorative manner. None are explained or justified. They are taken as axiomatic.

His thinking also displays symptoms of an ethical schizophrenia: on the one hand, he is morally neutral and infinitely indulgent with regard to non-Western, African culture; on the other hand, he is morally absolutist and infinitely unforgiving with regard to Western, British culture. The indulgence is evident in his treatment of human sacrifice in Benin. He pays almost no attention to it. There is one occasion when he nonchalantly admits that it might have happened, but only to brush it aside so that he can focus our attention on British atrocities: 'Quite probably the Oba made human sacrifices of slaves or prisoners, and quite possibly killed hostages he had taken when the Royal City came under rocket attack. But the sacking of Benin City was quite another thing.'[121] Otherwise, Hicks consistently insinuates that the reports were made-up fantasies: 'Each new story of the Oba's barbarity sought to outdo the last, to take the hyperbolic yarn spun by Richard Burton . . . to new levels of gothic schlock-horror.'[122] The only relevant entry in Hicks' index comprises 'sacrifice, *ideas of*'.[123]

Whereas the balm of indulgence is given the Edo, the acid of cynicism is poured relentlessly over the British. The abolition of the slave trade and slavery in the British Empire receives no credit at all. Instead, it is presented only as causing an 'intensification of a crisis for whiteness' that produced '[t]he ideology of militarist humanitarianism'.[124] What Hicks seems to be claiming here is that, having recognised the equal humanity of black Africans, the British needed to change the rationale for their colonial domination – from the sub-humanity of blacks to their moral degeneracy:

. . . as the status of black Africans as chattel to be raided, sold and displaced shifted, so a new ideology of race was needed to justify the project of European colonialism in Africa. It is in this context that the accusations began, primary among which was the blaming of slavery on Africans . . . anti-slavery became evidence of the moral degeneracy of Africans . . . By the 1890s, the ideology of projection had moved much further, becoming more than just propaganda – a belief system for a new kind of white supremacy. Whereas they had previously just used public anti-slavery sentiment to their own ends, now neo-imperialists accused kings and chiefs of imperialism ... Sentiments of anti-slavery and missionary Christianity were actively used to justify violence.[125]

Hicks expresses no moral concern at all about African slavery. Indeed, at one point he even allows the reader to suppose that Europeans introduced it to Africa: 'That most violent and purposeful of category mistakes, the mixing up of humanity and things, had come to West Africa with the slave trade – the commoditisation of people on an industrial scale.'[126] Instead, all his moral opprobrium is directed at the British because of their use of the cause of anti-slavery to justify the extension of their domination – 'the use of a "human rightist" justification for unprovoked regime change'.[127] The possibility that the eradication of African slavery might ever have required and justified British domination is simply never considered. 'Anti-slavery', according to Hicks, was only ever a 'pretext'.[128] And that was so in the case of Benin: 'the fact of slavery and slave-raiding existing within a British Protectorate was a major factor in the successful lobbying for the sacking of Benin City in 1897 – offering freedom for slaves was used as a means of creating a new social order after military operation [*sic*]'.[129] Observe how this view robs Africans of the dignity of moral agency and responsibility. What Africans do to each other is of no concern; it does not matter. All that matters is what whites do to blacks.[130] Whites remain centre-stage, albeit not in a good way.

In the light of these axioms, when Hicks turns to British action in relation to Benin in January and February 1897, he argues three things. The first is that the 'punitive' expedition in February was not in fact retaliatory, but had been decided upon in pursuit of commercial goals long before Phillips' expedition set off in January. '[S]ince the 1960s,' Hicks tells us, 'historians have increasingly understood the expedition to depose Oba [Overami] ... not as a retaliation, but to have been dictated by policy for a long time.'[131] To substantiate this claim, he cites four sources. Of these, A. F. C. Ryder's *Benin and the Europeans, 1485–1897* (1970) and Robert Home's *City of Blood Revisited* (1982) – the most recent source – do not in fact argue that pre-existing colonial policy 'dictated' – that is, pre-determined – the military assault on Benin.

That assault, Hicks argues, was part of a concerted British military campaign in East and West Africa from 1887 to 1900, 'a new phase in the use of military force justified as anti-slavery measures' that was inspired by the Brussels Anti-Slavery Conference of 1889–90.[132] The use of force against Benin had been contemplated long before January 1897. In May 1892 Consul-General Claude Maxwell MacDonald had written to the prime minister, Lord Salisbury, of the Oba's use of fetishes to restrict trade: 'I shall be surprised . . . if these barbarous practices which have been the custom of the country for centuries will be abandoned by the Priesthood without a severe struggle, and a display, and probable use of force on the part of the Oil Rivers Protectorate [later, the Niger Coast Protectorate] which however I should only recommend as a last extremity.' The following year, Vice-Consul Gallwey had written in his *Report on Benin District of Oil Rivers Protectorate for the Year Ending 31 July 1892* that '[a]nything in the shape of a punitory expedition, though it may eventually prove advisable, would paralyze trade for a very long period'.[133] And in May 1893 MacDonald had written again: 'Time and much patience will be required however before the resources of this district can be in any measure developed, the great stumbling-block to any immediate advance being the fetish reign of terror which exists throughout the Kingdom of Benin, and will require severe measures in the future before it can be stopped.' Hicks comments: 'the desirability and, indeed, the practicalities of a punitive expedition against the Kingdom of Benin were already being discussed, in, as it were, an anticipatory mode, in the months after the signing of the 1892 Treaty'.[134] That is misleading: necessity *in extremis* falls some considerable way short of 'desirability', contemplation does not amount to a decision, and both MacDonald and Gallwey urged patience and caution.

Hicks proceeds to argue that by the autumn of 1896 preparations for an attack on Benin in February 1897 'were clearly already well under way'. As evidence, he invokes a newspaper report in January 1897 of a survey of rivers and waterways by the Niger Coast Protectorate 'over a year ago' and the arrival of military officers participating in a

Royal Niger Company (RNC) expedition against an unknown target on the Niger river in November 1896. While the former hardly makes his case, the latter would, if the RNC's expedition could be tied to the Benin one. Since we know that the RNC *was* intent on military action, if the Benin expedition could be identified with it, then we could infer that the latter was intended, too – before Phillips and his comrades set off. Therefore, Hicks tries to persuade us to think of the two operations as a single 'joint action of the Company and the Protectorate'.[135] To that end, he observes that both Ralph Moor, the NCP's consul-general, and Sir George Goldie, the RNC's governor, were in London in November and December 1896 – hinting at collaboration without actually showing it.[136] Ten pages later he refers to 'sustained exchanges between Goldie and Moor, that took place after the Kirk Report recommended that the Company would be rolled into the Protectorate in some form or another' – without documenting the exchanges or reporting what they were about.[137] Yet Robert Home, whom he cites in support, actually makes it clear that Moor regarded Goldie as a rival, not a collaborator: 'Moor was a worried man, nervously watching his rivals jockeying for position' and fearing that, should its campaign against the Niger emirates of Bida and Ilorin succeed, the RNC might get to Benin first.[138] Hicks also writes of counter-insurgency operations undertaken by protectorate forces after the taking of Benin City 'in partnership' with the RNC.[139] One of the two sources he cites in substantiation is, again, Home. If we turn to the cited page (109), however, what we find is the very opposite of what Hicks tells us: not partnership at all, but bitter rivalry. Taking advantage of the political vacuum that the protectorate's toppling of the regime in Benin had created, the RNC intruded into its territory first to negotiate with the on-the-run Oba, and then to try and capture him. All of this was to the 'anger and chagrin' of Moor, who 'complained bitterly to the Foreign Office of this latest example of RNC poaching in Protectorate territory'.[140]

Aware that this thesis is vulnerable at this crucial point, Hicks moves to protect it, writing: 'Historians have emphasised the personal and political differences between the Company and the Government in this period, and it is certainly the case that decision making operated differently for the Company as compared with the Protectorate. But the Government had a common direction of travel ... the collaborative aspects should not be neglected.'[141] The alert reader will observe that the 'personal and political differences' that Home describes had nothing at all to do with 'decision making' processes, that 'a common direction of travel' does not amount to a joint operation and that Hicks has yet to establish any 'collaborative aspects'. On the very next page, he scores an own goal, when he reports that '[t]he Company's own desire to be involved in an action against the Oba of Benin ... continued into February, *although in the end they were kept out* of this part of the operations of this concerted military campaign'.[142] Since the assumption of a concerted campaign has yet to be proven, we should set it aside and note that what remains – the rejection of the RNC's desire to be involved – strongly implies that the action was not concerted at all. Hicks proceeds to score further own goals. He tells us that the two simultaneous operations 'were firmly detached from each other through the propaganda machines of Company and Protectorate' – without having already shown that they were operating in concert or explaining why the 'propaganda machines' felt the need to hide their purported concerting. He asserts that *both* parts of the supposedly 'coherent double-pronged campaign' had been sanctioned by the prime minister – when the Foreign Office's telegram to Phillips of 8 January expressly withheld permission for a military action against Benin in 1897, and when the prime minister and the secretary of state for foreign affairs were at that time the very same person.[143] And he urges upon us that 'Goldie even offered the services of his soldiers to the Protectorate's part of the campaign' – having just told us on the previous page that his offer was in fact refused.[144]

Hicks' first argument does not succeed: he does not make the case that military action against Benin in February had already been decided upon before Phillips' expedition in January. Hicks' second argument is that Phillips' expedition was just a ploy, its members were quite possibly armed and their deaths were only a 'supposed massacre'. The white men 'reportedly' took only revolvers. 'Various reports suggested that the expedition "offered a stout resistance",' he tells us – citing a single source, the *Daily Mail*. Gallwey's published recollection of '[a]bout a mile of road strewn with bodies' at the site of the massacre could be evidence of 'a . . . sustained two-way exchange' – rather than the widespread slaughter of unarmed carriers. Together this evidence '*might call into question* the unarmed status of the expedition', Hicks concludes – diffidently.[145] The diffidence is fitting, since the closest we have to first-hand testimony is unanimously against him. Captain Alan Boisragon, one of two survivors of the massacre, wrote that 'we were not carrying revolvers', which were all 'locked up in our boxes'. Bacon, the February expedition's intelligence officer, reported that 'no member of the expedition, at the express desire of Mr Phillips, wore any weapon, which were all locked up in their boxes'. And Henry Ling Roth, presumably informed by his brother, the February expedition's surgeon, reports that at the trial of those suspected of responsibility for the attack on Phillips, the three witnesses for the prosecution, Igbedio, Agamoye and Webari, 'all acknowledged that they knew beforehand that all the white men were unarmed'.[146] We could, of course, pour the acid of cynicism indiscriminately onto these sources, just because they are British and colonialist, but then we would also have to apply it to the *Daily Mail* and Captain Gallwey. Hicks then tells us that Home concluded that three of Phillips' white companions may have been taken to Benin City as hostages, where they 'perhaps lost their lives before or during the British attack of the subsequent month'.[147] This is both coy and inaccurate. What Home actually says is that an Itsekiri carrier testified that '*the day after the massacre*, he saw four white men sitting bound in the Oba's sacrificial compound, and the following day their heads were brought round with stick-gags in their mouths'.[148]

The third main line of argument that Hicks pursues is that, in the course of 'sacking' Benin, the British perpetrated atrocious violence and looting. He is disturbed by the vast asymmetry of military power, with the British using naval guns and Maxim machine-guns to wreak colonial 'ultraviolence' upon an enemy armed with, at best, muskets. He is also disturbed by what he implies was the indiscriminate bombardment and burning of towns or villages and the brutal use of expanding bullets.[149] He asserts that Edo deaths ran into the 'tens of thousands'.[150] Hicks does not seem to understand that the purpose of military endeavour is precisely to subdue the enemy by overwhelming him – that is, by achieving such an asymmetry of power that he either runs away or gives up. He also seems to think that the bombardment of areas where civilians are resident necessarily constitutes indiscriminate killing. In fact, the ethical principle of discrimination in warfare prohibits only the *intentional* killing of non-combatants: one should never make the killing of civilians one's prime purpose – say, in order to terrorise a population. However, if one supposes that enemy combatants are operating in a residential district, if it is important to dislodge or harass them and if there are no more 'surgical' means available, then one may attack a civilian district – just as the Allies bombed French towns during the invasion of Normandy in 1944. The criterion is that of military necessity, and its application is compatible with the killing of civilians on a large scale. In order to determine whether or not the British shelling of riverside villages in February 1897 was ethically indiscriminate, we need to know what the operational commander's rationale was. According to Boisragon, the intention of the two waterborne columns that flanked the main, landborne one was to '[draw] away the enemy's attention from the main attack'. Bacon confirms this military intention, but adds another, more dubious one: not only 'to harass and destroy towns and villages while the main operations lasted', but also 'to increase the punishment inflicted on the nation'.[151] This last aim would be indiscriminate, insofar as the damage done exceeded that required by the military purpose. Whether or not it actually did so is not clear and would be hard to determine. Certainly, Hicks does not determine it. Military necessity, not wanton brutality, was also the rationale for the use of expanding bullets, as his own footnote makes clear: the greater destructive force of expanding bullets was thought necessary to stop a charging enemy in his tracks.[152] As for the number of Edo casualties inflicted by the British, Hicks is right to say that it must have been higher than the several hundred caused in Benin City itself. 'But,' he asks, 'how to quantify the jungle deaths of an army of tens of thousands, the urban population, the ravaging of the countryside over weeks . . .?'[153] How, indeed. At the end of the chapter that begins, 'Some attempt at counting up the deaths must come first', he gives up, writing on the chapter's penultimate page, 'Let us hold back on fixing any number on the African casualties of the Benin atrocity at this point.'[154] Later, on page 114, he comes forward, and out of the unargued blue plucks the figure 'tens of thousands'.

When Hicks arrives at what happened in Benin City itself, he is unequivocal: the city was '[s]ystematically destroyed by fire, gun cotton and sledgehammers', its Royal Court 'burnt to the ground by British troops'. The fire of 21 February 'later claimed as accidental' was 'in fact probably just one that got out of control and so damaged stored goods in a mounting frenzy of demolition'.[155] Here he flies breezily in the face of the only first-hand testimony we have, which I presented above and which tells of targeted demolition for the purpose of military defence, of the care taken not to start an accidental conflagration, of the intention to use the city as the seat of a new government and of the surprise with which the fire of 21 February struck the startled British.[156] Benin did burn, but it was not sacked.[157]

Hicks' concluding, damning judgement is that '[t]he British atrocity at Benin City was a crime against humanity that mapped directly onto the three principal elements of the 1899 Hague Convention: the indiscriminate attack on human life in which tens of thousands died; the purposeful and proactive destruction of an ancient cultural, religious and royal site; and the looting of sacred artworks'.[158] I have explained why I think that it is not clear that the tactics employed in the attack were ethically indiscriminate, that Hicks' claim of tens of thousands of Edo dead lacks foundation, that the destruction of the city was not intentionally wanton and that the removal of property was not looting. Besides, the Hague Convention did not apply to the events in Benin in February 1897, for three reasons: it was signed in July 1899 and came into effect only on 4 September 1900; its provisions were 'only binding on the Contracting Powers, in case of war between two or more of them' (Preamble, Article 2), and the Oba of Benin was not a contracting party; and the Edo warriors did not fight 'in accordance with the laws and customs of war', as understood by the mainly European signatories (Annex, Article 1). The fighting in Benin was not subject to international law, only to moral law – as the British and the Edo, each in their own very different ways, understood it.

The concept of a 'crime against humanity' is of much later provenance than the Hague Conventions. According to the Rome Statute of 1998, which established the International Criminal Court, a 'crime against humanity' is one that is intentionally perpetrated against a civilian population either by the policy of a government or by a 'widespread and systematic' practice tolerated by it.[159] Of the eleven acts specified as kinds of this crime, none of them obviously describe what the British did in Benin in 1897. They did not, for example, subject the Edo to systematic extermination, enslavement or deportation. They did bombard and burn villages, but these tactics had a military purpose, may have been proportionate to it, and ceased once Benin City had been taken and the Oba deposed.

When all is said and done, then, my view of the Benin expedition of 1897 is this. Removing the obstruction of the freedom of Europeans and Africans to trade with the Edo in Benin was not sufficient just cause for taking the risks and incurring the costs of going to war, even if that obstruction violated the treaty of 1892. However, the removal and replacement of a political regime bound up with the gravely unjust practices of slavery and ritual human sacrifice were sufficient. Nevertheless, London, with all its many responsibilities at home and overseas, still wanted a decisive reason why it – rather than some other power – should assume the burdens of war, in order to liberate a remote people in West Africa. The slaughter of an unarmed embassy furnished it. When they went to war in February 1897, therefore, the British government intended primarily to retaliate for the massacre of Phillips' expedition, in order to maintain their regional authority and deter any repetition. The ending of the practices of slavery and human sacrifice, and the enabling of free trade with its civilising influence, were secondary intentions. War was a fitting – and in that sense, proportionate – means to achieve all of these aims. The tactic of using overwhelming force was also proportionate to the military purpose of subduing the enemy, and ending the bloodshed, as quickly as possible. The tactic of bombarding villages and towns might have been indiscriminate, insofar as it exceeded what was obviously required to subdue enemy combatants, but it is not clear that it did. After Benin City was taken, some buildings were demolished for defensive purposes. The subsequent general conflagration was an accident. The removal of artworks as spoils of war was customary and in accordance with British and international law at the time. Its intentions were mainly to reward the officers for their dangerous labours, to defray the costs of the operation and perhaps to relieve the plight of war-widows and -orphans. After a brief period of anarchy outside the city, a new native government under the supervision of a British political resident was installed.

The humanitarian motives for British retaliation and regime change may have been secondary, but they were not insincere. By 1 April, the new resident, Alfred Turner, had proclaimed that any slave who arrived in the deserted city before his master would become free, with the consequence that 'numerous slaves' rushed back. And by 18 May, he had prohibited slave-trading in the markets of Benin City. As a result, according to Philip Igbafe, 'a general emancipation of slaves followed in the wake of British occupation of Benin'. It may be that Turner's primary motive in making his proclamation was to repopulate the city and extend British authority, but, after the immediate grant of emancipation and the banning of the slave trade in 1897, the British persisted in the decades-long task of eradicating domestic slavery. In the achievement of this, the gradual social influence of the 'civilising seeds' of Western education and Christianity, 'which taught men freedom, justice, equality', played an important part. 'After 1900,' writes Igbafe, 'the British drive for . . . the abolition of slavery can be looked upon as a practical demonstration of their commitment to the principle of emancipation and manumission.'[160]

VII

Of all the many colonial wars fought by the British Empire, the Second Anglo-Boer War in South Africa involved the greatest imperial effort and was among the most controversial. Although it lasted less than half as long as the American War of Independence – running from October 1899 to May 1902 – it involved more than four times as many troops. It sucked in approximately 450,000 of them, including substantial contributions from Australia, Canada and New Zealand. Total British lethal casualties were about 22,000, the majority of them caused by disease.[161] Irish nationalists tended to support the Boers; African

Americans, however, supported the British.[162] So did most black South Africans, who 'saw Britain not as an oppressor, but instead as an actual or potential protector and liberator'. For, '[i]t was from Britain, the main source of their ideas about racial equality . . . that they expected help to come to improve their lot'.[163]

The British were fighting the two Boer republics of the Orange Free State and the Transvaal (otherwise known as the South African Republic), which had been established in the middle of the nineteenth century by migrants of mainly Dutch descent, who had trekked north from Cape Colony into the interior in order to escape British rule.[164] One of their main grievances was the racially egalitarian implication of the empire's decision to abolish slavery in 1833 – which led to the emancipation of more than 38,000 slaves in Cape Colony. The grievance was given frank expression by Anna Steenkamp, a sister of one of the leaders of the Great Trek of 1836. The Boers had left Cape Colony because of

> the shameful and unjust proceedings with reference to the freedom of our slaves – and yet it is not their freedom that drove us to such lengths, as their being placed on an equal footing with Christians, contrary to the laws of God, and the natural distinction of race and religion, so that it was intolerable for any decent Christian to bow down beneath such a yoke; wherefore we rather withdrew in order to preserve our doctrines in purity.[165]

Writing almost fifty years later in 1882, H. Rider Haggard observed that '[t]he Englishman and the Boer look at natives from a very different point of view. The Englishman, though he may not be very fond of him, at any rate regards the Kafir as a fellow human being with feelings like his own. The average Boer does not.'[166] From late 1901 a fifth of the Boers in the field – five thousand – fought with the British.[167] So did about twenty thousand Africans.[168] And among the Indian residents of Natal who volunteered to man a British ambulance corps was Mohandas Gandhi.[169]

The Boers were appalled that the British should deploy Africans against them – rather as American colonists were appalled when the

British deployed freed slaves against them. Early in his siege of Mafeking, the Boer General Piet Cronjé wrote to the besieged Colonel Robert Baden-Powell: 'It is understood that you have armed Bastards, Fingos and Baralongs against us – in this you have committed an enormous act of wickedness.'[170] In response, the Boers openly admitted killing armed Africans when they captured them, and, according to Thomas Pakenham, 'there is much unpublished evidence that they killed the unarmed ones, too'. Canon Farmer, a leading British missionary in the Transvaal, wrote in March 1901: 'I should be sorry to say anything that is unfair about the Boers. They look upon the Kaffirs as dogs & the killing of them is hardly a crime [– that is, the *Boers think that* the killing of Africans is "hardly a crime"]'.[171]

In the first, more conventional phase of the war the Boers bested the British, mainly because of their novel use of long-range, smokeless magazine rifles from concealed, entrenched positions and their enemy's slowness in changing their close-order tactics.[172] But the British adapted and, by developing such things as the creeping artillery barrage and – in the war's second, guerrilla phase – adopting a strategy of driving Boer commandos into a network of blockhouses linked by barbed wire, finally prevailed after more than two and a half years of increasingly brutal fighting.[173]

The causes of the war were a matter of controversy at the time and have remained so ever since. Perhaps the explanation most widely influential in the first half of the twentieth century was the one offered by J. A. Hobson, war correspondent for the *Manchester Guardian*: gold. In *The War in South Africa: Its Causes and Effects* (1900), Hobson argued that financial capitalists such as Cecil Rhodes – but 'of which the foreign Jew must be taken as the leading type'[174] – had manipulated the British into the war in order to maximise their profits by grabbing the Transvaal goldfields.[175] Those who have examined the historical detail, however, tend to find this thesis wanting.[176] For example, the South African-born historian G. H. L. Le May wrote in 1965 of the general view that the South African conflict had approximated 'the simple Marxist pattern of imperialist war', that '[t]he facts do not support this contention'. And on Hobson's thesis in particular he pronounced, 'The explanation of the war as a capitalists' conspiracy must be discarded; it is too smooth and rounded to fit easily into the jagged background of events and personalities.'[177] Three years later, Lewis H. Gann and Peter Duignan came to the same conclusion: 'Compared with . . . [the] great political issues, the economic questions were of only secondary importance. The British did not fight to make their mining concerns on the Witwatersrand safe against the exactions of unenlightened pastoralism.'[178] In 2003, Dennis Judd and Keith Surridge concurred, having this to say about the economic thesis:

> It was easy at the time, and has ever since remained a strong temptation, simply to attribute the outbreak of the war to the inexorable demands of capitalism and big business . . . In many ways it is compelling, certainly easier on the intellectual faculties, simply to accept the 'capitalist conspiracy' theory of the war, rather than to tease out all the ambivalence, confusion and paradox . . . It may also be that it is sometimes hard to abandon conspiracy theories, chiefly because of their inherent attractiveness – which owes much to the promise that they will unravel mysteries hitherto deliberately obscured by powerful, perhaps sinister forces. At any rate, historians as distinguished as Eric Hobsbawm have stuck to the view that 'whatever the ideology, the motive for the Boer war was gold'.[179]

The facts that tell against this view include the following. First, there is no evidence that Rhodes had any direct influence over the policy of the imperial government in the run-up to war. Next, the mining capitalists were not all of one mind: while some favoured the overthrow of the Transvaal's government, others feared the disruptive effects of war, not least on the supply of labour – rightly, as it turned out.[180] Further, since the Boer republic had already been comprehensively penetrated by largely British capital, business expertise and technological know-how, it is hard to see what could have been gained, economically, by invading it: 'Even if the British government needed secure access to gold bullion in order to maintain sterling as a great international currency, the Transvaal had to sell its gold on the open market – and hence why not to the United Kingdom – and there were, moreover, other suppliers of bullion worldwide.'[181] Most significant of all, there is no evidence that the man whose views and actions were most decisive in shaping British policy – Sir Alfred Milner, the high commissioner in South Africa – was primarily driven by the profit-maximising interests of the mine-owners. As Le May reported in 1995, 'I have not read any argument that alters my view that Milner was the principal architect of the war and that his motives were political not economic.'[182]

Milner was a very convinced British imperialist. In 1925, the year he died, he wrote in *The Times* newspaper: 'I am a Nationalist and not a Cosmopolitan ... A Nationalist is not a man who necessarily thinks his nation better than others, or is unwilling to learn from others. He does think that his duty is to his own nation and its development ... I am a British race patriot ... It is not the soil of England ... which is essential to arouse my patriotism, but ... the spiritual heritage, the principles, the aspirations, of the British race.'[183] (Note that for Milner 'race' meant neither place of birth nor skin colour. His grandfather was a German subject; his father, a resident in Germany; and he himself had been born at Giessen, north of Frankfurt-am-Main.) As in 1925, so in 1899, he genuinely believed in the 'world State' of the British Empire as a civilising force, bringing good government in the form of honest officials, efficient administration, the rule of law, agricultural modernisation and infrastructural improvement.[184] Crucially, it also involved a special solicitude for those at the bottom of the social heap, be they the poor of London's East End, the *fellahin* of the banks of the Nile, or black mine-workers in the Witwatersrand (the 'Rand').[185]

In South Africa, Milner was determined to secure British imperial supremacy. Thomas Pakenham attributes this to the fact that 'what he [Milner] was interested in was power. Not merely for himself, but for England and the English race'.[186] While some might take that to be morally damning, it is in fact banal. Anyone desiring to achieve something naturally wants the power to achieve it. Wanting power is, as such, morally neutral. In order to evaluate it, we need to know what Milner wanted to achieve through the establishment of supreme British power in South Africa. What were his goals? Most straightforwardly, he wanted to keep secure the empire's maritime facilities at Cape

Town, which he regarded as 'the most strategic point in the Empire, the possession of which is absolutely necessary to us as a great Eastern power'.[187] In addition, he wanted regional stability, because instability was a threat to life and prosperity and its management tended to require funding from London. Southern Africa in the last decade of the nineteenth century was unstable. It comprised two British colonies, two Boer republics and numerous African peoples within their shifting borders and outside them. Also operating outside were Boer adventurers, Arab slavers, the British South Africa Company, the Portuguese and the Germans. The scope for friction igniting into armed conflict between two of these bodies, and then embroiling the rest, therefore, was considerable. For that reason, British policy-makers had long wanted to bring the two Boer republics into an imperially ordered South African political union. However, whereas the Transvaal had teetered on the edge of bankruptcy in the late 1870s, by the late 1890s it was growing wealthy on the Rand's gold mines and using its wealth to buy sophisticated modern weaponry. This created the prospect of a political union that would not be a confederal dominion within the British Empire like Canada, but instead, after Afrikaners within the British colonies had been seduced into abandoning their loyalty to the Crown, a Boer-dominated United States of South Africa.

We might reasonably ask why this prospect was such a spectre in Milner's eyes. What would have been so terrible about it – apart from the loss of British prestige and a possible threat to the Royal Navy's access to the strategic dockyard at Simonstown? The answer lies in what the Union of South Africa actually became fifty years later, when it was dominated by the Boers: an *apartheid* state. While it would be exaggerating to claim that the welfare of black Africans was Milner's foremost concern in 1899, it was certainly a leading one. In a letter of November 1897, he stated that his work in South Africa had two main goals: first, to restore good relations between the Afrikaners and the English, and, second, to 'secure for the Natives . . . adequate and sufficient protection against oppression and wrong'. He continued:

> . . . if it were not for my having some conscience about the treatment of the blacks, I *personally* could win over the Dutch in the [Cape]

Colony and indeed in all of the South African dominions in my term of office, and that I could do without offending the English. You have only to sacrifice 'the n---er' absolutely and the game is easy . . . You say and say truly that self-government is the basis of our colonial policy and the keystone of colonial loyalty. That principle, fearlessly and unflinchingly applied, would make South Africa as loyal as Canada – but what would be the price? The abandonment of the black races, to whom you have promised protection, and the tolerance of a state of things in a self-governed state under the British flag, which we would never tolerate for a moment in India, in Egypt, or in any of the Crown Colonies.[188]

Since, in Milner's view, the British Empire must not abandon black Africans, and since the Transvaal's constitution affirmed that 'the *Volk* desire to permit no equality between people of colour and the white inhabitants, either in Church or State',[189] the former could not simply tolerate the latter and risk it becoming predominant in South Africa. As he wrote to Joseph Chamberlain, secretary of state for the colonies, in 1900: 'I do not think the reconciliation of the two [white] races hopeless, but the Dutch must be made to feel from the first that it is a question for them of a change of attitude or of political extinction. Either they must accept our flag and membership of the British Empire in good faith . . . or we shall have to keep up a system of autocratic rule till their opposition to the new order of things is completely broken.'[190]

Milner's conviction that the nettle in South Africa had to be grasped was further strengthened by the issue of the Transvaal's treatment of the approximately sixty thousand British subjects who had come to work in the Rand. Mixed race 'Cape Coloureds' were being abused by the Boer police.[191] Moreover, in 1890 the residence qualification for the franchise had been raised from five to fourteen years, to prevent Uitlanders ('outsiders') – mainly British immigrants – from becoming politically dominant, even though their taxes furnished the government with most of its revenue.[192] Then, in 1898, the Transvaal's chief justice, J. G. Kotzé, who had asserted a right of judicial review or 'testing right' over Volksraad (parliament) legislation permitting the expulsion of any foreigner considered to be 'a danger to the public peace and order', was summarily dismissed. In March 1899 21,000 Uitlanders petitioned the British government to intervene, and Milner talked up their grievances in order to impress the need for action upon London. He had long been of the view that either the Transvaal had to be persuaded to reform itself or there should be war, and he was willing to force the choice. As he had written to Chamberlain the previous year:

> There is no way out of the political troubles of S. Africa except reform in the Transvaal or war ... *Looking at the question from a purely S. African point of view*, I should be inclined to work up to a crisis, not indeed by looking about for causes of complaint or making a fuss about trifles, but by steadily and inflexibly pressing for the redress of substantial wrongs and injustices. It would not be difficult thus to work up an extremely strong *cumulative case*.[193]

The colonial secretary, however, was more cautious, insisting that if war was to come, the Transvaal would have to be the aggressor.[194] At the end of May Milner entered into face-to-face negotiations with the Transvaal's president, Paul Kruger, at Bloemfontein. Milner stressed that he was not seeking to 'swamp' the Boer population in their Volksraad and he proposed that the gold-mining districts of the Rand have seven out of twenty-eight seats; that is, no more than a quarter of the total – even though the 60,000 Uitlanders outnumbered the 30,000 Boer voters by two to one.[195] Yet Kruger was willing to contemplate no more than five seats and refused to reduce the residence qualification for the franchise to less than seven years – and even then only on condition that the British renounce their claim to imperial suzerainty and the concomitant right of intervention on behalf of British subjects. This was unacceptable to the Cabinet in London. By 2 September Kruger had come to think that war was inevitable and resolved to make a pre-emptive strike on Natal before any British reinforcements arrived. On 8 September London decided to increase the diplomatic pressure by dispatching a further 10,000 troops to bolster South Africa's garrison of 12,000, and news of this decision reached South Africa the following day. By the time the military reinforcements had arrived in Durban on 22 September, the expected British ultimatum had still not been received in Pretoria or Bloemfontein.[196] Without this and its proof of British aggression, President Steyn of the Orange Free State was unwilling to go to war. Nevertheless, on 9 October the Transvaal issued its own ultimatum and two days later Boer troops invaded the British colony of Natal.[197]

Should we conclude from this sequence of events, as some historians do, that the Second Anglo-Boer conflict was basically 'Milner's War' and that he was its prime mover?[198] The answer is yes, insofar as it is probable that the British Cabinet would have settled for a compromise had it not been for Milner's determination to force the issue and resolve it once and for all. As he wrote to Lord Roberts in June 1900, 'I precipitated a crisis which was inevitable before it was altogether too late.'[199] But the answer is no, insofar as Kruger was co-responsible. Had it not been for his refusal to yield any further in the negotiations during the summer of 1899, matters would not have escalated. Which of the two instances of intransigence deserves moral blame depends on how we evaluate what each was trying to achieve, and whether there were more prudent ways than war of trying to achieve it. On one side, Kruger sought to maintain Boer control over the Transvaal and thereby its independence from the British. But the ceding of a minority of parliamentary seats to the Uitlanders would not have lost that control. And, besides, independence is not its own justification. The Transvaal's independence involved the legal subordination of black Africans and other coloured peoples: it was constitutionally racist. On the other side, Milner sought to prevent the possibility that racist 'Krugerism' would come to dominate South Africa. There were no grounds for confidence that internal forces would drive reform; diplomacy had failed to extract sufficient concessions; and the development of gold-mining in the Rand made it likely that the unreformed status quo would grow stronger, not weaker. In Milner's eyes, therefore, it was a case of either going to war in 1899 or giving up altogether. I think he was right. War in 1899 was a last resort in a just cause.

The cause of the Boer War of 1899–1902 is one of its controversial features; the manner of its execution is another. In the second, guerrilla phase of the fighting (from May 1900) the British adopted the 'scorched earth' tactic of destroying the farms of Boer commandos, primarily in order to rob them of support and supplies. Many, including Milner, were sickened by the tactic. A related policy was also controversial: the setting up of 'camps of refuge' or 'concentration camps'. After Louis Botha, the wartime commander-in-chief of the Boer commandos, had declined a British offer to exclude all farms from military operations,[200] camps were established, initially to protect surrendered Boers, together with their families, against summary punishment by their former comrades, then to house the displaced families of Boers still fighting, but also to prevent civilians from communicating intelligence to the commandos in the towns, By August 1901 they housed almost 94,000 Boers and 24,500 of their black servants.[201] The inmates were given – free of charge – food rations, clothing, medical and nursing care, and (for children) education.[202] By October, however, a combination of disease (mainly measles), overcrowding, insanitary conditions, insufficiently balanced diet and inadequate planning was causing deaths at an annual rate of 344 per thousand.[203] In response to an alarming report from the social welfare campaigner Emily Hobhouse, the British government set up an official commission, comprising six women led by Millicent Fawcett, a prominent Liberal Unionist and leader of the women's suffrage movement. In December the Fawcett Commission delivered its own report, which was highly critical of conditions in the camps, attributing most of the blame to the authorities, but reserving some for the unhygienic failure of Boer women to ventilate their tents.[204] Following reforms in the administration of the camps, the mortality rate declined to 160 per thousand in January 1902, and then to 20 per thousand in May.[205] Nonetheless, over a period of almost two years somewhere between 18,000 and 26,000 Boers died in the camps, together with between 7,000 and 12,000 Africans – mainly from epidemics of measles and typhoid.[206]

In June 1901 Sir Henry Campbell-Bannerman, the leader of the Liberal Party, denounced the farm-burning and concentration camps as 'methods of barbarism'.[207] Were these tactics really as barbarous as Campbell-Bannerman's phrase alleged? 'Just war' ethics prescribes two principles in waging war: discrimination, which forbids the intentional killing of non-combatants; and proportionality, which requires that only such damage is done as is necessary to serve a suitably important military objective. The disquieting truth is that successful counter-insurgency against guerrillas almost invariably necessitates harsh measures that put civilians at risk. Unless counter-insurgent forces are so numerous that they can afford to guard villages and farms permanently – and they seldom are – they will have to stop insurgents using or intimidating civilians by more drastic means. Insofar as they were proportionate to this end, the burning of farms and the seizure of livestock and food supplies were justified by military necessity and so permissible, both morally and legally.[208] For sure, these measures had the effect of exposing civilians to harm – but then so did the Allied use of bombing and artillery in the invasion of Normandy, which, all told, killed 35,000 French non-combatants.[209] Notwithstanding their harshness, the burning of property and the seizure of goods were quite distinct, morally, from lining up innocent civilians in front of mass graves and intentionally slaughtering them. The establishment of the 'camps of refuge' shows that the farm-burning tactic was not intended to harm civilians. And the subsequent deaths of too many of the inmates was due to disease and poor conditions rather than execution, and to incompetence rather than intention. Once it was brought to London's attention, effective remedial action was taken.[210]

Both of the controversial tactics adopted were designed to bring to a swifter conclusion what had become a very bitter war, and, together with the network of blockhouses into which the last guerrillas were driven, they succeeded in their aim. However, while it is true that the death rate in the camps, even at its peak of 43 per cent, 'did not compare outrageously' with that of the poorest class in the worst slums of European cities of the nineteenth century, that rate was avoidably high in 1901.[211] We know that because it fell dramatically in 1902, when changes were made. Insofar as what was ended in 1902 could have been avoided in 1901, it should have been, and the failure to avoid it was culpable. That said, culpable negligence does not amount to intentional genocide, so any suggestion – such as Pakenham's – that General Kitchener's 'concentration camps' approximated the Nazi death camps of the 1940s, and that what happened in them was a 'holocaust', is ethically distorting.[212]

The war ended with the signing of the Treaty of Vereeniging on 31 May 1902. As we saw in Chapter 4, Article 8 of this peace agreement deferred the issue of the granting of the franchise to black Africans in the Boer republics on the same basis as in Cape Colony until 'after' the republics had been removed from post-war imperial supervision and granted confederal autonomy. Pakenham interpreted that as making 'mockery of Chamberlain's claim that one of Britain's war aims was to improve the status of Africans'.[213] Against this view, I have argued that it was a morally justifiable compromise that, recognising the limits of imperial power, aimed to avoid exacerbating Boer bitterness and undermining the peace in the short term, while holding onto the hope that demographic change and growing loyalty to the British Empire would gradually bring about a liberalisation of Boer culture in the long term.[214] In a speech he gave at the Drill Hall, Johannesburg, on 31 March 1904, Milner bravely declared that, regarding 'the colour question', he was 'in the opinion of the vast majority of the people in this room, a heretic on the subject . . . and an unrepentant heretic . . . I continue to hold the view that we got off the right lines in this matter when we threw over the principle of Mr Rhodes – equal rights for all civilised men'. Nevertheless, he was 'prepared to rely for the return to the true path *upon a gradual change in the opinion of the people of South Africa* . . . You may learn that the essence of wisdom . . . is discrimination; not to throw off all people of colour . . . into one indistinguishable heap – but to follow closely the difference of race, of circumstance, and of degree of civilisation, and to adapt your policy intelligently and sympathetically to the several requirements of each.'[215]

In the aftermath of the war Milner worked assiduously to build a generous peace that would provide the basis for the British Empire to win the hearts of the alienated Boers. Whereas before the war the Colonial Office had had £600,000 in total to cover all of its worldwide operations, Milner and Chamberlain secured a guaranteed loan of £35 million for investment in South Africa, which led to the construction of 'a grid-mesh of new railways and irrigation channels . . . as impressive as the ones built by Cromer in Egypt and the Sudan'.[216] In distributing relief, the imperial administration was careful not to discriminate on grounds of political sympathy.[217] In the judgement of one historian, 'The fabric of civilisation which the war had destroyed, Milner restored in a much more perfect form; his reconstruction schemes laid the material groundwork of Union. It was because of the enduring quality of this solid basis that the bold appeal to the heart which Campbell-Bannerman made by his generous grants of self-government reaped such a rich harvest.'[218] Botha, the former Boer military commander, repeatedly praised the improvements in agricultural techniques that Milner had introduced and the generous state funding he had secured to back their development. Another former guerrilla general, Jan Christian Smuts, considered the agreement whereby the Crown restored self-government to the Transvaal and the Orange Free State in 1906–7 to be 'one of the wisest political settlements ever made in the history of the English nation'.[219] Three years later the Boer republics joined the Union of South Africa as a dominion within the British Empire. And four years after that, Botha and Smuts together suppressed a Boer revolt in order to bring South Africa into the First World War on the British side: 'They had been so completely converted to British imperialism in its Liberal expression that they were willing to accept the responsibilities as well as the privileges of membership of the Empire.'[220]

So far, so good for Milner's strategy of long-term cultural and political change. Another important movement in that direction was the securing of equal voting rights for every 'British subject of European descent' in the South Africa Act 1909, clause 43 (c).[221] Unfortunately, Milner's attempts to increase the number of British immigrants, so as to shift the demography of South Africa gradually in favour of more liberal politics, failed. He had hoped that his land-settlement scheme would attract up to 10,000 immigrants to the Transvaal and Orange Free provinces. In the event, only about 1,300 men and their families came to settle.[222] The long-term consequence was that, while the Cape Province retained its colour-blind franchise, it was never extended to other parts of South Africa. Instead, it was qualified in 1936 and then abolished altogether in 1959.[223] Two years later South Africa left the British Commonwealth.

VIII

After the massacre at Amritsar, the British counter-insurgency operation that has attracted the greatest opprobrium is the repression of
the 'Mau Mau' uprising in Kenya from 1952 to 1960.[224] During the
eight-year 'Emergency', on the one hand, the rebels killed 32 European
settlers, 63 European members of the armed forces, 170 African
members and at least 1,800 African non-combatants, although many
hundreds more went missing. On the other hand, 11,503 rebels were
killed in combat, according to official figures, although David Anderson
thinks that the real number was probably more than 20,000. At least
150,000 Kikuyu spent time in a detention camp.[225]

As this set of figures hints, the conflict was as much between Africans
as it was between Africans and Europeans: 'The war did not simply
pit oppressive British forces against noble Kenyan nationalist rebels
. . . As many Kikuyu fought with the colonial government as did those
against it.'[226] By the end of 1954 Africans loyal to the British were
inflicting half of the rebels' casualties and, according to the Kenyan
historian Bethwell A. Ogot, they played 'the crucial role' in defeating
the uprising.[227] Members of the Mau Mau used violence to terrorise
other Africans into compliance, committing atrocities against native
loyalists, including the murder of nine African Christians on Christmas
Eve 1952 at Nyeri and the massacre of up to a hundred loyalists and
family members, mostly women, at Lari in March 1953.[228] During one
attack at Kandara in October 1952, 'three of the Tribal Police wives
and four of their children were hacked to pieces. The heads of the
four children were laid out in a row beside their disembowelled mothers.'[229] Yet the worst atrocity was committed by the loyalist chief, Njiri
wa Karanja, who, retaliating for the rebels' decapitation of his son,
perpetrated the massacre of about four hundred civilians at Mununga
in June 1953.

The causes of this bitter violence comprised an interlocking complex
of factors. Originally, British interests in East Africa lay in securing
the sea routes to India and the suppression of the Arab slave trade.
Then, partly to avoid an accidental collision with Germany and partly
to replace the financially unviable Imperial East Africa Company, Kenya

was declared a British protectorate in 1890. In the following decade
British involvement in the government of Egypt and the Sudan generated a further security interest in controlling the headwaters of the
Nile and a further humanitarian interest in containing the southward
spread of Islam. To these ends, the 'Uganda' railway had been built
from the coast to the shores of Lake Victoria by 1901, partly for military purposes, partly to discourage the revival of the slave trade in
Uganda and partly to facilitate trade. Since the construction and maintenance of the railway was expensive, the question arose of how to
pay for it. The only feasible answer was the development of European
agriculture in the Kenya highlands.[230]

Accordingly, the government designated certain limited areas as
open for European settlement, stipulating either that the land be unoccupied or that dispossessed Africans be compensated.[231] When the
first white settlers arrived in 1902 much of the land was unoccupied,
and local Kikuyu often assisted in building their houses and barns and
proceeded to work as labourers. In order to increase the supply of
wage-earning labour, a hut tax was instituted. Pushed by the need to
pay tax and pulled by the prospect of acquiring capital and livestock,
between 1904 and 1920 about seventy thousand people, mainly young
men, were attracted from central Kenya to the highlands. There they
took up squatter contracts, which allowed them to graze and cultivate
small areas for themselves, while providing up to 180 days of labour
per annum to a European farmer. 'In material terms,' writes David
Anderson, 'the squatters who went west did pretty well. Incomes were
relatively high, compared with those realized within the Kikuyu
reserves, and as the links with their kin back in central Kenya weakened
over the years, these pioneers found themselves freed from at least
some of the obligations of customary life.'[232]

However, while the settlers perceived the squatters as hired hands,
with no legal claim to the land they occupied, the squatters held that
they had a customary right to full ownership of land that they had
cleared for cultivation. In 1925 the courts backed the settlers with a
fateful judgment that resident labourers on European farms were
'tenants-at-will' and could be evicted without appeal. On the eve of
the Second World War, white farmers, whose economic viability had

generally been precarious, were intent on developing high-grade dairy and beef farming.[233] The war raised prices and, for the first time, gave settlers substantial capital for development. It also created a white manpower shortage, which in 1940 compelled the colonial administration to suspend its inclination to curb settler power and to cede control over squatter affairs to the settler district councils. In 1945 these councils passed local laws reducing squatter cultivation and banning their disease-prone cattle altogether, lest they infect settler herds. The consequence was that squatter incomes declined sharply, causing more than a hundred thousand Kikuyu to move back to central Kenya in 1946–52.[234]

The sudden influx of ex-squatters into the Kikuyu reserves exacerbated competition for, and litigation over, land, which was already intensifying because of rapid population growth on the back of medical triumphs over disease.[235] It also heightened social divisions among the Kikuyu. When they had left for the highlands, the squatters had abandoned their traditional obligations of labour. Partly for that reason, and partly because they themselves were inclined to increase their commercial profits by reneging on their traditional obligations to tenants, the chiefs and landed elders were not much more sympathetic to the plight of the squatter refugees than the white settlers.[236]

Aware of the growing agrarian crisis on the reserves, the colonial government responded by seeking to improve agricultural productivity by means of a campaign for soil conservation and improved land husbandry – a policy that the moderate nationalist Jomo Kenyatta praised.[237] Because the need was urgent, a new generation of young chiefs were given the authority to implement the necessary measures. This they did by using the traditional system of communal labour to build terraces. However, because the terraces were often too narrow, they were washed away every rainy season, making the demand on communal labour unrelenting. Moreover, the terracing frequently destroyed the most valuable crop, wattle, and the use of women to build them offended social custom. Consequently, it was in the areas where these modernising measures were most keenly felt that the Mau Mau rebellion won its greatest support.[238]

On 3 October 1952 the Mau Mau claimed their first European victim,

stabbing to death a woman near her home in Thika. Six days later
they assassinated Senior Chief Warihiu, a major ally of the colonial
administration. On 20 October, Governor Evelyn Baring – Lord
Cromer's son – declared a state of emergency. This gave him the legal
basis for deploying the army in aid of the civil power, in order to
forestall excessive violence by the settlers, whose attitudes clashed
with his own 'essentially liberal' views.[239] It also gave him the right to
exercise discretionary power in doing whatever he thought 'necessary
or expedient for securing the public safety, the defence of the territory,
the maintenance of public order and the suppression of mutiny, rebellion and riot'. This included detaining suspects without trial.[240]

By the end of 1954 the number of detainees reached a peak of 71,346,
declining to 19,575 by December 1957. Detainees were rehabilitated
by stages, moving along a 'pipeline' of camps of declining severity to
eventual release. Health conditions in the camps were sometimes very
poor, with one, built to house a population of 6,000 but in fact holding
16,000, suffering an outbreak of typhoid in 1954 that killed 115 inmates.
However, the colonial authorities did take steps to improve sanitation,
and in 1955 when tuberculosis struck camps in Central Province, those
infected were released to prevent further contagion. Nonetheless, by
1958 some had been held in the camps for six years, and in March
1959 when eighty-eight recalcitrant prisoners at Hola refused to do
manual labour on an experimental irrigation scheme, the decision was
made at a high level of the Kenya government, though perhaps not
the highest, to force them, with the result that (African) warders
clubbed eleven of them to death.[241] The story that the prisoners had
drowned or died from drinking excessive water in the intense heat
quickly spread from the camp to the British press and the House of
Commons. Just over a week later, when the autopsies had been
completed, an official statement was made, admitting evidence of death
by violence. Six months later on 1 September, the report of the Fairn
inquiry, which had been commissioned by the government in London,
brought the truth to light.[242]

Security forces did exploit the wide room for discretion permitted
them by the emergency regulations, though British troops less so than
members of the settler-dominated auxiliary Kenya Police Reserve

(KPR) and the Kikuyu Guards.[243] For example, they used aggressive methods of interrogation that would now be classified as 'torture' or 'inhuman and degrading treatment', but were not clearly so then. Upon being captured, a suspect would usually be subjected to an immediate tactical interrogation to obtain 'hot' information about the location and plans of any insurgents in the vicinity. While this did not always involve brutal treatment, it sometimes did. On one occasion an officer in the KPR tried to frighten a prisoner into revealing the whereabouts of a Mau Mau gang by firing a shot four inches above his head and threatening, 'The next one goes through your skull.' On other occasions, the Kenya police would place an upturned bucket on a prisoner's head and beat it with a metal instrument until he gave in.[244] There is evidence that some agents of the state did not merely exploit the law's latitude, but broke it, conducting summary executions. In April 1953, Baring reported to London that, in the preceding six months, 430 suspects had been shot while attempting to escape or resisting arrest. One Colonial Office official commented, 'I find it increasingly difficult to believe that in the present circumstances all the prisoners concerned would invariably be shot dead and none of them just wounded.'[245]

David Anderson has drawn attention to another gruesome feature of the repression of the Mau Mau rebellion: the unusually high number of convicted rebels who were hanged. Anderson counts a total of 1,090 between October 1952 and March 1958, which he claims was more than in all other British colonial emergencies after 1945 and more than double the executions of convicted terrorists in French Algeria. That may be so, but, on his own evidence, these were not summary executions. About 3,000 were accused of capital charges relating to Mau Mau activity. Of those, 1,499 were convicted and sentenced to hang; and of those, 160 lodged successful appeals and another 240 had their sentences commuted.[246] Bethwell Ogot comments that, in calling the executed men 'unacknowledged martyrs of the rebel cause', Anderson conflates martyrs with criminals hired to carry out assassinations.[247]

While in these cases there were, as Anderson shows, instances of judicial bias and corruption, tainted testimony, questionable evidence, confessions extracted under torture and apparently inconsistent judgments, the record of the judiciary during the Kenya Emergency shows that it was not generally or systemically corrupted by political bias. The courts did hold members of the security forces to account. By February 1954, of the 130 prosecutions brought against the police for brutality, with 40 cases still pending, 73 convictions had been secured.[248] That amounts to over 81 per cent of the cases tried. The attorney-general from 1953 to 1954, John Whyatt, was assiduous in defending the right of individuals to a fair trial. In 1954 the three senior judges sitting on Kenya's appeal court overturned the convictions for murder in the case of Bruxnell-Randall and, to use Anderson's own words, mounted 'a savage attack on the security forces in general . . . for disregard of legal process'.[249] And in December of the same year, Acting Justice Arthur Cram, who presided over the trial of those accused of murdering two Mau Mau suspects at the home guard post at Ruthagati, issued a judgment in which he savaged 'the corruption, dishonesty, and flagrant perjury' of all those connected with the defence of Muriu Wamai, and the judicial extortion by the local African court.[250] What is more, judges were not the only determined critics of abuse by agents of the state. General George Erskine, who commanded British forces in Kenya from June 1953 until May 1955, disapproved of the tendency of the Kenya Police Reserve, most of whom were white settlers, to resort quickly to physical force and resolved to impose tighter discipline on his troops.[251]

Given all the above, is it appropriate to say that the British waged a 'dirty war' in the Kenya Emergency? In one sense it is appropriate, since all war is dirty. Even wars that are – all things considered – morally justified will involve moments of the wrongful, disproportionate, unnecessary use of force. The Allies' crusade against Nazism certainly did: Allied units are known to have slaughtered German prisoners-of-war in more or less hot blood during the invasion of Normandy.[252] Just wars are seldom morally pure, but, then, little that human beings do is pure. Of all kinds of violent conflict, counter-insurgency is perhaps the most difficult to keep pure. This is because it typically involves anonymous insurgents who do not play by the rules, or whose rules are very different from those that constrain their uniformed opponents. Consequently, the latter perceive that the former are 'cheating', and almost nothing is more calculated to tempt disciplined troops to lose control than that. The only greater temptation is when the cheating takes the form of needless cruelty, mutilating contempt or mass atrocity.[253] Then righteous rage begs to be let loose, and if unleashed, the cycle of atrocity and counter-atrocity begins. This seems to have happened quite a lot during the Emergency in Kenya, especially in the first nine months before General Erskine took command. Not all of it was generated by rage at rebel atrocity, however. Some of it was motivated initially by settler racism, and much of it was permitted by police and home guards who had not been trained to discipline themselves. So the counter-insurgency contained considerable dirt.

However, it was not radically dirty insofar as the governor, the commander-in-chief and the senior judiciary in the colony, and the government in London, were determined to clean things up and to keep them that way.[254] The governor's resistance of further prosecutions of senior government officers responsible for the policy that led to the Hola killings, and the commander-in-chief's deflection of an inquiry into the army's conduct away from events before his arrival, for fear of undermining the morale of the administration and the security forces, do not gainsay that determination.[255] Moreover, in the case of Hola, London brought the truth to light within six months.[256] The rule of law – albeit very permissive law – was generally upheld, despite some serious failures: 'The British did conduct their counter-insurgency operations according to the rule of law . . . they did establish limits beyond which they did not go. They ensured that . . . they did not follow Nazi policies . . . and practice genocide in their colonies.'[257] That is the main reason why it is misleading to liken the Kenyan detention camps to Nazi 'concentration camps' or to the Soviet 'gulag', or to call the Ruthagati home guard post 'Kenya's Belsen'.[258] The other supporting reason is that it is out of proportion: 'In the mid-1950s, the real [Soviet] Gulag contained more than 2.5 million enslaved prisoners, more than thirty times the number detained in Kenya, and much higher mortality rates. We need to make sure we have language left to denounce the worst evils of all.'[259]

IX

In our review of the six most infamous cases of British imperial military violence, we have found one case (the First Opium War) where the British government's decision to go to war was totally unjustified, and two (the Second Anglo-Boer War and the Benin expedition) where it was justified. In three cases, we found instances of the disproportionate and indiscriminate use of violence (the Indian Mutiny, Amritsar and the early months of the Kenya Emergency), and in a fourth (the Boer War) an instance of culpable negligence in the administration of 'camps of refuge'. However, in all of those cases, the imperial and colonial governments repudiated the abuse and resolved to stop it. In that sense, the culpable violence or negligence was not symptomatic of a consistent, characteristically racist, colonial 'logic'. It was not essential or systemic. Moreover, in not one of these cases is it appropriate to assimilate British wrongdoing to Nazi genocide.

On the contrary, it would leave a very unbalanced impression, if we were to end our consideration of British imperial violence without recalling that the empire was at its most violent in the two world wars, in 1914-18 upholding international order by opposing Germany's unprovoked aggression against Belgium and France,[260] and in 1939-45 upholding international order by opposing the expansionist aggression of Germany's atrociously racist Nazi regime against Poland and France and its Japanese ally's expansionist aggression against China, Australasia and India. Indeed, between May 1940 and June 1941, the British Empire was the *only* military force – with the exception of Greece – in the field against Hitler. The Second World War

witnessed a coordinated global effort . . . the like of which will never be seen again. Hundreds of years of British imperial history and tradition and the networks, infrastructure, contacts, and institutions that it had forged were called to life by a decision taken at the imperial centre in London. This sent a current running throughout the overseas power centres of Empire from Cairo to Colombo to Canberra, and they sprang to life alongside Britain and mobilized their respective regions for war. It was a breath-taking spectacle and remains so to this day.[261]

In late 1941, the Eighth Army in North Africa 'was the most ethnically varied army to assemble in modern history'.[262] Only a quarter of it was British, the rest was imperial, drawn from Australia, India, New Zealand, South Africa, Southern Rhodesia, Basutoland, Bechuanaland, Ceylon, Cyprus, the Gambia, the Gold Coast, Kenya, Mauritius, Nigeria, Palestine, Rodrigues, Sierra Leone, the Seychelles, Swaziland, Tanganyika and Uganda. Meanwhile in the East the Fourteenth Army was composed of Indians from every corner of the Raj, Gurkhas from Nepal, Kenyans, Nigerians, Rhodesians and Somalis, as well as men from Kent and Cumberland. By 1945, Indians and Africans comprised 90 per cent of the troops. Indeed, the African contribution (37,000) was on a scale similar to the British (63,000), when compared to the Indian (498,000).[263] By the summer of 1945 58 per cent of South East Asia Command's personnel were Indian and 25 per cent African.[264] India alone recruited 2,581,726 men into the British imperial armed forces – whereas only 43,000 fought for the Japanese and 3,000 for Hitler in 1945.[265]

All of these colonial recruits were volunteers – although some volunteering was more voluntary than others. When recruiting parties arrived in African villages, for example, tribal elders or chiefs would determine who was to sign up.[266] Nonetheless, one son of a minor chief who was the first to volunteer later testified: 'We felt we were British, that we were safe under British administration. If they had trouble elsewhere, we went.'[267] And in 1942, Kofi Busia, a prominent Gold Coast intellectual who later became the prime minister of independent Ghana, wrote: 'There is not much doubt as to what would happen to the African under a German regime. Did Hitler himself not write of the Negro that "It is an act of criminal insanity to train a being who was only born a semi-ape?" Hitler himself has thus raised the racial question which has contributed to the loyal support that the colonies have to Britain. It has made the war a racial war which is Africa's as well as Britain's.'[268]

As in Africa, so in India the motives for volunteering were various. Recruits 'joined for many reasons, ranging from altruism, familial loyalty, the lure of regimental glory in the context of India's long martial traditions – not forgetting the fact that "many men enjoy soldiering"

– to material need; it was a well-paying job after all'.[269] Nevertheless, all of 'those who joined the Indian armed forces after December 1941 made a personal choice to support the government in the war against Japan. In so doing they were rejecting the offer of a competing [imperial Japanese] model for India based on the racial essentialism, violence, and barbarism they were able to witness, by virtue of the Indian press, in neighbouring, Japanese-occupied China.'[270] They may not have been fighting to preserve the British as their rulers, but they were fighting to preserve what the British had built, so that Indians could come to rule it.[271]

As Keith Jeffery has observed, 'The nature of British imperialism, with its peace-time free press, civil rights, habeas corpus, the cultivation of elites, and promises – however vague – of ultimate self-government, paid enormous dividends during the war.'[272]

CONCLUSION

On the Colonial Past

I

'To attempt to judge an empire,' wrote Margery Perham in 1961, 'would be rather like approaching an elephant with a tape-measure.'[1] Yet she wrote that as a rebuke to 'the cult of anti-colonialism' of her day, which 'is generally expressed in something like a ritual condemnation of imperialism which seldom shows much discrimination as between past and present, between one imperialism and another, or between the different aspects of their role'.[2] The fact that she issued such a rebuke implied that she thought the judgement being made by anti-colonialists to be wrong, which in turn implied that she thought she could make a better one. Instead of indiscriminate condemnation, she sought to offer a discriminating judgement, as the title of her Reith Lectures – 'The Colonial Reckoning' – suggests.

I shall seek to do the same here in the conclusion of this book. As we have seen, the subject of British colonialism alone is not only as vast as an elephant, but rather less coherent. So the task of making an overall moral judgement about it presents a major challenge. Yet it is a challenge that I and others like me have to face. What forces the challenge upon us is the fact that so many have evidently rushed to judgement and condemn (British) colonialism as a whole for its racist, rapacious, exploitative, violent 'logic', talking of 'colonialism' and 'slavery' in the same breath as if they were identical. Those of us who dissent from this judgement are bound to come up with a better, more complicated, more discriminate one.

Let me begin by drawing up a tally of the evils of British colonialism – and by 'evils' here I mean not only culpable wrongdoing or injustice, but also unintended harms. In the account offered in this book we have met: brutal slavery; the epidemic spread of devastating disease; economic and social disruption; the unjust displacement of natives by settlers; failures of colonial government to prevent settler abuse and famine; elements of racial alienation and racist contempt; policies of needlessly wholesale cultural suppression; miscarriages of justice; instances of unjustifiable military aggression and the indiscriminate and disproportionate use of force; and the failure to admit native talent to the higher echelons of colonial government on terms of equality quickly enough to forestall the build-up of nationalist resentment. All these evils are lamentable, and where culpable, they merit moral condemnation. None of them, however, amounts to genocide in the proper sense of the concerted, intentional killing of all the members of a people, the paradigm of which was the Nazi policy of implementing a 'Final Solution' to the 'problem' of the Jews. In the history of the British Empire, there was nothing morally equivalent to Nazi concentration or death camps, or to the Soviet Gulag.

II

Still, some claim that the contemporary British – whether in the form of their state, particular institutions or particular families – should make reparation for their colonial evils, especially that of slavery. The principle that those who have benefited from an injustice should either repair the damage or compensate its victim is moral common sense. No one doubts, for example, that after the Second World War Germany's government should have restored stolen property to its Jewish owners or compensated them for its loss. In those circumstances, the identities of the Jewish wronged and the Nazi wrongdoers, and the relationship between original victims and surviving family members, were all clear enough. And the harm done was definite and quantifiable. In these circumstances, reparation and compensation made good sense.

The passage of time, however, muddies the waters. As the moral philosopher Onora O'Neill has written: 'claims to compensation have to show that continuing loss or harm resulted from past injury. This is all too often impossible where harms have been caused by ancient or distant wrongs . . . Is everybody who descends (in part) from those who were once enslaved or colonised still being harmed by those now ancient and distant misdeeds? Can we offer a clear enough account of the causation of current harms to tell where compensation is owed? Can we show who ought to do the compensating?'[3] The riotous jungle of history overgrows and obscures the causal pathways. In the case of British slavery, the victims themselves are, of course, all long dead and – short of God, an afterlife and a Final Judgement – lie forever beyond the reach of compensation. As for their twenty-first-century descendants, their present condition, while owing something to the enslavement of their ancestors, also owes much to events and choices in the almost two hundred years since emancipation. Can we be sure that they would have been better off had their ancestors remained in West Africa – some as slaves and sacrificial funeral fodder? Are there not some descendants of slaves who now prosper rather more than some descendants of slave-owners? Have not some of the latter used their tainted inheritance for charitable purposes, perhaps even anti-slavery endeavours? And what, exactly, would proportionate compensation for the historic sufferings of slavery look like?[4]

Besides, if the intention is to right grave historic wrongs, why should *slavery* be the sole focus? The plight of medieval serfs or early industrial workers dwelling in urban slums may have been better than that of slaves toiling in the West Indies, but not very much better.[5] Moreover, why should *British* slavery be the focus? If the historic injustice of slavery is to be rectified, then it needs to be done fairly and across the board. If the British are to be presented with a bill for compensation, then so should the descendants of the inland African chiefs who sold other Africans to the slave-traders, as well as the descendants of the Arab slave-traders who sold the slaves to the Europeans on the coast.[6] They all profited too. And the British themselves should seek compensation from the descendants of the Barbary corsairs, who raided Cornwall in the 1600s and carted off whole villages into slavery on the

Mediterranean coast of North Africa. If the British, then the Americans, too, since, in its early years, the United States spent a fifth of its entire national budget in tribute to the pirate states of Algiers and Tripoli, in order to stop their raids on its ships and enslavement of their crews. Yesterday's oppressors were often the day before yesterday's victims. In a letter published in *The Times* some years ago, a former British diplomat recounted a conversation he had had shortly after Nigeria's independence with one of the country's new rulers. The ruler was pressing the case for Britain to compensate the Nigerians for decades of colonial oppression. After listening intently, the diplomat's turn to reply came. 'I entirely agree,' he said. 'And you shall have your compensation – just as soon as we get ours from the Romans.'[7]

III

These issues hardly make an appearance in Hilary McD. Beckles' case in *Britain's Black Debt: Reparations for Caribbean Slavery and Native Genocide*, which presents itself on the back cover as 'the first scholarly work that looks comprehensively at the reparations discussion in the Caribbean'.[8] Beckles' general view of British colonialism is expressed in his description of it as a 'criminal enrichment project'[9] and of its 'known features' as 'its terrorism of adults and ruthless exploitation of children; its maddening material poverty; and the racial brutality it bred within the prison known as the plantation'.[10] He claims that '[f]rom the West Indies, the British exported the financially successful model of African enslavement to the rest of the colonized world', and he refers to Queen Elizabeth II's apology in 1995 for 'the genocidal activities committed by the British' in New Zealand.[11] This description of British colonialism will seem wildly distorted to anyone who finds the account given in this book generally plausible. One symptom of Beckles' politically charged inaccuracy is that the royal apology he referred to was for the punitive confiscation of Māori lands in 1865, which, however wrong, was hardly genocide.

Against the claim that Africans themselves were deeply implicated in the slave trade, Beckles argues that they never reduced 'subordinate workers, political prisoners and others subject to criminal punishment' to the legal status of 'non-humans, perpetual property and reproductive chattels';[12] that this 'is the classic divide-and-rule defence in which victims are blamed for their victimization'; that '[t]he majority of African leaders over time opposed the slave trade' and '[f]or this they were destabilised and destroyed';[13] and that African chiefs were forced to raid for slaves under pain of attack and enslavement themselves.[14]

In response, I observe that the West African custom of burying 'servants' alive with their deceased master does rather imply a view of them as violently disposable property; that to blame African slave-traders is not to blame African slaves; that there are no historical grounds for the claim that African chiefs generally opposed the slave trade; and that, while it is possible that some chiefs felt themselves compelled by Europeans to raid for slaves, many of them were engaged in slave-raiding and trading for centuries before Europeans arrived on the scene.[15] The fact that, faced with the claim of African complicity, some West African states have withdrawn their support for the 'reparations movement' might be because of their recognition of the truth rather than because of Western intimidation, as Beckles speculates.[16]

On the issue of the extent to which Britain's wealth and power was built on the slave trade and slavery, Beckles is unequivocal: 'It is important for British society to acknowledge that its development as a nation-state, the transformation of its economy to sustainable industrialization, and its global standing as a super-power among nations were founded upon a crime against humanity in the form of racial chattel enslavement of African bodies and the global trafficking of these bodies for three hundred years.'[17] In adopting this view, he declares himself 'particularly indebted to Eric Williams, whose scholarship underpins much of this work'.[18] He is aware that Williams' thesis in *Capitalism and Slavery* has been criticised: 'Conservative . . . economic historians launched a crusade against it. In most cases . . . there were layers of ideology, distinctly Eurocentric and sometimes with racial undertones.'[19] Nevertheless, he argues that 'its continued capacity to stimulate further research speaks to its essential correctness'.[20] In defence of his position he invokes Robin Blackburn, former editor of the *New Left Review* and author of *The Making of New World Slavery: From the Baroque to the Modern, 1492–1800*, and indirectly through him the Marxist tradition of British historiography, with its leading lights, Eric Hobsbawm and Christopher Hill.[21] Such British scholars, steeped in the study of labour history and 'with a deep intellectual commitment to social justice', he tells us, have tended to treat the issues raised by Williams 'more fairly'. Knowing the tendency for capital to subject labour to a basic subsistence level, they have recognised the importance of African enslavement to the rise of industrial capitalism in general.[22] In addition to Marxist historians, Beckles also enlists some critics of Williams. The 'ardent critic' David Richardson, he argues, nonetheless 'essentially agreed with the fundamental correctness of Williams' research', when he wrote (in 1987) that 'Caribbean-based demands may have accounted for 12 per cent of the growth of English industrial output in the quarter century before 1776 . . . Although West Indian and related trades provided a more modest stimulus to the growth of British industrial production than Williams imagined, they nevertheless played a more prominent part in fostering industrial changes and export growth in Britain during the third quarter of the eighteenth century than most historians have assumed.'[23] And summarising Kenneth Morgan's position, Beckles writes, 'For Morgan, the slavery system was not the cause of British development. It was a "stimulus". Williams would not have disagreed.'[24]

Beckles' argument here is riddled with problems. First, he does not engage with the 'conservative' economic historians who disagreed with Williams – indeed, he does not even name them. Instead, he summarily dismisses their views as distorted by political 'ideology' (unlike his own) and by racism.

Second, the works of recognised experts on transatlantic slavery such as David Eltis, Seymour Drescher and David Brion Davis appear in his bibliography but receive no mention at all in the text. (It was Davis who declared of Williams' thesis in 2010 that it 'has now been wholly discredited by other scholars'.)[25]

Third, Beckles identifies himself with a Marxist-Leninist reading of colonial economics which, as we saw in Chapter 6, has not fared well when brought into contact with the historical data.[26]

Fourth, his claim that Richardson and Morgan end up confirming Williams' thesis is just not true. That thesis was not that the profits from the slave trade were merely an economic stimulus – no one denies that – but that they made 'an *enormous* contribution to Britain's industrial development' (the emphasis is mine).[27] That is Beckles' position, too: Britain's wealth and power were '*founded* upon a crime against humanity' (the emphasis is mine). In contrast, Richardson judges the contribution of the slave trade and slavery to be 'more modest' – 12 per cent is significant, but hardly enormous. And Morgan reckons that it would be 'incorrect' to claim that the profits from the trade were 'a major stimulus for industrialization in Britain', but rather that they played 'a significant, though not decisive part' in its evolution.[28]

Fifth and finally, Beckles is completely oblivious to the century and a half of costly British imperial endeavour in suppressing the slave trade and the institution of slavery worldwide.

IV

Notwithstanding the implausibility of Beckles' case, I do not mean to say that there are no colonial cases closely analogous to that of the Nazi theft of Jewish property, that is to say, where it is clear that a just law or treaty was broken, what right was violated, who held the right, who are the descendants of the right-holder and who should make good the loss. In such cases, reparation or compensation would make sense. However, many – perhaps most – cases where native peoples now assert historic rights to land allegedly stolen from their ancestors are not of that kind. The rights they assert are not legal, but moral. They cannot be legal, because when Europeans first arrived on the natives' shores, there was no international law that fixed what the native peoples held, and what the migrants could claim, by legal right. However, to talk of non-conventional, natural, moral rights misleads, because the very concept of a right – being originally legal – implies a fixity that does not exist.[29] Therefore, we should jettison talk of 'rights' in such cases, and talk of 'justice' instead. But justice varies according to circumstances. What is just in an abundant environment with a small population is not just in the same environment with a large population or depleted resources: 'entitlements are sensitive to circumstances' and the very same act of snatching that is unjust in one set of circumstances may not be unjust in another.[30]

What this means is that, even if there was an injustice done in the past, reversing it may not achieve justice in the present. For example, the historic theft of land meant a gravity of loss to my ancestor in 1800 that it cannot mean for me in 2020, now that I am supported by a welfare state.[31] Similarly, even if you now sit on the land stolen from my ancestor, simply returning it to me would do you an injustice, insofar as you have built a life and an economy on it and are not culpable for the original wrong. '[T]here have been huge changes since North America and Australasia were settled by white colonists,' writes the legal philosopher Jeremy Waldron. 'The population has increased manyfold, and most of the descendants of the colonists, unlike their ancestors, have nowhere else to go . . . the changes that have taken place over the past two hundred years mean that the costs of respecting primeval entitlements are much greater now than they were in 1800'.[32] Besides, trying to respect alleged primeval entitlements by rolling time backwards and restoring aboriginal land and self-government does not always benefit the natives. Some in Canada argue that such a policy continues to 'keep natives isolated and dependent, thus perpetuating existing social pathologies . . . [and] has resulted in a large amount of corruption where powerful families siphon off most of the resources while the majority remain mired in poverty and social dysfunction. Privileged leaders live in luxury and are paid huge salaries, while most aboriginal people rely on social assistance.'[33]

In the face of these intractable complications Waldron concludes that our focus should lie on addressing present injustices rather than trying to untangle historic injustices: 'it is the impulse to justice now that should lead the way . . . not the reparation of something whose wrongness is understood primarily in relation to conditions that no longer obtain. Entitlements . . . fade with time, counterfactuals . . . are impossible to verify, injustices . . . are overtaken by circumstances'.[34] Onora O'Neill agrees with him: 'Compensation is required for present harm caused by past wrongdoing, not simply for current disadvantage *however caused*. Unless we can trace the causal pathways, we cannot tell who has gained from ancestral wrongdoing, and should now shoulder the costs of compensating those whose present disadvantage was caused by past wrongdoing. It may therefore make more sense . . . to argue for a distributive – or redistributive – account of aspects of justice, which seeks action to redress present disadvantage, *whatever its origins*.'[35]

V

Whatever the debit column of British colonialism, there is a credit column, too, of which any fair ethical assessment must take account. There are plenty of natives who would nod in agreement with that claim. Four years after India had gained its independence, Nirad Chaudhuri prefaced *The Autobiography of an Unknown Indian* (1951) with this: 'Dedicated to the Memory of the British Empire in India which conferred subjecthood on us but withheld citizenship; to which yet every one of us threw out the challenge: "Civis Britannicus Sum" because all that was good and living within us was made, shaped, and quickened by the same British rule.'[36] Even though Chaudhuri mixed his admiration with sharp criticism, it lost him his job as a political commentator with All India Radio. Half a century later, a represent-ative of a more self-confident India could afford to be less touchy. In July 2005 the then prime minister of India, Manmohan Singh, was awarded an honorary degree by the University of Oxford. Upon receiving it, he said that, notwithstanding legitimate economic griev-ances,

India's experience with Britain had its beneficial consequences too. Our notions of the rule of law, of a Constitutional government, of a free press, of a professional civil service, of modern universities and research laboratories have all been fashioned in the crucible where an age-old civilization of India met the dominant Empire of the day. These are all elements which we still value and cherish. Our judiciary, our legal system, our bureaucracy and our police are all great institutions, derived from British-Indian administration and they have served our country exceedingly well. The idea of India as enshrined in our Constitution, with its emphasis on the principles of secularism, democracy, the rule of law and, above all, the equality of all human beings irrespective of caste, community, language or ethnicity, has deep roots in India's ancient culture and civilization. However, it is undeniable that the founding fathers of our Republic were also greatly influenced by the ideas associated with the age of enlightenment in Europe. Our Constitution remains a testimony to the enduring interplay between what is essentially Indian and what is very British in our intellectual heritage.[37]

More broadly, the credit column in the British imperial ledger contains the following items. If the empire initially presided over the slave trade and slavery, it renounced both in the name of basic human equality and then led endeavours to suppress them worldwide for a hundred and fifty years.[38] The empire also: moderated the disruptive impact of Western modernity upon very unmodern societies; promoted a worldwide free market that gave native producers and entrepreneurs new economic opportunities; created regional peace by imposing an overarching imperial authority on multiple, warring peoples;[39] perforce involved representatives of native peoples in the lower levels of government; sought to relieve the plight of the rural poor and protect them against rapacious landlords; provided a civil service and judiciary that was generally and extraordinarily incorrupt; developed public infrastructure, albeit usually through private investment; made foreign investment attractive by reducing the risks through establishing political stability and the rule of law; disseminated modern agricultural methods and medicine; stood against German aggression – first militarist, then Nazi – and for international law and order in the two world wars, helping to save both the Western and the non-Western world for liberal democracy; brought up three of the most prosperous and liberal states now on earth – Canada, Australia and New Zealand; gave birth to two more – the United States and Israel; evolved into a loose, consensual, multiracial international organisation, the (British) Commonwealth of Nations, which some states that never belonged to the British Empire have opted to join – Mozambique (1995) and Rwanda (2009); inspired by the ideal of the Commonwealth, helped to plan and realise first the League of Nations and then the United

Nations;[40] through the Commonwealth applied moral pressure to South Africa to abandon its policy of *apartheid*;[41] through the wartime anti-fascist alliance of 1939–45, evolved into an important part of the post-war Western alliance against Soviet and Chinese communism; and still has a significant afterlife in the Western military alliance of NATO, the intelligence alliance of the 'Five Eyes',[42] and influential economic development agencies such as the UK's British International Investment and Department for International Development.[43]

So the British Empire did good as well as evil. But did it do *more* good than evil? Several of those who advocate reparations for colonial evils think that it did more evil than good – but they assume so, without arguing their case.[44] They do not argue their case, I surmise, because they are uneasily aware that it cannot be easily argued. Nor can the counter-case. This is because the goods and evils that the empire caused, intentionally or not, are of such different kinds that they cannot be measured against one another. They are incommensurable. How much chalk is worth so much cheese? How much racism is worth so much immunisation against disease? How many unjustly killed people are worth the blessings of imperially imposed peace? How much humanitarian anti-slavery would make up for the evils of slavery? To ask these questions is immediately to expose their absurdity. Such varied good and evils cannot be sensibly reduced to a common currency and then weighed against each other, so that we can conclude that one set was more evil than another. Here, as often elsewhere, a utilitarian calculation cannot be conducted rationally.[45]

Given that *all* kinds of human rule produce a mixture of good and evil – even the Nazis built autobahns in Germany and the Fascists made the trains run on time in Italy – does it follow, therefore, that the moral difference between them is only a matter of degree, and that we cannot judge any of them to be, all things considered, wrong? No, it does not. We can try to discern central values or principles that were consistently expressed and concordant goals that were earnestly pursued and realised, more or less. If these values, principles and goals were gravely evil and immoral, we can then say that the rule was *systemically* unjust. And if it was not systemically unjust, then we can say that it was systemically just, whether more or less. The most obvious candidate for a systemically unjust regime is that of the Nazis in Germany in the 1930s and 1940s. Dominated by the mind of one man, its view of the world was violently racist and its aggressive, expansionist nationalism unburdened by moral scruple. The death factories devoted to 'processing' millions of Jews in the midst of the exigencies of war were not incidental to the regime; they expressed its resolute, crazed heart. It is no accident that the contemporary enemies of European and, especially, British colonialism try to assimilate or identify it with Nazism. For then we can all be sure that it was basically, essentially evil – notwithstanding all the colonial building of bridges and railways. Hence the claims of colonial 'genocide' in 1820s Tasmania and 1890s Matabeleland, of racist callousness towards starving natives on the western plains of Canada in the 1880s, of 'crimes against humanity' in Benin in 1897, and of 'concentration camps' in South Africa in the 1900s and Kenya in the 1950s. Moving in the same direction, if more subtly, are those historians who write of the racist or violent 'logic' of British colonialism, implying that racism and racist violence consistently characterised its central, driving force.[46]

However, as my moral analysis of the British Empire has shown, it is entirely inappropriate to liken it to Nazism. Nor was it *essentially* racist or disproportionately violent. Nor, with due respect to Marxist critics, was it *essentially* exploitative. From the early decades of the nineteenth century its natural, innocent concerns to promote trade and maintain strategic advantage were increasingly supplemented and tempered by Christian humanitarianism, a commitment to public service and a liberal vision of political life. As Margery Perham wrote with regard to Africa:

> No record can ever be made of all that was done, good, bad and indifferent, by Britain in her dozen or more African territories during the brief years of her tenure. The mosaic is too vast for its pattern to be seen at one time or from one viewpoint, and we are always brought back to the question of standards by which to judge Britain's record. There can be no doubt that, if the standard is to be the interests of the ruled, these have steadily counted for more as the period of empire continued. The existence of informed liberal opinion, the publicity of

debate, the use of commissions of inquiry to probe every serious problem and grave event, all helped to this end. The African colonies, as the latest acquisitions, have greatly benefited from this progression in virtue.[47]

Perham's point about the important role played by liberal traditions and institutions of free speech and political criticism was amplified by Lewis Gann and Peter Duignan, when they observed that the imperial system in general had 'a built-in capacity for self-criticism': 'Future historians will necessarily draw on the material accumulated by . . . commissions of inquiry, parliamentary debates, metropolitan blue books, and similar records which formed part of a self-corrective mechanism of a type unknown to earlier Matabele, Somali, or Arab conquerors; they played an important part in putting a stop to imperial abuses.'[48]

Also included in the liberal political vision was the good of self-government. As we have seen, all three Scottish governors of Calcutta, Bombay and Madras around 1820 recognised that British rule in India could not be permanent and should aim to enable the natives to govern themselves decently and then withdraw with a good grace. One of them, Sir John Malcolm, wrote in 1823: 'Let us, therefore, calmly proceed on a course of gradual improvement: and when our rule ceases, for cease it must (though probably at a remote period), as the natural consequence of our success in the diffusion of knowledge, we shall as a nation have the proud boast that we have preferred the civilisation to the continued subjection of India.'[49] By 1930 Canada, South Africa, Australia and New Zealand had become effectively self-governing. From 1919 the British were committed by the Government of India Act to widen Indian participation in government *en route* to the same political autonomy. This arrived in 1947 more abruptly and violently than was desirable, and it came to African colonies in the 1960s too quickly in the expert eyes of Perham. But she – and others like her – recognised that, once nationalism had taken hold among the natives, it could not long be resisted: 'once Africans had been fully stirred in racial self-consciousness and political aware-ness, prematurely though this may be in their own interests, there was little more that foreign rulers could do for them'.[50]

This was so mainly because colonial rule could not survive – as it could never have survived – without the widespread cooperation of natives. No doubt in some cases, this was elicited by fear. But fear is a motive in any society, where the threat of coercion that lies behind the law induces compliance, and not every such threat is unjustified. Besides, fear was certainly not the only motive for native cooperation – as is made clear by the testimonies of Charles Big Canoe and James Ashquabe in Canada, Babo of Karo and Chinua Achebe in Nigeria, Kofi Busia in the Gold Coast, Da'ud 'Abd al-Latif in the Sudan, Ahmad Lutfi al-Sayyid in Egypt, King Faisal in Iraq, Ram Mohan Roy and the Punjabi peasants who spoke to Charles Westwater in India, and Sun Yat-sen in Hong Kong. Recognising the good that colonial government did, native peoples often found it to be not only sufficiently legitimate, but the best available, even admirable and to be emulated. So, in the 1950s and 1960s several million Chinese voted with their feet, fled the lawless mainland and found refuge in the colony of Hong Kong.[51] Even now there are many Chinese in Hong Kong who, if given the choice, would prefer life in a gradually democratising, liberal, law-governed British colony to life under the arbitrary, repressive thumb of the Chinese regime in Beijing.[52]

EPILOGUE

On Anti-colonialism and the British Future

I

Not all contemporary anti-colonialists are propelled by humanitarian motives. The Chinese Communist Party, for example, likes to beat the drum about China's 'hundred years of humiliation' at the hands of Western powers, especially the British Empire, in order to excite nationalist feeling at home and manipulate liberal guilt abroad in the service of a rudely aggressive foreign policy. In contrast, anti-colonialists in today's West – whether post-colonialist academics or 'decolonising' activists – are apparently motivated by righteous anger at the demeaning and oppressive racism that, they believe, structures Western societies because of the toxic legacy of their colonial past.[1]

Whether that belief is accurate, however, is a moot point. For example, a 2018 report of the European Union Agency for Fundamental Rights found that the prevalence of racist harassment as perceived by people of African descent was lower in the UK than in any other EU country except Malta, and the prevalence of overall racial discrimination was the lowest in the UK bar none.[2] Moreover, the report of the UK government's Commission on Race and Ethnic Disparities, which was published in March 2021, argued that contemporary Britain is not in fact structurally racist.[3] However, whatever the truth about racism in today's Britain, this book shows that its roots do not lie in her colonial history. Notwithstanding the early period of degrading slavery and later elements of appalling racial prejudice, the British Empire was not essentially racist. It repudiated slavery in the name of a Christian vision of basic human equality, and from 1807 during the second half of its existence, it was centrally committed to emancipating slaves from the West Indies and Brazil, across Africa, to India and Australasia. As we have heard, when Frederick Douglass visited Britain from 1845 to 1847, he found 'a perfect absence' of the racial hatred that had pursued him in the United States. In the Second World War, the empire exhausted itself in opposing the murderously racist Nazi regime, against which, from May 1940 to June 1941, it was the only military power in the field (apart from Greece). And when, during that war the US Army arrived in Britain and asked the native British to accommodate its policy of racial segregation, local people indignantly refused and the secretary of state for the colonies vigorously objected.[4]

Anti-colonialists cannot be blamed for condemning racism, along with economic exploitation and wanton violence. But they can be blamed for letting their condemnations run out ahead of the data. Time and time again in this book, we have seen historians and others overegging the sins of British colonialism – whether Hilary Beckles on slavery; James Daschuk and the Truth and Reconciliation Commission of Canada on late-nineteenth-century and early twentieth-century Canada; Dan Hicks on 1897 Benin; Adekeye Adebajo on Rhodes in 1890s South Africa; Thomas Pakenham on the Second Anglo-Boer War; David Anderson and (far more so) Caroline Elkins on 1950s Kenya; William Dalrymple, Madhusree Mukerjee, Rudrangshu Mukherjee, Shashi Tharoor and Kim Wagner on the British Raj in India; Robert Hughes, Henry Reynolds (somewhat) and Lyndall Ryan on 1840s Tasmania; and the CWGC's Special Committee and David Olusoga on the imperial commemoration of the war dead worldwide after 1918.

As to why the condemnations have exceeded the evidence – as to their propelling motives – we can only speculate.[5] There is no doubt that, in some cases, material political interests have been active: Hilary Beckles' book, for example, is an argument for reparations. In other cases, mundane professional interests may have played a part. Like most other people, typical academics just want to get on in life, and, having no special endowment of moral courage, they are not extraordinarily inclined to suffer the costs of dissidence. So, observing that anti-colonialism is fashionable, opening doors to posts, promotions and grants, many academics will be content to go with the flow, signalling their subscription to the correct assumptions. Yet the intemperate, *ad personam* hostility that many anti-colonialists are wont to show dissenters suggests deeper, sometimes darker springs.[6]

II

There are, of course, the familiar human pleasures of crusading, of knowing that one is in the right, of occupying the moral high ground and casting the wicked down it. But the dangers of crusading are also familiar: the ugly arrogance of self-righteousness, impervious to correction and productive of high-handed abuse, even atrocity. Anti-colonialists readily recognise this in colonialists, but not in themselves. Sin always lies *over there*.

One reason for this attitude lies in the idea that the views and feelings of the oppressed – and of those who presume to take up their cause – are the first and last word, the final authority. They speak a truth that cannot be gainsaid. A seminal expression of this appears in a classic post-colonial text, Frantz Fanon's *The Wretched of the Earth*. Born in Martinique in 1925, Fanon had studied medicine in France, specialising in psychiatry, and was working in a hospital in Algeria when the nationalist uprising against the French erupted in 1954. The following year he himself joined the anti-colonial rebels. Not long afterwards, however, he was diagnosed with leukaemia and, having travelled to Bethesda, Maryland for medical treatment, died there in 1961. Shortly before his death he dictated and published *Les damnées de la terre* ('The Wretched of the Earth'), for which Jean-Paul Sartre wrote a preface and which went on to make a deep impression on the leadership of the Black Power movement in the US.[7] In one passage, Fanon asserts the view that the nationalist revolutionaries are the privileged possessors of the truth:

> . . . the community triumphs, and . . . it spreads its own light and its
> own reason . . . truth is the property of the national cause . . . The

native replies to the living lie of the colonial situation by an equal falsehood . . . Truth is that which hurries on the break-up of the colonialist regime; it is that which promotes the emergence of the nation; it is also all that protects the natives, and ruins the foreigners. In this colonialist context there is no truthful behaviour: and the good is quite simply that which is evil for 'them'. Thus we see the primary Manichaeism which governed colonial society is preserved intact during the period of decolonization; that is to say that the settler never ceases to be the enemy, the opponent, the foe that must be overthrown.[8]

As the needs of revolutionary liberation determine the 'truth', so black vitality throws off the shackles of European reason:

The concept of Negro-ism [négritude] . . . was the emotional if not the logical antithesis of that insult which the white man flung at humanity . . . The unconditional affirmation of African culture has succeeded the unconditional affirmation of European culture. On the whole, the poets of Negro-ism oppose the idea of old Europe to a young Africa, tiresome reasoning to lyricism, oppressive logic to high-stepping nature, and on the one side stiffness, ceremony, etiquette and scepticism, while on the other frankness, liveliness, liberty and – why not? – luxuriance; but also irresponsibility . . . In order to ensure his salvation and to escape from the supremacy of the white man's culture the native feels the need to turn backwards towards his unknown roots and to lose himself at whatever cost in his own barbarous people.[9]

Whatever its merits in restoring the self-respect of the colonised, this view amounts to a dogmatic revolutionary authoritarianism that dismisses contradictory reasons as reactionary rationalisations. And the cost, in the end, can be very high indeed – an illiberal totalitarianism that is incapable of self-correction and results in the likes of Stalin's purges of 1936–8, Mao's Cultural Revolution of 1966–76 and Pol Pot's 'killing fields' of 1975–9.

Fanon's own work displays a causal connection between revolutionary self-righteousness and the cavalier treatment of historical evidence. For alongside his assertion that truth is whatever serves the revolution, we find generalisations about European colonialism that owe more to ideological axioms than to a disciplined observation of historical data. Thus, he claims that European wealth 'has been founded on slavery, it has been nourished with the blood of slaves and it comes directly from the soil and from the subsoil of that under-developed world'.[10] Yet our discussion of Eric Williams' thesis in Chapter 2 has shown that this is very probably untrue. Next, Fanon writes that '[t]he colonial regime owes its legitimacy to force . . . And when in laying down precise methods the settler asks each member of the oppressing minority to shoot down thirty or 100 or 200 natives, he sees that nobody shows any indignation that the whole problem is to decide whether it can be done all at once or by stages'.[11] Yet our discussion of colonial government in Chapter 7 made clear that its legitimacy also usually rested on native cooperation, by no means all of it coerced. And our discussion of settler violence in Chapter 5 showed that not even in Tasmania were settlers generally disposed to exterminate the aboriginals. Regarding the Mau Mau uprising in Kenya, Fanon talks of 'the 200,000 victims of the repression'.[12] It is not clear that by 'victims' here, he means fatalities. But since the two other cases he mentions in the same sentence do concern fatalities – 'the 45,000 dead at Sétif . . . the 90,000 dead in Madagascar' – the impression lingers that the Kenyan victims were also killed. In fact, those killed by the security forces in the emergency numbered somewhere between 11,500 and 20,000 – that is, between 5.75 and 10 per cent of Fanon's figure. Finally, he claims that colonialism, which 'turns to the past of the oppressed people, and distorts, disfigures and destroys it', resulted in 'cultural obliteration'.[13] Yet in Chapter 3 we observed that, in the case of India and Java, ancient Hindu culture was rescued from oblivion, not obliterated, by British Orientalists.

The lack of historical scrupulousness can reasonably be attributed to the ideas that 'truth' is whatever the anti-colonialist revolution requires and that revolutionary vitality should be preferred to bour-geois reason. For those ideas make history no longer an authority that constrains what may be claimed, but merely an armoury to be ransacked in the interest of rhetorical advantage. Such an attitude has certainly been visible among the supporters of Rhodes Must Fall in particular and of 'decolonisation' in general. Symptoms have also appeared among some of the historians we have encountered. The problem with it is that it renders entirely unaccountable the revolutionary's assumptions and choice of means, placing them safely beyond criticism. The problem is that it is authoritarian.[14]

The influence of authoritarian ideas like Frantz Fanon's goes some way towards explaining the tendency of many anti-colonialists to treat historical data as political ammunition rather than intellectual constraints, and to propel the indictment of colonialism well beyond the evidence. Certainly, moral-political dogmatism is characteristic of the discipline – if 'discipline' is the apt word – of post-colonial studies. In his Introduction to the *Oxford Handbook* on the subject, Graham Huggan describes it as 'a committed mode of . . . knowledge . . . that dedicates itself to the service of human freedom in the context of a world historically conditioned by colonial relations of power'.[15] Yet the typical labourer in the post-colonial fields is neither a philosopher equipped to interrogate concepts such as 'freedom' and 'power', nor an ethicist equipped to evaluate them morally, nor an historian equipped to enter sympathetically into the strange world of the past.[16] Usually, the post-colonialist is a scholar of literature, who has taken her bearings wholesale from postmodern theorists, for whom the injustice of 'colonialism' is axiomatic.[17] As Huggan says, 'the colonizer versus the colonized' is 'the field's formative binary'.[18] It should not surprise, then, to find Stephen Howe reporting that 'most contemporary historians of empire . . . have tended to identify . . . postcolonial cultural theories . . . with an alleged disregard for historical specificity and precision'. Then, he comments: 'There was, it must be recognized, considerable warrant for such charges in the work of some of the key early postcolonialists . . . Too often, a handful of isolated colonial texts or incidents served as rather perfunctory prefaces to far-reaching declarations about a generalized "colonial situation". Three of the essential keywords of historical and social-scientific discourse seemed disconcertingly absent: "evidence", "context", and "explanation".'[19] In the light of what we have seen in this book, what Howe reports of some early post-colonialist leaders remains true of many of their followers today.

III

In addition to authoritarian ideas and dogmatic assumptions, another factor is propelling the anti-colonialists' over-reach. Many of those who indict the European or British colonial pasts are themselves European or British. To condemn one's own people might be right, but it ought also to be painful. One surely would not choose to do it, unless one felt it necessary. And yet exaggeration of colonialism's sins is often not at all reluctant, but wilful, even gleeful. Far from being resisted, it is embraced. The anti-colonialists *want* the worst to be true, and so they meet any suggestion to the contrary not with the eyes of curiosity, but the fist of aggression. But why? What is going on here, psychologically, even spiritually?

One plausible candidate is the operation of a degenerate Christian sensibility. For Christians, the paradoxical mark of the genuinely right-eous person is a profound awareness of their own unrighteousness. The saint is distinguished as the one who knows more deeply than others just what a sinner he really is. There is considerable virtue in this, of course, for it tempers self-righteousness with compassion for fellow sinners, forbidding the righteous to cast the unrighteous beyond the human pale. Yet, like all virtue, it is vulnerable to vice. For it can degenerate from genuine humility into a perverse bid for supreme self-righteousness, which exaggerates one's sins and broadcasts the display of repentance: holier-than-thou because more-sinful-than-thou. The Jesuit-educated French philosopher Pascal Bruckner captures this when he writes of contemporary, post-imperial Europe:

> This is the paternalism of the guilty conscience: seeing ourselves as the kings of infamy is still a way of staying on the crest of history. Since Freud we know that masochism is only a reversed sadism, a passion for domination turned against oneself. Europe is still messianic in a minor key . . . Barbarity is Europe's great pride, which it acknowledges only in itself; it denies that others are barbarous, finding attenuating circumstances for them (which is a way of denying them all responsi-bility).[20]

There is a self-obsessive quality to this attitude. While the rhetoric claims the mantle of the oppressed, the action ignores them. Thus highly privileged students and professors gather on the streets of Oxford to clamour for the downfall of the statue of a British imperialist who died in Cape Town well over a century ago. Meanwhile in today's South Africa the African National Congress loots the state, triples unemployment, sharpens economic inequality and riots when its leader is sentenced to gaol for refusing to answer charges of corruption.[21] And the Oxford protesters are silent. They fiddle in Oxford, while Africa burns. Bruckner captures this point, too:

> [B]y erecting lack of love for oneself into a leading principle, we lie to ourselves about ourselves and close ourselves to others . . . In Western self-hatred, the Other has no place. It is a narcissistic relationship in which the African, the Indian, and Arab are brought in as extras.[22]

Remember Dan Hicks' account of Benin: the wicked white colonialist fills the centre-stage, entirely obscuring black agency.[23] And the white post-colonialist gets to play champion of the oppressed.

IV

Anti-colonialism is not a reliable guide to Britain's colonial past, and it encourages us to draw the wrong lessons for the future. If it were true that the record of Britain's three-hundred-year career of using its imperial power to shape the world were a simple litany of oppression and atrocity, or one where its good effects were accidental to an essentially racist, exploitative and wantonly violent imperial project, then contemporary Britons would be justified in repudiating any lingering ambition to promote 'Western values' around the world, in jettisoning their expensive capability for projecting military force overseas, in forbearing from criticism of how others choose to conduct their political affairs and in doing penance for their manifold colonial sins. If the anti-colonialist narrative were true, Britain should abandon its post-1945 role as a main supporter of the US-dominated liberal world order and settle down instead to emulating penitent, virtually pacifist

Germany.[24] But, as this book has shown, the anti-colonialist narrative is not true.

Yes, the British Empire contained evils and injustices, some of them very grave and some of them culpable – but so does the history of any long-standing state. It was not essentially racist, exploitative or wantonly violent. It showed itself capable of correcting its sins and errors, and of learning from them. And, over time, it became increasingly motivated by Christian humanitarianism and intent upon preparing colonised peoples for liberal self-government. Indeed, ironically, much of what anti-colonialists clamour for from their academic armchairs, colonial officials were often hard at work trying to build. So if colonial history gives those who of us who identify ourselves with Britain cause for lament and shame, it also gives us cause for admiration and pride.

This is not a case of what anti-colonialists condescendingly dismiss as 'imperial nostalgia'.[25] Let me be clear: Britain's imperial moment has passed, once and for all. The conditions that occasioned it will not recur again, for good and for ill. So this is not about nostalgia. Rather, it is about discriminate identification with liberal, humanitarian principles and endeavours of the colonial past that deserve to be admired, owned and carried into the future. And it is about not letting what Elie Kedourie called 'the canker of imaginary guilt' cripple the self-confidence of the British – together with Canadians, Australians and New Zealanders – in their role as important pillars of the liberal international order.[26]

Notes

ACKNOWLEDGEMENTS

1   Gilley recounts the story that culminated in the ultimate cancellation of his article by the *Third World Quarterly* in 'How the Hate Mob Tried to Silence Me', *Standpoint*, December 2017/ January 2018: How the hate mob tried to silence me (pdx.edu). Nonetheless, 'The Case for Colonialism' can be found here: http://www.web.pdx.edu/~gilleyb/2_The%20case%20for%20coloni-alism_at2Oct2017.pdf. Subsequently, in October 2020, the Rowman & Littlefield Publishing Group cancelled the publication of Gilley's biography of Sir Alan Burns, together with his book series 'Problems of Anti-Colonialism' as he recounts here: An Academic Responds to his Cancellers.pdf (pdx.edu). Happily, Regnery Gateway had the courage to publish *The Last Imperialist: Sir Alan Burns' Epic Defense of the British Empire* in September 2021. The book series, however, remains on the shelf. In the spring of 2022 Gilley published 'The Case for Colonialism: A Response to My Critics' in *Academic Questions*: https://www.nas.org/academic-questions/35/1/the-case-for-colonialism-a-response-to-my-critics

INTRODUCTION

1   Nigel Biggar, 'Message to Students: Rhodes Was No Racist', *The Times,* 22 December 2015; 'Rhodes, Race, and the Abuse of History', *Standpoint*, March 2016.

2   Nigel Biggar, 'Don't Feel Guilty about Our Colonial History', *The Times*, 30 November 2017. This refers to Bruce Gilley, 'The Case for Colonialism', *Third World Quarterly* (September 2017) and draws from Gilley, 'Chinua Achebe on the Positive Legacies of Colonialism', *African Affairs*, 115/461 (October 2016).

3   See the website of the McDonald Centre for Theology, Ethics and Public Life: https://www.mcdonaldcentre.org.uk/ethics-and-empire.

4   The eminent imperial historian John Darwin, who designed the 'Ethics and Empire' project with me, has written that a 'propensity in human communities has been the accumulation of power on an extensive scale: the building of empires. Indeed, the difficulty of forming autonomous states on an ethnic basis,

against the gravitational pull of cultural or economic attraction (as well as disparities of military force), has been so great that empire (where different ethnic communities fall under a common ruler) has been the default mode of political organization throughout most of history. Imperial power has usually been the rule of the road' (*After Tamerlane: The Global History of Empire since 1405* [London: Allen Lane, 2007], p. 23). Krishan Kumar, who now helps to direct the 'Ethics and Empire' project, not only views empire as a fact of global political life, but thinks that there can be much to be said in its favour. Of his book, *Visions of Empire: How Five Imperial Regimes Shaped the World* (Princeton and Oxford: Princeton University Press, 2017), he writes: 'There are plenty of works lambasting empires, ferociously portraying their dark and often brutal side. I have tried to show them in a different light. I have tried to suggest that they have been ways of dealing with some of the most difficult and challenging problems in modern states, how to manage difference and diversity . . . What I find striking is less the mistakes and occasional brutalities of empire than a remarkable record of success, one that nation-states would be lucky to match' (ibid., pp. xv–xvi).

5   The journalist Sathnam Sanghera has espoused the conspiracy theory, which is popular on the left, that the 'culture wars' in Britain are basically an invention of Boris Johnson's Conservative government, which has stoked them for polit- ical advantage (*Empireland: How Imperialism Has Shaped Modern Britain* [London: Penguin, 2021], pp. 220–2). Well, no doubt the government does have an eye to political advantage, but to suppose that the present cultural conflict over colonialism, race and gender is all the government's nefarious doing is nonsense. Observe the genesis of my own modest role in it. In late November 2017 I published an article in *The Times* and early the following month I posted an online description of a research project, 'Ethics and Empire', which I had launched the previous July. My wife and I then left for Germany to celebrate our thirty-fifth wedding anniversary. That is when war broke out. Called to action by Dr (now Professor) Priyamvada Gopal of Cambridge University, who tweeted to her political allies, 'OMG. This is serious shit . . . We need to SHUT THIS DOWN' (13 December 2017, 8.45 a.m.), students and academics in Oxford and worldwide published three online denunciations of 'Ethics and Empire', spaced out over a week. None of them was addressed to me, and the third one was directed at my university, urging it to withdraw its support from my project. This campaign was accompanied and followed by very aggressive, provocative and personal tweeting, and among the most intemperate of the aggressors was Professor Kim Wagner – to whom, as it happens, Sanghera offered 'particular thanks' in the acknowledgements of his book (p. xii). In sum, this local front of the culture war developed because some academics and students decided to launch a personal and political attack on me, on the ground that I had said and done things of which they did not approve. The Conservative government had nothing to do with it. Indeed, Boris Johnson's government did not yet exist.

6   There is a word in English beginning with 'n', derived from the Latin word

for 'black', that has usually been deployed to express racist disdain or abuse for people with non-white skins. In the current cultural climate, it has become unsayable and unprintable, no matter what the context or the intent of the writer. In this book there are twelve occasions when it appears in quotations – either when its use is being reported by a third party or when it is being used ironically – or when I am referring to such uses. In every case, following the current practice of *The Times* (see, for example, 'Obituary: Richard Leakey', 3 January 2022), I have rendered it as 'n---er' or 'n---ers'.

7   In a 2006 book review of Paul Maylam's *The Cult of Rhodes: Remembering an Imperialist in Africa* (Cape Town: David Philip, 2005), Adebajo sought to substantiate Rhodes' alleged racism and genocidal intent by reporting him as saying 'I prefer land to n---ers'; 'the natives are like children. They are just emerging from barbarism'; and 'one should kill as many n---ers as possible' ('Worse than the Rest', *Times Literary Supplement*, 28 July 2006, p. 25). These 'quotations' were invoked in the petition presented by Rhodes Must Fall campaigners to Oriel College, Oxford in December 2015.

Appearances, however, deceived. For Adebajo had omitted to tell his readers that the first 'quotation' had been lifted from a novel by Olive Schreiner (*Trooper Peter Halket of Mashonaland* [London: Unwin, 1897]) – it is fiction. The second quotation is an accurate report of what Rhodes said in a parliamentary speech in 1894, but its full context, which Adebajo chose to withhold, makes it less than obviously racist: 'Now, I say the natives are children. They are just emerging from barbarism. They have human minds . . . we ought to do something for the minds and the brains that the Almighty has given them. *I do not believe that they are different from ourselves*' (Vindex, *Cecil Rhodes, His Political Life and Speeches, 1881–1900* [London: Chapman and Hall, 1900], pp. 383, 388. The emphasis is mine). The third quotation appears in none of Rhodes' several dozen biographies, including Maylam's. It seems to be a distortion of words attributed to Rhodes by Gordon Le Sueur, who had accompanied him during the Second Matabele War in 1896–7. According to Le Sueur, on asking an officer of the British South Africa Company's police how many casualties the enemy had suffered in a recent fight, Rhodes was told that there had been very few, since the Africans had thrown down their arms and begged for mercy. Rhodes responded, 'Well, you should not spare them. You should kill all you can, as it serves as a lesson to them when they talk things over at their fires at night' (Gordon Le Sueur, *Cecil Rhodes: The Man and His Work* [London: John Murray, 1913], p. 159: https://archive.org/details/cecilrhodesmanhi00lesurich/page/159). In other words, 'Next time don't give quarter, but kill all you can. Otherwise, they'll only come back to attack again.' Whatever moral evaluation one makes of this advice – given on the battlefield of a conflict undisciplined by any international laws of war – it is a world removed from a recommendation of a general policy of genocide aimed at black Africans. Note that the word 'n---ers' does not appear in Le Sueur's report; it only appears in Adebajo's.

The original investigation that first exposed Adebajo's misquotations was conducted by Madeline Briggs and reported in 'Misinformation in the Rhodes Campaign', *The Poor Print* (Oriel College's Student Newspaper), 11 January 2016: https://thepoorprint.com/2016/01/22/misinformation-in-the-rhodes-campagin/) [*sic*].

Writing in the *Sunday Telegraph* on 16 May 2021 (https://www.telegraph. co.uk/opinion/2021/05/15/letters-face-to-face-gp-appointments-vital-must-used-wisely/), Adebajo sought to rebut my criticism:

> Sir, Nigel Biggar erroneously accuses me of making up three quotes in a 2006 review of a book on Cecil Rhodes by Paul Maylam (*The Cult of Cecil Rhodes*) that appeared in the *Times Literary Supplement*. He says that the first quote, 'I prefer land to n---rs', was in a fictional 1897 novel by Olive Schreiner. But two renowned Rhodes biographers, Professor Maylam and Antony Thomas, have attributed this statement to Rhodes, as did a 1956 biographer, Felix Gross.
>
> Professor Biggar claims that a second Rhodes quote, 'The natives are children. They are just emerging from barbarism', was 'misleadingly torn from its proper context'. However, both Professor Maylam and the historian Stanlake Samkange confirmed these words as having been uttered by Rhodes in a racist July 1894 speech to the Cape parliament, which is available online.
>
> Finally, Professor Biggar claims that the quote, 'One should kill as many n---rs as possible', is 'a mixture of distortion and fabrication'. But it is cited by Professor Maylam.
>
> Perhaps Professor Biggar should stick to his own field of theology and not wade into tendentious history.

My response to this, which the *Sunday Telegraph* declined to publish, was as follows:

> Sir, Adekeye Adebajo objects to my claim that he has misquoted Cecil Rhodes (Comment, May 2; Letters, 16 May). First, he argues that the quotation, 'I prefer land to n---rs', was attributed to Rhodes by 'renowned biographers' Paul Maylam, Antony Thomas, and Felix Gross. Yet Maylam's book is not a biography, but a history of reception; and Thomas was a documentary film-maker, whose popular biography of Rhodes is not in the front rank. Besides, Thomas gives no source for the quotation. Maylam cites Gross, who references only hearsay from the disaffected Olive Schreiner. The only documentary source is Schreiner's 1897 novel, where the words are spoken by a character that looks like Rhodes. It's fiction.
>
> Regarding the second quotation, 'The natives are children. They are just emerging from barbarism', I complained that, torn out of context, it misleads. Professor Adebajo replies by saying that it appears in a 'racist' speech by Rhodes in 1894. It does appear in the speech, but, read in context, it is not racist. Immediately following the professor's selected words come these: 'They have human minds . . . We ought to do something for the minds and the brains that the Almighty has given them. I do not believe that they are different from ourselves'.

Third, Professor Adebajo again invokes Maylam's authority for the third quotation, 'One should kill as many n---rs as possible'. Yet this appears nowhere in Maylam's book.

My case stands.

8   Vindex, *Cecil Rhodes*, p. 388.

9   See Biggar, 'Rhodes, Race, and the Abuse of History'; and Chapter 3, note 17.

10 Aamna Mohdin, 'Protesters Rally in Oxford for Removal of Cecil Rhodes Statue', *Guardian*, 9 June 2020.

11 The priority of present politics over the historical truth is evident in a comment made to the press by Robert Gildea, a professor at Oxford University who specialises in twentieth-century French history. Referring to the statue overlooking Oxford's High Street, he said: 'Rhodes looks patronisingly down upon us. We celebrate and idolise him. He blocks our treatment of history, and therefore he should be taken down [Rhodes ser patroniserende ned på os. Vi fejrer ham og idoliserer ham. Ham blokerer for vores behandlung af historien, og derfor skal han tages ned]' (Jørgen Ullerup, 'Kulturkrigen raser på britiske universiteter', *Jyllands Posten*, 28 October 2021: https://jyllands-posten.dk/international/europa/ECE13372877/kulturkrigen-raser-paa-britiske-universiteter/). To Gildea, Rhodes symbolises a colonial mentality of white supremacism ('looks down patronisingly'), which still possesses the British ('We . . . idolise') and hinders the triumph of a 'progressive' reading of their past ('blocks our treatment of history'). The idol needs to be pulled down, so that the racist spell can be broken. The truth, however, is that Rhodes was neither a 'white supremacist' nor of a generally patronising disposition. Moreover, his statue was erected to honour him specifically as a college benefactor, not to celebrate everything he did. Further, were it not for the fuss that Professor Gildea and his political allies have worked up over the statue, hardly anyone would be aware of it. Further still, I have yet to meet – or read – anybody who idolises Rhodes.

12 As Pascal Bruckner has written, 'Isn't it astonishing that the first nations that abolished slavery, after having greatly profited by it, were also the only ones that are now the object of accusations and demands for reparations?' (*The Tyranny of Guilt: An Essay on Western Masochism*, trans. Steven Rendall [Princeton, NJ: Princeton University Press, 2010], p. 155).

13 So, for example, of the forty-four contributors to *The Oxford Handbook of Postcolonial Studies* (Oxford: Oxford University Press, 2013), twenty-four are scholars of literature, and only four are clearly historians.

14 Elleke Boehmer and Tom Holland, 'Are Empires Always Bad?', *Prospect* (December 2020), pp. 16–17. For further comment on Said and 'post-colonialism' in this book, see pp. 26–7, 76, 306n.16, 318–19n.74 and 327n.69.

15 Robert Musil, *The Man Without Qualities*, trans. Sophie Wilkins (London: Picador, 2017), p. 575.

16 Henry Kissinger, *On China* (London: Penguin, 2012), pp. 22ff.

17 Gideon Rachman, *Easternisation: War and Peace in the Asian Century* (London: Bodley Head, 2016), p. 61.

18 'China Ambassador to the UK: "Hong Kong Is No longer Under Colonial

Rule"', *Sky News*, 6 July 2020: https://www.youtube.com/watch?v=JQR28g-JxJIQ

19 See, for example, George Monbiot's five-minute online caricature of 'Western civilisation': https://youtu.be/UtBKDMN2U4s. Monbiot is a former BBC journalist and a present *Guardian* columnist.

20 In Nyasaland in the 1880s and 1890s the empire indirectly supported action against Arab slavers, latterly through the British South Africa Company. And guess who ran the BSAC? Cecil Rhodes.

21 In 2018 I was interviewed by Afua Hirsch for a Channel 4 programme. At the beginning of the interview, she asked me if members of my family had been involved in the British Empire, giving the impression that she supposed that no one would speak up for colonialism, unless he had a personal interest to defend. In fact, I have no direct family investment in the empire at all. My father almost emigrated to South Africa in the 1930s to grow oranges, but did not. Remotely, however, I probably do have colonial connections, insofar as people with my Scottish surname lent it to the Biggarsberg Mountains in KwaZulu-Natal, South Africa, to Biggar Lake in the Algonquin Park, Ontario, and to the township of Biggar in Saskatchewan, Canada.

22 James McDougall, Erin O'Halloran, Hussein Ahmed Hussein Omar, Peter Hill, et al. '"Ethics and Empire": An Open Letter from Oxford Scholars', *The Conversation*, 19 December 2017: https://theconversation.com/ethics-and-empire-an-open-letter-from-oxford-scholars-89333

23 See Chapter 2, sections II and III. Slavery has not always been what we assume it is. In his book *Slavery and Islam* (London: Oneworld Academic, 2019) Jonathan A. C. Brown presents the following scene (pp. 28–9). It is the 1500s and we are visiting a well-off home in Mecca. Our host sits drinking tea. Suddenly, he flies into a rage, shouting at a young man who is leaning down to speak to him, and hits him with a fly-swatter. Another, slightly older man rushes over and receives some instructions, together with some gold coins. Pointing to the man he has just smacked, our host exclaims, 'This disappointment. I know he wishes for my death!' Then, turning to the other man he has instructed, he adds, warmly, 'But you pray for my long life.' Curious to know who the two men are, we discreetly ask the older one. He tells us that his name is Saffron and that he has worked in this house for five years. In a year's time, however, he will have saved enough money to move out and start his own business. What about the younger man? 'Oh, that poor boy,' says Saffron, 'he'll be here till the old man dies.' The abused young man, it turns out, is our wealthy host's son. Saffron, on the other hand, authorised to act for his master in business affairs, is a trusted slave. And he is in the process of buying back his freedom by instalments. (Brown's historically informed fiction is based on Shaun Marmon, 'Domestic Slavery in the Mamluk Empire: A Preliminary Sketch', in Shaun Marmon, ed., *Slavery in the Islamic Middle East* [Princeton: Markus Wiener, 1999]). So, 'slavery' has not always lived down to our grim assumptions. Sometimes slaves have in fact been better off than contracted employees or even their master's own children. Indeed, sometimes they have

risen to positions of considerable wealth and power. From 1555 to 1579, for example, Soḳullu Meḥmed Pasha was grand vizier (or prime minister) of the Ottoman Empire during the reign of three sultans. He was married to a sultan's daughter and owned thousands of slaves. And yet he was himself a slave (Brown, *Slavery and Islam*, pp. 29–30; see also G. Veinstein, 'Soḳullu Meḥmed Pasha', in P. Bearman, Th. Bianquis, C. E. Bosworth, E. van Donzel, W. P. Heinrichs, eds, *Encyclopaedia of Islam*, 2nd edn [Leiden: Brill, 2012]).

24 G. H. Le May, *British Supremacy in South Africa, 1899–1907* (Oxford: Clarendon Press, 1965), p. 57.

25 Yves R. Simon, *The Ethiopian Campaign and French Political Thought*, ed. Anthony O. Simon, trans. Robert Royal (Notre Dame: University of Notre Dame, 2009), p. 55.

26 Reinhold Niebuhr (1892–1971) was an American Protestant theologian and public intellectual.

27 While Ireland was subject to English colonial rule in the medieval and early modern periods, it is a moot point whether or not it should be thought of as a colony in the eighteenth and nineteenth centuries. Until 1801 Ireland had its own parliament. In 1801 this was abolished, in order to dilute the political dominance of Protestant landowners. Thereafter, the Irish sent 100 MPs to Westminster, where they exercised considerable influence on British political life, most notably at the turn of the twentieth century. Numerous Irish participated in the running of the British Empire, not only as soldiers but also as administrators. As Krishan Kumar has commented, 'None of this sounds like the condition of a classic colony' (*Visions of Empire*, p. 318).

28 The term 'the British Commonwealth of Nations' was coined by Jan Smuts in 1917 (F. S. Crafford, *Jan Smuts: A Biography* [New York: Doubleday, 1943], p. 142).

1. MOTIVES, GOOD AND BAD

1 For the sake of clarity, let me explain here what I understand a motive to be. Etymologically, a motive is what *moves* someone to act – a reason for action. As such it can be either a 'push' factor or a 'pull' one. We can be pushed into action by a strong emotion or pulled by the attraction of a goal we want to achieve. Insofar as a motive is 'pulled' by a goal, it is closely related to an intention. An intention is a desire for a goal that has become crystallised into a plan to achieve it.

2 The 'improvised and provisional character' of the British Empire, whose '"command and control" . . . was always ramshackle and quite often chaotic', is one of the main themes of John Darwin's work (*Unfinished Empire: The Global Expansion of Britain* [London: Allen Lane, 2012], pp. xii, xiii). What he observes of the British Empire as a whole, Tirthankar Roy observes of the empire in India in particular: 'For the British Empire in India, which fundamentally changed in character from its early foundation by East India Company adventurers to being a Crown colony, in the process undergoing deep changes

in the composition of the ruling class, it is hard to pin down the colonisation project to one single motivation or even an identifiable group of decision-makers' ('The British Empire and the Economic Development of India, 1858–1947', *Revista de Historia Económica/ Journal of Iberian and Latin American Economic History*, 34/2 [2015], p. 213).

3   Richard Hooker, *The Works of That Learned and Judicious Mr Richard Hooker, etc.*, ed. John Keble, 3 vols, 6th edn (Oxford: Clarendon Press, 1874), Vol. I, Book III, Chapter 1.11, p. 347. See Nigel Biggar, 'Why the Establishment of the Church of England is Good for a Liberal Society', in Mark Chapman, Judith Maltby and William Whyte, eds, *The Established Church: Past, Present and Future* (London: T. & T. Clark, 2011).

4   David Gilmour, *The British in India: Three Centuries of Ambition and Experience* (London: Allen Lane, 2018), pp. 28–9.

5   John Malcolm, *Malcolm: Soldier, Diplomat, Ideologue of British India* (Edinburgh: John Donald, 2014). The account of Malcolm's early life can be found on pp. 9–17, and of Goethe's persistent interest in Malcolm's *History of Persia* on p. 359.

6   Tirthankar Roy, *An Economic History of India, 1707–1857*, 2nd edn (London: Routledge, 2021), p. 45.

7   Lawrence James, *Raj: The Making and Unmaking of British India* (London: Abacus, 1997), p. 11. The 'anarchy' from which northern India suffered in the wake of the attenuation of Mughal imperial authority was not so much the complete collapse of political institutions as the emergence of a multiplicity of rival, and often warring, states. Some of these states, however, were too weak to prevent the flourishing of stateless enclaves of brigands and pirates.

8   It is also an emerging theme, it seems, in contemporary Chinese empire. First of all, China has developed a strong commercial interest in buying raw materials – especially minerals, timber and oil – from African countries, especially since 1980. This has entailed an interest in the security from piracy of shipping in the Indian Ocean. Accordingly, in 2017 the Chinese People's Liberation Army opened its first overseas naval base in Djibouti between the Gulf of Aden and the Red Sea.

9   Roy, *Economic History of India, 1707–1857*, pp. 4–5. Roy's targets here are Shashi Tharoor in *Inglorious Empire: What the British Did to India* (London: Hurst, 2017) and William Dalrymple in *The Anarchy: The Relentless Rise of the East India Company* (London: Bloomsbury, 2019). On Tharoor's view that, combining 'the license to loot everything' with 'perfidy, chicanery and cupidity', the EIC extracted wealth from the native princes, and on Dalrymple's judgement that the British 'conquest' of India was the 'supreme act of corporate violence', Roy comments: 'Tharoor and Dalrymple are not sufficiently well informed to bat for the Indian warlords. Claims like theirs peddle sentiments – triumph or righteous outrage – but they are not correctly based on evidence and not reliable as history.'

10 Empires often begin when militarily skilled foreigners are invited to aid a local ruler against his enemies, and are then rewarded with local land. That is how

the Normans first established themselves in Ireland and southern Italy. It is also how the East India Company began to dominate India.

11 J. W. Kaye, *Life and Correspondence of Major-General Sir John Malcolm*, 2 vols (London: Smith, Elder & Co., 1856), vol. I, pp. 320–1.

12 *Journals and Diaries of the Assistants to the Agent and Governor-General North-West Frontier and Resident in Lahore, 1846–1849* (Allahabad, 1911), IV, pp. 1, 65–6; quoted by James, *Raj*, p. 114. Abbott gave his name to the city of Abbottabad, which is now best known as the site of Osama bin Laden's death in 2011.

13 James, *Raj*, p. 64.

14 Zareer Masani, 'Warren Hastings "Loved India a Little More than His Own Country"', *Open Magazine*, 6 April 2017: https://openthemagazine.com/essay/warren-hastings-loved-india-a-little-more-than-his-own-country/; 'How British Orientalists Were Responsible for Rediscovering Indian History', *The Wire*, 11 March 2018: https://thewire.in/history/how-british-orientalists-were-responsible-for-rediscovery-of-indian-history

15 William Dalrymple, *White Mughals: Love and Betrayal in Eighteenth-Century India* (London: Flamingo, 2003), p. 41.

16 I use the word 'disciples' advisedly, since sometimes their faith in Said is blind. For example, in her book *Insurgent Empire: Anticolonial Resistance and British Dissent* (London: Verso, 2019) Priyamvada Gopal invokes the authority of Said repeatedly without any hint of awareness that his thesis has attracted considerable criticism (see pp. 3, 9, 18, 26, 27, 29, 30). For an early skirmish in the war between Said and Bernard Lewis, see Bernard Lewis, 'The Question of Orientalism', *New York Review of Books*, 24 June 1982, and 'Orientalism: An Exchange', *New York Review of Books*, 12 August 1982. For a full-blown critique of Said, see Ibn Warraq, *Defending the West: A Critique of Edward Said's Orientalism* (New York: Prometheus, 2007). For an account of the controversy over *Orientalism* that tends to favour Said, see Zachary Lockman, *Contending Visions of the Middle East: The History and Politics of Orientalism*, 2nd edn (Cambridge: Cambridge University Press, 2010), Chapter 6. For a more even-handed account, see Dane Kennedy, *The Imperial History Wars: Debating the British Empire* (London: Bloomsbury, 2018), Chapter 1. For a recent critique of *Orientalism*, see Sameer Rahim, 'Disorientated: The Confusions of Edward Said', *Prospect*, June 2021: 'But [Said's] turning his argument into a totalising theory inevitably resulted in drastic simplifications. Arabists Robert Irwin and Daniel Martin Varisco have laid out the charges: ignoring German and Russian orientalists because those countries didn't have Middle Eastern empires; conflating philological studies like Edward Lane's Arabic lexicon and literary works by Goethe and Flaubert; and reducing the art of western orientalists to lascivious stereotypes, while missing its influence on Muslim painters like Osman Hamdi Bey. In jittery prose, the book has some curious asides – one scholar is said to have "ransacked" the oriental archives, when all he did was consult them. Remarkably, at the book's close Said retracts his own thesis: orientalist "scholars and critics," he writes, "are perfectly capable of freeing

themselves from the old ideological straitjacket". So, you might ask, what's your point?' (p. 69).

17 See also David Gilmour's comments on p. 76.

18 Victoria Glendinning, *Raffles and the Golden Opportunity, 1781–1826* (London: Profile, 2012), p. 37.

19 Nirad C. Chaudhuri, *The Autobiography of an Unknown Indian* (London: Picador, 1999), pp. 433–4.

20 Nirad C. Chaudhuri, *Thy Hand, Great Anarch! India 1921–1952* (London: Chatto and Windus, 1987), p. 675.

21 James, *Raj*, p. 120.

22 David Gilmour, *The Ruling Caste: Imperial Lives in the Victorian Raj* (London: John Murray, 2005), pp. 10–11.

23 James Belich, *Replenishing the Earth: The Settler Revolution and the Rise of the Anglo-World, 1783–1939* (Oxford: Oxford University Press, 2008), p. 126.

24 Ibid., pp. 80–1.

25 Ibid., pp. 128–33, 156–65. Belich reports that there is a 'vexed migration debate' (ibid., 131) among economic historians about what caused the explosion in British and Irish migration in the nineteenth century, in which 'pull' theories (the attraction of economic opportunities) 'currently have an edge on push theories' (ibid., p. 130): 'The dominant explanation for American migration as for others is the classic pull factor, rational choice, whereby people moved west for higher wages and better opportunities' (ibid., p. 132). To this, Belich himself adds two further factors: increased 'ease of transfer' (ibid., p. 132) and 'a great shift in attitudes to emigration' (ibid., p. 146).

26 Ibid., pp. 164, 558.

27 Tim Jeal, *Livingstone*, revised edn (New Haven and London: Yale University Press, 2013), pp. 2–3, 102–3, 219–25, 387. Livingstone also contemplated the cultivation of cotton on the Batoka Plateau (in what is now Zambia), with a view to reducing the dependence of British textile mills on cotton grown by American slaves (Niall Ferguson, *Empire: How Britain Made the Modern World* [London: Allen Lane, 2003], p. 135).

28 On its website, Anti-Slavery International declares: 'Over 180 years ago anti-slavery campaigners finally achieved what they had fought for over 60 years – abolishing a system of slavery in the British Empire. But the abolitionists . . . knew the job of ending slavery was far from complete, which is why . . . in 1839 . . . they founded the British and Foreign Anti-Slavery Society, in the 1990s renamed as Anti-Slavery International, to continue disrupting slavery in all its forms . . . We have achieved plenty throughout our history, from ending particular systems of slavery in Belgian Congo, Peru, and China, to playing a big part in passing all major anti-slavery conventions, to ending many forms of slavery in modern times, to outlawing the traditional form of sexual slavery in Niger only last month' (www.antislavery.org; accessed 7 December 2020).

29 James, *Raj*, p. 54.

30 Ibid., p. 151.

31 *The Private Journal of the Marquess of Hastings, K. G., Governor-General and*

Commander-in-Chief in India, ed. Marchioness of Bute, 2 vols, 2nd edn (London: Saunders & Otley, 1858), vol. I, p. 35; vol. II, pp. 101–2; quoted by James, *Raj*, p. 72.

32 Colin Newbury, 'Great Britain and the Partition of Africa, 1870–1914', in *The Oxford History of the British Empire*, 5 vols, Vol. III: 'The Nineteenth Century', ed. Andrew Porter (Oxford: Oxford University Press, 1999), p. 624.

33 Ronald Hyam, 'The Partition of Africa: Geopolitical and Internal Perspectives', in *Understanding the British Empire* (Cambridge: Cambridge University Press, 2010), p. 100.

34 Ibid., pp. 105, 107.

35 Ibid., p. 103.

36 Lord Salisbury, House of Commons, 10 July 1890, in *Hansard*, vol. 346 (1890), cols 1270–1: https://hansard.parliament.uk/Lords/1890-07-10/debates/4ed35c10-bcc3-4b86-8eac-9f1309cb26be/Anglo-GermanAgreementBill(No180).

37 Newbury, 'Great Britain and the Partition of Africa', p. 639.

38 Since Egypt was part of the Ottoman Empire, its ruler was a 'viceroy'. In fact, apart from the payment of tribute, it was an autonomous state.

39 Roger Owen, *Lord Cromer: Victorian Imperialist, Edwardian Proconsul* (Oxford: Oxford University Press, 2004), p. 125. Baring was made the Earl of Cromer in 1901 and is most widely known as 'Lord Cromer'.

40 Ibid., p. 114. Tigrane Pasha, the son-in-law of Nubar Pasha, Egypt's Armenian prime minister on three occasions, reported that Baring's defence of Egypt's rural population at the International Conference on Egyptian Finance in London in 1884 was much appreciated in Cairo (ibid., p. 207).

41 Ibid., p. 177.

42 Afaf Lutfi al-Sayyid, *Egypt and Cromer: A Study in Anglo-Egyptian Relations* (London: John Murray, 1968), p. 28. The author is the same person as Afaf Lutfi al-Sayyid-Marsot.

43 Baring (Cromer) to Iddesleigh, 24 October 1886, quoted by Lutfi al-Sayyid, *Egypt and Cromer*, p. 59.

44 The Earl of Cromer, *Modern Egypt*, 2 vols (London: Macmillan, 1908), vol. II, p. 128.

45 Ibid., p. 568.

46 Owen, *Lord Cromer*, pp. 329–30. Afaf Lutfi al-Sayyid-Marsot points out that 'native Egyptians' at the time comprised over 9 million out of a total population of 9,734,000. Nevertheless, she reports that Baring's view was 'accepted at face value by many people, including Egyptians themselves' (*Egypt and Cromer*, p. 148).

47 Owen, *Lord Cromer*, pp. xii, 400.

48 Ronald Storrs, *Orientations* (London: Nicholson & Watson, 1939), p. 89. Storrs worked under Cromer for three years before the latter resigned in 1907.

49 Owen, *Lord Cromer*, p. 348.

50 Al-Sayyid, *Egypt and Cromer*, pp. 128, 138.

51 Ibid., pp. 196, 202.

52 Keith Jeffery, *Field Marshal Sir Henry Wilson: A Political Soldier* (Oxford: Oxford University Press, 2008), p. 253. The hatred of which Wilson spoke was to kill him: he was assassinated by the IRA on the doorstep of his home in central London in 1922.

53 Jonathan Schneer, *The Balfour Declaration: The Origins of the Arab-Israeli Conflict* (London: Bloomsbury, 2010), pp. 134–5; Tom Segev, *One Palestine, Complete: Jews and Arabs under the British Mandate* (New York: Henry Holt, 1999), p. 41. However, if Shlomo Sand is to be believed, the Zionist vision bought by Balfour was a nationalist myth, in that Jews born and resident outside of Palestine had not, in general, spent the centuries yearning to 'return' there. Indeed, many eminent Jews in the nineteenth and early twentieth centuries were expressly *anti*-Zionist – including Balfour's own Cabinet colleague Edwin Montagu. It was not until the 1880s, when pogroms in Russia stimulated the mass migration of Jews westward, which in turn stimulated antisemitism in Central and Western Europe, that the Zionist search for a Jewish homeland began in earnest. Even then, the preferred location was not Palestine. In 1903 the Sixth Zionist Congress formally approved of Uganda in principle; and, when permitted by immigration policy in 1919–23, Eastern European Jews much preferred to emigrate to the United States. See Sand, *The Invention of the Land of Israel: From Holy Land to Homeland* (London: Verso, 2012), esp. pp. 161–5, 175, 183–5, 191–4.

54 Failing the continued British occupation of Egypt, Cyprus was thought a better military base than Palestine for securing the Canal (Segev, *One Palestine, Complete*, p. 198).

55 Schneer, *Balfour Declaration*, p. 84.

56 Segev, *One Palestine, Complete*, p. 92. Ronald Storrs, governor of Jerusalem from 1917 to 1926, made the same point more vividly when he wrote, 'The thinking Arabs regarded Article 6 [of the Mandate, stipulating that the British Administration shall encourage Jewish settlement] as Englishmen would regard instructions from a German conqueror for the settlement and development of the Duchy of Cornwall, of our Downs, commons and gold-courses, not by Germans, but by Italians "returning" as Roman legionaries' (*Orientations*, p. 370). Shortly before, he had identified the issue of principle: 'if there is no international statute of limitations and the pages of history could be turned back indefinitely, then let the Arabs "return" to Spain, which they had held quite as long and at least as effectively as the Jews had held Palestine' (ibid., p. 365).

57 Although the wording of the Balfour Declaration did give the British some room for political manoeuvre, it seems that Zionists never understood 'homeland' to mean anything other than 'state'. When asked why he had accepted the promise of a national home in Palestine, rather than holding out for a state, Chaim Weizmann replied, 'That is a tactical question' (Segev, *One Palestine, Complete*, p. 101). In July 1921 Balfour himself admitted that his declaration had always meant the eventual creation of a Jewish state – as its commitment to uphold only 'the civil and religious rights of existing non-Jewish communities

in Palestine', and not their political rights, tends to suggest. However, since Winston Churchill was surprised by the foreign secretary's admission, it seems that not all of Balfour's Cabinet colleagues shared his tacit understanding (ibid., p. 194).

58 Segev, *One Palestine, Complete*, pp. 233, 239. Let me make my intended meaning here clear. What I am drawing attention to is not Jewish prejudice against Arabs, but the predictable reaction of European town-dwellers to the lives of Palestinian peasants.

59 Schneer, *Balfour Declaration*, p. 342.

60 Sand, *Invention of the Land of Israel*, p. 119. Balfour had a reputation for 'intellectual nonchalance and . . . philosophical indifference to the mundane aspects of political life' (David Gilmour, *Curzon* [London: Macmillan, 1994], p. 232). 'Enraptured by great ideas, he was bored by the details needed to put them into practice' (ibid., p. 301). See also ibid., p. 503. He provides an example of why intellectuals can make for dangerous politicians.

61 Ali A. Allawi, *Faisal I of Iraq* (New Haven: Yale, 2014), p. 103. Allawi served as minister of trade, of defence and of finance in successive Iraqi governments between 2003 and 2006. He was reappointed minister of finance in May 2020. His excellent, judicious and much-lauded biography has the distinction among most Anglophone publications on the topic of drawing liberally on Arabic sources.

62 Segev, *One Palestine, Complete*, p. 334. Chancellor was Palestine's high commissioner from 1928 to 1931.

63 Storrs, *Orientations*, p. 352.

64 Segev, *One Palestine, Complete*, pp. 170-2, 270, 356, 514.

65 Given the possible implications for contemporary international politics of my reading of British policy in Palestine following the Balfour Declaration, let me make it clear that I believe that the present State of Israel has the right to exist. Israel is, in many respects, an extraordinarily successful, prosperous and liberal state that serves its citizens well. The fact that its origins were morally dubious is a characteristic that it shares with many states, and justice is seldom well served by trying to roll history back. Notwithstanding that, the question of how best to do justice in the present to the children and grandchildren of those Palestinian Arabs who were displaced and made stateless remains alive.

66 David R. Woodward, *Field Marshal Sir William Robertson: Chief of the Imperial General Staff in the Great War* (Westport, Conn.: Praeger, 1998), p. 113.

67 Charles Townshend is firmly insistent on this: 'oil was a secondary issue' (*When God Made Hell: The British Invasion of Mesopotamia and the Creation of Iraq, 1914–1921* [London: Faber and Faber, 2010], pp. xxi–ii, 141, 435, 506). Ali Allawi is more inclined to emphasise the role of oil (*Faisal I of Iraq*, p. 100). Dismissing as 'at best disingenuous' Lord Curzon's denial in 1923 that British policy was motivated by an interest in oil, Allawi writes that 'even though the world was awash with oil in 1925, the deposits in Iraq were potentially of immense strategic importance to Britain. Oil may not have loomed large in the protracted negotiations over Mosul, but it was certainly there in the background' (ibid., p. 454).

This, of course, concedes that oil was not a primary issue. Further, Townshend observes that 'the oil resources at Kirkuk [a subdivision of the *vilayet* or province of Mosul] *did not figure at all* in the Cabinet's discussions' (*When God Made Hell*, p. 506. The emphasis is mine). A 'background' issue that did not figure 'at all' does not even amount to a secondary factor. A background factor that is entirely passive is not a factor, but merely a feature of the hinterland.

68 The Sykes-Picot Agreement was largely overtaken by events: Russia surrendered its claim to Constantinople and territory east of it, removing the need for a French buffer in Syria. See Schneer, *Balfour Declaration*, Chapter 6, esp. 85–6.

69 Townshend, *When God Made Hell*, p. 404. Ali Allawi observes that the British 'were the only party that could take on the responsibility of government as the old order fell apart' (*Faisal I of Iraq*, p. 339).

70 Allawi, *Faisal I of Iraq*, p. xxii.

71 Ibid., p. 474.

72 Townshend, *When God Made Hell*, p. 14.

73 It is very widely held that the British promised Hussein that this Arab state would include Palestine, and that in later supporting the creation of a Jewish state there, they broke faith and betrayed his trust. The British undertakings to Hussein are contained in a set of correspondence between Sir Henry McMahon, high commissioner to Egypt, and the sharif in 1915–16. Exactly what the British promised has been the subject of heated controversy. Certainly, they did not explicitly promise that Palestine would be part of Hussein's state, since Palestine goes unmentioned in the correspondence. Moreover, it is very unlikely that McMahon would have intended to promise Acre, Haifa and Jaffa to the sharif, given the importance that the British and their French allies attached to controlling ports in the eastern Mediterranean. Further, the reciprocal undertakings did not amount to a treaty, since they were conditional upon the uncertain outcome of the war – as Hussein himself recognised in January 1918 (Elie Kedourie, *In the Anglo-Arab Labyrinth: The McMahon-Husayn Correspondence and Its Interpretations, 1914–1939*, 2nd edn [London: Frank Cass, 1976, 2000], p. 191; Allawi, *Faisal I of Iraq*, pp. 249–50). Further still, some of what Hussein himself promised was never realised: the revolt of Arab officers in Syria and Mesopotamia came to nothing.

The single outstanding authority on the McMahon-Hussein correspondence is Elie Kedourie's *In the Anglo-Arab Labyrinth*, which has been described by Avi Shlaim as 'the most definitive study' (*Israel and Palestine: Reappraisals, Revisions, Refutations* [London: Verso, 2009], p. 5). The noun in the main title of Kedourie's book is apt, since the text is forensically, mind-bendingly dense. For that reason, many reputable authors have chosen to bypass its conclusion that the story of British double-dealing is groundless: for example, it fails to achieve any mention in the indexes of Tom Segev's *One Palestine, Complete* (1999), Jonathan Schneer's *The Balfour Declaration* (2010), or Ali Allawi's *Faisal I of Iraq* (2014). James Barr, on the other hand, does use Kedourie's book to quote McMahon (*A Line in the Sand: Britain, France and the Struggle that Shaped the Middle East* [London: Simon & Schuster UK, 2011], pp. 25–6 n.15). However, instead of engaging with Kedourie's detailed historical argument, Barr rests content to perpetuate the ready-made myth of British perfidy.

74   Townshend, *When God Made Hell*, pp. 407, 409, 410.

75   Ibid., p. 475. According to Townshend, the widespread view that the R.A.F. used mustard-gas bombs during the rebellion is a myth (ibid., p. 476). No chemical ordnance was available there. See R. M. Douglas, 'Did Britain Use Chemical Weapons in Mandatory Iraq?', *Journal of Modern History*, 81/4 (2009).

76   Allawi, *Faisal I of Iraq*, p. 384.

77   Ibid., p. 399.

78   Ibid., pp. 518–19, 543.

79   'The Covenant of the League of Nations', Article 22: https://avalon.law.yale.edu/20th_century/leagcov.asp#art22 (accessed 7 December 2020).

80   Malcolm, *Malcolm*, p. 455.

81   Elphinstone wrote in 1819: 'The most desirable death for us to die of should be the improvement of the natives reaching such a pitch as would render it impossible for a foreign nation to retain the government' (2 July 1819, letter to Sir James Mackintosh; quoted in Malcolm, *Malcolm*, p. 455); and Malcolm wrote in 1823: 'Let us, therefore, calmly proceed on a course of gradual improvement: and when our rule ceases, for cease it must (though probably at a remote period), as the natural consequence of our success in the diffusion of knowledge, we shall as a nation have the proud boast that we have preferred the civilisation to the continued subjection of India. When our power is gone, our name will be revered; for we shall leave a moral monument more noble and imperishable than the hand of man ever constructed' (*A Memoir of Central India, Including Malwa and Adjoining Provinces*, 2 vols, vol. II [London: Kingsbury, Parbury and Allen, 1823; Cambridge: Cambridge University Press, 2011], p. 304).

2. FROM SLAVERY TO ANTI-SLAVERY

1   For an analysis of the differences between indentured servitude and slavery, see Jerome S. Handler and Matthew C. Reilly, 'Contesting "White Slavery" in the Caribbean: Enslaved Africans and European Indentured Servants in Seventeenth-Century Barbados', *New West Indian Guide*, 91 (2017), esp. pp. 38–45.

2   Jonathan A. C. Brown bravely conducts an original and searching analysis of the moral wrongness of 'slavery' in *Slavery and Islam*, pp. 15–65, 147–200.

3   In the Ottoman world, for example, slaves were sometimes better off than contracted employees or even their master's own children. See the Introduction, note 23.

4   David Ritchie, *Natural Rights: A Criticism of Some Ethical and Political Conceptions* (London: Swan Sonnenschein, 1895), p. 104.

5   See Leland Donald, *Aboriginal Slavery on the Northwest Coast of North America* (Berkeley and Los Angeles: University of California Press, 1997).

6   Robert C. Davis, *Christian Slaves, Muslim Masters: White Slavery in the*

Mediterranean, the Barbary Coast and Italy, 1500–1800 (London: Palgrave Macmillan, 2003). These figures do not include Europeans enslaved by other Mediterranean traders – for example, those based in Morocco. Davis' calculations are not based on records, which do not exist, but on what would be needed to replenish the slave population, given annual losses to death, escape, ransom and conversion to Islam. His unavoidably speculative conclusion has been met with some scepticism, for example, from Peter Earle, author of *Corsairs of Malta and Barbary* (London: Sidgwick & Jackson, 1970), and John Wright in *The Trans-Saharan Slave Trade* (London: Routledge, 2007). See Rory Carroll, 'New Book Reopens Old Arguments about Slave Raids on Europe', *Guardian*, 11 March 2004: https://www.theguardian.com/uk/2004/mar/11/highereducation.books

7   See Olivier Pétré-Grenouilleau, *Les traites négrières: essai d'histoire globale* (Paris: Editions Gallimard, 2004). Pétré-Grenouilleau has been described as 'one of the most . . . distinguished historians in France' (Joseph C. Miller, 'A Global History of the Slave Trade', *Journal of African History*, 49/2 [2008], p. 306). His book won the Prix de l'Essai de l'Académie Française and the Livre d'Histoire prize of the Senate of the French Republic.

8   N. Levtzion and J. F. P. Hopkins, eds, *Corpus of Early Arabic Sources for West African History* (Cambridge University Press, 1981), p. 52.

9   Robin Law, 'Human Sacrifice in Pre-Colonial Africa', *African Affairs*, 84/334 (January 1985), esp. pp. 57–8, 60, 61, 62, 70, 73, 74. Human sacrifice continued to be a part of royal funeral ceremonies in the Gold Coast as late as 1944 (Bruce Gilley, *The Last Imperialist: Sir Alan Burns' Epic Defense of the British Empire* [Washington, DC: Regnery Gateway, 2021], Chapter 9).

10   Stephen D. Behrendt, 'The Transatlantic Slave Trade', in Robert L. Paquette and Mark M. Smith, *The Oxford Handbook of Slavery in the Americas* (Oxford: Oxford University Press, 2010), p. 262, Table 11.1. David Richardson reports a slightly higher figure of over 3.4 million slaves exported by the British from Africa in the shorter period of 1662–1807 ('The British Empire and the Atlantic Slave Trade, 1660–1807', in *The Oxford History of the British Empire*, 5 vols, Vol. II: 'The Eighteenth Century', ed. P. J. Marshall, p. 441).

11   Frank Kitson, *Prince Rupert: Admiral and General-at-Sea* (London: Constable, 1999), p. 238. The Royal African Company was founded in 1672 but had its origins in the Company of Royal Adventurers Trading into Africa, which had been established in 1660.

12   Richardson, 'British Empire and the Atlantic Slave Trade, 1660–1807', pp. 444–5.

13   Olaudah Equiano, *The Interesting Narrative and Other Writings*, ed. Vincent Carretta, revised edn (New York: Penguin, 2003), p. 58; quoted by Adam Hochschild, *Bury the Chains: The British Struggle to Abolish Slavery* (London: Macmillan, 2005), p. 32.

14   Behrendt, 'Transatlantic Slave Trade', p. 260, citing Philip D. Curtin's *The Atlantic Slave Trade: A Census* (Madison: University of Wisconsin Press, 1969).

15   Richardson, 'British Empire and the Atlantic Slave Trade, 1660–1807', p. 454.

16 In 1788 Jamaica's assembly passed the Consolidated Slave Law, which was intended to keep families together (Kenneth Morgan, *Slavery and the British Empire: From Africa to America* [Oxford: Oxford University Press, 2007], p. 77).

17 Larry Gragg, *Englishmen Transplanted: The English Colonization of Barbados, 1627–1660* (Oxford: Oxford University Press, 2003), p. 129.

18 Morgan Godwyn, *The Negro's & Indians Advocate, Suing for Their Admission into the Church* . . . (London: J.D., 1680), quoted in Alden T. Vaughan, *Roots of American Racism: Essays on the Colonial Experience* (Oxford: Oxford University Press, 1995), p. 72.

19 Michael Craton, *Testing the Chains: Resistance to Slavery in the British West Indies* (Ithaca, NY: Cornell University Press, 1982), pp. 109–10.

20 Morgan, *Slavery and the British Empire*, p. 137.

21 Thomas Thistlewood, Folder 38, Box 7, Thomas Thistlewood Papers, James Marshall and Marie-Louise Osborn Collection, Beinecke Rare Book and Manuscript Library, Yale University; quoted by Helen McKee, 'From Violence to Alliance: Maroons and White Settlers in Jamaica, 1739–1795', *Slavery and Abolition*, 39/1 (2018), p. 39.

22 Morgan, *Slavery and the British Empire*, pp. 23–4, 113. See also Handler and Reilly, 'Contesting "White Slavery" in the Caribbean', pp. 38–45.

23 Trevor Burnard, 'British West Indies and Bermuda', in Paquette and Smith, *Oxford Handbook of Slavery in the Americas*, p. 143.

24 Morgan, *Slavery and the British Empire*, pp. 57, 60, 81.

25 Eric Williams, *Capitalism and Slavery* (Chapel Hill, NC: University of North Carolina Press, 1944), p. 105.

26 Ibid., pp. 105–6.

27 Roger Anstey, 'Capitalism and Slavery: A Critique', *Economic History Review*, New Series, 21/2 (August 1968).

28 Richardson, 'British Empire and the Atlantic Slave Trade, 1660–1807', p. 461. C. H. Feinstein argues that 'the economic profits of the [slave] trade were merely wasted in Africa, not funnelled into industry in Britain' (C. H. Feinstein, 'Capital Accumulation and the Industrial Revolution', in Roderick Floud and Donald McCloskey, eds, *The Economic History of Britain since 1700*, 1st edn, 2 vols [Cambridge: Cambridge University Press, 1981], Vol. I, pp. 99–100).

29 David Brion Davis, 'Foreword', in Seymour Drescher, *Econocide: British Slavery in the Era of Abolition*, 2nd edn (Chapel Hill, NC: University of North Carolina Press, 2010), p. xiv. While David Richardson reported recently that 'some' continue to advocate Williams' thesis that slavery was a major cause of British industrialisation, in the accompanying endnote he cites only one, quarter-of-a-century-old work – Robin Blackburn's 1998 *The Making of New World Slavery* (Richardson, *Principles and Agents: The British Slave Trade and its Abolition* [Newhaven, CT: Yale University Press, 2022], pp. 10, 274).

30 According to David Eltis and Stanley L. Engerman, one expression of this view is Robin Blackburn's *The Making of New World Slavery: From the Baroque to the Modern, 1492–1800* (London: Verso, 2010). See Eltis and Engerman, 'The

Importance of Slavery and the Slave Trade to Industrializing Britain', *Journal of Economic History*, 60/1 (March 2000), p. 124.

31   Eltis and Engerman, 'Importance of Slavery', p. 135.

32   Joel Mokyr, 'Editor's Introduction: The New Economic History and the Industrial Revolution', in Joel Mokyr, ed., *The British Industrial Revolution: An Economic Perspective*, 2nd edn (London: Routledge, 1999), pp. 49–50.

33   Morgan, *Slavery and the British Empire*, p. 83.

34   J. D. Fage, 'African Societies and the Atlantic Slave Trade', *Past and Present*, CXXV (1989), pp. 97–115.

35   Walter Rodney, 'African Slavery and Other Forms of Social Oppression on the Upper Guinea Coast in the Context of the Atlantic Slave Trade', *Journal of African History*, 7/3 (1966), p. 443: 'many of the forms of slavery and subjection present in Africa in the nineteenth and twentieth centuries and considered indigenous to that continent were in reality engendered by the Atlantic slave trade'.

36   Richardson, 'British Empire and the Atlantic Slave Trade, 1660–1807', p. 463.

37   McKee, 'From Violence to Alliance', p. 28.

38   Mavis C. Campbell, *The Maroons of Jamaica, 1655–1796* (Granby, Mass.: Bergin and Garvey, 1988), pp. 198–9: 'it is certain that the Maroons did keep slaves among themselves, though not on a large scale to be sure. Now what is to be said of a people who fought their way successfully out of slavery, just to turn around and to commence slaving others? Without attempting a moralistic reply, we can only remind ourselves that in almost all known slave societies, from antiquity to modern, slaves have been known to keep slaves. Furthermore, in most slave revolts – Spartacus's being the most outstanding – the rebels' aim was invariably to reverse the system and not to overthrow slavery as such.' Four years after his own manumission at the age of thirty-five, Toussaint Louverture, later the famous black leader of Haiti's successful slave revolt, owned at least one slave and rented a coffee plantation with thirteen slaves for two years in 1779–81 (Sudhir Hazareesingh, *Black Spartacus: The Epic Life of Toussaint Louverture* [London: Allen Lane, 2020], pp. 9, 30–1).

39   Charles Louis de Secondat, Baron de Montesquieu, *The Complete Works of M. De Montesquieu*, 4 vols, Vol. 1: *The Spirit of Laws* (London: T. Evans, 1777), Book XV, Chapter 1, p. 311.

40   Adam Smith, *The Theory of Moral Sentiments*, ed. Dugald Stewart (London: Henry G. Bohn, 1853), Part V, Chapter 2, p. 299. It seems that Smith was not alone in taking a romantic view of Africans. Kenneth Morgan refers to a 'stream of popular works [that] upheld the primitivism of Negroes as something to be admired for its simplicity, sincerity, and lack of worldly vices' (*Slavery and the British Empire*, p. 159).

41   John Wesley, *Thoughts upon Slavery* (London & Philadelphia: Joseph Cruckshank, 1774), title page and p. 56.

42   See note 13 of this chapter.

43   The Clapham Sect was a network of socially and politically prominent evangelical Anglicans, who laboured for various social reforms, including the

abolition of slavery, from the 1780s to the 1840s. Many of them worshipped at Holy Trinity Church on Clapham Common, London. Hence the name.

44 John Stauffer, 'Abolition and Antislavery', in Paquette and Smith, *Oxford Handbook of Slavery in the Americas*, p. 564.

45 Ibid., p. 563.

46 Morgan, *Slavery and the British Empire*, pp. 178–81. In the light of the American War of Independence, 1776–83, subsequent British governments can be forgiven for being reluctant to override colonial assemblies. If they pressed too hard, they risked the permanent loss of humanitarian influence. So, when urged to legislate for the likes of Jamaica in 1824, George Canning, foreign secretary, responded: 'no feeling of wounded pride, no motive of questionable expediency, nothing short of real and demonstrable necessity, shall induce me to moot the awful question of the transcendental power of parliament over every dependency of the British Crown. That transcendental power . . . ought to be kept back . . . It exists, but it should be veiled' (16 March 1824, House of Commons, cited in George R. Mellor, *British Imperial Trusteeship, 1783–1850* [London: Faber & Faber, 1951], p. 92). Nevertheless, the London government did consider suspending Jamaica's constitution and imposing direct Crown colony rule in 1838.

47 Howick to the Earl of Mulgrave, 7 July 1832; quoted by Hochschild, *Bury the Chains*, p. 344.

48 See Chapter 2, pp. 63–4.

49 Thomas Clarkson to Sir Thomas Fowell Buxton, 25 September 1833, Clarkson MSS, Henry E. Huntington Library, San Marino, California; quoted by Morgan, *Slavery and the British Empire*, p. 192.

50 Roger Anstey, *The Atlantic Slave Trade and British Abolition, 1760–1810* (London: Macmillan, 1975), pp. 51–3.

51 Davis, 'Foreword', in Drescher, *Econocide*, p. xv.

52 This was David Richardson's judgement in 2022, when he wrote that Williams' 'decline thesis no longer carries the weight in explaining abolition of the British slave trade that is sometimes assumed' (*Principles and Agents*, p. 11). Reporting without demur David Brion Davis's view that Williams' 'decline thesis' was vitiated by his 'narrow-minded cynicism' (ibid., pp. 11, 15), Richardson asserts unequivocally that British abolition occurred when the slave trade 'was at or close to its historic peak' (ibid., p. 2). For a summary of the historical debate provoked by Eric Williams' *Capitalism and Slavery*, see Gad Heuman, 'Slavery, The Slave Trade, and Abolition', in *The Oxford History of the British Empire*, 5 vols, Vol. V: 'Historiography', ed. Robin Winks, pp. 322–4. In 2021, perhaps eager to exploit a fresh market created by the Black Lives Matter campaign in the wake of the death of George Floyd the previous year, Penguin reissued Eric Williams' *Capitalism and Slavery*. Leading the book's contemporary plauditors is Sathnam Sanghera, who declares on the back cover, 'You cannot understand slavery or British Empire without it.' In truth, the predominant weight of historiography indicates that you will largely misunderstand both slavery and the empire with it.

53   Foreign and Commonwealth Office, *Slavery in Diplomacy: The Foreign Office and the Suppression of the Transatlantic Slave Trade*, History Note No. 17 (London: Foreign and Commonwealth Office, 2007), Chapter 2, esp. pp. v, 29 and 46: https://issuu.com/fcohistorians/docs/history_notes_cover_hphn_17

54   Cited by Andrew Porter, 'Trusteeship, Anti-Slavery, and Humanitarianism', in *Oxford History of the British Empire*, Vol. III, ed. Porter, p. 211.

55   David Eltis, *Economic Growth and the Ending of the Transatlantic Slave Trade* (Oxford: Oxford University Press, 1987), Table 2, pp. 92–3.

56   Leslie Bethell, *The Abolition of the Brazilian Slave Trade: Britain, Brazil and the Slave Trade Question, 1807–1869* (Cambridge: Cambridge University Press, 1979), p. 360.

57   Thomas Fowell Buxton, *The African Slave Trade and Its Remedy* (London: John Murray, 1839).

58   Michael W. Doyle, *Empires* (Ithaca: Cornell University Press, 1986), pp. 181, 185.

59   Basil S. Cave, 'The End of Slavery in Zanzibar and British East Africa', *Journal of the Royal African Society*, 9/33 (October 1909), pp. 20–33. Cave served as a British consul in British East Africa and Zanzibar, at rising grades, from 1891 to 1909. John Lonsdale appears to imply that, since the abolition of the legal status of slavery still left the freed slaves economically dependent on Arab landlords, it was of little account ('East Africa', in *The Oxford History of the British Empire*, 5 vols, Vol. IV: 'The Twentieth Century', eds Judith M. Brown and Wm. Roger Louis, p. 533). That would be so, however, only if the granting of legal rights against maltreatment counted for nothing.

60   Nancy Gardner Cassels, *Social Legislation of the East India Company: Public Justice versus Public Instruction* (New Delhi: SAGE Publications India, 2010), p. 173.

61   Indian Penal Code (1860), sections 367, 370, 371.

62   Glendinning, *Raffles and the Golden Opportunity*, pp. xv, 45, 121, 198–9.

63   The lower figure of £1.367 billion was reached by the following method: (1) take an estimate of the average peacetime defence spending by Britain in the nineteenth century of 2.5 per cent of GDP (B. R. Mitchell, *British Historical Statistics* [Cambridge: Cambridge University Press, 1988], p. 587); (2) assume that half of this (1.25 per cent) was directed at the Royal Navy (as both Professor Andrew Lambert of King's College London and Dr Stephen Prince, head of the Naval Historical Branch at the Ministry of Defence, have recommended to me in personal correspondence); (3) apply 1.25 per cent to the UK's 2019 GDP of £2,214 billion to reach a figure of £27,675,000,000, the equivalent total naval expenditure in 2019 values; (4) take the average percentage of naval manpower assigned to West Africa in the fifty-year period 1816–65 (4.94 per cent) as a proxy for the proportion of the Royal Navy's resources committed to anti-slave-trade operations in the Atlantic (following Eltis in *Economic Growth and the Ending of the Transatlantic Slave Trade*, p. 91); (5) apply (4) to (3) to reach a figure of £1,367,145,000 for the expenditure on anti-slave-trade operations in the Atlantic in 2019 values.
        The higher figure of £1.742 billion was reached by this method: (1) take the

average annual expenditure of £7,512,000 on the Royal Navy during the fifty-year period of 1816–65 (Mitchell, *British Historical Statistics*, pp. 587–8); (2) take the average percentage of naval manpower assigned to West Africa in the same period (4.94 per cent) as a proxy for the proportion of the Royal Navy's resources committed to anti-slave-trade operations in the Atlantic; (3) apply (2) to (1) to reach a figure of £371,093 as the average annual expenditure by the Royal Navy on suppressing the Atlantic slave trade; (4) enter the years 1816, 1826, 1836, 1846, 1856 and 1866 into the calculator on the MeasuringWorth. com website (https://www.measuringworth.com/calculators/ppoweruk/), and select the 'project' (for example, item of government expenditure) and 'economic cost' (per cent of GDP as an indicator of 'the importance of the item to society as a whole') options, to reach an average figure across those five years of £1,741,680,000 in 2019 values.

64 Eltis, *Economic Growth and the Ending of the Transatlantic Slave Trade*, pp. 96, 97.

65 Chaim D. Kaufmann and Robert A. Pape, 'Explaining Costly International Moral Action: Britain's Sixty-Year Campaign against the Atlantic Slave Trade', *International Organization*, 53/4 (Autumn 1999), pp. 634–7, esp. 636.

66 Ibid., p. 631.

67 It is true that the number of sugar plantations in Jamaica had been declining since the beginning of the century – from eight hundred and thirty in 1804 to six hundred and seventy in 1834, amounting to a reduction of 19 per cent over thirty years. However, after the abolition of the institution of slavery the decline sharpened markedly, showing a reduction of 51 per cent over twenty years from 1834 to 1854. These figures were supplied to me by Kenneth Morgan, in whose forthcoming book, *A Concise History of Jamaica* (Cambridge: Cambridge University Press, 2022), they appear.

68 One of the themes of Jeremy Black's *Slavery: A New Global History* (London: Constable and Robinson, 2011) is the relative military weakness of European powers in Africa. The assumption of 'African vulnerability', he writes 'is misplaced, indeed woefully so' (*Slavery*, p. 253).

69 Cave, 'End of Slavery in Zanzibar and British East Africa', p. 22.

70 Ibid., p. 32.

71 Cromer, *Modern Egypt*, Vol. II, pp. 495, 496–7, 499–500.

72 S. J. Braidwood, *Black Poor and White Philanthropists: London Blacks and the Foundation of the Sierra Leone Settlement, 1786–1791* (Liverpool: Liverpool University Press, 1994), p. 269. He continues: 'We noted earlier that the Sierra Leone expedition, seen as a forced deportation of blacks from Britain, formed the centre-piece of [Folarin] Shyllon's thesis that "racism has been the British way of life ever since the first blacks settled in Britain". Can the expedition be fairly described as "a concerted attempt . . . by the British Government and Britain's liberal establishment to rid Britain of her black population"? Evidence exists on both sides of the question and the present writer has tried to acknowledge this; but, when all has been taken into account, a very different picture emerges. There is no solid evidence that the motive of either the Committee

for the Relief of the Black Poor or of the Government in supporting the Sierra Leone venture was, as Shyllon asserts, to "preserve the purity of the English bloodstream". The Committee and the key individuals within the Government appear to have been motivated primarily by humanitarianism springing from Christian convictions, by gratitude felt towards the blacks as loyalists, and by abolitionist sympathies' (ibid., p. 269).

73 Stauffer, 'Abolition and Antislavery', p. 564.

74 Another considerable fly in the ointment of the anti-colonialists' story that a persistent 'colonial mentality' makes contemporary Britain systemically racist is Bernard Porter's thesis that the British people as a whole were typically indifferent to the British Empire (*The Absent-Minded Imperialists: Empire, Society, and Culture in Britain* [Oxford: Oxford University Press, 2004]). Krishan Kumar comments: 'The views of Porter and others are . . . valuable in questioning the sometimes mechanical assumptions of postcolonial scholars that the empire's impact on the metropolitan society . . . *must* have been as profound and pervasive as it was on the populations of the colonial peripheries. These things have to be shown, by whatever empirical means are to hand; and if the evidence is not there, or is thin, then it is right to challenge the post-colonial theorists (who with reference to their leader Edward Said, Porter provocatively called "Saidists")' (*Visions of Empire*, p. 320).

3. HUMAN EQUALITY, CULTURAL SUPERIORITY AND 'RACISM'

1 Egon Flaig, 'Faschistoider "Antikolonialismus" – Frantz Fanon', in *Die Niederlage der politischen Vernunft* (Springe: Zu Klampen Verlag, 2017), pp. 107–8. Flaig references Bernard Lewis, *Race and Slavery in the Middle East: An Historical Enquiry* (New York: Oxford University Press, 1990), pp. 43–53; R. Segal, *Islam's Black Slaves: The Other Black Diaspora* (New York: Farrar, Straus & Giroux, 2001), pp. 35–66; and D. M. Goldenberg, *The Curse of Ham: Race and Slavery in Early Judaism, Christianity, and Islam* (Princeton: Princeton University Press, 2003).

2 Gerald Hanley, *Warriors: Life and Death among the Somalis* (London: Eland, 1993), p. 187. This was first published as the opening half of *Warriors and Strangers* in 1971. Of Irish parentage, Hanley went to Kenya in 1934 at the age of eighteen, where he worked on a farm until 1939. At the outbreak of war, he joined the King's African Rifles and served in Somalia and Burma. In the 1950s he lived in India and Pakistan, where he married a Brahmin woman who had been adopted as a child by an Englishwoman.

3 Chinua Achebe, 'Africa's Tarnished Name' (1998), in *The Education of a British-Protected Child: Essays* (London: Penguin, 2009), p. 90, quoting from David Livingstone, *Missionary Travels and Researches in South Africa* (London: Ward Lock & Co., 1857).

4 David Lovatt Smith, *My Enemy: My Friend* (Nairobi: FOCCAM, 2000) p. 257. While there is much truth in what 'George' thinks about the aptness of native

African custom for surviving in an unforgiving environment, we should not romanticise it. For example, some Kikuyu agricultural practices caused soil exhaustion and erosion.

Although his book is a work of fiction, Lovatt Smith writes that '[m]any of the events that take place are based on historical incidents which occurred in the Kiambu and Fort Hall Districts of Kenya . . . I have been able to do this with help from copious notes, interrogation reports and Mau Mau documents and photographs which I have retained from that time, and I have referred to these extensively. A few of those people with whom I was associated at the time have also assisted me to ensure that I have the events as correct as possible, now, after more than forty years has elapsed' (ibid, p. 3).

5   Porter, 'Trusteeship, Anti-Slavery, and Humanitarianism', p. 216. See also John Gascoigne with Patricia Curthoys, *The Enlightenment and the Origins of European Australia* (Cambridge: Cambridge University Press, 2002), pp. 163–7; and Richard Price, *Making Empire: Colonial Encounters and the Creation of Imperial Rule in Nineteenth-Century Africa* (Cambridge: Cambridge University Press, 2008), Chapter 6.

6   Vindex, *Cecil Rhodes,* pp. 383, 388. The emphasis is mine. Although 'barbarism' and 'civilisation' are now widely assumed to be racist, three or four generations ago they were respectable, technical terms. In *Ancient Society* (New York: Henry Holt, 1877), Lewis H. Morgan, a pioneer of scientific anthropology, developed a theory of human progress that divides into three stages: 'savagery', 'barbarism' and 'civilisation'. Morgan's 'barbarism' roughly corresponds to what we now call the pre-historic Bronze and Iron Ages; it is not the lowest stage of human development. His theory influenced Karl Marx and Friedrich Engels.

Quoting an 1887 speech, William Beinart makes much of Rhodes' declared intention that Africans should be 'a subject race' ('Appendix A: Historical Appendix to the Report of the Oriel College Commission on the Rhodes Statue and Diversity within the College', in Oriel College, *Report of a Commission of Inquiry Established by Oriel College, Oxford into Issues Associated with Memorials to Cecil Rhodes* [Oxford: Oriel College, 2021], pp. 99, 100). However, he overlooks the crucial qualification that Rhodes made: 'Treat the natives as a subject people *as long as they continue in a state of barbarism and communal tenure*' (ibid., p. 100; my emphasis). See Nigel Biggar, 'A Critical Response to William Beinart, "Appendix A: Historical Appendix to the Report of the Oriel College Commission on the Rhodes Statue and Diversity within the College", in Oriel College, *Report of a Commission of Inquiry Established by Oriel College, Oxford into Issues Associated with Memorials to Cecil Rhodes* (Oxford: Oriel College, 2021)', p. 1, para. 2: https://www.mcdonaldcentre.org.uk/sites/default/files/content/files/beinart_appendix_a_response_by_nigel_biggar.pdf; https://historyreclaimed.co.uk/cecil-rhodes-a-critical-response-to-professor-william-beinart/.

7   As Beinart points out, Rhodes did support two pieces of legislation that tightened the conditions of eligibility for the franchise in such a way as to reduce the number of African voters – one in 1887 and one in 1892 ('Appendix A', pp.

99–100). However, he hints that this was a political compromise to appease the Afrikaner Bond and concedes that Rhodes did not reject black enfranchisement on principle: he was 'not opposed to a small measure of representation in the central colonial legislature for black people' (ibid., pp. 100–1). See Biggar, 'A Critical Response', p. 1, para. 3.

8   Robert I. Rotberg, *The Founder: Cecil Rhodes and the Pursuit of Power* (New York: Oxford University Press, 1988). p. 611. Beinart reports that Rhodes first deployed the slogan of 'equal rights for every civilised man south of the Zambesi' in 1896–7 with reference to members of the white working class in Cape Town ('Appendix A', p. 101). Nevertheless, it remains true that in 1898 he generalised it to apply to beyond whites (Biggar, 'A Critical Response', p. 1, para. 4).

9   J. S. Mill, *On Liberty*, ed. and intro. Gertrude Himmelfarb (London: Penguin, 1974), p. 69.

10   Henry Melvill, 'Sermon XIV: The Examination of Cain', *Sermons on Certain of the Less Prominent Facts and References in Sacred Story*, 2 vols (London: Francis & John Rivington, 1845), Vol. II, p. 374.

11   J. G. Lockhart and C. M. Woodhouse, *Rhodes* (London: Hodder and Stoughton, 1963), p. 415.

12   Covenant of the League of Nations (1919), Article 22.

13   Robert Calderisi substantiates his claim that Rhodes' 'most remarkable feature was an almost total lack of pretension' in *Cecil Rhodes and Other Statues: Dealing Plainly with the Past* (Columbus, Ohio: Gatekeeper press, 2021), p. 24.

14   In March 1896 the Ndebele attacked African 'Native Police' and settlers around Bulawayo, killing between 155 and 211 whites, including between 23 and 27 women and children. William Beinart comments: 'This evidence suggests that some constraint was shown [by the Ndebele]' ('Appendix A', p. 110). It might do, but only if we can be sure that the low number represents the presence of will rather than the lack of opportunity. I do not think we know that. The reasons for the uprising were several. One was the seizure of a large portion of native cattle by white settlers after the 1893 war, thus depriving Africans of much of their main source of food (ibid., pp. 105, 108). Another was a devastating outbreak of rinderpest and the consequent policy of slaughtering infected herds, which the natives perceived as spiteful (ibid., p. 109). And a third was the vindictive, sometimes murderous, conduct of the 'Native Police', who often came from peoples who had been incorporated into the Ndebele state and accorded the lowest social status (ibid., pp. 109, 110).

15   Terence Ranger, *Voices from the Rocks: Nature, Culture and History in the Matopos Hills of Zimbabwe* (Oxford: James Currey, 1999), pp. 79–86. Unfortunately, Rhodes' experiment in combining a regular supply of labour to white farmers with long-term security of land for blacks was not adopted by other white landowners, and Rhodes' own verbal guarantee of land security did not long survive his death in 1902. In 1903, the chief native commissioner's attempts to establish a stronger basis for African rights on Rhodes' estate failed, and by 1911 Africans were being evicted on a large scale (ibid., pp. 88–97).

16 Rotberg, *Founder*, pp. 570, 573.

17 This is a controversial point. Some biographers assert that by the word 'race' in his will Rhodes had in mind the distinction, not between white and black, but rather between British and Afrikaner. Certainly, it was the conflict between these last two that preoccupied him for most of his life. However, in 1896 two things happened to change his focus. First, his involvement in the abortive coup d'état in the Transvaal – the infamous 'Jameson Raid' – destroyed his credibility in the eyes of the Afrikaners, and with it any possibility of playing conciliator between them and the British. Second, after he had made peace with the Ndebele later in the same year, he told a companion that prosperity in South Africa depended on establishing 'complete confidence between the white and black races', and he vowed to make building that one of his main aims. After 1896, therefore, Rhodes was much more conscious of the conflict between whites and blacks. That is one reason to think that the word 'race' in his will does not refer simply to the distinction between British and Afrikaner. There are two further reasons. One is that the July 1899 will was drafted in England, where the word 'race' referred to ethnicity in general, and, without explicit qualification, cannot possibly be understood to refer to Afrikaner ethnicity in particular. The other reason is that this is how the first Rhodes Trustees understood the word. In 1907 the question of awarding a Rhodes Scholarship to an African American arose. Some Trustees were averse, fearing that white Scholars from the southern states of the USA would not appreciate being presented with a black *confrère*. Nevertheless, the Trustees felt bound by the terms of Rhodes' will not to permit colour to disqualify a candidate. So, it came about that, within five years of Rhodes' death, the first African American became a Rhodes Scholar.

18 Gilmour, *British in India*, p. 309.

19 Sepoys were Indian troops serving under British command.

20 James, *Raj*, p. 227.

21 Victoria, Queen of Great Britain, *The Letters of Queen Victoria, 1896–1901*, ed. George Earl Buckle, 9 vols, Vol. 9: '1896–1901' (Cambridge: Cambridge University Press, 2014), p. 251. The emphases are Victoria's.

22 Gilmour, *Ruling Caste*, p. 301.

23 Robert Bickers, *The Scramble for China: Foreign Devils in the Qing Empire, 1832–1914* (London: Allen Lane, 2011), p. 305: 'a sense of insecurity was a basic fact about colonial life; it was part of the equipment of the colonist, carried out in the mental baggage. It was best symbolized by the fact that British troops in India carried weapons into church services, a lesson in guardedness learnt the hard way in 1857.'

24 Paul Collier, *Exodus: Immigration and Multiculturalism in the 21st Century* (London: Allen Lane, 2013), Chapters 1 and 3.

25 Storrs, *Orientations*, pp. 72, 84. Afaf Lutfi al-Sayyid-Marsot agrees: 'With the increase in the number of British officials, their bonds of friendship with the Egyptians had weakened, for they now formed a colony of their own, and did not mingle with the natives. The new British officials had little knowledge of the Egyptians, and even less contact with them' (*Egypt and Cromer*, p. 140).

Edward Thompson makes the same numerical point about British officials in India after 1857, who became 'just sufficient in number to form a society of their own, aloof from the Indian population' (Edward Thompson and G. T. Garratt, *Rise and Fulfilment of British Rule in India* [London: Macmillan, 1934], p. 481).

26   Storrs, *Orientations*, p. 85.

27   Gilmour, *Ruling Caste*, p. 254.

28   Ibid., p. 252, referring to Edward W. Said, *Orientalism* (New York: Vintage, 1978), p. 11. What Gilmour writes of the ICS 'Orientalists' was also true of Sir Stamford Raffles, who established an EIC trading post at Singapore in 1819. Raffles so appreciated the value and beauty of Java's indigenous culture and its pre-Islamic Hindu heritage that he sought to recover it from oblivion by collecting antiquities and by writing *The History of Java* (1817) (Glendinning, *Raffles and the Golden Opportunity*, pp. xv, 169). In 1823 he founded the Singapore Institution, partly to enable the company's employees to learn the native languages. This still flourishes – renamed in 1868 as the 'Raffles Institution' – in the form of a secondary school that gained the highest number of admissions to the University of Cambridge in 2019 (https://www.under graduate.study.cam.ac.uk/sites/www.undergraduate.study.cam.ac.uk/files/ publications/undergraduate_admissions_by_apply_centre_2019_cycle.pdf).

29   Gilmour, *Ruling Caste*, pp. 256-7.

30   Thompson and Garratt, *Rise and Fulfilment of British Rule in India*, p. 475. Notwithstanding his view that British rule was good for India, Nirad Chaudhuri is withering in his criticism of the racist contempt for Indians typically shown by 'the local British' (*Thy Hand, Great Anarch!*, pp. 60-4, 65-7, 668-79).

31   Zareer Masani, *Indian Tales of the Raj* (London: BBC Books, 1997), p. 31. The story in Africa was sadly similar. Judging by fiction written by white authors with immediate experience of the colonial period, racism on the part of Europeans (and Asians) towards black Africans, whether in the form of passive indifference or active humiliation, was – while not universal – too common. Thus, in *Major Dane's Garden*, Margery Perham's 1926 novel about British Somaliland in the 1920s, Rhona, Colonel Cavell's new wife, learned that 'that she must not regard Somals as human beings . . . No one encouraged her to take an intelligent interest in the country or its life, human or animal . . . she came to regard Somaliland simply as an opportunity for her husband's career' (*Major Dane's Garden*, 2nd edn [London: Rex Collins, 1970], pp. 33, 122). Perham wrote her book 'soon after' spending a year in British Somaliland (ibid., 'Introduction').

In his story about the Mau Mau uprising in 1950s Kenya, David Lovatt Smith also attributes cultural indifference – in his case horribly fatal – to the settler, Philip Beare: 'Poor Philip! He was so totally out of touch with Africans, nor was he prepared to knuckle down and learn about them . . . He and his family would suffer the terrible consequences of his inability to adapt to African conditions, and his reluctance to learn about African people, amongst whom he had elected to live' (*My Enemy: My Friend*, pp. 42; see also pp. 48-57). The fictional Beare appears to have been modelled on the real Roger Ruck, who was brutally murdered along with his wife and six-year-old son on 24 January 1953 (David Anderson, *Histories of the Hanged: The Dirty War in Kenya and the End of Empire* [New York: W. W. Norton, 2005], pp. 93–5).

In Elspeth Huxley's Mau Mau novel, *A Thing to Love*, we read that the Kenyan nationalist Gitau 'had seen a European woman there [in a shop in Nairobi] and had gone up to ask her and this woman had turned on him and spoken in bad Swahili as if he were a thieving dog. "Go to the back, boy," she'd said in a voice like a saw, "and wait until the white folk have been served" . . . her injustice and spite rankled' (*A Thing to Love* [London: Chatto & Windus, 1954], pp. 103–4). Huxley lived in Kenya as a child and teenager from 1913 to 1925 and visited Africa frequently afterwards. In the mid-1930s she attended a course in anthropology at the London School of Economics, which was taught by Bronisław Malinowski. Among her fellow students was Jomo Kenyatta, whose *Facing Mount Kenya: The Tribal Life of the Gikuyu* (London: Secker and Warburg, 1938) may have informed her 1939 epic *Red Strangers* (London: Penguin, 1999), which tells the story of colonial expansion in Kenya from the viewpoint of three Kikuyu Africans. In 1960 she was appointed a member of the Advisory Commission for the Review of the Constitution of the Federation of Rhodesia and Nyasaland. See Mary Bull, 'Huxley (neé Grant), Elspeth Josceline', in *Oxford Dictionary of National Biography* (Oxford: Oxford University Press, 2004).

In Lovatt Smith's *My Enemy: My Friend*, the African teenager Thiong'o wa Kimani discovered that '[t]he older Europeans only gave him orders and told him what work they wanted him to do. They seldom talked in a friendly, social way or asked about his home or his family . . . She [Mrs Beare] never spoke freely or showed any real interest in his questions.' He also found that in an Asian shop 'he was of so little consequence . . . that his presence was not even worth acknowledging' (*My Enemy: My Friend*, pp. 5–6, 18).

To be fair, we should note that Asian prejudice against Africans was reciprocated, for in Gerald Hanley's novel *The Year of the Lion* (London: William Collins, 1953), we read: 'The African leered at the Indian, despising him . . . while he looked up to the white man, he looked down on the Indians' (pp. 19, 20).

32 Masani, *Indian Tales of the Raj*, pp. 56–7.

33 Ibid., p. 85.

34 M. K. Gandhi, *My Autobiography or The Story of My Experiments with Truth* (London: Penguin, 2001), Chapters 13–25. This was first published in two volumes in 1927 and 1929.

35 Ibid., *My Autobiography*, Chapter 33. Gandhi's experience of the contrast between Britain and South Africa was later echoed by Desmond Tutu's in the 1960s: 'It was in Britain that he [Tutu] first began to realise the intrinsic evil of apartheid. Police officers were polite. White people did not take precedence in queues. He visited Lord's, the Royal Albert Hall and the Travellers Club in Pall Mall. He lost the sense of inferiority most black South Africans felt in the

presence of whites, but that made his family's return to racially segregated South Africa in 1967 all the more jarring' (Obituary, 'Archbishop Desmond Tutu', *The Times*, 27 December 2021).

36 Curzon to St John Brodrick, 2 October 1903; quoted in Gilmour, *Curzon*, p. 171.

37 Gilmour, *Curzon*, p. 172.

38 Alfred Milner, *England in Egypt* (London: Edward Arnold, 1902), pp. 21–2.

39 Ibid., pp. 23, 358. The emphases are mine.

40 Owen, *Lord Cromer*, p. 221.

41 Milner, *England in Egypt*, pp. 318, 320–1, 328, 329.

42 Cromer to Sir Edward Grey, 3 March 1907; Cromer to Sir Edward Grey, 8 March 1907; quoted in Owen, *Lord Cromer*, p. 345.

43 Allawi, *Faisal I of Iraq*, p. 326. I say that the young man with whom Faisal spoke was 'probably' the Duke of Devonshire's eldest son, Edward Cavendish, because, while Faisal's description of him fits in almost all respects, Edward was not his father's only son.

44 Al-Sayyid, *Egypt and Cromer*, p. 75.

45 Ibid., p. 65. The emphasis is al-Sayyid's.

46 Cromer, *Modern Egypt*, Vol. II, pp. 179, 180, 180–1n.1. Roger Owen reports that Cromer's views on Islam were 'deeply offensive to most Muslims' (*Lord Cromer*, p. 355). However, his admiration for Muhammad Abdu and his vision of a reformed Islam indicates that Cromer's criticism was directed at features of traditional Islamic culture, rather than at Islam itself. Indeed, in *Modern Egypt*, he distinguishes between 'Islam, that noble monotheism' and the Islamic 'social system', which 'keeps women in a position of marked inferiority', 'tolerates slavery' and endorses polygamy, whose effects are 'baneful'. At the same time Cromer is sufficiently even-handed to observe that 'the annals of Islam are not stained by the history of an Inquisition' (*Modern Egypt*, pp. 132, 134, 136, 137–8, 157).

47 Milner, *England in Egypt*, pp. 326–7, 330–1.

48 Ibid., p. 359.

49 Edmund Burke, 'Speech on Fox's Bill, 1 December 1784', in *Writings and Speeches of Edmund Burke*, ed. Paul Langford et al., 9 vols (Oxford: Clarendon Press, 1981–2015), Vol. V: 'India: Madras and Bengal, 1774–1785', ed. P. J. Marshall (1981), p. 389.

50 Edmund Burke, 'Impeachment of Warren Hastings', *Writings and Speeches*, Vol. VI: 'The Launching of the Hastings Impeachment, 1786–1788', ed. P. J. Marshall (1991), p. 476.

51 James, *Raj*, pp. 201–2.

52 Sir John Malcolm, *Report of the Province of Malwa and Adjoining Districts* (Calcutta: Government Gazette Press, 1822), Appendix: 'Notes of Instructions to Assistants and Officers acting under the Orders of Major General Sir John Malcolm, G.C.B.', pp. xxiii–iv.

53 Strictly speaking, *'sati'* is the widow who dies and *'sahamarana'* ('dying in company') is the manner of her death (Thompson and Garratt, *Rise and*

Fulfilment of British Rule in India, p. 326). Thompson reported that the practice of *sati* still persisted in some parts as late as August 1932 (ibid., p. 329).

54 James, *Raj*, pp. 226, 280.

55 Bentinck's outlawing of *sati* was challenged in a petition to the Privy Council. Ram Mohan Roy travelled to England to lobby in favour of the ban, which was upheld in 1832. Unfortunately, Roy died the following year in what is now a suburb of Bristol, where he lies buried. He is credited with saying: '[T]hough it is impossible for a thinking man not to feel the evils of political subjection and dependence on a foreign people, yet when we reflect on the advantages which we have derived and may hope to derive from our connection with Great Britain, we may be reconciled to the present state of things which promises permanent benefits to our posterity. Besides security from foreign invaders and internal plunderers, let us ask ourselves whether we could have rescued ourselves from the stigma of female murder (burning of widows) but for the English? Whether we could have otherwise obtained the power of equalising ourselves with the rulers of the country in regard not only to civil but to criminal jurisprudence?' (Kartar Lalvani, *The Making of India: The Untold Story of British Enterprise* [London: Bloomsbury, 2016], pp. 1, 49). Accordingly, in 1823 Roy wrote to Lord Amherst, the governor-general, to protest against the EIC's policy of supporting traditional Sanskrit learning – 'the best calculated to keep this country in darkness' – and to urge it instead to promote the education of 'the natives of India in mathematics, natural philosophy, chemistry, anatomy, and other useful sciences, which the nations of Europe have carried to a degree of perfection that has raised them above the inhabitants of other parts of the world' ('Letter from Rammohun Roy to Lord Amherst, governor-general in council, dated 11 December 1823', in Lynn Zastoupil and Martin Moir, eds, *The Great Indian Education Debate: Documents Relating to the Orientalist-Anglicist Controversy, 1781–1843* (Richmond: Curzon, 1999), pp. 111, 113.

56 Anderson, *Histories of the Hanged*, p. 20; 'Women Missionaries and Colonial Silences in Kenya's Female "Circumcision" Controversy, 1906–1930', *English Historical Review*, CXXXIII, no. 565 (December 2018), pp. 1515–18.

57 Makau Mutua, *Human Rights: A Political and Cultural Critique* (Philadelphia: University of Pennsylvania Press, 2008), pp. 8, 84, 155–6.

58 Ponsonby to Palmerston, 27 December 1840, PRO, FO/195/108, quoted by Ehud R. Toledano in *Slavery and Abolition in the Ottoman Middle East* (Seattle: University of Washington, 1998), pp. 116–17. The emphasis is Ponsonby's.

59 El-Obaid Ahmed El-Obaid and Kwadwo Appiagyei-Atua, 'Human Rights in Africa – A New Perspective on Linking the Past to the Present', *McGill Law Journal*, 41 (1996), p. 850.

60 Makau wa Mutua, 'Limitations in Religious Rights: Problematizing Religious Freedom in the African Context', *Buffalo Human Rights Law Review*, 5 (1999), p. 75.

61 Mutua, *Human Rights*, pp. 115–16.

62 Mutua, 'Limitations in Religious Rights', pp. 75–6.

63   Ibid., p. 105.

64   Ibid., p. 86.

65   It is an irony that would probably not amuse Professor Mutua that his views overlap those of the colonial powers in the early 1950s, when they resisted the extension of 'human rights' to their colonies in the name of protecting traditional culture and the deeply rooted customs of native peoples against catastrophe (Roland Burke, *Decolonization and the Evolution of International Human Rights* [Philadelphia: University of Pennsylvania Press, 2010], pp. 115, 121). Thus, in the debate over the Special Colonial Application clause of the 1950 draft covenant on human rights, the Belgian delegate, M. Soudan, argued that to force human rights abruptly on less civilised peoples would be socially destructive (ibid., pp. 116–17). Roland Burke is cynical about the motives of the colonial delegations to the UN Third (Social, Humanitarian and Cultural Affairs) Committee, telling us that they 'feigned' reverence for traditional culture, because, '[e]ver anxious about stability and the limits of their policing power', they were disinclined to alienate traditional elites (ibid., pp. 114, 127). Since, as Burke himself tells us, the colonial powers usually regarded traditional culture as inferior, it is doubtful that they revered it much (ibid., pp. 114, 116–17). But they were certainly worried about political stability, and since instability often meant bloodshed, since anarchy threatens all forms of human good, and since it is the special moral responsibility of ruling authorities to prevent anarchy, their worry was well founded.

66   Baba of Karo, *Baba of Karo: A Woman of the Muslim Hausa*, transcribed and translated by Mary F. Smith (London: Faber & Faber, 1965), pp. 48–9, 50.

67   Mutua, 'Limitations in Religious Rights', pp. 101–2.

68   Mutua, *Human Rights*, p. 116.

69   Ronald Hyam reports that, inspired by the post-colonial 'speculations' of Edward Said, theoretical anthropologists in the early 1990s promoted the thesis that Christianity had been imposed on Africans by missionaries, who were 'cultural imperialists' misshaping African culture to conform to their own 'hegemonic world-view'. However, the reality was more complex, as historical ethnographers have always understood, and '[p]ost-colonial theory . . . bypassed . . . evidence of missionaries being manipulated' and '[i]n the rush to denounce "imperialism" . . . was strangely deaf to African "agency"' ('The View from Below: The African Response to Missionaries', in *Understanding the British Empire*, p. 183). With its message of the 'brotherhood of man' and 'equality before Christ', Christianity proved naturally attractive to African refugees, slaves, children, marginalised adults such as women and repressed teenagers such as girls fleeing circumcision (ibid., pp. 184, 192). Further, it was 'largely Africans who evangelised other Africans', the evangelists often being 'young men who were essentially rebels, young men who challenged the elders and consciously sought change' (ibid., p. 182). Further still, Western missionaries and Africans were engaged in a constant process of mutual give and take (ibid., pp. 183–4). Africans voted with their own feet: in 1900 there were about 9 million African Christians out of a total population of 100 million; by 1990 there were about 200 million out of 450 million (ibid., p. 178).

70   Ndabaningi Sithole, *African Nationalism* (Cape Town: Oxford University Press, 1959), p. 53. Brian Stanley confirms Sithole's last point, when he writes that '[c]ultural imperialism, the most hated of all forms of imperialism, in fact did more than any other to bring the empire to an end' (*The Bible and the Flag: Protestant Missions and British Imperialism in the Nineteenth and Twentieth Centuries* [Leicester: Apollos, 1990], p. 52). Stanley's book offers a balanced account of (Protestant) Christian missionary activity in the British Empire, and of relevant historiography (up to 1990).

71   Mutua, 'Limitations in Religious Rights', p. 103.

72   Ibid., pp. 96–7.

73   Burke, *Decolonization and the Evolution of International Human Rights*, p. 126.

74   I discuss more fully the question of how far human rights are 'Western' in *What's Wrong with Rights?* (Oxford: Oxford University Press, 2020), Chapter 8, from which the last four paragraphs have been lifted almost verbatim.

75   Chinua Achebe, 'The Education of a British-Protected Child' (1993), in *Education of a British-Protected Child*, p. 7.

76   Chinua Achebe, 'My Dad and Me' (1996), in *Education of a British-Protected Child*, p. 37.

77   Bernth Lindfors, *Conversations with Chinua Achebe* (Jackson, MS: University of Mississippi, 1997), pp. 66–7. There are some Africans who share neither Mutua's fierce loyalty to traditional culture nor even Achebe's wistfulness for it. In *A Curse from God* (1970), the Kenyan novelist S. N. Ngũbiah depicted polygamy, the treatment of women as property and circumcision in the most unflattering terms, obliquely challenging Jomo Kenyatta's argument for a return to Kikuyu tribal folkways (F. Hale, 'The Critique of Gĩkũyũ Religion and Culture in S. N. Ngũbiah's *A Curse from God*', *Acta Theologica*, 27/1 (2007).

78   Nasrin Pourhamrang, '*Things Fall Apart* Now More Famous Than Me, Says Chinua Achebe', *Daily Trust*, 8 September 2012: https://dailytrust.com/things-fall-apart-now-more-famous-than-me-says-chinua-achebe.

79   Commonwealth War Graves Commission (CWGC), *Report of the Special Committee to Review Historical Inequalities in Commemoration* (Maidenhead: CWGC, 2021), p. 6.

80   Ibid., pp. 6, 10.

81   Alexandra Topping, 'UK Failure to Commemorate Black and Asian War Dead Known "For Years"', *Guardian*, 22 April 2021; Mark Bridge, 'Apology Over Non-white War Dead Left Unnamed', *The Times*, 22 April 2021; BBC, 'Commonwealth War Graves: PM "Deeply Troubled" Over Racism', 22 April 2021: https://www.bbc.co.uk/news/uk-56840131; Al Jazeera, 'Britain's Unequal Troop Commemorations Due to "Pervasive Racism"', 22 April 2021: https://www.aljazeera.com/news/2021/4/22/britains-unequal-troop-commemorations-due-to-pervasive-racism

82   Topping, 'UK Failure to Commemorate'.

83   CWGC, *Report of the Special Committee*, pp. 8–9, 29.

84   Ibid., p. 21.

85 Ibid., p. 22.

86 Ibid., pp. 27, 39, 44.

87 Ibid., pp. 27, 30, 49.

88 Ibid., p. 30. The emphasis is mine.

89 James Hastings, *Encyclopedia of Religion and Ethics*, 13 vols (Edinburgh: T. & T. Clark, 1908–26), Vol. IV: 'Confirmation – Drama' (1914), s.v. 'Death and Disposal of the Dead (Introductory)', pp. 420, 422. It is noteworthy that in this Edwardian article we find an admirable instance of cultural *self*-criticism, when the author, E. Sidney Hartland, describes as 'barbarous' the medieval *European* custom of denying burial to a person who had died in debt until his creditors had been satisfied – a custom recorded as late as 1811 in Shoreditch (ibid., p. 420).

90 CWGC, *Report of the Special Committee*, p. 30.

91 Ibid., pp. 30, 33.

92 Ibid., p. 34.

93 While the report does not make unequivocally clear that the graves for the white South Africans and Europeans were individually marked, I have inferred that they were.

94 Ibid., pp. 31–2, 33–4.

95 Ibid., p. 26.

96 Ibid., p. 49.

97 Ibid., p. 21. The emphasis is mine.

98 Ibid., p. 49. The emphasis is mine.

99 Ibid., pp. 6, 31, 40, 49.

4. LAND, SETTLERS AND 'CONQUEST'

1 Despite its disturbing social implications, this moral principle was widely acknowledged in the 'natural law' tradition that thrived in late medieval and early modern Europe. See Nigel Biggar, *What's Wrong with Rights?*, pp. 37–8, 229–30.

2 Tracey Lindberg, 'The Doctrine of Discovery in Canada', in Robert J. Miller, Jacinta Ruru, Larissa Behrendt and Tracey Lindberg, *Discovering Indigenous Lands: The Doctrine of Discovery in the English Colonies* (Oxford: Oxford University Press, 2010), pp. 89, 90, 91.

3 Tom Flanagan, *First Nations? Second Thoughts*, 2nd edn (Montreal and Kingston: Queen's University Press, 2008), pp. 12–13. 'BP' or 'Before Present' is the most commonly used convention for carbon dating and means 'before 1950'. Since Flanagan's book is politically controversial in Canada, we should note that it won the 2001 Donner Prize for the best book on Canadian public policy, and the 2001 Donald Smiley Prize awarded by the Canadian Political Science Association for the best book on Canadian politics and government. My own judgement is that Flanagan thinks carefully and fairly, and writes with authority.

4 Flanagan, *First Nations? Second Thoughts*, p. 15.

5   Ibid., p. 6.

6   Georges Erasmus and Joe Sanders, 'Canadian History: An Aboriginal Perspective', in Diane Engelstad and John Bird, eds, *Nation to Nation: Aboriginal Sovereignty and the Future of Canada* (Concord, Ontario: Anansi, 1992), p. 4; quoted in Flanagan, *First Nations? Second Thoughts*, p. 23.

7   Flanagan, *First Nations? Second Thoughts*, p. 17.

8   Pekka Hämäläinen, *The Comanche Empire* (New Haven and London: Yale University Press, 2008), pp. 1–2.

9   Ibid., pp. 2, 14. Hämäläinen tells us that the 'Comanches were not . . . self-conscious imperialists, following a pre-meditated expansionist agenda, nor were they all-conquering militarists bent on subjugating other societies. They established their pre-eminence in stages, responding often in an ad hoc fashion to circumstances that on first inspection seem to have little to do with imperial power politics . . . Comanches exercised power on an imperial scale, but they did so without adopting an imperial ideology and without building a rigid, European-style empire' (ibid., p. 352). Hämäläinen operates here with a crude caricature of European empires. In fact, if the history of the British Empire is anything to go by, European empire was often quite as un-premeditated and ad hoc as the Comanche one, and no more (or less) 'bent on subjugating other societies'.

10   Flanagan, *First Nations? Second Thoughts*, pp. 18, 39.

11   Ibid., p. 19.

12   Ibid., p. 24. If anyone doubts Flanagan, because he is not an anthropologist, perhaps they will heed Hymie Rubinstein, who is one: 'Established social science has shown that the history of humanity, including the story of the pre-European inhabitants of the so-called New World, is a tale of migration, warfare, slavery, forced assimilation, and genocide . . . the first human settlers of what was for them a "new world" likely arrived from Asia about 2,500 years ago, spreading through the two continents in trickles and waves, displacing, absorbing, and eliminating the previous inhabitants as they competed for resources. The dynamic nature of the earliest peopling of the Americas is revealed by the archaeological record, which provides considerable evidence that these "first peoples" were engaged in inter-group warfare long before Europeans arrived. A well-documented example is the 14th-century Crow Creek massacre . . . Archaeologists have found the remains of nearly 500 victims killed during the massacre. Many skeletons showed signs of mutilation, including scalping, broken teeth, beheadings, and amputated limbs . . . many skeletons had old wounds that had healed, suggesting involvement in previous conflicts' ('Indigenous Exceptionalism and the TRC', in Rodney A. Clifton and Mark DeWolf, eds, *From Truth Comes Reconciliation: An Assessment of the Truth and Reconciliation Report* (Winnipeg: Frontier Centre for Public Policy, 2021), pp. 148, 150–1).

13   Ibid., p. 19. I observe that Flanagan's conclusion is confirmed by one politically hostile witness. James Daschuk, who, with some tendentiousness, blames the starvation of the native peoples of the western plains in the late 1870s and early

1880s partly upon the racist ideology of the government of John A. McDonald, nevertheless concedes that '[i]n many cases, the First Nations that entered into treaties with the crown [from the 1870s] were inheritors of the plains rather than inhabitants since prehistoric times' (*Clearing the Plains: Disease, Politics of Starvation, and the Loss of Aboriginal Life* [Regina: University of Regina Press, 2013], p. 183). I discuss Daschuk's critique of McDonald's government in Chapter 7, section V.

14   Adekeye Adebajo, 'Why Price Is Wrong Over Rhodes', *South African Sunday Independent*, 29 March 2015. He made the same claim four years earlier in 'Mandela and Rhodes, Africa's Saint and Sinner', *Independent Online*, 26 July 2011.

15   André Maurois summarises the situation well: 'Mashonaland was really a No Man's Land, a raiding ground for the Matabeles, a kind of reserve in which they went hunting when they wanted to sport and loot in the form of girls, cattle, and slave boys for herders' (*Cecil Rhodes*, trans. Rohan Wadham [London: Collins, 1953], p. 83). Maurois appears to be quoting someone else here, but he does not identify his source.

16   See pp. 115–16 later in this chapter.

17   William Beinart's case against Rhodes rests heavily on his view that the BSAC's entry into Ndebele territory in 1890 was 'an armed invasion' that resulted in 'violent conquest' ('Appendix A', pp. 103, 105, 118). I do not agree. Given the 'Rudd Concession' and Lobengula's initial acceptance of the company's presence, its entry did not clearly amount to an invasion. Moreover, the 'violent conquest' occurred three years later, only *after* the Ndebele assault on the Shona in and around Salisbury, which persuaded Rhodes that Lobengula had to be subdued.

18   In his account, Beinart tells us that in July 1893 'a sizeable Ndebele army moved eastward in order to assert authority over Shona communities who were living on or near settler farms around Salisbury. They did not threaten white settlers, but they did disrupt labour supplies and captured a limited amount of cattle. Jameson warned them to leave, which they did not' ('Appendix A', p. 106). This description is coy, overlooking the fact that 'asserting authority' in this case involved the killing of Shona within sight of the settlers, which, together with the refusal of the Ndebele to leave, surely gave the British good reason to *feel* threatened. It also fails to mention that, in approaching the white settlements, the Ndebele army was defying Lobengula, which implies that he had lost control of at least a significant portion of his own people. In that case, had Rhodes negotiated with him, as Beinart thinks he should have done (ibid., p. 106), it is doubtful that Lobengula would have been able to keep his side of any peace agreement.

19   Beinart tells us that Rhodes 'had no scruples about the violence used' ('Appendix A', p. 123). He is particularly disturbed by the BSAC's 'unbridled use . . . of the Maxim gun', especially the fact that it was used 'only by one side' (ibid., pp. 99, 106, 107). This implies that he thinks that fairness in war requires the opposing sides to be equal in strength. That, however, is a recipe for endless

war, since it is only when one side overpowers the other that the fighting will stop. The ultimate aim of military endeavour is to make the enemy lose the will to fight, and that is achieved by overwhelming them. Several other features of the BSAC's military tactics in the war of 1896-7 also disturb Beinart: the 'scorched earth' policy, the shooting of enemy soldiers in flight, and the exploding of dynamite in caves where women and children were known to be hiding (ibid., pp. 99, 105, 111, 112, 114, 115). First, the burning of villages and the destruction of grain stores may have been justified by military necessity, in that they deprived enemy troops of support and sustenance. A similar policy was adopted by the British Army against the Boers in the Second Anglo-Boer War of 1899-1902. Second, enemy soldiers who flee have not surrendered, and if their flight is successful, they will live to fight another day. Therefore, it is morally permissible to shoot enemy soldiers who are retreating, but who have not laid down their arms. Unfortunately, in conflicts such as those of 1893 and 1896-7, where the opponents represent very alien cultures and where there is no commonly recognised international law, there are no commonly recognised conventions for signalling and accepting surrender and sufficient trust to warrant the taking of risks is absent. Beinart tells us that '[i]mperial authorities tried to offer a qualified form of amnesty but it was clearly not trusted (or known)' (ibid., p. 112). Third, it is clear from Beinart's own account that the explosion of dynamite in caves was a last resort and not intended to slaughter civilians. He tells us that those hiding included 'armed men'; that at Intaba zikaMambo and Marandellas, when attempts were made to 'smoke out' the occupants, women and children who gave themselves up were not harmed; that dynamite was used on one occasion only when a chief responded to an invitation to surrender by killing two policemen, and on another only after the attempt at 'smoking out' had failed. As we see in Chapter 8, pp. 248-9, Dan Hicks expresses a similar, militarily naive view of British tactics in their invasion of Benin in 1897.

20 The phrase 'militarised state' is Beinart's ('Appendix A', p. 106).

21 W. A. Elliott, *Gold from the Quartz* (London Missionary Society, 1910), p. 81.

22 Quoted by David A. Nock and Celia Haig-Brown in 'Introduction', *With Good Intentions: Euro-Canadian and Aboriginal Relations in Colonial Canada* (Vancouver: University of British Columbia Press, 2006), pp. 14-15.

23 Flanagan, *First Nations? Second Thoughts*, pp. 40-2.

24 Louis Riel, address to the court, 1 August 1885, in George F. G. Stanley et al., *The Collected Writings of Louis Riel*, 5 vols (Edmonton: University of Alberta Press, 1985), Vol. 3, p. 548; quoted in Thomas Flanagan, *Riel and the Rebellion: 1885 Reconsidered*, 2nd edn (Toronto: University of Toronto Press, 2000), p. 95.

25 See Henry Reynolds, *The Law of the Land* (Victoria: Penguin, 1987), p. 12.

26 Flanagan, *First Nations? Second Thoughts*, p. 60.

27 While the 'doctrine of discovery' had been operative from the late fifteenth century, it was the subject of a seminal exposition in 1823 by Chief Justice John Marshall in the US Supreme Court ruling *Johnson v M'Intosh*. See Robert J. Miller, 'The Doctrine of Discovery', in Miller et al., *Discovering Indigenous Lands*, pp. 3-4.

28 Robert J. Miller, 'The Legal Adoption of Discovery in the United States', in Miller et al., *Discovering Indigenous Lands*, pp. 29–30. In fairness, I should report that Miller entertains the fashionable, 'critical' suspicion that 'the real motivation' behind these arrangements was exploitative and had little to do with respect for native rights. However, in all human likelihood the colonists' motivations were various, and Miller provides no evidence that the cynical ones were dominant.

29 Ibid., p. 45.

30 Ibid., p. 50.

31 Acadia was a colony of New France that, from 1604, comprised most of what are now the Maritime provinces of Canada, part of the province of Quebec, and part of the state of Maine in the United States.

32 Sarah Carter, 'Aboriginal People of Canada and the British Empire', in Phillip Buckner, ed., *Canada and the British Empire*, Oxford History of the British Empire Companion Series (Oxford: Oxford University Press, 2010), p. 202; J. R. Miller, *Shingwauk's Vision: A History of Native Residential Schools* (Toronto: University of Toronto Press, 1996), p. 97.

33 Ingeborg Marshall, *A History and Ethnography of the Beothuk* (Montreal & Kingston: McGill-Queen's University Press, 1996), p. 120; quoted in Carter, 'Aboriginal People of Canada and the British Empire', p. 203.

34 Carter, 'Aboriginal People of Canada and the British Empire', p. 204.

35 Donald B. Smith, 'Macdonald's Relationship with Aboriginal Peoples', in Patrice Dutil and Roger Hall, eds, *Macdonald at 200: New Reflections and Legacies* (Toronto: Dundurn, 2014), p. 61.

36 Carter, 'Aboriginal People of Canada and the British Empire', pp. 214–15.

37 Ibid., p. 215; Flanagan, *First Nations? Second Thoughts*, pp. 145–7; *Copy of Treaty No. 6 between Her Majesty the Queen and the Plain and Wood Cree Indians and Other Tribes of Indians* (Ottawa: Indigenous and Northern Affairs Canada, 1964), p. 4: http://www.trcm.ca/wp-content/uploads/PDFsTreaties/Treaty%206%20Text%20and%20Adhesions.pdf.

38 Daschuk, *Clearing the Plains*, p. xx. For a full explanation, see Chapter 7, section V.

39 Flanagan explains that '[l]ife in dense agricultural communities allowed diseases such as smallpox, influenza, and measles to leap from domesticated animal hosts to become crowd diseases of human beings. By early modern times, all societies of the Old World had acquired some resistance to these diseases, which became lethal when transferred to the inexperienced populations of the New World' (*First Nations? Second Thoughts*, p. 39).

40 Daschuk, *Clearing the Plains*, pp. xii, xv–xvi.

41 Michael King, *The Penguin History of New Zealand* (Rosedale, NZ: Penguin, 2003. Sydney, NSW: Accessible Publishing System PTY, 2010), pp. 7, 44, 47. King argues persuasively against what he calls the 'Great New Zealand Myth' of Polynesian discovery as early as the ninth century (ibid., pp. 32, 43, 48). While not an academic historian, Michael King held a D.Phil. in history from the University of Waikato and his bestselling book attracted a very positive review from K. R. Howe, professor of history at Massey University at Albany,

who described it as 'extraordinarily well informed in terms of modern research details', 'highly instructive for historians' and 'sophisticated history writing' (*New Zealand Herald*, 22 October 2003: https://www.nzherald.co.nz/lifestyle/ imichael-kingi-the-penguin-history-of-new-zealand/ T7BIDPOZEQWPFEDRQDR3JWL4RI/ [as at 7 June 2021]). King's *Penguin History* was the first to fully incorporate Māori history and experience.

42 King, *Penguin History*, pp. 4, 61, 67.
43 Ibid., pp. 83, 86–9, 93, 124, 149, 151.
44 Ibid., pp. 111, 127, 130, 139, 140.
45 Ibid., pp. 151–2.
46 Ibid., pp. 97, 156.
47 Ibid., p. 147. See also p. 149.
48 Ibid., pp. 156, 157, 161, 169–70.
49 Ibid., pp. 172–3.
50 Jacinta Ruru, 'Asserting the Doctrine of Discovery in Aotearoa New Zealand: 1840–1960s', in Miller et al., *Discovering Indigenous Lands*, p. 213; Claudia Orange, *The Treaty of Waitangi* (Wellington: Bridget Williams Books, 1987), p. 8. 'Paradoxically,' Robert Tombs writes, 'there was little appetite in London for adding to the empire, and some conquests were handed back. Parts of Indonesia were returned to Holland in 1824. The Ionian Islands were ceded to Greece. There was no attempt to regain Corsica, which had previously asked to join the empire, after its reoccupation by France in 1796. Later requests from inhabitants of Ethiopia, Mexico, Uruguay, Sarawak, Katanga and Morocco to join the empire were firmly turned down, and there was reluctance and delay in absorbing Fiji, New Guinea and Basutoland' (*The English and Their History* [London: Allen Lane, 2014], p. 541).
51 King, *Penguin History*, pp. 171, 178. Claudia Orange offers a measure of corroboration when she writes that some early New South Wales governors 'took an active interest' in mitigating the lawless maltreatment of Māori (*Treaty of Waitangi*, p. 8).
52 Orange, *Treaty of Waitangi*, pp. 17, 106–7, 108, 123.
53 Ibid., pp. 27–8.
54 'Lord Normanby', *New Zealand History* (Wellington, NZ: New Zealand Ministry for Culture and Heritage, 2017): https://nzhistory.govt.nz/people/ lord-normanby (as at 1 September 2020).
55 Orange, *Treaty of Waitangi*, pp. 132–4.
56 Ibid., p. 111.
57 Ibid., pp. 114–15.
58 Ibid., pp. 149–50.
59 Ibid., pp. 228–9.
60 By 1871 the Europeans or 'Pakeha' numbered 256, 393, while by 1874 the Māori had declined to 45,470 and were declining further (ibid., p. 185).
61 King, *Penguin History*, pp. 193, 201, 245.
62 Orange, *Treaty of Waitangi*, pp. 98–9.
63 Ibid., pp. 100, 102, 104.

64 Ibid., p. 115.

65 King, *Penguin History*, p. 249.

66 Ibid., p. 261. See James Belich, *The New Zealand Wars and the Victorian Interpretation of Racial Conflict* (Auckland: Auckland University Press, 2015).

67 King, *Penguin History*, p. 266.

68 Orange, *Treaty of Waitangi*, pp. 153–4.

69 Ibid., pp. 138–9, 160, 161.

70 Ibid., pp. 137, 139–40.

71 Ibid., pp. 202, 207.

72 King, *Penguin History*, pp. 183, 589, 606, 607.

73 Larissa Behrendt, 'The Doctrine of Discovery in Australia', in Miller et al., *Discovering Indigenous Lands*, p. 174.

74 Behrendt comments: 'They were of course wrong about this. The whole continent was populated and the pre-contact Aboriginal population has been estimated as being between 1 and 1.5 million people' (ibid., p. 175). It seems to me, however, that 1.5 million people – less than ten times the current population of Oxford – spread over Australia's almost 2 million habitable square miles still makes for a very sparse population of between 0.5 and 0.75 people per square mile. The habitation was even sparser, if Henry Reynolds is correct that a pre-contact population of up to 500,000 inhabited 1.544 million square miles, averaging 0.32 people per square mile (*Law of the Land*, pp. 10, 50).

75 Ann Curthoys, 'Indigenous Subjects', in Deryck M. Schreuder and Stuart Ward, eds, *Australia's Empire*, Oxford History of the British Empire Companion Series (Oxford: Oxford University Press, 2008), pp. 82–3. Whether or not the formal international legal doctrine of *terra nullius* had been formulated by the late eighteenth century and so could have informed British imperial policy-makers and colonial governors of that time, is a matter of dispute among historians. Whatever the case, Tom Flanagan argues that the Australian discussion has been mistaken to suppose that the doctrine of *terra nullius* is an argument about property rights, rather than one about sovereignty (*First Nations? Second Thoughts*, p. 57).

76 According to Henry Reynolds, 'Within a short time of the initial settlement it was known that the interior was not uninhabited . . . By the 1830s well-informed settlers knew that Australia was a patchwork of clearly defined tribal territories and that local blacks defended their territory against both Europeans and traditional enemies' (*Law of the Land*, p. 42; see also Chapter 3).

77 Curthoys, 'Indigenous Subjects', pp. 89–90. Writing to his successor in 1807, after six years as governor of New South Wales, Philip Gidley King expressed the view that he had 'ever considered them [the Aborigines] the real proprietors of the soil' (Reynolds, *Law of the Land*, p. 73). Such a view became increasingly common among colonial governors from 1821, as Henry Reynolds shows (ibid., pp. 87–8). Then he comments: 'The belief that the Aborigines were the original proprietors of Australia and had an interest in the soil took deep root in colonial society between 1820 and 1850' (ibid., p. 87).

78 Against Henry Reynolds, Bain Attwood argues that the in-principle Christian

humanitarianism of colonial officials was virtually annulled by 'the practical tasks of government in the service of empire' (*Empire and the Making of Native Title: Sovereignty, Property and Indigenous People* [Cambridge: University of Cambridge Press, 2020], p. 69):

> It is naïve to attribute the position the Colonial Office adopted on matters such as native people's interests in land to its principal figures' commitment to some high-minded religious, moral or legal principles. Their stances in such matters are best understood as the result of a complex mix of principle and expediency. While the Colonial Office's major players undoubtedly believed they had a duty to protect the interests of the native peoples, they were equally convinced that there were very real political factors that circumscribed any attempt on the part of the British government to uphold the interests the Aboriginal people might be deemed to have. This conviction owed a good deal to the Colonial Office's perception of the relative power of the imperial and colonial government, the settlers and the Aboriginal people, and especially of the force each could or could not wield . . . There is no evidence to suggest that Christian humanitarianism . . . made any substantial difference to the way native rights in land were treated in South Australia, though there can be no doubt that it helped to create a milieu in which the major British political players adopted a language of protection and that this promoted a considerable amount of talk about British duties and the rights of Aboriginal people, though it seems doubtful that these rights were ever conceived as anything more than a right to be protected (ibid., pp. 94–5).

Attwood's argument strains to imply a more pejorative picture than is warranted. First, moral principles ought to be adjusted to take account of circumstances, for if they were not so adjusted they would be imprudent, and imprudence is a moral vice. Those who want to realise humanitarian ideals in political affairs ought to consider carefully what is politically possible, else they risk realising nothing of the ideals at all. To present this, as Attwood does, as a mix of 'principle and expediency' is unfair, since 'expediency' carries the connotation of mere convenience, with an additional hint of cynical amorality. A fairer description would be to say that the Colonial Office's deliberations were a mixture of 'principle and practical or political possibility'.

Second, to say that the humanitarian colonial officials 'adopted a language' of protection, which promoted 'a considerable amount of talk' about 'duties' and 'rights' tends to imply that the talk was insincere and effected nothing. But that is not true, for practical steps were taken to protect the aborigines. Thus, in a letter to the Colonisation Commissioners in December 1835, Sir George Grey, writing on behalf of the Colonial Office, insisted that the boundaries of the colony of South Australia be extended only so far as to encompass 'vacant territory' and to avoid 'any act of injustice' towards aboriginal peoples 'whose proprietary right to the soil we have not the slightest ground for disputing'. Indeed, he required the Commissioners to extend the boundaries only so far as 'they can show, by some sufficient evidence, that the land is unoccupied, and that no earlier or preferable title exists' (ibid., p. 74). Commenting on this letter, Attwood complains that Grey did not positively state that any aboriginal peoples actually had rights to property in land, but merely entertained the possibility that some might have (ibid., p. 75). This is cavilling. The presumption of Grey's letter is clearly that only vacant territory may be colonised, that where land is occupied by aboriginals they have a prima facie proprietary right to it and that the burden of proof to the contrary lies with the colonisers.

Third, given that Attwood is not satisfied by the affirmation of a right of aborigines to protection against *further* violation of rights to property in land or by the view that aborigines should be recompensed for past violations by 'what was seen as the gifts of civilisation and Christianity' (ibid., p. 40), his residual complaint appears to be that the British colonisers did not seek to rectify past violations by restoring unjustly taken land to their rightful, aboriginal owners. This must be what he means when he writes that 'there is little evidence to suggest that any serious consideration was given to upholding the Aboriginal people's rights to property in land' (ibid.). He attributes this to 'the Colonial Office's perception of the relative power of the imperial and colonial government, the settlers and the Aboriginal people, and especially of the force each could or could not wield' (ibid., p. 95). In other words, colonial officials believed that there were practical, military and political constraints upon what they could do to rectify such unjust seizure of aboriginal land as had already taken place. Insofar as the officials' view had good grounds – and I think it did – it was realistic, not cynical.

79 House of Commons, *Report of the Parliamentary Select Committee on Aboriginal Tribes (British Settlements)*, reprinted for the Aborigines Protection Society (London: Ball, Chambers, and Hatchard, 1837), 'Suggestions', p. 126.

80 Arthur Keppel-Jones, *Rhodes and Rhodesia: The White Conquest of Zimbabwe, 1884–1902* (Montreal and Kingston: McGill-Queen's University Press, 1983), p. 77.

81 Carter, 'Aboriginal People of Canada and the British Empire', p. 204. The emphasis is mine.

82 Ibid., p. 215.

83 Tracey Lindberg, 'Contemporary Canadian Resonance of an Imperial Doctrine', Miller et al., *Discovering Indigenous Lands*, p. 168 n.221.

84 Lindberg, 'Doctrine of Discovery in Canada', p. 112.

85 Flanagan, *First Nations? Second Thoughts*, pp. 115–18.

86 Mark Whittow, *The Making of Byzantium, 600–1025* (Berkeley: University of California Press, 1996), p. 83.

87 Bruce Trigger, 'The Historians' Indian: Native Americans in Canadian Historical Writing from Charlevoix to the Present', *Canadian Historical Review*, 67/3 (1986), p. 336; quoted in Frances Widdowson and Albert Howard, *Disrobing the Aboriginal Industry: The Deception behind Indigenous Cultural Preservation* (Montreal & Kingston: McGill-Queen's University Press, 2008), p. 44.

88 Alexander von Gernet, *Oral Narratives and Aboriginal Pasts: An Interdisciplinary*

Review of the Literature on Oral Traditions and Oral Histories (Ottawa: Research and Analysis Directorate, Indian and Northern Affairs Canada, 1996), p. 20.

89 Eric Richards, *Britannia's Children: Emigration from England, Scotland, Wales and Ireland since 1600* (Hambledon: London and New York, 2004), p. 149. James Belich differs from Richards in thinking that British emigration in the nineteenth century was stimulated by a deliberately promoted settler ideology, and enhanced by the deliberate policy of both imperial and colonial governments (*Replenishing the Earth*, pp. 73, 190, 265, 283, 288, 406). Nonetheless, he describes Richards' book as 'the best recent work on British emigration' and he does not dissent from Richards' view that it was largely driven by private demand, not public stimulus.

90 Alan Taylor, *American Revolutions: A Continental History* (New York: W. W. Norton, 2016), pp. 61–2.

91 Ibid., p. 61.

92 Ibid., p. 75.

93 Alan Taylor regards the British prohibition of American settlers from the trans-Appalachian West as a cause of the subsequent revolutionary conflict equal to that of the imposition of taxes (ibid., pp. 6, 77).

94 Ibid., p. 251. Commissioned in 1786 by his former comrade-in-arms, Hugh Percy, later 2nd Duke of Northumberland, Joseph Brant's portrait now hangs in the National Portrait Gallery in Washington, DC.

95 Ibid., p. 7.

96 Ibid., p. 287.

97 Mark G. Hirsch, 'Illegal State Treaties', in Suzan Shown Harjo, ed., *Nation to Nation: Treaties between the United States and American Indian Nations* (Washington, DC: Smithsonian Institution, 2014), p. 66.

98 See Chapter 8, section VII for a fuller account of the origins and conduct of the Second Anglo-Boer War.

99 Thomas Pakenham, *The Boer War* (London: Weidenfeld and Nicolson, 1979), pp. 563–5. I take it that what is referred to here as 'Clause 9' in a draft of the treaty became Article 8 of the final version.

100 Pakenham's general disposition towards the British in South Africa oscillated between the sceptical and the scathing. As I will explain, both here and especially when I treat the Second Anglo-Boer War in Chapter 8, section VII, he is often unfair. Sometimes his unfairness lacked scruple. For example, Pakenham claimed that, when commanding Mafeking under siege from October 1899 to May 1900, Robert Baden-Powell had operated a racially biased food policy: 'The white garrison took part of the rations of the black garrison. And part of the black garrison was accordingly given the choice of starving to death in the town or running the gauntlet of the [besieging] Boers' (*Boer War*, p. 406). Tim Jeal spends seventeen pages of his by-no-means-uncritical biography of Baden-Powell dismantling this claim (*Baden-Powell* [London: Pimlico, 1989], pp. 260–77). At one point he lays out how Pakenham reversed the meaning of an excerpt from the testimony of a journalist, J. Emerson Neilly,

who had been present in Mafeking during the siege. Pakenham presented it thus:

> I saw them [Africans in the besieged town] fall down on the veldt and lie where they had fallen, too weak to go on their way. The sufferers were mostly little boys – mere infants ranging from four or five upwards . . . Hunger had them in its grip, and many of them were black spectres and living skeletons . . . their ribs literally breaking their shrivelled skin – men, women and children . . . Probably hundreds died from starvation or the diseases that always accompany famine. Certain it is that many were found dead on the veldt . . . words could not portray the scene of misery; five or six hundred human frameworks of both sexes and all ages . . . dressed in . . . tattered rags, standing in lines, each holding an old blackened can or beef tin, awaiting turn to crawl painfully up to the soup kitchen where the food was distributed (*Boer War*, p. 408).

Jeal then supplies the words that Pakenham chose to omit:

> Certain it is that many were found dead on the veldt, and others succumbed to hunger in the hospital. The Barolongs proper were not so badly off; the least fortunate were the strange Kaffirs who came in from the Transvaal as refugees when the war started, and the slaves and servants of the Barolong nation. When the Colonel [Baden-Powell] got to know of the state of affairs he instituted soup kitchens, where horses were boiled in huge cauldrons, and the savoury mess doled out in pints and quarts to all comers. Some of the people – those employed on works – paid for the food; the remainder, who were in the majority, obtained it free. One of those kitchens was established in the stadt [the Barolongs' community], and I several times went down there to see the unfortunate fed. [Words could not . . .] (Jeal, *Baden-Powell*, p. 270).

Jeal comments: 'The sentences cut from this Neilly quotation make it absolutely plain that nobody in need was being denied food by Baden-Powell. Yet Mr Pakenham claims that 2,000 people were denied food altogether.' (ibid.)

101 See G. B. Pyrah, *Imperial Policy and South Africa, 1902–10* (Oxford: Clarendon Press, 1955), Chapter IV: 'The Non-European Majority', esp. pp. 92–6; John Marlowe, *Milner: Apostle of Empire* (London: Hamish Hamilton, 1976), pp. 121–2, 132, 140; Terence H. O'Brien, *Milner: Viscount Milner of St James's and Cape Town, 1854–1925* (London: Constable, 1979), p. 220; Le May, *British Supremacy in South Africa*, p. 203.

102 Nowadays *Realpolitik* denotes nothing but the ruthless pursuit of power – as represented classically by Macchiavelli. Originally, however, it meant something quite different. It was coined in 1853 by Ludwig August von Rochau, a liberal who had been disillusioned by the crushing of the various attempts in Europe to establish liberal constitutions in 1848, which had invariably failed. (Europe's 1848 was rather like the Arab Spring, except that it expired within twelve months.) Von Rochau invented the word 'Realpolitik' to describe and recommend the pursuit of liberal constitutional goals by politically realistic – gradual

and patient – means. Originally, it meant the pursuit of liberal ends by politically canny, rather than politically stupid, means. Only later under Bismarck did its meaning degenerate into the ruthless pursuit of power in a social Darwinist struggle for survival. See John Bew, 'The Real Origins of Realpolitik', *The National Interest*, 130 (March/April 2014) and *Realpolitik: A History* (New York: Oxford University Press, 2016).

Saul Dubow, Smuts Professor of Commonwealth History at the University of Cambridge, follows Pakenham in judging that 'Britain reneged on its promises and allowed the Union of South Africa to be constituted in 1910 as a white supremacist state' ('Britain's Inglorious Tactics during the Boer War', *Daily Telegraph*, 12 August 2021). For reasons that I have given, I consider this morally simplistic and unfair.

103 Pakenham, *Boer War*, p. 576.

104 Elspeth Huxley alludes to this when she has one of her European characters observe the mood of Kikuyu members of the Home Guard after a battle during the Mau Mau uprising: 'These men were happy because they had killed. They had bloodied their spears and affirmed a manhood they were often forced to doubt because so many ways of proving it had been taken away. Like their fathers before them, they had slain their enemies, and at last felt themselves to be whole men' (*A Thing to Love*, p. 251). Gerald Hanley makes the same point when he writes of (fictional) Africans engaged in a Zebra hunt in the 1930s: 'They had not known how bored they were. Now, they were lit up with an almost sadistic energy, for this was all that was left for the spears to do in the world of wages and white men' (*The Year of the Lion*, p. 93).

105 According to Jared Diamond, when Europeans, who had become partly immune to germs spread from domesticated animals, came into contact with peoples who had had no previous exposure, 'epidemics resulted in which up to 99 percent of the previously unexposed population was killed. Germs thus acquired ultimately from domestic animals played decisive roles in the European conquests of Native Americans, Australians, South Africans, and Pacific Islanders' (*Guns, Germs and Steel: A Short History of Everybody for the Last 13,000 Years* [London: Vintage, 1998], p. 92). See also Chapter 11, 'The Lethal Gift of Livestock', ibid., pp. 195–214.

106 Judy Campbell, *Invisible Invaders: Smallpox and Other Diseases in Aboriginal Australia, 1780–1880* (Melbourne: Melbourne University Press, 2002). Campbell's book makes the most meticulous and ambitious argument in favour of an Indonesian source of the smallpox that afflicted Australian aboriginals. No one quarrels with her claim that the disease was introduced into northern and north-western Australia in the nineteenth century by Indonesian fishermen from Makassar on South Sulawesi. (See, for example, Michael J. Bennett, 'Smallpox and Cowpox under the Southern Cross: The Smallpox Epidemic of 1789 and the Advent of Vaccination in Colonial Australia', *Bulletin of the History of Medicine*, 83/1 [Spring 2009], p. 42.) What has been fiercely contested, however, is her argument, first, that the British could not have been responsible for the devastating outbreak of smallpox at Sydney Cove in south-eastern

Australia in April 1789, and that therefore, second, it must have – and could have – been caused by contagion from the Indonesian-infected north.

For the first part of her argument Campbell relied decisively on the work of Frank Fenner, the distinguished Australian virologist and principal author of *Smallpox and Its Eradication* (Geneva: World Health Organization, 1988), in holding that variolous (smallpox-infected) matter, brought in naval surgeons' bottles to Sydney Cove by the First Fleet in 1788, could not have remained infectious after enduring an eight-month sea voyage in high temperatures. However, while the 1976 tests reported by Fenner showed that the infectivity of variolous matter declines rapidly at 35°C or more, the historical data shows that the First Fleet never experienced temperatures so high (Christopher Warren, 'Could First Fleet Smallpox Infect Aborigines? A Note', *Aboriginal History*, 31 [2007], esp. pp. 155–6). Moreover, it seems that the tests had been conducted on the mildest form of smallpox, not the virulent form that struck the aborigines in 1789. From this Craig Mear reasonably infers 'that a liquid form of virus, kept in a sealed container, with no humidity and out of sunlight in the bottom, for instance, of a sea chest, would have been still infective enough to cause an epidemic . . .' ('The Origin of the Smallpox Outbreak in Sydney', *Journal of the Royal Australian Historical Society*, 94/1 [2008], p. 6 [in the printout from https://go.gale.com/ps/i.do?p=AONE&u=googlescholar&id=GALE|A505359630&v=2.1&it=r&sid=AONE&asid=e47b790d]).

Regarding the second part of Campbell's argument, Mear raises a number of objections that cast doubt on the feasibility of smallpox being communicated from northern to south-eastern Australia in 1789: the lack of evidence of a drastic drop in the numbers of aboriginal people in the north, which an epidemic there would have caused; the sparsity of aboriginal communities; and the time taken to travel between them: 'It is difficult to imagine small bands of perhaps twenty people, with up to fourteen or fifteen members increasingly stricken with smallpox being able or willing to travel anywhere to spread the virus . . . It is improbable that . . . sufferers could travel any great distance to infect others . . . To postulate that smallpox, which needs a large population to reproduce itself, could spread so far over such a long time, in groups which were by the nature of their existence small and fairly self-contained, moving contrary to existing trade routes and custom is drawing a very long bow . . . The spread of smallpox from northern to south-eastern Australia through trade was distinctly improbable' (ibid., pp. 8–9).

If Mear is correct – and his argument does seem cogent – then it becomes more likely that the British were the cause. We do know that the surgeons of the First Fleet had brought with them 'variolous matter in bottles', because a contemporary witness, Royal Marine Watkin Tench, tells us so (*Sydney's First Four Years*, intro. and annotated by L.F. Fitzhardinge [Sydney: Angus and Robertson, 1961], p. 146). However, while it is possible that the matter was still infective in April 1789, we cannot be sure that it was, since, apart from the temperatures prevalent during the voyage, we can only speculate about the conditions in which it was kept. What is more, we also know that the successful transport of variolous matter to Australasia was not assured at that time, since, three years later, in May 1792, Philip Gidley King, lieutenant-governor of Norfolk Island, wrote to Sir Joseph Banks that 'our rising generation will be much obliged to you *if any method can be devised* to send the smallpox matter, so as it may inoculate these young creatures [native children]' (Bennett, 'Smallpox and Cowpox', p. 50. The emphasis is mine).

Moreover, when the smallpox epidemic struck aboriginal people at Sydney Cove in 1789, it 'baffled and troubled [British] observers at the time . . . There was complete bewilderment regarding the source of the disease' (ibid., pp. 39, 44). And when he left the colony two and a half years later in December 1791, Tench observed that 'no solution' to the problem of provenance 'had been given' (ibid., p. 44).

Whereas Michael Bennett allows that the smallpox-infected matter 'could have been stolen or, more likely, discarded without any record' (ibid., p. 48), Christopher Warren develops a conspiracy theory. He observes that in 1788–9 the British settlement at Sydney Cove was under increasing pressure, suffering from a scarcity of food, marines and ammunition at a time of growing tension and violence with the aborigines (Christopher Warren, 'Smallpox at Sydney Cove – Who, When, Why?', *Journal of Australian Studies*, 38.1 [2014], pp. 69, 70–3). He notes that by the 1770s deploying smallpox had become 'an irregular military tactic' in North America, where General Gage had advocated it and Major Robert Donkin had commended it in his *Military Collections and Remarks* (1777), and he speculates that some of the First Fleet's marines may have learned of it there (ibid., p. 73). He also reports that whereas '[i]nitially' Eora aboriginal traditions 'probably associated smallpox with . . . men from a great distance', 'modern renditions' now associate it with local Europeans, and that one of these traditions has it that smallpox was spread by 'blankets with . . . a crown' (ibid., p. 74). On this basis, Warren concludes that it is probable that 'senior marines, possibly with assistance from a convict with access to medical supplies or, more likely, a surgeon' deliberately decided to infect the aborigines with variolous matter (ibid., p. 79).

However, several factors serve to reduce the probability of Warren's hypothesis. First, Elizabeth A. Fenn – upon whose work on biological warfare in eighteenth-century North America he relies – counted only two clear instances of the spread of smallpox being used as a military tactic: one (against native Americans) at Fort Pitt in 1763, the other (against American colonists) at Yorktown in 1783 ('Biological Warfare in Eighteenth-Century North America: Beyond Jeffrey Amherst', *Journal of American History*, 86/4 [March 2000], pp. 1558, 1572–3). Second, she observes that Donkin's advocacy appears only in an ironic footnote to a discussion of the use of bows and arrows – 'Dip arrows in matter of smallpox, and twang them at the American rebels . . .' – and that since this footnote had been carefully excised from all but three known copies of his book, it 'seems . . . that the excision took place . . . before the volume was widely distributed' (ibid., pp. 1577–8). Third, at least one of the marines present in Sydney in 1789, Watkin Tench, considered the idea of the deliberate infection of aboriginal people to be 'a supposition so wild as to be unworthy of consideration' (Tench, in *Sydney's First Four Years*, p. 146). And fourth, if the aboriginal tradition attributing the epidemic to infected blankets distributed by the British is a 'modern rendition' in the sense of a recent invention, it is historically worthless.

The truth is that we do not know what caused the outbreak at Sydney Cove in 1789. As the evidence now stands, a northern provenance seems unlikely, but a conspiracy among some 'senior marines' – without the knowledge of Governor Arthur Phillip and his close colleagues, whose response to the news of the epidemic was to try to aid the aborigines (Bennett, 'Smallpox and Cowpox', p. 43) – is merely circumstantial speculation. Writing in 2021, Peter Dowling summarises the current state of knowledge:

> Puzzling over the origin of the disease observed at Sydney Cove, several possibilities have been put forward by historians, including the accidental or deliberate release of variolous matter brought with the colonists of the First Fleet in January 1788; a visiting French squadron that arrived at Botany bay; seasonal fishermen reaching northern Australia from Makassar, where the disease was endemic; and a type of 'native pox' presumed to be an endemic disease of Australia. While many researchers have made articulate use of historical records, citing evidence for their particular case and in some cases speculating on evidence that does not exist, no one author or theory has in the end prevailed over the others. The question of origin of the 1789 smallpox epidemic among Australian Aboriginal people has remained unresolved. The limiting factor in the debate has been the historical records themselves, which show no conclusive evidence either way. (*Fatal Contact: How Epidemics Nearly Wiped Out Australia's First Peoples* [Clayton, Victoria: Monash University Publishing, 2021], p. 23)

107 Ronald Hyam, 'Partition of Africa', p. 99. Hyam's point here was anticipated by the Scottish moral philosopher David Ritchie, when he wrote in 1900 that '[t]ropical lands are apt to become black anarchies or white tyrannies; and in the interest of black and white alike the controlling hand of governments influenced by the ideas of temperate and civilized countries is absolutely necessary' ('War and Peace', *International Journal of Ethics*, 11 [January 1900], p. 158).

5. CULTURAL ASSIMILATION AND 'GENOCIDE'

1   For a history of the post-1945 policy of *apartheid* in South Africa, see Saul Dubow, *Apartheid, 1948–1994* (Oxford: Oxford University Press, 2014).

2   Thus, Jan Christian Smuts (1870–1950) – one-time Boer military opponent of the British in the Second Anglo-Boer War, twice prime minister of the Union of South Africa, and internationalist supporter of the British Commonwealth, the League of Nations and the United Nations – supported racial segregation in South Africa, but 'only . . . as part and parcel of the civilising mission' (Willem H. Gravett, 'Jan Christian Smuts (1870–1950) in Context: An Answer to

Mazower and Morefield', *The Round Table: Commonwealth Journal of International Affairs*, 106/3 [2017], p.270). 'Smuts did not claim that Africans were forever incapable of acculturation to Western standards or norms . . . Smuts recognised the universality of the human mind as a feature shared by peoples of all cultures . . . Smuts was adamantly and vociferously opposed to [the Nationalists' policy of] apartheid' (pp. 270–1).

3   John A. Macdonald in Canada, House of Commons, *Debates*, 5 May 1880, p. 1991; quoted in Smith, 'Macdonald's Relationship with Aboriginal Peoples', p. 72.

4   Alan C. Cairns, *Citizens Plus: Aboriginal Peoples and the Canadian State* (Vancouver: UBC Press, 2000), p. 48.

5   R. J. Surtees, 'The Development of an Indian Reserve Policy in Canada', *Ontario History*, 61 (1969), p. 92; quoted in Carter, 'Aboriginal People of Canada and the British Empire', p. 205.

6   Carter, 'Aboriginal People of Canada and the British Empire', p. 205.

7   Flanagan, *First Nations? Second Thoughts*, pp. 167–8.

8   Daschuk, *Clearing the Plains*, p. 183.

9   Flanagan, *First Nations? Second Thoughts*, pp. 169–70.

10   Theodore Binnema and Kevin Hutchings, 'The Emigrant and the Noble Savage: Sir Francis Bond Head's Romantic Approach to Aboriginal Policy in Upper Canada, 1836–1838', *Journal of Canadian Studies*, 39/1 (Winter 2005), p. 122; quoted in Carter, 'Aboriginal People of Canada and the British Empire', p. 206.

11   In 1837–8 there were two armed uprisings in Upper and Lower Canada, which were motivated by frustration at the lack of progress in securing the electoral representation of lawmakers and thereby greater self-government. The rebellions led to Lord Durham's *Report on the Affairs of British North America* in 1839, the uniting of the Colonies of Upper and Lower Canada in 1840, and the granting, nine years later, of 'responsible' government – that is, government accountable to an elected legislature.

12   Smith, 'Macdonald's Relationship with Aboriginal Peoples', pp. 67–8.

13   Ibid., pp. 77, 80. A 'status Indian' was someone registered as an Indian under the Indian Act of 1876.

14   Charles Big Canoe and James Ashquabe to Sir John Macdonald, not dated; quoted in Smith, 'Macdonald's Relationship with Aboriginal Peoples', p. 77. Big Canoe had taught himself to read and write English, farmed and kept cattle, and lived in a large framed house, on whose central table lay a book of hymns printed in both English and Ojibwa (ibid., pp. 77–8).

15   John A. Macdonald to Peter E. Jones, 31 August 1886; quoted in ibid., p. 79.

16   Rotberg, *Founder*, p. 222.

17   Ibid., pp. 360–1; Pyrah, *Imperial Policy and South Africa*, p. 89.

18   King, *Penguin History*, pp. 236, 305. King claims that this made New Zealand 'the first neo-European country in the world to give votes to its indigenous population' (ibid., p. 305). That is true only if Cape Colony does not count as a 'neo-European' country.

19   King, *Penguin History*, pp. 390–1.

20   Flanagan, *First Nations? Second Thoughts*, p. 172.

21 Daschuk, *Clearing the Plains*, pp. 115–16.

22 Ibid., p. xxi.

23 As J. R. Miller has written, rising concern in Christian humanitarian circles in Britain about the deleterious effects upon natives of colonisation was 'critically important' to the motivation and intention that impelled the launching of the schools (*Shingwauk's Vision*, p. 63).

24 Ibid., p. 81.

25 Ibid., p. 84.

26 Ibid., pp. 76, 79, 80, 84.

27 Truth and Reconciliation Commission of Canada [TRCC], *Final Report. Summary: Honouring the Truth, Reconciling for the Future* (Toronto: TRC of Canada, 2015), pp. 60, 62. The introduction of compulsory attendance needs to be put in the context of the increasing acceptance of the idea of universal public schooling and of compulsion as the means to realise it. In the 1870s both Ontario and British Columbia had introduced laws obliging all parents to send their children to school under certain conditions, and '[b]y 1910, most provinces had introduced compulsory school legislation for children who fell under their jurisdiction' (Nina Green, Brian Giesbrecht and Tom Flanagan, 'They Were Not Forced', *Dorchester Review*, 21 April 2022, p. 4, 'Compulsory Attendance': https://www.dorchesterreview.ca/blogs/news/they-were-not-forced).

28 Patrice Dutil, 'Not Guilty: Sir John A. Macdonald and the Genocide Fetish', *Dorchester Review*, 10/2 (Autumn-Winter 2020), p. 15; Miller, *Shingwauk's Vision*, pp. 171, 424.

29 Miller, *Shingwauk's Vision*, p. 300.

30 Ibid., p. 424: 'the evidence is overwhelming that a great deal of the sexual exploitation and violence perpetrated on male, and in rare instances female, students was the work of older students'.

31 Ibid., p. 114.

32 Ibid., pp. 118, 142, 171. In New Zealand, native regard for residential schools appears to have been somewhat different. The 1847 Educational Ordinance encouraged the setting up of English-language industrial boarding schools to 'civilise' Māori children by removing them from their 'primitive' native cultures. However, as Māori resistance against settlers mounted in the late 1850s, they began to abandon these schools (Andrea Smith, *Indigenous Peoples and Boarding Schools: A Comparative Study* [New York: United Nations Permanent Forum on Indigenous Issues, 2009], p. 15). In 1867 the Native Schools Act provided village day-schools, in which '[a]t the specific request of Maori parents, the medium of instruction . . . was English' (King, *Penguin History*, p. 276).

33 Miller, *Shingwauk's Vision*, pp. 205, 428.

34 Ibid., p. 429. In this section, I have relied very heavily on Miller's book, partly because it was recommended to me by several Canadian historians as the standard work on the topic of the history of the residential schools, and partly because of the intellectual quality of the work itself. For Miller is scrupulous in displaying all of the data, even when they go against the grain of his own

interpretation, which allows the reader to see when that interpretation runs out ahead of its supporting evidence. Because the *Final Report* of the Truth and Reconciliation Commission of Canada does not display the same scrupulousness, I have not relied on it much at all. For further explanation of my judgement of the *Final Report*, see note 67 of this chapter below.

35 Widdowson and Howard, *Disrobing the Aboriginal Industry*, p. 25.

36 For example, by Chief Darrell Boissoneau (Miller, *Shingwauk's Vision*, p. 9).

37 TRCC, *Final Report. Summary*, p. 1.

38 Widdowson and Howard, *Disrobing the Aboriginal Industry*, p. 25.

39 On 27 May 2021 the southern British Columbia Nation of Tk'emlúps te Secwépemc announced the discovery of the remains of 215 children in the grounds of the former Kamloops Indian Residential School. Chief Judy Wilson of the nearby Neskonlith Indian band alluded to 'atrocities' and 'mass graves', while the Southern Chiefs Organization Grand Chief Jerry Daniels spoke of 'genocide' (Jana G. Pruden, 'Discovery of Children's Remains at Kamloops Residential School "Stark Example of Violence" Inflicted Upon Indigenous Peoples', [Toronto] *Globe and Mail*, 28 May 2021: https://www.theglobeand mail.com/canada/article-bodies-found-at-kamloops-residential-school-site-in-bc/). Talk of a 'mass gravesite' or 'mass graves' then appeared in press coverage by the *Globe and Mail* (Andrea Woo and Jeffrey Jones, 'Discovery of Remains of 215 Children at Former Kamloops Residential School Prompts Calls from Indigenous Leaders to Investigate All Sites', [Toronto] *Globe and Mail*, 30 May 2021: https://www.theglobeandmail.com/canada/article-calls-for-action-follows-discovery-of-childrens-remains-at-kamloops/; '"Mass Graves Do Not Belong in Any School." Readers React to the Discovery of the Remains of 215 Children at a Residential School in B.C., Plus Other Letters to the Editor': https://www. theglobeandmail.com/opinion/letters/article-june-1-mass-graves do-not-belong -in-any-school-readers-react-to-the/), *New York Times* (Ian Austen, '"Horrible History": Mass Grave of Indigenous Children Reported in Canada', *New York Times*, 29 May 2021: https://www.nytimes.com/2021/05/28/world/canada/ kamloops-mass-grave-residential-schools.html), and Al Jazeera (Jillian Kestler D'Amours, 'Canada: Calls Grow to Uncover More Residential School Mass Graves', Al Jazeera, 3 June 2021: https://www.aljazeera.com/news/2021/6/3/ canada-calls-grow-uncover-more-residential-school-mass-graves). Subsequently, statues of Queen Victoria and Queen Elizabeth II were toppled and several Roman Catholic churches were vandalised or burned down (Nick Allen, 'No. 10 Condemns Toppling of Queen Elizabeth II and Victoria Statues in Canada', *Daily Telegraph*, 2 July 2021: https://www.telegraph.co.uk/world-news/2021/ 07/02/queen-elizabeth-ii-victoria-statues-ripped-protesters-canada/; Rozina Sabur, 'Churches Burned Down as Anger Over "Cultural Genocide" Sweeps Canada', *Daily Telegraph*, 24 July 2021: https://www.telegraph.co.uk/ world-news/2021/07/24/churches-burned-anger-cultural-genocide-indigenous-children/).

In fact, what had been discovered were not mass graves at all, but unmarked graves in known cemeteries (Jana G. Pruden and Mike Hager, 'Anthropologist

Explains How She Concluded 200 Children Were Buried at the Kamloops Residential School', [Toronto] *Globe and Mail*, 15 July 2021: https://www.theglobeandmail.com/canada/article-kamloops-residential-school-un-marked-graves-discovery-update/). Whether the Kamloops graves had always been unmarked or whether their original wooden markers had disintegrated has not been determined. Certainly, speaking of the Catholic cemetery near the Marieval Indian Residential School in Saskatchewan, Chief Cadmus Delorme of the Cowessess First Nation was careful to insist that it was not a mass grave site, but contained the individual graves of both children and adults – some of them non-indigenous – whose markers were no longer extant (Globe Staff, 'Kamloops, St Eugene's, Marieval: What We Know About Residential Schools' Unmarked Graves So Far', [Toronto] *Globe and Mail*, 6 July 2021: https://www.theglobeandmail.com/canada/article-residential-schools-unmarked-graves-st-eugenes-marieval-kamloops/; Mark Taylor, 'Cowessess First Nation Places Solar Lights to Illuminate 751 Unmarked Graves at Former Residential School Site', [Toronto] *Globe and Mail*, 26 June 2021: https://www.theglobe-andmail.com/canada/article-cowessess-first-nation-place-solar-lights-next-to-each-unmarked-grave/). The cemeteries had long been untended and allowed to deteriorate, perhaps because native peoples – especially those who had not been Christianised – were unaccustomed to burying their dead and marking their graves.

Nor did the 'discovery' of unmarked graves amount to news. The TRCC included a 'Missing Children and Unmarked Burials Project', whose findings had been published in Volume 4 of its *Final Report* in 2015 (http://www.trc.ca/assets/pdf/Volume_4_Missing_Children_English_Web.pdf).

Since the graves have only been located by ground-penetrating radar and have not (yet) been exhumed, we do not know what caused the death of those buried. Talk of 'mass graves', 'atrocities' and 'genocide' presumes murder, but the TRCC's report did not document any deaths by violent means. The most likely cause was disease, especially tuberculosis or the Spanish flu of 1918–19 (*Final Report. Summary*, pp. 93, 99). The report documented the deaths of 3,200 pupils at the residential schools during 1869–1965, which amounts to 2.1 per cent of the total of 150,000. The annual average of fatalities during that period was 33 across the whole of the residential school system (*Final Report. Summary*, p. 92), although the death rate before 1910 was often three times the rate after that date (ibid., p. 91). In August 2021, the website of the 'Missing Children Project' of the National Centre for Truth and Reconciliation at the University of Manitoba claimed that 'more than 4,100 children who died of disease or accident while attending a residential school'. That figure amounts to 2.7 per cent of the total and an annual average of 42 deaths. While the 'Missing Children Project' no longer appears on the centre's website, its claim was reported in this newspaper article: 'Read the Truth and Reconciliation Commission of Canada's final report', *Kamloops This Week*, 1 June 2021 (https://www.kamloopsthisweek.com/local-news/read-the-truth-and-reconciliation-commission-of-canadas-final-report-4448533).

When the announcement of the 'discovery' of the 215 unmarked graves at Kamloops was made at the end of May 2021, Chief Rosanne Casimir said that a full report would be released the following month. In the middle of July, however, Racelle Kooy, speaking for the Tk'emlúps te Secwépemc, said that a full copy of the report 'would not be released to the public and media' (Pruden and Hager, 'Anthropologist Explains How She Concluded 200 Children Were Buried at the Kamloops Residential School').

According to Tom Flanagan:

All the major elements of the story are either false or highly exaggerated. First, no unmarked graves have been discovered at Kamloops or elsewhere. GPR has located hundreds of soil disturbances, but none of these has been excavated, so it is not known whether they are burial sites, let alone children's graves . . . Second, there are no 'missing children' . . . the legend of missing children arose from a failure of TRC researchers to cross-reference the vast number of historical documents about residential schools and the children who attended them . . . Third, . . . [s]cholars generally agree that more students attended day schools on Indian reserves than went away to residential schools . . . It wasn't until 1920 that school attendance was made compulsory for Indian children, and enforcement was often lax . . . How could the fake news story of unmarked graves, with its attendant legends of missing children ripped from the arms of their mothers, have gained such wide currency among political and media elites? The short answer is that it fits perfectly into the progressive narrative of white supremacy, of the white majority in Canada oppressing racial minorities . . . the claims of unmarked graves are a new money-maker. ('The Truth About Canada's Indian Graves: The Indigenous Industry Is Thriving Off Fake News', *UnHerd*, 29 June 2022: https://unherd.com/2022/06/the-truth-about-canadas-indian-graves/)

40 Miller, *Shingwauk's Vision*, p. 341.

41 See Donald B. Smith and J. R. Miller, 'No Genocide: It's Not the Right Word for the History Books', *Literary Review of Canada* (October 2019): https://reviewcanada.ca/magazine/2019/10/no-genocide/). Miller was among the fifty Canadian historians who signed an Open Letter in August 2021 protesting against the Canadian Historical Association's claim that 'the existing historical scholarship' makes it 'abundantly clear' that Canada's treatment of indigenous peoples was genocidal. 'There are no grounds', the Letter states, 'for such a claim that purports to represent the views of all of Canada's professional historians' ('Open Letter: Historians Rally vs "Genocide" Myth', *Dorchester Review*, 12 August 2021: https://www.dorchesterreview.ca/blogs/news/historians-rally-vs-genocide-myth). The other signatories included Margaret MacMillan, Emeritus Professor of International History at the University of Oxford.

42 Miller, *Shingwauk's Vision*, p. 186. See further, J. R. Miller, *Residential Schools and Reconciliation: Canada Confronts its History* (Toronto: University of Toronto Press, 2017), pp. 232, 234; Gerry Bowler, 'Is the Final Report of the TRC Good History?', in Clifton and DeWolf, *From Truth Comes Reconciliation: An Assessment*

of the Truth and Reconciliation Report, pp. 139–40; and Rubinstein, 'Indigenous Exceptionalism and the TRC', in ibid., pp. 163–4.

43 Miller, *Shingwauk's Vision*, pp. 185, 186, 436.

44 See Bowler, 'Is the Final Report of the TRC Good History?', p. 128.

45 Miller, *Shingwauk's Vision*, pp. 8, 9, 10, 85, 178, 179, 191, 192.

46 Ibid., pp. 10, 408, 431: the Indians sought practical instruction and useful learning, 'not the suppression of languages, the denigration of Aboriginal culture, and the forceful indoctrination of Christian beliefs that the schools transmitted'.

47 Ibid., p. 153.

48 Ibid., pp. 185, 414.

49 Colin Kidd, *The Forging of Races: Race and Scripture in the Protestant Atlantic World, 1600–2000* (Cambridge: Cambridge University Press, 2006), p. 26.

50 Glen Williams, *Blood Must Tell: Debating Race and Identity in the Canadian House of Commons, 1880–1925* (Ottawa: willowBX Press, 2014), pp. 27, 29.

51 Miller, *Shingwauk's Vision*, p. 153.

52 Ibid., pp. 187, 188.

53 Ibid., pp. 173, 199, 204.

54 But this was also true, according to my own experience, of Scottish primary schools of the late 1950s and English boarding schools of the early 1960s. Miller is alert to this, writing that 'at least some of the problems of harsh treatment, emotional deprivation, and inadequate food were experienced by the inmates of most custodial educational establishments, such as private boarding schools for non-Native children in Canada, the United Kingdom, and elsewhere' (ibid., p. 290).

55 Ibid., pp. 200, 201, 202.

56 Ibid., pp. 157, 253.

57 Ibid., pp. 118–19.

58 Ibid., p. 252. Miller writes: 'The theory behind this practice was that the young men were refining their agricultural skills through practical application, but the youths were obviously a cheap source of labour at a time of peak demand for hands' (ibid., p. 256). He seems to imply that, because the native pupils' practical endeavours provided cheap labour, they could not also be a form of practical education. But he does not explain why they could not be both at the same time.

59 Ibid., pp. 126–7, 167.

60 Ibid., pp. 128, 131, 132.

61 Ibid., pp. 174, 176.

62 Ibid., p. 140.

63 TRCC, *Final Report. Summary*, p. 91.

64 Miller, *Shingwauk's Vision*, pp. 143, 422.

65 Ibid., pp. 125, 423.

66 See Chapter 7, note 69.

67 I said in note 34 above that I have not relied much on the Truth and Reconciliation Commission of Canada's *Final Report*, because its presentation of the evidence

is not scrupulously even-handed. Let me explain with reference to the report's summary volume. First of all, it refers to all former pupils tendentiously as 'Survivors', encouraging the reader to assume that all such pupils read their experience in terms of surviving the oppression of their schools, whereas we know from Miller that many did not and do not read their experience in this way. Second, while the report mentions the testimony of former staff or their children in defence of the schools, it does so only to say that 'Survivors' 'found it very difficult to listen to' it (ibid., p. 14). Third, of the exonerating testimony of former pupils, which Miller faithfully records, the report makes no mention at all. Fourth, the report relies decisively – and uncritically – on 'the truth of lived experiences as told to us by Survivors and others' (ibid., p. 12). The notions that 'lived experience' is never pure, but always interpreted; that the interpretation might be misshapen by an interest in exploiting the political power of victimhood; or that it might not tell the truth at all – these notions are never allowed to intrude. Indeed, they are dismissed as racist. Regarding the refusal of Crown counsel to prosecute alleged crimes in the schools without corroborating evidence, the report comments: 'This approach was based on an unwillingness to take the complainant's own evidence as sufficient to justify a prosecution. It betrays an unwillingness to take the evidence of Aboriginal people as being worthy of belief' (ibid., p. 166). It does no such thing; it merely recognises that, since testimony can be fraudulent, it should not be taken at face value. Fifth, the interpretation of the history of the residential schools is placed within a history of colonialism that descends into caricature. Thus, in the section entitled 'The Imperial context' we read: 'Empires were established militarily . . . Colonies were established to be exploited economically . . . To gain control of the land of Indigenous people, colonists . . . waged wars of extinction' (ibid., p. 45). Sixth, this section contains thirty-two references, of which a remarkable quarter are devoted to a single, minor volume: Stephen Howe's *Empire: A Very Short Introduction* (Oxford: Oxford University Press, 2002). Seventh, the report makes assertions about the specific histories of the colonisation of Canada and the residential schools that are either untrue or misleading. It tells us that the native peoples 'did not need to be "civilized" . . . [They] had systems that were complete unto themselves and met their needs' (ibid., p. 49). And yet, as we have seen, many natives recognised that their traditional way of life was no longer sustainable and acknowledged the need to undergo a measure of assimilation to the dominating European culture. Then, the report tells us that children were sent to residential schools, 'not to educate them, but primarily to break their link to their culture and identity' (ibid., p. 2). But it later admits that 'the industrial schools were intended to prepare First Nations people for integration into Canadian society by teaching them basic trades, particularly farming' (ibid., p. 57). Next, it tells us that the original mission of civilising native peoples 'was replaced in the nineteenth century by a racism that chose to cloak itself in the language of science, and held that the peoples of the world had differing abilities' (ibid., p. 47). But biological racism never replaced the Christian humanitarianism that espoused basic racial equality and the possibility of native development; it merely rivalled it. Were that not so, the *raison d'être* of the residential schools would have evaporated. Finally, the report opens its chapter 'The history' with a piece of imaginative fiction: 'It can start with a knock on the door one morning . . . The officials have arrived and the children must go. For tens of thousands of Aboriginal children for over a century, this was the beginning of their residential schooling. They were torn from their parents . . . Then, they were hurled into a strange and frightening place, one in which their parents and culture would be demeaned and oppressed' (ibid., p. 38). And yet residential schooling was entirely voluntary until 1894, and voluntary as a rule until 1920, as the report goes on to admit (ibid., pp. 60, 62). All of my comments up to this point have concerned the summary volume of the TRCC. The TRCC's first volume on the history of residential schools, which covers the period up until 1939, offers, of course, a much fuller account than the summary (*Final Report*, Vol. 1: 'Canada's Residential Schools: The History, Part 1, Origins to 1939' [Montreal and Kingston: McGill-Queen's University Press, 2015]). Yet the fuller volume shares in the flaws of the summary one. It, too, tends to caricature the phenomenon of European colonialism: 'Each European empire gathered together a set of colonies, usually by force or the threat of force, into an unequal political union. The imperial homeland dominated and exploited the colonies . . . the idea of a . . . *Pax Britannica* . . . is largely a myth'. (ibid., pp. 11, 12). It, too, invokes Stephen Howe's *Very Short Introduction* considerably more than any other book (fourteen times) in its chapter on colonialism in general (ibid., pp. 739–43). And it, too, misinforms us that in the nineteenth century 'scientific racism' simply 'replaced' the basically egalitarian view that native peoples were capable of civilisation (ibid., p. 18). I observe that Patrice Dutil, professor in the Department of Politics and Administration at Ryerson University, Toronto, concurs with my judgement. Writing of the TRCC's first volume on the history of residential schools, he comments that '[i]t barely pretends to be an academic document . . . the TRC's report does not, technically or literally speaking, constitute "history". The study makes no attempt to put things in perspective, to show how practice evolved or to compare the Canadian experience with that of other countries' (Dutil, 'Not Guilty', p. 15). Gerry Bowler, professor emeritus of history at the University of Manitoba, agrees: 'So, is the Final Report of the Truth and Reconciliation Commission good history? No, it is not; it fails at a fundamental level. No undergraduate student would be allowed to get away with making extraordinary claims without backing them up by reference to their sources. Far too often, we are told of genocide or other atrocities without so much as a single footnote to indicate the basis of the conclusion . . . The [report's] conclusions were overtly determined from the investigation, testimonies were made in violation of the canons of oral history, many of the authors saw themselves as crusaders righting ancient wrongs, and fundamental questions were left unasked and unanswered' ('Is the Final Report of the TCD Good History?', p. 141). In sum, I have not relied upon the Truth and Reconciliation Commission's report, because it is not reliable.

68 Widdowson and Howard, *Disrobing the Aboriginal Industry*, pp. 25–6.

69 Tom Lawson appears to disagree, since he equates 'progress' with 'eradication' and 'genocide' (*The Last Man: A British Genocide in Tasmania* [London: Bloomsbury, 2021], pp. 22, 125) and views the British attempt to share the benefits of modern civilisation with the aboriginal peoples as 'an attack on difference and the magnificent variety of the human race and human cultures' (ibid, p. 27).

70 According to Diamond Jenness (1886–1969), Canada's most famous anthropologist, 'Tools of stone still formed the basis of all [aboriginal] material culture, and they were not farther advanced economically than the inhabitants of England two thousand years before Christ' (*Indians of Canada* [1932], p. 33); quoted by Flanagan, *First Nations? Second Thoughts*, p. 37.

71 I cannot agree with those who argue that 'there is no qualitative difference between mass murder and cultural genocide, because the latter destroys the indigenous systems of meaning and ultimately the survivors' will to live, resulting ultimately in widespread death' (A. Dirk Moses, 'Conceptual Blockages and Definitional Dilemmas in the "Racial Century": Genocides of Indigenous Peoples and the Holocaust', in A. Dirk Moses and Dan Stone, *Colonialism and Genocide* [Abingdon: Routledge, 2007], p. 166). The destruction of someone's cultural 'system of meaning' can indeed be gravely disorienting. It can drive some to despair and thence to suicide; but it can also drive others to adapt. Dirk Moses appears to agree with me (ibid., p. 169). On this, Tom Lawson equivocates. While making an explicit distinction between mass murder on the one hand and cultural suppression and ethnic relocation on the other, he blurs it repeatedly by his choice of language. So he states unequivocally that the British government and its agents never 'explicitly planned the physical destruction of indigenous Tasmanians' (*Last Man*, p. 14) and that 'there was self-evidently no worked-through and unifying aim of putting to death the existing communities on the part of "white settlers", their descendants or the British, colonial or Australian governments' (ibid., p. 17). Yet he describes the widespread belief or fear that the aboriginal peoples 'were expiring' and 'doomed to be wiped from the face of the earth' as 'extermination discourse' (ibid., pp. 42, 204). The word 'exterminate', however, means to 'annihilate' and it connotes a deliberate action. One does not 'exterminate' by accident. Further, Lawson describes the attempt to corral and relocate certain tribes by means of the 'Black Line' as having 'the clear goal of the eradication of particular ethnic and linguistic group in a defined region' (ibid., p. 18). But the word 'eradicate' means to 'destroy completely', which is not the same as 'to relocate', even forcibly. The same kind of oblique erasing of the distinction between intentional mass murder and a policy of cultural assimilation can be found in Lyndall Ryan, whom Lawson quotes here: 'from the outset the British in effect were trying to eliminate the Aborigines by killing the parents, abducting their children and transforming them into white people' (*Tasmanian Aborigines: A History since 1803* [Crows Nest, NSW: Allen & Unwin, 2012], p. 49; quoted in Lawson, *Last Man*, p. 4). First, to do something 'in effect' is not to do it deliberately. Yet one cannot 'try' to do something accidentally. So was it deliberate or was it not? Had it been deliberate, I assume

that Ryan would not have written 'in effect'. Second, to transform people is not exactly to 'eliminate' them, unless one assumes that cultural identity is the very same as life itself. But, since people do in fact change their cultural identities without actually dying, that is a false assumption. Third, Ryan's sentence implies that the British generally killed aboriginal parents in order to re-educate their children, thus associating the policy of cultural assimilation with murder. If that is true, I have read it nowhere else.

72 Robert Hughes, *The Fatal Shore: The Epic of Australia's Founding* (New York: Vintage, 1986), p. 120.

73 I say 'near extinction' because, while it was long assumed that the Tasmanian aborigines had become completely extinct by the 1840s, there are now about 30,000 'mixed race' Tasmanians who identify themselves as aboriginal and who therefore resist claims of 'genocide'.

74 Alan Atkinson, 'Conquest', in Schreuder and Ward, *Australia's Empire*, p. 46.

75 Keith Windschuttle, *Fabrication of Aboriginal History*, 2 vols., Vol. 1, 'Van Diemen's Land, 1803–1847' (Sydney: Macleay Press, 2002). Volume Two has not yet appeared. Since Windschuttle is not a professional academic and some historians have therefore been inclined to dismiss him as a 'tabloid historian' (Bain Attwood, 'Old News from a Tabloid Historian', *The Australian*, 6 January 2003, p. 13), we should note that Ann Curthoys has numbered *The Fabrication of Aboriginal History* among 'the key works on this aspect of Tasmanian history' ('Raphaël Lemkin's "Tasmania": An Introduction', in Moses and Stone, *Colonialism and Genocide*, p. 73 n.19). Curthoys is an Australian Research Council professorial fellow at the University of Sydney, and was invited to contribute a chapter on 'Indigenous Subjects' to the volume on Australia in the Oxford History of the British Empire Companion Series. See Chapter 4, note 75.

76 Keith Windschuttle, 'Doctored Evidence and Invented Incidents in Aboriginal Historiography', in Bain Attwood and S. G. Foster, eds, *Frontier Conflict: The Australian Experience* (Canberra: National Museum of Australia, 2003), p. 106.

77 Bain Attwood, *Telling the Truth about Aboriginal History* (Allen & Unwin, 2005), p. 162.

78 Geoffrey Blainey, 'The Fabrication of Aboriginal History, Volume 1: Book Review', *New Criterion*, 21/8 (April 2003), pp. 79–82. (Since I was able to locate only an online copy, I have not been able to identify the original pagination of the quotations. The material I have quoted here, however, appears on pages 1 and 2 of the online printout.) The historians to whom Blainey's criticism refers are Brian Plomley, Lyndall Ryan and Henry Reynolds. It bolsters the general thrust of Windschuttle's thesis, if not all of its details, that the last of these, Reynolds, had himself written in 1995 that '[t]here is a tendency among writers sympathetic to the Aborigines to exaggerate the numbers killed in order to emphasise the brutality of the colonial encounter' (*The Fate of a Free People* [Ringwood: Penguin, 1995], p. 77). Reynolds himself thinks that Ryan's figure of 700 aboriginal deaths is 'probably too high', and opts instead for 250–400 (ibid., pp. 76, 81–2). The strained tendentiousness of some of Ryan's reasoning is visible in this passage: 'By matching these three pieces of evidence [of killings

of whites by aboriginals and the dispatch of soldiers to stop them], and the fact that fewer Aborigines were in the area the following year, I surmised that a massacre of Aborigines had taken place in the location identified in the Land Commissioners' Journals and had been hushed up. The fact that so many stock-keepers and shepherds had been killed in this area led me to believe that their mates had joined the military and field police as a vigilante group in this action, as was customary . . . I am even more convinced of my conclusion, because no reports of the actual personnel of the parties sent out by Police Magistrate Smith have ever been found' ('Who is the Fabricator?' in Robert Manne, ed., *Whitewash: On Keith Windschuttle's Fabrication of Aboriginal History* [Melbourne: Black Inc. Agenda, 2003], pp. 238–9).

79 Blainey, 'Fabrication of Aboriginal History', p. 3 of the online printout.

80 Flood, *Original Australians*, pp. 66–7.

81 Geoffrey Blainey, *Triumph of the Nomads: A History of Ancient Australia* (London: Macmillan, 1975), p. 106.

82 Ibid., p. 109. It is true that Blainey's source here comes from mainland Australia, not Tasmania. However, I am not aware of any good reason to suppose that what was true of mainland aborigines was not also true of Tasmanian ones. The anthropologist Peter Sutton has reviewed Blainey's argument and, notwithstanding one qualification, confirms it (Peter Sutton, *The Politics of Suffering: Indigenous Australia and the End of the Liberal Consensus* [Melbourne: University of Melbourne Press, 2009], pp. 91–2).

83 Windschuttle, *Fabrication of Aboriginal History*, pp. 50, 110.

84 Ibid., p. 111. For example, Brian Plomley, *Aboriginal/Settler Clash in Van Diemen's Land* (Launceston: Queen Victoria Museum and Art Gallery, 1992), p. 13: 'Between 1803 and 1823 there was no concerted effort by the Aborigines to drive the settlers from the lands they had appropriated.'

85 Windschuttle, *Fabrication of Aboriginal History*, p. 101.

86 Ibid., p. 99.

87 Ibid., p. 114.

88 Ibid., pp. 106, 110.

89 Thus, Plomley qualified his statement in note 84 above by adding that there were clashes in the north 'because the settlers were occupying lands upon which the natives depended for their food supply' (*Aboriginal/Settler Clash*, p. 13).

90 Belich, *Replenishing the Earth*, p. 268.

91 Ibid., pp. 269, 271.

92 John Connor, 'British Frontier Warfare Logistics and the "Black Line", Van Diemen's Land (Tasmania), 1830', in *War in History*, 9/2 (2002), pp. 156–7.

93 Reynolds, *An Indelible Stain?*, p. 76, quoting A. Bell-Fialkoff, *Ethnic Cleansing* (New York: St Martin's, 1996), p. 3.

94 Henry Reynolds, *Frontier: Aborigines, Settlers, and the Land* (Sydney: Allen & Unwin, 1987), p. 29.

95 Governor Arthur, Memorandum, Sorrell Camp, 20 November 1830, in *British Parliamentary Papers: Colonies: Australia*, Vol. 4: 'Correspondence and Papers Relating to the Government and Affairs of the Australian Colonies, 1830–36'

(Shannon: Irish University Press, 1970), p. 244; quoted in Windschuttle, *Fabrication of Aboriginal History*, pp. 182–3.

96 Windschuttle, *Fabrication of Aboriginal History*, p. 169.

97 Arthur to Murray, 20 November 1830, in *British Parliamentary Papers: Colonies: Australia*, Vol. 4, p. 231; quoted in ibid., pp. 172–3.

98 Lyndall Ryan, *Tasmanian Aborigines*, p. 140. Tim Rowse, emeritus professor in the Institute for Culture and Society, Western Sydney University, has reflected on the motives of aboriginal collaboration with the British in nineteenth-century New South Wales, Queensland and the Northern Territory in 'The Moral World of the Native Mounted Police', *Law and History*, 5/1 (January 2018).

99 Arthur to Henry Bathurst, secretary of state for war and the colonies, 7 November 1816, National Archives CO 123/25.

100 Government Notice, No. 160, 19 August 1830, in *British Parliamentary Papers: Colonies: Australia*, Vol. 4, p. 233. Arthur's humanitarian intentions were entirely in line with consistent British colonial policy toward the Tasmanian aboriginals since 1803. See Raphaël Lemkin, 'Tasmania', ed. Ann Curthoys, in Moses and Stone, *Colonialism and Genocide*, pp. 75–7, 88, 89.

101 Government Notice, No. 161, 20 August 1830, in *British Parliamentary Papers: Colonies: Australia*, Vol. 4, pp. 233–4. Lyndall Ryan repeats the assertion made by the historian Henry Melville in 1835 that no settler was ever in fact brought to court for offences of assaulting or killing aboriginals (*Aboriginal Tasmanians*, 2nd edn [St Leonards, NSW: Allen & Unwin, 1981], p. 88), as does Sharon Morgan (*Land Settlement in Early Tasmania: Creating an Antipodean England* [Cambridge: Cambridge University Press, 1992]). However, Windschuttle reminds us that Brian Plomley had pointed out in 1966 that the first case of a convict convicted and punished by the supreme court of Van Diemen's Land for the manslaughter of an aboriginal occurred in May 1824, with a second following in November. How many other such cases there were we do not know, since we lack a comprehensive analysis of the contemporary press (*Fabrication of Aboriginal History*, p. 191).

102 Reynolds, *An Indelible Stain?*, p. 85.

103 Reynolds, *Frontier*, p. 55.

104 Reynolds, *An Indelible Stain?*, pp. 71–2.

105 Reynolds, *Frontier*, p. 55.

106 The Committee for the Care and Treatment of Captured Aborigines was commissioned by Governor Arthur and ran from February 1830 to September 1833. It became known as the 'Aborigines Committee' or the 'Broughton Committee', after its chairman, Archdeacon William Broughton.

107 Curr to Charles Arthur, 28 April 1830; quoted in Windschuttle, *Fabrication of Aboriginal History*, pp. 302–3. Charles Arthur was the lieutenant-governor's aide-de-camp. The emphasis is Curr's.

108 Windschuttle, *Fabrication of Aboriginal History*, p. 307. See also pp. 303–8.

109 Brian Plomley, ed., *Friendly Mission: The Tasmanian Journals and Papers of George Augustus Robinson 1829–1834* (Kingsgrove, NSW: Tasmanian Historical Research Association, 1966), p. 98.

110 Windschuttle, *Fabrication of Aboriginal History*, pp. 326–42. Tom Lawson implies that exterminationist sentiment was ascendant among the settlers, writing of 'the desire to exterminate that abounded in the settler community' (*Last Man*, p. 52) and of 'the policy of extermination currently being pursued by much of the rest of the settler population' (ibid., p. 74). Had he engaged with Windschuttle, instead of dismissing him on political grounds (ibid., p. 16), he might have been more cautious.

111 Archives Office of Tasmania, Hobart, Colonial Secretary's Office papers, CSO 1/323/7578, pp. 370–1; quoted in Windschuttle, *Fabrication of Aboriginal History*, pp. 332–3.

112 Ibid., pp. 334, 338–9, 340.

113 Ibid., pp. 298–9. See Stuart Piggin, *Evangelical Christianity in Australia: Spirit, Word and World* (Melbourne: Oxford University Press, 1996), p. viii: 'Evangelicalism was the official Christianity brought to Australia with the First Fleet . . . Wilberforce's evangelicalism . . . was a warm, practical, humanitarian movement which focused on commitment to the world . . . The vision of a redeemed criminal class, a converted Aboriginal race . . . was large, even grand.'

114 Gascoigne and Curthoys, *Enlightenment and the Origins of European Australia*, p. 152. They write: 'The theme that racial differences were almost literally skin deep frequently recurred in discussions of the character of Aboriginal society' (p. 150).

115 Ibid., p. 155.

116 James Boyce, 'Fantasy Island', in Manne, *Whitewash*, pp. 34, 37.

117 Keith Windschuttle, 'The Fabrication of Aboriginal History', lecture at the Sydney Institute, 11 February 2003, *The Sydney Papers*, Summer 2003, p. 26.

118 Atkinson, 'Conquest', p. 46.

119 Windschuttle, *Fabrication of Aboriginal History*, pp. 224–5.

120 For example, Clive Turnbull, 'Tasmania: The Ultimate Solution', in F. S. Stevens, *Racism: The Australian Experience*, 2 vols, Vol. 2: 'Black versus White' (Sydney: ANZ Book Company, 1972), p. 230; Lloyd Robson, *A History of Tasmania*, Vol. 1: 'Van Diemen's Land from the Earliest Times to 1855' (Melbourne: Oxford University Press, 1983), p. 220: the Flinders Island reservation was the world's 'first concentration camp'; and Hughes, *Fatal Shore*, p. 423.

121 Reynolds, *Fate of a Free People*, pp. 175, 187, 188. Although Windschuttle differs from Reynolds about Robinson, he agrees that the colonial government was assiduous in providing for the needs of the aboriginals (*Fabrication of Aboriginal History*, pp. 239–41).

122 Windschuttle, *Fabrication of Aboriginal History*, pp. 237–8, 242.

123 Reynolds argues that the death rate on Flinders Island 'was not atypical of the situation during the first generation of Aboriginal reserves and missions' (*Fate of a Free People*, p. 186).

124 Sathnam Sanghera describes as 'casual, stomach-churning' my view – as summarised in a paragraph of a newspaper article – that what happened in early

colonial Tasmania did not amount to genocide (*Empireland*, p. 194). Readers may compare his account (ibid., pp. 149–51) with mine, and judge for themselves which of the two is more casual. Had he shown any curiosity about the reasons for my view and asked me, I would have shared a draft of this section of my book with him. But he did not ask, preferring instead to rely on the authority of Kehinde Andrews (ibid., pp. 305–6 n.1), who believes that '[t]he British Empire was far worse than the Nazis' (Nicola Woolcock, 'Cambridge College Named after Winston Churchill Debates His "Backward" Views on Race', *The Times*, 11 February 2021: https://www.thetimes.co.uk/article/cambridge-college-named-for-sir-winston-churchill-to-debate-his-backward-views-on-race-dzdrd-j29n. For a critique, see Andrew Roberts and Zewditu Gebreyohanes, '*The Racial Consequences of Mr Churchill*': A Review (London: Policy Exchange, 2021), p.14). Sanghera also complains, with a hint of exasperation, about my 'endless newspaper columns' – which is surely an odd thing for a professional journalist to complain about.

Nonetheless, *Empireland* is engaging, lively, thoughtful, full of fascinating detail, and, most of all, comprises important personal testimony about how Britain's imperial legacy looks and feels to a contemporary British Sikh. Its account of imperial history, however, is generally superficial and, notwithstanding intermittent nuance, tends heavily towards condemnation. So, for example, while Sanghera admits that the empire (inadvertently) bequeathed 'a certain tradition of anti-racism' (*Empireland*, pp. 161, 221), he tells us that it was characterised by 'racial extremism' and that 'we are institutionally racist as a nation . . . [because] our society grew out of the racist institution of British Empire' (ibid., p. 169).

125 Russell Thornton, *American Indian Holocaust and Survival* (Norman and London: University of Oklahoma Press, 1987), p. xvi; quoted in Moses, 'Conceptual Blockages and Definitional Dilemmas', p. 158.

126 Antoon A. Leenaars et al., 'Genocide and Suicide among Indigenous People: The North Meets the South', *Canadian Journal of Native Studies*, 19/2 (1999), p. 338; quoted in Moses, 'Conceptual Blockages and Definitional Dilemmas', p. 158.

127 The emphasis is mine.

128 Reynolds, *An Indelible Stain?*, p. 85. In the conclusion to his book, Reynolds considers the charge that federal and state governments in Australia perpetrated 'cultural genocide' through the policy of the forced removal of aboriginal children from their families into government- or church-run institutions between 1905 and the early 1970s. The rationale for the policy was the assumption that the pure-blooded aboriginal population was in rapid and terminal decline, but that mixed-race children could be saved by being assimilated to mainstream, European society. Estimates of the number of children involved range from 20,000 to more than 100,000. Some have argued that such a policy amounted to the destruction of the aboriginal people *as a people* and therefore amounts to a cultural form of 'genocide'. Tom Lawson is one such, describing policies undoubtedly intended to help aboriginal peoples adapt culturally, in order to

survive, as genocidal: 'The logic of the British presence in Tasmania, and indeed on continental Australia, looked forward to and indeed demanded a future free of the original owners of the soil. It is only the idea of genocide, incorporating both cultural and physical destruction, that can fully capture the totality of the project to undermine and destroy indigenous populations and culture' (*Last Man*, p. 23). Reynolds, however, rightly resists this line of thinking, holding that the issue of intention is 'critical' (*An Indelible Stain?*, p. 174). He observes that Raphaël Lemkin, who coined the term 'genocide' and pioneered the drafting of the Genocide Convention in the 1940s, distinguished between, on the one hand, 'cultural genocide' *aiming at* the annihilation of the cultural life of a group and using drastic methods to achieve it, and, on the other, a policy *aiming at* assimilation and using only moderate coercion (ibid., p. 175). Reynolds also observes that the proposal to include 'cultural genocide' in the 1948 Convention on the Prevention and Punishment of the Crime of Genocide was eventually rejected (ibid., p. 176). I note that Donald B. Smith and J. R. Miller take a similar position on the application of 'cultural genocide' to the assimilationist policies of Canadian governments, starting with that of John A. Macdonald (Smith and Miller, 'No Genocide').

129 The longstanding belief that the Tasmanian aboriginals were entirely wiped out is now disputed by those who claim reparations, especially the restoration of allegedly stolen land.

130 For example, Norbert Finzsch, '"It Is Scarcely Possible to Conceive that Human Beings Could Be So Hideous and Loathsome": Discourses of Genocide in Eighteenth- and Nineteenth-century America and Australia', in Moses and Stone, *Colonialism and Genocide*, p. 19: 'the wilful blindness to or impotent disapproval of . . . unauthorized settler actions on the part of colonial author-ities can be construed as an implicit intention to destroy the indigenes, despite the fact that they were often in thrall [*sic*] to humanitarian ideals of just treat-ment of the "natives". For the fact is that . . . such enlightened humanitarians were prepared to accept, if in an agonized or resigned manner, the "inevitable extinction" of the aboriginal peoples. After all, how could they justify halting the march of progress in the form of colonization in order to save such abject creatures?' Wilful blindness is indeed among the things that can vitiate an act, as is malicious intention. But they are not the same thing.

131 Lawson, *Last Man*, p. 23.

132 This is the title of Asa Briggs' famous book, *The Age of Improvement, 1783–1867* (London: Longmans, 1960, 2000).

133 Lawson acknowledges this: 'The Colonial Office consistently believed that colonial development was the means of saving indigenous peoples . . . Indeed, it was in fact widely assumed that if the intentions of British colonialism had been maintained, indigenous peoples would have thrived under the 'amity and kindness' of benign imperial rule . . . Humanitarian voices . . . argued consist-ently that colonialism needed to be conducted in the correct spirit in order that it might benefit indigenous populations too' (*Last Man*, pp. 204, 205).

134 I cannot quite agree with Dirk Moses, when he writes: 'Certainly, colonialism

NOTES

in Australia, as elsewhere, could not be halted in the manner of flicking a light
switch. The Colonial Office . . . was only a small part of a massive state apparatus. But only a miserably attenuated concept of intention would absolve it in
these circumstance [sic]. The rhetoric of inevitability also served to mask choices
open to policymakers, choices they were not prepared to entertain because
they fundamentally approved of the civilizing process in which they were
engaged . . . Where genocide was not explicitly intended, then it was implicitly,
in the sense of the silent condoning, sometimes agonized acceptance, of events
held to be somehow "inevitable"' (Moses, 'Conceptual Blockages and
Definitional Dilemmas', p. 174). The imperial and colonial governments had
good reasons to doubt that colonisation could be halted and reversed by 1825,
but they strove to ameliorate the evils it entailed. So they were guilty neither
of intending genocide nor of complacently condoning or accepting it. Whether
the aboriginals' encounter with the modern world would have been better
managed by another people at a later time, we shall never know. But we have
no good reason to be sure that it would have been.

135 House of Commons, *Report of the Parliamentary Select Committee on Aboriginal
Tribes*, 'Conclusion', pp. 105–6; Margery Perham, *The Colonial Reckoning*, The
Reith Lectures 1961 (London: Collins, 1961), p. 107.

136 During the 1930s the British did try to restrict the mass immigration of
Jewish settlers to Palestine – especially after the Arab Revolt of 1936–9.
However, Palestine was within relatively easy reach of Britain, being just
under four thousand nautical miles distant (compared to New Zealand's
fourteen and a half thousand miles). Moreover, the Palestinian coastline was
only about two hundred miles long (compared to Canada's twenty-two
thousand miles). Even so, Britain's attempt to control Zionist immigration
brought down on its head ferocious condemnation. In 1939 the government
published a White Paper, proposing to limit immigration to 75,000 over a
five-year period, unless the Arabs should consent to more. In response,
Jewish demonstrators in Palestine compared the White Paper to the
Nuremberg Laws and Malcolm MacDonald, the colonial secretary, to Hitler
(Segev, *One Palestine, Complete*, p. 441).

6. FREE TRADE, INVESTMENT AND 'EXPLOITATION'

1 D. K. Fieldhouse, *The West and the Third World* (Oxford: Blackwell, 1999),
pp. 127–8. In this chapter I depend quite heavily on Fieldhouse's work, which
the imperial historian John Darwin, the economic historian Tirthankar Roy
and the development economist Paul Collier all recommended to me as authoritative.

2 James, *Raj*, p. 39. It may be, however, that James exaggerates the EIC's rapacity.
Nirad Chaudhuri reports this: 'On 17 May 1766, when British rule in Bengal
had not even been consolidated, the Directors of the East India Company,
supposed to be a body of rapacious traders, wrote to their agents in Calcutta:
"It is now more immediately our interest and duty to protect and cherish the

inhabitants, and to give no occasion to look on every Englishman as their natural enemy." This was written to explain their refusal to permit monopoly of certain trades to their factors in Bengal' (*Thy Hand, Great Anarch!*, pp. 778–9).

3   Tirthankar Roy, 'Inglorious Empire: What the British Did to India', a review of Shashi Tharoor's *Inglorious Empire*, *Cambridge Review of International Affairs*, 31/1 (2018), p. 136. The claim that the Marathas committed genocide is Roy's.

4   See Chapter 1, section II.

5   Franklin and Mary Wickwire, *Cornwallis: The Imperial Years* (Chapel Hill: University of North Carolina Press, 1980), p. 72.

6   James, *Raj*, p. 193.

7   Malcolm, *Malcolm*, p. 424. Tirthankar Roy confirms Malcolm's perception, when he writes that the EIC's aim of 'demilitarizing' the countryside was '[o]verall . . . successful', creating the conditions for smoother market integration and the revival of agricultural trade in the eastern Gangetic plain (*Economic History of India, 1707–1857*, p. 65).

8   By contrast, the French Empire was the most consistently protectionist, especially from the early 1920s to the 1950s, sheltering infant colonial industries, providing them with a secure market and encouraging metropolitan investment in a stable environment (Fieldhouse, *West and the Third World*, pp. 25–7).

9   Fieldhouse, *West and the Third World*, pp. 44–7.

10 Bill Warren, *Imperialism: Pioneer of Capitalism*, ed. J. Sender (London: NLB-Verso Editions, 1980), p. 131. Tirthankar Roy also observes that, '[i]f there was a fall in textile employment there was a rise in employment in indigo, opium, and saltpetre. However, we do not know if the latter compensated for the former' (*The Economic History of India, 1857–1947* [Delhi: Oxford University Press, 2000, 2006, 2011, 2020], p. 43).

11 Indians ended up running businesses in Britain. For example, Dwarkanath Tagore – the grandfather of the famous Rabindranath – went into business with British partners, was guest of honour at the 1842 Eisteddfod in Wales and now lies buried in Kensal Green Cemetery in London (James, *Raj*, p. 280).

12 Fieldhouse, *West and the Third World*, p. 94.

13 Ibid., p. 96.

14 Ibid., p. 77.

15 Owen, *Lord Cromer*, p. 83.

16 Gilmour, *Ruling Caste*, p. 9. See also Tirthankar Roy in note 86 below.

17 Owen, *Lord Cromer*, p. 313. Writing of the period after the First World War, Fieldhouse indirectly supports Cromer's position: there were 'strong and disinterested economic arguments against artificially stimulated local industries . . . [which] would largely benefit the protected producer – initially, probably expatriate – at the expense of the poor consumer. Because they would be relatively inefficient, there would be negative value added. In much of tropical Africa, indeed, these predictions proved true after independence' (*West and the Third World*, p. 85).

18 Owen, *Lord Cromer*, pp. 311–12. Afaf Lutfi al-Sayyid-Marsot agrees with this reading of Cromer in *Egypt and Cromer*, pp. 138–9.

19 C. van Onselen, *Chibaro: African Mine Labour in Southern Rhodesia, 1900–1933* (London: 1975), pp. 87–8.

20 Vindex, *Cecil Rhodes*, pp. 374–5.

21 Rotberg, *Founder*, p. 471.

22 A. R. Dilley, 'The Economics of Empire', in Sarah Stockwell, ed., *The British Empire: Themes and Perspectives* (Oxford: Blackwell, 2008), p. 113. This bears out the general thesis of L. H. Gann and Peter Duignan that '[e]conomic history . . . suggests that the importance of tax pressure as a means of mobilizing labor progressively diminishes with the expansion of a country's economy, giving way to more positive economic incentives' (*Burden of Empire: An Appraisal of Western Colonialism in Africa South of the Sahara* [London: Pall Mall, 1968], p. 380). Ndabaningi Sithole presents the new economy of wage-earning, even in the form of mining, as an attraction to African men: 'With the new freedom from tribal wars, men soon found something else to do . . . Many mines for gold, diamonds, chrome, asbestos, copper, and uranium were opened, and to these thousands, and afterwards millions, of Africans flocked to work, or to have adventure' (*African Nationalism*, pp. 67–8).

23 Onselen, *Chibaro*, pp. 78, 92.

24 Ibid., p. 36.

25 William Beinart describes the compounds as 'racially restrictive', even though he acknowledges that they were not imposed on all African workers ('Appendix A', pp. 99, 103).

26 Gardner F. Williams, *The Diamond Mines of South Africa: Some Account of Their Rise and Development* (New York: Macmillan, 1902; Cambridge: Cambridge University Press, 2011), pp. 413, 416.

27 Rotberg, *Founder*, p. 220. Rotberg refers the reader to Josiah Wright Matthews, *Incwadi Yami: Or Twenty Years' Personal Experience in South Africa* (New York, 1887), p. 218; and James Bryce, *Impressions of South Africa* (New York, 1898), p. 204.

28 John Tengu Jabavu, *Imvo Zabantsundu*, 5 June 1906; quoted by H. J. Simons and R. E. Simons in *Class and Colour in South Africa, 1850-1950* (Harmondsworth: Penguin, 1969), p. 46.

29 Patrick Harries, *Work, Culture, and Identity: Migrant Laborers in Mozambique and South Africa, c. 1860–1910*, Social History of Africa series, ed. Allen Isaacman and Jean Hay (Portsmouth, NH: Heinemann; London: James Currey; Johannesberg: Witwatersrand University Press, 1994), pp. 68–9. Harries was professor of African history at the University of Basel until his death in 2015. His book was very well received. For example, James Derrick described it as 'an exemplary study' in *African Affairs*, 94/376 (July 1995); William Worger, as 'a welcome contribution' in the *American Historical Review*, 100/5 (December 1995); Kathleen Sheldon, as a 'path-breaking study' in *Africa Studies Review*, 38/2 (September 1995); and Tshidiso Maloka, as 'a crucial contribution' in the *Journal of Historical Sociology*, 10/2 (1996).

30 Harries, *Work, Culture, and Identity*, p. 78.
31 Onselen, *Chibaro*, pp. 35, 37, 38, 39, 49.
32 Ibid., pp. 43, 50 (Table B), 63–4. The alarming 1906 figure of 75.94 deaths per thousand comprises one of 65.91 for deaths by disease and another of 9.03 for deaths by accident. In Britain the 1906 rate of coal miners' deaths by accident was 1.29. In Southern Rhodesia, this rate decreased the following year by over half to 3.91 and thereafter never exceeded 4.92. Within five years (by 1911) the mortality rate for disease had been halved to 28.62, and within a decade (by 1916) it had been reduced by two-thirds to 22.48. While the 80 per cent improvement between 1906 and 1933 represents a very considerable reduction in the overall mortality rate, some might still consider it too high. Whether that is so depends, of course, upon which norm it is being measured against. When the portion of the 1933 mortality rate of African miners in Southern Rhodesia attributable to deaths by accident alone (2.30 per thousand) is compared to the equivalent figure for coal miners in Britain (1.03), it is more than double (Durham Mining Museum, 'Statistics: Table 1: Fatal Accidents at all Mines from 1873 to 1953, distinguishing the principal causes': http://www.dmm.org.uk/stats/index.htm). However, the rate of deaths of US miners attributable to all causes (accidents and disease) in 1930–2 was considerably higher than that of its British equivalent, and even in 1950 it was still about double the British one (Philip E. Enterline, 'Mortality Rates Among Coal Miners', *American Journal of Public Health*, 54/5 [1964], pp. 765–6, 767). One source appears to show the 1933 US mortality rate for miners dying from accidents alone as approximately 2.5 (Mark J. Perry, 'Chart of the Day: Coal Mining Deaths in the US, 1900-2013', American Enterprise Institute, 15 May 2014: https://www.aei.org/carpe-diem/chart-of-the-day-coal-mining-deaths-in-the-us-1900-2013/). If that is correct, the corresponding Rhodesian rate was about the same or even slightly lower. By far the greater part (9.2 per thousand or 80 per cent) of the overall Rhodesian rate (11.50) was due to death by disease. That proportion is not extraordinary when compared with the statistics of deaths of US miners in 1950: out of a total of 3,047 deaths from disease or accidents at work, 85 per cent was caused by disease (Enterline, 'Mortality Rates', pp. 763–4). How the rate of African miners in Southern Rhodesia dying from disease in 1933 compares with the rate of the African population in general, I do not know. But I note that from 1930–7 just under half (48.6 per cent) of African miners' deaths from disease was attributable to pneumonia (Ravai Marindo, 'Death Colonized: Historical Adult Mortality in Rhodesia (Zimbabwe)', *Zambezia*, XXVI/ii [1999], p. 159, Table 9) and that the annual Colonial Report for Northern Rhodesia in 1930 commented that 'though the death-rate [of African miners] from pneumonia may seem high, it must be remembered that this disease heads the list of causes of death in ordinary village life' (*Northern Rhodesia Report for 1930*, No. 1561 [London: HMSO, 1932], p. 40). Patrick Harries corroborates this when he writes that '[p]neumonia had always been a major cause of death during the cold winter months' (*Work, Culture, and Identity*, p. 77).

33 Ferguson, *Empire*, p. 74.

34 As I discovered when walking along it around Princeton in April 2015.

35 Pyrah, *Imperial Policy and South Africa*, p. 191.

36 Bridglal Pachai, 'Indentured Chinese Immigrant Labour on the Witwatersrand Goldfields', *India Quarterly*, 21/1 (January-March 1965), pp. 59, 65. On the eve of the arrival of the Chinese labourers, the number of miners needed was estimated at 197,000, while the number available was 68,280.

37 Le May, *British Supremacy in South Africa*, p. 161. The emphasis is Milner's.

38 Peter Richardson, 'The Recruiting of Chinese Indentured Labour for the South African Gold Mines, 1903-1908', *Journal of African History*, XVIII/1 (1977), p. 86.

39 Pachai, 'Indentured Chinese Immigrant Labour', p. 69.

40 Pyrah, *Imperial Policy and South Africa*, p. 192; Pachai, 'Indentured Chinese Immigrant Labour', pp. 63-4, 75-7.

41 Pachai, 'Indentured Chinese Immigrant Labour', p. 80. According to Kartar Lalvani, it is estimated that of the more than 150,000 indentured male labourers who had arrived in South Africa from India since 1860, only 25 per cent opted to return home (Lalvani, *Making of India*, p. 396).

42 T. M. Devine, *The Scottish Clearances: A History of the Dispossessed 1600–1900* (London: Allen Lane, 2018), p. 157. See also pp. 12, 127, 129, 319, 331, 336.

43 Ibid., p. 163.

44 See Chapter 2, pp. 59–60. The abolition of the Atlantic slave trade in 1807 is correlated with – and probably caused – the West African expansion of the production of agricultural and forestry products for internal as well as overseas markets (Gareth Austin, 'The Economics of Colonialism in Africa', in Célestin Monga and Justin Yifu Lin, eds, *The Oxford Handbook of Africa and Economics*, 2 vols, Vol. 1: 'Context and Concepts' [Oxford: Oxford University Press, 2015], p. 524).

45 B. Berman and J. Lonsdale, *Unhappy Valley: Conflict in Kenya and Africa*, 2 vols, Vol. 1: 'State and Class' (London: James Currey, 1992), pp. 132, 186: *pace* Marxist 'dependency' theory, historical research shows that Africans and other colonial peoples were not simply the 'passive receptors of external forces'.

46 Fieldhouse, *West and the Third World*, p. 180. Here Fieldhouse appears to be summarising Berman and Lonsdale, *Unhappy Valley*, Vol. 1, Chapter 8: 'Up from Structuralism', but he actually ranges beyond them. Still, Berman and Lonsdale do write that '[f]rom the very beginning elements of various African societies were willing to cooperate for the own anticipated advantage both within their own communities or over neighbouring societies . . . At least some of the dominated were able to bargain for and manipulate the system to gain substantial benefits from the European agents of the metropole.' (ibid., pp. 192–3).

47 Austin, 'Economics of Colonialism in Africa', p. 525.

48 Ibid., p. 527; F. N. Howe, 'The Early Introduction of Cocoa to West Africa', *African Affairs*, 45/180 (July 1946), pp. 152-3. Writing about cocoa production in the Gold Coast, R. H. Green and S. H. Hymer have commented: 'In numerous

instances . . . African farmers have rapidly accepted new crops and new techniques and have shown a high propensity to innovate, to accept risk, and to invest well in advance of returns. The sharp increases in the production of export crops show this to be true. Between 1919 and 1959, exports of Ghana (Gold Coast) rose 838 per cent, those of Nigeria 955 per cent, and those of (former) French West Africa 1,031 per cent' ('Cocoa in the Gold Coast: A Study in the Relations between African Farmers and Agricultural Experts', *Journal of Economic History*, 26/3 [September 1966], p. 299).

49   Colin Bundy, *The Rise and Fall of the South African Peasantry*, 2nd edn (Cape Town and Johannesburg: David Philip, 1988), p. 67; Belich, *Replenishing the Earth*, p. 383.

50   Bundy, *Rise and Fall of the South African Peasantry*, p. 45; Norman Etherington, 'African Economic Experiments in Colonial Natal, 1845–1880', in Bill Guest and John M. Sellars, eds, *Enterprise and Exploitation in a Victorian Colony: Aspects of the Economic and Social History of Natal* (Pietermaritzburg: University of Natal Press, 1985), p. 275; quoted in Belich, *Replenishing the Earth*, p. 385.

51   Austin, 'Economics of Colonialism in Africa', pp. 530–1, Tables 27.4 and 27.5.

52   Fieldhouse, *West and the Third World*, pp. 129, 166.

53   Ibid., p. 146.

54   Pachai, 'Indentured Chinese Immigrant Labour', p. 60.

55   Belich, *Replenishing the Earth*, p. 382.

56   See note 36 above in this chapter.

57   Dudley Baines, *Migration in a Mature Economy: Emigration and Internal Migration in England and Wales, 1861–1900* (Cambridge: Cambridge University Press, 1985), p. 63, Table 3.3.

58   In April 1903 Milner, then governor of the Transvaal and Orange River Colony, wrote to Joseph Chamberlain: 'The Mines have exhausted their efforts, by higher wages, better recruiting and *much better arrangements in every respect* – food, clothing, sanitation, etc. – to get natives, but though they have got *some thousands more* these are not nearly enough' (Cecil Headlam, ed., *The Milner Papers*, 2 vols (London: Cassell, 1931), Vol. II, p. 465; quoted in O'Brien, *Milner*, p. 210. The emphasis is Milner's).

59   Niall Ferguson, 'British Imperialism Revised: The Costs and Benefits of "Anglobalization"', Development Research Institute Working Paper Series, No. 2, April 2003 (New York: New York University, 2003), pp. 12–13; P. J. Cain and A. G. Hopkins, *British Imperialism, 1688–2015*, 3rd edn (London: Routledge, 2016), p. 474; P. J. Cain, 'Economics and Empire: The Metropolitan Context', in *Oxford History of the British Empire*, Vol. III, ed. Porter, p. 48, Table 2.6.

60   Dilley, 'Economics of Empire', p. 103, referring to Cain, 'Economics and Empire', p. 48, Table 2.6.

61   Cain and Hopkins, *British Imperialism*, p. 474, Table 18.7.

62   Fieldhouse, *West and the Third World*, p. 84; Austin, 'Economics of Colonialism in Africa', p. 528.

63   Dilley, 'Economics of Empire', p. 114; K. Dike Nworah, 'The Politics of Lever's

West African Concessions, 1908–1913', *International Journal of African Historical Studies*, 5/2 (1972), pp. 251–2.

64 Ferguson, 'British Imperialism Revised', pp. 7–9. Sir Alan Burns, who served as a colonial administrator in the Bahamas, British Honduras, Nigeria and the Gold Coast confirmed Ferguson's plausible speculation, when he wrote: 'It is useful to compare conditions in present and former colonial territories with those countries which have never "suffered" from colonialism. In these latter countries capital has been shy of the risks involved under inefficient and unstable government' ('Colonialism Before and After' [unpublished manuscript, c.1973], p. 114; quoted by Bruce Gilley, *Last Imperialist*, p. 73).

65 Fieldhouse, *West and the Third World*, p. 23.

66 Ibid., p. 75.

67 Joseph Chamberlain, 'Mr. Chamberlain on Trade', *The Times*, 1 April 1895, p. 11.

68 Fieldhouse, *West and the Third World*, p. 81.

69 Ibid., p. 76.

70 The colonial government's support of native resistance to capitalist development, partly out of idealisation of peasant culture and partly out of fear of political unrest, is a prominent theme in G. B. Kay, *The Political Economy of Ghana: A Collection of Documents and Statistics, 1900–1960* (Cambridge: Cambridge University Press, 1972).

71 L. G. Reynolds, *Economic Growth in the Third World: 1850–1980* (New Haven and London: Yale University Press, 1985); Fieldhouse, *West and the Third World*, p. 167. Reynolds' 'balance-sheet' is as follows. To its credit, colonialism clarified territorial boundaries and provided internal peace; stimulated new and old export crops, encouraging the pursuit of comparative advantage in the global market; provided the beginnings of a modern infrastructure, especially communications; and took steps to prevent famine evolving out of scarcity. On the debit side, it typically presided over a drain of profits from colonies to the imperial metropolis via investors and trading companies; export production was wont to generate enclaves, especially around plantations and mines; retained profits from the modern sector tended to generate income inequalities; domestic handicrafts were left unprotected from foreign competition; there was no promotion of modern industry, not least because government revenues depended heavily on import duties; educational provision was very limited, especially at secondary and tertiary levels; and colonial governments encouraged immigration from India to fill intermediate roles between the top echelon of Europeans and the mass of native workers, creating a three-tier division of labour (ibid.). As indicated in what I have written so far, I am inclined to doubt that the export of a portion of the profits is necessarily a drain, that income inequalities between native peoples in the modern economy and those in the traditional economy need be unjust, that domestic handicrafts should have been protected, that the development of modern industry should have been promoted by governments rather than permitted by the free transfer of technology and skills, that a hierarchical division of labour according to skills (rather than race) is wrong, and

that immigrants from India (or China) were wont to perform 'superior' work to that of Africans.

72 Fieldhouse, *West and the Third World*, p. 167. I note that the Marxist economist Bill Warren agrees with Reynolds' conclusion. See note 81 below in this chapter.

73 Gann and Duignan, *Burden of Empire*, p. 367. Warren also asserts what Gann and Duignan show. See note 81 below.

74 Tharoor is an MP in India's lower house, the Lok Sabha, having served as a minister in two governments and as an under-secretary-general of the UN.

75 Fieldhouse, *West and the Third World*, p. 35.

76 David Washbrook, 'The Indian Economy and the British Empire', in Douglas M. Peers and Nandini Gooptu, eds, *India and the British Empire*, Oxford History of the British Empire Companion Series (Oxford: Oxford University Press, 2012), p. 45.

77 Washbrook, 'Indian Economy and the British Empire', pp. 51–2.

78 Roy, 'Inglorious Empire', p. 135. Roy, professor of economic history at the London School of Economics and author of *The Economic History of India, 1857–1947*, observes that Tharoor omitted to mention any of these historians. His overall judgement of Tharoor's book is this: 'Few professional historians think that the British Empire ruled India with India's best interests in mind. Yet, few would consider Tharoor's dark narrative an accurate depiction of one of the most complex 200-year episodes in world history' (ibid., p. 135). Roy passes a similar judgement on Jon Wilson, now professor in modern history at King's College, London, when he wrote: 'Ruled by Muslims before the British, India was a prosperous, rapidly commercialising society . . . British rule pauperised India' ('False and Dangerous', *Guardian*, 8 February 2003: https://www.theguardian.com/education/2003/feb/08/highereducation.britishidentity). 'Wilson does not say where the data to show this came from,' Roy comments. 'Statistical studies now available dispute both claims . . . It is safe to say that the [East India] Company's state rise made *almost* no difference to the average Indian' (*Economic History of India, 1707–1857*, p. 12).

79 Roy, 'Inglorious Empire', p. 135. Tharoor's dates and figures are not identical to Roy's, but their meaning is the same (Tharoor, *Inglorious Empire*, pp. 216–17, 230–1).

80 In 1750 China was responsible for an estimated 32.8 per cent of world manufacturing output, India 24.5 per cent, Germany 2.9 per cent and Britain 1.9 per cent. By 1913 Britain's share had ballooned to 13.6 per cent and Germany's to 14.8, while China's had collapsed to 3.6 and India's to 1.4 (B. R. Tomlinson, 'Economics and Empire: The Periphery and the Imperial Economy', in *Oxford History of the British Empire*, Vol. III, ed. Porter, p. 69, Table 3.8).

81 Roy, 'British Empire and the Economic Development of India', pp. 211–12. Roy comments that 'pessimistic' Marxism, which views colonialism primarily in terms of the extraction of native surplus, has 'not been altogether successful' in refuting the 'optimistic' classical Marxist view that global capitalism was a source of innovation and productivity gains that were widely shared between colonist and colonised regions (ibid.). David Fieldhouse agrees: the pessimism

of the neo-Marxists was 'remarkably unfocused and uninformed' and 'fed on dogma rather than knowledge' (*West and the Third World*, p. 54). He also gives us a summary of the views of Bill Warren, a rare 'optimistic' Marxist who argued that colonialism was necessary for the genesis of Third World development (ibid., pp. 169–73). In this he followed Marx himself (ibid., pp. 42–7). As expressed in Chapter 6 of *Imperialism: Pioneer of Capitalism*, Warren believed that colonial governments provided at least three major benefits. First, they brought considerable improvements in health through Western medicine and anti-famine measures, which caused greater longevity, a bigger market and greater consumption – as is shown by a comparison of the records of independent Liberia, Ethiopia and Thailand with other African and Asian countries under colonial rule. Second, foreign trade led to the importation of incentive goods, which were crucial in stimulating production in the poorer levels of society. *Pace* the conventional argument, these imports caused only a relative decline in local handicrafts, since there was in fact 'an *absolute* rise in the volume and number of items of traditional production, because the market underwent a massive expansion during this period' (ibid., p. 131). Third, colonial schools had a vital role 'in dissolving traditional outlooks in a manner which, however, traumatic, could only facilitate individualism, rationality, and a democratic outlook' (ibid., p. 135). On the alleged debits in the economic record of colonialism, Warren's views were: that the repatriation of profits by Western capitalists did not constitute a net drain, since they amounted to only a portion of the value added in the host country, leaving a substantial benefit; that the growth of commodity exports during the nineteenth century was largely a spontaneous reaction by native producers to the expanding European market, and that specialisation in agricultural exports could be an adequate basis for modern, industrial development – as was the case in Latin America, the United States and the British settler colonies; that, whatever the defects of colonial economic management (artificially low wages, infrastructure skewed to serve the export trade, and the blocking of native industrial development in the interests of foreign trading companies), the colonial transition to commodity production for the international market was likely to have better consequences than the continuation of earlier pre-capitalist modes of production. In sum, notwithstanding its coercion – which could be good or bad – and its disadvantageous bias towards the selfish interests of metropolitan and settler capitalists, colonialism was a necessary stage in the development of some Third World countries.

82 Roy, 'British Empire and the Economic Development of India', pp. 215–16.
83 Ibid., p. 213.
84 Against Marxist historians who claim that it was colonial rule that caused peasants to be subject to increasing indebtedness and impoverishment, Roy argues that the historical record is 'too mixed and differentiated for any generalisation to be sustained' and that there is 'no compelling evidence' to show that agricultural yields were higher and rising before colonialism or in areas not directly subject to colonial rule (Ibid., pp. 222, 223). Nevertheless, he finds

sufficient empirical evidence to claim that the 'nationalist dream, the thesis of prosperous workers falling into poverty is rejected by the best time-series data on wages that we now have. The dataset shows that agricultural labourers saw a slow betterment of their level of living in the early nineteenth century' (*Economic History of India, 1707–1857*, p. 139).

85 From 1865 to 1914, the estimated volume of foreign trade to and from India 'more than doubled' and the estimated ratio of foreign trade in national income increased from 8–10 per cent to 20 per cent (Roy, 'British Empire and the Economic Development of India', p. 224).

86 By 1914 the fourth largest cotton textile mill industry in the world, financed and managed by Indians, had emerged in Bombay. Factory employment rates between 1850 and 1940 were 'comparable with those of other emerging economies at the time, Japan and imperial Russia, and considerably more impressive than the patchy and uneven industrialisation in the rest of the contemporary tropical world' (Ibid., p. 225).

87 Roy, 'Inglorious Empire', p. 136. Between 1880 and 1914 India's large-scale industrial production grew by 4–5 per cent annually, a rate comparable with Germany's (Ronald Findlay and Kevin H. O'Rourke, *Power and Plenty: Trade, War, and the World Economy in the Second Millennium* [Princeton: Princeton University Press, 2007], p. 422).

88 Roy, 'Inglorious Empire', p. 137.

89 James, *Raj*, p. 184.

90 Patrick K. O'Brien, 'The Costs and Benefits of British Imperialism, 1846–1914', *Past and Present*, 120 (1988); invoked by Roy in 'Inglorious Empire', p. 135. One issue raised in the 'drain' debate is how much of Britain's surplus represented 'legitimate' payments for services provided to India, which promoted the latter's growth and could not have been obtained elsewhere as cheaply. In what David Washbrook calls 'the most careful of recent considerations', G. Balachandran (*India and the World Economy, 1850–1950* [Delhi: Oxford University Press, 2003]) estimated the 'drain' at no more than 1–1.25 per cent of India's GDP, 'a substantial amount but hardly the difference between a transition from "tradition" to "modernity"'. Further, Angus Maddison ('Dutch Income from Indonesia, 1700–1939', *Modern Asian Studies*, 23/4 [1989]) has shown that, relative to their GDPs, the direct flow of resources from India to Britain was 'extremely low' compared to other contemporary colonial empires, amounting to only a tenth of the flow between Java and the Netherlands (Washbrook, 'Indian Economy and the British Empire', pp. 49–50). Maddison estimates that the 'drain' of capital from India to Britain between 1868 and 1930 was between 0.9 and 1.3 per cent of Indian national income (*The World Economy: A Millennial Perspective* [Paris: OECD, 2001], p. 87, Table 2-21b).

91 Roy in 'Inglorious Empire', pp. 135–6.

92 Washbrook, 'Indian Economy and the British Empire', pp. 50, 57.

93 Roy, 'Inglorious Empire', p. 136. Roy refers to Patrick K. O'Brien and Leandro Prados de la Escosura, 'The Costs and Benefits for Europeans from Their Empires Overseas', *Revista de Historia Economica*, 16:1 (1998); and Lance

Davis and Robert Huttenback, *Mammon and the Pursuit of Empire: The Political Economy of British Imperialism, 1860–1912* (Cambridge: Cambridge University Press, 1986). David Washbrook comments that, since very little private British capital was invested in India, if India was the jewel in the British imperial crown, 'this was very much not because of the profits earned directly from it' ('Indian Economy and the British Empire', p. 58).

94 Roy, 'British Empire and the Economic Development of India', p. 228.

95 Ibid., p. 226.

96 Roy, *Economic History of India, 1707–1857*, pp. 12–13.

97 Roy, 'British Empire and the Economic Development of India', pp. 219, 229: 'The record of the Empire in creating public goods was marked by a lack of sustained commitment . . . The 19th century famines were reminders of how badly the government performed as a guardian of welfare.'

98 Ibid., pp. 216, 219–20.

99 Ibid., p. 132.

100 According to Tirthankar Roy in personal correspondence with the author, 2 October 2020.

101 After witnessing the effects of the famine of 1833, Arthur Cotton saw developing irrigation as a moral duty: 'His canals, aqueducts and dams along the Cauvery and Godavari rivers . . . enormously increased the prosperity of the adjacent farmland. In 1987, forty years after Independence, a statue in his honour was erected in the state of Andhra Pradesh' (Gilmour, *British in India*, pp. 212–13).

102 Lalvani, *Making of India*, pp. 116–27.

103 Ibid., p. 124.

104 Gilmour, *Ruling Caste*, p. 9.

105 From 23.06 million acres in 1885 to 53.73 million in 1939 (Roy, *Economic History of India, 1857–1947*, p. 258, Table 5.6).

106 Ferguson, *Empire*, p. 216.

107 Lalvani, *Making of India*, p. 142. David Gilmour acknowledges that, by raising the water table, canals in some places may have caused the spread of saline deposits and consequent damage to crops. However, this affected only 'a minuscule proportion of the land' and, in his estimation, the harm done cannot outweigh the enormous benefits produced by the multiplication of irrigated land by a factor of eight (*Ruling Caste*, p. 9).

108 Dave Donaldson, 'Railroads of the Raj: Estimating the Impact of Transportation Infrastructure', *American Economic Review*, 108/4–5 (2018), p. 931.

109 Lalvani, *Making of India*, pp. 21, 160, 161, 199, 222.

110 Nobutaka Ike, 'The Pattern of Railway Development in Japan', *Far Eastern Quarterly*, 14/2 (Feb. 1955), Table 2, p. 223.

111 E-Tu Zen Sun, 'The Pattern of Railway Development in China', *Far Eastern Quarterly*, 14/2 (Feb. 1955), p. 179.

112 R. K. Ray, 'Introduction', in R. K. Ray, ed., *Entrepreneurship and Industry in India, 1800–1947* (Delhi: Oxford University Press, 1992), p. 47. Curzon also gave the Tatas a guarantee that the government would buy 20,000 tons of steel per annum for ten years at import prices.

113　Fieldhouse, *West and the Third World*, pp. 153–4.

114　Ibid., pp. 150–1. What is true of Australia applied to all British colonial governments in the financially turbulent period between the two world wars. Whereas
'[t]here were defaults by numerous independent debtor countries including
Argentina, Brazil, Chile, Mexico, Japan, Russia, and Turkey . . . all [British]
colonial governments weathered the storms and stresses of the interwar period
without resorting to default . . . Colonial administrators tended to favor sound
money, balanced budgets, and openness to trade – precisely the things that
reassured investors' (Niall Ferguson and Moritz Schularick, 'The Empire Effect:
The Determinants of Country Risk in the First Age of Globalization, 1880–1913',
Journal of Economic History, 66/2 [June 2006], p. 307).

115　Avner Offer, 'Costs and Benefits, Prosperity, and Security, 1870–1914', in *Oxford
History of the British Empire*, Vol. III, ed. Porter, p. 709; Fieldhouse, *West and
the Third World*, p. 143.

116　Judging by the views expressed by their fictional settlers and officials, some
literary Britons with experience of colonial East Africa lamented the loss of
pre-modern Africa, even as they recognised its inexorability. For example, Gerald
Hanley in *The Year of the Lion* (1953): 'He [Jervis] joined that band of white
men which would never again be sure whether it wanted an Africa of literate
and progressive people geared to the wheels of the West, or like this one before
him in its tribal prime, laughing, in touch with and understanding the Africa of
the forest, and the beast.' (p. 77); 'The doctor could not quite convey his sympathy
for this Africa which was soon to be sick before its death and then its rebirth
among the tractors and the buses and the rational life . . . "Do you think we
should have come here, Doc?" Jervis asked. "Should have? What's the good of
thinking about that? We're here. That's all about it. The question is what to do.
Do we simply take a look round, examine the tribal system, pronounce it useless
in the modern world, and so smash it up? Or do we keep it, nurse it, change
the worst bits and see the African of the future grateful we saved it for him?
What do we do? Do we wreck it all now and try to make an imitation white
man, or do we go slowly? That's the problem"' (pp. 156, 159). For another
example, take David Lovatt Smith in *My Enemy: My Friend* (2000), where the
elderly Kikuyu Kinyanjui says to the settler Frank Harris: 'in a few short years
my whole life has been turned upside down', and Frank observes to himself
how 'the march of progress trampled everything and everyone who got in its
way' and how Kinyanjui and his people 'were being wrenched through a thousand years of evolution in just one generation' (pp. 195, 202).

117　Sithole, *African Nationalism*, p. 72.

118　Fieldhouse, *West and the Third World*, p. 168.

119　R. von Albertini with Albert Wirz, *European Colonial Rule, 1880–1940: The
Impact of the West on India, Southeast Asia, and Africa*, trans. John G.
Williamson (Oxford: Clio, 1982), p. 507.

120　According to Niall Ferguson, English common law gave investors stronger legal
protection than French civil law ('British Imperialism Revised', p. 9).

121　Cain and Hopkins, *British Imperialism*, p. 628 n.5.

122 Roy, *Economic History of India, 1707–1857*, p. 176.
123 Fieldhouse, *West and the Third World*, pp. 221–2, 350.
124 Ibid., p. 350.

7. GOVERNMENT, LEGITIMACY AND NATIONALISM

1 Ferguson, *Empire*, pp. 167–73.
2 Fieldhouse, *West and the Third World*, p. 78.
3 The Representation of the People (Equal Franchise) Act 1928 gave women electoral equality with men. The Representation of the People Act 1918 had granted men aged twenty-one and over the vote, but only women aged thirty and over.
4 Indeed, according to Paul Collier, democratic elections can sometimes be a political liability, increasing the likelihood of political violence: 'democratic elections cannot possibly, *in themselves*, be a solution to the problem of violence or to the larger problem of decent government. In themselves, they are a recipe for driving political leadership into the gutter . . . In promoting elections, the rich, liberal democracies have basically missed the point. We want to make the bottom billion look like us, but we forget how we got to where we now are' (*Wars, Guns, and Votes: Democracy in Dangerous Places* [London: Vintage, 2010], pp. 40, 49. See also, more broadly, Chapter 1).
5 Winston Churchill, House of Commons, 11 November 1947.
6 James, *Raj*, p. 119.
7 Leela Visaria and Pravin Visaria, 'Part I. V. Population (1757–1947)', *The Cambridge Economic History of India*, ed. Dharma Kumar and Meghnad Desai, 2 vols, Vol. 2: 'c.1757–c.1970' (Cambridge: Cambridge University Press, 1983), p. 466, Table 5.1.
8 James, *Raj*, p. 120.
9 Gilmour, *Ruling Caste*, p. 11.
10 Meanwhile, during the British 'occupation' of Egypt circa 1890, there were a mere 366 Britons employed by the Egyptian government, only 39 of whom occupied high positions, and backed by a small garrison of 5,000 troops (Owen, *Lord Cromer*, p. 241).
11 A. H. M. Kirk-Greene, 'The Thin White Line: The Size of the British Colonial Service in Africa', *African Affairs*, 79/314 (January 1980), pp. 35, 38, 39. Gareth Austin reckons that the ratios were in fact even lower, since the censuses on which Kirk-Greene based his figures under-counted ('Economics of Colonialism in Africa', p. 526).
12 Frederick Lugard, *The Dual Mandate in British Tropical Africa* (Edinburgh: Blackwood, 1922).
13 Perham, *Colonial Reckoning*, pp. 57–8. Perham commented that '[w]hen . . . the intelligentsia of Lagos asked Lugard to recognise them as the leaders and spokesmen of Nigeria, he could answer truly enough that most of them had never been more than a few dozen miles inland and that all the hundred or so rulers of the vast hinterland had never so much as heard of them' (ibid., p. 113).

Perham's remarkable life is well narrated in Brad Faught's *Into Africa: The Imperial Life of Margery Perham* (London: I. B. Tauris, 2012).

14 Perham, *Colonial Reckoning*, p. 34.

15 Gilmour, *Ruling Caste*, p. 194. Mortimer Durand is best known for the 'Durand Line', marking the border between Afghanistan and Pakistan (or British India, as it was then), which he agreed with the Emir of Afghanistan, Abdur Rahman Khan, in 1893.

16 Gilmour, *British in India*, p. 183; James, *Raj*, p. 183.

17 Gilmour, *Ruling Caste*, p. 47.

18 Ibid., p. 129.

19 Owen, *Lord Cromer*, p. 69.

20 Ibid., p. 146.

21 James, *Raj*, pp. 431–2.

22 House of Commons, *Debates*, Vol. 97, cc. 1695–7 (20 August 1917).

23 Writing in 1904, Lord Milner expressed the same view: 'Representative government has its merits – no doubt – but the influence of representative assemblies, organised upon the party system, upon administration – 'government' in the true sense of the word – is almost uniformly bad' (Le May, *British Supremacy*, p. 10).

24 Earl of Cromer, 'The Government of Subject Races', in *Political and Literary Essays, 1908–1913* (London: Macmillan, 1913), pp. 28, 53. This essay was originally published in the *Edinburgh Review* (January 1908).

25 Ibid., pp. 28, 52.

26 Denis Judd and Keith Surridge, *The Boer War* (London: John Murray, 2002), p. 86.

27 The assumption prevailed in that the qualified franchise was not withdrawn from black Africans before South Africa acquired the status of a dominion in 1910 and, with it, effective independence in domestic policy. Up until then the Afrikaner Bond sought on several occasions to restrict the black franchise – with limited success, according to Farai Nyika and Johan Fourie ('Black Disenfranchisement in the Cape Colony, c.1887–1909: Challenging the Numbers', *Journal of Southern African Studies*, 46/3 [2020]) – but they never sought simply to abolish it. In 1936 the South African Parliament passed the Representation of Natives Act, which removed black voters in the Cape from the common voters' roll and placed them on a separate roll, allowing them to elect only three members to the House of Assembly. The Act also provided for four indirectly elected white senators to represent black people all over the country. Qualified coloured voters in the Cape remained on the common roll. In 1959 the Promotion of Bantu Self-Government Act turned traditional tribal lands into eight independent African states or 'Bantustans' and abolished the right of black Africans to vote in elections to the South African Parliament. In 1968 the Separate Representation of Voters Amendment Act abolished the remaining parliamentary representation for coloured people. In 1970 the Black Homeland Citizenship Act assigned Africans citizenship of their Bantustan, while removing their citizenship of South Africa.

28 Rotberg, *Founder*, p. 618. The proposed legislation referred to here was the 1899
    Parliamentary Registration Law Amendment bill. While it is true that, in promoting
    what would become the 1894 Glen Grey Act, Rhodes supported a certain disen-
    franchisement of black Africans, he did so not for racist reasons, but as a political
    compromise designed to promote reconciliation between Briton and Afrikaner.

29 Rotberg, *Founder*, p. 611.

30 Smith, 'Macdonald's Relationship with Aboriginal Peoples', pp. 77, 80. A 'status
    Indian' was someone registered as an Indian under the Indian Act of 1876.
    Early in 1885 Macdonald had intended to extend the federal franchise to all
    status Indians on equal terms with British subjects, but in the wake of the
    North-West Rebellion in the spring, the legislation was restricted to Indians
    east of Manitoba. In 1898 the Liberal government of Wilfred Laurier withdrew
    what the Macdonald government had granted, so as to deprive the Conservatives
    of Indian electoral support. Status Indians did not regain the federal vote until
    1960. It should be noted that since acquisition of the federal vote meant the
    loss of the rights of status Indians, including exemption from taxation, many
    native people did not seek it.

31 John A. Macdonald to Peter E. Jones, 31 August 1886; quoted in Smith,
    'Macdonald's Relationship with Aboriginal Peoples', p. 79. Macdonald's view
    of native Canadians was equivocal. On the one hand, he said such things as,
    'we cannot change the barbarian, the savage, into a civilised man' (House of
    Commons, Ottawa, 6 July 1885; quoted in Williams, *Blood Must Tell*, p. 147).
    On the other hand, he supported the conditional extension of the franchise to
    Indians, and he envisaged native MPs in the House of Commons in due course.
    Glen Williams describes the former as an expression of 'biological determinism'
    (ibid., pp. 146, 267). I doubt that, because it seems to me more an expression
    of practical pessimism regarding the Indians of the west, intensified in the light
    of their violence during the recent North-West Rebellion, than an expression of
    theoretical conviction. Had that pessimism sunk as deep as biological deter-
    minism, Macdonald would not have entertained any hope at all of the civilisation
    of Indians. But he did entertain it, albeit in a very chastened fashion: 'There is
    only one way – patience, patience, patience. We see what patience has done in
    the older Provinces. Look at the Province of Ontario. The Indian is still an
    Indian. His color is the same, but he is law-abiding, he is a peaceful man . . . In
    the course of ages – it is a slow process – they will be absorbed in the country'
    (House of Commons, Ottawa, 10 June 1885; ibid., p. 151); 'All we can hope for
    is to wean them, by slow degrees, from their nomadic habits, which have almost
    become an instinct, and by slow degrees absorb them or settle them on the land'
    (House of Commons, Ottawa, 5 May 1880; ibid., p. 147).

32 Lawrence James, *The Rise and Fall of the British Empire* (London: Abacus,
    1994), p. 296.

33 David Throup, 'The Origins of Mau Mau', *African Affairs*, 84/336 (July 1985),
    pp. 401–2.

34 Lonsdale, 'East Africa', p. 541. See also David French, *The British Way in
    Counter-Insurgency, 1945–1967* (Oxford: Oxford University Press, 2011), pp.

192, 195. When considering the late economic and political development of Kenya – and other colonies in West and East Africa – the observation of L. H. Gann and Peter Duignan should be borne in mind: 'The vast majority of African people experienced imperial tutelage for no more than the lifetime of a single grandmother. Even this brief period was in practice further curtailed by two world wars and a world slump.' (*Burden of Empire*, p. 372).

35 Amartya Sen, 'Food, Economics, and Entitlements', in Jean Drèze and Amartya Sen, *The Political Economy of Hunger*, Vol. 1: 'Entitlement and Well-being' (Oxford: Oxford University Press, 1991), p. 42. Sen's main argument, however, is that the main cause of people dying of famine is often not the lack of available food, but the lack of cash with which to buy it. The solution, therefore, is the provision of 'cash-relief'.

36 Cobden to Henry Ashworth, 12 April 1842; quoted by Martin Lynn in 'British Policy, Trade, and Informal Empire in the Mid-Nineteenth Century', in *Oxford History of the British Empire*, Vol. III, ed. Porter, p. 104.

37 Louise A. Tilly, 'Food Entitlement, Famine, and Conflict', *Journal of Interdisciplinary History*, 14/2 (Autumn 1983), p. 342. Tilly reports Sen's argument that Adam Smith's faith in the market mechanism for marrying demand with supply failed to address the problem of 'meeting a need that has not been translated into effective demand because of lack of market-based entitlement and shortage of purchasing power' (Sen, *Poverty and Famines: An Essay on Entitlement and Deprivation* [Oxford: Oxford University Press, 1983], pp. 160, 161).

38 Roy Foster, *Modern Ireland, 1600–1972* (London: Penguin, 1988), pp. 323–4.

39 See John Mitchel, *An Apology for the British Government in Ireland* (Dublin: Irish National Publishing Association, 1860), and Paul Bew's report of it in *Ireland: The Politics of Enmity, 1789–2006* (Oxford: Oxford University Press, 2007), p. 209.

40 Bew, *Ireland*, p. 197.

41 Cormac Ó Gráda, *Black '47 and Beyond: The Great Irish Famine in History, Economy, and Memory* (Princeton: Princeton University Press, 1999), p. 124. *Pace* Amartya Sen, Ó Gráda argues that 'though official neglect and endemic injustice played their part in Ireland in 1846 and 1847, there is no denying that the Irish famine was, at least in those years, also a classic case of food shortage' – and not just a case of the poor distribution of available food (ibid., pp. 123–4).

42 Foster, *Modern Ireland*, p. 325.

43 Bew, *Ireland*, pp. 203, 205.

44 Jennifer Hart, 'Sir Charles Trevelyan at the Treasury', *English Historical Review*, 75/294 (January 1960), p. 99. Paul Bew argued as far back as 1999 that Hart's reading of Trevelyan was based on a misrepresentation of a letter he had written to Father Mathew in October 1846 ('A Case of Compassion Fatigue', *Spectator*, 13 March 1999, pp. 37–8). See Bew, *Ireland*, p. 197 n.106. Five years later, Robin Haines devoted seven pages to dismantling Hart's misreading in *Charles Trevelyan and the Great Irish Famine* (Dublin: Four Courts Press, 2004), pp. 3–9. In correspondence with the author on 12 October 2020, Bew reported

that 'no one has gone to the source to say that we got it wrong'. Laura Trevelyan gives a useful summary of the controversy about her ancestor's role in the Irish famine in *A Very British Family: The Trevelyans and Their World* (London: I. B. Tauris, 2006), pp. 37–47.

45 Haines, *Charles Trevelyan*, p. 4.

46 Charles Trevelyan, *The Irish Crisis* (London: Longman, Brown, Green, and Longmans, 1848), p. 201.

47 Bew, *Ireland*, pp. 179, 210.

48 'More Alms for the "Destitute Irish"', *The Nation*, 16 October 1847; quoted in Bew, *Ireland*, p. 199.

49 *The Nation*, 8 November 1845; quoted in Bew, *Ireland*, pp. 177–8.

50 Foster, *Modern Ireland*, p. 327.

51 Although some landlords went to costly lengths to relieve local distress, 'by and large, the class who possessed most did least' (Foster, *Modern Ireland*, p. 330).

52 Bew, *Ireland*, p. 191.

53 A. M. Sullivan, *New Ireland* (Philadelphia: Lippincott, 1878), p. 86.

54 Dutil, 'Not Guilty', p. 9.

55 Daschuk, *Clearing the Plains*, pp. 108, 184.

56 James Daschuk, 'When Canada Used Hunger to Clear the West', [Toronto] *Globe and Mail*, 19 July 2013. Ironically, *Clearing the Plains* was awarded the Sir John A. Macdonald Prize. In 2018 the Canadian Historical Association removed Macdonald's name from the prize.

57 Daschuk attributes the collapse of the bison stocks to the introduction of cattle, which competed for forage and spread disease: 'The ecological significance of the introduction of cattle cannot be overstated' (ibid., p. 102).

58 Ibid., pp. xix, xxi.

59 Ibid., p. 123.

60 Ibid., pp. 157–8.

61 Ibid., p. 116.

62 Ibid., p. xxi.

63 Ibid., p. 186.

64 *Copy of Treaty No. 6*, p. 4. The emphasis is mine.

65 Daschuk, *Clearing the Plains*, p. 184.

66 Ibid., p. 117.

67 Ibid., p. 123. It is true that Macdonald also said, '[W]e are doing all we can, by refusing food until the Indians are on the verge of starvation, to reduce the expense'. However shockingly callous this sounds, Macdonald had to yield to parliamentary pressure from his Liberal opponents to reduce expenditure, as Daschuk recognises: 'Political pressure from the opposition Liberals was an important factor in constraining government expenditures on the Indian population' and in causing the Conservative Government to emphasise the work-for-rations policy (ibid., p. 133.)

68 Ibid., p. 128. In 1883 expenditure on food relief was cut from $607,235 to $530,982 (ibid., p. 134).

69 Ged Martin, 'The Department of Indian Affairs in the Dominion of Canada
    Budget, 1882', https://www.gedmartin.net/martinalia-mainmenu-3/312-
    indian-affairs-1882-budget (2020), page 12 of the print-out. Martin, emeritus
    professor of history and former director of the Centre for Canadian Studies at
    the University of Edinburgh, argues that in 1882 the Dominion of Canada's
    'spending on Aboriginal people, notably those in severe distress on the prairies,
    represented a substantial segment of overall government expenditure' (ibid., p. 1).
    To illustrate how tightly constrained was the spending power of the Canadian
    government in 1882, he relays J. R. Miller's observation that the United States
    spent more each year on frontier wars during the 1870s than the total (annual)
    Ottawa budget (ibid., p. 4). He estimates a net figure for government expend-
    iture in 1882 of $21.573 million (ibid., p. 3). Of this, $9.227 million was spent
    servicing debt, which was essential for maintaining public credit, and a further
    $3.531 million was spent on subsidies for the provinces, which was obliged by
    the terms of confederation in 1867. Of only four other items exceeding $1 million,
    spending on Indian Affairs ($1.107 million) was one (ibid., p. 4). This was more
    than the spending on civil government ($0.946 million), militia and defence
    ($0.754 million), and the administration of justice ($0.582 million) (ibid., p. 5).
    The cost of pensioning, training and providing emergency support to native
    people equalled 12.16 per cent of non-debt and non-subsidy spending – 'a
    remarkably heavy burden at the time' (ibid., p. 6). Of the dominion government's
    response to the crisis in the Treaty 7 area (approximately 130,000 square kilo-
    metres of land from the Rocky Mountains to the west, the Cypress Hills to
    the east, the Red Deer River to the north and the US border to the south),
    Martin writes:

    > The urgency of the operation may be seen in allocation figures reported to
    > the Auditor General. The Department had begun with $102,000 earmarked
    > for emergency relief. It soon needed a further parliamentary grant of $327,139.
    > It says something for the humanity of Canada's MPs that [Sir Leonard
    > Tilley, the finance minister] could announce this large item with the simple
    > statement: 'I need scarcely enter upon any explanation of the circumstances
    > under which this additional expenditure was made necessary for the current
    > year.' When this large outlay still did not prove adequate, Ottawa resorted
    > to the device of a Governor-General's warrant, which authorised the expend-
    > iture of $94,702, and would be subject to retrospective approval. Even with
    > this blizzard of cash, there was an overspend of $39,310 (ibid., p. 8).

    Patrice Dutil tells basically the same story, albeit with different figures ('Not
    Guilty', pp. 13–14).

70 Daschuk, *Clearing the Plains*, p. 183. See pages 107–8 of this book for an account
    of the 'Numbered Treaties'.
71 Ibid., p. 125.
72 Ibid., p. 115.
73 Ibid., p. 184. Yet at the same time Daschuk chides the dominion government
    for having 'had no contingencies for the unexpected disruption' (ibid., p. 135).

74 According to Brad Faught, professor of history at Tyndale University, Toronto, in correspondence with the author, 13 September 2020.

75 Dutil, 'Not Guilty', pp. 13–14. Daschuk sometimes provides an estimate of the number of native peoples who died from disease – for example, 3,512 for the victims of the smallpox epidemic of 1869–70 (*Clearing the Plains*, p. 82). But with regard to native starvation on the western plains in 1879–83, he gives only death rates, not a number of the total deaths.

76 A. P. MacDonnell, *Report on the Food-grain Supply and Statistical Review of the Relief Operations in the Distressed Districts of Behar and Bengal during the Famine of 1873–74* (Calcutta: Bengal Secretariat Press, 1876). Unfortunately, there is no documentary evidence in this report of Irish inspiration for MacDonnell's intense interest in famine relief, since it contains only one reference to Ireland (and its population density) on page 127. There is no reference at all to Ireland in the 1901 report of the Indian Famine Commission, which MacDonnell chaired.

77 Gilmour, *Ruling Caste*, p. 118.

78 Ibid., pp. 114–16.

79 Tirthankar Roy, *How British Rule Changed India's Economy: The Paradox of the Raj* (Cham, Switzerland: Palgrave Pivot, 2019), p. 130.

80 See James, *Raj*, p. 579: 'There might have been just enough food available if there had been effective machinery in place for rationing, the control of distribution and, above all, a willingness to cooperate among peasant farmers and entrepreneurs. None existed.' But see Roy's dissident view in note 82 below.

81 According to S. Y. Padmanabhan, the outbreak of rice disease in Bengal in October 1942 was similar in its unprecedented nature to the potato blight in Ireland in the 1840s: 'Though administrative failures were immediately responsible for this human suffering, the principal cause of the short crop production of 1942 was the epidemic of helminthosporium disease which attacked the rice crop in that year . . . Nothing as devastating . . . has been recorded in plant pathological literature' ('The Great Bengal Famine', *Annual Review of Phytopathology*, 11 [September 1973], p. 11).

82 Barney White-Spunner, *Partition: The Story of Indian Independence and the Creation of Pakistan in 1947* (London: Simon & Schuster, 2017), pp. 40–1. Amartya Sen has observed: 'The current supply [of rice] for 1943 was only about 5 per cent lower than the average of the preceding five years. It was, in fact, 13 per cent *higher* than in 1941, and there was, of course, no famine in 1941' (Amartya Sen, *Poverty and Famines: An Essay on Entitlement and Deprivation* (Oxford: Oxford University Press, 1983, p. 58. The emphasis is Sen's). He has also observed that the Bengal Famine occurred in boom conditions, with a massive expansion of war-related economic activity, albeit one that favoured the urban over the rural labouring classes ('Food, Economics, and Entitlements', p. 38). Roy disputes Sen's claim, arguing that the size of the Bengal harvest 'probably fell' (*How British Rule Changed India's Economy*, p. 129).

83 A secondary problem was bias in the distribution of famine relief caused by

Hindu prejudice against Muslims and those of low caste (Abhijit Sarkar, 'Fed by Famine: The Hindu Mahasabha's Politics of Religion, Caste, and Relief in Response to the Great Bengal Famine, 1943-1944', *Modern Asian Studies*, 54/6 [2020]).

84 James, *Raj*, pp. 579–80. When he arrived to take up the viceroyalty in October 1943, Lord Wavell found the 'Bengal administration a mass of corruption and dishonesty from top to bottom' and 'that the pilfering and misappropriation of food grains was now on such a scale as to make relief measure largely ineffective' (Wavell to Amery, 8 November 1943, in Nicholas Mansergh and E. W. R. Lumby, eds, *Constitutional Relations between Britain and India: The Transfer of Power, 1942–7*, 12 vols (1970–83), Vol. IV: 'The Bengal Famine and the New Viceroyalty, 15 June 1943–31 August 1944' (London: HMSO, 1970), No. 213. See also Lance Brennan in 'Government Famine Relief in Bengal, 1943', *Journal of Asian Studies*, 47/3 (August 1988), pp. 555, 557.

85 Wavell to Amery, 1 November 1943, in Mansergh and Lumby, *The Transfer of Power*, vol. IV, pp. 432–3.

86 Madhusree Mukerjee, a science journalist, accuses Churchill in *Churchill's Secret War: The British Empire and the Ravaging of India during World War II* (New York: Basic Books, 2010), while Tirthankar Roy, the economic historian, exonerates him in *How British Rule Changed India's Economy*, pp. 129–30. 'The Cabinet took decisions,' writes Roy, 'in the knowledge that the Axis powers were sinking one ship every day and had sunk around a million tons of shipping in 1942' (ibid.). See also Zareer Masani, 'Churchill and the Genocide Myth', *The Critic*, 13 (December 2020), pp. 38–40; James Holland, *Burma '44: The Battle that Turned Britain's War in the East* (London: Bantam Press, 2016), p. 113; and James Holland, *Sicily '43: The First Assault on Fortress Europe* (London: Bantam Press, 2020), pp. 42, 47.

87 Cormac Ó Gráda, '"Sufficiency and Sufficiency and Sufficiency": Revisiting the Great Bengal Famine of 1943-44', in *Eating People Is Wrong, and Other Essays on Famine, Its Past and Its Future* (Princeton: Princeton University Press, 2015), p. 90: '. . . the lack of political will to divert foodstuffs from the war effort rather than speculation . . . was mainly responsible for the famine. Those in authority at the time knew that there was a shortfall but kept quiet about it. The War Cabinet in London chose not to act on it. Winston Churchill's lack of empathy for India and "all to do with it" mattered.' However, Roy counters that there is 'little evidence that Churchill's personal views about Indians influenced the policies of the War Cabinet' and that the Cabinet believed what it was told – that there was no shortage (*How British Rule Changed India's Economy*, pp. 129-130).

88 White-Spunner, *Partition*, p. 45; Roy, *How British Rule Changed India's Economy*, pp. 129–30.

89 James, *Raj*, p. 581.

90 Hugh F. Kearney, 'The Great Famine: Legend and Reality', in *Studies: An Irish Quarterly Review*, 46/182 (Summer 1957), pp. 187–8. Kearney is in fact articulating the implied collective conclusion of *The Great Famine*, eds, R. Dudley

Edwards and T. Desmond Williams (Dublin: Browne and Nolan, 1956).

91 Roy, *How British Rule Changed India's Economy*, pp. 129–30. Wavell believed that Suhrawardy 'siphoned money from every project that was undertaken to ease the famine, and awarded to his associates contracts for warehousing, the sale of grain to governments, and transportation' (Thomas Keneally, *Three Famines: Starvation and Politics* [New York: Public Affairs, 2011], p. 97).

92 Owen, *Lord Cromer*, p. 348.

93 Al-Sayyid, *Egypt and Cromer*, p. 86.

94 Margery Perham asserted this point more generally: 'When Britain is criticised for not having begun this or that social service in Africa at some early date it is often forgotten that it was only gradually in Britain herself that such functions were regarded as proper to the State' (*Colonial Reckoning*, p. 120).

95 Referring to British colonial Africa as a whole, Perham wrote that 'in the earlier decades of this [twentieth] century Africans in many if not most parts, were indifferent or suspicious about Western education. Often there was real hostility. This was especially true of female education' (ibid., p. 18).

96 Owen, *Lord Cromer*, pp. 314–15.

97 See pp. 209–11 and note 139 in this chapter.

98 Lalvani, *Making of India*, pp. 371–2.

99 Ibid., pp. 373, 376.

100 Masani, *Indian Tales of the Raj*, p. 89.

101 Achebe, 'Education of a British-Protected Child', pp. 19, 21.

102 Appollos O. Nwauwa, 'The British Establishment of Universities in Tropical Africa, 1920–1948: A Reaction against the Spread of American "Radical" Influence', *Cahiers d'études africaines*, 33/130 (1993). It seems that the journal misspelled Professor Nwauwa's first name, which is 'Apollos'.

103 The British-owned Chinese language newspaper *Shenbao* had been founded in 1872 and from the safety of Hong Kong an entirely Chinese-owned newspaper, the *Tsun-wan yat-po*, explicitly criticised Chinese imperial policy and proposed reforms from 1874 (Robert Bickers, *Out of China: How the Chinese Ended the Era of Western Domination* [London: Allen Lane, 2017], p. 299).

104 Sun's speech was delivered in English on 20 February 1923. Since there is no extant record of it in English, this quotation was taken from a version that was reconstructed from a Chinese translation and newspaper reports in the *South China Morning Post*, 21 February 1923, and published online by the Research Centre for Translation at the Chinese University of Hong Kong: https://www.cuhk.edu.hk/rct/pdf/e_outputs/b2930/v29&30P042.pdf

There is a bitter irony in the fact that Sun is held up today as a revolutionary hero by the Chinese Communist Party (CCP), which celebrated the 150th anniversary of his birth in 2016. It was the British colony of Hong Kong's refusal to extradite him that saved Sun from a Qing imperial prison or worse. Yet it was the CCP's attempt in 2019 to get the Hong Kong legislature to pass a bill enabling extradition between Hong Kong and the Chinese mainland that marked the beginning of a wider suppression of the liberal legacy of British colonial rule. Sun is surely turning in his grave.

105 This was not simply the result of colonial masters wanting to keep power in their alien hands. Later in the twentieth century, at least, one major opponent of democratisation in Hong Kong was the Chinese business community (Jonathan Dimbleby, *The Last Governor: Chris Patten and the Handover of Hong Kong* [Barnsley: Pen & Sword, 1997, 2018], p. 107).

106 Chinua Achebe, *There Was a Country: A Personal History of Biafra* (New York: Penguin, 2012).

107 Ibid., pp. 43–4.

108 Ibid., p. 36.

109 Chinua Achebe in an interview, 'Voice of Nigeria', *West Africa*, 24 February 1962, p. 201; quoted in Ezenwa-Ohaeto, *Chinua Achebe: A Biography* (Oxford: James Currey, 1997), p. 88.

110 Perham, *Colonial Reckoning*, pp. 125, 126, 128.

111 P. J. Cain, 'Character, "Ordered Liberty" and the Mission to Civilise: British Moral Justification of Empire, 1870–1914', in *Journal of Imperial and Commonwealth History*, 40/5 (December 2012), p. 575 n.84, quoting Gormley in Aida Edemariam, 'Brendan Gormley: "I Wasn't Very Charitable"', *Guardian*, 23 January 2010: 'I think the colonial period, and the aid period, in 100 years, are going to be re-evaluated. A lot of the dedication and commitment in little colonial district offices – they went there for years, they learned the language – they were actually much closer to the community than a lot of aid workers. I think history might give us [in the international aid business] quite a hard judgment.'

112 Robert O. Collins and Francis M. Deng, eds, *The British in the Sudan, 1898–1956* (London: Macmillan, 1984), pp. 216, 241 n.1.

113 'Covenanted' officials in the Indian Civil Service comprised Britons occupying the higher administrative echelons, while 'uncovenanted' officials comprised Indians in the lower echelons.

114 Gilmour, *British in India*, p. 40; here Gilmour is quoting the *Tribune*, 7 June 1898. The *Tribune* is an English-language newspaper that was founded in Lahore in 1881 by Sardar Dyal Singh Majithia. See also Gilmour, *Ruling Caste*, p. 149.

115 Ibid., p. 168; Fred Leventhal and Peter Stansky, *Leonard Woolf: Bloomsbury Socialist* (Oxford: Oxford University Press, 2019), p. 42.

116 Ibid., pp. 41–2.

117 Charles Westwater, letter to *The Tablet*, 29 March 2003, p. 15.

118 Lalvani, *Making of India*, p. 42.

119 Nirad Chaudhuri agrees: 'So I declared that empires could be and were, so far as any human phenomenon can be, both moral and beneficial . . . imperialism could be justified on the ground on which St Thomas Aquinas justified the exercise of authority of all kinds, which he said was moral if it was for the subject's good or the common good' (*Thy Hand, Great Anarch!*, p. 777).

120 Michael Hechter, *Alien Rule* (Cambridge: Cambridge University Press, 2013), pp. 36–7, 38 n.31, 39 n.34. See also Bickers, *Scramble for China*, pp. 192–204.

121 Hechter, *Alien Rule*, p. 2. See also pp. 3, 6.

122 Roy Foster appears to endorse this view. Without demur, he paraphrases the
constitutional nationalist leader John Redmond as saying that 'by 1900 the
struggle over the land was effectively won, and it could be argued that the form
of British government was neither unduly oppressive nor unrepresentative:
indeed, the prospect of Britain granting self-government or "Home Rule", to
Ireland seemed inevitable' (*Vivid Faces: The Revolutionary Generation in
Ireland, 1890–1923* [London: Allen Lane, 2014], pp. 25–6. He also reports the
revolutionary Sean O'Faolain as making the point, in retrospect, that 'by 1916,
the panoply of Irish historical grievances, used as the rationalization for armed
resistance, had become "purely emotional impulses"' (ibid., p. 27). And of many
of the 'revolutionary generation' he comments, 'These young people came
from backgrounds of privilege but recalled living under a sense of national
oppression – which hardly fitted the objective conditions of their lives' (ibid.,
p. 327).

123 So claimed Kevin Myers in 'Never, Never, Never . . . Imagine that Our History
Is Now Behind Us', *Irish Independent*, 31 May 2007. For substantiation at the
level of local government, see Virginia Crossman, 'Epilogue: Breakdown: 1892–
1922' in *Politics, Law and Order in Nineteenth-century Ireland* (Dublin: Gill
and Macmillan, 1996), pp. 182–92; and Terence Dooley, 'Introduction' in *The
Plight of Monaghan Protestants, 1912–1926* (Maynooth Studies in Irish Local
History; Dublin: Irish Academic Press, 2000), pp. 7–19.

124 I owe these data to a report mainly based on the 1901 census, which was
provided in personal correspondence by Professor W. E. Vaughan, a leading
scholar of the history of Ireland in the nineteenth century at Trinity College,
Dublin.

125 See J. J. Lee, *Ireland, 1912–1985: Politics and Society* (Cambridge: Cambridge
University Press, 1989), p. 513, Table 12.

126 Desmond FitzGerald, *Desmond's Rising: Memoirs 1913 to Easter 1916* (Dublin:
Liberties Press, revised edn, 2006), pp. 58–9, 88. Desmond was the father of
Garret FitzGerald, who served as taoiseach (prime minister) of Ireland twice
in the 1980s.

127 Foster, *Modern Ireland*, p. 483.

128 Charles Townshend, *Easter 1916: The Irish Rebellion* (London: Allen Lane,
2005), p. 269; see also pp. 265–7.

129 See ibid., Chapter 10, 'Punishment'.

130 Peter Godwin, *Mukiwa: A White Boy in Africa* (London: Picador, 2007),
p. 205. I am grateful to Dermot O'Callaghan for giving me this remarkable book
in January 2016 in St Patrick's Cathedral, Dublin, just after I had delivered a
lecture arguing that the Easter Rising a hundred years before had been morally
unjustified. At the time, I was not sure why he had given it; now I know.

131 Godwin, *Mukiwa*, pp. 258–9.

132 Ibid., p. 296.

133 Al-Sayyid, *Egypt and Cromer*, p. 171.

134 Owen, *Lord Cromer*, pp. 335–41.

135 Al-Sayyid, *Egypt and Cromer*, p. 169.

136 Ibid., p. 191.

137 L. S. Rathore, 'Political Ideas of Jawaharlal Nehru: Some Reflections', *Indian Journal of Political Science*, 46/4 (October–December 1985), pp. 452, 463.

138 Elie Kedourie, *Nationalism*, 4th edn (Oxford: Blackwell, 1993), p. 96.

139 Al-Sayyid, *Egypt and Cromer*, p. 139. The same applied in India. When giving evidence to the Disorders Inquiry Committee in 1919, Mahatma Gandhi himself said of 'the half-educated youth of the country': 'Take a boy who has passed to the High School and has little knowledge of English, still less a knowledge of English history. He reads newspapers which he only half understands and feeds on his own predilections instead of checking them.' One instance was Hans Raj, the twenty-three-year-old who organised the fateful assembly in the Jallianwala Bagh in Amritsar on 13 April 1919 (see Chapter 8, pp. 227–8). Although he had passed the exam for entry to university, he went through a series of jobs before ending up as a commission agent for stationery and medicine. Comments Kim Wagner: 'like so many other young Indian men, [he had] failed to secure the respectable livelihood that he expected from his education' (*Amritsar 1919: An Empire of Fear and the Making of a Massacre* [New Haven: Yale, 2019], pp. 50–1).

140 Al-Sayyid, *Egypt and Cromer*, pp. 161, 184.

141 Tom Garvin, *Nationalist Revolutionaries in Ireland, 1858–1928* (Dublin: Gill and Macmillan, 1987), p. 49.

142 Foster, *Vivid Faces*, p. xxi.

143 Peter Hart, *The I.R.A. and Its Enemies: Violence and Community in Cork, 1916–1923* (Oxford: Clarendon Press, 1998), pp. 169, 170. Hart is quoting here from the obituary of Liam Hoare, captain of Gurtroe Company (Cork 1) in the *Irish Times*, 9 March 1918.

144 Foster, *Vivid Faces*, p. 8.

145 James, *Raj*, pp. 351–2.

146 Ibid., pp. 349–52; Gilmour, *Ruling Caste*, pp. 132–4; Owen, *Lord Cromer*, pp. 175–6.

147 Krishan Kumar observes that the French Empire was better than the British at integrating native peoples into the ruling elite, quoting the British anthropologist Lucy Mair, who wrote in 1936 that '[t]his [more favourable French] attitude toward the educated native arouses the bitter envy of his counterpart in neighbouring British colonies' (*Visions of Empire*, p. 436).

148 Al-Sayyid, *Egypt and Cromer*, p. 140.

149 Nwauwa, 'British Establishment of Universities in Tropical Africa', p. 248.

150 Ibid., p. 259, quoting J. Flint, *Nigeria and Ghana* (Englewood Cliffs, NJ: Prentice-Hall, 1966), p. 160.

151 Ibid., pp. 259–60.

152 Augustine Birrell, 'On Nationality' (1890), in Augustine Birrell, *Self-Selected Essays: A Second Series* (London: Thomas Nelson, 1916), pp. 248–9.

153 Chaudhuri, *Thy Hand, Great Anarch!*, p. 674.

154 Al-Sayyid, *Egypt and Cromer*, pp. 71–2, 141.

155 Perham, *Colonial Reckoning*, pp. 38–9.

156 T. E. Lawrence, *Seven Pillars of Wisdom: A Triumph* (London: Folio Society, 2000), p. 66. Of course, the eloquence may have been more Lawrence's than Faisal's.

157 See Chapter 1, p. 41.

158 Perham, *Colonial Reckoning*, pp. 71, 79.

159 Sir Alan Burns shared Perham's dismay at the excessive, counterproductive pace of decolonisation, but he blamed it more on the United Nations, the United States and weak British governments than on native nationalists (Gilley, *Last Imperialist*, Chapters 10, 11 and 12). Writing in about 1973, he commented: 'All that we have to regret is that we left our work unfinished and that to some extent we deserted our friends. The British colonial service asked only for time, time to lay the foundations securely, and time was denied us' ('Colonialism Before and After', p. 97; quoted in Gilley, *Last Imperialist*, p. 252).

160 John Plamenatz, *On Alien Rule and Self Government* (London: Longmans, 1960), p. 3.

161 Ibid., p. 22.

162 Ibid., p. 69.

163 Ibid., p. 83.

8. JUSTIFIED FORCE AND 'PERVASIVE VIOLENCE'

1 The most recent and comprehensive instance of advocacy of this charge can be found in Caroline Elkins' *Legacy of Violence: A History of the British Empire* (New York: Alfred A. Knopf, 2022). The case that Elkins makes is a poor one, fundamentally because her accounts of political legitimacy and of the ethics of political violence are staggeringly naive – just like Elleke Boehmer's, as found on page 5 of this book. Elkins' simplistic view is that British colonial rule, being imposed by force, was illegitimate, and that therefore no use of violence by colonial authorities could have been morally justified. 'What we do know is that all empires were violent,' she writes. 'Coercion was central to initial acts of conquest and to the maintenance of rule over non-consenting peoples' (*Legacy of Violence*, p. 23). But *all* states depend on violent force or the threat of it. Moreover, judging by what we have seen of the British case, empire did *not* always begin with conquest. Further, it often *did* command – or come to command – the consent of the peoples it ruled.

In addition to political theoretical and ethical naivety, Elkins' work suffers from what even a sympathetic reviewer, Sunil Khilnani, has been moved to call her 'nuance-vaporising ideological apparatus'. Among other things, this causes her to fail to notice that liberal imperialism generated not only colonial paternalism, but also resistance to colonial authoritarianism ('The British Empire Was Much Worse Than You Realize', *New Yorker*, 28 March 2022, page 10 of the online print-out). 'The ungainly truth,' Khilnani warns, 'is that liberal thought has been a resource for repression and resistance alike, and theories of imperial power impatient with this ambiguity may not withstand the scrutiny

they deserve' (ibid., page 11). Moving in a similar direction, John Darwin criticises Elkins' reductionism. '[T]wo generations of scholarship have been
dedicated,' he writes,

> to showing the enormous complexity and diversity of colonial societies, and
> the multiple ways in which they responded to British and other colonial
> rulers. Colonial rule meant different things to different people, and different
> peoples. Co-operation – or, as it is sometimes termed 'collaboration' –
> extended far more widely than a tiny elite . . . [W]e should not assume too
> readily that violence and terror were the norm in colonial governance, if
> only because few colonies had the means to fund them . . . And 'A history
> of the British Empire' – the subtitle of this book – should also remind us
> that it engaged colonial peoples in many ways other than by violence: reli-
> giously, educationally, architecturally, philosophically, medically, scientifically
> and through ideas about law and – perhaps surprisingly – justice. Much of
> this has survived. Even as we reject the morality of colonialism, it is too
> reductionist to see its legacy as simply or mainly one of violence. ('Lowering
> the Flag: How the British Justified Imperial Violence to Themselves', in
> *Times Literary Supplement*, No. 6211 [15 April 2022], p. 8).

Elkins' prosecutorial zeal makes her an unreliable reporter and interpreter
of the historical data. I will substantiate this claim in relation to her treatment
of the Second Anglo-Boer War and the Mau Mau rebellion in notes 165, 176,
188, 212, 225, 227 and 257 below. Meanwhile, here is what Bruce Gilley has to
say about her account of the communist insurgency in Malaya in 1948:

> There, according to Elkins, Henry Gurney oversaw 'a police state' with the
> alarming ability to arrest criminals, levy fines, and impose 'the death sentence
> for a range of offenses', including terrorism. The leader of the insurgency, known
> as Chin Peng (actually, his name was Ong Boon Hua), was a freedom fighter,
> in her telling. The 41,000 native policemen and 250,000 native auxiliaries who
> signed up to combat the insurgency were not evidence of the legitimacy of
> colonial rule. Rather, they showed that 'Britain was throwing massive weight
> behind the forces of law and order'. The British wanted to cling to Malaya 'for
> economic resources' such as tin and rubber, not to save the people of Malaya
> from communism. Odd that one of Gurney's major policies was the creation
> of a pan-ethnic Independence of Malaya Party. Clever ploy.
>
> In fact, Ong's domestic support was nil beyond a small band of Chinese
> radicals who, as he later wrote in his memoirs, were motivated by 'Chinese
> patriotism' and 'international socialism'. This had zero appeal to the Malay,
> Indian, and even Chinese communities in the colony. Ong's jungle fighters
> ambushed Gurney's car north of Kuala Lumpur in 1951. Gurney died in a
> hail of bullets, drawing fire from his driver and wife, who hid in a culvert
> with his dead body until help arrived. 'Dead in one of the empire's remote,
> roadside gutters', in the enthusiastic telling of Elkins. He had it coming,
> after all. A 'trademark mustache punctuated his ever-present scowl'. The
> day of his assassination, he was heading for 'a weekend of colonial leisure'

in a 'Rolls-Royce' with 'crown insignia'. Presumably, the graduate students gathered on the library floor for colonial horrors story hour are expected to gasp with each salacious detail. Levying fines! A mustachioed scowl! Colonial leisure (whatever that is)!

Ong was eventually exfiltrated to Beijing via North Korea in 1960 as his movement collapsed into ideological schism and Stalinist purges. For Elkins, it appears a great pity that his movement did not succeed. Anyone taking potshots at the Tommies is, in her view, always on the side of justice. Were Elkins to ask a Malaysian or Singaporean today, she would find those poor ex-subjects still laboring under the violent 'colonial' idea that not being taken over by a communist tyranny was a good thing. A leader of Malaya from the Indian community who would become independent Malaysia's ambassador to the United Nations, Radhakrishna Ramani, said this of Gurney's death at the time: 'This should not merely be the end of another great man. This must be the beginning of a renewed determination to steel our hearts and strengthen our hands to end such dastardly crimes forever, and with the greatest possible speed.' Ramani represented the people of Malaya. Ong did not. You won't find Ramani mentioned in Elkins's book. She is too busy relishing the thought of Gurney's riddled corpse in a gutter. ('A History of Colonialism That's More Angry Than Accurate', *Washington Examiner*, 24 February 2022.)

The military historian Robert Lyman concurs, dismissing Elkins' claim that Britain fought to prevent Malaya's independence as 'a blatant lie, which any reading of a reputable history book would reveal' ('Violence Against History', *The Critic*, 2 October 2022: https://thecritic.co.uk/violence-against-history/).

2   For a clear and thoughtful exposition of the 'just war' tradition, see A. J. Coates, *The Ethics of War* (Manchester: Manchester University Press, 1997). See also Nigel Biggar, *In Defence of War* (Oxford: Oxford University Press, 2013).

3   John Darwin, 'Imperial History by the Book: A Roundtable on John Darwin's *The Empire Project*: Reply', *Journal of British Studies*, 54/4 (Oct. 2015), p. 994.

4   I did consider including in this list the American War of Independence. That, of course, was a very important instance of British imperial belligerency, even if its scale was much smaller than that of the Second Anglo-Boer War. However, although it is widely assumed that the imperial cause was unjust, and the American 'patriot' cause just, both sides could command some moral justification. And although imperial troops did sometimes commit atrocities, so did patriots, and the fighting was not generally characterised by violations of the laws of war as understood at the time. Therefore, even if the war is usually reckoned not to redound to the British Empire's credit, it is not an instance of imperial violence that is widely supposed to demonstrate the empire's essential evil.

5   Bickers, *Scramble for China*, p. 29. See also Julia Lovell, *The Opium War: Drugs, Dreams and the Making of China* (London: Picador, 2011), Chapter 1.

6   Ibid., p. 74. The Yao were a non-Han, aboriginal people who 'in anger at the depredations of neighbouring Han communities who competed with them for scarce resources, rose and struck out at the Qing' in 1832 (ibid., pp. 73–4).

7 Bickers argues that the Cabinet's decision was not taken primarily to enforce the illegal trade or to secure reparations, but for 'honour' (ibid., pp. 80–1).

8 Ibid., p. 396: 'We are not accustomed to taking honour seriously, but if we are to understand the course of the scramble [for China in the nineteenth century] we must.'

9 Ibid., pp. 21–2. Some have argued that the Chinese term commonly used for foreigners was not well translated by the English word 'barbarian', with its negative connotations (ibid., p. 49). Robert Bickers certainly thinks that misunderstanding played no small part in generating conflict: 'Mutual incomprehension and deliberate misrepresentation alike infected relations between the Qing and the Western world. Honour matters in this story, dignity too. The Sino-foreign conundrum seemed partly to derive from the simple impossibility of each side according the other sufficient dignity, or understanding when the other felt wronged, or else in perceiving slight when none was offered' (ibid., p. 15).

10 Frank Dikötter, Lars Laamann and Xun Zhou, 'China, British Imperialism, and the Myth of the "Opium Plague"', in James H. Mills and Patricia Barton, eds, *Drugs and Empires: Essays in Modern Imperialism and Intoxication, c. 1500–c. 1930* (London: Palgrave, 2007), p. 26. As reported, Dikötter has said: 'The traditional view is that the opium trade between India and China was created by the evil British to create widespread dependence and profits from the Chinese people. In fact, the trade had been in existence for a long time as the medicinal and social benefits of opium were widely incorporated into Chinese society. The British only responded to a market that was already there: the wars that followed were about trade alone, and had little to do with British military expansion' (John Crace, 'The Empire Strikes Back', *Guardian Education*, 4 January 2003, p. 15: https://www.theguardian.com/education/2003/jan/14/highereducation.news).

11 Bickers, *Scramble for China*, p. 83.

12 William Gladstone, House of Commons, in *Hansard*, 8 April 1840, columns 800–820.

13 Julia Lovell makes the same point (*The Opium War*, p. 346). The estimate of at least 45 million deaths consequent upon the Great Leap Forward is Frank Dikötter's (*Mao's Great Famine: The History of China's Most Devastating Catastrophe, 1958–62* [London: Bloomsbury, 2010], p. xii). These were caused by an inextricable mixture of vulnerabilities caused by government policy and then exploited by natural disasters. The estimate of at least 400,000 deaths consequent upon the Cultural Revolution is reported as 'widely accepted' by Maurice Meisner (*Mao's China and After: A History of the People's Republic*, 3rd edn [New York: Free Press, 1999], p. 354); that of 3 million comes from Jung Chang and Jon Halliday (*Mao: The Unknown Story* [London: Jonathan Cape, 2005], p. 569).

14 The revolt of 1857 has attracted a variety of names, each representing a different view of its motives. The 'Sepoy Mutiny' implies that the provoking grievances were strictly those that affected mercenary troops. The 'Indian Mutiny' broadens the scope a little further, but still denotes the event as, basically, a mutiny. The 'Great Rebellion' or the 'Revolt of 1857' abandon military moorings altogether,

and the 'First War of Indian Independence' expands the rebellion into an expression of Indian nationalism. On the latter, Lawrence James has commented: 'Indian historians have endeavoured to present the 1857 Mutiny as a proto-war of national independence, despite its confinement to the northern regions of the country . . . Wherever [the Mutineers] were free to create systems of government, the tendency was towards restoration and particularism . . . Individually and collectively Indians were not bent upon the creation of a unified nation state' (*Raj*, pp. 271, 272). My own view is that what began as a mutiny mainly stoked by the professional grievances of mercenary soldiers came to encompass a wider range of religious and political resentments, but remained far short of being an expression of incipient Indian nationalist consciousness. Of all the options I think that the 'Indian Mutiny' is the most accurate and the least misleading.

15 Saul David, *The Indian Mutiny 1857* (London: Viking, 2002), pp. 23–4, 28, 31–2; James, *Raj*, pp. 206–7, 237, 273.

16 See Chapter 3, pp. 75–6.

17 David, *Indian Mutiny*, pp. 38–9, 40.

18 James, *Raj*, pp. 235, 269: 'Every examination of the events of 1857 comes back to this fact: that the rank and file of the Bengal army imagined that they were about to be made Christians.'

19 Ibid., p. 297.

20 Roy, *Economic History of India, 1707–1857*, pp. 2, 11, 167.

21 James, *Raj*, p. 268.

22 Barbara English, 'The Kanpur Massacres in India in the Revolt of 1857', *Past and Present*, 142 (February, 1994), p. 169.

23 See Biggar, *In Defence of War*, pp. 85–8.

24 R. H. Vetch, 'Havelock, Sir Henry', in *Dictionary of National Biography* (1891): 'The influence exercised by Havelock over his troops, and the admirable discipline he maintained, are strikingly shown by the behaviour of the men on entering Cawnpore. The pitifulness of the scene presented by the remains of their murdered fellow-countrymen exasperated them to madness, but the firm hand of their commander held them in check, and even marauding was put down with a strong arm.' I thank Dr Nicholas Wood for alerting me to Havelock's role. See Nicholas J. Wood, 'Henry Havelock, History and Hagiography: Some 21st century (Baptist) Reflections on a 19th Century (Baptist) Hero' (not yet published).

25 John Clark Marshman, *Memoirs of Major-General Sir Henry Havelock, K.C.B.*, 3rd edn (London: Longmans, Green, Reader, and Dyer, 1867), p. 323.

26 In some cases, at least, British talk of vengeance exceeded its practice. Alfred Lyall, a magistrate in the North-Western Provinces, was given a year's special authority to imprison and execute murderers. He did hang several – all of them killers of other Indians rather than Europeans – 'but, like many of his colleagues, he was more bloodthirsty in spirit than in action. Officials cried out for vengeance, he reported, but became "utterly unable to act when they saw a wretched villain before them begging for his life"' (Gilmour, *Ruling Caste*, pp. 15, 87).

27 Rudrangshu Mukherjee, '"Satan Let Loose upon Earth": The Kanpur Massacres

in India in the Revolt of 1857', *Past and Present*, 128 (August 1990), pp. 93–4; 'Reply', *Past and Present*, 142 (February 1994), p. 183. The emphases are mine.

28 English, 'The Kanpur Massacres', p. 171. In my own judgement, the defence of his position that Mukherjee offers in his 'Reply' of February 1994 does not succeed in deflecting English's criticisms.

29 John William Kaye, *A History of the Sepoy War in India, 1857–1858*, 3 vols (London: W. H. Allen, 1876), Vol. II, pp. 270–1.

30 David, *Indian Mutiny*, p. 237.

31 Ibid., p. 239. The emphases are Queen Victoria's.

32 Christopher Herbert, *War of No Pity: The Indian Mutiny and Victorian Trauma* (Princeton: Princeton University Press, 2008), p. 16.

33 House of Commons, *East India (Proclamations)* (London: HMSO, 1908), p. 2: http://www.csas.ed.ac.uk/mutiny/confpapers/Queen%27sProclamation. pdf (accessed 3 November 2020).

34 Nigel Collett, *The Butcher of Amritsar: General Reginald Dyer* (London: Hambledon & London, 2005), pp. 261, 263; Nick Lloyd, *The Amritsar Massacre: The Untold Story of One Fateful Day* (London: I. B. Tauris, 2011), pp. 168, 171, 179, 180. Collett (p. 261) gives 10–15 minutes as the estimated length of time of the shooting, while Lloyd (p. 179) gives 6–10 minutes. The casualty figures cited here are those given by the Disorders Inquiry Committee, known as the Hunter Committee, in its report of 1920. The Indian National Congress claimed approximately 1,000 dead and more than 1,500 wounded. Collett reports estimates of over 500 dead ('A Muse Abused: The Politicizing of the Amritsar Massacre', *Asian Review of Books*, 17 July 2012: http://asianreviewofbooks.com/ content/archived-article/?articleID=1310); Zareer Masani reports 'best estimates' of 500–600 killed and roughly three times that wounded ('Amritsar: Beginning of the End of Empire', *Standpoint*, April 2019, p. 34).

35 Lloyd, *Amritsar Massacre*, p. 20.

36 Ibid., pp. 9–10.

37 Collett, *Butcher of Amritsar*, p. 219; Lloyd, *Amritsar Massacre*, p. 28.

38 Collett, *Butcher of Amritsar*, pp. 220–1; Lloyd, *Amritsar Massacre*, pp. 35, 41. Lloyd comments that while the Rowlatt Act was among the causes of the popular unrest, 'little was known of [its] exact provisions and [it was] not widely read' (ibid., p. 127). Kim Wagner agrees (*Amritsar 1919*, p. 51).

39 David Arnold, 'Death and the Modern Empire: The 1918–19 Influenza Epidemic in India', *Transactions of the Royal Historical Society*, 29 (2019), p. 181.

40 Lloyd, *Amritsar Massacre*, pp. 32–4.

41 Ibid., pp. 48–54.

42 Collett, *Butcher of Amritsar*, pp. 233–4.

43 Ibid., pp. 238, 246; Wagner, *Amritsar 1919*, pp. 71, 110–11, 142, 149, 156, 157.

44 Collett, *Butcher of Amritsar*, pp. 252–3.

45 Wagner, *Amritsar 1919*, p. 147.

46 Collett, *Butcher of Amritsar*, pp. 326, 423.

47 Ibid., pp. 33, 38.

48 Ibid., p. 337. See also pp. 255, 325, 328.

49 Lloyd, *Amritsar Massacre*, pp. 181–2.

50 Collett, *Butcher of Amritsar*, pp. 321, 387.

51 Ibid., pp. 331, 396.

52 Ibid., pp. 355–6. Collett reports that 'not one expert military writer on imperial policing and counter-insurgency, from Dyer's day to the present, has been able to bring himself to acquit Dyer of both a breach of law and of a catastrophic failure of judgment' (ibid., p. 442).

53 Lloyd, *Amritsar Massacre*, p. 164.

54 Collett, *Butcher of Amritsar*, p. 382. Wagner argues that Churchill was being 'disingenuous' in his repudiation of 'frightfulness', since a few months later he 'initiated the indiscriminate policy of brutal reprisals in Ireland' (*Amritsar, 1919*, p. 252). In support he cites Richard Toye, *Churchill's Empire: The World that Made Him and the World He Made* (London: Macmillan, 2010) and Charles Townshend, *The British Campaign in Ireland, 1919–1921: The Development of Political and Military Policies* (Oxford: Oxford University Press, 1975) (ibid., p. 301). Personal correspondence during 29 November to 1 December 2020 with Professor Townshend and Dr William Sheehan (author of *A Hard Local War: The British Army and the Guerrilla War in Cork, 1919–1921* [Cheltenham: History Press, 2011]) suggests that Wagner's judgement is inaccurate and uncharitable. Taking 'reprisal' to mean a more or less immediate retaliatory response to an attack, Townshend stated that 'it can be confidently said that Churchill did not instigate or approve of indiscriminate reprisals'. All official reprisals were 'highly discriminate' and involved the destruction of property rather than the killing of people. However, Churchill 'probably favoured targeted assassination'. Dr Sheehan adds that British officers engaged in such assassinations reported directly to Churchill and that the targets were both active members of the IRA and those providing logistical support. An assassination is not quite a reprisal, and a *targeted* assassination is, by definition, discriminate.

55 Collett, *Butcher of Amritsar*, pp. 392, 408.

56 Masani, 'Amritsar: Beginning of the End of Empire', p. 36.

57 Collett, *Butcher of Amritsar*, pp. 322, 387, 390.

58 Ibid., pp. 399–401.

59 Ibid., p. 345.

60 Edward Thompson, who was a vocal advocate of India's progress to self-government and entertained both Gandhi and Nehru at his Oxford home (Peter J. Conradi, *A Very English Hero: The Making of Frank Thompson* [London: Bloomsbury, 2012], pp. 96–9), concluded that Indian opinion had mistaken the meaning of the 'Amritsar Massacre'. In 1932 he wrote: 'Over a dozen years I have met an exceptional number of men who were close to what happened and have known intimately protagonists of both sides . . . I have never doubted that General Dyer's action saved the Punjab from a revolt, with its attendant horrors. Nor have I ever doubted that it did irreparable mischief to the Raj, and that he shot away more than he preserved. His deed was appalling . . . Yet we may dismiss once for all the belief that he was anti-Indian or a man naturally cruel.

The man who "kept on seeing" what had happened was neither of these things ... The story of the last dozen years would have been immeasurably happier had we realized that Jalianwalabagh was the scene of a mistake and not of calculated brutality' (*A Letter from India* [London: Faber & Faber, 1932], pp. 101, 103, 104).

61 Kim Wagner locates the event of 13 April 1919 in the context of 'the structural dynamics' of colonial rule in India, interpreting it as the expression of a consistent 'colonial mentality' (*Amritsar 1919*, pp. xvii, xxi). This mentality was haunted by the Indian Mutiny, acutely sensitive to the fragility of British rule, and so prone to explosions of disproportionate, indiscriminate, exemplary violence designed to terrorise the population into acquiescence. The unconstrained repression of the mutiny 'remained a blueprint for the maintenance of colonial control' (ibid., pp. 6, 16, 254). Wagner seeks to substantiate his thesis by identifying the presence of the spectre of 1857 in British reactions to the 'Kuka outbreak' of 1872, the riots in the Punjab of 1907 and the disturbances in Amritsar in 1919.

In 1872, after capturing sixty-eight members of a Sikh revivalist sect who had perpetrated a series of murderous attacks on Muslims in the Punjab, Deputy Commissioner J. L. Cowan summarily executed sixty-eight prisoners by blowing them from guns, arguing that 'to prevent the spreading of the disease, it is absolutely necessary that repressive measures should be prompt and stern ... this incipient insurrection must be stamped out at once' (ibid., p. 8). Counting against this being an expression of Wagner's consistent 'colonial mentality' are the following points: the evidence of Cowan being motivated by the memory of 1857 is entirely circumstantial; his action was not indiscriminate, since it comprised punishment of sectarian murderers; nor was it clearly disproportionate, since it aimed to deter further attacks of which there were rumours; nonetheless, the viceroy, Lord Napier, refused to condone Cowan's action, overriding the support given him by the lieutenant-governor of the Punjab; the reaction in Britain was marked by incredulity, since '[r]ecent events had changed the way people in Britain perceived such brutality within the Empire'; and Cowan was removed from his post (ibid., pp. 7–9).

With regard to the British reaction to unrest in 1907, Wagner's thesis depends almost entirely on circumstantial evidence, with the one exception of the testimony of the viceroy, Lord Minto, who observed 'a nervous hysterical Anglo-Indian feeling', and wrote to his wife, 'The recollections of the Mutiny have shed a great influence over both Europeans and Natives.' (ibid., p. 13).

As for the Amritsar massacre itself, it is clear that General Dyer believed that the authority of British rule in the Punjab was at stake, and that he perceived (probably correctly) that the crowd assembled in the Jallianwala Bagh posed a deliberately defiant challenge to that authority. It is reasonable to suppose that his perception of *this* crowd was coloured by the recently murderous conduct of other crowds in the same city. It is therefore not reasonable to expect him to have assumed that *this* crowd was unarmed and non-violent. It is also relevant that his force was small in number and the crowd appeared (and was), by comparison, very large, and that he did not know that the reason that the crowd did not disperse quickly was that most of the exits were blocked. Nonetheless, he could have afforded to give a verbal warning, then a command to fire warning shots and then not to keep firing continuously for up to fifteen minutes. If he had reason not to consider his action indiscriminate – perceiving the crowd to be openly defiant of the law and as violent as other crowds had recently been – it was still disproportionate. Was this because, haunted by the Indian Mutiny, he regarded those gathered in the Jallianwala Bagh 'in racialised terms and amenable only to the language of brute force', and, following the 'blueprint' of 1857, decided to punish them with 'indiscriminate violence' (ibid., pp. 236, 253-4)? No, since he did not think his action was indiscriminate and since there is no evidence that he acted as he did *because they were Indians* rather than *because they were openly defying the law and (as he perceived it) potentially violent*.

Besides, in the closing pages of his book Wagner abruptly qualifies his thesis, when he writes that, '[w]hile British rule in India was *not essentially* maintained through terror and spectacles of violence, the same cannot be said for the borderlands of the Raj, nor of the ever-expanding frontiers of the Empire' (ibid., p. 256; the emphasis is mine). In the end, therefore, Wagner admits that there were at least two colonial mentalities, and that, insofar as the one he tries to argue for actually existed, it was – literally – peripheral.

On another occasion, Wagner's attempt to make the case that colonial violence was pervasively 'racialised' also fails. Against his thesis Huw Bennett et al. have argued that the British use of expanding bullets was not determined by racism but by the military need to disable adversaries who did not subscribe to the convention of war 'that combatants should fall out of action once wounded' (Huw Bennett, Michael Finch, Andrei Mamolea and David Morgan-Owen, 'Studying Mars and Clio: Or How Not to Write about the Ethics of Military Conduct and Military History', *History Workshop Journal*, 88 [Autumn 2019], p. 275). Wagner has responded by arguing that the British developed expanding bullets 'exclusively for use in "savage warfare"', that is, 'against non-white enemies' ('Expanding Bullets and Savage Warfare', *History Workshop Journal*, 88 [Autumn 2019], p. 281). Yet this misses the crucial issue, which is whether 'savage' refers to non-white enemies who are less than fully human and therefore less worthy of restraint, or to the 'fanatical' mode by which certain non-whites wage war and that requires more destructive force to stop. That is, was the choice of expanding bullets determined by racist contempt or by military necessity and proportion? Wagner's own article provides plenty of evidence that it was the latter.

The claim that British rule in India was 'pervasively' or 'essentially' violent – and therefore illegitimate – is a recurrent one. We have heard it not only from Kim Wagner, but also from Rudrangshu Mukherjee. It is also made by Jon Wilson, who characterises the Raj as prone to extreme violence caused by chronic anxiety (*India Conquered: Britain's Raj and the Chaos of Empire* [London: Simon & Schuster, 2016]). In the light of what we have seen of the

Raj in the course of this book, this seems simplistic, and several reviewers of Wilson's book have found it so: Joshua Ehrlich, 'Review Article: Anxiety, Chaos, and the Raj', *Historical Journal*, 63/3 (June 2020); David Gilmour, 'Colonial Conundrums', *Literary Review*, August 2016; and Zareer Masani, 'Britain's Raj and the Chaos of Empire', *History Today*, 67/4 (April 2017).

62   Collett, *Butcher of Amritsar*, pp. 76, 440.

63   Ibid., p. 439.

64   Nick Lloyd notes that, in 1934, Charles Gwynn complained in *Imperial Policing* that it is perhaps 'widely felt that an officer who takes strong action which he genuinely considers is necessitated by the circumstances cannot rely on the support of the Government' (Lloyd, *Amritsar Massacre*, p. 201). See also Masani, 'Amritsar: Beginning of the End of Empire', p. 37. Margery Perham suggests that Amritsar did constrain colonial governors in post-1945 Africa in their use of armed force: 'The governor may have genuine fears for minorities . . . Is he to stand aside, and, in some territories, see the moderate, the loyal, and even the indifferent, intimidated; their houses burned, perhaps; the law flouted; the economy halted? He may remember all that followed Amritsar and will allow no shooting except as an utterly last resource' (*Colonial Reckoning*, p. 65).

65   Collett, *Butcher of Amritsar*, pp. 203, 216, 349, 422.

66   Dabinderjit Singh, 'The Truth behind the Amritsar Massacre', *politics.co.uk*, 16 January 2014: https://www.politics.co.uk/comment-analysis/2014/01/16/the-truth-behind-the-amritsar-massacre In June 2014 the British foreign secretary, William Hague, reported claims that as many as 3,000 people had been killed: https://www.bbc.co.uk/news/uk-26027631

67   Lloyd, *Amritsar Massacre*, pp. 206–7.

68   Robert Home, *City of Blood Revisited: A New Look at the Benin Expedition of 1897* (London: Rex Collings, 1982), pp. 93, 95–7.

69   Home, *City of Blood Revisited*, p. 100. Home's estimate of 2,000 items is conservative. In 1919 Felix von Luschan estimated 2,400 items. In 1982 Philip Dark reckoned perhaps 4,000 or more. In 2020 Dan Hicks tentatively speculated 'quite possibly 10,000 bronzes, ivories, and other objects'. Ten pages later his 'quite possibly' suddenly becomes a 'probably' (Dan Hicks, *The Brutish Museums: The Benin Bronzes, Cultural Violence and Cultural Restitution* [London: Pluto Press, 2020], pp. 136, 147).

According to Eric Edwards of the Pitt Rivers Museum in Oxford, '[m]anillas (which were a traditional African exchange medium) were originally metal bracelets or armlets. Later forms were made of copper, bronze, or brass open rings . . . Eventually manillas became known as slave trade money after they were used by Europeans to acquire slaves. The slave trade in question was that to England and the Americas prior to 1807. Furthermore, Dutch traders ". . . bought slaves against payment in rough grey copper armlets which had to be very well made, otherwise the natives rejected them by the hundred" [C. K. Meek, *Law and Authority in a Nigerian Tribe: A Study in Indirect Rule* (London: Oxford University Press, 1937), p. 5]. A slave cost about 12 to 15 brass manillas in the 1490s . . . smaller pattern Popo Manillas, which were too small to wear as bracelets, were manufactured in Birmingham solely for the slave trade' ('Object Biographies', in *Rethinking Pitt-Rivers:* http://web.prm.ox.ac.uk/rpr/index.php/objectbiographies/78-manilla/).

70 H. Ling Roth, *Great Benin: Its Customs, Arts, and Horrors* (Halifax: F. King, 1903), Appendix III: 'The Surrender and Trial of the King', esp. pp. xiv, xvi: 'The Consul-General [Sir R. D. R. Moor] opened the proceedings by stating that the palaver was not about the late fighting, because it was quite right that the natives should fight for their country, but that it was about the massacre of the unarmed white men of Phillips' peaceful expedition. The palaver would be managed native fashion, that is, according to native custom and law, and not according to white man's law. The first thing to settle was to find out who instigated the massacre, whether the king or the chiefs? . . . The prisoners were allowed to cross-examine, but the evidence of the three chief witnesses was not upset on any material point . . . [Moor judged that] as the king and some others had for some years been under the impression that the white man was coming with war, there was a natural doubt in their minds, when Phillips' party came, as to whether it meant war; as to defend their country was a proper thing, he would give the king and chiefs the benefit of doubt; but as regards the chiefs who were present at the massacre, after learning that the white man was not bringing war, there could be no doubt in their case.' It is not clear who H. Ling Roth's source was. I presume that it was his brother F. N. Roth, who served as the expedition's surgeon.

71 Home, *City of Blood Revisited*, pp. 109, 112, 121–2.

72 R. H. Bacon, *Benin: The City of Blood* (London: Edward Arnold, 1897), pp. 13, 79, 80, 87–8, 92–3.

73 Bacon, *Benin*, pp. 13, 89–90, 93.

74 F. N. Roth, 'Diary of a Surgeon with the Benin Punitive Expedition by F. N. Roth, M.R.C.S.', in Ling Roth, *Great Benin*, Appendix II, pp. ix–x. Captains Alan Boisragon and Henry Gallwey, also eyewitnesses, corroborated the testimony of Bacon and Roth in *The Benin Massacre* (London: Methuen, 1897), pp. 180–1, 185, 187, 188 and 'Nigeria in the "Nineties"', *Journal of the Royal African Society*, 29/115 (April 1930), pp. 240–2.

75 Philip A. Igbafe, 'The Fall of Benin: A Reassessment', *Journal of African History*, 11/3 (1970), pp. 391, 398.

76 Home, *City of Blood Revisited*, p. 99. He writes that the British met the results of human sacrifices on their approach to the city; that Itsekiri slaves were observed being beheaded during the fighting; that seven still-living slaves – all of them carriers from Phillips' mission – were pulled from the burial pits; that outside the city walls lay nearly two hundred bodies, some showing the marks of violent death, of criminals, paupers and aliens lacking relatives to take them away; and that the heads of two white men were found lying at the foot of a crucifixion tree (ibid., pp. 80, 86, 87). Home's own writing generally inspires confidence because of the breadth of its information, its command of detail and its usual dispassion – with one rare exception that I will comment on shortly. He interviewed the four last surviving naval members of the expedition,

as well as a contemporaneous Benin chief, in the 1960s (ibid., pp. xi, 130).

77 Ibid., p. 103. In an article on human sacrifice in pre-colonial West Africa, Robin Law observes how detailed studies such as Home's 'have demonstrated how grossly exaggerated reports of human sacrifices' in Benin were used to justify the use of military force against it ('Human Sacrifice in Pre-Colonial West Africa', *African Affairs*, 84/334 [January 1985], p. 55). To be more exact: the eyewitness reports did not exaggerate what they saw; they mistook the scale of killing as normal.

78 Home, *City of Blood Revisited*, p. 103.

79 Law, 'Human Sacrifice in Pre-Colonial West Africa', p. 66.

80 Home, *City of Blood Revisited*, pp. 16, 17, 103.

81 Olatunji Ojo, 'Slavery and Human Sacrifice in Yorubaland: Ondo, *c.* 1870–94', *Journal of African History*, 46/3 (2005), p. 394. Ojo argues that it was the British military expedition of 1886 and their military occupation of Ibadan in 1893 that ended the practice of human sacrifice in Yorubaland, which lay immediately to the west of the kingdom of Benin (ibid., pp. 400, 402, 404).

82 Thomas Uwadiale Obinyan, 'The Annexation of Benin', *Journal of Black Studies*, 19/1 (September 1988), p. 37.

83 Igbafe, 'Fall of Benin', pp. 399, 400. Elsewhere in his article Igbafe takes a more nuanced position; namely, that British hostility to Benin was 'largely' due to its obstruction of trade and that humanitarian considerations were not 'foremost' in British officials' minds (ibid., pp. 186, 388, 391). Igbafe's article is invariably cited in subsequent discussions of the Benin expedition.

84 Ling Roth, *Great Benin*, Appendix I: 'The Treaty Made with the King of Benin', pp. i–ii. Gallwey changed his surname to 'Galway' in 1913.

85 Hicks, *Brutish Museums*, pp. 89–90.

86 Home, *City of Blood Revisited*, p. 34.

87 Ibid., p. 35: 'if the Oba refused to see them, the affront to British prestige would make it almost impossible for the Foreign Office not to sanction an armed solution.' This implies that in January 1897 Phillips believed that the Foreign Office still needed persuading to sanction military intervention. Hicks cites Home's account of Phillips' motivation without demur (*Brutish Museums*, p. 97), even though it stands in some tension with his own argument that the Foreign Office had already decided in favour of intervention by the end of the previous month.

88 Boisragon, who had accompanied Phillips on his expedition and was one of two white survivors, wrote that 'it was by trying to see if he couldn't stop such a state of things [that is, the practice of human sacrifice], by peaceful measures first of all, that poor Phillips and all our dear comrades lost their lives' (*Benin Massacre*, pp. 188–9). Bacon echoed this view when he mused, 'would not a gallant man like Phillips probably think that the presence of his mission might restrain the blood-lust of the King and Ju-Ju priests, and perhaps save some poor creatures from an untimely death?' (*Benin*, p. 17). Philip Igbafe dismisses this humanitarian account of Phillips' motivation, asserting that the Ague festival, which the Oba was celebrating, 'did not involve human sacrifices' ('Fall of Benin', p. 396 n.62). But Kathy Curnow, in effect, contradicts his unargued

assertion in her detailed account of the Ague ceremony, where she states that it did in fact involve human sacrifices ('The Art of Fasting: Benin's Ague Ceremony', *African Arts*, 30/4 [Autumn 1997], p. 46).

89 Home, *City of Blood Revisited*, pp. 7, 27, 33–6, 38, 40, 41, 44, 45, 46, 87; Bacon, *Benin*, p. 17.

90 Ibid., p. 50: 'Ministers and officials of the government were not amused that they had been manoeuvred against their wishes into a war with Benin . . . Moor was summoned from his lodgings to the Foreign Office by Curzon and the senior civil servant Sanderson. He probably had an uncomfortable interview.'

91 Ibid., p. 15. In case the idea of trade as a civilising force should strike the reader as odd, I should point out that the claim is commonly made today by those who argue for engagement with authoritarian regimes. For example, '. . . Germany holds to the aspirational axiom of *Wandel durch Handel*, change through trade. The argument, familiar to any official dealing with Germany for the past half-century is that commercial links with authoritarian regimes can sow the seed of liberal reform from within' (Roger Boyes, 'Germany Is Falling Out of Love with America', *The Times*, 27 January 2021, p. 24).

92 Ling Roth, *Great Benin*, Appendix I, pp. i–ii.

93 For example, see Obinyan, 'Annexation of Benin', p. 38; and, most recently, Dan Hicks, *Brutish Museums*.

94 Home, *City of Blood Revisited*, pp. 10–11, 30–1.

95 C. W. Newbury, *British Policy Towards West Africa: Select Documents, 1875–1914* (Oxford: Clarendon Press, 1971), p. 147 n.2. It is not crystal clear from Newbury's account which expedition is being referred to, but the context suggests that it is the military one that Phillips was asking permission to launch.

96 According to correspondence between the Foreign Office and Moor in late December 1896, which is cited by J. C. Anene in *Southern Nigeria in Transition, 1885–1906* (Cambridge: Cambridge University Press, 1966), pp. 190–1.

97 Hicks finds the timing of this telegram – fifty-three days after Phillips had written and five days after he had been killed – 'extremely odd' and suspects 'time-juggling' and 'forging', casting doubt on the appearance that the Foreign Office 'supposedly' cancelled the expedition at all (*Brutish Museums*, pp. 94–7). This reader, however, found himself unable to grasp what Hicks is claiming about the motive of this speculative conspiracy.

98 Moor to Foreign Office, 26 December 1896; cited in A. F. C. Ryder, *Benin and the Europeans, 1485–1897* (London: Longman, 1977), p. 280. Ryder's account tells a consistent story of London's inclination to restrain Moor: 'an unconvinced Foreign Office still preached caution'; 'the pacific means advocated by Lord Salisbury [the prime minister]' (ibid., pp. 282, 284).

99 Home, *City of Blood Revisited*, pp. 27, 29, 30.

100 After he retired as high commissioner for the Southern Nigeria Protectorate on the ground of ill health in 1903, Moor was never offered any official post in the Colonial Office. Six years later, at the age of forty-nine, he committed suicide at home in London. His entry in the *Oxford Dictionary of National Biography* records that, after the Benin expedition, 'Moor remained very ready to use

armed force, notably in the Aro expedition of 1901, but his commitment to economic development is acknowledged by Nigerian historians . . . The forestry department which he founded served the cause of conservation by supervising and controlling the tapping of wild rubber and the felling of hardwoods' (John D. Hargreaves, 'Moor, Sir Ralph Denham Rayment', *Oxford Dictionary of National Biography* [2004]: https://www.oxforddnb.com/view/10.1093/ref:odnb/9780198614128.001.0001/odnb-9780198614128-e-35086).

101 Home, *City of Blood Revisited*, pp. 100–1, 102.

102 Bacon, *Benin*, pp. 102, 104.

103 Home agrees with this when he writes that 'compounds which might be of military importance if the Edo mounted a retaliatory attack were destroyed' (*City of Blood Revisited*, p. 88).

104 Bacon, *Benin*, p. 105.

105 Ibid., p. 104.

106 Home, *City of Blood Revisited*, p. 89. See also William Fagg, 'Le pillage qui n'eut jamais lieu/ Benin: The Sack that Never Was', *Art Tribal*, special issue: 'Art Royal du Benin' (Geneva: Musée Barbier-Mueller, 1992), p. 38. Fagg's article first appeared as a chapter in Flora Kaplan, ed., *Images of Power: Art of the Royal Court of Benin* (New York: New York University, 1981).

107 Bacon, *Benin*, pp. 106, 108.

108 For example, Surgeon Roth's diary has this entry: 'About 3pm a good breeze sprang up, and whilst this was blowing, two carriers carelessly set fire to a hut . . . The wind blew stronger, and the fire increased frightfully, the flames passing from house to house.' ('Diary of a Surgeon', p. xii). See also Admiral Rawson's dispatches to London, 27 February 1897, in the *London Gazette*, 7 May 1897, para. 42: https://translanth.hypotheses.org/ueber/rawson-moor, and Henry Gallwey, 'Nigeria in the "Nineties"', p. 242.

109 Igbafe, 'Fall of Benin', p. 398.

110 Ryder, *Benin and the Europeans*, p. 290 n.2: 'Fortunately most of the magnificent brass objects belonging to the palace had been gathered together in a place of safety after the fall of the city, and so escaped destruction when parts of the palace were blown up or burned.'

111 Bacon, *Benin*, p. 108.

112 Hicks, *Brutish Museums*, p. 141. It seems that African carriers did loot, albeit at a trivial level. As Captain Walker went on to record: 'The whole camp is strewn with loot. mostly cloths, beads etc, and all the carriers are decked out in the most extraordinary garments' (ibid., pp. 141–2).

113 Ibid., pp. 11, 12.

114 Home, *City of Blood Revisited*, p. 101.

115 Fagg, 'Le pillage qui n'eut jamais lieu', p. 39.

116 Hicks doubts Fagg (*Brutish Museums*, pp. 142–3). But the practice of devoting the money raised by the sale of the spoils of war to the relief of war-widows and wounded was well established. For example, after the siege of Bhurtpore in 1826, when the prize money was divided, the officers present gave the sum of £1,000 to the widows of each of the four European officers killed, and £1,000

to be divided among the widows and orphans of the European soldiers killed (James Grant, *British Battles on Land and Sea* [London: Cassell, 1885], p. 575). I have been told that the refusal of the British commander Lord Combermere to follow suite with his own portion created a scandal at the time, although I have not been able to find documentary corroboration of this.

117 Hicks, *Brutish Museums*, pp. 90, 143.

118 Wayne Sandholtz, *Prohibiting Plunder: How Norms Change* (New York: Oxford University Press, 2007), p. 97.

119 For bibliographical details, see note 69 above in this chapter.

120 Hicks, *Brutish Museums*, pp. xiii, 4, 15, 21, 33, 55.

121 Ibid., p. 46.

122 Ibid., p. 39. Sir Richard Francis Burton (1821–90) was a multilingual British soldier, explorer and scholar, whose works and letters were frequently critical of British colonial policies.

123 Ibid., p. 336. The emphasis is mine.

124 Ibid., pp. 43, 53.

125 Ibid., pp. 44, 45.

126 Ibid., p. 33. To be fair, it is not clear here which slave trade Hicks is referring to. However, since the European trade is the only one he discusses, and since 'industrial' and 'commoditisation' connote capitalism, he leaves the reader with the impression that the slave trade was originally Western. I assume that he knows that that is not true.

127 Ibid., p. 84.

128 Ibid., pp. 48, 63, 81.

129 Ibid., p. 44.

130 Regarding this point, it is notable that Hicks rejects Nick Thomas' view of the colonial encounter as one of 'entanglement', highlighting indigenous agency and rejecting the post-colonial assumption of 'the imposition of the West upon the rest' (ibid., p. 27).

131 Ibid., p. 40.

132 Ibid., pp. 53, 63.

133 Hicks implies that the only reason Gallwey urged caution was a concern 'about the potential impact on profits' (ibid., p. 68). He omits to refer to another item in his own bibliography, an earlier lecture given by Gallwey to the Royal Geographical Society in December 1892, in which he cautioned against a punitive expedition in non-commercial, humanitarian terms: 'Human sacrifices are of frequent occurrence, and the rule is one of terror . . . It is, however, to be hoped that now this country is under Her Majesty's protection these terrible practices will be put an end to, though it must take time. Punitive measures are all very well in their way, but in a country like Benin the effect would probably be to drive the natives into the bush, and make them greater savages than ever; one cannot reasonably hope to abolish in a short time customs that have been in practice for centuries' ('Journeys in the Benin Country, West Africa', *Geographical Journal* 1/2 [February 1893], p. 129).

134 Hicks, *Brutish Museums*, pp. 67–9.

135 Ibid., p. 100.

136 Ibid., p. 91.

137 Ibid., p. 101. The 'Kirk Report' refers to the report of Sir John Kirk's *Enquiry into Outrage Committed on Brass People by Royal Niger Company* (London: HMSO, 1896).

138 Home, *City of Blood Revisited*, pp. 28–9. Hicks cites p. 26 of Home's book in support of his suggestion that the military officers gathering on the Niger river in November 1896 to take part in the RNC's imminent expedition 'against an unknown target' (in fact the Bida and Ilorin emirates 250 miles north of Benin) had something to do with the Protectorate's February 1897 expedition (*Brutish Museums*, p. 85). In fact, what Home tells us on that page is that Gallwey's successor as vice-consul was Major Peter Copland-Crawford, who, although he supported an aggressive Benin policy 'opposed the RNC'.

139 Hicks, *Brutish Museums*, p. 132.

140 Home, *City of Blood Revisited*, p. 109.

141 Hicks, *Brutish Museums*, p. 100.

142 Ibid., p. 101.

143 Ibid., pp. 101, 102. The emphasis is mine. Lord Salisbury combined the two positions of prime minister and foreign secretary from 29 June 1895 to 12 November 1900.

144 Ibid., pp. 101, 102.

145 Ibid., pp. 46, 92–3. The emphasis is mine.

146 Boisragon, *Benin Massacre*, pp. 78–9, 100; Bacon, *Benin*, p. 17; Ling Roth, *Great Benin*, Appendix III, p. xiv.

147 Hicks, *Brutish Museums*, p. 93, citing Home, *City of Blood Revisited*, pp. 45–6.

148 Home, *City of Blood Revisited*, p. 46. The emphasis is mine.

149 Hicks, *Brutish Museums*, pp. 4, 10, 11, 111, 123, 124. He acknowledges Kim Wagner's 'expert input' on the subject of expanding bullets. See note 61 above in this chapter.

150 Ibid., p. 114.

151 Boisragon, *Benin Massacre*, p. 171; Bacon, *Benin*, p. 115; quoted in Hicks, *Brutish Museums*, p. 111.

152 Hicks, *Brutish Museums*, p. 265 n.28. See also note 61 above in this chapter.

153 Ibid., p. 121.

154 Ibid., pp. 115, 126.

155 Ibid., pp. 7, 128, 131.

156 Even the first-hand testimony that Hicks himself quotes points to a military rationale for the demolition. The diary of Captain Herbert Walker recorded the agenda: '*Strong defensive post, with stockade to be constructed.* King's house and all surrounding will eventually be destroyed and no building allowed on the same site.' And of chief Ojumo's house and compound, Walker writes: '*Thought possible that the enemy might have rallied there*, but we found the place deserted, destroyed the "Ju-Ju" shrines and set the whole on fire'. Hicks presents this as evidence of 'systematic destruction', which it was (ibid., p. 133. The emphases are mine). But it was not indiscriminately systematic.

157 William Fagg was rightly scathing about the claim that Benin was 'sacked': 'There are certain phrases which are very useful in distinguishing between historians and would-be, pseudo-, or *ex parte* historians, who of course are not entitled to the name at all. One of these is "the Sack of Benin" . . .' ('Le pillage qui n'eut jamais lieu', p. 37).

158 Ibid., p. 114.

159 Rome Statute of the International Criminal Court, Article 7: https://treaties. un.org/doc/Treaties/1998/07/19980717%2006-33%20PM/Ch_XVIII_10p.pdf

160 Philip Igbafe, 'Slavery and Emancipation in Benin, 1897–1945', *Journal of African History*, XVI/3 (1975), pp. 417–18, 428.

161 Pakenham, *Boer War*, p. 572.

162 Kathleen Burk, *The Lion and the Eagle: The Interaction of the British and American Empires, 1783–1972* (London: Bloomsbury, 2018), p. 356.

163 Christopher Saunders, 'African Attitudes to Britain and the Empire before and after the South African War', in Donal Lowry, ed., *The South African War Reappraised* (Manchester: Manchester University Press, 2000), p. 140. Saunders continues: 'While evidence of the attitudes of non-elite Africans is difficult to find, there are a few indications that non-elite views were less pro-British than those of the elite. In the most important available source for African attitudes, the African newspapers of the time, however, the discourse is almost entirely pro-imperial . . . For the westernised African elite which began to emerge at the Cape from the 1870s, Britain was associated, not only with power and wealth, but as importantly with Christianity, the ending of the slave trade and the emancipation of the slaves . . . Looking to Britain as a counterpoise to local [white] racial power, the African elite was able to point out how unjustly Africans were being ruled . . . In that sense, African pro-imperialism was a kind of anti-colonialism' (ibid., pp. 141, 143). See also Peter Warwick, *Black People and the South African War*, African Studies Series (Cambridge: Cambridge University Press, 1983), pp. 110–14. A prime example of such a Westernised African was the remarkable Sol. T. Plaatje, who, as magistrate's interpreter, liaised between the British civil authorities and the African majority inside Mafeking during the famous siege of 1899–1900. (The diary he kept during the siege was discovered in 1969 and published as *The Boer War Diary of Sol. T. Plaatje: An African at Mafeking*, ed. John L. Comaroff [London: Macmillan, 1973].) 'Like other educated Africans,' writes Neil Parsons, Plaatje 'came out of the [Second Boer] war optimistic that the British would enfranchise all educated and propertied males in the defeated Boer colonies (Transvaal and the Orange Free State) without regard to race' ('Introduction', in Sol. T. Plaatje, *Native Life in South Africa, Before and Since the European War and the Boer Rebellion*: https://www. sahistory.org.za/sites/default/files/Native%20Life%20in%20South%20Africa_0. pdf). The decision of the British government, during the peace negotiations, not to insist on extending the black franchise to the Boer republics before restoring them to self-government was a severe disappointment to the black elite. And the subsequent, racially discriminatory policies of the government of the Union of South Africa, especially the Native Land Act of 1913, dismayed them.

Even so, Plaatje and others like him continued to appeal to the imperial government in London for redress, as he recounts in his book *Native Life in South Africa*, ed. and intro. Brian Willen (London: Longman, 1987), especially Chapter 15.

164 As G. H. L. Le May put it, the Boer (or 'farmer' in English) was the migrant species of the more sedentary Afrikaner. Afrikaners were resident in Cape Colony, would have spoken and written both English and high Dutch, and were typically more politically liberal than the Boer Voortrekkers, who made the pioneering trek northward. See Le May, *The Afrikaners: An Historical Interpretation* (Oxford: Blackwell, 1995), p. 6. For simplicity's sake I will refer to those fighting the British as 'Boer'.

165 Judd and Surridge, *Boer War*, p. 21. Caroline Elkins tells her readers that 'the Afrikaners (or Boers) had fought for decades to sever themselves from British rule and its direct assaults on their way of life' (*Legacy of Violence*, p. 81). She omits to point out that that 'way of life' included biological racism and a belief in permanent white racial supremacy, and that the main reason that the Boers had trekked out of Cape Colony in the 1830s was the British Empire's decision to abolish slavery in the name of basic human equality. Instead, she refers coyly and neutrally to Boer 'conceptions of race and labour that contested emancipation', reserving her only hint of disapproval for the 'the mid-Victorian [British] imperialists' who regarded those conceptions as 'anachronistic' (ibid.). Whereas throughout her book, Elkins expresses relentless moral indignation against the alleged racism of the imperial British, here she indulges the racism of the Boer trekkers. The implication is clear: what Elkins really objects to is not racism, but the British. Barnaby Crowcroft makes a similar point about Elkins' attitude towards violence: 'Her treatment of Malaya's communist insurgency suggests that she is not particularly exercised by violence when it is committed by ideological *confrères*' ('Bombastic Lecture on the Evil Empire', *The Critic*, June 2022, p. 69).

166 H. Rider Haggard, *Cetywayo and His White Neighbours: or Remarks on Recent Events in Zululand, Natal, and the Transvaal* (London: Kegan Paul, Trench, Trübner, 1906), p. 100. To be fair about Boer attitudes to Africans, we should take note of Sir Bartle Frere's different judgement in 1879: '[The Boers'] general feeling seems to me much like that of the less educated class of farmers in remote districts of our own country [England] towards the labouring class; it is hard and unsympathetic, but not intentionally cruel feeling. There are, of course, terrible exceptions in South Africa as elsewhere on the outskirts of civilization, where there is a chronic kind of race antagonism; but as regards the Native races within the Colonial border, the tendency of the Boer farmer is generally not to "bully" the natives who are his workpeople but to treat them often, I think, with more real kindness than they would experience from European employers of the ruder class; certainly the Dutch, as a rule, seem to me to retain the voluntary services of their native servants for longer periods, and with less occasional friction, than English colonists of the same class' (Le May, *Afrikaners*, p. 81).

167 Pakenham, *Boer War*, p. 571; Judd and Surridge, *Boer War*, p. 96.

168 Pakenham, *Boer War*, pp. 547–8.

169 Ibid., p. 225. Gandhi wrote afterwards that '[t]he relations formed with the whites during the war were of the sweetest' and that ordinary British soldiers were 'friendly and thankful' (*Autobiography*, 1982, pp. 203–5; quoted in Judd and Surridge, *Boer War*, p. 85).

170 Pakenham, *Boer War*, p. 396.

171 Ibid., p. 573. See also p. 534.

172 Ibid., pp. 179, 180, 231, 234, 257; Judd and Surridge, *Boer War*, p. 63.

173 I once met a man who had fought in the war. As a teenager in the late 1960s, I accompanied my mother as she delivered 'meals-on-wheels' to pensioners in Castle-Douglas, Scotland. On entering the living room of an elderly, mustachioed gentleman on Queen St, I recognised the large painting over the mantlepiece as a depiction of some scene in the Boer War. On asking him about it, I learned that he had served as an under-age drummer boy.

174 J. A. Hobson, *The War in South Africa: Its Causes and Effects* (London: Nisbet, 1900), p. 189.

175 According to Iain R. Smith, 'Hobson's book about the South African War has tended to be regarded with embarrassment by commentators on the prolific output of this wide-ranging and influential thinker because of its crude "conspiracy plot" explanation and its obvious role as a polemic.' Nevertheless, 'despite repeated attempts to rebut it, it has continued to exercise great influence' – most notably via Lenin. Yet, '[o]nce historians were able to test this hypothesis against the evidence . . . the "Hobson thesis" about the origins of the war . . . had to be abandoned. No convincing evidence has been found to support the idea that the British government acted at the behest of mine-magnates or capitalists with a stake in the Transvaal during the mounting crisis with Kruger's government which resulted in war. Nor did the British government go to war "to secure for the mines a cheap, adequate supply of labour" – another of J. A. Hobson's assertions which has reverberated down the century' ('A Century of Controversy over Origins', in Lowry, *The South African War Reappraised*, pp. 28, 29, 31).

176 Anyone who relies on Caroline Elkins' account of the Boer War in *Legacy of Violence: A History of the British Empire* will have no idea that Hobson's thesis is controversial and that historians far more expert than him have concluded that the British motivation for going to war had little or nothing to do with gold. Elkins simply reports as fact that '[t]o maintain its position as the world's banker and, with it, global economic dominance Britain had to ensure the steady flow of gold', referencing the Marxist historian Eric Hobsbawm and the New Left thinker Tom Nairn (*Legacy of Violence*, p. 81).

177 Le May, *British Supremacy in South Africa*, pp. 27, 29. Because of his one-time mane of bright-red hair, Godfrey Hugh Lancelot Le May was called 'Copper' when he taught me at Worcester College, Oxford in 1974–5.

178 Gann and Duignan, *Burden of Empire*, p. 36. They explain: 'The Transvaal government . . . did not threaten British gold investments on the Witwatersrand; nor did the mining companies have sufficient cause to stir up hostilities because

of the financial burdens laid upon them by Boer corruption and red tape. The
Transvaal administration could usually be "squared"; its financial demands
were not nearly so heavy as the charges laid upon mining concerns by the
British South Africa Company's government in neighbouring Rhodesia' (ibid.,
pp. 36–7).

179 Judd and Surridge, *Boer War*, pp. 221–2.

180 Smith, 'A Century of Controversy over Origins', in Lowry, *The South African
War Reappraised*, pp. 33, 37: the idea 'that there was a capitalist conspiracy
behind the resort to war in 1899' has

> not stood the test of the extensive work of R. V. Kubicek in the archives of the
> mining companies. He concluded that the business interests and priorities of
> the cosmopolitan capitalists involved in gold-mining in South Africa were
> different from the imperial interests of the British government and frequently
> out of step with them, and that the last thing the capitalists wanted or needed
> in 1899 was a war . . . The common assumption (which owes much to Marxist
> ideas about class interest) that the mine-magnates acted as a monolithic body
> and must have had a coherent political stance . . . squares ill with the different
> views between firms – and even between different members of the same firm
> – which emerges from the archives . . . the mine-magnates were . . . in all sorts
> of ways, in competition with each other.

To this, Smith adds the general methodological observation that '[t]he danger
with historical interpretations which are reached without the testing and
time-consuming work in the archives is that they may reflect little more than
the transient theoretical preoccupations of their authors' (ibid., p. 23). Among
these 'theoretical preoccupations' in the twentieth century was 'a materialist
approach with regard to questions of historical causation' (ibid., p. 34).

181 Judd and Surridge, *Boer War*, p. 223.

182 Le May, *Afrikaners*, p. 110. Saul Dubow appeals to the 'large body of historical
opinion' that 'holds that the real motivation of mining magnates like Rhodes
was to gain control of the huge gold wealth of the Transvaal' ('Britain's Inglorious
Tactics during the Boer War'). As I have shown, there are several considerable
historians who doubt Hobson's thesis and reckon that the mining interests of
Rhodes and others did not determine British policy. For the reasons given, I
think they are correct.

It is true that Thomas Pakenham claimed in 1979 to have found evidence
of 'an informal alliance' between Milner and the firm of Wernher-Beit, the
dominant Rand mining house, and argued that 'contrary to the accepted view
of later historians, [these capitalists] were . . . active partners with Milner in
the making of the war'. The aim of this 'secret alliance', apparently, was to
reduce the cost of African labour on the Rand, which they blamed on the
incompetence and corruption of the Transvaal's government (*Boer War*, p. 259;
see also p. 430). Elsewhere, Pakenham softened his claim, saying only that
'[i]t was this secret alliance . . . that *gave Milner the strength* to precipitate the
war' (ibid., pp. xvi–xvii; the emphasis is mine). This vaguer claim suggests that

the capitalist alliance stiffened Milner's resolve rather than provided him with his leading reasons. However, against Pakenham's conspiracy theory stand the following facts, which imply that Milner was not in the pocket of the mining capitalists. In May 1902 he appointed a commission to investigate and report on the living and working conditions of Africans in the Rand mines. Shocked by the report, he instructed the mine-owners to make improvements in diet, sanitation, medical facilities, habitation and working conditions. According to G. B. Pyrah, 'Milner, all credit to him, refused to purchase efficiency at the cost of native health, in spite of the dire need for revenue . . . Milner was no tool of the capitalists . . . The High Commissioner cherished the mines only because they supplied the means of financing, in part, his policy of reconstruction; they formed to him a means to an end' (*Imperial Policy and South Africa*, pp. 187–8). Accordingly, in June 1902 Milner doubled the pre-war tax on mining profits to 10 per cent (ibid., p. 207). It would have been highly unusual if this had pleased the capitalists.

What is true of Milner is true of colonial government generally. As L. H. Gann and Peter Duignan wrote:

> Even in a backward and relatively undifferentiated economy like that of Northern Rhodesia, the state machinery throughout the colonial period responded to pressures infinitely more complex than the real or imagined machinations of copper magnates. A British governor had to consider the interests of farmers and traders, of civil servants and railway men. He received instructions from London based on political and economic considerations at home that far transcended local interests; he also tried to satisfy demands from missionaries and humanitarians; last but not least, he was animated by a spirit of public service which aimed at making the state an impartial arbiter between competing interests and an instrument for public welfare as a whole. (*Burden of Empire*, p. 66.)

183 Lord Milner, 'Key to My Position', *The Times*, 27 July 1925; quoted in Marlowe, *Milner*, p. 364.

184 Marlowe, *Milner*, pp. 38–9.

185 Throughout his adult life, Milner was committed to social reform and improvement. As an undergraduate at Balliol College, Oxford he came under the influence of the political philosopher T. H. Green, who espoused the view that the state should be active in fostering an environment where individuals can flourish and that privileged members of society should make sacrifices to aid the weaker (Richard Symonds, *Oxford and Empire: The Last Lost Cause?* [London: Macmillan, 1986], pp. 29, 41). Consequently, '[h]e went down from Oxford in 1879 imbued with notions of public service' (Colin Newbury, 'Milner, Alfred, Viscount Milner', *Oxford Dictionary of National Biography* [2008], p. 2: https://www.oxforddnb.com/view/10.1093/ref:odnb/9780198614128.001.0001/ odnb-9780198614128-e-35037?print=pdf). In 1882 he gave a series of lectures on 'Socialism' to the Tower Hamlets University Extension Society. The following year he began to make regular visits to Whitechapel to learn of conditions in London's East End, where he supported the social welfare efforts of a local

parish. When he was thirty-one years old, he stood as a Liberal candidate in the 1885 general election campaign, advocating free elementary education and the liberalisation of land laws (O'Brien, *Milner*, pp. 46, 50, 61, 246). Some months after arriving in South Africa in 1897, he wrote that the press had reported 'nothing except that Mrs Hanbury Williams [the wife of his military secretary] had kissed a black child as well as a white one . . . I think she was right. Most white people in South Africa think she was wrong' (Milner to Glazebrook, 29 September 1897, in J. E. Wrench, *Alfred Lord Milner: The Man of No Illusions, 1854–1925* [London: Eyre and Spottiswoode, 1958], p. 182). As note 182 above records, Milner took steps to improve the working conditions of African miners in 1902. The view that he was oblivious to the welfare of Africans and a tool of the Rand capitalists was, in G. B. Pyrah's eyes, 'grotesque': 'Milner always retained his socialistic bias, and he did some of his best work for the natives by reforming the pass laws and compelling the mine-owners to institute improvements in native living and working conditions on the Rand. He reduced flogging as a penalty, and never ceased to regard as most important the appointment of honourable and capable men as magistrates and native commissioners' (*Imperial Policy and South Africa*, p. 96).

186 Pakenham, *Boer War*, p. 20.

187 Marlowe, *Milner*, p. 39.

188 Milner to H. H. Asquith, 18 November 1897; quoted in Le May, *British Supremacy*, p. 12. Caroline Elkins quotes Milner as saying, 'You have only to sacrifice "the n---er" absolutely and the game is easy . . .', but abstracts the quotation from its context, so as to make it imply that Milner was advocating the sacrifice of justice for black Africans. 'For Milner,' she writes, 'no great principles were involved in so-called native protections. The question was one of national self-interest, and coercion had to be deployed when necessary in order to achieve a racially defined British Empire whose economy was tethered to imperial state power' (*Legacy of Violence*, p. 83). This is entirely false.

The promise of protection had been made to black Africans in the terms of the 1884 Convention of London, by which Britain had recognised the Transvaal's conditional independence. On the one hand, this agreement surrendered Britain's rights as 'Suzerain' to intervene via the person of a British resident to 'take such steps for the protection of the persons and property of Natives as are consistent with the laws of the land' and to be the final arbiter in case of 'any encroachments . . . made by Transvaal residents upon the land of such Natives', which had been affirmed by Article XVIII of the 1881 Convention of Pretoria at the end of the First Anglo-Boer War (G. W. Eybers, ed., *Select Constitutional Documents Illustrating South African History, 1795–1910* [London: Routledge, 1918], p. 460). On the other hand, Article 8 of the 1884 Convention banned 'slavery or apprenticeship partaking of slavery', while Article 19 affirmed the rights of native Africans to buy land, to enjoy access to the courts and to freedom of movement within the state under a pass system (Eybers, *Select Constitutional Documents*, p. 472; see also p. 274). Those rights, according to Vernon Bogdanor, had been ignored by the Boers (*The Strange Survival of Liberal Britain: Politics and Power before the First World War* [Hull: Biteback, 2022], p. 163).

Quoting from a letter of Milner to Percy Fitzpatrick on 28 November 1899, Pakenham reports that Milner 'claimed' that there were two great principles in his work in South Africa: the first was to '"secure for the Natives . . . protection against oppression and wrong"'; the second was 'to secure the loyalty of the Uitlanders, who were determined to keep the natives oppressed'. Then he comments, 'this second principle, of course, took priority for the time being, even if the ultimate solution was to see the natives "justly governed"' (*Boer War*, p. 120). The 'of course' is unfairly cynical, for if Milner could not retain the loyalty of native-born Britons in the Transvaal, his long-term plan of changing the demography in favour of the British and thereby of liberalising Afrikaner culture could never succeed. His priority was justified.

189 Le May, *Afrikaners*, p. 55.

190 Ibid., p. 130.

191 Pakenham, who is generally unsympathetic to the British case, concedes that '[t]he case against the Zarps [Boer police] for persecuting the Cape Coloureds was in fact legally (and morally) a strong one' (*Boer War*, p. 50).

192 Bogdanor, *Strange Survival of Liberal Britain*, p. 163. Bogdanor also reports on page 174 that, in May 1899, Sir Henry de Villiers, the *Afrikaner* chief justice of the Cape, declared himself 'quite certain that if in 1881 [during the negotiations that produced the Convention of Pretoria] it had been known to my fellow-Commissioners that the President [of the Transvaal] would adopt his retrogressive policy [over the franchise], neither President Brand [then President of the Orange Free State] nor I would ever have induced them to consent to the Convention'. Instead, they would have advised the British government to resume war.

193 Milner to Chamberlain, 23 February 1898, in Le May, *British Supremacy*, pp. 12–13. The emphases are Milner's.

194 Pakenham, *Boer War*, pp. 23–4.

195 Pakenham, *Boer War*, pp. 49, 66–7. Pakenham tells us that Milner protested that he did not intend to 'swamp' the Boers and that he held out only for a quarter of the Volksraad's seats for the Uitlanders. Pakenham does not draw the inference, however, that this implies that Kruger's concern about the loss of Boer independence was overwrought. I thank Vernon Bogdanor for bringing my attention to this important point (*Strange Survival of Liberal Britain,* pp. 180, 181).

196 Le May reports that the British ultimatum had been sanctioned by the Cabinet on 29 September, but had not been delivered by 9 October, when the Boer ultimatum was given to the British agent in Pretoria (*British Supremacy in South Africa*, p. 26). The reason for the delay in the delivery of the British ultimatum is not clear. However, if it is true that it was sent by steamship rather than telegraph, as Byron Farwell reports in *The Great Boer War* (London: Allen Lane, 1977), then the delay must have been deliberate. It is

commonly – and reasonably – assumed that this was because Chamberlain and Milner wanted the Boers to make the first, aggressive move, which would render the war easier to sell at home. But what would the British have done, if the Boers had not played the role of aggressor? Is it clear that they would have attacked anyway? I have not been able to pin down the answer to those questions.

197 Pakenham, *Boer War*, pp. 102–3.

198 G. H. L. Le May entitled the first chapter of *British Supremacy in South Africa*, 'Sir Alfred Milner's War', and Thomas Pakenham entitled Part I of *The Boer War*, 'Milner's War'.

199 Milner to Lord Roberts, 6 June 1900, in Le May, *British Supremacy*, p. 1.

200 T. G. Otte, *Statesman of Europe: A Life of Sir Edward Grey* (London: Allen Lane, 2020), pp. 169–70.

201 Pakenham, *Boer War*, pp. 495, 510.

202 Bogdanor, *Strange Survival of Liberal Britain*, p. 263.

203 Judd and Surridge, *Boer War*, p. 194; Bogdanor, *Strange Survival of Liberal Britain*, p. 263.

204 Pakenham, *Boer War*, p. 517. Dr Alec Kay, who had worked in the camps, reported that '[t]he Boers in the camps often depend on home remedies, with deplorable results. Inflammation of the lungs and enteric fever are frequently treated by the stomach of a sheep or a goat which has been killed at the bedside of a patient being placed hot and bloody over the chest or abdomen; cow-dung poultices are a favourite remedy for many skin diseases; lice are given for jaundice; and crushed bugs for convulsions in children. These are common remedies in everyday use on the farms' (quoted in Judd and Surridge, *Boer War*, p. 195).

205 Le May, *British Supremacy*, p. 109.

206 Le May, *Afrikaners*, p. 118; Pakenham, *Boer War*, p. 518.

207 In fact, Campbell-Bannerman was not the first to describe the policy of burning farms as 'barbarous'. Eight months earlier, Milner had done so in a letter to Chamberlain (John Wilson, *CB: A Life of Sir Henry Campbell-Bannerman* [London: Constable, 1973], p. 350). After his use of the phrase 'methods of barbarism' had attracted criticism, Campbell-Bannerman used a debate in the House of Commons to specify what he had meant. He was not accusing anyone of 'intentional cruelty' in the policy of farm-burning and concentration camps. Moreover, he said, 'I have never said a word that would imply cruelty or even indifference on the part of the officers or men in the British Army. It is the whole system which they have to carry out that I consider, to use a word which I have already applied to it, barbarous' (in Hansard, *House of Commons Debate*, Vol. 95, 17 June 1901: https://api.parliament.uk/historic-hansard/commons/1901/jun/17/south-african-war-mortality-in-camps-of [accessed 9 August 2021]).

208 Britain was a state party to the Hague Convention (II) with Respect to the Laws and Customs of War on Land, which it signed on 29 July 1899 and which came into force on 4 September 1900. According to Article 23 of the Convention, 'it is especially prohibited: . . . To destroy or seize the enemy's property, *unless*

such destruction or seizure be imperatively demanded by the necessities of war' (Mary Ellen O'Connell, *International Law and the Use of Force: Documentary Supplement*, 2nd edn [New York: Thomson Reuters/ Foundation Press, 2009], p. 59. The emphasis is mine). Besides, the Convention's Regulations Respecting the Laws and Customs of War on Land, according to Article 2, were 'only binding on the Contracting Parties, in case of war between two or more of them' (ibid., p. 54). The South African (or Transvaal) Republic and the Orange Free State, with which Britain fought the Second Anglo-Boer War, were independent states, but were neither party to the Convention nor supporting signatories of it.

209 Antony Beevor, *D-Day: The Battle for Normandy* (London: Viking, 2009), p. 519.

210 Moreover, the tactic of indiscriminate farm-burning was abandoned in November 1900, largely due to the intervention of Milner and Chamberlain (Bogdanor, *Strange Survival of Liberal Britain*, pp. 262–3). Dubow argues that the British use of concentration camps 'amounted to a war on women and children' ('Britain's Inglorious Tactics during the Boer War'). While the negligence of the British military authorities was culpable, it did not amount to intentional killing. Dubow obscures the moral distinction. The concentration camps in South Africa were no more a 'war on women and children' than the inadvertent killing of French women and children by Allied bombing during the Normandy invasion in 1944.

211 Le May, *British Supremacy*, p. 110.

212 See Pakenham, *Boer War*, p. xvii: 'The conscience of Britain was stirred by the holocaust in the [concentration] camps, just as the conscience of America was stirred by the holocaust in Vietnam.' Caroline Elkins describes Kitchener's blockhouse and concentration camp strategy as 'an all-out assault on an entire civilian population' (*Legacy of Violence*, p. 85), claims that he made women and children 'legitimate targets of violence', and asserts that 'Kitchener's forces had to either capture the "infested" Afrikaner population or kill them' (ibid. p. 87). Thus, she clearly insinuates that Kitchener intended to use violence indiscriminately and, indeed, genocidally. Nothing that I have read elsewhere supports this insinuation. Indeed, Elkins herself rows back from it when she writes, '*Whether the civilian deaths were a deliberate or an unintended consequence of Kitchener's war plans,* the establishment of the British concentration camps in South Africa represented the first time a single ethnic group had been targeted en masse for detention or deportation' (ibid. The emphasis is mine). (The 'first time' in what? The history of the world? Hardly. Quite apart from the forcible deportation of populations in ancient times – famously, of the population of Jerusalem to Babylon in 597 BC – the Spanish had used concentration camps in Cuba on the eve of the Spanish-American War of 1898, and the Americans had copied them in their counter-insurgency campaign from late 1899 in the Philippine-American War of 1899–1902.)

213 Pakenham, *Boer War*, pp. 563–5.

214 See Chapter 4, pp. 119–22. Le May and Pyrah both appreciate that the genuine

desire of Milner and other Liberals to defend and promote native welfare and status faced real political and practical obstacles. Le May quotes Milner as opposing, on prudential grounds, any attempt to impose the extension of the Cape franchise of black voters on the Boer: 'It would be very unfortunate to raise the question of native voters. There would be practically none in the Transvaal, and for the sake of a theory it would be unwise to start with a conflict with the Whites . . . If necessary, the thing could possibly be brought about *sub silentio*' (*British Supremacy*, p. 77). Le May also reports that the Colonial Office considered whether native populations could be effectively protected by clauses written into a constitution and decided that they could not. They also discussed indirect sanctions, such as reserving part of the colonial revenue for direct expenditure on non-whites, but concluded that that had been tried and had failed in Natal, New Zealand and Western Australia (ibid., p. 203). Pyrah writes: 'The Liberals . . . believed that to try to force upon South Africans British ideas and solutions would only rile those people, who would in turn regard the natives with the more profound hostility, thus impairing whatever hopes there might be of tranquillity between black and white. While not oblivious to native interests, the Liberals found themselves in a predicament from which there lay no ideal outlet. They perforce chose the lesser of two evils. Where they had a strong and honourable case, in the matter of the Protectorates, they in no way receded from their obligations; where native affairs formed a question of internal politics within the South African States, they refused to exercise any sort of pressure on the colonial Governments, hoping rather that the passage of time and accumulation of experience would act as a solvent on South African opinion' (*Imperial Policy and South Africa*, p. 137).

215 Marlowe, *Milner*, pp. 153–4. The emphasis is mine.

216 Pakenham, *Boer War*, p. 575.

217 Pyrah, *Imperial Policy and South Africa*, p. 214.

218 Ibid., pp. 235–6.

219 J. C. Smuts, *Jan Christian Smuts* (London: Cassell, 1952), p. 98.

220 Pyrah, *Imperial Policy and South Africa*, pp. 215, 230. See also Le May, *Afrikaners*, p. 141.

221 The South Africa Act, 1909, *American Journal of International Law*, 4 (1910), 'Official Documents', 43 (c): https://ia801901.us.archive.org/0/items/jstor-2212266/2212266.pdf. To be precise, the vote was accorded to British subjects of European descent who were male and at least twenty-one years old.

222 Pyrah, *Imperial Policy and South Africa*, p. 200.

223 See Dubow, *Apartheid, 1948–1994*.

224 Quite what 'Mau Mau' meant is uncertain and has been subject to a variety of interpretations. Some rebels preferred to refer to themselves as members of the Kenya Land and Freedom Army.

225 John Blacker, 'The Demography of Mau Mau: Fertility and Mortality in the 1950s: A Demographer's Viewpoint', *African Affairs*, 106 (April 2007), p, 226; Anderson, *Histories of the Hanged*, pp. 4–5; Daniel Branch, *Defeating Mau Mau, Creating Kenya: Counterinsurgency, Civil War, and Decolonization*

(Cambridge: Cambridge University Press, 2009), p. 5. Based on the compara-
tively low growth rate of the Kikuyu population from 1948 to 1962, Caroline
Elkins estimated that up to 300,000 Kikuyu may have disappeared during the
Emergency (*Imperial Reckoning: The Untold Story of Britain's Gulag in Kenya*
[New York: Henry Holt & Co., 2005]. p. 366). However, Pascal James Imperato
argues that this figure is based on flawed deductions from the 1948 and 1962
censuses ('Differing Perspectives on Mau Mau', *African Studies Review*, 48/3
[December 2005], p. 150). Blacker substantiates Imperato's claim in 'The
Demography of Mau Mau'. In her latest book's account of the Mau Mau conflict,
Elkins does not repeat her claim (*Legacy of Violence*, pp.546–79).

226 Branch, *Defeating Mau Mau*, pp. xii, 5.
227 Branch, *Defeating Mau Mau*, pp. xii, 5; Bethwell A. Ogot, 'Review Article:
Britain's Gulag', *Journal of African History*, 46/3 (2005), p. 499. Branch criticises Elkins' *Imperial Reckoning* for barely mentioning African loyalists, and
he observes that while it was awarded a Pulitzer Prize in 2006, '[a]mong
academics, the book has been less well received. The methodology behind
some of the most contentious claims have been called into question. Moreover,
respected figures from within the fields of imperial and African history have
fiercely criticised Elkins' arguments' (*Defeating Mau Mau*, p. xv). Along the
same lines, but more strongly, Ogot describes Elkins' 2005 account of the Mau
Mau uprising as a conflict between anti-colonial nationalists and colonial collaborators as 'simplistic', is severely sceptical of her reliance on oral testimony, at
one point accuses her of dishonesty, and finds little in her book that is 'untold'
('Review Article: Britain's Gulag', pp. 493, 494, 498). In contrast to David
Anderson's 'highly perceptive and complex history', he writes, 'Elkins's book
is just another inside story of prison, camp life, barbed-wire village, of torture
and shooting and starvation, of the vileness of the secret police and the Home
Guard and the men who gave them their orders, a kind of case for the prosecution. She portrays the Mau Mau war as an unequal conflict between the
British colonial forces and their lackeys in Kenya on one side, and Mau Mau
fighters on the other side. This is too simple' (ibid., p. 495).
    In *Legacy of Violence*, Elkins does make mention of Kikuyu loyalists, and
describes the conflict as a civil war (pp. 547–8, 566–7). Yet she claims that, by
the end of 1955, the British colonial government had managed 'to detain nearly
the entire Kikuyu population' – without offering any explicit calculation
(p. 563). This could be taken to imply that the loyalists were a tiny, insignificant
minority, whereas, in fact, according to Branch, as many Kikuyu fought with
the colonial government as against it (*Defeating Mau Mau*, p. xii). Elkins also
repeats the alleged oral testimony that Ogot found to be 'dishonest' in her
earlier book, without offering any defence (*Legacy of Violence*, pp. 556–7).

228 African Christians tended to oppose the Mau Mau rebellion, not least because
of its violence (Sithole, *African Nationalism*, p. 56).
229 W. H. [Tommy] Thompson, 'The Outbreak of Mau Mau in Fort Hall', in John
Johnson, ed., *Colony to Nation: British Administrators in Kenya, 1940–1963*
(London: Erskine Press, 2002), p. 195.

230 James, *Rise and Fall of the British Empire*, pp. 293–5; Hyam, 'Partition of Africa', pp. 100, 101, 109, 112; Lonsdale, 'East Africa', pp. 532–3; John Lonsdale, 'The Conquest State of Kenya, 1893–1905' in Berman and Lonsdale, *Unhappy Valley*, 'State and Class', pp. 16, 19, 25.

231 White settlers in Kenya came to own only a fifth of the useable land, leaving most of African agriculture in place (Lonsdale, 'East Africa', p. 534). Margery Perham claims that the Kenya highlands, where the white settlers staked their claims, were 'almost uninhabited', and that the amount of inhabited land taken from Africans was 'a very small proportion of the whole' (*Colonial Reckoning*, p. 94).

232 Anderson, *Histories of the Hanged*, p. 24.

233 Margery Perham wrote sympathetically of the settlers in 1961, that '[s]ettlement could succeed only at the cost of long, very practical and scientific experiment in types of soil, of seed, of livestock, and in very hard-bought experience of the fickle climate', and that 'the farmers have committed themselves, their resources and their families to Africa' (*Colonial Reckoning*, pp. 91, 92). The theme of settler hardship is a recurrent one in novels about colonial East Africa. For example, in *A Thing to Love*, Elspeth Huxley, whose parents had been settlers, wrote this: 'The Colonel's farming career had been like a game of snakes and ladders, heavily beset with snakes. Every time he had approached his goal, he had struck a slump, or a plague of locusts, or a drought, or an outbreak of disease, and back he had slid almost to his starting-point' (p. 142); and in *The Year of the Lion*, Gerald Hanley wrote along the same lines: '"Listen," Browning said, serious, his pose gone. "Being a settler in this country is a bloody hard thing. This country is a museum, a museum containing every damned animal disease that's ever been known to man. They kill your beasts like flies when they come. Wait and see. Then, if you grow corn or maize or some other thing, there are locusts. Never seen 'em yet, eh? Well, wait. You'll see 'em all right. You need a bloody bank account like Henry Ford to keep going"' (p. 78).

234 Anderson, *Histories of the Hanged*, pp. 23–6; Throup, 'Origins of Mau Mau', pp. 413, 415.

235 Anderson, *Histories of the Hanged*, pp. 30–1; Lonsdale, 'East Africa', pp. 536, 540.

236 Anderson, *Histories of the Hanged*, p, 32; Branch, *Defeating Mau Mau*, pp. 17, 30, 33, 35.

237 Kenyatta became the first prime minister of an independent Kenya in 1963.

238 Anderson, *Histories of the Hanged*, p. 32; Lonsdale, 'East Africa', p. 540; Throup, 'Origins of Mau Mau', pp. 411, 421–7. In contrast, Mau Mau found little support in the non-Kikuyu districts of Meru and Embu, where the colonial regime's experiments had succeeded in establishing African peasant production of coffee, a high-value cash crop, on broad-based terraces. This not only entailed far less labour in preserving the terraces, but offered a tangible reward for work on soil conservation (Throup, 'Origins of Mau Mau', pp. 427–8).

239 Anderson, *Histories of the Hanged*, pp. 62, 85; Anthony Clayton, 'Baring,

(Charles) Evelyn, first Baron Howick of Glendale', *Oxford Dictionary of National Biography* (2006): https://www.oxforddnb.com/view/10.1093/ref:odnb/9780198614128.001.0001/odnb-9780198614128-e-30789.

240 French, *British Way in Counter-Insurgency*, pp. 74, 77, 79.

241 Anderson, *Histories of the Hanged*, pp. 313–14, 319, 321, 326–7; French, *British Way in Counter-Insurgency*, p. 163. According to Willoughby Thompson, the local district officer and magistrate summoned to the camp in the aftermath of the violence, the decision to force the 'hard-core' detainees to work had been taken 'at the highest level' of the Kenya government, including the governor himself (W. H. [Tommy] Thompson, 'Trouble at Hola', in Johnson, *Colony to Nation*, p. 208). Charles Douglas-Home disputes this, however, arguing that the 'Cowan Plan' to use 'compelling force' on recalcitrant detainees had been decided by the ministers of defence and African affairs and the commissioner of prisons only, and was not put before the governor's Ministerial Security Council (*Evelyn Baring: The Last Proconsul* [London: Collins, 1978], pp. 291, 295). According to Thompson, most of the warders at Hola were Nandi, 'haughty warrior stock' disposed to be 'totally contemptuous' of the Kikuyu detainees. Besides, since the 'hard-core' among the latter were in the habit of throwing their latrine buckets at, and sometimes over, the warders, the latter had a bone to pick with them. 'Told in bad Swahili to take a tough line,' Thompson reports, 'the Nandi took their chance. Out came the truncheons and old scores were settled. Prison Officers on the spot lost control and it was at least five minutes before any order was re-established . . . The whole thing was as simple as that. There were no political machinations and no sinister designs' (ibid.).

242 Anderson, *Histories of the Hanged*, pp, 326–7, 328. Anderson reports that Thompson told him in June 1999 that, from an interview with Baring the day after the killings, he believed that the governor knew that the report of the killings as drownings initially released and transmitted to London was 'a lie' (ibid., p. 326–7). In an account published four years later, Thompson wrote that, when he had first arrived at the camp, he was told that the prisoners had collapsed in the heat, whereupon the panicking guards had doused them with buckets of water. He immediately radioed Nairobi to urge that a senior CID officer, the commissioner of prisons and the chief native commissioner make their way to Hola immediately. When he got off the radio, he discovered that the prison officer in charge at the camp had disobeyed his instructions and confirmed the initial story of deaths by drowning. This then appeared on the front pages of British newspapers and was repeated in the House of Commons. The following day (4 March 1959) Thompson was interviewed by Governor Baring, who in a direct phone call to the secretary of state for the colonies, Alan Lennox-Boyd, in London, was 'told that it would be politically unwise to alter the story' since it would put the minister 'in an untenable position in the House'. Baring then issued a statement 'to the effect that senior officers were on the spot gathering evidence and that a further press notice would be issued in due course'. Thus was the Kenya government 'panicked . . . into making

what I can only describe as a daft statement of what was taken as confirmation and resulted in a dreadful tangle of deceit' (Thompson, 'Trouble at Hola', pp. 206-9).

However, to say that Baring *knew* that the original story was a lie when he rang London is probably unfair. He may well have strongly suspected that it was untrue, but he could not have been sure. And when, later the same day, three senior officers from the Prisons, Defence and African Departments, just returned from Hola, all told him that the deaths had *not* been caused by violence, he probably became even less sure (Douglas-Home, *Evelyn Baring*, pp. 289-90). So, by Thompson's own account, he prevaricated and played for time. Eight days later, when the autopsies had been completed, another official statement was made, which admitted evidence of violence, and a week after that an inquest opened (ibid., p. 290). Since the coroner reported that there was insufficient evidence on which to base a charge against any individual warder, the attorney-general, Eric Griffith-Jones, started disciplinary proceedings against the camp commandant and his deputy, who were both suspended from duty. The commandant was found guilty of failures and retired from the service without loss of gratuity (ibid., pp. 293-4).

243 Godfrey Muriuki, '*Counter-Insurgency in Kenya, 1952-60: A Study of Military Operations against Mau Mau*, by Anthony Clayton', *African Affairs*, 77/307 (April 1978), p. 262.

244 French, *British Way in Counter-Insurgency*, pp. 157-8, 172.

245 Ibid., p. 156. General George Erskine, who commanded British forces in Kenya from June 1953 to May 1955, wrote in December 1953: 'There is no doubt from Oct[ober] 1952 until last June there was a great deal of indiscriminate shooting by Army and Police. I am quite certain prisoners were beaten to extract information. It is a short step from beating to torture and I am now sure, although it has taken me some time to realise it, that torture was a feature of many police posts. I do not believe the regular police were heavily involved although some of them may have been. The real trouble came from the Kenya settler dressed as KPR or in Kenya Reg[imen]t. This example tended to spread and was whipped up by such events as the Lari Massacre and every European murder' (Erskine to Head, 10 December 1953, quoted in French, *British Way in Counter-Insurgency*, p. 169). As David French writes, from this 'it is reasonable to conclude that he was reporting what had indeed happened' (ibid., pp. 146-7).

246 Anderson, *Histories of the Hanged*, pp. 6-7, 291.

247 Ogot, 'Review Article: Britain's Gulag', p. 503.

248 French, *British Way in Counter-Insurgency*, pp. 140-1.

249 Anderson, *Histories of the Hanged*, pp. 114-15; Ogot, 'Review Article: Britain's Gulag', p. 502.

250 Anderson, *Histories of the Hanged*, pp. 301-5.

251 Ibid., p. 85; Huw Bennett, 'Erskine, Sir George Watkin Eben James (1899-1965)', *Oxford Dictionary of National Biography*: https://www.oxforddnb.com/view/10.1093/ref:odnb/9780198614128.001.0001/odnb-9780198614128-e-97289 (accessed on 13 November 2020). When Captain Griffiths of the King's African

Rifles was court-martialled on the charge of murdering two forest workers but found not guilty on a technicality, Erskine was dismayed and insisted that he be retried on a lesser charge. According to David French, this 'may serve as testimony to [Erskine's] determination to ensure the good behaviour of all members of the security forces' (French, *British Way in Counter-Insurgency*, p. 168). Huw Bennett, however, argues that Erskine's initial determination to reform the British Army's conduct weakened as he 'came to believe . . . in the strategic effectiveness of repression' (*Fighting the Mau Mau: The British Army and Counter-Insurgency in the Kenya Emergency* [Cambridge: Cambridge University Press, 2013], p. 267). Yet he also tells us that '[c]lear elements of restraint were present in military policy from 1952 to 1956 . . ..Repeated efforts were made by GHQ to instil and maintain a disciplined fighting force . . . The influence of the minimum force concept can certainly be traced in actual practice on operations . . . Prisoners in military hands could often expect to receive humane treatment . . . As General Erskine declared the day after arriving in Kenya, he believed in justice' (ibid., pp. 264–5). Bennett's two sets of claims can be reconciled, if we suppose that while Erskine never ceased to expect his troops to act justly, he came to think, in the light of the need for swiftly successful counter-insurgency, that justice can accommodate more brutality than he had first thought. He might well have been correct: the ethical prohibition of the intentional killing of the innocent and the disproportionate killing or harm of anyone can still permit a great detail of lethal force, and lethal force, however well disciplined, is never gentle. Bennett observes that, while 'the current debate in military circles tends to assume that warfare is perfectible to a humane standard', 'it may be that counter-insurgencies will always be brutal' (ibid., p. 286). That is probably true, provided we do not assume that brutality must be unrestrained.

252 Beevor, *D-Day*, pp. 68, 180, 393, 438.

253 See Biggar, *In Defence of War*, pp. 85–8.

254 Daniel Branch argues, in relation to the Kenya Emergency, that when 'state perpetrated violence' 'recurs with great frequency', it should be understood not as occasional aberrations but as part of the state's 'operating *logic*' (Branch, *Defeating Mau Mau*, p. 87; the emphasis is mine). 'Logic' implies a central, sustained, driving force. This is wrong, first of all because it fails to discriminate between morally different kinds of state violence; second, because the frequency of abuse by agents of the state may be symptomatic of its lack of control rather than its inner logic; and third, because those in charge of Kenya's colonial state in fact sought to rein the violence in.

255 For Governor Baring's resistance to further prosecutions, see Douglas-Home, *Evelyn Baring*, pp. 295–8.

When, in the wake of the Griffiths case mentioned in note 251 above, an inquiry was held into the conduct of the army, General Erskine successfully insisted that it not consider events before his arrival in June 1953. David French comments: 'The inquiry was not a complete whitewash. But it was certainly not as thorough, penetrating, or revealing as it might have been . . . The authorities . . . had to walk a fine line between maintaining the rule of law as defined by emergency regulations on the one hand, and not undermining the morale of the security forces by punishing those who broke them' (*British Way in Counter-Insurgency*, pp. 168, 169, 171).

256 The unlawful killings at Hola took place on 3 March 1959; the Fairn report was published on 1 September 1959. I note that one Kenyan historian broadly confirms my conclusion. Describing Anthony Clayton's view, Godfrey Muriuki writes: 'The author argues that excesses were minimized by several factors. The Attorney General was against malpractices by the Security Forces, a factor which led to his removal. The judiciary upheld its standards under very difficult conditions. And ultimately the British Parliament acted as an effective watchdog throughout the period.' Then Muriuki comments, 'Most of the author's conclusions are sound and well-documented' ('*Counter-Insurgency in Kenya*', p. 263).

257 French, *British Way in Counter-Insurgency*, pp. 74, 82. One of the serious failures appears to have been the handling of the 'emergency' in Nyasaland in 1959. While the ('Devlin') *Report of the Nyasaland Commission of Inquiry* exonerated the colonial government from criticism for its decision to declare an emergency and assume emergency powers, it found 'at every level of the administration an indifference to and misuse of the law', going so far as to conclude that 'Nyasaland is – no doubt temporarily – a police state' (Brian Simpson, 'The Devlin Commission (1959): Colonialism, Emergencies, and the Rule of Law', *Oxford Journal of Legal Studies*, 22/1 [2002], pp. 18, 30, 37). However, in a subsequent letter, Lord Devlin explained to his correspondent: 'I agree that "the police state" was an unfortunate phrase to have used. What we meant by it was the police were given and were using extremely wide powers against which the individual was denied the ordinary protection of courts of law . . . we did not mean that Gestapo methods were being employed' (ibid., p. 45).

David French is inclined to be scathing about the doctrine of 'minimum force', observing that it could comprise a great deal of force indeed. He quotes Christopher Soames, the secretary of state for war, as saying in 1958 about the Cyprus Emergency both that '[i]t is known by every soldier in Cyprus that, whatever action he is called upon to take, he has to do it with the minimum of force', but that '[w]e must never forget that the role of the security forces is to conquer terrorism, and there will be many incidents when the minimum force necessary will be quite a lot of force'. French comments: 'Anyone reading . . . listening to Soames might think that the troops were operating in Wonderland under the command of the Mad Hatter' (*British Way in Counter-Insurgency*, pp. 84–5). That is unfair. What is the minimum necessary force is bound to depend on the prevailing circumstances, and according to those circumstances, it could be little or great. Nevertheless, the requirement of minimality is a constraint, for without it the quantity of force would be even greater, no matter what the circumstances.

Caroline Elkins is also scathing about appeals to military necessity: 'Necessity. Minimum use of force. Any degree of force necessary. Such excruciating nomenclature exercises didn't change the fact that Britain was violating the ethos of postwar international humanitarian law, which sought to reduce the suffering that British forces were inflicting to defeat colonial insurgencies' (*Legacy of Violence*, p. 565). For this, she coins the phrase, 'legalized lawlessness' (ibid., p. 566). First of all, we should observe that Elkins implicitly confirms French's claim that the British did generally maintain the rule of law, albeit permissively conceived: what they did was 'legalized'. Second, it is not clear whether Elkins is referring here to International Humanitarian Law (otherwise known as the 'Law of Armed Conflict' or the 'Laws of War') or to International Human Rights Law. These are distinct bodies of law, but in the index to her book she does not distinguish them, listing only the former, but not the latter. Third, the intention of International Humanitarian Law – its 'ethos'? – is not simply 'to reduce the suffering' inflicted by military forces, but to limit it to what is militarily necessary. And finally, the phrase 'legalized lawlessness' is, literally, nonsense. It may be that something that is legal should not be. But so long as it is legal, it cannot be 'lawless' in the sense of being beyond the law.

258 Marshall S. Clough was the first to refer to a 'Kenyan gulag' (*Mau Mau Memoirs: History, Memory and Politics* [Boulder, CO: Lynne Rienner, 1997]), and the London-based Federal Independence Party first coined the name 'Kenya's Belsen'. But David Anderson adopts them both in *Histories of the Hanged* without any obvious reservation (pp. 305, 312, 315). Elkins repeatedly makes the Soviet and Nazi comparisons in *The Untold Story of Britain's Gulag in Kenya*, Chapter 5 and pp. 147, 153, 171, 181, 335.

259 Ronald Hyam, *Britain's Declining Empire: The Road to Decolonisation, 1918–1968* (Cambridge: Cambridge University Press, 2006), p. 192 n.111.

260 Biggar, *In Defence of War*, pp. 129–44; 'Was Britain Right to Go to War in 1914?', *Standpoint*, 27 August 2013; 'Cards on the Table: A Flawed, Candid History of Britain and the Great War', *Australian Book Review*, March 2015; 'Proportionality: Lessons from the Somme', *Soundings*, 101/3 (2018), pp. 197–205.

261 Ashley Jackson, *The British Empire and the Second World War* (London: Hambledon Continuum, 2006), p. 526.

262 Jackson, *British Empire and the Second World War*, p. 2.

263 Robert Lyman, *A War of Empires: Japan, India, Burma, and Britain, 1941–45* (Oxford: Osprey, 2021), pp. 488, 494, 507–8 (Appendix 3). According to Robert Lyman in an email of 2 January 2021, '[t]he Japanese regarded the Africans to be the best jungle fighters in 14 Army'. Gerald Hanley, who commanded Somali troops in the Fourteenth Army in Burma wrote: 'it was not till I got to the Fourteenth Army in Burma, with its many races, that I saw what the British Empire might have been, despite the fears felt by those upstairs in London about the servants downstairs' (*Warriors*, pp. 90–1).

264 Jackson, *British Empire and the Second World War*, p. 2. Even if I had not read about the imperial nature of Britain's war-effort in 1939–45, I would have known about it from my Scottish father's experience. Serving in an anti-aircraft unit

in Italy, he found himself north of Florence in September and October 1944. Probably in Borgo San Lorenzo, he was accosted by a jeep-load of Americans, who, because of his deep tan, mistook him for an Indian. They were trying to make contact with the nearby 8th Indian Infantry Division.

265 The figure of 2,581,726 recruits to British imperial armed forces in 1939–45 comes from Bisheshwar Prasad, ed., *The Official History of the Indian Armed Forces in the Second World War, 1939–1945*, 24 vols (1953–66), Vol. 17: 'India and the War' (New Delhi: Government of India, 1966), p. 258; the figures of 43,000 Indians fighting for the Japanese in the Indian National Army and 3,000 for Hitler's Indian Foreign Legion in 1945 come from Nicholas Mansergh, E. W. R. Lumby and Penderel Moon, *Constitutional Relations between Britain and India: The Transfer of Power, 1942–1947*, 12 vols (1970–83), Vol. 6: 'The Post-war Phase: New Moves by the Labour Government, 1 August 1945–22 March 1946' (London: HMSO, 1976), p. 369, Annexure I to No. 154.

266 I owe thanks to Robert Lyman and Ashley Jackson for their advice on these matters. In some tension with this account is David Killingray's claim that, while '[u]ndoubtedly some [of the more than half a million Africans who entered the armed forces in the Second World War] came as "volunteers" . . . most came as conscripts through a variety of means involving force' ('Labour Exploitation for Military Campaigns in British Colonial Africa, 1870–1945', *Journal of Contemporary History*, 24/3 [July 1989], p. 490). Still, there were material attractions, for '[d]uring the 1939–45 war, the physical treatment and welfare provision for military labour were vastly different from those experienced in the Great War. Men conscripted into the pioneer battalions enjoyed relatively high standards of materi-al comfort compared to their normal expectations in civilian life' (ibid., p. 493; see also pp. 495, 498). Whatever the kind, degree and extent of force, if Gerald Hanley's witness is to be believed, some African troops positively relished the prospect of a fight: 'When [in Burma] the Somali battalion, after a shattering artillery bombardment from the Japanese guns, finally attacked with the bayonet, they went headlong and their [British] officers could not keep up with them. One of them who was decorated for bravery in that battle, a Degoyida from the northern frontier of Somali Kenya, told me that he enjoyed it, and that he admired the way the Japanese infantry liked to stand and fight it out' (*Warriors*, p. 188).

267 Christopher Somerville, *Our War: How the British Commonwealth Fought the Second World War* (London: Weidenfeld & Nicolson, 1998), pp. 4, 35.

268 Kofi Busia, *West Africans and the Issues of War* (London: Sheldon Press, 1942), p. 11; quoted in Gilley, *Last Imperialist*, p. 144.

269 Lyman, *War of Empires*, p. 31.

270 Ibid. Anyone who doubts that Indians had good reason to fight for India under British colonial rule against 'liberation' by Japanese imperialism should consider Chinua Achebe's observation, when he wrote in 1991 that 'the depth of bitterness' of Koreans at Japanese colonial rule 'was more profound than anything one encounters in Africa today' ('Teaching *Things Fall Apart*' [1991], in *Education of a British-Protected Child*, p. 128). Niall Ferguson confirms this point, when he

writes that '[t]he Rape of Nanking reveals precisely what the leading alternative to British rule in Asia stood for' (*Empire*, p. 332). What happened when Japanese troops seized the capital of the Republic of China at Nanking in late 1937 is highly controversial. According to Chinese orthodoxy, the number of civilian Chinese killed is 300,000 (David Askew, 'New Research on the Nanking Incident', *Asia-Pacific Journal*, 2/7 [13 July 2004], p. 17). But, according to Askew, the Japanese discussion is 'the most sophisticated' (pp. 6–7) and among Japanese scholars estimates of the number of Chinese killed vary from zero to nearly 200,000; the proportions of those killed who were combatants, combatant-deserters, and civilians are disputed; and the period over which the killings took place ranges from six to twelve weeks between November 1937 and March 1938 (ibid., pp. 8–10). Nonetheless, there seems to be little reason to doubt that the execution of prisoners-of-war and the killing of civilians took place on a scale involving several tens of thousands, maybe even more than one-hundred thousand.

271 Lyman, *War of Empires*, pp. 31, 32, 487, 497–8, 501.
272 Keith Jeffery, 'The Second World War', in *Oxford History of the British Empire*, Vol. IV, eds Brown and Louis, p. 307.

CONCLUSION: ON THE COLONIAL PAST

1 Perham, *Colonial Reckoning*, p. 102.
2 Ibid., p. 14.
3 Onora O'Neill, 'Rights to Compensation', in *Justice across Boundaries: Whose Obligations?* (Cambridge: Cambridge University Press, 2016), p. 51.
4 According to World Bank data, in 2020 life expectancy in post-slavery Barbados was 24 years higher than in post-slave-trading Nigeria, literacy (in Barbados in 2014) was almost 40 per cent higher (than in Nigeria in 2018), and GNI per capita in $international 482 per cent higher (https://databank.worldbank.org/views/reports/reportwidget.aspx?Report_Name=CountryProfile&Id=b450fd57&tbar=y&dd=y&inf=n&zm=n&country=BRB; https://databank.worldbank.org/views/reports/reportwidget.aspx?Report_Name=CountryProfile&Id=b450fd57&tbar=y&dd=y&inf=n&zm=n&country=NGA; accessed 4 September 2022). Eric A. Posner and Adrian Vermeule analyse the difficulty of 'netting out' the benefits and costs of the wrong of slavery: slaves benefited from European enslavement insofar as the alternative was slaughter back home by an enemy; many wrongdoers passed their unjust profits to descendants who made sacrifices for the sake of slaves; some descendants of slaves are also the descendants of slave-masters and would not exist but for slavery ('Reparations for Slavery and Other Historical Injustices', 103 *Columbia Law Review* 689 [2003], pp. 702, 708, 740). Mark Milke summarises the general problem eloquently: 'At some point, too many waves really have crashed onto the shore of our collective histories and retreated, and any effect from deeds committed long ago removed with the receding tide ... Beyond clear lines of theft to thief, slaveholder to slave, or murderer to those who perished, entire countries and their populations alive today would be caught in impossible calculations if the working assumption

for justice is that an act from the distant past can be partly remedied with compensation today, or even that it should serve as the basis for active discrimination between groups today . . . the further one travels down historical paths long overgrown by the thickets of newer generations, peoples, immigrants, and other possible causes for today's observed effects, the more impossible it is to begin, never mind finish, such calculations. Beyond tight provable links between harm and harmed in recent generations and decades, it is otherwise preferable to avoid the impossible calculations that seek cosmic justice from the dead. Let them – and us – rest in peace' (*The Victim Cult: How the Grievance Culture Hurts Everyone and Wrecks Civilizations* [Parksville, BC: Thomas and Black, 2019], pp. 237, 246).

5   As Richard Vernon puts it, the list of all those who suffered at the hands of 'the states of the eighteenth, nineteenth and twentieth centuries, whose failures of responsibility were almost universally appalling', is long and includes women, children, industrial workers, religious minorities, soldiers and sailors (*Historical Redress: Must We Pay for the Past?* [London: Continuum, 2012], pp. 108–9). Out of all the eligible candidates, how can we justify selecting slaves?

6   John Torpey reports that in the Organisation of African Unity summit of 1993, which was convened to consider the African reparations campaign, '[t]he role of North Africans and Middle Easterners – not to mention sub-Saharan Africans themselves – in the slave trade threatened to muddy the historical waters' ('Making Whole What Has Been Smashed: Reflections on Reparations', *Journal of Modern History*, 73/2 [June 2001], p. 353). See also Adaobi Tricia Nwaubani, 'My Great-Grandfather, the African Slave-Trader', *New Yorker*, 15 July 2018: 'African intellectuals tend to blame the West for the slave trade, but I knew that white traders couldn't have loaded their ships without help from Africans like my great-grandfather. I read arguments for paying reparations to the descendants of American slaves and wondered whether someone might soon expect my family to contribute' (https://www.newyorker.com/culture/personal-history/my-great-grandfather-the-nigerian-slave-trader).

7   Unfortunately, I have been unable to identify the date of the letter's publication. The same point was made memorably in an episode of the incomparable television series *The West Wing*, where Josh Lyman, the White House's Deputy Chief of Staff, is talking to Jeff Breckenridge, an African American lawyer who is pressing the case for reparations for slavery. Says Lyman: 'You know, Jeff, I'd love to give you the money. I really would. But I'm a little short of cash right now. It seems the SS officer forgot to give my grandfather his wallet back when he let him out of Birkenau' (Torpey, 'Making Whole What Has Been Smashed', p. 356).

8   Hilary McD. Beckles, *Britain's Black Debt: Reparations for Caribbean Slavery and Native Genocide* (Kingston, Jamaica: University of West Indies Press, 2013).

9   Ibid., p. xvii.

10   Ibid., p. 2.

11   Ibid., pp. 3, 12.

12   Ibid., p. 18.

13 Ibid., p. 168.

14 Ibid., pp. 181–2.

15 In private correspondence during 2–5 December 2020, I raised Beckles' claim that most African chiefs opposed the slave trade, and that those who collaborated did so under duress, with Professor Kenneth Morgan, an economic and social historian of the transatlantic slave trade. Morgan commented, 'I have never seen any African historian support such a view.' He also observed that the authority that Beckles cites on the issue, Hugh Thomas, 'was not a slave-trade historian or an Africanist'. The Beninese historian Abiola Félix Iroko confirms Morgan's view: 'When the slave trade was abolished, Africans were against abolition. King Kosoko of Lagos was against abolition at the time . . . Of those who were sold and had offspring . . . [s]ome returned home . . . [and] became, in turn, slaveholders and bought slaves for their correspondents who remained in Brazil. Africans resumed this trade after abolition' ('Historian: "Africans Must Be Condemned for the Slave Trade"', interview with Abiola Félix Iroko on Benin Web TV, *Free West Media*, 28 July 2020: https://freew estmedia.com/2020/07/28/historian-africans-must-be-condemned-for-the-slave-trade/ [accessed 29 June 2021]). Concurrent, too, is the view of the dissident intellectual from the Ivory Coast, and winner of the Nelson Mandela Prize for Literature in 2017, Ernest Tigori: 'this [slave] trade happened strictly between local leaders and European merchants, as European governments had not yet set foot in Africa. In the seventeenth and eighteenth centuries, Africa included powerful kingdoms such as Ashanti, Dahomey, Kongo, and the notion that they could have been forced by mere merchants to sell their people to slavery against their will is simply ludicrous' (Raymond Ibrahim, '"I'm Saddened by the White Man's Emasculation": An African Sets the Record Straight', *PJ Media*, 15 January 2020: https://pjmedia.com/columns/raymond-ibrahim/2020/01/15/ im-saddened-by-the-white-mans-emasculation-an-african-sets-the-record-straight-n123156 [accessed 29 June 2021]). See also Finn Fuglestad, S*lave Traders by Invitation: West Africa's Slave Coast in the Precolonial Era* (London: Hurst, 2018).

16 Beckles, *Britain's Black Debt*, p. 168.

17 Ibid., p. 23; see also pp. 82, 84.

18 Ibid., p. xiv.

19 Ibid., p. 101.

20 Ibid., p. 4.

21 Robin Blackburn, *The Making of New World Slavery: From the Baroque to the Modern, 1492–1800* (London: Verso, 1997). Blackburn is emeritus professor in the department of sociology at the University of Essex.

22 Beckles, *Britain's Black Debt*, pp. 101–2.

23 Ibid., p. 105.

24 Ibid., p. 106.

25 See Chapter 2, p. 52.

26 Beckles prefaces each of his fifteen chapters with a quotation. One of these is of Jeremy Corbyn, four of Diane Abbott and two of Dawn Butler. Corbyn was

leader of the Labour Opposition from 2015–20, and Abbott and Butler both served in his Shadow Cabinet.

27 See Chapter 2, p. 51.

28 See Chapter 2, p. 53.

29 See Nigel Biggar, *What's Wrong with Rights?*, pp. 121–31. Out of my examination of natural rights in general I concluded that it is best not to talk of natural, moral rights at all, since they connote a stability and fixity that does not exist apart from conventional law and its supportive institutions. I note that David Lyons entirely concurs with regard to natives' assertion of historic rights to land. He argues that 'moral rights to land are inherently unstable or variable with circumstances' and that when migrants land on the shores of a native people, what share of goods the former may justly claim and what the latter justly owe is not determinate: '[o]ne cannot say, a priori, what form such sharing would have to take . . . property rights themselves, and not just their exercise or contents, are relative to circumstances' ('The New Indian Claims and Original Rights to Land', *Social Theory and Practice*, 4/3 [Fall 1977], pp. 263, 269).

30 Jeremy Waldron, 'Superseding Historic Injustice', *Ethics*, 103/1 (October 1992), pp. 20, 23.

31 Jeremy Waldron, 'Redressing Historic Injustice', *University of Toronto Law Journal*, 52 (2002), p. 148.

32 Waldron, 'Superseding Historic Injustice', p.26.

33 Widdowson and Howard, *Disrobing the Aboriginal Industry*, pp. 8–9.

34 Waldron, 'Superseding Historic Injustice', p. 27.

35 O'Neill, 'Rights to Compensation', p. 52; the emphases are O'Neill's. The political philosopher David Miller and the political scientist Alan C. Cairns concur. Miller writes: 'Thus we might think that colonial nations have special remedial responsibilities to their impoverished former colonies without delving into contested questions such as whether colonialism unjustly enriched the metropolis at the expense of the periphery' (*National Responsibility and Global Justice* [Oxford: Oxford University Press, 2007], pp. 139–40). Cairns reports, with approval, that Canada's prime minister, Pierre Trudeau, resisted attempts at redress for past injustice, quoting President John F. Kennedy in 1972: 'We will be just in our time. This is all we can do. We must be just today' (*Citizens Plus*, p. 52).

36 Chaudhuri, *The Autobiography of an Unknown Indian* (London: Macmillan, 1951). The dedication was omitted from the 1999 Picador edition, apparently without the author's permission. Chaudhuri has been described as 'India's most distinguished writer of English prose in the 20th century' ('Obituary: Nirad C. Chaudhuri', *Independent*, 3 August 1999). The Indo-Trinidadian man of letters V. S. Naipaul judged his *Autobiography* to be 'maybe the one great book to have come out of the Indo-British encounter' (*The Overcrowded Barracoon and Other Articles* [London: Andre Deutsch, 1972], p. 59); the South African woman of letters Doris Lessing reckoned it 'one of the great books of the twentieth century' (*Time Bites: Views and Reviews* [New York: HarperCollins, 2004], p. 214); and the Indo-British novelist Salman Rushdie lauded it as 'a

masterpiece' (Salman Rushdie and Elizabeth West, eds, *Vintage Book of Indian Writing 1947–97* [London: Vintage, 1997], p. xvii). Predictably, however, Chaudhuri's scepticism of Indian nationalism and part-admiration of the British Empire was not popular in newly independent India, where he was forced out of his job as a political commentator on All India Radio and deprived of his pension. In 1970 Chaudhuri and his wife moved to north Oxford, where he died in 1999.

37 Manmohan Singh, address in acceptance of honorary degree from Oxford University, 8 July 2005: https://mea.gov.in/Speeches-Statements.htm?dtl/2623/Address+}by+Prime+Minister+Dr+Manmohan+Singh+in+acceptance+of+Honorary+Degree+from+Oxford+University

38 Denmark banned the transatlantic slave trade in 1792 and was the first European state to do so. However, it was only in 1847 that it resolved to phase out the institution of slavery in its colonial possessions over a twelve-year period. France initially banned slavery throughout its empire in 1794, then reinstated it under Napoleon in 1802 and only finally abolished it in 1848.

39 The pacifying effect of an overarching imperial authority was something that native peoples could appreciate. After Cetshwayo's Zulu kingdom had been defeated in 1879, the British high commissioner divided it into twelve mini-kingdoms, but London then refused to take imperial responsibility for over-seeing them. As a consequence, the Zulu were prone to conflict among themselves and vulnerable to Boer incursions. In 1911 Rider Haggard wrote in his diary reports of two remarks made by Zulu chiefs to British representatives during *indabas* or formal conferences: 'You defeated us but you are not ruling as you should do' and 'We are left orphaned' (H. Rider Haggard, *Diary of an African Journey. The Return of Rider Haggard*, ed. and intro. Stephen Coan [Pietermaritzburg: University of Natal Press, 2000], pp. 185, 293). Observing this state of affairs, the bishop of Zululand pleaded with Lord Granville, the colonial secretary, 'For God's sake, my lord, in common justice and mercy, take over the whole land *and rule it*' (Haggard, *Cetywayo and His White Neighbours*, p. xxxix. The emphasis is the bishop's). If natives were sensible of the evils of the absence of effective imperial rule, we can reasonably infer that they must also have been sensible of the benefits of its presence. See also ibid., pp. xvii, xxv, xxxi, xxxiv, 45, 50; and Saul David, *Zulu: The Heroism and Tragedy of the Zulu War of 1879* (London: Penguin, 2004), pp. 366, 372–3.

40 Kumar, *Visions of Empire*, pp. 365–8. See also Mark Mazower, *No Enchanted Palace: The End of Empire and the Ideological Origins of the United Nations* (Princeton: Princeton University Press, 2009). Mazower argues that the British Empire was 'one of the key places where thinking about international organi-zation emerged', and that 'the UN [was] essentially a further chapter in the history of world organization inaugurated by the League and linked through that to the question of empire and the visions of global order that emerged out of the British Empire in particular in its final decades' (ibid., pp. 13–14).

41 While most members of the Commonwealth favoured economic sanctions against the *apartheid* regime as a means of pressure, Britain (Mrs Thatcher) did not.

42 The 'Five Eyes' is an international alliance for cooperation in signals intelligence between Australia, Canada, New Zealand, the United Kingdom and the United States. It is based on the United Kingdom – United States of America (UKUSA) Agreement of 1946, which was a development of an informal wartime agreement in 1941.

43 Describing itself as 'the world's first development financial institution', British International Investment began life as the Colonial Development Corporation, which was founded in 1948 'to do good without losing money'. In 2019 it had a portfolio of investments – mainly in former colonies such as India, Nigeria, South Africa and Kenya – worth £4.7 billion. In November 2021 the CDC Group was rebranded as 'British International Investment'. The UK government's Department for International Development (DFiD) grew out of the Overseas Development Ministry, which was created in 1964 to combine the overseas aid operations of several government departments, including those of the Colonial Office. In 2018/19 DFiD managed the delivery of £11 billion, and of the top twenty recipients of bilateral 'official development assistance' fourteen were former members of the British Empire (Foreign, Commonwealth and Development Office, *Statistics on International Development: Final UK Aid Spend 2019* [London: FCDO, September 2020], p. 5). In September 2020 DFiD was merged with the Foreign Office into the Foreign, Commonwealth and Development Office.

44 For example, the political theorist Daniel Butt takes his cue from Jürgen Osterhammel's historically dubious, stipulative definition of colonialism as 'a relationship of domination between an indigenous (or forcibly imported) majority and a minority of foreign invaders', in which fundamental decisions affecting the lives of the colonised people are made by the colonial rulers in pursuit of 'interests that are often defined in a distant metropolis'. Butt then comments that 'it is nowadays commonplace to maintain that the domination that [colonized peoples] suffered at the hand of the colonizing power was unjust' ('Repairing Historical Wrongs and the End of Empire', *Social and Legal Studies*, 21/2 [2012], p. 228). The political scientist Richard Vernon asserts, without argument, that '[t]he *harm* done by both slavery and colonialism is both immense and undeniable . . . The *benefits received* (and retained) from slavery and colonialism are very much harder to establish clearly' (*Historical Redress*, p. 45. The emphases are Vernon's).

45 I observe that Brian Simpson agrees with me. Referring to Harold Macmillan's audit of the colonial empire in 1957, he wrote: 'This exercise in cost benefit analysis failed, as all such attempts do in relation to factors incapable of quantification, to provide crystal clear guidance' ('Devlin Commission', p. 33).

46 When, led by James McDougall, fifty-eight Oxford academics published an online denunciation of my 'Ethics and Empire' project in December 2017, they attributed to me an 'absurd "balance-sheet"' approach to assessing the British Empire ('"Ethics and Empire": An Open Letter from Oxford Scholars'). At the time, I was perplexed, since, as I explained in my riposte (https://www.

mcdonaldcentre.org.uk/sites/default/files/content/heres_my_reply_to_those_
who_condemn_my_project_on_ethics_and_empire_comment_the_times_
the_sun.pdf; https://www.thetimes.co.uk/article/heres-my-reply-to-those-who-
condemn-my-project-on-ethics-and-empire-cw5f2z80x) and have explained
again here, I have long been sceptical of cost-benefit calculations. Now I think
I understand my critics better. What they were arguing was that, since the
British Empire was essentially racist, exploitative and disproportionately violent
– like the Nazi regime – no good achievement, however great, can compensate.
My difference from them, therefore, is that I do not accept that the empire was
essentially any of those things.

47 Perham, *Colonial Reckoning*, p. 130.

48 Gann and Duignan, *Burden of Empire*, p. 372.

49 Malcolm, *A Memoir of Central India*, p. 304. See p. 43 of this book.

50 Perham, *Colonial Reckoning*, p. 71.

51 The same phenomenon of people from a non-colonised or post-colonial state
choosing to migrate to a British colony was visible in the Caribbean in the
1920s, when many Haitians found the colonial Bahamas preferable to the
republican land of their birth (Gilley, *Last Imperialist*, p. 73).

52 The Canadian public policy analyst and newspaper columnist Mark Milke
reports this: 'When I first visited Hong Kong in 2013, almost every politician,
civil servant, and business leader I met emphasized three priorities they wanted
the territory to retain vis-à-vis the regime in Beijing: 1) capitalism; 2) the rule
of law, including the British legal code; and 3) Hong Kong's strong anti-cor-
ruption stance that dated from reforms in the 1970s . . . Relevant to debates in
the West over colonialism and ongoing allegations of imperial guilt, Hong
Kong's leaders were uninterested in such sensitivities, but in the opposite. They
wanted critical vestiges of past British colonialism and ideas strengthened, not
abandoned. To wit, in 2019, when Hong Kong protesters rallied against even
more interference from Beijing, protesters in Hong Kong raised a British flag'
(*Victim Cult*, p. 115).

EPILOGUE: ON ANTI-COLONIALISM AND
THE BRITISH FUTURE

1 Let me explain here how far 'decolonisation' makes good sense to me. Its original and most natural home is in former colonies. So when the Kenyan novelist
and playwright Ngũgĩ wa Thiong'o argued in *Decolonising the Mind: The Politics
of Language and African Literature* (Woodbridge and Nairobi: James Currey
and East African Educational Publishers, 1986) that African literature should be
written in African languages such as his own Gikuyu, rather than in English, it
makes obvious good sense. When transferred to Britain, if 'decolonisation' means
correcting the neglect in school curricula of the history of immigration and the
contribution of immigrants, that should be done. And if there are important
texts that have been excluded from reading lists, *just because* of prejudice against
the race of their authors, they should be included. All that makes good sense.

'Decolonisation', however, usually means much more, and here I begin to dissent. Typically, it means an opposition to 'Euro-centricity' and a correlative insistence on shifting attention to non-European histories and cultures. Yet a certain Euro-centricity in British education is entirely justified. Britain is not Anywhere. It is located in north-west Europe, has a particular history and has developed particular institutions and traditions. It is vitally important, therefore, that school education should focus on helping budding citizens understand the immediate cultural and political environment for which they are about to become directly responsible. Typically, 'decolonisation' also assumes that Britain is a systemically racist country; that its systemic racism is based on a sense of essential and permanent European or Western cultural superiority; and that this mentality is a product of our colonial history. It will be clear from what I have written in the book that I disagree with all of this. For an African critique of 'decolonisation', see Olúfémi Táíwò, *Against Decolonisation: Taking African Agency Seriously* (London: Hurst, 2022). Táíwò is a better philosopher than he is a historian, however. Thus, for example, he writes that whereas the French and Portuguese 'held out to their subjects the promise of full citizenship if they "assimilated"', the British 'never did' (ibid., p. 17). That is not so. Since 1853 the franchise in Cape Colony was available to black Africans on the same conditions as whites.

2   European Union Agency for Fundamental Rights, *Being Black in the EU: Summary of the Second European Union Minorities and Discrimination Survey* (Vienna: EUAFR, 2019), pp. 2, 3, 7, 9.

3   Commission on Race and Ethnic Disparities, *The Report* (London: HMSO, 2021), pp. 8, 36, 77. Referred to variously as the 'CRED' or (after its chair, Dr Tony Sewell) the 'Sewell' report, it is controversial, of course, and has been angrily dismissed by *Guardian* journalists and left-wing activists, among others, often by appeal to the 'lived experience' of 'Black people'. 'Lived experience', however, is never pure; it is always interpreted, and not all interpretations are accurate. But even where the interpretation is accurate, it represents the accurate experience only of some individuals. The commission's report, however, looks beyond the perceptions of particular individuals to hard, social scientific data, in order to ground reliable generalisations. Moreover, it takes explicit pains to disaggregate 'Black, Asian, and Minority Ethnic' or 'BAME' people, observing that the situation of, say, Chinese Britons is often dramatically different from that of Black Caribbean Britons. Of the nine commissioners, all but one was non-white. Their report is very well written, conceptually precise, driven by the data, nuanced and thorough. For a judicious comparison of the Sewell report with the subsequent counter-report of the Runnymede Trust, *Race and Racism in England*, see John Root, 'Runnymede vs Sewell?', in *Out of Many, One People*, no. 40, 27 July 2021: https://johnroot.substack.com/p/runnymede-vs-sewell-40-27072021. The Sewell report wins, hands down.

4   See Christopher Thorne, 'Britain and the Black GIs: Racial Issues and Anglo-American Relations in 1942', in *Border Crossings: Studies in International History* (Oxford: Blackwell, 1988), pp. 259–74; David Reynolds, 'The Churchill Government and the Black American Troops in Britain during World War II',

in *Transactions of the Royal Historical Society*, Fifth Series, 35 (1985), pp. 113–33; and David Reynolds, *Rich Relations: The American Occupation of Britain, 1942–1945* (London: HarperCollins, 1995), chapters 14 and 18. The British reaction was not all of a piece, of course. Some Cabinet ministers, for example, argued in favour of respecting, and even replicating, the American 'color-bar'. Significantly, it was the secretary of state for the colonies who 'deplored the idea of seeking to guide British citizens into the ways of the Americans. Such a move, he felt, was likely to cause serious resentment among coloured people already in Britain, as well as those in the colonies; it could also lead to a reaction among the general public "gravely prejudicial to Anglo-American relations"' (Thorne, 'Britain and the Black GIs', p. 266).

5   Writing sixty years ago in 1962, Gabriel Marcel, the French Catholic philosopher, observed the tendency of the left to manipulate colonial history to suit its ideological prejudices, driven by a hidden passion: 'I consider the man of the left to be almost always someone who treats the past very casually and who, in particular, does not hesitate to manipulate it according to a number of preformed ideas. I find this extremely clear, for example, with regard to the problem of colonisation . . . What strikes me about the man of the left is a certain lack of reflection – with exceptions, of course. The great danger which threatens the man of the left is to succumb to the mirage of ideology. What I often discover in the man of the left is a kind of abstract thought which is in reality at the service of a passion that cannot be confessed' ('Je crois que l'homme de gauche est presque toujours quelqu'un qui traite le passé avec beaucoup de désinvolture et qui, en particulier, n'hésite pas à le manipuler suivant un certain nombre d'idées préformées. Je trouve cela extrêmement net par exemple pour le problème de la colonisation . . . Ce qui me frappe chez l'homme de gauche, c'est une certaine carence de la réflexion. Avec des exceptions, bien évidemment. Le grand danger qui menace l'homme de gauche, c'est de succomber au mirage de l'idéologie. Ce que je découvre souvent chez l'homme de gauche, c'est une sorte de pensée abstraite qui est en réalité au service d'une passion qui ne s'avoue pas') ('Qu'est-ce qu'un homme de droite?', *Arts* (1962): http://www.gabriel-marcel.com/articles&textes/homme_droite.php).

6   One example has been provided by Priyamvada Gopal, then reader in postcolonial and related literatures at the University of Cambridge, now promoted to professor: see Nigel Biggar, 'Vile Abuse Is Now Tolerated in Our Universities', *The Times*, 10 April 2018: https://www.thetimes.co.uk/article/vile-abuse-is-now-tolerated-in-our-universities-xqnbpl7ft (accessed 21 July 2021); Sumantra Maitra, '"If I Want to Hold Seminars on the Topic of Empire, I Will Do So Privately": An Interview with Nigel Biggar', *Quillette*, 7 June 2018: https://quillette.com/2018/06/07/want-hold-seminars-topic-empire-will-privately-interview-nigel-biggar/ (accessed 21 July 2021); Nigel Biggar, 'Cambridge and the Exclusion of Jordan Peterson', *TheArticle*, 2 April 2019: https://www.thearticle.com/cambridge-and-the-exclusion-of-jordan-peterson (accessed 21 July 2021); 'Cambridge Has Double Standards on Free Speech', *The Times*, 4 April 2019: https://www.thetimes.co.uk/article/cambridge-has-double-standards-on-free-

speech-7cl2d6qgr (accessed 21 July 2021); and 'The Naked Emperors of British Academia', *Standpoint*, 18 September 2019: https://standpointmag.co.uk/the-naked-emperors-of-british-academia/ (accessed 21 July 2021). Another example has been given by Richard Drayton, Rhodes professor of imperial history at King's College London in 'Biggar vs Little Britain: God, War, Union, Brexit and Empire in Twenty-First Century Conservative Ideology', in Stuart Ward and Astrid Rasch, eds, *Embers of Empire in Brexit Britain* (London: Bloomsbury, 2019): https://kclpure.kcl.ac.uk/portal/files/111209748/978135011 3800_CH14.pdf (accessed 21 July 2021). For my response, see Nigel Biggar, 'The Drayton Icon and Intellectual Vice', in *Quillette*, 27 August 2019: https://quillette.com/2019/08/27/the-drayton-icon-and-intellectual-vice/ (accessed 21 July 2021).

7   In his preface, Sartre is absolutely cynical about the gap between the French colonists' humanist ideals and their racist methods. '[O]ur humanism,' he wrote, '. . . was nothing but an ideology of lies, a perfect justification for pillage . . . the European has only been able to become a man through creating slaves and monsters . . . in the notion of the human race we found an abstract assumption of universality which served as cover for the most realistic practices . . . we had no mission at all' (Preface in Frantz Fanon, *The Wretched of the Earth*, trans. Constance Farrington [London: Penguin, 1967], p. 21). Sartre also waxed lyrical about the humanising effects of nationalist violence:

> by this mad fury, by this bitterness and spleen, by their ever-present desire to kill us . . . they [the native rebels] have become men . . . The native cures himself of colonial neurosis by thrusting out the settler through force of arms. When his rage boils over, he rediscovers his lost innocence and he comes to know himself in that he himself creates his self . . . The rebel's weapon is the proof of his humanity. For in the first days of the revolt you must kill: to shoot down a European is to kill two birds with one stone, to destroy an oppressor and the man he oppresses at the same time: there remain a dead man, and a free man . . . The child of violence, at every moment he draws from it his humanity. We were men at his expense, he makes himself man at ours . . . violence . . . can heal the wounds that it has inflicted (ibid., pp. 15, 18, 19, 20, 25).

8   Fanon, *Wretched of the Earth*, pp. 37, 39.
9   Ibid., pp. 171, 175.
10 Ibid., p. 76.
11 Ibid., pp. 66–7.
12 Ibid., p. 62.
13 Ibid., pp. 169, 190.
14 In Fanon's case, this authoritarianism acquired fascistic qualities. He shared Sartre's fascination with the cathartic power of revolutionary violence:

> Decolonization is the veritable creation of new men . . . 'The last shall be first and the first last'. Decolonization is the putting into practice of this sentence . . . this will only come to pass after a murderous and decisive

struggle . . . this narrow [colonial] world [can only be turned upside down by] absolute violence . . . The colonized man finds his freedom in and through violence . . . The poetry of [Aimé] Césaire takes on in this precise aspect of violence a prophetic significance. We may recall one of the most decisive pages of his tragedy where the Rebel (indeed!) explains his conduct: . . . 'I struck, and the blood spurted; that is the only baptism that I remember today' . . . For the native, life can only spring up again out of the rotting corpse of the settler (ibid., pp. 28, 29, 35, 68, 69, 73).

In the light of this almost aesthetic fascination with violence, and the preference for 'barbarous' vitality and irresponsibility over civilised reason and restraint, Egon Flaig was not being sensationalist when he described Fanon's anticolonialism as 'fascistoid' (Flaig, 'Faschistoider "Antikolonialismus" – Frantz Fanon', pp. 103, 131).

15 Graham Huggan, ed., *The Oxford Handbook of Postcolonial Studies* (Oxford: Oxford University Press, 2013), p. 1.

16 For example, literature furnished twenty-four of the forty-four contributors to the *Oxford Handbook*, history four, political science and anthropology four, and philosophy one.

17 Dane Kennedy concurs, cautioning that, despite its title, 'postcolonial theory', 'much of it is less engaged in developing a body of theory than in making gestures of obeisance to it' (*The Imperial History Wars: Debating the British Empire* [London: Bloomsbury, 2018], p. 9

18 Huggan, *Oxford Handbook of Postcolonial Studies*, p. 15.

19 Stephen Howe, 'Imperial Histories, Postcolonial Theories', in Huggan, *Oxford Handbook of Postcolonial Studies*, p. 163. Kennedy documents the generally hostile stance to post-colonial theory taken by contributors to the *Oxford History of the British Empire*, which was published in 1998–9 (*Imperial History Wars*, pp. 32, 36–7).

20 Bruckner, *Tyranny of Guilt*, pp. 34, 35.

21 R. W. Johnson, 'Orgy of Looting and Corruption Has Destroyed Mandela's Dream', *The Times*, 17 July 2021.

22 Bruckner, *Tyranny of Guilt*, pp. 100–1.

23 See Chapter 8, pp. 242–52.

24 This is the option that Bruckner fears for Europe: 'the duty to repent forbids the Western bloc, which is eternally guilty, to judge or combat other systems, other states, other religions. Our past crimes command us to keep our mouths closed . . . Reserve and neutrality will redeem us. No longer participating, no longer getting involved in the affairs of our time, except perhaps by approving of those whom we formerly oppressed. In this way, two different Wests will be defined: the good one, that of the old Europe that withdraws and keeps quiet, and the bad one, that of the United States that intervenes and meddles in everything . . . Europe is in danger of becoming the Pontius Pilate of nations . . . On the whole, the Old World prefers guilt to responsibility' (Bruckner, *Tyranny of Guilt*, pp. 3, 90, 98).

25 For one of a myriad of examples, see the online notice posted by the Centre

for Global History at the University of Oxford, which declares its boycott of my 'Ethics and Empire' project: https://global.history.ox.ac.uk/article/empires-and-colonialism#/ (accessed 29 July 2021)

26 Arguing in contradiction of the belief that Britain had betrayed the Arabs during the First World War, which had infected the British Foreign Office, Elie Kedourie commented: 'No doubt, great Powers do commit great crimes, but a great Power is not always and necessarily in the wrong; and the canker of imaginary guilt even the greatest Power can ill withstand' (*Into the Anglo-Arab Labyrinth*, p. 220).

Bibliography

Achebe, Chinua. 'Africa's Tarnished Name' (1998). In *The Education of a British-Protected Child.*

_____. 'My Dad and Me' (1996). In *The Education of a British-Protected Child.*

_____. 'Teaching *Things Fall Apart*' (1991). In *The Education of a British-Protected Child.*

_____. 'The Education of a British-Protected Child' (1993). In *The Education of a British-Protected Child.*

_____. *The Education of a British-Protected Child: Essays.* London: Penguin, 2009.

_____. *There Was a Country: A Personal History of Biafra.* New York: Penguin, 2012.

Adebajo, Adekeye. 'Mandela and Rhodes, Africa's Saint and Sinner'. *Independent Online*, 26 July 2011.

_____. 'What Rhodes Said'. In *Sunday Telegraph*, 16 May 2021.

_____. 'Why Price Is Wrong Over Rhodes'. In *South African Sunday Independent*, 29 March 2015.

_____. 'Worse than the Rest'. In *Times Literary Supplement*, 28 July 2006.

Al Jazeera. 'Britain's Unequal Troop Commemorations Due to "Pervasive Racism"', 22 April 2021: https://www.aljazeera.com/news/2021/4/22/britains-unequal-troop-commemorations-due-to-pervasive-racism

Al-Sayyid, Afaf Lutfi. *Egypt and Cromer: A Study in Anglo-Egyptian Relations.* London: John Murray, 1968.

Albertini, R. von with Albert Wirz. *European Colonial Rule, 1880–1940: The Impact of the West on India, Southeast Asia, and Africa.* Trans. John G. Williamson. Oxford: Clio, 1982.

Allawi, Ali A. *Faisal I of Iraq.* New Haven: Yale, 2014.

Allen, Nick. 'No. 10 Condemns Toppling of Queen Elizabeth II and Victoria Statues in Canada'. In *Daily Telegraph*, 2 July 2021: https://www.telegraph.co.uk/world-news/2021/07/02/queen-elizabeth-ii-victoria-statues-ripped-protesters-canada/.

Anderson, David. *Histories of the Hanged: The Dirty War in Kenya and the End of Empire.* New York: W. W. Norton, 2005.

_____. 'Women Missionaries and Colonial Silences in Kenya's Female "Circumcision" Controversy, 1906–1930'. In *English Historical Review*, CXXXIII, no. 565 (December 2018).

Anene, J. C. *Southern Nigeria in Transition, 1885–1906*. Cambridge: Cambridge University Press, 1966.

Anstey, Roger. 'Capitalism and Slavery: A Critique'. In *Economic History Review*, New Series, 21/2 (August 1968).

_____. *The Atlantic Slave Trade and British Abolition, 1760–1810*. London: Macmillan, 1975.

Arnold, David. 'Death and the Modern Empire: The 1918–19 Influenza Epidemic in India'. In *Transactions of the Royal Historical Society*, 29 (2019).

Askew, David. 'New Research on the Nanking Incident'. In *Asia-Pacific Journal*, 2/7 (13 July 2004).

Atkinson, Alan. 'Conquest'. In Schreuder and Ward, *Australia's Empire*.

Attwood, Bain. *Empire and the Making of Native Title: Sovereignty, Property, and Indigenous People*. Cambridge: Cambridge University Press, 2020.

_____. 'Old News from a Tabloid Historian'. In *The Australian*, 6 January 2003.

_____. *Telling the Truth about Aboriginal History*. Crows Nest, NSW: Allen and Unwin, 2005.

_____ and S. G. Foster, eds. *Frontier Conflict: The Australian Experience*. Canberra: National Museum of Australia, 2003.

Austen, Ian. '"Horrible History": Mass Grave of Indigenous Children Reported in Canada'. In *New York Times*, 29 May 2021: https://www.nytimes. com/2021/05/28/world/canada/kamloops-mass-grave-residential-schools.html

Austin, Gareth. 'The Economics of Colonialism in Africa'. In Monga and Lin, *The Oxford Handbook of Africa and Economics*.

Baba, of Karo. *Baba of Karo: A Woman of the Muslim Hausa*. Transcribed and trans. Mary F. Smith. London: Faber & Faber, 1965.

Bacon, R. H. *Benin: The City of Blood*. London: Edward Arnold, 1897.

Baines, Dudley. *Migration in a Mature Economy: Emigration and Internal Migration in England and Wales, 1861–1900*. Cambridge: Cambridge University Press, 1985.

Balachandran, G. *India and the World Economy, 1850–1950*. Delhi: Oxford University Press, 2003.

Barr, James. *A Line in the Sand: Britain, France, and the Struggle that Shaped the Middle East*. London: Simon & Schuster UK, 2011.

BBC. 'Commonwealth War Graves: PM "Deeply Troubled" Over Racism', 22 April 2021: https://www.bbc.co.uk/news/uk-56840131

_____. 'Golden Temple Attack: UK Advised India But Impact "Limited"', 7 June 2014: https://www.bbc.co.uk/news/uk-26027631

Beckles, Hilary McD. *Britain's Black Debt: Reparations for Caribbean Slavery and Native Genocide*. Kingston, Jamaica: University of West Indies Press, 2013.

Beevor, Antony. *D-Day: The Battle for Normandy*. London: Viking, 2009.

Behrendt, Larissa. 'The Doctrine of Discovery in Australia'. In Miller et al., *Discovering Indigenous Lands*.

Behrendt, Stephen D. 'The Transatlantic Slave Trade'. In Paquette and Smith, *Oxford Handbook of Slavery in the Americas*.

Beinart, William. 'Appendix A: Historical Appendix to the Report of the Oriel College Commission on the Rhodes Statue and Diversity within the College'. In Oriel College, *Report of a Commission of Inquiry Established by Oriel College, Oxford into Issues Associated with Memorials to Cecil Rhodes*. Oxford: Oriel College, 2021.

Belich, James. *The New Zealand Wars and the Victorian Interpretation of Racial Conflict*. Auckland: Auckland University Press, 2015.

_____. *Replenishing the Earth: The Settler Revolution and the Rise of the Anglo-World, 1783–1939*. Oxford: Oxford University Press, 2008.

Bell-Fialkoff, A. *Ethnic Cleansing*. New York: St Martin's, 1996.

Bennett, Huw. 'Erskine, Sir George Watkin Eben James (1899–1965)'. In *Oxford Dictionary of National Biography*: https://www.oxforddnb.com/view/10.1093/ref:odnb/9780198614128.001.0001/odnb-9780198614128-e-97289.

_____. *Fighting the Mau Mau: The British Army and Counter-Insurgency in the Kenya Emergency*. Cambridge: Cambridge University Press, 2013.

_____, Michael Finch, Andrei Mamolea and David Morgan-Owen. 'Studying Mars and Clio: Or How Not to Write about the Ethics of Military Conduct and Military History'. In *History Workshop Journal*, 88 (Autumn 2019).

Bennett, Michael J. 'Smallpox and Cowpox under the Southern Cross: The Smallpox Epidemic of 1789 and the Advent of Vaccination in Colonial Australia'. In *Bulletin of the History of Medicine*, 83/1 (Spring 2009).

Berman, B. and J. Lonsdale. *Unhappy Valley: Conflict in Kenya and Africa*. 2 vols. Vol. 1: 'State and Class'. London: James Currey, 1992.

Bethell, Leslie. *The Abolition of the Brazilian Slave Trade: Britain, Brazil and the Slave Trade Question, 1807–1869*. Cambridge: Cambridge University Press, 1979.

Bew, John. *Realpolitik: A History*. New York: Oxford University Press, 2016.

_____. 'The Real Origins of Realpolitik'. In *The National Interest*, 130 (March/April 2014).

Bew, Paul. 'A Case of Compassion Fatigue'. In *Spectator*, 13 March 1999.

_____. *Ireland: The Politics of Enmity, 1789–2006*. Oxford: Oxford University Press, 2007.

Bickers, Robert. *Out of China: How the Chinese Ended the Era of Western Domination*. London: Allen Lane, 2017.

_____. *The Scramble for China: Foreign Devils in the Qing Empire, 1832–1914*. London: Allen Lane, 2011.

Biggar, Nigel. 'A Critical Response to William Beinart, "Appendix A: Historical Appendix to the Report of the Oriel College Commission on the Rhodes Statue and Diversity within the College", in *Oriel College, Report of a Commission of*

Inquiry Established by Oriel College, Oxford into Issues Associated with Memorials to Cecil Rhodes (Oxford: Oriel College, 2021)': https://www.mcdonaldcentre.org.uk/sites/default/files/content/files/beinart_appendix_a_response_by_nigel_biggar.pdf; https://historyreclaimed.co.uk/cecil-rhodes-a-critical-response-to-professor-william-beinart/.

————. 'A Response to Adekeye Adebajo', unpublished.

————. 'Cambridge and the Exclusion of Jordan Peterson'. In *TheArticle*, 2 April 2019: https://www.thearticle.com/cambridge-and-the-exclusion-of-jordan-peterson

————. 'Cambridge Has Double Standards on Free Speech'. In *The Times*, 4 April 2019: https://www.thetimes.co.uk/article/cambridge-has-double-standards-on-free-speech-7cl2d6qgr

————. 'Cards on the Table: A Flawed, Candid History of Britain and the Great War'. In *Australian Book Review*, March 2015.

————. 'Don't Feel Guilty About Our Colonial History'. In *The Times*, 30 November 2017.

————. 'Here's My Reply to Those Who Condemn My Project on Ethics and Empire'. In *The Times*, 23 December 2017: https://www.thetimes.co.uk/article/heres-my-reply-to-those-who-condemn-my-project-on-ethics-and-empire-cw5f2z80x

————. *In Defence of War*. Oxford: Oxford University Press, 2013.

————. 'Message to Students: Rhodes Was No Racist'. In *The Times*, 22 December 2015.

————. 'Proportionality: Lessons from the Somme'. In *Soundings*, 101/3 (2018).

————. 'Rhodes, Race, and the Abuse of History'. In *Standpoint*, March 2016.

————. 'The Drayton Icon and Intellectual Vice'. In *Quillette*, 27 August 2019: https://quillette.com/2019/08/27/the-drayton-icon-and-intellectual-vice/

————. 'The Naked Emperors of British Academia'. In *Standpoint*, 18 September 2019: https://standpointmag.co.uk/the-naked-emperors-of-british-academia/

————. 'Vile Abuse Is Now Tolerated in Our Universities'. In *The Times*, 10 April 2018: https://www.thetimes.co.uk/article/vile-abuse-is-now-tolerated-in-our-universities-xqnbpl7ft

————. 'Was Britain Right to Go to War in 1914?'. In *Standpoint*, 27 August 2013.

————. *What's Wrong with Rights?* Oxford: Oxford University Press, 2020.

————. 'Why the Establishment of the Church of England is Good for a Liberal Society'. In *The Established Church: Past, Present and Future*. Mark Chapman, Judith Maltby and William Whyte, eds. London: T. & T. Clark, 2011.

Binnema, Theodore and Kevin Hutchings. 'The Emigrant and the Noble Savage: Sir Francis Bond Head's Romantic Approach to Aboriginal Policy in Upper Canada, 1836–1838'. In *Journal of Canadian Studies*, 39/1 (Winter 2005).

Birrell, Augustine. 'On Nationality' (1890). In Birrell, *Self-Selected Essays: A Second Series*. London: Thomas Nelson, 1916.

Black, Jeremy. *Slavery: A New Global History*. London: Constable and Robinson, 2011.

Blackburn, Robin. *The Making of New World Slavery: From the Baroque to the Modern, 1492–1800*. London: Verso, 1997.

Blacker, John. 'The Demography of Mau Mau: Fertility and Mortality in the 1950s: A Demographer's Viewpoint'. In *African Affairs*, 106 (April 2007).

Blainey, Geoffrey. 'The Fabrication of Aboriginal History, Volume 1: Book Review'. In *New Criterion*, 21/8 (April 2003).

————. *Triumph of the Nomads: A History of Ancient Australia*. London: Macmillan, 1975.

Boehmer, Elleke and Tom Holland, 'Are Empires Always Bad?', *Prospect* (December 2020).

Bogdanor, Vernon. *The Strange Survival of Liberal Britain: Politics and Power before the First World War*. Hull: Biteback, 2022.

Boisragon, Alan. *The Benin Massacre*. London: Methuen, 1897.

Bowler, Gerry. 'Is the Final Report of the TRC Good History?' In Clifton and DeWolf, *From Truth Comes Reconciliation: An Assessment of the Truth and Reconciliation Report*.

Boyce, James. 'Fantasy Island', in Manne, *Whitewash*.

Boyes, Roger. 'Germany Is Falling Out of Love with America', *The Times*, 27 January 2021.

Braidwood, S. J. *Black Poor and White Philanthropists: London Blacks and the Foundation of the Sierra Leone Settlement, 1786–1791*. Liverpool: Liverpool University Press, 1994.

Branch, Daniel. *Defeating Mau Mau, Creating Kenya: Counterinsurgency, Civil War, and Decolonization*. Cambridge: Cambridge University Press, 2009.

Brennan, Lance. 'Government Famine Relief in Bengal, 1943'. In *Journal of Asian Studies*, 47/3 (August 1988).

Bridge, Mark. 'Apology Over Non-white War Dead Left Unnamed'. In *The Times*, 22 April 2021.

Briggs, Asa. *The Age of Improvement, 1783–1867*. London: Longmans, 1960, 2000.

Briggs, Madeline. 'Misinformation in the Rhodes Campaign'. In *The Poor Print* (Oriel College's Student Newspaper), 11 January 2016: https://thepoorprint. com/2016/01/22/misinformation-in-the-rhodes-campagin/) [*sic*].

British Parliamentary Papers: Colonies: Australia. Vol. 4: 'Correspondence and Papers Relating to the Government and Affairs of the Australian Colonies, 1830–36'. Shannon: Irish University Press, 1970.

Brown, Jonathan A. C. *Slavery and Islam*. London: Oneworld Academic, 2019.

Brown, Judith M. and Wm. Roger Louis, eds. *The Oxford History of the British Empire*. 5 vols. Vol. IV: 'The Twentieth Century'. Oxford: Oxford University Press, 1999.

Bruckner, Pascal. *The Tyranny of Guilt: An Essay on Western Masochism*. Trans. Steven Rendall. Princeton, NJ: Princeton University Press, 2010.

Buckner, Phillip, ed. *Canada and the British Empire*. Oxford History of the British Empire Companion Series. Oxford: Oxford University Press, 2010.

Bundy, Colin. *The Rise and Fall of the South African Peasantry*. 2nd edn. Cape Town and Johannesburg: David Philip, 1988.

Burk, Kathleen. *The Lion and the Eagle: The Interaction of the British and American Empires, 1783–1972*. London: Bloomsbury, 2018.

Burke, Edmund. 'Impeachment of Warren Hastings'. In *Writings and Speeches*, Vol. VI: 'The Launching of the Hastings Impeachment, 1786–1788', ed. P. J. Marshall (1991).

————. 'Speech on Fox's Bill, 1 December 1784'. In *Writings and Speeches*, Vol. V: 'India: Madras and Bengal, 1774–1785', ed. P. J. Marshall (1981).

————. *Writings and Speeches of Edmund Burke*. Ed. Paul Langford et al. 9 vols. Oxford: Clarendon Press, 1981–2015).

Burke, Roland. *Decolonization and the Evolution of International Human Rights*. Philadelphia: University of Pennsylvania Press, 2010.

Burnard, Trevor. 'British West Indies and Bermuda'. In Paquette and Smith, *Oxford Handbook of Slavery in the Americas*.

Burns, Alan. *Colonialism Before and After*. Unpublished, *c*.1973.

Butlin, Noel. *Our Original Aggression*. Sydney: Allen & Unwin, 1983.

Butt, Daniel. 'Repairing Historical Wrongs and the End of Empire'. In *Social and Legal Studies*, 21/2 (2012).

Buxton, Thomas Fowell. *The African Slave Trade and Its Remedy*. London: John Murray, 1839.

Cain, P. J. 'Character, "Ordered Liberty" and the Mission to Civilise: British Moral Justification of Empire, 1870–1914', special issue on 'Empire and Humanitarianism', *Journal of Imperial and Commonwealth History*, 40/5 (December 2012).

————. 'Economics and Empire: The Metropolitan Context'. In Porter, *The Oxford History of the British Empire*, Vol. III.

———— and A. G. Hopkins. *British Imperialism, 1688–2015*. 3rd edn. London: Routledge, 2016.

Cairns, Alan C. *Citizens Plus. Aboriginal Peoples and the Canadian State*. Vancouver: University of British Columbia Press, 2000.

Calderisi, Robert. *Cecil Rhodes and Other Statues: Dealing Plainly with the Past*. Columbus, Ohio: Gatekeeper Press, 2021.

Cambridge, University of. 'Applications, Offers & Acceptances by UCAS Apply Centre 2019': https://www.undergraduate.study.cam.ac.uk/sites/www.undergraduate. study.cam.ac.uk/files/publications/undergraduate_admissions_by_apply_ centre_2019_cycle.pdf.

Campbell, Judy. *Invisible Invaders: Smallpox and other Diseases in Aboriginal Australia, 1780–1880*. Melbourne: Melbourne University Press, 2002.

Campbell, Mavis. C. *The Maroons of Jamaica, 1655-1796.* Granby, Mass.: Bergin and Garvey, 1988.

Canny, Nicholas, ed. *The Oxford History of the British Empire.* 5 vols. Vol. I: 'The Origins of Empire'. Oxford: Oxford University Press, 1998.

Carroll, Rory. 'New Book Reopens Old Arguments about Slave Raids on Europe'. In *Guardian*, 11 March 2004: https://www.theguardian.com/uk/2004/mar/11/highereducation.books

Carter, Sarah. 'Aboriginal People of Canada and the British Empire'. In Buckner, *Canada and the British Empire.*

Cassels, Nancy Gardner. *Social Legislation of the East India Company: Public Justice versus Public Instruction.* New Delhi: SAGE Publications India, 2010.

Cave, Basil S. 'The End of Slavery in Zanzibar and British East Africa'. In *Journal of the Royal African Society*, 9/33 (October 1909).

Chamberlain, Joseph. 'Mr. Chamberlain on Trade'. In *The Times*, 1 April 1895.

Chang, Jung and Jon Halliday. *Mao: The Unknown Story.* London: Jonathan Cape, 2005.

Chaudhuri, Nirad C. *The Autobiography of an Unknown Indian.* London: Picador, 1999.

_____. *Thy Hand, Great Anarch! India 1921-1952.* London: Chatto & Windus, 1987.

Clayton, Anthony. 'Baring, (Charles) Evelyn, first Baron Howick of Glendale'. In *Oxford Dictionary of National Biography* (2006): https://www.oxforddnb.com/view/10.1093/ref:odnb/9780198614128.001.0001/odnb-9780198614128-e-30789.

Clifton, Rodney A; and Mark DeWolf, eds. *From Truth Comes Reconciliation: An Assessment of the Truth and Reconciliation Report.* Winnipeg: Frontier Centre for Public Policy, 2021.

Clough, Marshall S. *Mau Mau Memoirs: History, Memory and Politics.* Boulder, CO: Lynne Rienner, 1997.

Coates, A. J. *The Ethics of War.* Manchester: Manchester University Press, 1997.

Collett, Nigel. 'A Muse Abused: The Politicizing of the Amritsar Massacre'. In *Asian Review of Books*, 17 July 2012: http://asianreviewofbooks.com/content/archived-article/?articleID=1310).

_____. *The Butcher of Amritsar: General Reginald Dyer.* London: Hambledon & London, 2005.

Collier, Paul. *Exodus: Immigration and Multiculturalism in the 21st Century.* London: Allen Lane, 2013.

_____. *Wars, Guns, and Votes: Democracy in Dangerous Places.* London: Vintage, 2010.

Collins, Robert O. and Francis M. Deng, eds. *The British in the Sudan, 1898-1956.* London: Macmillan, 1984.

Commission on Race and Ethnic Disparities, *The Report.* London: HMSO, 2021.

Commonwealth War Graves Commission, *Report of the Special Committee to*

Review Historical Inequalities in Commemoration. Maidenhead: CWGC, 2021.

Connor, John. 'British Frontier Warfare Logistics and the "Black Line", Van Diemen's Land (Tasmania), 1830'. In *War in History*, 9/2 (2002).

Conradi, Peter J. *A Very English Hero: The Making of Frank Thompson*. London: Bloomsbury, 2012.

Copy of Treaty No. 6 between Her Majesty the Queen and the Plain and Wood Cree Indians and Other Tribes of Indians. Ottawa: Indigenous and Northern Affairs Canada, 1964: http://www.trcm.ca/wp-content/uploads/PDFsTreaties/Treaty%206%20Text%20and%20Adhesions.pdf.

Crace, John. 'The Empire Strikes Back', *Guardian Education*, 4 January 2003: https://www.theguardian.com/education/2003/jan/14/highereducation.news.

Crafford, F. S. *Jan Smuts: A Biography*. New York: Doubleday, 1943.

Craton, Michael. *Testing the Chains: Resistance to Slavery in the British West Indies*. Ithaca, NY: Cornell University Press, 1982.

Cromer, Earl of. *Political and Literary Essays, 1908–1913*. London: Macmillan, 1913.

_____. *Modern Egypt*. 2 vols. London: Macmillan, 1908.

_____. 'The Government of Subject Races'. In Cromer, *Political and Literary Essays*.

Crossman, Virginia. *Politics, Law and Order in Nineteenth-century Ireland*. Dublin: Gill and Macmillan, 1996.

Crowcroft, Barnaby. 'Bombastic Lecture on the Evil Empire'. In *The Critic*, June 2022.

Curnow, Kathy. 'The Art of Fasting: Benin's Ague Ceremony'. In *African Arts*, 30/4 (Autumn 1997).

Curthoys, Ann. 'Indigenous Subjects'. In Schreuder and Ward, *Australia's Empire*.

_____. 'Raphaël Lemkin's "Tasmania": An Introduction'. In Moses and Stone, *Colonialism and Genocide*.

Curtin, Philip D. *The Atlantic Slave Trade: A Census*. Madison: University of Wisconsin Press, 1969.

Dalrymple, William. 'Robert Clive Was a Vicious Asset-stripper. His Statue Has No Place in Whitehall', *Guardian*, 11 June 2020

_____. *The Anarchy: The Relentless Rise of the East India Company*. London: Bloomsbury, 2019.

_____. *White Mughals: Love and Betrayal in Eighteenth-century India*. London: Flamingo, 2003.

Darwin, John. *After Tamerlane: The Global History of Empire since 1405*. London: Allen Lane, 2007.

_____. 'Imperial History by the Book: A Roundtable on John Darwin's *The Empire Project*: Reply'. In *Journal of British Studies*, 54/4 (Oct. 2015).

_____. 'Lowering the Flag. How the British Justified Imperial Violence to Themselves'. In *Times Literary Supplement*, No. 6211 (15 April 2022).

_____. *Unfinished Empire: The Global Expansion of Britain*. London: Allen Lane, 2012.

Daschuk, James. *Clearing the Plains: Disease, Politics of Starvation, and the Loss of Aboriginal Life*. Regina: University of Regina Press, 2013.

_____. 'When Canada Used Hunger to Clear the West', [Toronto] *Globe and Mail*, 19 July 2013.

David, Saul. *The Indian Mutiny 1857*. London: Viking, 2002.

_____. *Zulu: The Heroism and Tragedy of the Zulu War of 1879*. London: Penguin, 2004.

Davis, David Brion. 'Foreword'. In Drescher, *Econocide*.

Davis, Lance and Robert Huttenback. *Mammon and the Pursuit of Empire: The Political Economy of British Imperialism, 1860–1912*. Cambridge: Cambridge University Press, 1986.

Davis, Robert C. *Christian Slaves, Muslim Masters: White Slavery in the Mediterranean, the Barbary Coast and Italy, 1500–1800*. London: Palgrave Macmillan, 2003.

Deng, Francis M. 'In the Eyes of the Ruled'. In Collins and Deng, eds, *The British in the Sudan*.

Devine, T. M. *The Scottish Clearances: A History of the Dispossessed 1600–1900*. London: Allen Lane, 2018.

Diamond, Jared. *Guns, Germs, and Steel: A Short History of Everybody for the Last 13,000 Years*. London: Vintage, 1998.

Dikötter, Frank. *Mao's Great Famine: The History of China's Most Devastating Catastrophe, 1958–62*. London: Bloomsbury, 2010.

_____, Lars Laamann and Xun Zhou. 'China, British Imperialism, and the Myth of the "Opium Plague"'. In Mills and Barton, *Drugs and Empires*.

Dilley, A. R. 'The Economics of Empire'. In Stockwell, *The British Empire*.

Dimbleby, Jonathan. *The Last Governor: Chris Patten and the Handover of Hong Kong*. Barnsley: Pen & Sword, 1997, 2018.

Donald, Leland. *Aboriginal Slavery on the Northwest Coast of North America*. Berkeley and Los Angeles: University of California Press, 1997.

Donaldson, Dave. 'Railroads of the Raj: Estimating the Impact of Transportation Infrastructure'. In *American Economic Review*, 108/4–5 (2018).

Dooley, Terence. *The Plight of Monaghan Protestants, 1912–1926*. Maynooth Studies in Irish Local History. Dublin: Irish Academic Press, 2000.

Douglas, R. M. 'Did Britain Use Chemical Weapons in Mandatory Iraq?'. In *Journal of Modern History*, 81/4 (2009).

Douglas-Home, Charles. *Evelyn Baring: The Last Proconsul*. London: Collins, 1978.

Dowling, Peter. *Fatal Contact: How Epidemics Nearly Wiped Out Australia's First Peoples*. Clayton, Victoria: Monash University Publishing, 2021.

Doyle, Michael W. *Empires*. Ithaca: Cornell University Press, 1986.

Drayton, Richard. 'Biggar vs Little Britain: God, War, Union, Brexit and Empire in Twenty-First Century Conservative Ideology'. In Stuart Ward and Astrid Rasch, eds, *Embers of Empire in Brexit Britain*. London: Bloomsbury, 2019.

Drescher, Seymour. *Econocide: British Slavery in the Era of Abolition*. 2nd edn. Chapel Hill, NC: University of North Carolina Press, 2010.

Drèze, Jean and Amartya Sen. *The Political Economy of Hunger*. Vol. 1: 'Entitlement and Well-being'. Oxford: Oxford University Press, 1991.

Dubow, Saul. *Apartheid, 1948–1994*. Oxford: Oxford University Press, 2014.

_____. 'Britain's Inglorious Tactics during the Boer War'. In *Daily Telegraph*, 12 August 2021.

Dudley Edwards, R. and T. Desmond Williams, eds. *The Great Famine*. Dublin: Browne and Nolan, 1956.

Durham Mining Museum. 'Statistics: Table 1: Fatal Accidents at all Mines from 1873 to 1953, Distinguishing the Principal Causes': http://www.dmm.org.uk/stats/index.htm

Dutil, Patrice. 'Not Guilty: Sir John A. Macdonald and the Genocide Fetish'. In *Dorchester Review*, 10/2 (Autumn-Winter 2020).

_____ and Roger Hall, eds. *Macdonald at 200: New Reflections and Legacies*. Toronto: Dundurn, 2014.

Earle, Peter. *Corsairs of Malta and Barbary*. London: Sidgwick & Jackson, 1970.

Edemariam, Aida. 'Brendan Gormley: "I Wasn't Very Charitable"'. In *Guardian*, 23 January 2020.

Edwards, Eric. 'Object Biographies'. In *Rethinking Pitt-Rivers*: http://web.prm.ox.ac.uk/rpr/index.php/objectbiographies/78-manilla/

Ehrlich, Joshua. 'Review Article: Anxiety, Chaos, and the Raj'. In *Historical Journal*, 63/3 (June 2020).

Elkins, Caroline. *Imperial Reckoning: The Untold Story of Britain's Gulag in Kenya*. New York: Henry Holt & Co., 2005.

_____. *Legacy of Violence: A History of the British Empire*. New York: Alfred A. Knopf, 2022.

Elliott, W. A. *Gold from the Quartz*. London Missionary Society, 1910.

El-Obaid, El-Obaid Ahmed; and Kwadwo Appiagyei-Atua. 'Human Rights in Africa – a New Perspective on Linking the Past to the Present'. In *McGill Law Journal*, 41 (1996).

Eltis, David. *Economic Growth and the Ending of the Transatlantic Slave Trade*. Oxford: Oxford University Press, 1987.

Eltis, David and Stanley L. Engerman. 'The Importance of Slavery and the Slave Trade to Industrializing Britain'. In *Journal of Economic History*, 60/1 (March 2000).

Engelstad, Diane and John Bird, eds. *Nation to Nation: Aboriginal Sovereignty and the Future of Canada*. Concord, Ontario: Anansi, 1992.

English, Barbara. 'The Kanpur Massacres in India in the Revolt of 1857'. In *Past and Present*, 142 (Feb, 1994).

Enterline, Philip E. 'Mortality Rates Among Coal Miners'. In *American Journal of Public Health*, 54/5 (May 1964).

Equiano, Olaudah. *The Interesting Narrative and Other Writings*. Ed. Vincent Carretta. Revised edn. New York: Penguin, 2003.

Erasmus, Georges and Joe Sanders. 'Canadian History: An Aboriginal Perspective'. In Engelstad and Bird, *Nation to Nation*.

Etherington, Norman. 'African Economic Experiments in Colonial Natal, 1845–1880'. In Guest and Sellars, *Enterprise and Exploitation in a Victorian Colony*.

European Union Agency for Fundamental Rights. *Being Black in the EU: Summary of the Second European Union Minorities and Discrimination Survey*. Vienna: EUAFR, 2019.

Eybers, G. W., ed. *Select Constitutional Documents Illustrating South African History, 1795–1910*. London: Routledge, 1918.

Ezenwa-Ohaeto. *Chinua Achebe: A Biography*. Oxford: James Currey, 1997.

Fage, J. D. 'African Societies and the Atlantic Slave Trade'. In *Past and Present*, CXXV (1989).

Fagg, William. 'Le pillage qui n'eut jamais lieu/Benin: The Sack that Never Was'. In *Art Tribal*, special issue: 'Art Royal du Benin'. Geneva: Musée Barbier-Mueller, 1992.

Fanon, Frantz. *The Wretched of the Earth*. Preface by Jean-Paul Sartre. Trans. Constance Farrington. London: Penguin, 1967.

Farwell, Byron. *The Great Boer War*. London: Allen Lane, 1977.

Faught, Brad. *Into Africa: The Imperial Life of Margery Perham*. London: I. B. Tauris, 2012.

Feinstein, C. H. 'Capital Accumulation and the Industrial Revolution'. In Floud and McCloskey, *Economic History of Britain since 1700*.

Fenn, Elizabeth A. 'Biological Warfare in Eighteenth-Century North America: Beyond Jeffrey Amherst'. In *Journal of American History*, 86/4 (March 2000).

Fenner, F. and D. A. Henderson, I. Arita, Z. Jesek and I. D. Ladnyi. *Smallpox and Its Eradication*. Geneva: World Health Organization, 1988.

Ferguson, Niall. 'British Imperialism Revised: The Costs and Benefits of "Anglobalization"'. Development Research Institute Working Paper Series, No. 2, April 2003. New York: New York University, 2003.

_____. *Empire: How Britain Made the Modern World*. London: Allen Lane, 2003.

_____ and Moritz Schularick. 'The Empire Effect: The Determinants of Country Risk in the First Age of Globalization, 1880–1913'. In *Journal of Economic History*, 66/2 (June 2006).

Fieldhouse, D. K. *The West and the Third World*. Oxford: Blackwell, 1999.

Findlay, Ronald and Kevin H. O'Rourke. *Power and Plenty: Trade, War, and the World Economy in the Second Millennium*. Princeton: Princeton University Press, 2007.

Finzsch, Norbert. '"It Is Scarcely Possible to Conceive that Human Beings Could Be So Hideous and Loathsome": Discourses of Genocide in Eighteenth- and Nineteenth-century America and Australia'. In Moses and Stone, *Colonialism and Genocide*.

FitzGerald, Desmond. *Desmond's Rising: Memoirs 1913 to Easter 1916.* Revised edn. Dublin: Liberties Press, 2006.

Flaig, Egon. 'Faschistoider "Antikolonialismus" – Frantz Fanon'. In *Die Niederlage der politischen Vernunft.* Springe: Zu Klampen Verlag, 2017.

Flanagan, Thomas (Tom). *First Nations? Second Thoughts.* 2nd edn. Montreal and Kingston: Queen's University Press, 2008.

_____. *Riel and the Rebellion: 1885 Reconsidered.* 2nd edn. Toronto: University of Toronto Press, 2000.

_____. 'The Truth About Canada's Indian Graves: The Indigenous Industry Is Thriving Off Fake News', *UnHerd*, 29 June 2022: https://unherd.com/2022/06/the-truth-about-canadas-indian-graves/.

Flint, J. *Nigeria and Ghana.* Englewood Cliffs, NJ: Prentice-Hall, 1966.

Flood, Josephine. *The Original Australians: Story of the Aboriginal People.* Crows Nest, NSW: Allen & Unwin, 2006.

Floud, Roderick and Donald McCloskey, eds. *The Economic History of Britain since 1700.* 1st edn. 2 vols. Cambridge: Cambridge University Press, 1981.

Foreign and Commonwealth Office. *Slavery in Diplomacy: The Foreign Office and the Suppression of the Transatlantic Slave Trade.* History Note No. 17. London: Foreign and Commonwealth Office, 2007: https://issuu.com/fcohistorians/docs/history_notes_cover_hphn_17

Foreign, Commonwealth and Development Office. *Statistics on International Development: Final UK Aid Spend 2019.* London: FCDO, September 2020.

Foster, Roy. *Modern Ireland, 1600–1972.* London: Penguin, 1988.

_____. *Vivid Faces: The Revolutionary Generation in Ireland, 1890–1923.* London: Allen Lane, 2014.

Free West Media. 'Historian: "Africans Must Be Condemned for the Slave Trade"'. Interview with Abiola Félix Iroko on Benin Web TV. *Free West Media*, 28 July 2020: https://freewestmedia.com/2020/07/28/historian-africans-must-be-condemned-for-the-slave-trade/

French, David. *The British Way in Counter-Insurgency, 1945–1967.* Oxford: Oxford University Press, 2011.

Fuglestad, Finn. *Slave Traders by Invitation: West Africa's Slave Coast in the Precolonial Era.* London: Hurst, 2018.

Gallwey, Henry L. 'Journeys in the Benin Country, West Africa'. In *Geographical Journal* 1/2 (February 1893).

_____. 'Nigeria in the "Nineties"'. In *Journal of the Royal African Society*, 29/115 (April 1930).

Gandhi, M. K. *My Autobiography or The Story of My Experiments with Truth.* London: Penguin, 2001.

Gann, L. H. and Peter Duignan. *Burden of Empire: An Appraisal of Western Colonialism in Africa South of the Sahara.* London: Pall Mall, 1968.

Garvin, Tom. *Nationalist Revolutionaries in Ireland, 1858–1928.* Dublin: Gill and Macmillan, 1987.

Gascoigne, John with Patricia Curthoys. *The Enlightenment and the Origins of European Australia.* Cambridge: Cambridge University Press, 2002.

Gernet, Alexander von. *Oral Narratives and Aboriginal Pasts: An Interdisciplinary Review of the Literature on Oral Traditions and Oral Histories.* Ottawa: Research and Analysis Directorate, Indian and Northern Affairs Canada, 1996.

Gilley, Bruce. 'A History of Colonialism That's More Angry than Accurate'. In *Washington Examiner*, 24 February 2022: https://www.washingtonexaminer.com/opinion/a-history-of-colonialism-thats-more-angry-than-accurate

_____. 'An Academic Responds to his Cancellers'. In *American Conservative*, 9 October 2020: An Academic Responds to his Cancellers.pdf (pdx.edu).

_____. 'Chinua Achebe on the Positive Legacies of Colonialism'. In *African Affairs*, 115/461 (October 2016).

_____. 'How the Hate Mob Tried to Silence Me', *Standpoint*, December 2017/ January 2018: How the hate mob tried to silence me (pdx.edu).

_____. 'The Case for Colonialism'. In *Third World Quarterly* (September 2017): http://www.web.pdx.edu/~gilleyb/2_The%20case%20for%20colonialism_at2Oct2017.pdf.

_____. 'The Case for Colonialism: A Response to My Critics'. In *Academic Questions*, Spring 2022: https://www.nas.org/academic-questions/35/1/the-case-for-colonialism-a-response-to-my-critics

_____. *The Last Imperialist: Sir Alan Burns' Epic Defense of the British Empire.* Washington, DC: Regnery Gateway, 2021.

Gilmour, David. 'Colonial Conundrums'. In *Literary Review*, August 2016.

_____. *Curzon.* London: Macmillan, 1994.

_____. *The British in India: Three Centuries of Ambition and Experience.* London: Allen Lane, 2018.

_____. *The Ruling Caste: Imperial Lives in the Victorian Raj.* London: John Murray, 2005.

Glendinning, Victoria. *Raffles and the Golden Opportunity, 1781–1826.* London: Profile, 2012.

Godwin, Peter. *Mukiwa: A White Boy in Africa.* London: Picador, 2007.

Godwyn, Morgan. *The Negro's & Indians Advocate, Suing for Their Admission into the Church . . .* London: J.D., 1680.

Globe and Mail. 'Kamloops, St Eugene's, Marieval: What We Know about Residential Schools' Unmarked Graves So Far'. In [Toronto] *Globe and Mail*, 6 July 2021: https://www.theglobeandmail.com/canada/article-residential-schools-unmarked-graves-st-eugenes-marieval-kamloops/.

_____. '"Mass Graves Do Not Belong in Any School." Readers React to the Discovery of the Remains of 215 Children at a Residential School in B.C., Plus Other Letters to the Editor'. In [Toronto] *Globe and Mail*, 1 June 2021: https://www.theglobeandmail.com/opinion/letters/article-june-1-mass-graves-do-not-belong-in-any-school-readers-react-to-the/.

Goldenberg, D. M. *The Curse of Ham: Race and Slavery in Early Judaism, Christianity, and Islam.* Princeton: Princeton University Press, 2003.

Gopal, Priyamvada. *Insurgent Empire: Anti-colonial Resistance and British Dissent.* London: Verso, 2019.

Gragg, Larry. *Englishmen Transplanted: The English Colonization of Barbados, 1627–1660.* Oxford: Oxford University Press, 2003.

Grant, James. *British Battles on Land and Sea.* London: Cassell, 1885.

Gravett, Willem H. 'Jan Christian Smuts (1870–1950) in Context: An Answer to Mazower and Morefield'. In *The Round Table: Commonwealth Journal of International Affairs*, 106/3 (2017).

Green, Nina, Brian Giesbrecht and Tom Flanagan. 'They Were Not Forced'. In *Dorchester Review*, 21 April 2022: https://www.dorchesterreview.ca/blogs/news/they-were-not-forced

Green, R. H. and S. H. Hymer. 'Cocoa in the Gold Coast: A Study in the Relations between African Farmers and Agricultural Experts'. In *Journal of Economic History*, 26/3 (September 1966).

Guest, Bill and John M. Sellars, eds. *Enterprise and Exploitation in a Victorian Colony: Aspects of the Economic and Social History of Natal.* Pietermaritzburg: University of Natal Press, 1985.

Haggard, H. Rider. *Cetywayo and His White Neighbours: or Remarks on Recent Events in Zululand, Natal, and the Transvaal.* London: Kegan Paul, Trench, Trübner, 1906.

————. *Diary of an African Journey. The Return of Rider Haggard.* Ed. and intro. Stephen Coan. Pietermaritzburg: University of Natal Press, 2000.

Haines, Robin. *Charles Trevelyan and the Great Irish Famine.* Dublin: Four Courts Press, 2004.

Hale, F. 'The Critique of Gĩkũyũ Religion and Culture in S. N. Ngũbiah's *A Curse from God*'. In *Acta Theologica*, 27/1 (2007).

Hämäläinen, Pekka. *The Comanche Empire.* New Haven and London: Yale University Press, 2008.

Handler, Jerome S. and Matthew C. Reilly. 'Contesting "White Slavery" in the Caribbean: Enslaved Africans and European Indentured Servants in Seventeenth-Century Barbados'. In *New West Indian Guide*, 91 (2017).

Hanley, Gerald. *The Year of the Lion.* London: William Collins, 1953.

————. *Warriors: Life and Death among the Somalis.* London: Eland, 1 993.

Hansard. *House of Commons Debate.* Vol. 95, 17 June 1901: https://api.parliament.uk/historic-hansard/commons/1901/jun/17/south-african-war-mortality-in-camps-of (accessed 9 August 2021).

Hargreaves, John D. 'Moor, Sir Ralph Denham Rayment'. In *Oxford Dictionary of National Biography.* Oxford: Oxford University Press, 2004: https://www.oxforddnb.com/view/10.1093/ref:odnb/9780198614128.001.0001/odnb-9780198614128-e-35086).

Harjo, Suzan Shown, ed. *Nation to Nation: Treaties between the United States and American Indian Nations*. Washington, DC: Smithsonian Institution, 2014.

Harries, Patrick. *Work, Culture, and Identity: Migrant Laborers in Mozambique and South Africa, c. 1860–1910*. Social History of Africa series, ed. Allen Isaacman and Jean Hay. Portsmouth, NH: Heinemann; London: James Currey; Johannesburg: Witwatersrand University Press, 1994.

Hart, Jennifer. 'Sir Charles Trevelyan at the Treasury'. In *English Historical Review*, 75/294 (January 1960).

Hart, Peter. *The I.R.A. and Its Enemies: Violence and Community in Cork, 1916–1923*. Oxford: Clarendon Press, 1998.

Hartland, E. Sidney. 'Death and Disposal of the Dead (Introductory)'. In Hastings, *Encyclopedia of Religion and Ethics*, Vol. IV: 'Confirmation – Drama' (1914).

Hastings, James. *Encyclopedia of Religion and Ethics*. 13 vols. Edinburgh: T. & T. Clark, 1908–26.

Hastings, Marquess of. *The Private Journal of the Marquess of Hastings, K. G., Governor-General and Commander-in-Chief in India*. Ed. Marchioness of Bute. 2 vols. 2nd edn. London: Saunders & Otley, 1858.

Hazareesingh, Sudhir. *Black Spartacus: The Epic Life of Toussaint Louverture*. London: Allen Lane, 2020.

Headlam, Cecil, ed. *The Milner Papers*. 2 vols. London: Cassell, 1931.

Hechter, Michael. *Alien Rule*. Cambridge: Cambridge University Press, 2013.

Herbert, Christopher. *War of No Pity: The Indian Mutiny and Victorian Trauma*. Princeton: Princeton University Press, 2008.

Heuman, Gad. 'Slavery, The Slave Trade, and Abolition'. In Winks, *The Oxford History of the British Empire*, Vol. V.

Hicks, Dan. *The Brutish Museums: The Benin Bronzes, Cultural Violence and Cultural Restitution*. London: Pluto Press, 2020.

Hirsch, Mark G. 'Illegal State Treaties'. In Harjo, *Nation to Nation*.

Hobson, J. A. *The War in South Africa: Its Causes and Effects*. London: Nisbet, 1900.

Hochschild, Adam. *Bury the Chains: The British Struggle to Abolish Slavery*. London: Macmillan, 2005.

Holland, James. *Burma '44: The Battle that Turned Britain's War in the East*. London: Bantam Press, 2016.

_____. *Sicily '43: The First Assault on Fortress Europe*. London: Bantam Press, 2020.

Home, Robert. *City of Blood Revisited: A New Look at the Benin Expedition of 1897*. London: Rex Collings, 1982.

Hooker, Richard. *The Works of That Learned and Judicious Mr Richard Hooker, etc*. Ed. John Keble. 3 vols. 6th edn. Oxford: Clarendon Press, 1874.

House of Commons, *East India (Proclamations)*. London: HMSO, 1908: http://www.csas.ed.ac.uk/mutiny/confpapers/Queen%27sProclamation.pdf.

_____. *Report of the Parliamentary Select Committee on Aboriginal Tribes*

(British Settlements). Reprinted for the Aborigines Protection Society. London: Ball, Chambers, and Hatchard, 1837.

Howe, F. N. 'The Early Introduction of Cocoa to West Africa'. In *African Affairs*, 45/180 (July 1946).

Howe, K. R. 'Michael King, *The Penguin History of New Zealand*', a review, in the *New Zealand Herald*, 22 October 2003: https://www.nzherald.co.nz/lifestyle/imichael-kingi-the-penguin-history-of-new-zealand/ T7BIDPOZEQWPFEDRQDR3JWL4RI/ (as at 7 June 2021).

Howe, Stephen. 'Imperial Histories, Postcolonial Theories'. In Huggan, *The Oxford Handbook of Postcolonial Studies*.

Huggan, Graham, ed. 'Introduction'. In *The Oxford Handbook of Postcolonial Studies*.

_____. *The Oxford Handbook of Postcolonial Studies*. Oxford: Oxford University Press, 2013.

Hughes, Robert. *The Fatal Shore: The Epic of Australia's Founding*. New York: Vintage, 1986.

Huxley, Elspeth. *A Thing to Love*. Chatto & Windus, 1954.

_____. *Red Strangers*. London: Penguin, 1939.

Hyam, Ronald. *Britain's Declining Empire: The Road to Decolonisation, 1918–1968*. Cambridge: Cambridge University Press, 2006.

_____. 'The Partition of Africa: Geopolitical and Internal Perspectives'. In Hyam, *Understanding the British Empire*.

_____. 'The View from Below: The African Response to Missionaries'. In *Understanding the British Empire*.

_____. *Understanding the British Empire*. Cambridge: Cambridge University Press, 2010.

Ibrahim, Raymond. '"I'm Saddened by the White Man's Emasculation": An African Sets the Record Straight'. *PJ Media*, 15 January 2020: https://pjmedia.com/columns/raymond-ibrahim/2020/01/15/im-saddened-by-the-white-mans-emasculation-an-african-sets-the-record-straight-n123156

Igbafe, Philip A. 'The Fall of Benin: A Reassessment'. In *Journal of African History*, 11/3 (1970).

_____. 'Slavery and Emancipation in Benin, 1897–1945'. In *Journal of African History*, XVI/3 (1975).

Ike, Nobutaka. 'The Pattern of Railway Development in Japan'. In *Far Eastern Quarterly*, 14/2 (Feb. 1955).

Imperato, Pascal James. 'Differing Perspectives on Mau Mau'. In *African Studies Review*, 48/3 (December 2005).

Independent. 'Obituary: Nirad C. Chaudhuri'. In *Independent*, 3 August 1999.

Jackson, Ashley. *The British Empire and the Second World War*. London: Hambledon Continuum, 2006.

James, Lawrence. *Raj: The Making and Unmaking of British India*. London: Abacus, 1997.

_____. *The Rise and Fall of the British Empire*. London: Abacus, 1994.

Jeal, Tim. *Baden-Powell*. London: Pimlico, 1989.

_____. *Livingstone*. Revised edn. New Haven and London: Yale University Press, 2013.

Jeffery, Keith. *Field Marshal Sir Henry Wilson: A Political Soldier*. Oxford: Oxford University Press, 2008.

_____. 'The Second World War'. In Brown and Louis, *Oxford History of the British Empire*, vol. IV.

Jenness, Diamond. *Indians of Canada*. Ottawa: National Museum of Canada, 1932.

Johnson, John, ed. *Colony to Nation: British Administrators in Kenya, 1940–1963*. London: Banham: Erskine Press, 2002.

Johnson, R. W. 'Orgy of Looting and Corruption Has Destroyed Mandela's Dream'. *The Times*, 17 July 2021.

Journals and Diaries of the Assistants to the Agent and Governor-General North-West Frontier and Resident in Lahore, 1846–1849. Allahabad: Pioneer Press, 1911.

Judd, Denis and Keith Surridge. *The Boer War*. London: John Murray, 2002.

Kaplan, Flora, ed., *Images of Power: Art of the Royal Court of Benin* (New York: New York University, 1981).

Kaufmann, Chaim D. and Robert A. Pape. 'Explaining Costly International Moral Action: Britain's Sixty-Year Campaign against the Atlantic Slave Trade'. In *International Organization*, 53/4 (Autumn 1999).

Kay, G. B. *The Political Economy of Ghana: A Collection of Documents and Statistics, 1900–1960*. Cambridge: Cambridge University Press, 1972.

Kaye, J. W. *A History of the Sepoy War in India, 1857–1858*. 3 vols. London: W. H. Allen, 1876.

_____. *Life and Correspondence of Major-General Sir John Malcolm*, 2 vols. London, 1856.

Kearney, Hugh F. 'The Great Famine: Legend and Reality'. In *Studies: An Irish Quarterly Review*, 46/182 (Summer 1957).

Kedourie, Elie. *In the Anglo-Arab Labyrinth: The McMahon-Husayn Correspondence and Its Interpretations, 1914–1939*. 2nd edn. London: Frank Cass, 1976, 2000.

_____. *Nationalism*. 4th edn. Oxford: Blackwell, 1993.

Keneally, Thomas. *Three Famines: Starvation and Politics*. New York: Public Affairs, 2011.

Kennedy, Dane. *The Imperial History Wars: Debating the British Empire*. London: Bloomsbury, 2018.

Kenyatta, Jomo. *Facing Mount Kenya: The Tribal Life of the Gikuyu*. London: Secker and Warburg, 1938.

Keppel-Jones, Arthur. *Rhodes and Rhodesia: The White Conquest of Zimbabwe, 1884–1902*. Montreal and Kingston: McGill-Queen's University Press, 1983.

Kestler D'Amours, Jillian. 'Canada: Calls Grow to Uncover More Residential

School Mass Graves'. In *Al Jazeera*, 3 June 2021: https://www.aljazeera.com/news/2021/6/3/canada-calls-grow-uncover-more-residential-school-mass-graves.

Khilnani, Sunil. 'The British Empire Was Much Worse Than You Realize'. In *New Yorker*, 4 April 2022.

Kidd, Colin. *The Forging of Races: Race and Scripture in the Protestant Atlantic World, 1600–2000.* Cambridge: Cambridge University Press, 2006.

Killingray, David. 'Labour Exploitation for Military Campaigns in British Colonial Africa, 1870–1945'. In *Journal of Contemporary History*, 24/3 (July 1989).

_____. 'Military and Labour Recruitment in the Gold Coast during the Second World War'. In *Journal of African History*, 23/1 (1982).

King, Michael. *The Penguin History of New Zealand.* Rosedale, NZ: Penguin, 2003. Sydney, NSW: Accessible Publishing System PTY, 2010.

Kirk, Sir John. *Enquiry into Outrage Committed on Brass People by Royal Niger Company.* London: HMSO, 1896.

Kirk-Greene, A. H. M. 'The Thin White Line: The Size of the British Colonial Service in Africa'. In *African Affairs*, 79/314 (January 1980).

Kissinger, Henry. *On China.* London: Penguin, 2012.

Kitson, Frank. *Prince Rupert: Admiral and General-at-Sea.* London: Constable, 1999.

Kumar, Dharma and Meghnad Desai, eds. *The Cambridge Economic History of India.* 2 vols. Vol. 2: 'c.1757–c.1970'. Cambridge: Cambridge University Press, 1983.

Kumar, Krishan. *Visions of Empire: How Five Imperial Regimes Shaped the World.* Princeton and Oxford: Princeton University Press, 2017.

Lalvani, Kartar. *The Making of India: The Untold Story of British Enterprise.* London: Bloomsbury, 2016.

Law, Robin. 'Human Sacrifice in Pre-Colonial West Africa'. In *African Affairs*, 84/334 (January 1985).

Lawrence, T. E. *Seven Pillars of Wisdom: A Triumph.* London: Folio Society, 2000.

Lawson, Tom. *The Last Man: A British Genocide in Tasmania.* London: Bloomsbury, 2021.

Le May, G. H. L. *British Supremacy in South Africa, 1899–1907.* Oxford: Clarendon Press, 1965.

_____. *The Afrikaners: An Historical Interpretation.* Oxford: Blackwell, 1995.

Le Sueur, Gordon. *Cecil Rhodes: The Man and His Work.* London: John Murray, 1913.

Lee, J. J. *Ireland, 1912–1985: Politics and Society.* Cambridge: Cambridge University Press, 1989.

Leenaars, Antoon A., et al. 'Genocide and Suicide among Indigenous People: The North Meets the South'. In *Canadian Journal of Native Studies*, 19/2 (1999).

Lemkin, Raphaël. 'Tasmania'. Ed. Ann Curthoys. In Moses and Stone, *Colonialism and Genocide.*

Lessing, Doris. *Time Bites: Views and Reviews.* New York: HarperCollins, 2004.

Leventhal, Fred and Peter Stansky. *Leonard Woolf: Bloomsbury Socialist.* Oxford: University Press, 2019.

Levtzion, N. and J. F. P. Hopkins, eds. *Corpus of Early Arabic Sources for West African History.* Cambridge University Press, 1981.

Lewis Bernard, 'An Exchange'. In *New York Review of Books*, 12 August 1982.

––––––––. *Race and Slavery in the Middle East. An Historical Enquiry.* New York: Oxford University Press, 1990.

––––––––. 'The Question of Orientalism'. In *New York Review of Books*, 24 June 1982.

Lindberg, Tracey. 'Contemporary Canadian Resonance of an Imperial Doctrine'. In Miller et al., *Discovering Indigenous Lands.*

––––––––. 'The Doctrine of Discovery in Canada'. In Miller et al., *Discovering Indigenous Lands*

Lindfors, Bernth. *Conversations with Chinua Achebe.* Jackson, MS: University of Mississippi, 1997.

Livingstone, David. *Missionary Travels and Researches in South Africa.* London: Ward Lock & Co., 1857.

Lloyd, Nick. *The Amritsar Massacre: The Untold Story of One Fateful Day.* London: I. B. Tauris, 2011.

Lockhart, J. G. and C. M. Woodhouse. *Rhodes.* London: Hodder and Stoughton, 1963.

Lockman, Zachary. *Contending Visions of the Middle East: The History and Politics of Orientalism.* 2nd edn. Cambridge: Cambridge University Press, 2010.

Lonsdale, John. 'East Africa'. In Brown and Louis, *Oxford History of the British Empire*, Vol. IV.

––––––––. 'The Conquest State of Kenya, 1893–1905'. In Berman and Lonsdale, *Unhappy Valley.*

Louis, William Roger, ed. *The Oxford History of the British Empire.* 5 vols. Oxford: Oxford University Press, 1998–2001.

Lovatt Smith, David. *My Enemy: My Friend.* Nairobi: FOCCAM, 2000.

Lovell, Julia. *The Opium War: Drugs, Dreams and the Making of China.* London: Picador, 2011.

Lowry, Donal, ed. 'Introduction: Not Just a "Tea-time War"'. In Lowry, *The South African War Reappraised.*

––––––––. *The South African War Reappraised.* Manchester: Manchester University Press, 2000.

Lugard, Frederick. *The Dual Mandate in British Tropical Africa.* Edinburgh: Blackwood, 1922.

Lyman, Robert. *A War of Empires: Japan, India, Burma, and Britain, 1941–45.* Oxford: Osprey, 2021.

_____. 'Violence Against History', *The Critic*, 2 October 2022: https://thecritic.co.uk/violence-against-history/.

Lynn, Martin. 'British Policy, Trade, and Informal Empire in the Mid-Nineteenth Century'. In Porter, *Oxford History of the British Empire*, Vol. III.

Lyons, David. 'The New Indian Claims and Original Rights to Land'. In *Social Theory and Practice*, 4/3/ (Fall 1977).

MacDonnell, A. P. *Report on the Food-grain Supply and Statistical Review of the Relief Operations in the Distressed Districts of Behar and Bengal during the Famine of 1873-74*. Calcutta: Bengal Secretariat Press, 1876.

McDougall, James, Erin O'Halloran, Hussein Ahmed Hussein Omar, Peter Hill et al. '"Ethics and Empire": An Open Letter from Oxford Scholars'. In *The Conversation*, 19 December 2017: https://theconversation.com/ethics-and-empire-an-open-letter-from-oxford-scholars-89333

McKee, Helen. 'From Violence to Alliance: Maroons and White Settlers in Jamaica, 1739-1795'. *In Slavery and Abolition*, 39/1 (2018).

Maddison, Angus. 'Dutch Income from Indonesia, 1700-1939'. In *Modern Asian Studies*, 23/4 (1989).

_____. *The World Economy: A Millennial Perspective*. Paris: OECD, 2001.

Maitra, Sumantra. '"If I Want to Hold Seminars on the Topic of Empire, I will Do So Privately": An Interview with Nigel Biggar'. In *Quillette*, 7 June 2018: https://quillette.com/2018/06/07/want-hold-seminars-topic-empire-will-privately-interview-nigel-biggar/

Malcolm, John. *Malcolm: Soldier, Diplomat, Ideologue of British India*. Edinburgh: John Donald, 2014.

Malcolm, Sir John. *A Memoir of Central India, including Malwa and Adjoining Provinces*. 2 vols. London: Kingsbury, Parbury, and Allen, 1823; Cambridge: Cambridge University Press, 2011.

_____. *Report of the Province of Malwa and Adjoining Districts*. Calcutta: Government Gazette Press, 1822.

Manne, Robert, ed. *Whitewash. On Keith Windschuttle's Fabrication of Aboriginal History*. Melbourne: Black Inc. Agenda, 2003.

Mansergh, Nicholas and E. W. R. Lumby, eds. *Constitutional Relations between Britain and India: The Transfer of Power, 1942-7*. 12 vols. (1970-83). Vol. IV: 'The Bengal Famine and the New Viceroyalty, 15 June 1943-31 August 1944'. London: HMSO, 1973.

_____, E. W. R. Lumby and Penderel Moon, eds. *Constitutional Relations between Britain and India: The Transfer of Power, 1942-1947*, 12 vols (1970-83). Vol. VI: 'The Post-war Phase: New Moves by the Labour Government, 1 August 1945-22 March 1946'. London: HMSO, 1976.

Marcel, Gabriel. 'Qu-est-ce qu'un homme de droite?'. In *Arts* (1962): http://www.gabriel-marcel.com/articles&textes/homme_droite.php

Marindo, Ravai. 'Death Colonized: Historical Adult Mortality in Rhodesia (Zimbabwe)'. In *Zambezia*, XXVI/ii (1999).

Marlowe, John. *Milner: Apostle of Empire*. London: Hamish Hamilton, 1976.

Marmon, Shaun. 'Domestic Slavery in the Mamluk Empire: A Preliminary Sketch'. In Shaun Marmon, ed., *Slavery in the Islamic Middle East*. Princeton: Markus Wiener, 1999.

Marshall, Ingeborg. *A History and Ethnography of the Beothuk*. Montreal & Kingston: McGill-Queen's University Press, 1996.

Marshall, P. J.; and Alaine Low, eds. *The Oxford History of the British Empire*. 5 vols. Vol. II: 'The Eighteenth Century'. Oxford: Oxford University Press, 1998.

Marshman, John Clark. *Memoirs of Major-General Sir Henry Havelock, K.C.B.* 3rd edn. London: Longmans, Green, Reader, and Dyer, 1867.

Martin, Ged. 'The Department of Indian Affairs in the Dominion of Canada Budget, 1882': https://www.gedmartin.net/martinalia-mainmenu-3/312-indian-affairs-1882-budget.

Masani, Zareer. 'Amritsar: Beginning of the End of Empire'. *Standpoint*, April 2019.

_____. 'Britain's Raj and the Chaos of Empire'. In *History Today*, 67/4 (April 2017).

_____. 'Churchill and the Genocide Myth'. In *The Critic*, 13 (December 2020).

_____. 'How British Orientalists Were Responsible for Rediscovering Indian History'. In *The Wire*, 11 March 2018: https://thewire.in/history/how-british-orientalists-were-responsible-for-rediscovery-of-indian-history.

_____. *Indian Tales of the Raj*. London: BBC Books, 1997.

_____. 'Warren Hastings "Loved India a Little More than his Own Country"'. In *Open Magazine*, 6 April 2017: https://openthemagazine.com/essay/warren-hastings-loved-india-a-little-more-than-his-own-country/.

Maurois, André. *Cecil Rhodes*. Trans. Rohan Wadham. London: Collins, 1953.

Maylam, Paul. *The Cult of Rhodes: Remembering an Imperialist in Africa*. Cape Town: David Philip, 2005.

Mazower, Mark. *No Enchanted Palace: The End of Empire and the Ideological Origins of the United Nations*. Princeton: Princeton University Press, 2009.

Mear, Craig. 'The Origin of the Smallpox Outbreak in Sydney'. In *Journal of the Royal Australian Historical Society*, 94/1 (2008): https://go.gale.com/ps/i.do?p=AONE&u=googlescholar&id=GALE|A505359630&v=2.1&it=r&sid=AONE&asid=e47b790d

Meek, C. K. *Law and Authority in a Nigerian Tribe: A Study in Indirect Rule*. London: Oxford University Press, 1937.

Meisner, Maurice. *Mao's China and After: A History of the People's Republic*. 3rd edn. New York: Free Press, 1999.

Mellor, R. *British Imperial Trusteeship, 1783–1850*. London: Faber & Faber, 1951.

Melvill, Henry. 'Sermon XIV: The Examination of Cain'. *Sermons on Certain of the Less Prominent Facts and References in Sacred Story*. 2 vols. London: Francis & John Rivington, 1845.

Milke, Mark. *The Victim Cult: How the Grievance Culture Hurts Everyone and Wrecks Civilizations*. Parksville, BC: Thomas and Black, 2019.

Mill, J. S. *On Liberty*. Ed. and intro. Gertrude Himmelfarb. London: Penguin, 1974.

Miller, David. *National Responsibility and Global Justice*. Oxford: Oxford University Press, 2007.

Miller, Joseph C. 'A Global History of the Slave Trade'. In *Journal of African History*, 49/2 (2008).

Miller, J. R. *Residential Schools and Reconciliation: Canada Confronts Its History*. Toronto: University of Toronto Press, 2017.

_____. *Shingwauk's Vision: A History of Native Residential Schools*. Toronto: University of Toronto Press, 1996.

_____ et al. 'Open Letter: Historians Rally vs "Genocide" Myth'. In *Dorchester Review*, 12 August 2021: https://www.dorchesterreview.ca/blogs/news/historians-rally-vs-genocide-myth

Miller, Robert J. 'The Doctrine of Discovery'. In Miller et al., *Discovering Indigenous Lands*.

_____. 'The Legal Adoption of Discovery in the United States'. In Miller et al., *Discovering Indigenous Lands*.

_____, Jacinta Ruru, Larissa Behrendt and Tracey Lindberg. *Discovering Indigenous Lands: The Doctrine of Discovery in the English Colonies*. Oxford: Oxford University Press, 2010.

Mills, James H. and Patricia Barton, eds. *Drugs and Empires: Essays in Modern Imperialism and Intoxication, c.1500–c.1930*. London: Palgrave, 2007.

Milner, Alfred. *England in Egypt*. London: Edward Arnold, 1902.

Mitchel, John. *An Apology for the British Government in Ireland*. Dublin: Irish National Publishing Association, 1860.

Mitchell, B. R. *British Historical Statistics*. Cambridge: Cambridge University Press, 1988.

Mohdin, Aamna. 'Protesters Rally in Oxford for Removal of Cecil Rhodes Statue'. In *Guardian*, 9 June 2020.

Mokyr, Joel. 'Editor's Introduction: The New Economic History and the Industrial Revolution'. In Joel Mokyr, ed., *The British Industrial Revolution: An Economic Perspective*, 2nd edn. London: Routledge, 1999.

Monbiot, George. 'The True Legacy of Christopher Columbus: "Western Civilisation"': https://youtu.be/UtBKDMN2U4s.

Monga, Célestin and Justin Yifu Lin, eds. *The Oxford Handbook of Africa and Economics*. 2 vols. Vol. 1: 'Context and Concepts'. Oxford: Oxford University Press, 2015.

Montesquieu, Charles Louis de Secondat, Baron de. *The Complete Works of M. De Montesquieu*. 4 vols. Vol. 1: *The Spirit of Laws*. London: T. Evans, 1777.

Morgan, Kenneth. *A Concise History of Jamaica*. Cambridge: Cambridge University Press, 2022.

_____. *Slavery and the British Empire: From Africa to America*. Oxford: Oxford University Press, 2007.

Morgan, Sharon. *Land Settlement in Early Tasmania: Creating an Antipodean England*. Cambridge: Cambridge University Press, 1992.

Moses, A. Dirk. 'Conceptual Blockages and Definitional Dilemmas in the "Racial Century": Genocides of Indigenous Peoples and the Holocaust'. In Moses and Stone, *Colonialism and Genocide*.

_____ and Dan Stone. *Colonialism and Genocide*. Abingdon: Routledge, 2007.

Mukerjee, Madhusree. *Churchill's Secret War: The British Empire and the Ravaging of India during World War II*. New York: Basic Books, 2010.

Mukherjee, Rudrangshu. '"Satan Let Loose upon Earth": The Kanpur Massacres in India in the Revolt of 1857'. In *Past and Present*, 128 (August 1990).

_____. 'Reply'. *Past and Present*, 142 (February 1994).

Muriuki, Godfrey. '*Counter-Insurgency in Kenya, 1952–60: A Study of Military Operations against Mau Mau*, by Anthony Clayton'. In *African Affairs*, 77/307 (April 1978).

Musil, Robert. *The Man Without Qualities*. Trans. Sophie Wilkins. London: Picador, 2017.

Mutua, Makau wa. *Human Rights: A Political and Cultural Critique*. Philadelphia: University of Pennsylvania Press, 2008.

_____. 'Limitations in Religious Rights: Problematizing Religious Freedom in the African Context'. In *Buffalo Human Rights Law Review*, 5 (1999).

Myers, Kevin. 'Never, Never, Never . . . Imagine that Our History Is Now Behind Us'. In *Irish Independent*, 31 May 2007.

Naipaul, V. S. *The Overcrowded Barracoon and Other Articles*. London: Andre Deutsch, 1972.

New Zealand Ministry for Culture and Heritage. 'Lord Normanby'. In *New Zealand History*. Wellington, NZ: New Zealand Ministry for Culture and Heritage, 2017: https://nzhistory.govt.nz/people/lord-normanby

Newbury, Colin (C. W.). *British Policy Towards West Africa: Select Documents, 1875–1914*. Oxford: Clarendon Press, 1971.

_____. 'Great Britain and the Partition of Africa, 1870–1914'. In Porter, *Oxford History of the British Empire*, Vol. III.

_____. 'Milner, Alfred, Viscount Milner'. In *Oxford Dictionary of National Biography*. Oxford: Oxford University Press, 2008: https://www.oxforddnb.com/view/10.1093/ref:odnb/9780198614128.001.0001/odnb-9780198614128-e-35037?print=pdf)

Nock, David A. and Celia Haig-Brown. *With Good Intentions: Euro-Canadian and Aboriginal Relations in Colonial Canada*. Vancouver: University of British Columbia Press, 2006.

Northern Rhodesia Report for 1930. No. 1561. London: HMSO, 1932.

Nwaubani, Adaobi Tricia. 'My Great-Grandfather, the African Slave-Trader'. In *New Yorker*, 15 July 2018: https://www.newyorker.com/culture/personal-history/my-great-grandfather-the-nigerian-slave-trader

Nwauwa, Appollos O. 'The British Establishment of Universities in Tropical

Africa, 1920–1948: A Reaction against the Spread of American "Radical" Influence'. In *Cahiers d'études africaines*, 33/130 (1993).

Nworah, K. Dike. 'The Politics of Lever's West African Concessions, 1908–1913'. In *International Journal of African Historical Studies*, 5/2 (1972).

Nyika, Farai and Johan Fourie. 'Black Disenfranchisement in the Cape Colony, c.1887–1909: Challenging the Numbers'. In *Journal of Southern African Studies*, 46/3 (2020).

Obinyan, Thomas Uwadiale. 'The Annexation of Benin'. In *Journal of Black Studies*, 19/1 (September 1988).

O'Brien, Patrick K. 'The Costs and Benefits of British Imperialism, 1846–1914'. In *Past and Present*, 120 (1988).

_____ and Leandro Prados de la Escosura. 'The Costs and Benefits for Europeans from Their Empires Overseas'. In *Revista de Historia Economica*, 16:1 (1998).

O'Brien, Terence H. *Milner: Viscount Milner of St James's and Cape Town, 1854–1925*. London: Constable, 1979.

O'Connell, Mary Ellen. *International Law and the Use of Force: Documentary Supplement*. 2nd edition. New York: Thomson Reuters/ Foundation Press, 2009.

Offer, Avner. 'Costs and Benefits, Prosperity, and Security, 1870–1914'. In Porter, *Oxford History of the British Empire*, Vol. III: 'The Nineteenth Century'.

Ogot, Bethwell A. 'Review Article: Britain's Gulag'. In *Journal of African History*, 46/3 (2005).

Ó Gráda, Cormac. *Black '47 and Beyond: The Great Irish Famine in History, Economy, and Memory*. Princeton: Princeton University Press, 1999.

_____. *Eating People Is Wrong, and Other Essays on Famine, Its Past and Its Future*. Princeton: Princeton University Press, 2015.

_____. '"Sufficiency and Sufficiency and Sufficiency": Revisiting the Great Bengal Famine of 1943–44'. In Ó Gráda, *Eating People Is Wrong*.

Ojo, Olatunji. 'Slavery and Human Sacrifice in Yorubaland: Ondo, c.1870–94'. In *Journal of African History*, 46/3 (2005).

O'Neill, Onora. 'Rights to Compensation', in *Justice across Boundaries: Whose Obligations?* Cambridge: Cambridge University Press, 2016.

Onselen, C. van. *Chibaro: African Mine Labour in Southern Rhodesia, 1900–1933*. London: 1975.

Orange, Claudia. *The Treaty of Waitangi*. Wellington, NZ: Bridget Williams Books, 1987.

Otte, T. G. *Statesman of Europe: A Life of Sir Edward Grey*. London: Allen Lane, 2020.

Owen, Roger. *Lord Cromer: Victorian Imperialist, Edwardian Proconsul*. Oxford: Oxford University Press, 2004.

Pachai, Bridglal. 'Indentured Chinese Immigrant Labour on the Witwatersrand Goldfields'. In *India Quarterly*, 21/1 (January-March 1965).

Padmanabhan, S. Y. 'The Great Bengal Famine'. In *Annual Review of Phytopathology*, 11 (September 1973).

Pakenham, Thomas. *The Boer War*. London: Weidenfeld and Nicolson, 1979.

Paquette, Robert L. and Mark M. Smith. *The Oxford Handbook of Slavery in the Americas*. Oxford: Oxford University Press, 2010.

Parsons, Neil. 'Introduction'. In Sol T. Plaatje, *Native Life in South Africa, before and since the European War and the Boer Rebellion*.

Peers, Douglas M. and Nandini Gooptu, eds. *India and the British Empire*. Oxford History of the British Empire Companion Series. Oxford: Oxford University Press, 2012.

Perham, Margery. *Major Dane's Garden*, 2nd edn. London: Rex Collins, 1970.

————. *The Colonial Reckoning*. The Reith Lectures 1961. London: Collins, 1961.

Pétré-Grenouilleau, Olivier. *Les traites négrières: essai d'histoire globale*. Paris: Editions Gallimard, 2004.

Piggin, Stuart. *Evangelical Christianity in Australia: Spirit, Word, and World*. Melbourne: Oxford University Press, 1996.

Plaatje, Sol T. *The Boer War Diary of Sol. T. Plaatje: An African at Mafeking*. Ed. John L. Comaroff. London: Cardinal, 1976.

————. *Native Life in South Africa*. London: Longman, 1987.

————. *Native Life in South Africa, Before and Since the European War and the Boer Rebellion:* https://www.sahistory.org.za/sites/default/files/Native%20 Life%20in%20South%20Africa_0.pdf

Plamenatz, John. *On Alien Rule and Self Government*. London: Longmans, 1960.

Plomley, Brian. *Aboriginal/Settler Clash in Van Diemen's Land*. Launceston: Queen Victoria Museum and Art Gallery, 1992.

————, ed. *Friendly Mission. The Tasmanian Journals and Papers of George Augustus Robinson 1829–1834*. Kingsgrove, NSW: Tasmanian Historical Research Association, 1966.

Porter, Andrew, ed. *The Oxford History of the British Empire*. 5 vols. Vol. III: 'The Nineteenth Century'. Oxford: Oxford University Press, 1999.

————. 'Trusteeship, Anti-Slavery, and Humanitarianism'. In Porter, *Oxford History of the British Empire*, Vol. III: 'The Nineteenth Century'.

Porter, Bernard. *The Absent-Minded Imperialists: Empire, Society, and Culture in Britain*. Oxford: Oxford University Press, 2004.

Posner, Eric A. and Adrian Vermeule. 'Reparations for Slavery and Other Historical Injustices'. In *Columbia Law Review* 103/689 (2003).

Pourhamrang, Nasrin. '*Things Fall Apart* Now More Famous than Me, Says Chinua Achebe'. In *Daily Trust*, 8 September 2012: https://dailytrust.com/ things-fall-apart-now-more-famous-than-me-says-chinua-achebe.

Prasad, Bisheshwar, ed. *The Official History of the Indian Armed Forces in the Second World War, 1939–1945*. 24 vols (1953–1966). Vol. 17: 'India and the War'. New Delhi: Government of India, 1966.

Price, Richard. *Making Empire: Colonial Encounters and the Creation of Imperial Rule in Nineteenth-Century Africa*. Cambridge: Cambridge University Press, 2008.

Pruden, Jana G. 'Discovery of Children's Remains at Kamloops Residential School "Stark Example of Violence" Inflicted upon Indigenous Peoples'. In [Toronto] *Globe and Mail*, 28 May 2021: https://www.theglobeandmail.com/canada/article-bodies-found-at-kamloops-residential-school-site-in-bc/.

_____ and Mike Hager. 'Anthropologist Explains How She Concluded 200 Children Were Buried at the Kamloops Residential School'. In [Toronto] *Globe and Mail*, 15 July 2021: https://www.theglobeandmail.com/canada/article-kamloops-residential-school-unmarked-graves-discovery-update/.

Pyrah, G. B. *Imperial Policy and South Africa, 1902–10*. Oxford: Clarendon Press, 1955.

Quinault, Roland. 'Gladstone and Slavery'. In *Historical Journal*, 52/2 (June 2009).

Rachman, Gideon. *Easternisation: War and Peace in the Asian Century*. London: Bodley Head, 2016.

Rahim, Sameer. 'Disorientated: The Confusions of Edward Said'. In *Prospect*, June 2021.

Ranger, Terence. *Voices from the Rocks. Nature, Culture, and History in the Matopos Hills of Zimbabwe*. Oxford: James Currey, 1999.

Rathore, L. S. 'Political Ideas of Jawaharlal Nehru: Some Reflections'. In *Indian Journal of Political Science*, 46/4 (Oct.–Dec. 1985).

Rawson, Admiral Harry. Dispatches to London, 27 February 1897. In *London Gazette*, 7 May 1897: https://translanth.hypotheses.org/ueber/rawson-moor

Ray, R. K., ed. *Entrepreneurship and Industry in India, 1800–1947*. Delhi: Oxford University Press, 1992.

Reynolds, David. 'The Churchill Government and the Black American Troops in Britain during World War II'. In *Transactions of the Royal Historical Society*, Fifth Series, 35 (1985).

_____. *Rich Relations: The American Occupation of Britain, 1942–1945*. London: HarperCollins, 1995.

Reynolds, Henry. *An Indelible Stain? The Question of Genocide in Australia's History*. Ringwood: Viking, 2001.

_____. *Frontier: Aborigines, Settlers, and the Land*. Sydney: Allen & Unwin, 1987.

_____. *The Fate of a Free People*. Ringwood: Penguin, 1995.

_____. *The Law of the Land*. Victoria: Penguin, 1987.

Reynolds, L. G. *Economic Growth in the Third World: 1850–1980*. New Haven and London: Yale University Press, 1985.

Richards, Eric. *Britannia's Children: Emigration from England, Scotland, Wales, and Ireland since 1600*. Hambledon: London and New York, 2004.

Richardson, David. *Principles and Agents: The British Slave Trade and its Abolition*. Newhaven, CT: Yale University Press, 2022.

_____. 'The British Empire and the Atlantic Slave Trade, 1660–1807'. In Marshall, ed., *Oxford History of the British Empire*, 5 vols, Vol. II: 'The Eighteenth Century'.

Richardson, Peter. 'The Recruiting of Chinese Indentured Labour for the South African Gold Mines, 1903–1908'. In *Journal of African History*, XVIII/1 (1977).

Riel, Louis. 'Address to the Court, 1 August 1885'. In Stanley et al., *Collected Writings of Louis Riel.*

Ritchie, David. *Natural Rights: A Criticism of Some Ethical and Political Conceptions.* London: Swan Sonnenschein, 1895.

Roberts, Andrew and Zewditu Gebreyohanes. *'The Racial Consequences of Mr Churchill': A Review.* London: Policy Exchange, 2021.

Robson, Lloyd. *A History of Tasmania.* Vol. 1: 'Van Diemen's Land from the Earliest Times to 1855'. Melbourne: Oxford University Press, 1983.

Rodney, Walter. 'African Slavery and Other Forms of Social Oppression on the Upper Guinea Coast in the Context of the Atlantic Slave Trade'. In *Journal of African History*, 7/3 (1966).

Rome Statute of the International Criminal Court: https://treaties.un.org/doc/ Treaties/1998/07/19980717%2006-33%20PM/Ch_XVIII_10p.pdf

Root, John. 'Runnymede vs Sewell?'. In *Out of Many, One People*, no. 40, 27 July 2021: https://johnroot.substack.com/p/runnymede-vs-sewell-40-27072021

Rotberg, Robert I. *The Founder. Cecil Rhodes and the Pursuit of Power.* New York: Oxford University Press, 1988.

Roth, H. Ling. *Great Benin: Its Customs, Arts, and Horrors.* Halifax: F. King, 1903.

Rowse, Tim. 'The Moral World of the Native Mounted Police'. In *Law and History*, 5/1 (2018).

Roy, Ram Mohun. 'Letter from Rammohun Roy to Lord Amherst, Governor-General in Council, dated 11 December 1823'. In *The Great Indian Education Debate: Documents Relating to the Orientalist-Anglicist Controversy, 1781–1843.* Ed. Lynn Zastoupil and Martin Moir. Richmond: Curzon, 1999.

Roy, Tirthankar. *An Economic History of India, 1707–1857.* 2nd edn. London: Routledge, 2021.

_____. *How British Rule Changed India's Economy: The Paradox of the Raj.* Cham, Switzerland: Palgrave Pivot, 2019.

_____. '"Inglorious Empire: What the British Did to India", a Review of Shashi Tharoor's *Inglorious Empire'*. In *Cambridge Review of International Affairs*, 31/1 (2018).

_____. 'The British Empire and the Economic Development of India, 1858–1947'. In *Revista de Historia Económica/ Journal of Iberian and Latin American Economic History*, 34/2 (2015).

_____. *The Economic History of India, 1857–1947.* Delhi: Oxford University Press, 2000, 2006, 2011, 2020.

Rubinstein, Hymie. 'Indigenous Exceptionalism and the TRC'. In Clifton and DeWolf, *From Truth Comes Reconciliation.*

Ruru, Jacinta. 'Asserting the Doctrine of Discovery in Aotearoa New Zealand: 1840–1960s'. In Miller et al., *Discovering Indigenous Lands*.

Rushdie, Salman and Elizabeth West, eds. *Vintage Book of Indian Writing 1947–97*. London: Vintage, 1997.

Ryan, Lyndall. *Tasmanian Aborigines: A History since 1803*. Crows Nest, NSW: Allen and Unwin, 2012.

————. *The Aboriginal Tasmanians*. 2nd edn. St Leonards, NSW: Allen & Unwin, 1981.

————. 'Who is the Fabricator?'. In Manne, *Whitewash*.

Ryder, A. F. C. *Benin and the Europeans, 1485–1897*. London: Longman, 1977.

Sabur, Rozina. 'Churches Burned Down as Anger Over "Cultural Genocide" Sweeps Canada'. In *Daily Telegraph*, 24 July 2021: https://www.telegraph.co.uk/world-news/2021/07/24/churches-burned-anger-cultural-genocide-indigenous-children/

Said, Edward W. *Orientalism*. New York: Vintage, 1978.

Salisbury, Lord. 'Speech', House of Commons, 10 July 1890. In *Hansard*, Vol. 346 (1890): https://hansard.parliament.uk/Lords/1890-07-10/debates/4ed35c10bcc3-4b86-8eac-9f1309cb26be/Anglo-GermanAgreementBill(No180).

Sand, Shlomo. *The Invention of the Land of Israel: From Holy Land to Homeland*. London: Verso, 2012.

Sandholtz, Wayne. *Prohibiting Plunder: How Norms Change*. New York: Oxford University Press, 2007.

Sanghera, Sathnam. *Empireland: How Imperialism Has Shaped Modern Britain*. London: Penguin, 2021.

Sarkar, Abhijit. 'Fed by Famine: The Hindu Mahasabha's Politics of Religion, Caste, and Relief in Response to the Great Bengal Famine, 1943–1944'. In *Modern Asian Studies*, 54/6 (2020).

Sartre, Jean-Paul. 'Preface'. In Fanon, *Wretched of the Earth*.

Saunders, Christopher. 'African Attitudes to Britain and the Empire before and after the South African War'. In Lowry, *South African War Reappraised*.

Schneer, Jonathan. *The Balfour Declaration: The Origins of the Arab-Israeli Conflict*. London: Bloomsbury, 2010.

Schreiner, Olive. *Trooper Peter Halket of Mashonaland*. London: Unwin, 1897.

Schreuder, Deryck M. and Stuart Ward, eds. *Australia's Empire*. Oxford History of the British Empire Companion Series. Oxford: Oxford University Press, 2008.

Segal, R. *Islam's Black Slaves. The Other Black Diaspora*. New York: Farrar, Straus & Giroux, 2001.

Segev, Tom. *One Palestine, Complete: Jews and Arabs under the British Mandate*. New York: Henry Holt, 1999.

Sen, Amartya. 'Food, Economics, and Entitlements'. In Drèze and Sen, *Political Economy of Hunger*, Vol. 1.

_____. *Poverty and Famines: An Essay on Entitlement and Deprivation.* Oxford: Oxford University Press, 1983.

Sheehan, William. *A Hard Local War: The British Army and the Guerrilla War in Cork, 1919–1921.* Cheltenham: History Press, 2011.

Shlaim, Avi. *Israel and Palestine: Reappraisals, Revisions, Refutations.* London: Verso, 2009.

Simon, Yves R. *The Ethiopian Campaign and French Political Thought.* Ed. Anthony O. Simon; trans. Robert Royal. Notre Dame: University of Notre Dame, 2009.

Simons, H. J. and R. E. Simons. *Class and Colour in South Africa, 1850–1950.* Harmondsworth: Penguin 1969.

Singh, Dabinderjit. 'The Truth behind the Amritsar Massacre'. In *politics.co.uk*, 16 January 2014: https://www.politics.co.uk/comment-analysis/2014/01/16/the-truth-behind-the-amritsar-massacre

Singh, Manmohan. 'Address in Acceptance of Honorary Degree from Oxford University, 8 July 2005': https://mea.gov.in/Speeches-Statements.htm?dtl/2623/Address+by+Prime+Minister+Dr+Manmohan+Singh+in+acceptance+of+Honorary+Degree +from+Oxford+University

Sithole, Ndabaningi. *African Nationalism.* Cape Town: Oxford University Press, 1959.

Sky News. 'China Ambassador to the UK: "Hong Kong is no longer under colonial rule"'. In *Sky News,* 6 July 2020: https://www.youtube.com/watch?v=JQR28gJxJIQ

Smith, Adam. *The Theory of Moral Sentiments.* Ed. Dugald Stewart. London: Henry G. Bohn, 1853.

Smith, Andrea. *Indigenous Peoples and Boarding Schools: A Comparative Study.* New York: United Nations Permanent Forum on Indigenous Issues, 2009.

Smith, Donald B. 'Macdonald's Relationship with Aboriginal Peoples'. In Dutil and Hall, *Macdonald at 200.*

_____ and J. R. Miller. 'No Genocide: It's Not the Right Word for the History Books'. *Literary Review of Canada* (October 2019): https://reviewcanada.ca/magazine/2019/10/no-genocide/).

Smith, Iain. 'A Century of Controversy Over Origins'. In Lowry, *South African War Reappraised.*

Smuts, J. C. *Jan Christian Smuts.* London: Cassell, 1952.

Somerville, Christopher. *Our War: How the British Commonwealth Fought the Second World War.* London: Weidenfeld & Nicolson, 1998.

South Africa Act, 1909. In *American Journal of International Law*, 4 (1910), 'Official Documents', 43 (c): https://ia801901.us.archive.org/0/items/jstor-2212266/2212266.pdf.

Stanley, Brian. *The Bible and the Flag: Protestant Missions and British Imperialism in the Nineteenth and Twentieth Centuries.* Leicester: Apollos, 1990.

Stanley, George F. G. *The Collected Writings of Louis Riel.* 5 vols. Edmonton: University of Alberta Press, 1985.

Stauffer, John. 'Abolition and Antislavery'. In Paquette and Smith, *Oxford Handbook of Slavery in the Americas.*

Stevens, F. S. *Racism: The Australian Experience.* 2 vols. Vol. 2: 'Black versus White'. Sydney: ANZ Book Company, 1972.

Stockwell, Sarah, ed. *The British Empire: Themes and Perspectives.* Oxford: Blackwell, 2008.

Storrs, Ronald. *Orientations.* London: Nicholson & Watson, 1939.

Sullivan, A. M. *New Ireland.* Philadelphia: Lippincott, 1878.

Sun, E-Tu Zen. 'The Pattern of Railway Development in China'. In *Far Eastern Quarterly*, 14/2 (Feb. 1955).

Surtees, R. J. 'The Development of an Indian Reserve Policy in Canada'. In *Ontario History*, 61 (1969).

Sutton, Peter. *The Politics of Suffering: Indigenous Australia and the End of the Liberal Consensus.* Melbourne: University of Melbourne Press, 2009.

Symonds, Richard. *Oxford and Empire: The Last Lost Cause?* London: Macmillan, 1986.

Táíwò, Olúfémi. *Against Decolonisation: Taking African Agency Seriously.* London: Hurst, 2022.

Taylor, Alan. *American Revolutions: A Continental History.* New York: W. W. Norton, 2016.

Taylor, Mark. 'Cowessess First Nation Places Solar Lights to Illuminate 751 Unmarked Graves at Former Residential School Site'. In [Toronto] *Globe and Mail*, 26 June 2021: https://www.theglobeandmail.com/canada/article-cowes sess-first-nation-place-solar-lights-next-to-each-unmarked-grave/.

Tench, Watkin. *Sydney's First Four Years: being a reprint of A narrative of the expedition to Botany Bay, and A complete account of the settlement at Port Jackson.* Intro. and annotated by L. F. Fitzhardinge. Sydney: Angus and Robertson, 1961.

Tharoor, Shashi. *Inglorious Empire: What the British Did to India.* London: Hurst, 2017.

Thiong'o, Ngũgĩ wa. *Decolonising the Mind: The Politics of Language in African Literature.* Nairobi: James Currey, 1986.

Thompson, Edward. *A Letter from India.* London: Faber & Faber, 1932.

_____ and G. T. Garratt. *Rise and Fulfilment of British Rule in India.* London: Macmillan, 1934.

Thompson, W. H. [Tommy]. 'The Outbreak of Mau Mau in Fort Hall'. In Johnson, *Colony to Nation.*

Thorne, Christopher. *Border Crossings: Studies in International History.* Oxford: Blackwell, 1988.

_____. 'Britain and the Black GIs: Racial Issues and Anglo-American Relations in 1942'. In *Border Crossings.*

Thornton, Russell. *American Indian Holocaust and Survival*. Norman and London: University of Oklahoma Press, 1987.

Tilly, Louise A. 'Food Entitlement, Famine, and Conflict'. In *Journal of Interdisciplinary History*, 14/2 (Autumn 1983).

Toledano, Ehud R. *Slavery and Abolition in the Ottoman Middle East*. Seattle: University of Washington, 1998.

Tombs, Robert. *The English and Their History*. London: Allen Lane, 2014.

Tomlinson, B. R. 'Economics and Empire: The Periphery and the Imperial Economy'. In Porter, *Oxford History of the British Empire*, Vol. III.

Topping, Alexandra. 'UK Failure to Commemorate Black and Asian War Dead Known "For Years"'. In *Guardian*, 22 April 2021.

Torpey, John. 'Making Whole What Has Been Smashed: Reflections on Reparations'. In *Journal of Modern History*, 73/2 (June 2001).

Townshend, Charles. *Easter 1916: The Irish Rebellion*. London: Allen Lane, 2005.

————. *The British Campaign in Ireland, 1919–1921: The Development of Political and Military Policies*. Oxford: Oxford University Press, 1975.

————. *When God Made Hell: The British Invasion of Mesopotamia and the Creation of Iraq, 1914–1921*. London: Faber and Faber, 2010.

Toye, Richard. *Churchill's Empire: The World that Made Him and the World He Made*. London: Macmillan, 2010.

Trevelyan, Charles. *The Irish Crisis*. London: Longman, Brown, Green, and Longmans, 1848.

Trevelyan, Laura. *A Very British Family: The Trevelyans and Their World*. London: I. B. Tauris, 2006.

Trigger, Bruce. 'The Historians' Indian: Native Americans in Canadian Historical Writing from Charlevoix to the Present'. In *Canadian Historical Review*, 67/3 (1986).

Truth and Reconciliation Commission of Canada. *Honouring the Truth, Reconciling for the Future*. Summary of the Final Report. Toronto: Lorimer, 2015.

————. *Final Report*. Vol. 1: 'Canada's Residential Schools: The History, Part 1, Origins to 1939'. Montreal and Kingston: McGill-Queen's University Press, 2015.

————. *Final Report*. Vol. 4: 'Canada's Residential Schools: Missing Children and Unmarked Burials'. Montreal and Kingston: McGill-Queen's University Press, 2015.

————. 'Missing Children Project': http://www.trc.ca/events-and-projects/missing-children-project.html (accessed 1 August 2021).

Turnbull, Clive. 'Tasmania: The Ultimate Solution'. In Stevens, *Racism*.

Tutu, Archbishop Desmond: 'Obituary'. In *The Times*, 27 December 2021.

Ullerup, Jørgen. 'Kulturkrigen raser på britiske universiteter'. In *Jyllands Posten*, 28 October 2021: https://jyllands-posten.dk/international/europa/ECE13372877/kulturkrigen-raser-paa-britiske-universiteter/).

Vaughan, Alden T. *Roots of American Racism: Essays on the Colonial Experience.* Oxford: Oxford University Press, 1995.

Veinstein, G. 'Soḳullu Meḥmed Pasha'. In P. Bearman, Th. Bianquis, C. E. Bosworth, E. van Donzel, W. P. Heinrichs, eds, *Encyclopedia of Islam.* 2nd edn. Leiden: Brill, 2012.

Vernon, Richard. *Historical Redress: Must We Pay for the Past?* London: Continuum, 2012.

Vetch, R. H. 'Havelock, Sir Henry'. In *Dictionary of National Biography.* Oxford: Oxford University Press, 1891.

Victoria, Queen of Great Britain. *The Letters of Queen Victoria, 1896–1901.* Ed. George Earl Buckle. 9 vols. Vol. 9: '1896–1901'. First edition, 1932. Cambridge: Cambridge University Press, 2014.

Vindex. *Cecil Rhodes, his Political Life and Speeches, 1881–1900.* London: Chapman and Hall, 1900.

Visaria, Leela and Pravin Visaria. 'I.V. Population (1757–1947)'. In Kumar and Desai, *Cambridge Economic History of India,* Vol. 2.

Wagner, Kim A. *Amritsar 1919: An Empire of Fear and the Making of a Massacre.* New Haven: Yale, 2019.

_____. 'Expanding Bullets and Savage Warfare'. In *History Workshop Journal,* 88 (Autumn 2019).

Waldron, Jeremy. 'Redressing Historic Injustice'. In *University of Toronto Law Journal,* 52 (2002).

_____. 'Superseding Historic Injustice'. In *Ethics,* 103/1 (October 1992).

Warraq, Ibn. *Defending the West: A Critique of Edward Said's Orientalism.* New York: Prometheus, 2007.

Warren, Bill. *Imperialism: Pioneer of Capitalism.* Ed. J. Sender. London: NLB-Verso Editions, 1980.

Warren, Christopher. 'Could First Fleet Smallpox Infect Aborigines? A Note'. In *Aboriginal History,* 31 (2007).

_____. 'Smallpox at Sydney Cove – Who, When, Why?'. In *Journal of Australian Studies,* 38.1 (2014).

Warwick, Peter. *Black People and the South African War, 1899–1902.* African Studies Series. Cambridge: Cambridge University Press, 1983.

Washbrook, David. 'The Indian Economy and the British Empire'. In Peers and Gooptu, *India and the British Empire.*

Wesley, John. *Thoughts upon Slavery.* London & Philadelphia: Joseph Cruckshank, 1774.

Westwater Charles. 'Letter'. In *The Tablet,* 29 March 2003.

White-Spunner, Barney. *Partition: The Story of Indian Independence and the Creation of Pakistan in 1947.* London: Simon & Schuster, 2017.

Whittow, Mark. *The Making of Byzantium, 600–1025.* Berkeley: University of California Press, 1996.

Wickwire, Franklin and Mary. *Cornwallis: The Imperial Years.* Chapel Hill: University of North Carolina Press, 1980.

Widdowson, Frances and Albert Howard. *Disrobing the Aboriginal Industry: The Deception behind Indigenous Cultural Preservation.* Montreal & Kingston: McGill-Queen's University Press 2008.

Williams, Eric. *Capitalism and Slavery.* Chapel Hill, NC: University of North Carolina Press, 1944; and London: Penguin, 2021.

Williams, Gardner F. *The Diamond Mines of South Africa: Some Account of Their Rise and Development.* New York: Macmillan, 1902; Cambridge: Cambridge University Press, 2011.

Williams, Glen. *Blood Must Tell: Debating Race and Identity in the Canadian House of Commons, 1880–1925.* Ottawa: willowBX Press, 2014.

Wilson, John. *CB: A Life of Sir Henry Campbell-Bannerman.* London: Constable, 1973.

Wilson, Jon. 'False and Dangerous'. In *Guardian*, 8 February 2003: https://www.theguardian.com/education/2003/feb/08/highereducation.britishidentity)

_____. *India Conquered: Britain's Raj and the Chaos of Empire.* London: Simon & Schuster, 2016.

Windschuttle, Keith. 'Doctored Evidence and Invented Incidents in Aboriginal Historiography'. In Attwood and Foster, *Frontier Conflict*.

_____. *The Fabrication of Aboriginal History.* 2 vols. Vol. 1: 'Van Diemen's Land, 1803–1847'. Sydney: Macleay Press, 2002.

_____. 'The Fabrication of Aboriginal History'. Lecture at the Sydney Institute, 11 February 2003. *The Sydney Papers*, Summer 2003.

Winks, Robin W., ed. *The Oxford History of the British Empire.* 5 vols. Vol. V: 'Historiography'. Oxford: Oxford University Press, 1999.

Woo, Andrea and Jeffrey Jones. 'Discovery of Remains of 215 Children at Former Kamloops Residential School Prompts Calls from Indigenous Leaders to Investigate All Sites', [Toronto] *Globe and Mail*, 30 May 2021: https://www.theglobeandmail.com/canada/article-calls-for-action-follows-discovery-of-childrens-remains-at-kamloops/

Wood, Nicholas J. 'Henry Havelock, History and Hagiography: Some 21st century (Baptist) Reflections on a Nineteenth Century (Baptist) Hero'. Unpublished.

Woodward, David R. *Field Marshal Sir William Robertson: Chief of the Imperial General Staff in the Great War.* Westport, Conn.: Praeger, 1998.

Woolcock, Nicola. 'Cambridge College Named after Winston Churchill Debates His "Backward" Views on Race'. In *The Times*, 11 February 2021: https://www.thetimes.co.uk/article/cambridge-college-named-for-sir-winston-churchill-to-debate-his-backward-views-on-race-dzdrdj29n

World Bank. 'Country Profile: Barbados, 2022': https://databank.worldbank.org/views/reports/reportwidget.aspx?Report_Name=CountryProfile&Id=b450fd57&tbar=y&dd=y&inf=n&zm=n&country=BRB.

_____. 'Country Profile: Nigeria, 2022': https://databank.worldbank.org/views/reports/reportwidget.aspx?Report_Name=CountryProfile&Id=b450fd57&tbar=y&dd=y&inf=n&zm=n&country=NGA.

Wrench, J. E. *Alfred Lord Milner: The Man of No Illusions, 1854–1925*. London: Eyre and Spottiswoode, 1958.

Wright, John. *The Trans-Saharan Slave Trade*. London: Routledge, 2007.

Yat-sen, Sun. 'Address at the University of Hong Kong, 20 February 1923'. In *South China Morning Post*, 21 February 1923: https://www.cuhk.edu.hk/rct/pdf/e_outputs/b2930/v29&30P042.pdf.

Index